Bent Greve (Ed.)
De Gruyter Handbook of Contemporary Welfare States

De Gruyter Contemporary Social Sciences Handbooks

—

Volume 1

De Gruyter Handbook of Contemporary Welfare States

Edited by
Bent Greve

DE GRUYTER

ISBN 978-3-11-072470-7
e-ISBN (PDF) 978-3-11-072176-8
e-ISBN (EPUB) 978-3-11-072182-9
ISSN 2747-9269

Library of Congress Control Number: 2022936927

Bibliographic information published by the Deutsche Nationalbibliothek
The Deutsche Nationalbibliothek lists this publication in the Deutsche Nationalbibliografie;
detailed bibliographic data are available on the Internet at http://dnb.dnb.de.

Cover image: Rawpixel / iStock / Getty Images Plus
Typesetting: jürgen ullrich typosatz, Nördlingen

www.degruyter.com

Contents

Part III **Issues and challenges**

Part IV **Future research needs**

Part I **Research methods**

Bent Greve

1 Contemporary welfare states and their challenges

Abstract: This first chapter of the book takes the "temperature" of contemporary welfare states, while also trying to assess the strength of the challenges for different types of welfare regimes. It will also point to future opportunities – with the accompanying uncertainty – and in which areas more information is needed. Besides discussing central challenges for welfare states in the years to come the chapter also gives a short overview of each of the chapters in the book.

Keywords: challenges, welfare state, welfare state regimes, crisis, inequality

1.1 Introduction

Welfare states have evolved and developed over at least the last 150 years, although not with all countries at all times following the same path, implying that they are still very diverse in structure, universality and generosity. There was a golden age of welfare state growth shortly after the Second World War, which lasted until around 1973. Then after the oil-price shock in the 1970s welfare states have, at least since the OECD's path-breaking book (OECD 1981), been argued to be in crisis. This argument has been followed up with discussions on the dismantling of welfare states (Pierson 1994) or an era of permanent austerity (Pierson 2001). The debates on whether welfare states are in crisis continued after the financial crisis, causing further changes, often under the label of austerity and retrenchment in the literature. Albeit the data do not, in general, confirm that this has actually taken place looking at overall spending on welfare state policies (Greve 2020), the data also indicate that there can be areas within welfare states where retrenchment has taken place, depending on the legitimacy of different parts of the welfare states.

Over the years, the factors that were either expected to have, or are having, an impact on this development have been many and varied. For the same reasons, these factors have not been of similar strength across countries and welfare states. However, there are some common trends that have influenced, and can be expected to influence, contemporary welfare states' development in the years to come. These include aspects of globalisation, regionalisation, new technology, demography, voters' expectation and the re-structuring of societies. There are, however, also new challenges to welfare states. The financial crisis showed the vulnerability of welfare states' economic systems, but also that the ability to have a stable economy influences the options and ability to continue and be able to afford a welfare state.

https://doi.org/10.1515/9783110721768-001

The recent COVID-19 crisis has demonstrated a double pressure on welfare states, including whether there is a strong need for higher spending in several areas at the same time – in this case, health and the economy – when there is also strong pressure on the sustainability of the welfare state, or at least part hereof, at play. This combined with increasing economic inequality has implied both economic and political problems in a number of countries, thereby creating new variants of the existing and possible crises in the future. Each crisis, including the assessment of whether it is, in fact, a crisis, may vary according to ideology, but also how the individual country is positioned in relation to solving it. The changes in 2009 seemingly opened the way for discussion on the role of the market, and the COVID-19 crisis showed the need for state intervention in a Keynesian way to ensure the necessary demand was available in order to reduce the potential negative impact on societal development of the restrictions imposed in order to cope with the pandemic. At the same time, a number of the aspects already mentioned continue to be possible threats and pressures on welfare states – such as demographic change and the development of new technology.

This book thus takes the "temperature" of contemporary welfare states, while also trying to assess the strength of the challenges for different types of welfare regimes. It will also point to future opportunities – with the accompanying uncertainty – and in which areas more information is needed.

In section 1.2, a further elaboration of the possible challenges is presented, whereas section 1.3 gives a short overview of each of the chapters in the book. Lastly, section 1.4. concludes the chapter.

1.2 Core challenges for welfare states

For a number of years, the core challenges for welfare states in the developed world have been globalisation and changes in demography, with a growing number of persons permanently outside the labour market due to retirement. Increasing regional diversity in a number of countries is also a challenge.

This has resulted in pressure on welfare states, especially in relation to pension expenditure, where a number of reforms have been implemented in many countries (Ebbinghaus 2021), as has withdrawing earlier liberal reforms (Bridgen 2019), with a higher degree of inequality as a consequence (Hinrichs 2021). Overall, the focus in pension reforms has been on increasing the retirement age, changes from defined benefits to defined contributions, changes to the rules on indexations, etc. At the same time as this pressure in relation to reducing spending on income transfers and attempts to reduce the public expenditure pressure by increasing number of pensioners, there has also been, in a combination of demographic changes and expectations among citizens, an increased desire for increases in services in relation to health and elderly care (OECD 2021).

Furthermore, health and long-term care often have widespread support among populations, which is generally the case in all countries (OECD 2021), and the legitimacy of welfare states is thus challenged in the sense that disappointment among the population that has expected, for example, the best and latest health care, which is not met, risks delegitimising the welfare state. Health care is also a field where we want to spend more as we get richer (as individuals or countries).

While the globalisation of production has increased the pressure, especially on the unskilled labour force's options to get a job (Acemoglu and Restrepo 2017), higher migration has also been seen as a pressure on welfare states. Within the EU, the free movement of labour has been perceived as a threat to native workers, with slogans such as "they take our jobs" (Chomsky 2007; Greve 2019) being used. This reflects that even if there are no overall job losses, there may be distributional aspects of labour market turnover that can contribute to a change in the perception of what welfare states can and perhaps cannot do. This is an indication of one of the issues that has contributed to the increase in the level of inequality. Change on the labour market is thereby a new and strong item on the agenda for the development of welfare states (Greve 2021).

In addition, not only does globalisation influence the labour market, but new technology (including use of platforms, automation, artificial intelligence) is also a challenge, and although there is disagreement about the extent and consequences of this (Greve 2017; Frey 2019), especially people without the appropriate education and qualifications will constantly and to a greater extent be at risk of losing their jobs, and thus, in many countries, often their financial safety net as well (OECD 2019a). Even if there have not been direct cuts in the level of benefits in many countries, the benefits have not always continued to keep pace with real increases in wages on the labour markets and thereby, relatively speaking, they have been in decline. New technology has also contributed to the fact that the middle class in particular has been under pressure (Palier 2019) and has only to a lesser extent than higher income groups, if at all, seen a real improvement in the last 20–30 years, and with the prospect that their children will not get better positions than themselves (OECD 2019b).

In combination with the above challenges, there may be unexpected and sudden challenges, as clearly shown by the financial crisis in 2008/9 and the outbreak of COVID-19 in 2020. In situations such as these, there is the need to lessen the risk of having to reduce spending in welfare areas and thereby the relative decline. In fact, governments need to put money aside for a rainy day. In other words, permanent and high government debt can lead to a risk that if the real interest rate is high, spending will have to be reduced in other areas to cope with crises that, like these, can increase costs for either income transfers and/or the provision of welfare services.

In particular, the financing of welfare states can be put under pressure by global companies' ability to plan their taxation, for example, by relocating their business in search of the lowest taxes. This is aggravated by the uncertainty about the taxation of platforms, and welfare states with the greatest risk of sudden and major changes will be those with large deficits if a shock happens. Gaps in public finances and large government debt can be due to an unwillingness or inability to collect the necessary taxes or duties, or a constantly higher consumption than the income generated by taxes and duties. Therefore, the argument that lowering taxes and duties will benefit everyone due to higher economic activity, might mainly cause pressure on the ability to finance welfare states in the future.

Lastly, the higher level of inequality is a new pressure on welfare states due to its impact on the degree of social cohesion, as well as rising conflicts, on what are the most important aspects of welfare states' development. The risk of a high level of inequality, as well as poverty and its impact on society, is even described as risking "deaths of despair" (Case and Deaton 2020). This is further in line with the stronger focus on welfare services, such as more day-care for children, as part of a social investment approach in recent years, which then has implied a pressure on benefit systems. It is also important to be aware of the way in which this influences contemporary development, given that it might imply a conflict between different groups in individual countries. Overall, this also points towards a need not only to look into the new risks in welfare states, but also to keep an eye on the old risks.

1.3 Overview of the chapters

The book is divided into four parts. The first part will deal with the research methods used to understand and grasp the challenges for contemporary welfare states. This will include how to measure changes, as well looking into the issue of evidence-based social policy in welfare states.

In order to set out the background for, and an understanding of, the challenges, the second part will give a presentation on a number of welfare regimes, in the context that the challenges might vary due to history, economy and demography, among other things.

The third part will investigate a number of possible issues that are already, or might become, a challenge for the welfare states not only in the short term, but also further into the future, see more below.

The fourth and last part will show the future research needs and concludes with what we know about possible challenges and upcoming avenues for the welfare states.

Chapter 2 by Ciccia reviews the rich and vibrant area of research on the determinants of welfare state change. It identifies four families of theories based on the nature of the factors considered – macro-structures, institutions, actors, and individual preferences and attitudes – and the way their influence is conceptualised. It shows that in time we have witnessed both increased heterogeneity in the ways welfare state change is conceptualised and measured, and an increased integration between theoretical perspectives.

Chapter 3 by Andersen and Smith discusses the important issue and possible contradiction between evidence and policymaking, including raising the question of what is considered as valid evidence for decision making. Furthermore, the lack of clarity of what comprises evidence, combined with policymakers naturally being free to choose when making their decisions, implies both that best knowledge is not always used, and perhaps mainly used when policymakers agree with the advice.

The second part consists of Chapters 4–10. These chapters present the challenges in different types of welfare states. As one would expect, there are differences, but also similarities. The policies chosen are different, and there are a number of path-dependency elements witnessed within the chapters.

This starts with a chapter (Chapter 4) by van Gerven, on the Nordic welfare states, known especially for universality, a high degree of equality and generosity. However, in recent years the Nordic Model has undergone many changes. These include a stronger focus on forced activation in the active labour market policy and, in some areas, marketisation. In some of the Nordic countries, the changes also include higher levels of inequality, which overall might imply a deviation from the traditional understanding of the content of the Nordic Model.

Chapter 5 by Wiß focuses on the continental model and shows both the core characteristics of the model as well as current reform trends. On the one hand, this includes stability in the historical understanding of the model with a high degree of social insurance, but on the other hand, new elements such as a focus on services, including day-care for children, thereby indicating both path-breaking and path-dependent developments. The chapter also includes core data comparing different welfare regime clusters.

Chapter 6 on liberal welfare states by Heins and Dukelow gives an overview of the main characteristics of the liberal welfare regime, and links these key features and recent policy trends to the contemporary issues of migration, digitalisation, climate change and the COVID-19 pandemic. The chapter shows that liberal welfare states, despite important within-regime differences, have reacted to the COVID-19 crisis with a stronger degree of state intervention than could be expected from their underlying liberal principles, but also that high degrees of inequality are continuing.

Chapter 7 on Southern Europe by Natili and Jessoula indicates changes in the way the Southern European welfare model can be understood, but also the impact of historical development here. However, also that there are still strong challenges as a consequence of both the financial crisis in 2008/2009 and the COVID-19 crisis. The chapter shows that the main bulk of spending in these countries goes to old age people and survivors, implying less developed social protection and services in other parts of the welfare state.

Chapter 8 on Eastern Europe by Hrast and Dobrotić also points towards both similarities and differences in the approach of the welfare state's role in Eastern European countries, including that there is a very large degree of difference in the level of inequality among these countries. Further, it is the countries that have been in transition towards new types of societies for a long time that have differences in the types of welfare provided.

Chapter 9 by Li investigates the development of social policy in China, including challenges such as marketisation, demographic ageing, urbanisation, poverty and growing inequality. The answer to these challenges is less clear – albeit giving up the one child policy, new social insurances and attempts to reduce poverty, which have taken place are seen as central, given the economic growth in China.

South-East Asia by Hong is presented in Chapter 10. Here it is argued that even if being a late-comer to social policy, comprehensive welfare states with a focus on classical issues such as health care and labour market policy have been developed, as well as a strong emphasis on education as a driver for future growth.

The third part consists of Chapters 11–24, and looks into a variety of topics having an impact on contemporary welfare states' developments. Together, they should help in forming a picture of the changes, the reason for them and their consequences in different types of welfare states.

Chapter 11 by Trein focuses on one of the large spending areas of welfare state policies: health. The chapter shows that despite the systems for emergent treatment being not that different across countries, there are still strong variations in the size of the health care sector as well as inequality with regard to health. Preventative measures still only have a more limited role in the health care systems.

COVID-19 and its consequences on welfare states are covered in two chapters – Chapters 12 and 13 – but are also briefly referred to in other chapters.

Chapter 12 by Moreira and Béland looks into COVID-19 as a special case for societal development, and how it has influenced national economies as well as the life situation of individuals and families. It also presents data showing the numbers of COVID-19 cases, deaths and excess mortality across countries, as well as three ideal typical strategies used to cope with COVID-19. Lastly, the variations in fiscal responses to the crisis are shown.

Chapter 13 by Antenucci, Salvati and Tridico argues that there has been a stronger tendency for more intervention, especially using Italy as a case to present several changes not only in labour market policy, but also economic support to the vulnerable. Underlining the strengths and weaknesses of the Italian social security system in the pandemic, they argue for reforms to make the system more resilient to shocks, through the increase of its degree of universality.

Chapter 14 by Lopes and Poškutė investigates a social policy field with a strong expectation of growing pressure on welfare states due to demographic changes. They further point to the wide variety of long-term care systems in Europe, varying from strong state involvement to a strong reliance on the civil society and voluntary work. This raises issues on coverage and support to the most vulnerable in the years to come.

Chapter 15 by Vlachantoni focuses on an important aspect related both to inequality and living standards for those who have left the labour market and are dependent on public pensions. It shows a picture of a large number of changes in pension systems as well as indicating that especially the fund-based pension systems imply a risk of higher inequalities in the pension system.

Chapter 16 by Lutz and Knotz disentangles the complex relationship between the welfare state and international migration, focusing on the question of how migration affects the legitimacy of the welfare state as an institution. The chapter argues that the legitimacy of welfare state institutions rests on both their problem-solving capacity as well as public support – and that migration is needed to maintain the former, but can negatively affect the latter in some key respects. The chapter also shows, however, that a generous welfare state and open migration do not necessarily exclude each other and that welfare states face risks from having too many as well as having too few immigrants.

Chapter 17 by Thompson looks at education, an issue often neglected in welfare state analysis, despite its growing importance in several ways. The chapter especially looks at early school leavers and the situation in different types of welfare states, but also how this has repercussions on equality and inequality, as well as the stratification of societies.

Inequality has been a rising issue in many welfare states, and this is the focus in Chapter 18 by Greve. Although the development has not been the same in all countries, it is important to be aware of the consequence of inequality for societal development. The options to deal with inequality are discussed, but at the end of the day, however, it is a political decision as to what to do with inequality and what level of inequality is seen as acceptable.

Chapter 19 by Hussain analyses poverty in a European context using EU-SILC data from 2009–2019 divided into five different welfare regimes. The analysis shows that the variation in the number of people living in relative poverty does not follow the classical welfare state analysis and understanding of regimes, but that there can be strong variations within a regime, such as the case in the Eastern European welfare regime.

Chapter 20 by Greve shows how employment and unemployment have different impacts in European countries, but also that the changes underway might challenge who has access to social protection as a consequence of new technology. New technology, at the same time, implies a risk of fewer jobs as well as a stronger split between citizens in the access to income and job-security in a number of countries.

Chapter 21 by Bridgen and Schoyen discusses a new element in welfare states development, environmental sustainability. They present various ways of understanding how to cope with the environmental challenges in the years to come, as well as reflecting upon the possible impact on welfare states' future options.

Chapter 22 by Fitzi discusses what populism is, which has been an increasingly discussed topic, and how this can and might influence welfare states' development. Populism also influences the legitimacy of welfare states, and whether or not this implies a pessimistic or optimistic view on welfare states' development is open for interpretation, and even more so due to the consequences of COVID-19 on the demand for health care intervention.

Behavioural public policy, as discussed in Chapter 23 by Cartwright, is a relatively new field in social science. The chapter shows how Nudge might work to support people to behave in what is seen as a societally more optimal way. It does this by using, as an example, how to get people to pay tax. Other examples are also given, such as Save More Tomorrow. It can be argued to be a new way of managing societal development, albeit one not necessarily without problems.

Chapter 24 by Liu looks into the global inequality by analysing the North–South divide. Despite there having been a reduction in the degree of global inequality, the variations are still large and strong. The chapter shows that this is not only an issue of economic inequality, but also of differences in other spheres of inequality. Lastly, it discusses possible international instruments to contribute in a global way to more equal societies, although also showing that this is not simple.

Incentives have been a strong economic issue in many welfare states, as discussed in Chapter 25 by Shin. The focus is especially on incentives to take up a job, or work more, including discussions on in-work-benefits, as well as the possible interaction between the tax and benefit systems on the marginal change in disposable income when being unemployed and having an especially low income type of job.

The fourth part is, in fact, also the concluding chapter (Chapter 26). Overall, the chapter shows that there are a number of commonalities as well as differences across welfare states, across policy fields all in all, indicating that welfare states will continue to be a very important part of societies' development, and, without welfare states, inequality in a number of areas will continue to be high and thereby, in fact, making societies less well functioning than if welfare states continue to play a central role for societal development.

1.4 Summing-up

This book provides an overview of the current challenges and changes both in various welfare regimes and in a number of key welfare state areas. The picture is varied and filled with exceptions to general rules.

Nevertheless, a clear aspect is that welfare states will continue to be central for the good life of citizens in most countries. Although the weighting may vary from area to area, the degree of personal and collective responsibility will vary, and despite continued support for large parts of the welfare state, there will be areas where support is less strong. The struggles over where the money should be spent and where it is best spent will continue, just as populist currents will try to move money to what they consider best. It might further still vary across countries, partly reflecting historical traditions, but also variations in the legitimacy of the welfare states as well as economic options in different countries.

Therefore, continued research in order to understand and explain different welfare states, different topics and variations remains important.

References

Acemoglu, Daron, and Pascual Restrepo. 2017. "Robots and Jobs: Evidence from US Labor Markets." MIT Department of Economics Working Paper No. 17-04. *SSRN*. https://doi.org/10.2139/ssrn. 2940245.

Bridgen, Paul. 2019. "The Retrenchment of Public Pension Provision in the Liberal World of Welfare during the Age of Austerity – and its Unexpected Reversal, 1980–2017." *Social Policy & Administration* 53 (1), 16–33.

Case, Anne, and Angus Deaton. 2020. *Deaths of Despair and the Future of Capitalism*. Princeton, NJ: Princeton University Press.

Chomsky, Aviva. 2007. *"They Take Our Jobs!": And 20 Other Myths about Immigration*. Boston: Beacon Press.

Ebbinghaus, Bernhard. 2021. "Inequalities and Poverty Risks in Old Age across Europe: The Double-Edged Income Effect of Pension Systems." *Social Policy & Administration* 55 (3), 440–455.

Frey, Carl Benedikt. 2019. *The Technology Trap: Capital, Labor, and Power in the Age of Automation*. Princeton, NJ: Princeton University Press. Kindle edition.

Greve, Bent. 2017. *Technology and the Future of Work. The Impact on Labour Markets and Welfare States*. Cheltenham: Edward Elgar.

Greve, Bent. 2019. *Welfare, Populism and Welfare Chauvinism*. Bristol: Policy Press.

Greve, Bent. 2020. *Austerity, Retrenchment and the Welfare State. Truth of Fiction?* Cheltenham: Edward Elgar.

Greve, Bent. 2021. *Multidimensional Inequalities. International Perspectives Across Welfare States*. Berlin: De Gruyter.

Hinrichs, Karl. 2021. "Recent Pension Reforms in Europe: More Challenges, New Directions. An Overview." *Social Policy & Administration* 55 (3): 409–422.

OECD. 1981. *The Welfare State in Crisis*. Paris: OECD.

OECD. 2019a. *OECD Employment Outlook 2019: The Future of Work*. Paris: OECD.

OECD. 2019b. *Under Pressure: The Squeezed Middle Class*. Paris: OECD Publishing.

OECD. 2021. *Main Findings from the 2020 Risks That Matter Survey*. Paris: OECD Publishing https://doi.org/10.1787/b9e85cf5-en.

Palier, Bruno. 2019. "Work, Social Protection and the Middle Classes: What Future in the Digital Age?" *International Social Security Review* 72 (3), 113–133.

Pierson, P. 1994. *Dismantling the Welfare State?: Reagan, Thatcher and the Politics of Retrenchment*. Cambridge Studies in Comparative Politics. Cambridge: Cambridge University Press.

Pierson, Paul. 2001. "Coping With Permanent Austerity Welfare State Restructuring in Affluent Democracies." In *The New Politics of the Welfare State*, edited by Paul Pierson, 410–456. Oxford: Oxford University Press.

Rossella Ciccia

2 Four families of theories to understand welfare state change

Abstract: This chapter provides an overview of different theoretical approaches used to investigate welfare state change with a particular emphasis on cross-national analysis of Western Europe and North America. It distinguishes four families of theories based on the nature of the factors they consider – macro-structures, institutions, actors, individual preferences and attitudes – and the way their influence is conceptualised – as either the environment, filters and interactions, engine or micro-foundations of welfare states. By analysing developments over time, the chapter shows that we have witnessed to both an increased heterogeneity in the ways welfare state change is conceptualised and measured, and a growing integration of theoretical perspectives. In sum, theoretical advancement in this field has occurred less through the falsification and rejection of existing theories than through a process of integration, layering, refinement, and contextualisation whereby new theories have been used to complement and specify older ones and their field of applicability. This development has coincided with a shift away from grand theorising about the state and social conflict to greater emphasis on middle-range theories providing explanation for well-delimited instances of change concerning particular economic forms, periods, sectors or types of reforms.

Keywords: change, welfare state, social policy, macro, ideas, power, institutions, partisan politics, public opinion, political parties

2.1 Introduction

Explaining welfare state change is one of the big questions addressed by social policy scholars and is intimately connected to the development of the field of welfare state studies. How to conceptualise welfare state change is the object of ongoing discussions which span across such different issues as the level of the analysis (Bannink and Hoogenboom 2007; Ciccia 2017; Hinrichs 2000), the nature of change itself (Capano 2009; Green-Pedersen 2004) and the way to operationalise it (Clasen and Siegel 2007; Kühner 2007). The extent of disagreement is large and often encompasses even basic definitions. However, for reasons of space these debates cannot be reviewed here. For our purpose, welfare state change is broadly defined as any processes relating to the development, consolidation and restructuring of the way states protect individuals against a range of social risks that have come historically to be viewed as legitimate sources of entitlement to public resources. These processes can affect the whole of the welfare state, but also more limitedly specific policy areas or even instruments.

https://doi.org/10.1515/9783110721768-002

The aim of this chapter is to provide an overview of the different theoretical approaches used to investigate welfare state change with a particular emphasis on cross-national comparative analysis of Western Europe and North America. For analytical purposes, the chapter classifies extant theories in four families: 1) macro-structures; 2) institutions; 3) actors; and 4) individual preferences and attitudes. This distinction is based on the prominence afforded to different types of factors and the way their influence on the welfare state is conceptualised. The first family looks at the "environment" in which welfare states operate and points to the role of macro-structural transformations and changing socio-economic contexts. The second family turns the gaze to the state to analyse how political institutions and formal procedural rules filter the effect of the macro-context and social and political mobilisations. Several ideational approaches also tend to fall within this group. The third family focuses on the meso-level of organisations and political actors, their behaviour and strategies as the main drivers of change. The last family analyses public attitudes and electoral preferences with the aim of providing an account of the micro-foundations of the legitimacy of welfare states. Before discussing each family, it is important to emphasise that they have not developed in strict chronological order, rather they have often overlapped and are not always mutually exclusive. Nonetheless, each tends to privilege the analysis of a particular historical period and they can be subdivided based on their focus on either the post-war period of sustained expansion of welfare states, or their maturation in post-1970s.

2.2 Theory family one: the "environment" of social policy

While many countries already had some rudimentary form of social policy, the consolidation of modern nation states in the nineteenth and twentieth centuries gave new prominence to social policies. Between the late 1970s and 1990s, the main puzzle to be solved was why welfare developed at different rates and reached different levels of spending (Skocpol and Amenta 1986; Myles and Quadagno 2002).

The theories used to answer this question generally focused on macro historical phenomena creating both the conditions and the need for state intervention. These processes could be economic in nature as in the logic of industrialism (Wilensky 1975) and capitalist development (Gough 1979; Offe 1984), political as in the consolidation of mass democracy (Marshall 1950), or both as in theories of modernisation (Flora and Heidenheimer 1981). These theories all shared a neo-functionalist understanding of the dynamics of welfare state expansion which put the emphasis on the evolving nature of the "environment" in which welfare states operated. In this view, the growth of the welfare state was conceived as the inevitable outcome of the emergence of new social needs and the economic and political resources generated by large socio-economic transformations and their correlates (e.g. ageing populations, family change, rising productivity). This process would ultimately lead to the convergence of welfare states. From this perspective, politics was not a prominent explanatory factor. Faced with comparable levels of demands and resources, welfare programmes would develop independently of the balance of power among political forces. Another shared characteristic of these theories is their focus on an undifferentiated notion of the welfare state, often operationalised as welfare effort, i.e. aggregate social spending on income-maintenance programmes.

These theories have been widely criticised for their emphasis on impersonal socio-economic forces and the lack of attention to how the issues they generated were picked up by political actors initiating the reforms. The assumption that social policies were simply a response to social needs rendered them unfit to explain differences in national programmatic profiles or among countries with similar levels of development. Nonetheless, their insight remains of considerable importance and the set of factors they identify are widely acknowledged as a baseline of conditions for welfare state expansion (Skocpol and Amenta 1986; Pierson 1991). While these theories find limited applicability today, other contemporary perspectives follow similar heuristics. Prominent examples are studies that focus on the effect of exogenous shocks – for instance, economic crises (Farnsworth and Irving 2011; Greve 2020; Starke, Kaasch, and Hooren 2014) or globalisation (Swank 2002) – but differently from studies in the earlier period they draw on a more diverse set of explanatory factors.

The new social risks (NSR) perspective with its emphasis on the new social needs produced by the transition to post-industrial economies and associated family and labour market changes is one such example. The range of social risks considered is long and varied but among them stand out those relating to work–life balance, skill formation and labour market dualisation (Bonoli 2005; Taylor-Gooby 2004). Thus, family and education policies – and services – which had remained at the margin in studies of the welfare settlement, now come to the fore. Similar to theories in the earlier period, the idea that the main input for reforming the welfare state comes from changing socio-economic contexts lies at the heart of this approach. However, the NSR also shows some important points of departure from previous neo-functionalist accounts. First, it does not postulate convergence, but rather views change as occurring through various mechanisms of adaptation, and welfare states as set on different trajectories because of differences in their institutional contexts (Bonoli 2007). Drawing on institutionalist perspectives (family two), NSR posits that existing social policies and the pattern of interests they produce play a fundamental role in shaping reform strategies and the capacity of welfare states to adapt to changing socio-economic contexts (Taylor-Gooby 2004; Armingeon and Bonoli 2006). Second, it affords some salience to political actors, particularly in the form of policy preferences of those social groups most affected by new social risks (women, young and low-skilled individuals). However, it remains pessimistic about their ability to influence policymaking given their heterogeneous composition and limited representation in the electoral arena (Bonoli

2005). The NSR approach increasingly draws on the "new politics" perspective to conceptualise the influence of political actors (family three).

2.3 Theory family two: states and institutions as filters and interactions

The point of departure of studies in the second family is its emphasis on how the organisation of the state shapes welfare states by filtering and interacting with both larger macro-structural factors and social and political mobilisation. These theories challenge the view of the state as neutral arbiter of the competition among social groups, and rather share an interest in the many ways in which the features of governments and polities influence access to policymaking and hence reform patterns (Immergut 2006). Theoretically, several of these works are located within historical institutionalism; methodologically, they tend to privilege comparative historical analysis of one or a small number of cases. Despite these shared characteristics, this family remains heterogeneous with regard to the specific factors that are the focus of the analysis.

One approach (often referred to as "state-centred") highlights the apparatus of the state and the activities of relatively independent bureaucrats as the main cause of both cross-national differences and the expansion of welfare states through time (Heclo 1974; Orloff and Skocpol 1984; Weir and Skocpol 1985). These works reconceptualise the state from an arena of social conflict to an actor with the autonomy to set its own goals and different capacity to realise them (Orloff 1993; Skocpol 1992). Such an approach recognises the centrality of social and political actors but views them as conditioned by the institutional configuration of the state and previously enacted policies. An important contribution of this body of research is the conceptualisation of policy feedback, that is, the idea that once policies are in place, they change the politics of subsequent policy change by altering the patterns of group conflict through which reform occurs (Weir and Skocpol 1985; Skocpol 1992; Pierson 1993). These works paved the way for the analysis of slow-moving causal processes of welfare state transformation that occur through path dependence or gradual and incremental institutional change (Streeck and Thelen 2005).

A second approach has instead focused on institutional rules and procedures. While some of these studies look at broad welfare state dynamics, they generally privilege the analysis of specific policy sectors (Immergut 1992; Thelen 2004; Steinmo 1993). The core claim of these studies is that the way the formal institutions of governments are designed fundamentally alters the mechanisms by which social pressures are transmitted to policymakers, resulting in different patterns of reform. Immergut (1992) has put forward the concept veto points – defined by the interactions of constitutional rules and electoral results – to formalise the analysis of this dynamic process. As stated by Immergut (1992, 243) "political institutions can be thought as the outermost frame of political conflict". Thus, while they do not determine reform outputs, they do significantly shape trajectories of policymaking by altering the power of particular actors to influence reforms, their strategic calculations and political behaviour.

A third approach focuses instead on the role of ideational institutions (Béland 2005; Blyth 2002; Hall 1989; Jenson 2009; Rothstein 1998; Schmidt and Thatcher 2013). Heclo's pioneering study (1974), which claimed that pension policy in Britain and Sweden had been shaped by civil servants "puzzling" over problems, was among the first to identify the relevance of policy learning effects. Despite this early formulation, attention to ideational factors represent a later addition to this family, and the various works that can be placed here show fundamental disagreement about core concepts (Béland and Cox 2010; Campbell 2002). Under the broad umbrella of ideational analyses, we find such different things as norms, frames, discourses or policy paradigms, pointing at different ways in which ideas can transform welfare states. Scholarship emphasising the role of gender norms in the construction and evolution of welfare states is often also implicitly or explicitly ideational (Adams and Padamsee 2001). The contributions of this research are too vast and diverse to do them justice here, but they all share an interest in the way that ideas alter the cognitive frameworks of socio-political actors and are used performatively to influence patterns of support for welfare measures.[1]

Institutionalist perspectives have made several contributions to knowledge, and concepts such as policy feedback and path dependence are now routinely used in analyses of welfare state change. However, authors located in this family easily concede that "the state certainly does not become everything" (Skocpol 1985, 7) and that the effects of political institutions are best considered as interaction effects (Immergut 2010), and thus cannot predict reform outputs without consideration of the policy actors (family 3) and the characteristics of the broader socio-economic context (family 1). However, they also contend that explanations that focus on the latter determinants will remain unsuccessful until they include an examination of the political institutions that makes them relevant (Immergut 1992). The insight of institutionalist and state-centric perspectives has deeply influenced contemporary theorising on the welfare state, and even actor-centred theories such as those emphasising partisanship, now acknowledge that the preferences and strategies of political actors are significantly constrained by the broader institutional context of policymaking (Beramendi et al. 2015; Starke, Kaasch, and Hooren 2014). Thus, at the centre of present debates is not so much the issue whether it is institutions or actors that matter, but rather if it is more productive for the analysis to begin from the institutional context, or from the preferences and strategies of political actors.

---

1 On this point, see also the section on Theory family four.

2.4 Theory family three: actors as the engine of change

The third family of theories considers political and social actors as the main drivers of change. At its origin it developed as a response to neo-functionalist approaches and their neglect of political processes in the articulation of social needs (family one). This body of research focuses prominently on the strategies and behaviours of political parties, but it has also included other actors, particularly trade unions, employers' organisations, businesses and other private interests (Anderson 2001; Gingrich 2011; Ebbinghaus and Manow 2004; Hall and Soskice 2001; Mares 2003; Martin and Swank 2012; Naczyk 2013; Swenson 1997). Attention to political factors also brought greater attention to the striking diversity of welfare states across industrialised nations (Esping-Andersen 1990; Sainsbury 1999). The core statement of these theories is that politics matters, but the ways it does is the object of disagreement. In particular, it has become commonplace to distinguish between an old politics of the golden age of welfare state expansion (1945–1975), and a new politics of the subsequent age of austerity.[2]

The power resource theory (PRT) (Korpi 1983; Huber and Stephens 2001) is probably the most credited account for the period of expansion. This theory views the growth of welfare states as the result of distributive struggles among classes. Its starting point is that class is the dominant cleavage in capitalist societies, and that the power resources of the working class – in the form of socially (unions) and politically (social-democratic parties) organised interests – determines the level of universalism and generosity of welfare states (Kersbergen and Vis 2014). Recognising that the strength of the Left alone has historically proven insufficient to the expansion of social rights, Esping-Andersen (1990) further expanded PRT to include the history of cross-class coalitions as the decisive cause of variation in welfare state arrangements. Thus, according to this perspective, the reach and redistributive capacity of welfare states is a function of the strength of working-class political mobilisation and the incorporation of the middle classes in the pro-welfare coalition.

While PRT still provides the main explanation for cross-national differences in social programmes during the so-called golden age, subsequent works have updated several of its assumptions to address some limitations. First, studies have extended the focus from social-democracy to also consider other party families, including Christian-democratic, right-wing and more recently populist parties (van Kersbergen 1995; Greve 2021; Jensen 2014). Secondly, they have moved beyond the assumption typical of PRT of political institutions as mere arenas for conflict to investigate the ways they condition and alter the strategic calculations of partisan actors (Beramendi et al. 2015;

---

2 For a critique of this periodisation see Wincott (2013).

Gingrich 2011; Häusermann 2010). Finally, other studies have questioned the idea that political ideology predetermines the policy preferences of political parties and rather explains them in light of shifting socio-economic cleavages, electoral competition and forms of party-voters linkages (Green-Pedersen 2001; Häusermann, Picot, and Geering 2013; Morgan 2013) – a point which will be further developed by theory family four.

A more fundamental critique to PRT has come instead from the Paul Pierson's work (1996, 2001) on the New Politics of the welfare state. Pierson contended that the politics of retrenchment differs in fundamental ways from the old politics of expansion. In an age of permanent austerity, political parties have become increasingly concerned with avoiding being blamed by the electorate for unpopular reforms. An additional obstacle to retrenchment comes from changes in the institutional context. Drawing on historical institutionalism, Pierson argued that the creation of large social programmes in the previous period generated major impediments to welfare state change in the form of mechanisms of increasing returns and policy feedback (Pierson 1993). These mechanisms are to be found at the level of both voters and interest groups benefiting from existing schemes and opposing major cutbacks. Therefore, the new politics suggests a resilience of the welfare arrangement of the golden age, still change is possible because political parties can adopt various strategies – obfuscation, compensation, division – to implement cutbacks. This process of retrenchment by stealth will more likely assume the form of incremental change.

The publication of this work stirred considerable debates in the late 1990s and early 2000s about the continued relevance of partisan politics (Allan and Scruggs 2004; Kittel and Obinger 2003; Korpi and Palme 2003) and the supposed stability of welfare states (Häusermann 2010; Palier 2010), and more recently on the use of blame avoidance strategies (Vis 2016; Jensen et al. 2018). The new politics thesis has produced an enduring influence on the field, particularly in the prominence afforded to electoral politics and the view of political parties as vote-seeking rational actors and welfare states as shaped by various forms of policy feedbacks (Béland and Schlager 2019; Hacker and Pierson 2019) defined in the interaction between political parties and the electorate (Jensen, Wenzelburger, and Zohlnhöfer 2019; Starke 2021).

The idea of a temporal discontinuity in the constellations of actors and political mechanisms shaping the transformation of welfare states after the heydays of the golden age is now generally accepted, and the distinction between an old and new politics widely used (Green-Pedersen and Haverland 2002; Starke 2021). Political actors, their behaviours and strategies are central in contemporary theorising of welfare state change, and this is probably both one of the most populous family of theories and the one where disagreement is more frequent. However, in time we have also witnessed a narrowing down of the scope of analyses from a broader set of actors and social processes to an understanding of the politics of reforms as essentially electoral politics. In particular, fewer studies today investigate the influence of business groups, interest groups and protest movements that had been included in earlier studies of welfare state expansion (Piven and Cloward 1979; Quadagno 1992; Amenta 2006).

2.5 Theory family four: the micro-foundations of welfare states

Do mass policy preferences influence welfare states' outputs and trajectories in advanced democracies (Brooks and Manza 2006)? The two approaches used to answer this question, focus on either public attitudes or electoral preferences with an underlying concern for the legitimacy of welfare states, conceptualised as a sort of responsiveness to citizens' preferences. Methodologically, these studies generally implement quantitative analysis of large surveys, theoretically they draw on a diverse set of established traditions which emphasise either the sociological or political underpinnings of welfare states' legitimacy.

The first approach is rooted in sociological traditions of study of public attitudes and investigates the determinants of support for the welfare state, often in the form of either preference for redistribution (Blekesaune and Quadagno 2003; Ebbinghaus and Naumann 2017; Mau 2004; Svallfors 1997; Taylor-Gooby 1985) or the perceived deservingness of welfare beneficiaries (Kangas 1997; van Oorschot 2000; Larsen 2008; Sachweh 2019). The privileged level of analysis is the whole of the welfare state, but a few studies also look at support for specific sectors (Chung and Meuleman 2017; Busemeyer, Garritzmann, and Neimanns 2020). Explanations for cross-national differences include combinations of individual-level factors (socio-demographic characteristics, ideological positions) and features of the macro context such as norms and values but also the feedback effect produced by existing welfare institutions. This research has produced great innovations in the ways welfare states are conceptualised and attitudes measured (Taylor-Gooby et al. 2020). However, and with few exceptions, these studies do not directly engage with the question of how mass preferences relate to political parties' positions and legislative initiatives, which constitutes instead the focus of the other body of literature analysed here.

The second approach is firmly located in comparative political economy traditions. Its starting point is also cross-national differences in preferences for redistribution, particularly in its relation to levels of inequalities and welfare institutions (Gingrich and Ansell 2012; Kenworthy and McCall 2008; Lupu and Pontusson 2011; Rehm 2016). A particular focus of a growing number of these studies is the way that socio-structural transformation typical of the post-industrial era (e.g. new occupational and demographic structures) have transformed classic social cleavages, voting behaviours and political parties' positions. Differently from political theories in earlier periods (family three), these studies do not assume that political parties have ideologically predetermined programmatic stances, rather in the post-industrial era the partisan politics of welfare states is shaped by two interrelated transformations: 1) in the dimensions of political conflict and the underlying distribution of preferences (Gingrich and Häusermann 2015; Häusermann and Kriesi 2015; Oesch 2008; Vlandas 2021); and 2) in the mechanisms linking citizens' preferences to political parties

(Kitschelt 2000; Kitschelt and Rehm 2015). By connecting studies of electoral politics and welfare states, this research aims to provide a more complex picture of how individual preferences are formed and if and how they relate to political parties' policy positions.

Family four shows an affinity with both partisan (family three) and institutional (family two) – including ideational – theories of which they try to establish the micro-foundations in public attitudes and electoral preferences. For instance, by testing and refining assumptions on policy feedback and interest-representation by political parties (Häusermann, Picot and Geering 2013; Kumlin and Stadelmann-Steffen 2014). They also often draw from family one to show the macro foundations (particularly, in changing labour market and occupational structures) of the reconfiguration of mass preferences, and hence of the pro-welfare state coalition in post-industrial economies. This scholarship has made several original contributions to knowledge on welfare state change particularly with regard to the interplay of individual and macro-level factors, and the democratic basis of the legitimacy of welfare states. However, it also shows some of the biases of other families such as the emphasis on party politics and limited attention to other forms of expression of political preference beyond the ballot box and the role of intermediary organisations in aggregating and shaping preferences (Kriesi et al. 2020; Ciccia and Guzman-Concha 2021). Moreover, it tends to privilege questions relating to the formation and distribution of preferences, while mechanisms linking preferences to political actors and policy outputs have so far received less attention.

2.6 Conclusions

What drives welfare state change? This chapter offered a non-exhaustive review of that vibrant area of scholarship which addresses this question. Several decades of intensive research have produced a large number of theories and concepts which have been subject to constant refinement in order to explain anomalies, sectoral and regional specificities and temporal developments. This chapter grouped these theories in four families based on the nature of the factors considered and the way their influence is conceptualised. In 2003 Edwin Amenta (2003, 115) wrote that theoretical advancement in social policy research had been spurred by the presence of a "relatively high agreement on what was to be explained – the adoption and expansion of major social programs – but relative disagreement among theoretical perspectives". The review presented here shows that while this statement is still broadly valid today, there is both growing disagreement about the definition of what is to be explained and increased convergence about what explains it.

The conceptualisation and measurement of welfare state change are still highly debated, and in time attention has shifted from the whole of the welfare state (measured as welfare effort or social rights to income-transfer programmes) to the level of sectors and single instances of reform and the inclusion of a wider set of policy areas (e.g. family policies, education and healthcare). Whereas functionalist and power re-source theories worked with an undifferentiated notion of the welfare state, institu-tionalist perspectives brought to the fore the importance of sectoral dynamics and constellations of actors. Micro-foundational analyses have also tended to privilege a holistic view of the welfare state as preferences for redistribution or aggregate social spending, although they have sometimes also focused on specific programmes, parti-cularly childcare and education. At the same time, studies have shown that what counts as change varies radically based on both the extent and pace of reforms (Palier 2010; Streeck and Thelen 2005). In sum, the conceptualisation and measurement of welfare state change have become increasingly heterogeneous, which accounts for both the generation of new theories and a level of disagreement – and incommensur-ability – between perspectives.

Despite these differences, dissimilarities between theoretical approaches are be-coming increasingly more a matter of degrees of emphasis on particular sets of factors than a clash between world views. Ontological and epistemological differences remain between some of these perspectives, but a general consensus seems to have emerged around a basic set of assumptions. The majority of social policy scholars today would probably agree that macro-structural transformations and exogenous events such as crises generate both the need and opportunities for reforms. Few would also deny that the way these inputs set welfare states on different paths depends on political actors, and that their preferences and behaviours are altered by existing institutions and the welfare state structures in which they operate – although they may start to disagree about the exact nature of those actors and the institutions that matter most.

We should also acknowledge that boundaries between families are not clear-cut and several works can be placed in two or more of these perspectives. For instance, theories of partisanship have evolved to consider the constraining influence of the in-stitutional context (Beramendi et al. 2015; Starke, Kaasch, and Hooren 2014). Simi-larly, the starting point of much micro-foundational analyses is the consideration of both the socio-structural and institutional foundations of shifting mass preferences, political cleavages and party systems (Gingrich and Häusermann 2015; Häusermann and Kriesi 2015). Explanations that draw on a single set of factors are today not only rare but considered as inadequate. We have witnessed a proliferation of middle-range theories which draw on two or more of the families described here to develop an ex-planation of well-delimited instances of change such as post-industrial economies, easy vs. unpopular reforms, specific forms of welfare regimes and social policy sec-tors. In sum, theoretical advancement has generally occurred less through the falsifi-cation and rejection of existing theories than through a process of integration, layer-ing, refinement and contextualisation whereby new approaches have been used to complement and specify older ones and their field of applicability.

References

Adams, Julia, and Tasleem J. Padamsee. 2001. "Signs and Regimes: Rereading Feminist Work on Welfare States." *Social Politics: International Studies in Gender, State & Society* 8 (1), 1–23.

Allan, James P., and Lyle Scruggs. 2004. "Political Partisanship and Welfare State Reform in Advanced Industrial Societies." *American Journal of Political Science* 48 (3), 496–512.

Amenta, Edwin. 2003. "What We Know About the Development of Social Policy: Comparative and Historical Research in Comparative and Historical Perspective." In *Comparative Historical Analysis in the Social Sciences*, edited by J. Mahoney and D. Rueschemeyer, 91–130. Cambridge: Cambridge University Press.

Amenta, Edwin. 2006. *When Movements Matter: The Townsend Plan and the Rise of Social Security*. Princeton, NJ: Princeton University Press.

Anderson, Karen M. 2001. "The Politics of Retrenchment in a Social Democratic Welfare State: Reform of Swedish Pensions and Unemployment Insurance." *Comparative Political Studies* 34 (9), 1063–1091.

Armingeon, Klaus, and Giuliano Bonoli (eds.) 2006. *The Politics of Post-Industrial Welfare States: Adapting Post-War Social Policies to New Social Risks*. London and New York: Routledge.

Bannink, Duco, and Marcel Hoogenboom. 2007. "Hidden Change: Disaggregation of Welfare State Regimes for Greater Insight into Welfare State Change." *Journal of European Social Policy* 17 (1), 19–32.

Béland, Daniel. 2005. "Ideas and Social Policy: An Institutionalist Perspective." *Social Policy & Administration* 39 (1), 1–18.

Béland, Daniel, and Robert H. Cox. 2010. *Ideas and Politics in Social Science Research*. Oxford: Oxford University Press.

Béland, Daniel, and Edella Schlager. 2019. "Varieties of Policy Feedback Research: Looking Backward, Moving Forward." *Policy Studies Journal* 47 (2), 184–205.

Beramendi, Pablo, Silja Häusermann, Herbert Kitschelt, and Hanspeter Kriesi (eds.) 2015. *The Politics of Advanced Capitalism*. Cambridge: Cambridge University Press.

Blekesaune, Morten, and Jill Quadagno. 2003. "Public Attitudes toward Welfare State Policies: A Comparative Analysis of 24 Nations." *European Sociological Review* 19 (5), 415–427.

Blyth, Mark. 2002. *Great Transformations: Economic Ideas and Institutional Change in the Twentieth Century*. Cambridge: Cambridge University Press.

Bonoli, Giuliano. 2005. "The Politics of the New Social Policies: Providing Coverage Against New Social Risks in Mature Welfare States." *Policy & Politics* 33 (3), 431–449.

Bonoli, Giuliano. 2007. "Time Matters: Postindustrialization, New Social Risks, and Welfare State Adaptation in Advanced Industrial Democracies." *Comparative Political Studies* 40 (5), 495–520.

Brooks, Clem, and Jeff Manza. 2006. "Social Policy Responsiveness in Developed Democracies." *American Sociological Review* 71 (3), 474–494.

Busemeyer, Marius R., Julian L. Garritzmann, and Erik Neimanns. 2020 *A Loud but Noisy Signal? Public Opinion and Education Reform in Western Europe*. Cambridge: Cambridge University Press.

Campbell, John L. 2002. "Ideas, Politics, and Public Policy." *Annual Review of Sociology* 28 (1), 21–38.

Capano, Giliberto. 2009. "Understanding Policy Change as an Epistemological and Theoretical Problem." *Journal of Comparative Policy Analysis: Research and Practice* 11 (1), 7–31.

Chung, Heejung, and Bart Meuleman. 2017. "European Parents' Attitudes Towards Public Childcare Provision: The Role of Current Provisions, Interests and Ideologies." *European Societies* 19 (1), 49–68.

Ciccia, Rossella. 2017. "A Two-Step Approach for the Analysis of Hybrids in Comparative Social Policy Analysis: A Nuanced Typology of Childcare between Policies and Regimes." *Quality & Quantity* 51 (6), 2761–2780.

Ciccia, Rossella, and César Guzman-Concha. 2021. "Protest and Social Policies for Outsiders: The Expansion of Social Pensions in Latin America." *Journal of Social Policy*, 1–22. https://doi.org/10.1017/S0047279421000623.

Clasen, Jochen, and Nico A. Siegel (eds.) 2007. *Investigating Welfare State Change: The Dependent Variable Problem in Comparative Analysis*. Cheltenham: Edward Elgar Publishing.

Ebbinghaus, Bernhard, and Philip Manow. 2004. *Comparing Welfare Capitalism: Social Policy and Political Economy in Europe, Japan and the USA*. London and New York: Routledge.

Ebbinghaus, Bernhard, and Elias Naumann (eds.) 2017. *Welfare State Reforms Seen from Below: Comparing Public Attitudes and Organized Interests in Britain and Germany*. Basingstoke: Palgrave.

Esping-Andersen, Gøsta. 1990. *The Three Worlds of Welfare Capitalism*. Cambridge: Polity Press.

Farnsworth, Kevin, and Zoë Irving (eds.) 2011. S*ocial Policy in Challenging Times: Economic Crisis and Welfare Systems*. Bristol: Policy Press.

Flora, Peter, and Arnold J. Heidenheimer. 1981. *The Development of Welfare States in Europe and America*. New Brunswick, NJ: Transaction Publishers.

Gingrich, Jane R. 2011. *Making Markets in the Welfare State: The Politics of Varying Market Reforms*. Cambridge: Cambridge University Press.

Gingrich, Jane, and Ben Ansell. 2012. "Preferences in Context: Micro Preferences, Macro Contexts, and the Demand for Social Policy." *Comparative Political Studies* 45 (12), 1624–1654.

Gingrich, Jane, and Silja Häusermann. 2015. "The Decline of the Working-Class Vote, the Reconfiguration of the Welfare Support Coalition and Consequences for the Welfare State." *Journal of European Social Policy* 25 (1), 50–75.

Gough, Ian. 1979. *The Political Economy of the Welfare State*. London: Macmillan.

Green-Pedersen, Christoffer. 2001. "Welfare-State Retrenchment in Denmark and the Netherlands, 1982–1998." *Comparative Political Studies* 34 (9), 963–985.

Green-Pedersen, Christoffer. 2004. "The Dependent Variable Problem Within the Study of Welfare State Retrenchment: Defining the Problem and Looking for Solutions." *Journal of Comparative Policy Analysis: Research and Practice* 6 (1), 3–14.

Green-Pedersen, Christoffer, and Markus Haverland. 2002. "Review Essay: The New Politics and Scholarship of the Welfare State." *Journal of European Social Policy* 12 (1), 43–51.

Greve, Bent. 2020. *Austerity, Retrenchment and the Welfare State: Truth or Fiction?* Cheltenham: Edward Elgar Publishing.

Greve, Bent (ed.) 2021. *Handbook on Austerity, Populism and the Welfare State*. Cheltenham: Edward Elgar Publishing.

Hacker, Jacob S., and Paul Pierson. 2019. "Policy Feedback in an Age of Polarization." *The ANNALS of the American Academy of Political and Social Science* 685 (1), 8–28.

Hall, Peter A. 1989. *The Political Power of Economic Ideas*. Princeton, NJ: Princeton University Press.

Hall, Peter A., and David Soskice. 2001. V*arieties of Capitalism: The Institutional Basis of Competitive Advantage*. Oxford: Oxford University Press.

Häusermann, Silja. 2010. *The Politics of Welfare State Reform in Continental Europe: Modernization in Hard Times*. Cambridge: Cambridge University Press.

Häusermann, Silja, and Hanspeter Kriesi. 2015. "What Do Voters Want? Dimensions and Configurations in Individual-level Preferences and Party Choice." In *The Politics of Advanced Capitalism*, edited by Pablo Beramendi, Silja Häusermann, Herbert Kitschelt, and Hanspeter Kriesi, 202–230. Cambridge: Cambridge University Press.

Häusermann, Silja, Georg Picot, and Dominik Geering. 2013. "Review Article: Rethinking Party Politics and the Welfare State – Recent Advances in the Literature." *British Journal of Political Science* 43 (1), 221–240.

Heclo, Hugh. 1974. *Modern Social Politics in Britain and Sweden*. New Haven, CT: Yale University Press.

Hinrichs, Karl. 2000. "Elephants on the Move. Patterns of Public Pension Reform in OECD Countries." *European Review* 8 (3), 353–378.

Huber, Evelyne, and John D. Stephens. 2001. *Development and Crisis of the Welfare State: Parties and Policies in Global Markets*. Chicago: University of Chicago Press.

Immergut, Ellen M. 1992. *Health Politics: Interests and Institutions in Western Europe*. Cambridge: Cambridge University Press.

Immergut, Ellen M. 2006. "Institutional Constraints on Policy." In *The Oxford Handbook of Public Policy*, edited by Robert E. Goodin, Michael Moran, and Martin Rein, 557–571. Oxford: Oxford University Press.

Immergut, Ellen M. 2010. "Political Institutions." In *The Oxford Handbook of the Welfare State*, edited by Francis G. Castles, Stephan Leibfried, Jane Lewis, Herbert Obinger, and Christopher Pierson, 227–240. Oxford: Oxford University Press.

Jensen, Carsten. 2014. *The Right and the Welfare State*. Oxford: Oxford University Press.

Jensen, Carsten, Christoph Arndt, Seonghui Lee, and Georg Wenzelburger. 2018. "Policy Instruments and Welfare State Reform." *Journal of European Social Policy* 28 (2), 161–176.

Jensen, Carsten, Georg Wenzelburger, and Reimut Zohlnhöfer. 2019. "Dismantling the Welfare State? After Twenty-Five Years: What Have We Learned and What Should We Learn?" *Journal of European Social Policy* 29 (5), 681–691.

Jenson, Jane. 2009. "Lost in Translation: The Social Investment Perspective and Gender Equality." *Social Politics: International Studies in Gender, State & Society* 16 (4), 446–483.

Kangas, Olli E. 1997. "Self-Interest and the Common Good: The Impact of Norms, Selfishness and Context in Social Policy Opinions." *The Journal of Socio-Economics* 26 (5), 475–494.

Kenworthy, Lane, and Leslie McCall. 2008. "Inequality, Public Opinion and Redistribution." *Socio-Economic Review* 6 (1), 35–68.

Kersbergen, Kees van. 1995. *Social Capitalism: A Study of Christian Democracy and the Welfare State*. London: Routledge.

Kersbergen, Kees van, and Barbara Vis. 2014. *Comparative Welfare State Politics*. New York: Cambridge University Press.

Kitschelt, Herbert. 2000. "Linkages Between Citizens and Politicians in Democratic Polities." *Comparative Political Studies* 33 (6–7), 845–879.

Kitschelt, Herbert, and Philipp Rehm. 2015. "Party Alignments: Change and Continuity." In *The Politics of Advanced Capitalism*, edited by Pablo Beramendi, Silja Häusermann, Herbert Kitschelt, and Hanspeter Kriesi, 179–201. Cambridge: Cambridge University Press.

Kittel, Bernhard, and Herbert Obinger. 2003. "Political Parties, Institutions, and the Dynamics of Social Expenditure in Times of Austerity." *Journal of European Public Policy* 10 (1), 20–45.

Korpi, Walter. 1983. *The Democratic Class Struggle*. London: Routledge.

Korpi, Walter, and Joakim Palme. 2003. "New Politics and Class Politics in the Context of Austerity and Globalization: Welfare State Regress in 18 Countries, 1975–95." *American Political Science Review* 97 (3), 425–446.

Kriesi, Hanspeter, Jasmine Lorenzini, Bruno Wüest, and Silja Häusermann (eds.) 2020. *Contention in Times of Crisis: Recession and Political Protest in Thirty European Countries*. Cambridge: Cambridge University Press.

Kühner, Stefan. 2007. "Country-Level Comparisons of Welfare State Change Measures: Another Facet of the Dependent Variable Problem Within the Comparative Analysis of the Welfare State?" *Journal of European Social Policy* 17 (1), 5–18.

Kumlin, Staffan, and Isabelle Stadelmann-Steffen (eds.) 2014. *How Welfare States Shape the Democratic Public: Policy Feedback, Participation, Voting, and Attitudes*. Cheltenham: Edward Elgar Publishing.

Larsen, Christian A. 2008. "The Institutional Logic of Welfare Attitudes: How Welfare Regimes Influence Public Support." *Comparative Political Studies* 41 (2), 145–168.

Lupu, Noam, and Jonas Pontusson. 2011. "The Structure of Inequality and the Politics of Redistribution." *American Political Science Review* 105 (2), 316–336.

Mares, Isabela. 2003. *The Politics of Social Risk: Business and Welfare State Development*. Cambridge: Cambridge University Press.

Marshall, T. H. 1950. *Citizenship and Social Class*. Cambridge: Cambridge University Press.

Martin, Cathie Jo, and Duane Swank. 2012. *The Political Construction of Business Interests: Coordination, Growth, and Equality*. Cambridge: Cambridge University Press.

Mau, Steffen. 2004. *The Moral Economy of Welfare States: Britain and Germany Compared*. London: Routledge.

Morgan, Kimberly J. 2013. "Path Shifting of the Welfare State: Electoral Competition and the Expansion of Work-Family Policies in Western Europe." *World Politics* 65 (1), 73–115.

Myles, John, and Jill Quadagno. 2002. "Political Theories of the Welfare State." *Social Service Review* 76 (1), 34–57.

Naczyk, Marek. 2013. "Agents of Privatization? Business Groups and the Rise of Pension Funds in Continental Europe." *Socio-Economic Review* 11 (3), 441–469.

Oesch, Daniel. 2008. "Explaining Workers' Support for Right-Wing Populist Parties in Western Europe: Evidence from Austria, Belgium, France, Norway, and Switzerland." *International Political Science Review* 29 (3), 349–373.

Offe, Claus. 1984. *Contradictions of the Welfare State*. Cambridge, MA: MIT Press.

Oorschot, W. van. 2000. "Who Should Get What, and Why? On Deservingness Criteria and the Conditionality of Solidarity Among the Public." *Policy & Politics* 28 (1), 33–48.

Orloff, Ann S. 1993. *The Politics of Pensions: A Comparative Analysis of Britain, Canada, and the United States, 1880–1940*. Madison, WI: University of Wisconsin Press.

Orloff, Ann S. and Theda Skocpol. 1984. "Why Not Equal Protection? Explaining the Politics of Public Social Spending in Britain, 1900–1911, and the United States, 1880s–1920." *American Sociological Review* 49 (6), 726–750.

Palier, Bruno (ed.) 2010. *A Long Goodbye to Bismarck? The Politics of Welfare Reforms in Continental Europe*. Amsterdam: Amsterdam University Press.

Pierson, Christopher. 1991. *Beyond the Welfare State? The New Political Economy of Welfare*. Cambridge: Polity Press.

Pierson, Paul. 1993. "When Effect Becomes Cause: Policy Feedback and Political Change." *World Politics* 45 (4), 595–628.

Pierson, Paul. 1996. "The New Politics of the Welfare State." *World Politics* 48 (2) 143–179.

Pierson, Paul. 2001. *The New Politics of the Welfare State*. Oxford: Oxford University Press on Demand.

Piven, Frances F., and Richard Cloward. 1979. *Poor People's Movements: Why They Succeed, How They Fail*. New York: Vintage.

Quadagno, Jill. 1992. "Social Movements and State Transformation: Labor Unions and Racial Conflict in the War on Poverty." *American Sociological Review* 57 (5), 616–634.

Rehm, Philipp. 2016. *Risk Inequality and Welfare States: Social Policy Preferences, Development, and Dynamics*. Cambridge: Cambridge University Press.

Rothstein, Bo. 1998. *Just Institutions Matter: The Moral and Political Logic of the Universal Welfare State*. Cambridge: Cambridge University Press.

Sachweh, Patrick. 2019. "Crisis Experiences and Welfare Attitudes During the Great Recession: A Comparative Study on the UK, Germany and Sweden." *Acta Sociologica* 62 (2), 135–151.

Sainsbury, Diane. 1999. *Gender and Welfare State Regimes*. Oxford: Oxford University Press.

Schmidt, Vivien A., and Mark Thatcher (eds.) 2013. *Resilient Liberalism in Europe's Political Economy*. Cambridge: Cambridge University Press.

Skocpol, Theda. 1985. "Bringing the State Back In: Strategies of Analysis in Current Research." In *Bringing the State Back In*, edited by Dietrich Rueschemeyer, Peter B. Evans, and Theda Skocpol, 3–38. Cambridge: Cambridge University Press.

Skocpol, Theda. 1992. *Protecting Soldiers and Mothers: The Political Origins of Social Policy in the United States*. Cambridge, MA: Harvard University Press.

Skocpol, Theda, and Edwin Amenta. 1986. "States and Social Policies." *Annual Review of Sociology* 12 (1), 131–157.

Starke, Peter. 2021. "Handbook on Austerity, Retrenchment and the Welfare State." In *The Politics of Retrenchment*, edited by Bent Greve, 25–40. Cheltenham, UK and Northampton, MA: Edward Elgar.

Starke, Peter, Alexandra Kaasch, and Franca van Hooren. 2014. "Political Parties and Social Policy Responses to Global Economic Crises: Constrained Partisanship in Mature Welfare States." *Journal of Social Policy* 43 (2), 225–246.

Steinmo, Sven. (1993) *Taxation and Democracy: Swedish, British and American Approaches to Financing the Modern State*. New Haven, CT: Yale University Press.

Streeck, Wolfgang, and Kathleen Thelen (eds.) 2005. *Beyond Continuity: Institutional Change in Advanced Political Economies*. Oxford: Oxford University Press.

Svallfors, Stefan. 1997. "Worlds of Welfare and Attitudes to Redistribution: A Comparison of Eight Western Nations." *European Sociological Review* 13 (3), 283–304.

Swank, Duane. 2002. *Global Capital, Political Institutions, and Policy Change in Developed Welfare States*. Cambridge: Cambridge University Press.

Swenson, Peter. 1997. "Arranged Alliance: Business Interests in the New Deal." *Politics & Society* 25 (1), 66–116.

Taylor-Gooby, Peter. 1985. "Attitudes to Welfare." *Journal of Social Policy* 14 (1), 73–81.

Taylor-Gooby, Peter, ed. (2004) *New Risks, New Welfare: The Transformation of the European Welfare State*. Oxford: Oxford University Press.

Taylor-Gooby, Peter, Jan-Ocko Heuer, Heejung Chung, Benjamin Leruth, Steffen Mau, and Katharina Zimmermann. 2020. "Regimes, Social Risks and the Welfare Mix: Unpacking Attitudes to Pensions and Childcare in Germany and the UK Through Deliberative Forums." *Journal of Social Policy* 49 (1), 61–79.

Thelen, Kathleen. 2004. *How Institutions Evolve: The Political Economy of Skills in Germany, Britain, the United States, and Japan*. Cambridge: Cambridge University Press.

Vis, Barbara. 2016. "Taking Stock of the Comparative Literature on the Role of Blame Avoidance Strategies in Social Policy Reform." *Journal of Comparative Policy Analysis: Research and Practice* 18 (2), 122–137.

Vlandas, Tim. 2021. "The Political Economy of Individual-Level Support for the Basic Income in Europe." *Journal of European Social Policy* 31 (1), 62–77.

Weir, Margaret, and Theda Skocpol. 1985. "State Structures and the Possibilities for 'Keynesian' Responses to the Great Depression in Sweden, Britain, and the United States." In *Bringing the State Back In*, edited by Peter Evans, Dietrich Rueschemeyer, and Theda Skocpol, 107–164. Cambridge: Cambridge University Press.

Wilensky, Harold L. 1975. *The Welfare State and Equality: Structural and Ideological Roots of Public Expenditures*. Berkeley and Los Angeles, CA: University of California Press.

Wincott, Daniel. 2013. "The (Golden) Age of the Welfare State: Interrogating a Conventional Wisdom." *Public Administration* 91 (4), 806–822.

Niklas Andreas Andersen and Katherine Smith

3 Evidence-Based Policy-Making

Abstract: The idea that public policies might usefully be improved by evidence (or, more strongly put, that policies ought to be evidence-based) is long-standing. However, official commitments to "Evidence-Based Policy-Making" (EBPM) are more recent, dating back to policy developments in the US and the UK in the 1990s. Since then, a vast research literature on EBPM has emerged. However, due to the rather fragmented nature of this literature and a general lack of cross-fertilisation, a number of fundamental questions remain unresolved. Questions about what constitutes "evidence"; what role evidence can and should play in policymaking processes and how the quest for EBPM affects the democratic legitimacy of policy-making.

In the current chapter, we do not attempt to resolve these questions, but we argue that a first step is to further more comparative analysis on whether, how and why EBPM is playing out differently in contrasting geo-political contexts. The chapter thus briefly outlines how ideas and practices relating to EBPM have evolved in two different groups of welfare states: first, liberal welfare states, including the UK and the US, in which the idea of evidence-based policy has its philosophical foundations; and, second, the Nordic/social democratic welfare states, some of the earliest adopters and translators of the idea.

The chapter concludes by highlighting the need for moving beyond an unattainable search for universally applicable mechanisms to increase evidence use, towards more complex and context specific understandings of how states can improve their approaches to using evidence, with a view to both improving policy outcomes *and* enhancing the democratic legitimacy of policymaking.

Keywords: Evidence-Based Policy-Making, welfare regimes, knowledge utilization, democratic legitimacy

3.1 Introduction – what is Evidence-Based Policy-Making?

The idea that knowledge (rather than opinions, values or power) should be the primary basis of policymaking has been continually resurfacing since the inception of the State itself – from Plato's "philosopher kings" (Plato 2007) to Henri de Saint-Simon's nineteenth-century notion of the "administrative state" (Saint-Simon 1964). In the twentieth century, this idea played a key part in the technocratic ideals of post-war policymaking in the USA (Fischer 1990). In recent decades, this idea has again gained traction via the concept of Evidence-Based Policy-Making (EBPM). Since the 1990s, we have witnessed:

https://doi.org/10.1515/9783110721768-003

- The proliferation of an international evidence-use movement (Hansen and Rieper 2009);
- An increasing promotion of political reforms under the heading of Evidence-Based Policy (EBP); and
- The emergence of a whole new research-field exploring the interplay between evidence and policy, including new academic journals (e.g. *Evidence and Policy* and *Implementation Science*).

These developments are all testament to the fact that EBPM, as an idea, has broad appeal and few opponents (Davey Smith, Ebrahim, and Frankel 2001). Although there were examples of governments distancing themselves from claims to be "evidence-based" in the first two decades of the twenty-first century (see, for example, Wells 2018), the COVID-19 pandemic has firmly resurrected the notion that policies are best led by science (e.g. Sasse, Haddon, and Nice 2020). As well as sounding reassuring in a crisis, part of the appeal of EBPM is perhaps its lack of clarity; the majority of relevant literature, whether it is promoting (e.g. Bogenschneider and Corbett 2010), criticising (e.g. Greenhalgh and Russell 2009) or describing (Nutley et al. 2019) EBPM, does not provide a definition beyond the commonsensical goal of enhancing evidence use in policymaking. There are, of course, exceptions, such as the following, slightly more detailed definition that: "objective knowledge from scientific research including rigorous evaluation studies should occupy a central place in policy decision making" (Head 2015). However, here, three pivotal questions remain unanswered:

1) What is "objective knowledge from scientific research" (i.e. what counts as "evidence")?;
2) What does it mean to "occupy a central place in policy decision making" (i.e. how do we define a policymaking process as evidence-*based*)? and
3) How does EBPM relate to the democratic legitimacy of political decision-making?

These three questions remain at the centre of debates around EBPM. Key proponents have borrowed heavily from the terminology of Evidence-Based Medicine, implying a conception of evidence as a form of knowledge concerning the effectiveness of interventions (ideally derived from Randomised Controlled Trials – RCTs); a definition which retains some dominance (e.g. Haynes et al. 2012. The following extract, from a report by the Behavioural Insights Team within the UK Government, is illustrative of this:

> Randomised controlled trials (RCTs) are the best way of determining whether a policy is working. They are now used extensively in international development, medicine, and business to identify which policy, drug or sales method is most effective. [...] However, RCTs are not routinely used to test the effectiveness of public policy interventions in the UK. We think that they should be. (Haynes et al. 2012, 4)

However, this rather narrow, positivist conceptualisation of evidence has sparked a large, critical literature arguing for a much broader range of research-based and non research-based knowledge to be considered as "evidence" (Parkhurst and Abey-singhe 2016; Stanhope and Dunn 2011). For example, in 2018, Deaton and Cartwright wrote a seminal article arguing that the value of RCTs was more limited than many acknowledged, concluding that "RCTs can play a role in building scientific knowledge and useful predictions but they can only do so as part of a cumulative program, combining with other methods, including conceptual and theoretical development, to discover not 'what works', but 'why things work'" (Deaton and Cartwright 2018, 2). Their article is not critical of RCTs *per se* but of what the authors call "magical thinking" about the power of RCTs, arguing that, in reality: "What methods are best to use and in what combinations depends on the exact question at stake, the kind of background assumptions that can be acceptably employed, and what the costs are of different kinds of mistakes' (Deaton and Cartwright 2018, 33). Using similar reasoning, Trish Greenhalgh has cautioned that efforts to adhere to a model of EBPM that employs an overly narrow hierarchy of evidence may risk undermining responses to COVID-19: "where the cost of inaction is counted in the grim mortality figures announced daily, implementing new policy interventions in the absence of randomised trial evidence has become both a scientific and moral imperative" (Greenhalgh 2020, unpaginated).

Similar differences are prevalent around the second question of what it means for policymaking processes to be evidence-based. Much of the EBPM literature suggests the evidence-agenda was born from an optimistic, idealised notion of policymaking (Cairney 2019). This was perhaps most famously articulated by Campbell's (1969) call to treat policy "*reforms as experiments*", that is policymakers should merely choose the ends (i.e. the societal problems they wish to solve), then let researchers design and test the means (i.e. the specific programs and interventions to solve the problems). Although few EBPM proponents have advanced quite such a bold proposal, much of the founding literature shares an understanding of EBPM as a rational and linear process that involves testing different interventions and adopting the most effective. This understanding has been criticised from both an empirical and a normative perspective (Botterill and Hindmoor 2012; Newman 2017; Sanderson 2009). Empirically, idealised notions of EBPM have been repeatedly criticised for setting the bar so high that any analysis of real-life policymaking will inevitably find policies are *not* evidence-based. Normatively, even if policymaking could feasibly be evidence-based, some note that the approach is not necessarily desirable since policymaking has to balance other legitimate concerns, not all of which can be answered with evidence (e.g. Stewart et al. 2020). In response, there have been shifts towards broader, more realistic framings of the role of evidence in policymaking, often signaled via a terminological change from evidence-*based* to evidence-*informed* (Nutley et al. 2019).

Linked to this is the third question; how EBPM relates to the legitimacy of democratic engagement in political decision-making (whether via voting in elections, responding to consultation or proactive advocacy and protest). As Geoff Mulgan (former advisor to Tony Blair, UK Prime Minister 1997–2007) argues, in democratically elected countries, "the people, and the politicians who represent them, have every right to ignore evidence" (Mulgan 2005, 224). A recent special issue of the journal *Evidence and Policy* exploring this issue argues that "there remain clear and pressing tensions between commitments to EBP, and the need for citizen engagement with those policies" (Stewart et al. 2020, 199; see also Saltelli and Giampietro 2017).

In this chapter, we do not propose any definite answers to these three questions, since our interest is in understanding how the idea of EBPM has played out over time, across distinct welfare contexts in this increasingly varied field. Instead, we elucidate some of the differing perspectives on, and experiences of, EBPM in ways that highlight contextual distinctions over time and between different types of welfare states. We argue that the field has generally moved towards a more inclusive understanding of evidence and a less stringent approach to conceptualising what research use in policy settings can (and ought, ideally, to) look like. However, more positivist and instrumental understandings of EBPM have not disappeared and debates about the democratic legitimacy of EBPM continue to shape the field.

These discussions remain especially relevant in our current situation. The last decade has seen the global rise of populism and so-called "post-truth politics", which some scholars see as a direct response and opposition to a hitherto dominant technocratic rationality of governments (Esmark 2020; Mudde and Kaltwasser 2017). As part of this, we have repeatedly witnessed the implementation of policies which appear to go against prevailing evidence (e.g. the austerity policies implemented across Europe, following the financial crash of 2008, involved substantially reducing welfare spending, despite evidence highlighting the likelihood that this would lead to negative population impacts – Quaglio et al. 2013). And while the current COVID-19 pandemic has illustrated the need for high-quality evidence in policymaking, it has also highlighted many of the persistent challenges related to EBPM (e.g. the often inconclusive nature of evidence and the tension between the need for swift political action and the time-consuming process of producing high-quality, scientifically robust evidence – Greenhalgh 2020).

3.2 Key ideas within the EBPM literature

Years before the mantra of EBPM was adopted by policymakers in the UK, Australia, Canada and elsewhere (Cabinet Office 1999; Cabinet Office 2000; Canadian Academy of Health Sciences 2009; Rudd 2008), policymakers in the USA (and, to a degree, the UK) were experimenting with efforts to improve the utilisation of research in policy (Weiss 1977). These earlier efforts to achieve research-informed policy stimulated a large literature exploring the relationship between science and policy (e.g. Blume 1977; Bulmer 1982; Caplan 1979; Weiss 1977; 1979; 1982). Many of the ideas put forth by this literature would later be repeated in the new field of EBPM (often without direct references to this older literature, as the early proponents of EBPM seemed more occupied with the field of Evidence-Based Medicine than the substantial research- and evaluation-utilisation literature within the social sciences). The ideas in these various models are summarised in Figure 3.1.

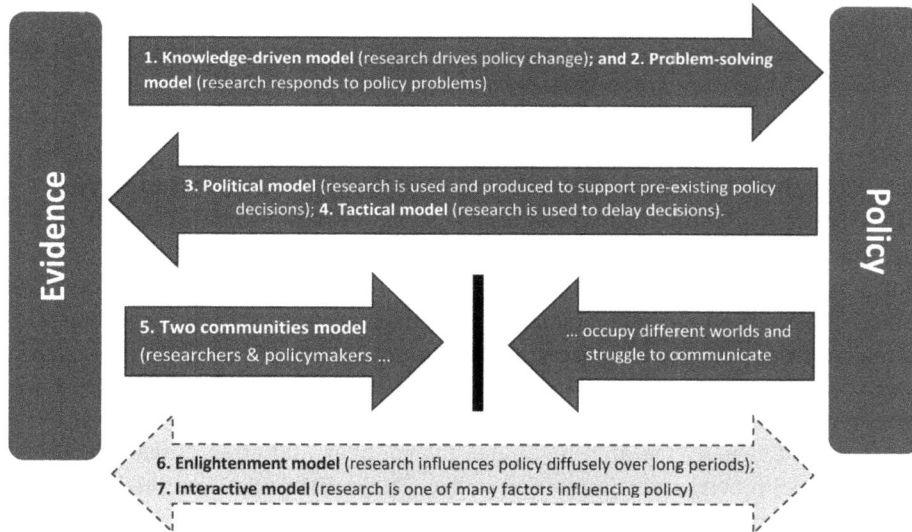

Figure 3.1: Visual summary of early models of the relationship between evidence and policy.

Models 1 and 2 summarise the simplest way of thinking about the relationship between evidence and policy, depicting a direct, linear connection in which evidence either drives policy change (the "knowledge-driven model"), or provides direct solutions to policy problems (Davies, Nutley, and Smith 2000; Weiss 1979). In both cases, knowledge is utilised by policymakers in an "instrumental" manner (Knorr 1977; Weiss 1980). Although there have been occasional examples of research feeding into policy in this manner, such simple models have been consistently discredited for failing to capture the intricacies and complexities of the actual relationship between evidence and policy (see Nutley and Davies 2000; Nutley, Walter, and Davies 2007). Nevertheless, these models were implied by some of the first proponents of EBPM and continue to serve as an ideal within parts of the literature.

The other five models in Figure 3.1 are linked by suggesting that policymakers rarely utilise research in the direct, instrumental depiction in models 1 and 2. The "political" model, for example, highlights the dominance of political values and ideologies within policy. From this perspective, research is only likely to play a role in policy if it is consistent with dominant political perspectives or agendas. The "tactical model" suggests a similarly symbolic approach to evidence in which policymakers encourage/fund research activity with the aim of delaying awkward decisions or distracting attention (Davies, Nutley, and Smith 2000).

Model 5, developed by Caplan in 1979, represents a more structural (less political) approach to explaining the difficulties in achieving evidence-based policy. Here, a key barrier to using evidence in policy is the cultural gap between researchers (the "producers") and policymakers (the "users"). Whilst not always referring to Caplan's (1979) work directly, many contemporary assessments of the limited use of research in policy and practice mirror Caplan's observations and promote solutions involving bringing the "two communities" closer together.

The final two models imply the influence of research on policy is necessarily looser and more limited than Models 1 or 2. Model 6 captures Weiss's (1977) account of the "enlightenment" function of research in policy, which involves research achieving diffuse conceptual (rather than direct instrumental) influence. In this model, bodies of research gradually change the way actors think about particular issues, over long periods. Finally, model 7 tries to reflect Donnison's (1972) account of policymaking processes as highly chaotic and complex, with policymakers seeking (and receiving) information from a variety of sources, including practitioners, journalists and interest groups, as well as academic researchers. In this model, research ideas travel back and forth between a variety of groups, transforming over time, often unpredictably.

Overall, this early research highlights the complex and often difficult nature of the relationship between research and policy. These difficulties informed questions among researchers and policymakers about the viability of using academic research in policy during the 1970s–1980s.

3.2.1 Current debates on EPBM – Old wine in new bottles?

The emergence of EBPM as a policy idea during the 1990s prompted a renewed academic interest in the relationship between research and policy (e.g. Black 2001; Burrows and Bradshaw 2001; Nutley, Walter and Davies 2007; Sanderson 2009; Young et al. 2002). Perhaps unsurprisingly, given Miller's (1980) assessment that there is a capacity within academia to be continually "re-inventing the broken wheel", this new body of work did not always appear to build directly on the earlier academic work. Rather, much of this literature implied an idealised version of models 1 and 2, in which research could (and should) produce utilisable grounds for policy decisions (e.g. Macintyre et al. 2001; Young et al. 2002). This led Parsons to argue that the commitment to EBPM marked:

> not so much a step forward as a step backwards: a return to the quest for a positivist yellow brick road leading to a promised policy dry ground – somewhere, over Charles Lindblom – where we can know 'what works' and from which government can exercise strategic guidance. (Parsons 2002, 45)

Perhaps unsurprisingly, given the complexities highlighted in earlier work, empirical assessments of the extent to which policies reflected available evidence found highly selective use of evidence, despite commitments to EBPM (e.g. Katikireddi et al. 2011; Naughton 2005). Academic activity once again sought to explain the persistent disjuncture between research and policy, reintroducing more complex accounts of this relationship. This included drawing attention to Weiss' (1977, 1979) arguments about the "enlightenment" function of research (e.g. Hird 2005; Petticrew et al. 2004; Young et al. 2002) and developing new, related ideas (e.g. Radaelli's 1995 concept of "knowledge creep").

For others, however, Caplan's (1979) account of "two communities" appears to have been more appealing, with various contemporary assessments of the limited use of research in policy focusing on a need to overcome institutional and cultural "gaps" between researchers and policymakers (e.g. Lomas 2000; Wimbush et al. 2005). This has informed arguments for work to achieve shared understandings, and increase interaction, between researchers and policymakers (e.g. Lomas 2000; Lavis 2006). The idea here appears to be that research would be more frequently employed by policymakers if only they could better access and understand it (and if researchers produced more relevant, responsive research). These approaches also stress the need to improve mechanisms of communication and levels of trust between researchers and policymakers.

Several reviews of knowledge transfer studies attempt to synthesise what we know about research use in policy (Innvær et al. 2002; Mitton et al. 2007; Nutley, Walter, and Davies 2007). These reviews highlight challenges around the accessibility and timeliness of research, a lack of policy incentives to use research, and a lack of understanding and trust between researchers and policymakers. Their recommendations tend to focus on mechanisms for *increasing* the chances that particular research projects will be employed by policymakers, which is distinct from trying to *improve* the quality of the research used in policymaking (which might involve mechanisms to *limit* the influence of poorer quality or less relevant research). Interestingly, only two of the reviews suggest the *quality* of the research was important for enhancing policy impact (Innvær et al. 2002; Nutley, Walter, and Davies 2007). The recommendations in many of these reviews are remarkably similar to those reviewed by Weiss in 1990:

> Most advice to policy researchers over the years has been geared towards that ubiquitous benevolent despot, the decision maker. Homilies have poured forth: identify the key decision maker; talk to her/him in person; be sure that research addresses the questions he/she raises; involve her/him in the research process; communicate results early and often; write in simple words and short summaries; be sure the results and the recommendations drawn from them are feasible within the constraints of the institutional system; be aware of the problems that may occur in implementing the recommendations and help the decision maker foresee and avoid them. And so on. Policy researchers have been repeatedly lectured to make themselves and their findings 'user friendly' to the decision maker. (Weiss 1990, 98)

This raises questions about the progress of scholarship in this area. Moreover, Weiss (1990) was already critical, concluding that such advice "has not worked very well", partly because research alone "is almost never convincing or comprehensive enough to be the sole source of policy advice" and partly because, "there are always issues that research doesn't cover". We add three further critiques of much of the recent scholarship on evidence and policy. First, policymakers and researchers each tend to be depicted as relatively homogenous groups. This seems questionable when there are so many accounts of the fractured and disjointed (even acrimonious) nature of re-lations *within* both academic research and policy (e.g. Bartley 1992; Gieryn 1983; Kava-nagh and Richards 2001). Second, it often appears to be assumed that it is possible for research to respond directly to policymakers' questions and concerns, despite chal-lenges to this idea (e.g. Petticrew et al. 2004; Whitehead et al. 2004). Third, such ap-proaches often fail to acknowledge the ideologies and interests shaping both policy and research (Rein 1980), which mean policymakers and researchers might disagree on the very issues that warrant research or on which methodologies provide valuable insights (Hammersley 2003).

These limitations help explain why the three fundamental questions presented in the introduction remain unresolved. Academic research is often fractured into distinct "camps" with widely diverging views on what constitutes "good research" (e.g. Col-lyer and Smith 2020) which makes it impossible to agree what constitutes evidence in EBPM. If research is unable to directly answer complex policy-questions with much certainty, how far should we go in efforts to ensure policies are evidence-*based*? And if research agendas are shaped by ideologies and interests, should we afford non-elected researchers more influence on policies than elected politicians or the general public? These questions challenge the dominant assumption within a great deal of the EBPM scholarship; that use of evidence in policy is *a priori* positive and so should be actively pursued. Instead, we argue for the need to better understand the contextual, divergent and contingent nature of evidence-use with a view to improving the role of research in policymaking (rather than simply increasing the research reaching policy discussions). A first step is to consider how the very idea of EBPM differs between countries.

3.3 Current/future challenges and promises of EBP in the development of welfare states

3.3.1 Comparing EBPM across welfare state regime types

Given the almost commonsensical nature of the idea of EBPM, it is unsurprising that the idea has proliferated across welfare states in the last two decades. However, when looking at the elusiveness of the concept and our unanswered questions, it is perhaps less obvious that the idea should fare equally well across diverse welfare settings. Here, we compare the international reach and divergence of EBPM as an idea in liberal welfare regimes (focusing on the US and UK) and social democratic welfare regimes (focusing on Norway, Denmark and Sweden (Esping-Andersen, 1991)). In some ways, the US, UK and the three Scandinavian countries can all be considered frontrunners in the uptake of ideas, methods and organisations associated with EBPM, albeit in different ways. The US was, and remains, the dominant exponent of the ideal of systematically evaluating policy programs through experimental or quasi-experimental methods. The New Labour government in the UK was the earliest example of a government actively promoting and formally labelling its own approach as "evidence-based policymaking", while the Scandinavian countries were the first to form their own national or regional variants of emerging international collaborations of evidence-producing organisations.

However, different patterns seem to emerge if we look beyond the initial uptake of the idea of EBPM and instead focus on the subsequent promotion and reception of the ideas. Indeed, there seems to be a marked difference between the liberal welfare states and the social democratic welfare states concerning whether and how politicians promote the idea of EPBM. The UK, especially under New Labour governments (1997–2010), were perhaps the most explicit of any administration in using the EBPM terminology, while the US has arguably been most active in promoting the central tenets of a positivist vision of EBPM (i.e. basing policies on rigorous quantitative evidence) via legislation. Although we can identify an original impetus with the Clinton administrations of the 1990s, this focus has persisted, even continuing under the recent Trump administration via the signing of the Foundations for Evidence-Based Policymaking Act. Of course the specific approaches of the Blair- and the Clinton-led administrations have to be understood in the context of the post-ideological political climate of the 1990s, where many centre-left governments tried to reinvent themselves as less socialist/social democratic and more rational and pragmatic. However, the comparison with the Scandinavian countries also suggests that the active promotion of EBPM by politicians is at least partly informed by other factors. In Scandinavian contexts, politicians have generally been much less vocal in their support of EBPM and the promotion of EBPM here has often been driven more by research institutes and other evidence-producing organisations than by policymakers. Even when some Scandinavian governments began to adopt EBPM ideas, this was often driven more by civil servants in the central administration than by elected politicians. This suggests a difference in political culture between the liberal and the social democratic welfare states, with the public support for policies in Scandinavian countries perhaps being less dependent on the idea they are "evidence-based". Indeed, in 2016, evaluation researcher, Evert Vedung, argued that "the evidence-wave will soon recede" in Nordic contexts, since he felt "the evidence-wave does not fit well with the Nordic administrative culture, which is built on dialogue, argumentation, deliberation and participation" (Vedung 2016 – Author's own translation). The findings of recent studies on the evidence movement in Scandinavia supports Vedung's prediction (Elvbakken and Hansen 2019; Møller 2017; Møller, Elvbakken, and Hansen 2019), finding that evidence-producing organisations became less influential in Scandinavia over the past decade. Alongside this, the notion of evidence has been broadened to include the knowledge of frontline professionals, such as social workers and school-teachers. Prior to the pandemic, a study of the evidence-agenda in the field of social policy in Denmark even suggests that so many negative connotations have been attributed to the term "evidence" that the Ministry of Social Affairs no longer uses this term in official communications (Møller 2017).

There are also important differences when looking at the implementation and reception of the idea of EBPM, both within and among the regime clusters. In the US, we see some of the foundations of EBPM (notably policy initiatives being designed and rolled out to facilitate rigorous quantitative assessment via RCTs and cost-benefit analyses) having been implemented ahead of the conception of EBPM as a term. In both the UK and Scandinavia, this way of making policies evaluable remains much less prevalent even now, despite official commitment to EBPM. This difference is likely to relate to divergent research traditions as well as different ideas around both what constitutes welfare policies and what "good" policymaking involves. The dominance of quantitative methods and a (neo)positivist approach is much more prevalent in the social sciences of the US than in the UK or Scandinavia, suggesting some of the differences between the US and elsewhere may be explained by cultural-disciplinary differences in research. At the same time, the time-limited, targeted nature of many US welfare policies, and the emphasis on achieving specific behavioural changes, also makes American welfare policies much more amenable to RCTs and cost-benefit analyses. Such experimental methods are more difficult to apply to the universal and rights-based nature of many welfare policies in social democratic welfare states, where the intended outcomes are often broader. The similarities between the Scandinavian countries and the UK here underline challenges around placing this country firmly within the liberal welfare states regime type (see also Bambra 2005).

Looking at the reception and, especially, critiques of EBPM, there are notable differences regarding *who* the opponents are and *what* their critique is based on and, here, the differences do appear to align with the welfare regime categorisation of the US and UK as liberal, and Denmark, Norway and Sweden as social democratic. In these liberal welfare states, critique seems to come mainly from within the research-community and the basis of this critique is often centred on the narrow notion of evidence and the simplified understanding of the research-policy relationship (cf. question 1 and 2 of the introduction). In Scandinavian contexts, there has been much outspoken critique of EBPM and this has come not only from researchers but also (indeed, largely) from the welfare professions (teachers, social workers etc.). Here, as the quotation from Evert Vedung (see above) highlights, critiques are not only about the nature of evidence and policymaking, but also the democratic legitimacy of EBPM. In these social democratic welfare regimes, EBPM has not only been criticised for bypassing the chain of accountability in a representative democracy but, more importantly, for neglecting the importance of deliberation and participation from non-experts.

This difference in the nature of the critique of EBPM may also help explain the difference among the countries regarding the current promotion of this idea. The UK and the US remain the most vocal official supporters of EBPM (despite direct challenges to the research claims of experts in both contexts prior to the COVID-19 pandemic and, in the US, prior to the election of President Biden). In the US, the norm of using a narrow set of experimental and quantitative methods to assess policy-interventions seem so ingrained in the political institutions that it is seldom debated, which perhaps explains why President Trump, who was often portrayed as an opponent to scientific research (Sharfstein 2017), nonetheless signed the Foundations for Evidence-Based Policymaking Act. In Scandinavia on the other hand, the term "evidence-based" is often used less openly by politicians – perhaps unsurprisingly given the critical reception of the idea by many public employees (see above). Instead, the evidence-based knowledge is increasingly inscribed into governance arrangements in ways that promote EBPM ideas as technical tools, less open to public scrutiny (Andersen 2021).

There are, of course, several caveats to the comparison sketched out in this chapter. First, we have only focused on two welfare regime types (and just five countries within these). Second, the scope of this chapter only allows for a very general comparison. To determine if there are systematic differences in the uptake of EBPM across welfare regime-types necessitates both the inclusion of countries from other regime-types as well as more in-depth, comparative analysis of the different cases (analysis which is currently lacking in the scholarship on evidence and policy). Finally, we are cautious as to whether regime-typology is a sensible starting point for comparing EBPM across countries. Since Esping-Andersen's seminal work, many researchers have criticised the typology for simplistically downplaying differences within regime-types (see, for example Emmenegger et al. 2015; Powell, Yörük, and Bargu 2020). A few countries (such as the US and Sweden) are widely accepted as ideal typical examples of specific regime-types but many others (including the UK) are harder to place. Moreover, our analysis implies that the explanatory factors of Esping-Andersen's typology (universalism and de-commodification) may be less important for EBPM than countries' political culture and institutions. The differences we sketch out in this chapter are therefore tentative and employed mainly to highlight the potential of comparative research around EBPM. The lack of comparative empirical studies of EBPM marks an important blind spot in current scholarship (Smith et al. 2019) which may be directly impeding scholarship and policy work around EBPM.

3.3.2 What are the issues that EBPM could potentially address?

The promise of EBPM, in terms of the issues it might address, depend on the answers to the three questions we outlined at the start of the chapter. If, for example, the answer to question 1 is that the "evidence" in EBPM is narrowly defined to quantitative, experimental data and analysis (as has been the case in the US) then the potential applicability of EBPM is reduced, especially in contexts (such as Scandinavia) where many social policies are rights-based and universal. Employed in this narrow way, EBPM can potentially aid policymakers only in deciding whether to pursue (or terminate) policy interventions that are amenable to quantitative, experimental evaluation. If, on the other hand, we take a far more inclusive approach to defining "evidence" and include, for example, opinion polls, qualitative data capturing lived experiences, professional opinions, etc. then the potential applicability of EBPM becomes far greater. However, this expansion then raises questions about the extent to which EBPM differs from general knowledge utilisation in policymaking.

The answer to question 1 directly impacts on the answer to question 2, what EBPM looks like, although this is also necessarily shaped by the contextual specificities of policymaking, as we have highlighted via our comparison between EBPM in the US, UK and Scandinavian contexts. Our analysis suggests that EBPM in the US involves embedding a positivist approach within (restricted strands of) policymaking, via mandatory requirements to employ tools such as cost-benefit analysis and mechanisms that help promote the utility, availability and accessibility of quantitative, experimental evidence and data. In the US (and, to some extent, the UK) these developments intersect with commitments to "open government" and the push for greater transparency around the scientific advice that is informing policy decisions. In this context, EBPM potentially offers a means of opening the "black box" of policymaking to public and expert scrutiny. In contrast, the resistance to EBPM among some researchers and professionals within social democratic countries (which relates, very directly, to the issues of legitimacy raised by question 3 in our introduction) appears to be informing a much subtler approach, in which selected tools of EBPM are built into governance arrangements in ways that deliberately seek to avoid public attention. All of this is likely to limit the issues that EBPM can feasibly address in Scandinavian contexts to policy developments that are not traditionally shaped via strong professional engagement or extensive democratic deliberation.

3.4 Conclusion

There is little doubt, as we illustrate here, that EBPM remains a contested concept but precisely why it is contested, or what is being contested, appears to vary by context. The scholarship surrounding EBPM is somewhat frustrating for at least three reasons: (1) there is a lack of definitional clarity, which results in different people using the same terms to refer to distinct ideas, while the same terms can be interpreted differently in diverse contexts; (2) perhaps because of this, there appears to be only limited and piecemeal learning across different bodies of relevant work, whether over time or between distinct policy issues (e.g. health and education), and the three questions we set out in the introduction all remain open to discussion; and (3) a lack of comparative analysis means there only limited insights into how and why EBPM is playing out differently in contrasting geo-political contexts. The current COVID-19 pandemic context underlines both the crucial role that scientific evidence can play in guiding policy and the limits to an EBPM ideal that embodies a hierarchy of evidence placing meta-analyses of RCTs at the pinnacle. In our view, this points to a pressing need to move beyond an unattainable search for universally applicable mechanisms to increase evidence use, towards more complex and context specific understandings of how states can improve their approaches to using evidence, with a view to both improving policy outcomes *and* enhancing the democratic legitimacy of policymaking.

References

Andersen, Niklas A., 2021. "The Technocratic Rationality of Governance –The Case of the Danish Employment Services." *Critical Policy Studies* 15 (4), 425–443.

Bambra, Clare. 2005. "Worlds of Welfare and the Health Care Discrepancy." *Social Policy and Society* 4 (1), 31–41.

Bartley, Mel. 1992. *Authorities and Partisans: Debate on Unemployment and Health*. Edinburgh: Edinburgh University Press.

Black, Nick. 2001. "Evidence Based Policy: Proceed With Care." *BMJ* 323 (7307), 275–280.

Blume, Stuart S. 1977. "Policy as Theory: A Framework for Understanding the Contribution of Social Science to Welfare Policy." *Acta Sociologica* 20 (3), 247–262.

Boaz, Annette, Huw Davies, Alec Fraser, and Sandra Nutley (eds.) 2019. *What Works Now? Evidence-Informed Policy and Practice*. Bristol: Policy Press.

Bogenschneider, Karen, and Thomas J. Corbett. 2010. *Evidence-Based Policymaking: Insights from Policy-Minded Researchers and Research-Minded Policymakers*. New York: Routledge.

Botterill, Linda C., and Andrew Hindmoor. 2012. "Turtles All the Way Down: Bounded Rationality in an Evidence-Based Age." *Policy Studies* 33 (5), 367–379.

Bulmer, Martin. 1982. "Models of the Relationship between Knowledge and Policy." In *The Uses of Social Research: Social Investigation in Public Policymaking*, by Martin Bulmer, 30–49. London: Allen and Unwin.

Burrows, Roger, and Jonathan Bradshaw. 2001. "Evidence-Based Policy and Practice." *Environment and Planning A* 33 (8), 1345–1348.

Cabinet Office. 1999. *Modernising Government* (White Paper). London: The Stationery Office.

Cabinet Office. 2000. *Wiring It Up: Whitehall's Management of Cross-Cutting Policies and Services: A Performance and Innovation Unit report*. London: Cabinet Office.

Cairney, Paul. 2019. "Evidence and Policy Making." In *What Works Now? Evidence-Informed Policy and Practice*, edited by Annette Boaz, Huw Davies, Alec Fraser, and Sandra Nutley, 21–40. Bristol: Policy Press.

Campbell, Donald T. 1969. "Reforms as Experiments." *American Psychologist* 24 (4), 409–429.

Canadian Academy of Health Sciences (2009) *Making an Impact – A Preferred Framework and Indicators to Measure Returns on Investment in Health Research*. URL: http://www.cahs-acss.ca/e/pdfs/ROI_FullReport.pdf.

Caplan, Nathan. 1979. "The Two-Communities Theory and Knowledge Utilization." *American Behavioral Scientist* 22 (3), 459–470.

Collyer, Taya A., and Katherine E. Smith. 2020. "An Atlas of Health Inequalities and Health Disparities Research: 'How is this all getting done in silos, and why?'." *Social Science and Medicine*, 264, 113330. https://doi.org/10.1016/j.socscimed.2020.113330

Davey Smith, George, Shah Ebrahim, and Stephen Frankel. 2001. "How Policy Informs the Evidence." *BMJ* 322 (7280), 184–185.

Davies, Huw T. O., Sandra M. Nutley, and Peter C. Smith (eds.). 2000 *What Works? Evidence-Based Policy and Practice in Public Services*. Bristol: Policy Press.

Deaton, Angus, and Nancy Cartwright. 2018. "Understanding and Misunderstanding Randomized Controlled Trials." *Social Science and Medicine* 210, 2–21.

Donnison, David. 1972. "Research for Policy." *Minerva* 10 (4), 519–536.

Elvbakken, Kari T., and Hanne F. Hansen. 2019. "Evidence Producing Organizations: Organizational Translation of Traveling Evaluation Ideas." *Evaluation* 25 (3), 261–276.

Emmenegger, Patrick, Jon Kvist, Paul Marx, and Klaus Petersen. 2015. "Three Worlds of Welfare Capitalism: The Making of a Classic." *Journal of European Social Policy* 25 (1), 3–13.

Esmark, Anders. 2020. *The New Technocracy*. Bristol: Policy Press.

Esping-Andersen, Gøsta. 1991. *The Three Worlds of Welfare Capitalism* (2nd ed.). Cambridge: Polity Press.

Fischer, Frank. 1990. *Technocracy and the Politics of Expertise*. Newbury Park, CA: Sage Publications.

Gieryn, Thomas F. 1983. "Boundary-Work and the Demarcation of Science from Non-Science: Strains and Interests in Professional Ideologies of Scientists." *American Sociological Review* 48 (6), 781–795.

Greenhalgh, Trisha, and Jill Russell. 2009. "Evidence-Based Policymaking – A Critique." *Perspectives in Biology and Medicine* 52 (2), 304–318.

Greenhalgh, Trisha. 2020. "Will COVID-19 Be Evidence-Based Medicine's Nemesis?" *PLoS Med* 17(6): e1003266. https://doi.org/10.1371/journal.pmed.1003266.

Hammersley, Martyn. 2003. "Social Research Today: Some Dilemmas and Distinctions." *Qualitative Social Work* 2 (1), 25–44.

Hansen, Hanne F., and Olaf Rieper. 2009. "The Evidence Movement: The Development and Consequences of Methodologies in Review Practices." *Evaluation* 15 (2), 141–163.

Haynes, Laura, Owain Service, Ben Goldacre, and David Torgerson. 2012. *Test, Learn, Adapt: Developing Public Policy with Randomised Controlled Trials*. London: Cabinet Office Behavioural Insights Team.

Head, Brian. 2015. "Policy Analysis and Public Sector Capacity." In *Policy Analysis in Australia*, edited by Brian Head and Kate Crowley, 53–67. Bristol: Policy Press.

Hird, John A. 2005. "Policy Analysis for What? The Effectiveness of Nonpartisan Policy Research Organizations." *Policy Studies Journal* 33 (1), 83–105.

Innvær, Simon, Gunn Vist, Mari Trommald, and Andrew Oxman. 2002. "Health Policy-Makers' Perceptions of Their Use of Evidence: A Systematic Review." *Journal of Health Services Research and Policy* 7 (4), 239–244.

Katikireddi, Srinivasa V., Martin Higgins, Lyndal Bond, Chris Bonell, and Sally Macintyre. 2011. "How Evidence Based is English Public Health Policy?" *BMJ* 343:d7310.

Kavanagh, D., and D. Richards. 2001. "Departmentalism and Joined-Up Government: Back to the Future?" *Parliamentary Affairs* 54 (1), 1–18.

Knorr, Karin. 1977. "Policymakers' Use of Social Science Knowledge: Symbolic or Instrumental?" In *Using Social Research in Public Policy*, edited by Carol H. Weiss, 165–182. Lexington, MA: Lexington-Heath.

Lavis, John N. 2006. "Research, Public Policymaking, and Knowledge-Translation Processes: Canadian Efforts to Build Bridges." *The Journal of Continuing Education in the Health Professions* 26 (1), 37–45.

Lomas, J. 2000. "Using 'Linkage and Exchange' to Move Research into Policy at a Canadian Foundation." *Health Affairs* 19 (3), 236–240.

Macintyre, S., I. Chalmers, R. Horton, and R. Smith. 2001. "Using Evidence to Inform Health Policy: Case Study." *BMJ* 322 (7280), 222–225.

Miller, S. M. 1980. "Reinventing the Broken Wheel." *Social Policy* 10 (5), 2–3.

Mitton, Craig, Carol E. Adair, Emily McKenzie, Scott B. Patten, and Brenca Waye Perry. 2007. "Knowledge Transfer and Exchange: Review and Synthesis of the Literature." *The Milbank Quarterly* 85 (4), 729–768.

Møller, Anne M. 2017. "Evidensdagsordenens metamorfoser i dansk socialpolitik." Politik 20 (2), 68–87.

Møller, Anne M., Kari-Tove Elvbakken, and Hanne F. Hansen. 2019. "Using Evidence in Scandinavia." In *What Works Now? Evidence-Informed Policy and Practice*, edited by Annette Boaz, Huw Davies, Alec Fraser, and Sandra Nutley Boaz, 321–335. Bristol: Policy Press

Mudde, Cas, and Cristóbal Rovira Kaltwasser. 2017. *Populism: A Very Short Introduction*. Oxford: Oxford University Press.

Mulgan, Geoff. 2005. "Government, Knowledge and the Business of Policy Making: The Potential and Limits of Evidence-Based Policy." *Evidence and Policy* 1 (2), 215–226.

Naughton, Michael. 2005. "'Evidence-based policy' and the Government of the Criminal Justice System – Only If the Evidence Fits!" *Critical Social Policy* 25 (1), 47–69.

Newman, Joshua. 2017. "Deconstructing the Debate Over Evidence-Based Policy." *Critical Policy Studies* 11 (2), 211–226.

Nutley, Sandra, and Huw T. O. Davies. 2000. "Making a Reality of Evidence-Based Practice." In *What Works? Evidence-Based Policy & Practice in Public Services*, edited by Hugh T. O. Davies, Sandra Nutley, and Peter C. Smith, 317–350. Bristol: Policy Press.

Nutley, Sandra M., Isabel Walter, and Huw T. O. Davies. 2007. *Using Evidence: How Research Can Inform Public Services*. Bristol: Policy Press.

Parkhurst, Justin. O., and Sudeepa Abeysinghe. 2016. "What Constitutes Good Evidence for Public Health and Social Policy-Making? From Hierarchies to Appropriateness." *Social Epistemology* 30 (5–6), 665–679.

Parsons, Wayne. 2002. "From Muddling Through to Muddling Up – Evidence Based Policy Making and the Modernisation of British Government." *Public Policy and Administration* 17 (3), 43–60.

Petticrew, Mark, Margaret Whitehead, Sally J. Macintyre, Hilary Graham, and Matt Egan. 2004. "Evidence for Public Health Policy on Inequalities: 1: The Reality According to Policymakers." *Journal of Epidemiology and Community Health* 58, 811–816.

Plato. 2007. *The Republic*. London: Penguin Books.

Powell, Mark, Erdem Yörük, and Ali Bargu. 2020. "Thirty Years of the *Three Worlds of Welfare Capitalism*: A Review of Reviews." *Social Policy and Administration* 54 (1), 60–87.

Quaglio, GianLuca, Theodoros Karapiperis, Lieve Van Woensel, Elleke Arnold, and David McDaid. 2013. "Austerity and Health in Europe." *Health Policy* 113 (1–2), 13–19.

Radaelli, Claudio M. 1995. "The Role of Knowledge in the Policy Process." *Journal of European Public Policy* 2 (2), 159–183.

Rein, Martin. 1980. "Methodology for the Study of the Interplay Between Social Science and Social Policy." *International Social Science Journal* xxii (2), 361–368.

Rudd, K. 2008. *Address to Heads of Agencies and members of Senior Executive Service*. Canberra: Australian Public Service Commission.

Saint-Simon, Henri de. (1964) *Social Organization, the Science of Man and Other Writings*. New York: Harper Torch.

Saltelli, Andrea and Mario Giampietro. 2017. "What is Wrong with Evidence Based Policy, and How Can It Be Improved?" *Futures* 91, 62–71.

Sanderson, Ian. 2009. "Intelligent Policy Making for a Complex World: Pragmatism, Evidence and Learning." *Political Studies* 57 (4), 699–719.

Sasse, Tom, Catherine Haddon, and Alex Nice. 2020. *Science Advice in a Crisis*. London: Institute of Government. https://www.instituteforgovernment.org.uk/sites/default/files/publications/science-advice-crisis_0.pdf

Sharfstein, Joshua M. 2017. "Science and the Trump Administration". *JAMA* 318 (14), 1312–1313.

Smith, Katherine E., Mark Pearson, William Allen, Melanie Barwick, Caitlin Farrell, Mark Hardy, Blane Harvey, Anita Kothari, Zachary Neal, and Arnaldo Pellini. 2019. "Building and Diversifying Our Interdisciplinary Giants: Moving Scholarship on Evidence and Policy Forward." *Evidence and Policy* 15 (4), 455–460.

Stanhope, Victoria, and Kerry Dunn. 2011. "The Curious Case of Housing First: The Limits of Evidence Based Policy." *International Journal of Law and Psychiatry* 34 (4), 275–282.

Stewart, Ellen, Jennifer Smith-Merry, Marc Geddes, and Justyna Bandola-Gill. 2020. "Opening Up Evidence-Based Policy: Exploring Citizen and Service User Expertise." *Evidence and Policy* 16 (2), 199–208.

Vedung, Evert. 2016. "Fire Evalueringsbølger." In *Evaluering af offentlig politik og administration*, edited by Thomas Bredgaard, 37–68. Copenhagen: Hans Reitzels Forlag.

Wells, Peter. 2018. "Evidence Based Policy Making in an Age of Austerity." *People, Place and Policy* 11 (3), 175–183.

Weiss, Carol. 1977. "Research for Policy's Sake: The Enlightenment Function of Social Research." *Policy Analysis* 3, 531–547.

Weiss, Carol. 1979. "The Many Meanings of Research Utilization." *Public Administration Review* 39 (5), 426–431.

Weiss, Carol, ed. 1980. *Social Science Research and Decision-Making*. New York: Columbia University Press.

Weiss, Carol H. 1982. "Policy Research in the Context of Diffuse Decision Making." *The Journal of Higher Education* 53 (6), 619–639.

Weiss, C. 1990. "The Uneasy Partnership Endures: Social Science and Government." In *Social Scientists, Policy, and the State*, edited by Stephen Brooks and Alain-G. Gagnon, 97–111. New York: Praeger.

Whitehead, Margaret, Mark Petticrew, Hilary Graham, Sally J. Macintyre, Clare Bambra, and Matt Egan. 2004 "Evidence for Public Health Policy on Inequalities 2: Assembling the Evidence Jigsaw." *Journal of Epidemiology and Community Health* 58 (10), 817–821.

Wimbush, Erica, Helen Harper, Daniel Wight, Laurence Gruer, Matthew Lowther, Shirley Fraser, and Jack Gordon. 2005. "Evidence, Policy and Practice: Developing Collaborative Approaches in Scotland." *Evidence and Policy* 1 (3), 391–407.

Young, Ken, Deborah Ashby, Annette Boaz, and Lesley Grayson. 2002. "Social Science and the Evidence-Based Policy Movement." *Social Policy and Society* 1 (3), 215–224.

Part II Welfare regimes

Part II Wetlands

Minna van Gerven

4 Nordic welfare states: up to challenge?

Abstract: This chapter analyses the extent to which the contemporary Nordic model is up to the challenge in the current economic and demographic landscape. The chapter first theorises the Nordic welfare states by discussing the four ingredients of the Nordic model: 1) universal welfare state provision, 2) extensive public services, 3) high labour market participation, and 4) gender equality in politics and practices. These dimensions are then empirically investigated by analysing the key welfare state indicators for the last 10 years (2010–2020) in Sweden, Denmark, Norway, Finland and Iceland. The analysis confirms the specificity of Nordic welfare states when compared to the EU27 or OECD averages. In general, the Nordic countries continue to entail generous systems of welfare provision and public services and fuel high labour market participation and gender equality. Yet, there are cracks in the contemporary Nordic model that suggest that universalism may not always be compatible with changing world. The future of the Nordic model seems to be up to the challenge, but it needs to fit with new social and economic conditions and to mitigate income and social inequalities, to continue to be effective also in the coming decades.

Keywords: Nordic welfare states, Nordic model, universalism, public services, labour market participation, gender equality, inequality, Sweden, Finland, Denmark, Norway, Iceland

4.1 Introduction

Numerous accounts describe and analyse "The Nordic Model" (Kosonen 1998; Stephens 1996; Greve 2004; 2018, Kettunen et al. 2015; Kautto et al. 2001; Dahl 2012; Kautto and Kvist 2002; Kildal and Kuhnle 2007; Kuhle 2019; Kvist and Saari 2007; Kvist and Greve 2011; etc.) and show how the Nordic model entails generous universalist welfare state provision, extensive public services, high labour market participation, and strong ideology and practice of gender equality. The Nordic uniqueness is typically contrasted and constructed in relation to other European welfare states, most famously in the context of the Esping-Andersen (1990) welfare state regime typology. Although Esping-Andersen's take was largely based on Sweden, the other Nordic countries (including Denmark, Norway, Finland and Iceland) constitute the exclusive membership of the "triple-A welfare states". Or the "Good" welfare state, referring to Manow's (2004) "Good, Bad, and Ugly" typology inspired by the classic spaghetti western film. "The Nordic model", although inducing different meanings by different people (Kuisma 2016), has become a fashion brand and export product (for example to China see van Gerven and Yang 2017). Yet, the preservation of the Nordic model in the

https://doi.org/10.1515/9783110721768-004

current economic and demographic landscape is challenging. High spending combined with an ageing population threatens the long-term sustainability of the European welfare systems (see e.g. Schubert, Villota, and Kuhlmann 2016). This chapter analyses to what extent the contemporary Nordic model is up to the challenge.

4.2 Teasing out the Nordic Model

The recipe for the Nordic model commonly comprises the following four ingredients: 1) universal welfare state provision, 2) extensive public services, 3) high labour market participation, and 4) gender equality in politics and practices.

4.2.1 Universal welfare state provision

Much of the splendour of the Nordic model is based on its strong manifestation of *universalism*. Universalism has various dimensions and meanings (Anttonen et al. 2012; Anttonen 2002). In the context of the welfare state, universalism refers to a specific mechanism of redistribution and services covering all citizens without tangible requirements of need or past activities (see e.g. Kildal and Kuhnle 2007). Universality embraces an idea of inclusive membership and, unlike contribution-based systems (such as Bismarckian/employment-based and Beveridgean/national insurance), universalist models aim at guaranteeing equal rights. It does not entail a clear reciprocal relationship between the giver and the receiver and, in this way, universalism hinges on de-commodification, where welfare rights are not strongly tied to labour market participation (Esping-Andersen 1990). With this understanding, universalism is commonly contrasted with liberal selective welfare states (Anttonen et al. 2012), where eligibility is determined by means (Rothstein 1998) and/or by income test (Korpi and Palme 1998).

The question of whether the universalist model is a "leaky bucket" (Okun 1975) or an "irrigation system" (Korpi 1985) for prosperity and economic growth remains at the centre of lively academic discussion. In the seminal article, Korpi and Palme (1998) highlighted the greater redistributive success of universal welfare states in comparison to those countries with targeted programmes. A contemporary understanding tends to support the general understanding that more equal societies fare better (Wilkinson and Pickett 2009; Acemoglu and Robinson 2012). Although universalism underlining equality may suggest superiority of the Nordic model to other models, contrasting universal states with targeted systems and defining universalism as an antonym for targeting is problematic. Van Oorschot and Roosma (2015) have made a valid point suggesting that the dichotomy between universality and targeting "is a *matter of degree, not of essence*" (p. 8). For example, a child benefit provided to all households is a prime example of universalism by design, but in practice, child benefit system is highly targeted in its effects. The system aims to improve the well-being of a selected population, in this case, households with children (see also Jacques and Noël 2018). The universality of the Nordic model demonstrates the difficulty of fitting ideal types with real-world practices. As Boldersen and Mabbett (1995, 119) almost three decades ago suggested, the complexity of national social systems, driven by the diversity of national systems (including universal, contribution-based and means-tested benefit under one policy domain) and many functional equivalents, makes welfare systems "mongrels" rather than "thoroughbreds".

Recently the universalism of the Nordic Model has been questioned in the light of reforms increasing responsibilities and activation for the citizens (Hansen 2019; Johansson and Hvinden 2007) and targeting the redistribution to those most in need (Saikkonen and Ylikännö 2020; van Gerven and Nygård 2017). Therefore, universalism, as a core feature of the Nordic model, indicating the strength and persistence of shared ideals (Kuisma 2016; Béland et al. 2014; Béland 2009) of redistributing wealth to all citizens needs to be re-evaluated.

4.2.2 Public services

The Nordic exceptionalism also includes a strong reliance on public delivery of goods and services. Manifested as "peculiar stateness" of the Nordic countries (Pedersen and Kuhnle 2017, 4), state and local government share the responsibility of regulation and provision of taxation-based cash benefits as well as public services. Szebehely and Meagher (2018, 295–296) have identified six dimensions of universal social services in elderly care, but these dimensions easily lend themselves to understanding the Nordic public services more broadly. First, the Nordic states have established a legislated right to public services. A good example here is the individual right of children to childcare. Second, the rule-based rights covering all residents (or at least the entire category of the population). Third, the services are financed through general taxes, whereby risks are collectively shared. Fourth and fifth, public services are widely used (universal) and they are considered of good quality (for instance public education).

The defining feature of the Nordic model has been the public spending in kind, generating a strong network of public or semi-public services. The strong state-led interventions have been legitimated by their objectives to promote citizen equality (see also Pedersen and Kuhnle 2017). Public services extend far beyond the "core" services of health care and education and cover a wide range of preventive and mitigating social services. The feasibility of the large public sector has remained a point of concern (Lindbeck 1997), but at the same time, it is legitimated through its impact on the overall economy via investments in health, education and training. Whether the universalist model is still expected to "crowd out private insurance by providing good social services to all" (Korpi and Palme 1998), is questioned in studies discussing privatisation and marketisation. Marketisation has transformed the many traditional areas of the public sector, including elderly care, household services and employment services (Brennan et al. 2012; Anttonen and Häikiö 2011; van Berkel and van der Aa 2005). Szebehely and Meagher (2018) for instance state that marketisation has led to de-universalisation in the context of elderly care services in Finland, Sweden, Denmark and Norway.

4.2.3 High labour market participation

Although the Nordic countries are successful in generating high employment and keeping unemployment low, they are, however, vulnerable to external shocks as small open economies (Katzenstein 1985). The countries rely heavily on exports, and during economic shocks (like economic recession or the current COVID-19 crisis and closing of borders) strengthening export and businesses and maintaining competitiveness has been crucial. Trade unions and corporatism have played an important role in organising social security and supporting workers in the labour market during these economic cycles. The capability of Keynesian economics has indeed been questioned in the age of the global economy, but the Nordic Model remains to support labour demand with extensive fiscal policy and active labour market policies (Greve et al. 2021) and combines generous unemployment benefits with the promotion of training, subsidised jobs and public support to return to employment. The priority of full employment, once central on the political agenda, has faded in the last decades, but the Nordic model remains committed to high employment for both genders.

Preceding the European Union's approach (van Gerven and Beckers 2009), and with the lead of Sweden, the Nordic countries were among the first to make the turn to active labour market policies in the 1990s. The Nordic activation model originated in the Swedish Rehn-Meinder model from the 1950s that combined Keynesian economic thinking with active labour market policies and state intervention in attempting to achieve full employment, economic growth and income equality. Based on OECD ALMP spending data, Bonoli (2009) still identifies a specific Nordic model of activation that puts "most emphasis on human capital investment, somewhat less on facilitating labour market re-entry and very little on direct job creation" (Bonoli 2009, 63). While prioritising training and social investment, Bonoli (2009, 63) sees the Nordic model to be less punitive in its approach to labour promotion than for instance the workfare-induced liberal model. However, more recent research posits that a series of activation reforms in the Nordic states has led to considerably stricter benefit conditions for job seekers in the Nordic countries (Knotz 2020), or even shift to "workfare" in some Nordic countries (Denmark, but also Sweden and Finland) (Hultqvist and Nørup 2017).

4.2.4 Gender equality

Nordic welfare state: A woman's best friend. Or, as Ruth Lister (2009) asks, a Nordic Nirvana? These kinds of expressions are used to describe the egalitarian Nordic model advancing the equal treatment of men and women. Nordic models are seen to be family-friendly, providing generous family leave arrangements for both parents, combined with the universal, free or heavily subsidised childcare system, providing high-quality care for children. The core aspect behind the family policy is the promotion of gender equality for women (Teigen and Skjeie 2017). The public childcare system has been central, but gender equality is also promoted through (free) access to health, comprehensive public old-age care services as well as free education from pre-school to university. These arrangements have enabled women to pursue an independent career on (more or less) equal terms with men (Orloff 2001; Lewis 2006). At the same time, the expansion of the public sector (jobs) and female labour market participation have indeed mutually reinforced each other. The Nordic model's gender equality aims are seen to inspire the development of the European social investment model (Hemerijck 2012) and European gender equality (Stratigaki 2004).

4.3 Trends from the last 10 years

In international comparisons, the Nordic countries score high with various indicators, such as democracy, rule of law, income inequality, or – the factor causing many media headings – happiness (Martela et al. 2020). Many commentators explain the success to relate to the high performance of the welfare states (e.g. Martela et al. 2020). This section presents the welfare state achievements in Sweden, Denmark, Norway, Finland and Iceland as measured by key welfare state indicators for the last 10 years (2010–2020) for the four theoretical aspects of the Nordic model described earlier.

4.3.1 Generous welfare state

The Nordic model covers a wide range of risks in a life cycle. Table 4.1 below indicates the social spending trends from the 1980s onwards.

Table 4.1: Trend of overall social spending as percentage of GDP between 1980 and 2019 in Nordic countries and OECD average (OECD 2021).

	1980	1990	2000	2010	2019
Country					
Denmark	20	21.9	23.8	29.6	28.3
Finland	18	23.3	22.6	27.4	29.1
Iceland	NA	13.3	14.5	16.4	17.4
Norway	16	21,6	20.4	22.1	25.3
Sweden	24	26.9	26.5	25.9	25.5
OECD Total	15	16.5	17.5	20.6	20.0

All Nordic countries, except Iceland, are well above the OECD average in total spending. Sweden, Denmark and Finland are among the top four spenders. The absence of Norway from the top group is often explained by the fact that GDP, due to the country's oil and gas resources, is exceptionally high. The spending has increased in all countries, with a noteworthy exception of Sweden. Sweden lost its top position in the 2010s, as Finland and Denmark currently spend the most. In the last 10 years, the spending has decreased only in Denmark and Sweden, as it is increasing elsewhere, especially in Finland, where the spending is expected to increase considerably due to population ageing in the coming decade.

Table 4.2: Trends in replacement rates in unemployment benefits 2010–2022 (OECD 2021).

Single, no children	2010	2015	2019	2020
Finland	64	73	66	66
Denmark	85	85	85	83
Iceland	82	77	79	80
Norway	72	67	68	68
Sweden	68	68	71	69
OECD – Total	67	67	68	

Table 4.2: (continued)

Couple, with children	2010	2015	2019	2020
Finland	85	89	85	85
Denmark	94	94	94	94
Iceland	92	91	93	92
Norway	88	88	88	88
Sweden	87	84	89	88
OECD – Total	86	86	86	

Another important indicator of generosity is the social benefit replacement rate. The peak of the Nordic model in terms of benefit generosity was in the late 1980s and ever since, the Nordic countries are converging towards the OECD average (Kangas and Saloniemi 2013, 30). The comparison of the trend shows divergence, where Finland, Sweden and Norway tend to be in line with the OECD average, whereas Denmark and Iceland are well above the OECD average. Pedersen and Kuhnle (2017) – while using different (CWED) data and distinguishing between various social security benefits – have similar findings to Table 4.2: Denmark, Iceland (and Norway) score constantly higher with replacement rates, where Sweden and Finland score (just) around (or under) OECD average. Although the trend has been reasonably stable, the low basic generosity of minimum benefits raises (for singles) questions of the eroding of a universalist model in Finland, Sweden, and to an extent Norway (see also Pedersen and Kuhnle 2017).

Table 4.3: Cluster Table on core indicators of poverty and inequality (Eurostat 2021; OECD 2021).

Poverty and inequality	SE	DK	NO	FI	IS	EU
Gini coefficient (in 2013) and most recent	(0.268–) 0.280	(0.254–) 0.264	(0.252–) 0.262	(0.262–) 0.269	(0.240–) 0.250	
At the risk of poverty % after social transfers (TESSI010) 2019	17.1	12.5	12.7	11.6	8.8 (in 2018)	16.5 (EU27)
In-work-poverty % in 2019 ILC_IW01 2019 18–64	7.7	6.3	6.4	2.9	7.3 (in 2018)	9.0 (EU 27)
Share of children aged less than 18 years at risk of poverty or social exclusion, 2019	23.1	13.2	16	14.3	12.8	22.5

Table 4.3 above shows the rise of poverty and inequality in the last decades but the Gini coefficients in the Nordic states are relatively similar and they are low (to start with) in comparison to many European countries (0.301 for France, 0.289 for Germany, 0.366 for the UK for 2018 (Eurostat 2021). The largest outlier is Sweden, where the risks of poverty and child poverty are higher than in other Nordic countries. The position of Sweden – the archetypical example of the Nordic model – is striking and raises concerns about inequality and exclusion in the "most inclusive" welfare state.

4.3.2 Public services

The Nordic peculiarity is analysed below in Table 4.4 by breaking social spending down into social transfers and benefits in kind.

Table 4.4: Trends of social spending in the Nordic countries in social transfers and benefits in kind, in percentages of GDP, 2010 and 2017 (OECD 2021).

	in cash 2010	in cash in 2017	in kind 2010	in kind 2017
Country				
Denmark	13.1	13.2	14.5	14.0
Finland	16.4	17.5	9.9	11.1
Iceland	6.7	6.8	9.6	9.1
Norway	11.1	12.8	10.4	12.0
Sweden	11.7	10.8	13.1	14.0
OECD Total	12.0	11.5	8.0	8.0

Supporting the claims made earlier in section 4.3.1. – with exception of Iceland – all Nordic countries have spending above or around the OECD average. There is some variation: spending has increased in Norway and in Finland, remained almost the same in Denmark and Iceland, and decreased in Sweden. The difference to OECD is seen in spending in kind, where the Nordic countries spend more than the OECD average. The spending in kind has increased in Norway, Sweden and Finland, and decreased a little in Denmark and Iceland. This suggests, however, that public services remain a typical feature of the Nordic model in the 2010s.

4.3.3 Labour market

Table 4.5 below indicates that employment rates are high, while all Nordic countries have higher employment rates than the EU average.

Table 4.5: Core indicators in employment and ALMP (Eurostat 2021, OECD 2021).

Employment	SE	DK	NO	FI	IS	EU
Employment rate, 20–64, % of population in 2010 and 2019	78.1–>82.1	74.9–>78.3	79.6–>79.5	73–>77.2	80.6–>85.9	67.8–>73.1
Female employment rate, 20–64, % of population, by gender in 2010 and 2019	75–>79.7	72–>74.7	76.9–>76.8	71.5–>75.8	77.6–>83	61.2–>67.3
Female part-time employment as percentage of the total employment	40.3–>32.5	37.4–>33.9	42.4–>37.7	19–>21.3	34.5–>34.1	29.6–>29.9
Long-term unem-ployed (12 months or more) as percentage of the active population	0.9	0.8	0.8	1.2	–	2.8 (EU27)
*Public spending on labour markets (benefits and services), total, % of GDP, 2000–2018	1.8–>1.6	3.8–>2.9	1.1–>0.8	2.7–>2.2		

The total employment is particularly high in Iceland and Sweden (above 80 %), but all Nordic countries beat the EU average when it comes to female employment. In the 2010s, the employment rate of Nordic women has grown, being highest in Iceland and lowest in Finland. Part-time employment is less common in Finland than in the neighbouring countries, but the average working hours of women do not drastically vary between countries (FI 34.5, SE 34.8, DK 31.1, IS 35, NO 31.2 in comparison to 34.1 EU27). Long-term unemployment is lower than the EU average and all Nordic countries (data on Iceland missing) spend generously on active labour market policies. Denmark and Finland are leading the region in these latest figures, Norway the laggard. The Danes indeed invested heavily in activation policy in the mid-1990s, under the flagship Flexicurity (Kvist and Pedersen 2007). In the recent decade, the Danes spent less, yet they remain the highest spenders in ALMP in the Nordic countries. Regarding the types of interventions utilised, OECD data suggest that Nordic states still focus more on "training first" rather than "work first" approach to activation (Martin 2015, 21) and although benefit conditions in the Nordic countries have been made more restrictive, the punitive approach relating sanctions rules remains softer than that of utilised in the Anglo-Saxon countries (Knotz 2020: 127)

4.3.4 Gender equality

Table 4.6 below shows that the gender employment gap, the difference between the employment rates of men and women aged 15–64 is well below the EU average in all Nordic countries: with Finland being the clear frontrunner here. When viewing the gender pay gap indicator, the Finnish triumph becomes less convincing. The gender pay gap, measured as a percentage of average gross hourly earnings of men, is above the EU average in Finland, where other Nordic countries (Denmark, Norway and Iceland) locate themselves around EU average, or below it (Sweden). These findings illustrate the "welfare-state p aradox" (Teigen and Skjeie 2017), where equality-oriented welfare states, such as Nordic welfare states, tend to have highly gender-segregated labour markets.

Table 4.6: Core indicators of gender equality in Nordic welfare states in 2019 and 2020 (Eurostat 2021, EIGE 2021).

Gender equality	SE	DK	NO	FI	IS	EU
Gender employment gap, 2019	4.7	7.2	5.2	2.7	5.6	11.7 (EU27)
Unadjusted gender pay gap, % of average gross hourly earnings of men in 2019	11.8	14	13.2 (2018)	16.6	13.8 (2018)	14.1
EIGE gender equality index	83.8	77.4	NA	74.7	NA	67.9

Although many Nordic states are currently run by female political leaders, most notably, in Finland where the Marin administration started their term with an all-female, 30+ aged government, many authors (Teigen and Skjeie 2017; Dahl 2012) have identified the gender gaps in representation in political and elites. By 2020, none of the Nordic countries has achieved a full gender parity in national assemblies nor has the female representation on corporate boards stabilised to an equal division of men and women (Teigen and Skjeie 2017, 17–18). When measured with the Gender equality index monitored by the European Institute for Gender Equality, The Nordic countries, however, do well. The GEI index uses a scale of 1 to 100, where 1 is for total inequality and 100 is for total equality and the scores denote the gaps between women and men on their levels of achievement in six core domains – work, money, knowledge, time, power and health. Here Nordic countries score well above the EU average and hold up the top four positions: with Sweden and Denmark on the top, and Finland following France as number 4.

4.4 Where do we stand now? The political struggle of the Nordic Model

Although the welfare state performance has not eroded significantly (with the exemption of the increase of child poverty in Sweden and Norway), the political developments in the past may cast darker shadows over the Nordic Model. These shadows are not yet easily captured by the aggregated welfare state performance indicators and require a more detailed and critical discussion.

Although the Nordic welfare states are seen as the bastion of social democracy, neoliberal politics from the 1990s onwards are seen to have weakened the ideals and practices of universalism (Lodemel and Moreira 2014; van Aerschot 2013). The omnipotent rise of active citizenship puts a stronger emphasis on individualism and meritocracy. Activation reforms underline responsibilities above solidarity and weaken the collective risk-sharing and national (universal) responses (Hansen 2019). At the same time, growing diversity challenges the traditional understanding of universalism and social citizenship. Anttonen et al. (2021) suggest that the "diversity blind" Nordic universal programmes are ill-suited for such diversification of societies with respect to ethnicity, religion and lifestyles. In a similar manner, Thelen (2013) talks about a different kind of universalism to characterise Denmark's new flexicurity model with a particularly virulent strain of anti-immigrant sentiment" (pp. 198–199). These debates are unmasking increasing welfare chauvinism (van der Waal et al. 2010; de Koster, Achterberg, and van der Waal 2013) that questions the basic notions of collective risk-sharing and universalism. Indeed, the notion of the universalist welfare state – rooted in sovereign countries and territories and covering homogenous populations – may be incompatible with the diversity of transnational societies in the twenty-first century (Greve 2021; 2014) and extending the cosmopolitan world views (van Gerven and Ossewaarde 2012). As Kangas and Saloniemi (2013) have pointed out, we may need to rethink universalism in the context of differentiated needs. New political choices are needed to solve the grand societal challenges, such as climate change and building of an eco-friendly and sustainable welfare state (Gough 2016; Berg and Saikkonen 2019) or addressing the inequalities of the digital-driven welfare states (Alston 2019; van Gerven forthcoming 2022).

Social citizenship has been upgraded to "active" (social) citizenship 2.0., where rights to social transfers and public services are more strongly related to individuals' responsibilities as active citizens. At the same time, minimum income schemes have been eroded (especially in Finland and Sweden) and have become more targeted (Kuivalainen and Niemelä 2010). Although universalism may be indeed more an issue of the decree, than of the essence (van Oorschot and Roosma 2015), the recent policy measures lowering minimum income benefits (sometimes by politics of non-decision e.g. by freezing the indexation) erode the universalism and polarise welfare state protection between labour market insiders and labour market outsiders. Activation for these vulnerable groups is no longer an issue of preparing them – via demand-led policies such as fostering life-long learning and training-based ALMP – but rather an instrumental return to the labour market with the "help" of stricter (behavioural) conditions and fewer rights.

The high spending in benefits in kind also does not mean that the quality and access to public services remains the same. Ageing of the population will lead to rising public spending and lower tax revenues, therefore affecting the funding base of the Nordic model. Finland, a country with the highest spending already, will face the fastest rise of the old-age dependence rate in the Nordic countries. This, like in other Nordic countries, will fuel the political sentiments to raise taxes and/or cut down services. These challenges may also erode gender equality if welfare cuts lead to an increase of informal care for the aged relatives. This will impose a triple bind for Nordic women, as they will not only be required to reconcile work and family (child/ren) responsibilities but now also take up (new) tasks of caring for elderly parents.

Many see marketisation as a deliberate political choice and a consequence of the dominance of (neo) liberal values that endangers the Nordic model (Kananen 2016). Nordic states have opted for marketisation and increased the room for private for-profit providers in the last decades (Anttonen and Karsio 2017; Szebehely and Meagher 2018). The marketisation has been particularly strong in-home care and elderly services, and particularly Sweden and Finland have increased the role of for-profit production to fill in the gaps that state retrieval in the 1990s recession left behind. In comparison, in Norway and Denmark marketisation has increased less (Anttonen and Karsio 2017: 228). At the same time, the role of non-profit providers in this sector has been growing in all countries, sometimes as a competitor of for-profit organisations or as a collaborator with the public sector (in collaborative partnerships). Marketisation can erode the Nordic model by transforming it towards a two-tier service system, where the better-off use private services and others have to use the public ones (Mathew Puthenparambil, Kröger, and Van Aerschot 2017). A similar development is the rise of occupational welfare or fiscal welfare (Greve 2018), which fuels polarisation between the rich using private health care services and the poor being reliant on public services, or the rise of funded occupational and personal pensions. Such developments may undermine the universalistic Nordic principles, increase inequalities and worsen the existing public services in the long run.

4.5 Conclusion

The chapter shows the specificity of Nordic welfare states (including Sweden, Denmark, Norway, Finland and Iceland), especially when compared to the EU27 or OECD averages. In general, the Nordic countries entail generous systems of welfare provision and public services and fuel high labour market participation. Furthermore, the Nordic Model fosters gender equality that aims at mitigating income and social inequalities.

Results also show country variations. Iceland differs with lower levels of social spending but is otherwise converging towards other Nordic states with respect to high employment levels, low inequality and high gender equality. Finland shows increasing social spending, but is also catching up with the Nordic levels of employment and spending in ALMPs. Perhaps the most remarkable development is that in Sweden where the recent rise of inequalities, especially with respect to child poverty and risk-of-poverty rates, pose worrisome questions about the future of equality and equal opportunities in the home country of the Nordic model. Denmark stands out particularly regarding high social spending but the decrease in spending in ALMP in recent years shows a departure from the country's prominence in activation. Norway spends the least on ALMP, but is otherwise very close to "average" Nordic, but with staggering signs of higher levels of child poverty.

The established welfare institutions have mitigated the negative effects of the financial crisis of the last decades, as well as the recent COVID-19 pandemic, where the public transfers and services have shown their effects as automatic stabilisers. The Nordic model seems not to have departed from its social democratic roots but, at the same time, the leadership of the "exceptional" Nordic model is not growing. Rather it is declining (e.g. regarding inequality and towards stronger meritocracy) as other countries catch up (e.g. gender equality). This casts shadows of concern in developments of the "post-universal" welfare states in the future, if the issues of inequality and polarisation are not addressed.

The Nordic Model needs to be adjusted in the future to fit with new social and economic conditions. The Nordic commitment to universalism with the strong responsibility of the state in administering welfare and wellbeing for the citizens seems to persevere for now, but the cracks in the contemporary Nordic model that suggest that universalism may not always be compatible with a changing world. The future of the Nordic model is not without challenges, but for now, Nordic countries seem to be up to the challenge.

References

Acemoglu, Daron, and James Robinson. 2012. *Why Nations Fail*. New York: Crown.

Aerschot, Paul van. 2013. *Activation Policies and the Protection of Individual Rights: A Critical Assessment of the Situation in Denmark, Finland and Sweden*. Farnham: Ashgate.

Alston, Philip. 2019. "Extreme Poverty and Human Rights." *Ga /74/493 ̣7564* (October), 1–23. http://statements.unmeetings.org/media2/21999189/sr-extreme-poverty-ga-3rd-cttee-statement-f.pdf.

Anttonen, Anneli. 2002. "Universalism and Social Policy: A Nordic-Feminist Revaluation." *NORA – Nordic Journal of Feminist and Gender Research* 10 (2), 71–80.

Anttonen, Anneli, and Liisa Haïkïö. 2011. "Care 'Going Market': Finnish Elderly-Care Policies in Transition." *Nordic Journal of Social Research*, 2. https://doi.org/10.7577/njsr. 2050.

Anttonen, Anneli, Liisa Häikiö, Kolbeinn Stefánsson, and Jorma Sipilä. 2012. "Universalism and the Challenge of Diversity." In *Welfare State, Universalism and Diversity*, edited by Anneli Anttonen, Liisa Häikiö, and Kolbeinn Stefánsson, 1–15. Cheltenham: Edward Elgar Publishing.

Anttonen, Anneli, and Olli Karsio. 2017. "How Marketisation Is Changing the Nordic Model of Care for Older People." In *Social Services Disrupted: Changes, Challenges and Policy Implications for Europe in Times of Austerity*, edited by Flavia Martinelli, Anneli Anttonen, and Margitta Mätzke, 219–238. Cheltenham: Edward Elgar Publishing.

Béland, Daniel. 2009. "Ideas, Institutions, and Policy Change." *Journal of European Public Policy* 16 (5), 701–718.

Béland, Daniel, Paula Blomqvist, Jørgen Goul Andersen, Joakim Palme, and Alex Waddan. 2014. "The Universal Decline of Universality? Social Policy Change in Canada, Denmark, Sweden and the UK." *Social Policy and Administration* 48 (7), 739–756.

Berg, Monika, and Paula Saikkonen. 2019. "The Eco-Social Nordic Welfare State – a Distant Dream or a Possible Future?" In *The Relational Nordic Welfare State: Between Utiopia and Ideology*, edited by Sakari Hänninen, Kirsi-Marja Lehtelä, and Paula Saikkonen, 162–183. Cheltenham: Edward Elgar Publishing.

Berkel, Rik van, and Paul van der Aa. 2005. "The Marketization of Activation Services: A Modern Panacea? Some Lessons from the Dutch Experience." *Journal of European Social Policy* 15 (4), 329–343.

Bolderson, Helen, and Deborah Mabbett. 1995. "Mongrels or Thoroughbreds: A Cross-National Look at Social Security Systems." *European Journal of Political Research* 28 (1), 119–139.

Bonoli, Giuliano. 2009. "Varieties of Social Investment in Labour Market Policy." In *What Future for Social Investment?*, edited by Nathalie Morel, Bruno Palier, and Joakim Palme, 55–66. Stockholm: Institute for Futures Studies Research Report.

Brennan, Deborah, Bettina Cass, Susan Himmelweit, and Marta Szebehely. 2012. "The Marketisation of Care: Rationales and Consequences in Nordic and Liberal Care Regimes." *Journal of European Social Policy* 22 (4), 377–391.

Dahl, Hanne Marlene. 2012. "Neo-Liberalism Meets the Nordic Welfare State – Gaps and Silences." *NORA – Nordic Journal of Feminist and Gender Research* 20 (4), 283–288.

EIGE. 2021. *Gender Equality Index 2020*. Available at https://eige.europa.eu/publications/gender-equality-index-2020-key-findings-eu. Accessed on 07 April 2021.

Esping-Andersen, Gøsta. 1990. *The Three Worlds of Welfare Capitalism*. Princeton, NJ: Princeton University Press.

Eurostat. 2021. *Labour Force Survey Database*. https://ec.europa.eu/eurostat/data/database. Accessed on 07 April 2021

Gerven, Minna van. forthcoming in 2022. "Social Policy in the Digital Age: Towards a Digital Welfare State?" In *Changing European Societies – The Role for Social Policy*, edited by Mara Yerkes, Kenneth Nelson, and Rense Nieuwenhuis. Cheltenham: Edward Elgar.

Gerven, Minna van, and Mieke Beckers. 2009. "Unemployment Protection Reform in Belgium, Finland, the Netherlands and the UK. Policy Learning through Open Coordination?" In *Changing European Employment and Welfare Regimes: The Influence of the Open Method of Coordination on National Labour Market and Welfare Reforms*, edited by Jonathan Zeitlin and Martin Heidenreich, 61–83. London: Routledge.

Gerven, Minna van, and Mikael Nygård. 2017. "Equal Treatment, Labor Promotion, or Social Investment? Reconciliation Policy in Finnish and Dutch Coalition Programs 1995–2016." *European Policy Analysis* 3 (1), 125–145.

Gerven, Minna van, and Marinus Ossewaarde. 2012. "The Welfare State's Making of Cosmopolitan Europe: Individualization of Social Rights as European Integration." *European Societies* 14 (1), 35–55

Gerven, Minna van, and Weiguo Yang. 2017. "Teaching the Dragon? The Diffusion of European Unions's Social and Employment Policies to China." In *Managing International Connectivity, Diversity of Learning and Changing Labour Markets*, edited by Ka Ho Mok, 245–261. Singapore: Springer.

Gough, Ian. 2016. "Welfare States and Environmental States: A Comparative Analysis." *Environmental Politics* 25 (1), 24–47.

Greve, Bent. 2004. "Are the Nordic Welfare States Still Distinct?" *Social Policy & Administration* 38 (2), 115–118.

Greve, Bent. 2014. "Free Movement as a Threat for Universal Welfare States?" *European Review* 22 (3), 388–402.

Greve, Bent. 2018. "At the Heart of the Nordic Occupational Welfare Model: Occupational Welfare Trajectories in Sweden and Denmark." *Social Policy & Administration* 52 (2), 508–518.

Greve, Bent. 2021. *Handbook on Austerity, Populism and the Welfare State*. Cheltenham: Edward Elgar.

Greve, Bent, Paula Blomquist, Bjørn Hvinden, and Minna van Gerven. 2021. "Nordic Welfare States— Still Standing or Changed by the COVID-19 Crisis?" *Social Policy and Administration* 55 (2), 295–311.

Hansen, Magnus Paulsen. 2019. *The Moral Economy of Activation: Ideas, Politics and Policies*. Bristol: Policy Press.

Hemerijck, Anton. 2012. *Changing Welfare States*. Oxford: Oxford University Press.

Hultqvist, Sara, and Iben Nørup. 2017. "Consequences of Activation Policy Targeting Young Adults with Health-Related Problems in Sweden and Denmark." *Journal of Poverty and Social Justice*, 25 (2), 147–161.

Jacques, Olivier, and Alain Noël. 2018. "The Case for Welfare State Universalism, or the Lasting Relevance of the Paradox of Redistribution." *Journal of European Social Policy* 28 (1), 70–85.

Johansson, Håkan, and Bjørn Hvinden. 2007. "Re-Activating the Nordic Welfare States: Do We Find a Distinct Universalistic Model?" *International Journal of Sociology and Social Policy* 27 (7/8), 334–346.

Kananen, Johannes. 2016. *The Nordic Welfare State in Three Eras: From Emancipation to Discipline*. London and New York: Routledge.

Kangas, Olli, and Antti Saloniemi. 2013. *Historical Making, Present and Future Challenges for the Nordic Welfare State Model in Finland*. Oslo: Fafo.

Katzenstein, P. 1985. *Small States in World Markets: Industrial Policy in Europe*. Ithaca, NY: Cornell University Press.

Kautto, Mikko, Johan Fritzell, Bjørn Hvinden, Jon Kvist, and Hannu Uusitalo. 2001. *Nordic Welfare States in the European Context*. London and New York: Routledge.

Kautto, Mikko, and Jon Kvist. 2002. "Parallel Trends, Persistent Diversity: Nordic Welfare States in the European and Global Context." *Global Social Policy* 2 (2), 189–208.

Kettunen, Pauli, Urban Lundberg, Mirja Österberg, and Klaus Petersen. 2015. "The Nordic Model and the Rise and Fall of Nordic Cooperation." In *Nordic Cooperation: A European Region in Transition*, edited by Johan Strang, 69–91. London and New York: Routledge.

Kildal, Nanna, and Stein Kuhnle. 2007. *Normative Foundations of the Welfare State: The Nordic Experience*. London and New York: Routledge.

Knotz, Carlo Michael. 2020. "Does Demanding Activation Work? A Comparative Analysis of the Effects of Unemployment Benefit Conditionality on Employment in 21 Advanced Economies, 1980– 2012." *European Sociological Review* 36 (1), 121–135.

Korpi, Walter. 1985. "Economic Growth and the Welfare State: Leaky Bucket or Irrigation System?" *European Sociological Review* 1 (2), 97–118.

Korpi, Walter, and Joakim Palme. 1998. "The Paradox of Redistribution and Strategies of Equality: Welfare State Institutions, Inequality, and Poverty in the Western Countries." *American Sociological Review* 63, 661–687.

Kosonen, Pekka. 1998. *Pohjoismaiset Mallit Murroksessa*. Tampere: Vastapaino.

Koster, Willem de, Peter Achterberg, and Jeroen van der Waal. 2013. "The New Right and the Welfare State: The Electoral Relevance of Welfare Chauvinism and Welfare Populism in the Netherlands." *International Political Science Review* 34 (1), 3–20.

Kuhnle, Stein. 2019. "Welfare States with Nordic Characteristics." In *Ageing Welfare and Social Policy*, edited by Jason L Powell and Sheying Chen, 3–14. Cham: Springer.

Kuisma, Mikko. 2016. "Oscillating Meanings of the Nordic Model: Ideas and the Welfare State in Finland and Sweden." *Critical Policy Studies* 11 (4), 433–454.

Kuivalainen, Susan, and Mikko Niemelä. 2010. "From Universalism to Selectivism: The Ideational Turn of the Antipoverty Policies in Finland." *Journal of European Social Policy* 20 (3), 263–276.

Kvist, Jon, and Bent Greve. 2011. "Has the Nordic Welfare Model Been Transformed?" *Social Policy and Administration* 45 (2), 146–160.

Kvist, Jon, and Lisbeth Pedersen. 2007. "Danish Labour Market Activation Policies." *National Institute Economic Review* 202, 99–112.

Kvist, Jon, and Juho Saari. 2007. *The Europeanisation of Social Protection*. Bristol: Policy Press.

Lewis, Jane. 2006. "Work/Family Reconciliation, Equal Opportunities and Social Policies: The Interpretation of Policy Trajectories at the EU Level and the Meaning of Gender Equality." *Journal of European Public Policy* 13 (3), 420–437.

Lindbeck, Assar. 1997. "The Swedish Experiment." *Journal of Economic Issues* 35 (3), 1273–1319.

Lister, R. 2009. "A Nordic Nirvana? Gender, Citizenship, and Social Justice in the Nordic Welfare States." *Social Politics: International Studies in Gender, State & Society* 16 (2), 242–278.

Lodemel, Ivar, and Amilcar Moreira. 2014. *Activation or Workfare? Governance and the Neo-Liberal Convergence*. Oxford: Oxford University Press.

Manow, Philip. 2004. "The Good, the Bad, and the Ugly Esping-Andersen's Regime Typology and the Religious Roots of the Western Welfare." *MPIfG Working Paper no. 04/3*. Cologne: Max Planck Institute for the Study of Societies.

Martela, Frank, Bent Greve, Bo Rothstein, and Juho Saari. 2020. "The Nordic Exceptionalism: What Explains Why the Nordic Countries Are Constantly Among the Happiest in the World." *World Happiness Report 2020*, 128–145. http://happiness-report.s3.amazonaws.com/2020/WHR20_Ch7.pdf.

Martin, John P. 2015. "Activation and Active Labour Market Policies in OECD Countries: Stylised Facts and Evidence on Their Effectiveness." *IZA Journal of Labor Policy* 4 (1). https://doi.org/10.1186/s40173-015-0032-y.

Mathew Puthenparambil, Jiby, Teppo Kröger, and Lina Van Aerschot. 2017. "Users of Home-Care Services in a Nordic Welfare State under Marketisation: The Rich, the Poor and the Sick." *Health and Social Care in the Community* 25 (1), 54–64.

OECD. 2021. *Social Spending (Indicator)*. https://www.oecd-ilibrary.org/social-issues-migration-health/social-spending/indicator/english_7497563b-en. Accessed on 07 April 2021.

Okun, Arthur M. 1975. *Equality and Efficiency: The Big Tradeoff*. Washington, DC: Brookings Institution Press.

Oorschot, Wim van, and Femke Roosma. 2015. "The Social Legitimacy of Differently Targeted Benefits." In *The Social Legitimacy of Targeted Welfare: New Perspectives on Popular Welfare Deservingness Opinions*, edited by Wim van Oorschot, Femke Roosma, Bart Meuleman, and Tim Reeskens, 1–39. Cheltenham: Edward Elgar Publishing.

Orloff, Ann Shola. 2001. "Equality, Employment and State Social Policies: A Gendered Perspective." In *What Future for Social Security*, edited by Jochen Clasen, 69–86. The Hague: Kluwer Law International.

Pedersen, Axel West, and Stein Kuhnle. 2017. "The Nordic Welfare State Model: 1 Introduction: The Concept of a 'Nordic Model.'" In *The Nordic Models in Political Science: Challenged, but Still Viable?*, edited by Oddbjørn Knutsen, 249–272. Bergen: Fagbokforlaget.

Rothstein, Bo. 1998. *Just Institutions Matter. The Moral and Political Logic of the Universal Welfare State. Theories of Institutional Design*. Cambridge: Cambridge University Press.

Saikkonen, Paula, and Minna Ylikännö. 2020. "Is There Room for Targeting within Universalism? Finnish Social Assistance Recipients as Social Citizens." *Social Inclusion* 8 (1), 145–154.

Schubert, Klaus, Paloma de Villota, and Johanna Kuhlmann. 2016. *Challenges to European Welfare Systems*. Cham: Springer.

Stephens, John D. 1996. "The Scandinavian Welfare States: Achievements, Crisis, and Prospects." In *Welfare State in Transition*, edited by Gøsta Esping-Andersen, 32–65. London: Sage.

Stratigaki, Maria. 2004. "The Cooptation of Gender Concepts in EU Policies: The Case of 'Reconciliation of Work and Family.'" *Social Politics: International Studies in Gender, State & Society* 11 (1), 30–56.

Szebehely, Marta, and Gabrielle Meagher. 2018. "Nordic Eldercare – Weak Universalism Becoming Weaker?" *Journal of European Social Policy* 28 (3), 294–308.

Teigen, Mari, and Hege Skjeie. 2017. "The Nordic Gender Equality Model." In *The Nordic Models in Political Science. Challenged, but Still Viable?*, edited by Oddbjørn Knutsen, 125–147. Bergen: Fagbokforlaget.

Thelen, Kathleen. 2013. *Varieties of Liberalization and the New Politics of Social Solidarity*. Cambridge: Cambridge University Press.

Waal, Jeroen van der, Peter Achterberg, Dick Houtman, Willem de Koster, and Katerina Manevska. 2010. "'Some Are More Equal than Others': Economic Egalitarianism and Welfare Chauvinism in the Netherlands." *Journal of European Social Policy* 20 (4), 350–363.

Wilkinson, Richard, and Kate Pickett. 2009. *The Spirit Level. Why Equality Is Better for Everyone*. London: Allen Lane.

Tobias Wiß

5 Continental European welfare states

Abstract: This chapter deals with the welfare states of Continental European countries. The 1970s defined the golden era of welfare states with very generous benefit levels and high expenditure, but since then dysfunctionalities have emerged over time creating pressure for adaption. After an overview of the origins of social protection, the chapter investigates empirically to what extent Continental European welfare states (still) differ from the welfare state of other countries and how reform trends look like in selected social policy fields. Despite major challenges due to ageing, less stable labour markets, financial and economic crises as well as the COVID-19 pandemic, the building blocks of Continental European welfare states such as the dominating role of social insurance schemes and employment-related social rights are still intact. They still have much in common and are to certain degrees still different from the other welfare states. However, recent reforms containing both liberal and social-democratic elements, such as retrenchment in public pension schemes and for long-term unemployed on the one hand and more work/family policies and non-contributory universalistic benefits on the other hand, might indicate slow endogenous changes with the long-term potential to undermine the original character of Continental European welfare states.

Keywords: Bismarck, conservative welfare state, Continental Europe, social insurance schemes, welfare reforms, welfare state

5.1 Introduction

This chapter deals with the welfare states of Continental European countries, whose common institutional characteristics are the production of welfare based on social insurance schemes with earnings-related benefits linked to employment. Their main aim is status maintenance for people with lifelong full-employment in times without own income such as during periods of sickness, unemployment and retirement. Such a strong status preservation orientation tends to reproduce social stratification and reduces inequalities only to a limited degree. The principle of subsidiarity also characterises Continental European welfare states (CEWS), in that the responsibility for welfare provision and benefits lies first and foremost with the family, religious organisations and other communities. The state takes on responsibility only if such institutions fail or are not capable of guaranteeing basic welfare.

The 1970s defined the golden era of CEWS with very generous benefit levels and high expenditure. However, dysfunctionalities have emerged over time creating new challenges for CEWS, even within some of their building blocks such as the male breadwinner model, life-long working careers and full employment.

https://doi.org/10.1515/9783110721768-005

This chapter gives first an overview of the origins of social protection. Second, it investigates empirically to what extent CEWS (still) differ from the welfare state of other countries. The third part looks at major challenges such as ageing, gender inequalities and less stable employment careers as well as reform trends in selected social policy fields that aim to mitigate these challenges.

5.2 The origins of Continental European welfare states

CEWS are often described as a conservative-corporatist model of welfare production (Esping-Andersen 1990) or the Bismarckian welfare model (Palier 2010a). However, we need to acknowledge that, depending on theoretical concepts, measurements and (available) data, the literature does not always subsume the same set of countries under these labels. Furthermore, a country only rarely fits perfectly to one welfare regime, being often characterised by a mix of welfare state institutions and social policy programmes.

In his original welfare capitalism typology, Esping-Andersen (1990) groups Austria, Belgium, France, Germany and Italy into the conservative-corporatist welfare regime and the Netherlands to the Social-Democratic regime. The book chapter on Continental Western Europe by Palier (2010b) treats Austria, Belgium, France, Germany and the Netherlands as one group. Clegg extends this list of countries to Luxembourg and Switzerland for his 2019 study (Clegg 2019). In the following, I therefore consider Austria, Belgium, France, Germany and the Netherlands as CEWS. I exclude Italy, because it has been more often characterised as a Southern European or Mediterranean regime (Bonoli 1997; Ferrera 1996; Leibfried 1992), and Switzerland, because its social insurance scheme is not as important as in the other CEWS (Palier 2010b) and it scored zero on the degree of conservativism in the cumulated index of Esping-Andersen (1990). I also exclude Luxembourg, because it is not covered by the core contributions of Esping-Andersen (1990) and Palier (2010b; 2010a). I retain the Netherlands because, despite a high degree on the socialism index in Esping-Andersen's welfare capitalism typology (1990), it has a medium degree of conservativism and is considered conservative or Bismarckian by several studies (Cantillon, Seeleib-Kaiser, and Veen 2021; Castles and Mitchell 1993; Clegg 2019; Gingrich and Häusermann 2015; Palier 2010b; 2010a; Schröder 2009).

The introduction of social policy programmes was not unique for CEWS. However, in contrast to market-based welfare benefits in the United States and state-led national insurances in the United Kingdom and many Nordic countries, self-administered social insurance schemes providing earnings-related benefits based on employment were the preferred choice in CEWS (Palier 2010b).

The first statutory social insurance schemes are associated with the introduction of the sickness insurance (1883), work accident insurance (1884) and the old-age insurance scheme (1889) by chancellor Otto von Bismarck in Germany. The literature offers three main explanations for their introduction. The first makes socio-economic developments responsible for their introduction as well as for their recalibration (Flora and Heidenheimer 1981; Pierson 2001; Wilensky 1975). Processes of industrialisation and urbanisation led to workers selling their labour force in exchange for wages, making them dependent on their employers and no longer protected against social risks such as unemployment, sickness and old-age previously covered by landowners and family members.

The second theory focuses on the power resources of organised labour. According to Korpi (1983) and Esping-Andersen (1990), the mobilisation and organisation of the working class in trade unions and their cooperation with labour parties exerted pressure on governments and employers to improve working conditions and to introduce social policy programmes for (male) workers in the industry.

Finally, the introduction and expansion of social insurance schemes has been explained with the conservative and religious motives of governors and their strategy to pacify the working class guaranteeing social peace (Hennock 2007; Huber and Stephens 2001; van Kersbergen 1995; van Kersbergen and Manow 2009).

5.3 Characteristics of Continental European welfare states

This second part investigates empirically to what extent CEWS (still) differ in their core characteristics from other countries. After the analysis of social expenses and the importance of social contributions for the financing of benefits, it shows the crumbling power of social partners who administer social insurance schemes. Afterwards, we look at the level of earnings-related benefits in four social insurance schemes and conclude with the blurring dominance of male breadwinner norms. Box-and-whisker plots graphically show the results. It should be noted that the central box of the following plots represents values within the lower and upper quartiles (25 to 75 percentile), showing the median (middle line) and mean (cross). The whiskers below and above the box display the minimum and maximum values, respectively.

Figure 5.1 shows that social protection expenditures in CEWS amounts on average to 28.7 % in 2017 and are rather high in comparison with other European welfare states. Only Northern European countries have a slightly higher level (29.6 %). Especially Eastern European countries as well as the UK and Ireland spend much less on social protection. However, all country groups increased their social expenditures between 1997 and 2017.[1] The small size of the boxplots for CEWS additionally indicate a very homogenous group.

---

[1] All data in this chapter refer to the most recent available years with information for all countries compared to 20 years earlier or the earliest available years.

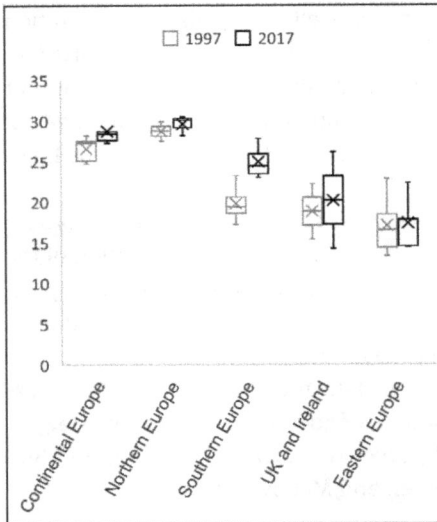

Figure 5.1: Expenses for social protection (% GDP).
Source: Eurostat [spr_exp_sum].
Notes: Continental Europe: Austria, Belgium, France, Germany and the Netherlands; Northern Europe: Denmark, Finland and Sweden; Southern Europe: Greece, Italy, Portugal and Spain; Eastern Europe: Czechia, Latvia, Lithuania, Slovenia and Slovakia (only countries with available data for 1997 and 2017 are included).

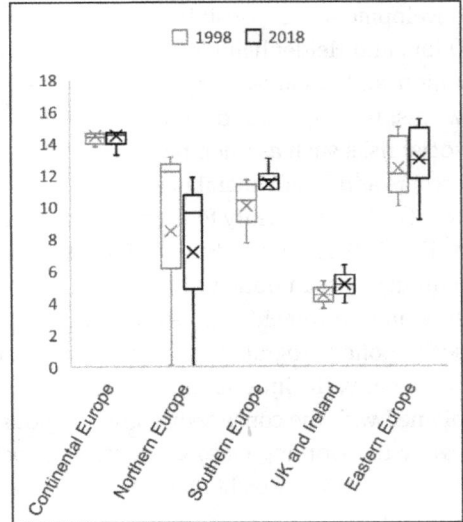

Figure 5.2: Tax revenue of social contributions of the general government as % of total revenue (% GDP).
Source: OECD Revenue Statistics.
Notes: Country groups as in Figure 5.1 except that Estonia, Hungary and Poland are additional countries for Eastern Europe (only countries with available data for 1998 and 2018 are included).

Compulsory social insurance schemes covering the risks of sickness, work accidents, unemployment and old age as the main source of welfare provision in CEWS are responsible for high social protection expenses. While the level of benefits and contributions remain in the hands of governments, their administration is carried by employees' and employers' representatives (i.e. trade unions and employer associations). Social insurance schemes are financed by earnings-related contributions of employers and employees. According to the OECD Revenue Statistics for 2018, Austria, Germany and the Netherlands have parity contributions (ratio of 1.0–1.2), employers in Belgium pay twice, and those in the Netherlands even three times the contributions of employees. Figure 5.2 reveals that the share of revenues from social contributions is exceptionally high in 2018 (14.5 % of GDP), with almost no change from 1998. As in Figure 5.1, small boxplots indicate homogeneity within CEWS regarding the financing of social protection by social contributions. Additional federal grants to social insurance schemes often cover vertical redistributive elements (e.g. for pensions in Germany and Austria).

The heritage of the statutory social insurance scheme's predecessors is still visible in the fragmentation of social insurance schemes along occupational groups. Germany, for example, still has more than 100 health insurance schemes, and pension insurance schemes in many CEWS distinguish, for example, blue-collar from white-collar workers and/or private from public sector employees. France and the Netherlands also have separate (quasi-)mandatory occupational pension schemes for different employee groups or sectors of employment.

The social partners play a key role in the administration of social insurance schemes and for wage negotiations (Ebbinghaus 2010). Figures 5.3 and 5.4 reveal that the power resources of trade unions in CEWS are based on widespread collective bargaining coverage, i.e. the share of employees covered by collective agreements, rather than on trade union density, i.e. the share of employees who are trade union members. Only every fourth employee (24 %) in CEWS was member of a trade union in 2019, similar to the liberal countries UK and Ireland (24 %) and much lower compared to Northern European countries (Figure 5.3). Belgium (49 %) and Austria (26 %) have considerable higher shares of trade union members than Germany (16 %), the Netherlands (15 %) and France (11 %). In contrast, collective bargaining coverage in 2018/19 in CEWS (84 %) was as high as in Northern European countries (86 %), albeit with large variation (from 98 % in Austria and France to only 54 % in Germany) (Figure 5.4).

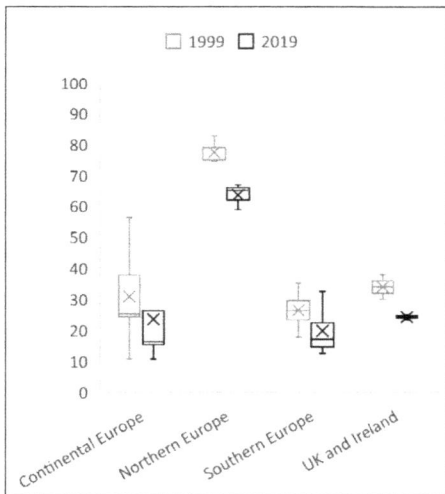

Figure 5.3 Trade union density (% employees). *Source*: OECD and AIAS 2021. *Notes*: Continental Europe: Austria, Belgium, France, Germany and the Netherlands; Northern Europe: Denmark, Finland and Sweden; Southern Europe: Greece, Italy, Portugal and Spain (the values of France shown as 2019 are for 2016, the values of Greece shown as 1999 are for 1998 and as 2019 are for 2016, the values of Portugal shown as 1999 are for 1997 and as 2019 are for 2016). Due to missing data, no results are shown for Eastern European countries.

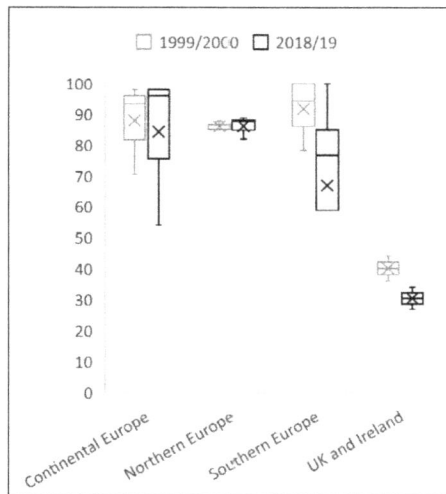

Figure 5.4: Collective bargaining coverage (% employees). *Source*: OECD and AIAS 2021. *Notes*: Continental Europe: Austria, Belgium, France, Germany and the Netherlands; Northern Europe: Denmark, Finland and Sweden; Southern Europe: Greece, Italy, Portugal and Spain (the values of France shown as 1999/2000 are for 1997 and the values of Finland, Sweden, Greece and Ireland shown as 2018/19 are for 2017). Due to missing data, no results are shown for Eastern European countries.

Regarding the benefits of social insurance schemes, CEWS provide mainly employment-related social rights and wage-related benefits, i.e. they depend on individual or the partner's employment. Entitlements require minimum periods of social contributions (e.g. 15 years minimum contributory period for pension benefits and one year of employment for unemployment benefits entitlement in Germany). The Social Insurance Entitlements dataset provides data for replacement rates of the four social policy fields pensions, unemployment, health, and work-related accidents (Figures 5.5–5.8) as part of the Social Policy Indicator (SPIN) database (Nelson et al. 2020). This is one of very few sources including comparative and longitudinal information on benefit entitlements for a range of social policy fields.

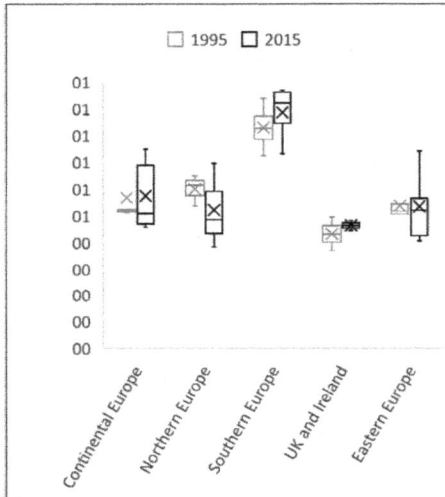

Figure 5.5: Net annual replacement rate for average single production worker (old-age pension benefits).
Source: Nelson et al. 2020.
Notes: Continental Europe: Austria, Belgium, France, Germany and the Netherlands; Northern Europe: Denmark, Finland and Sweden; Southern Europe: Greece, Italy, Portugal and Spain; Eastern Europe: Bulgaria, Czechia, Estonia, Hungary, Latvia, Lithuania, Poland, Slovenia and Slovakia (the values of Eastern Europe shown as 1995 are for 2005).

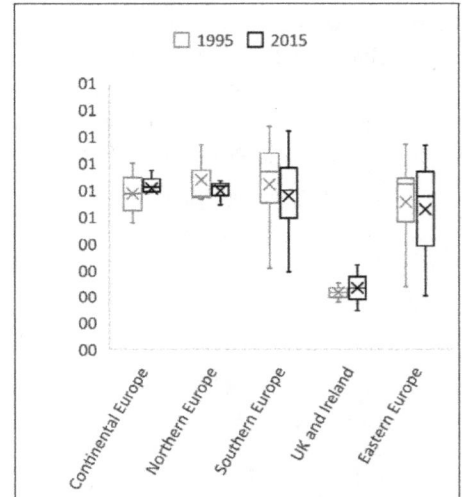

Figure 5.6: Net replacement (average after 1 and 26 weeks) for average single production worker (unemployment benefits).
Source: Nelson et al. 2020.
Notes: see notes for Figure 5.5.

CEWS show the second highest level of public pension benefits (after Southern European countries) in 2015 (Figure 5.5). The net annual replacement rate for an average single production worker in 2015 in CEWS was 57 %. The public pension system is most generous in Austria (75 %) and Belgium (69 %) and least in Germany (47 %) and the Netherlands (46 %). The low replacement in the Netherlands is due to the universal flat-rate basic pension scheme that is topped up by compulsory occupational pensions resulting in exceptionally high benefit levels (Anderson 2011). While Belgium increased the benefit levels between 1995 and 2015, Germany experienced a reduction from 52 % in 1995 to 47 % in 2015.

Compared with the other country groups, CEWS have the highest unemployment benefits for short-term unemployed (Figure 5.6), which could be related to firm and industry-specific skill requirements in coordinated market economies (Hall and Soskice 2001). As employees with specific skills have higher unemployment risks than employees with general skills, countries whose economy is based on such employees provide more generous unemployment benefits (Estevez-Abe, Iversen, and Soskice 2001; Iversen 2005). The net replacement for an average single production worker in CEWS in 2015, calculated as the average of benefits after 1 and 26 weeks of unemployment, was 61 %, slightly higher than in 1995 (59 %). With a reduction of unemployment benefits in Germany and the Netherlands and their increase in Belgium, CEWS became more similar over time (smaller boxplot in 2015) in this respect.

The net replacement for an average single production worker in 2015 for sickness benefits in CEWS was 80 %, not much different from their level in 1995 (Figure 5.7). The most generous sickness insurance schemes are found in Austria, Germany and Belgium (92 %–95 % replacement rate).

The benefit levels of work-related accident insurance schemes in 2015 in CEWS are second only to Eastern European countries' level (Figure 5.8). The net replacement for an average single production worker in 2015 was 88 % (1995: 87 %) (Figure 5.8). Similar to sickness benefits, work-related accident benefits are higher in Austria, Germany and Belgium (92 %–100 % replacement rate) compared to France (84 %) and the Netherlands (64 %).

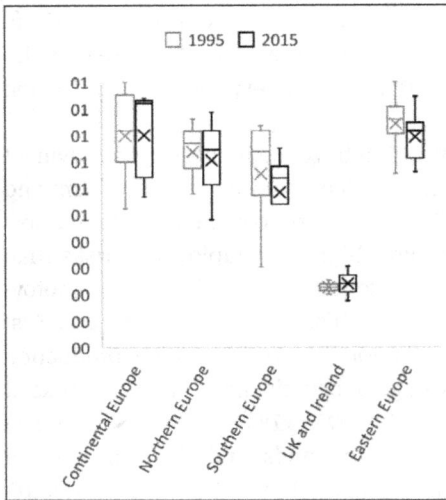

Figure 5.7: Net replacement rate (average after 1 and 26 weeks) for average single production worker (sickness benefits).
Source: Nelson et al. 2020.
Notes: see notes for Figure 5.5.

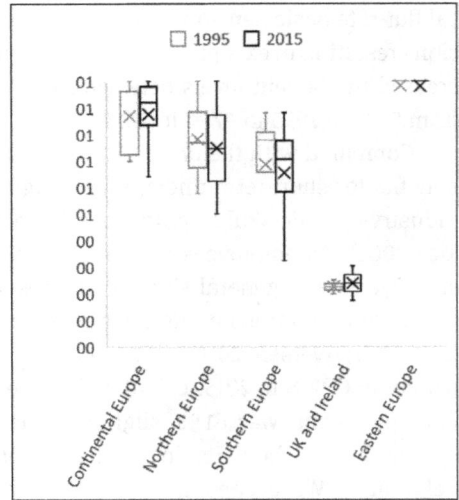

Figure 5.8: Net replacement rate (average after 1 and 26 weeks) for average single production worker (accident benefits).
Source: Nelson et al. 2020.
Notes: see notes for Figure 5.5.

Across all social insurance schemes, benefit levels in CEWS did not change much between 1995 and 2015. Across countries, we find remarkable variation for pension and sickness benefits, while replacement rates are very similar for unemployment and work-related accident insurance schemes.

As the last core characteristic of CEWS in this section, status preservation based on lifelong full employment and the (catholic) principle of subsidiarity produces family structures where men are the breadwinners and women are responsible for caring for children and older people (Lewis 1992). However, France has been an example of a modified male-breadwinner model thanks to women's high full-time employment rates and redistribution towards families with children (Lewis 1992). The male breadwinner model is linked to weak or limited de-familisation (independence of women from gender- and generation specific duties). We therefore find large overlaps between welfare regimes and different family policy models (Wiß and Greve 2020), with CEWS not always falling in the same group or cluster (for an overview and discussion of family policy concepts, see Lohmann and Zagel 2016).

A good measure for the male breadwinner norm, one of the (former) core characteristics of CEWS, is the survey question on whether men should have more rights to jobs than women when jobs are scarce (Gonalons-Pons and Gangl 2021) (Figure 5.9) and whether a pre-school child is likely to suffer if his/her mother works (Figure 10). Only 10 % of the respondents in CEWS in 2017/18 agree that men should have more rights to jobs than women when jobs are scarce (Figure 5.9), putting them in between the other country groups. The large decrease of 12 percentage points of the male breadwinner norm in CEWS between 1999 and 2017/18 is striking. Across countries, male breadwinner norms are more widespread in Austria (14 %) and France (12 %), despite the latter's modified male breadwinner model (see above), than in Germany (9 %) and the Netherlands (6 %). The results are very similar for the other question, although Austrians are much more sympathetic to this (47 %) than their Dutch counterparts (21 %).

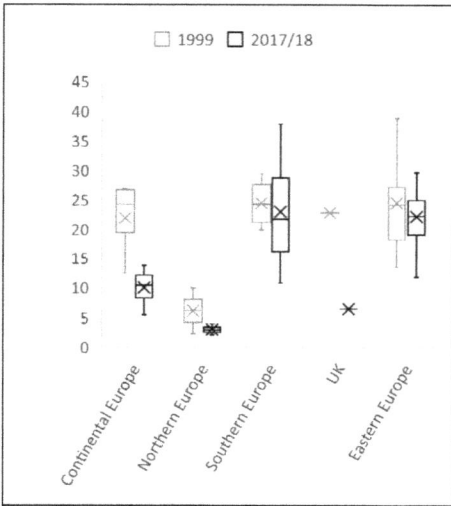

Figure 5.9: Male breadwinner norms I: scarce jobs.
Sources: EVS 2015 and EVS/WVS 2021.
Notes: Share of population that agrees on "When jobs are scarce, men have more right to a job than women." Continental Europe: Austria, France, Germany and the Netherlands; Northern Europe: Denmark, Finland and Sweden; Southern Europe: Greece, Italy, Portugal and Spain; Eastern Europe: Bulgaria, Czechia, Estonia, Hungary, Lithuania, Poland, Slovenia and Slovakia (the values of Finland shown as 1999 are for 2000 and the values of Portugal shown as 2017/18 are for 2020).

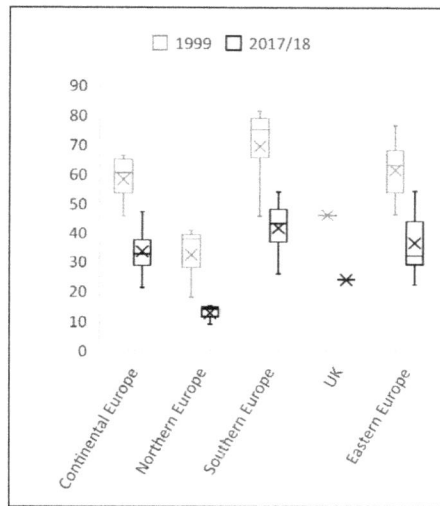

Figure 5.10: Male breadwinner norms II: children suffer.
Sources: EVS 2015 and EVS/WVS 2021.
Notes: Share of population that agrees on "A pre-school child is likely to suffer if his or her mother works." Continental Europe: Austria, France, Germany and the Netherlands; Northern Europe: Denmark, Finland and Sweden; Southern Europe: Greece, Italy, Portugal and Spain; Eastern Europe: Bulgaria, Czechia, Estonia, Lithuania, Poland, Slovenia and Slovakia (the values of Austria shown as 1999 are for 2008, the values of Finland shown as 1999 are for 2000 and the values of Portugal shown as 2017/18 are for 2020).

5.4 Contemporary challenges and reform trends

CEWS assume that people enter the labour market directly after school and work full-time with the same employer until retirement. However, nowadays career patterns and people's preferences are often more diverse, creating contribution gaps that may result in larger inequalities and endanger democracy: the legitimacy of a welfare state suffers when it does not produce proper outcomes.

5.4.1 Longevity and pensions

A higher life expectancy means that a) people spend more time in retirement which makes pension systems more costly and b) there is potentially more time to receive health and care-related services and benefits which burdens employment-based contributions when health and long-term care are predominantly financed via social insurance schemes. Higher retirement ages and/or lower benefits seem to be a more likely response than the shift to funded pensions, because people would need to pay contributions to finance current pensioners' benefits and at the same time contribute to their own funded pension plans (double-payment problem). The number of years a newborn is expected to live increased between 1995 and 2000 and 2015 and 2020 on average by 3.4 years for women (5.2 years for men) in CEWS, with the lowest life expectancy in Germany and the highest in France (the Netherlands for men). Projections expect a further increase of 6.5 years for women and men until 2045–2050 (Wittgenstein Centre for Demography and Global Human Capital 2018).

As a first reaction to this, Austria, Belgium, Germany and France implemented reforms within the public pension schemes in the 1990s and 2000s aiming at preserving their Bismarckian character. In line with the equivalence principle, they established a stronger link between contributions and benefits from which labour market insiders with stable full-time employment careers profit. Furthermore, Germany replaced the defined benefit calculation with point based notional-defined contributions considering the whole employment career; Austria extended the reference period for the calculation of benefits from the last (and usually best) five years prior to retirement to 40 years with contributions; and early retirement paths have been (partially) closed in all countries (Hinrichs 2021). However, these incremental reforms have often been supplemented with more radical retrenchment, higher statutory retirement ages (except for men in Austria) and a more important role for funded occupational and personal pensions (Ebbinghaus 2011; Hinrichs 2021). An exception is the Netherlands with its universal basic pension providing flat-rate benefits and a long tradition of (quasi-)mandatory funded occupational pensions based on collective agreements and strong union involvement (Anderson 2011). However, even funded occupational pensions are faced with retrenchment, such as lower benefit indexation and the shift from final-salary to average-salary defined benefit plans in the Netherlands (Wiß 2019) and lower return guarantees in Germany and Belgium.

5.4.2 Atypical employment, poverty and inequality

Working career interruptions and atypical employment are a further major challenge for CEWS whose benefits depend on long full-time employment careers. According to the OECD Labour Market Statistics, employment rates in 2020 in all CEWS, measured as the ratio of employed persons to the working age population (15–64 years), was significantly higher compared to 20 years ago. However, atypical employment was often responsible for employment growth. The share of part-time employment in 2019 exceeded 20 % in Austria, Germany and the Netherlands (with a strong increase in the last 20 years) and is below the EU average only in France (OECD Labour Market Statistics). Temporary employment is also on the rise with a particularly high incidence in the Netherlands and France (OECD Labour Market Statistics).

An indicator for less stable labour markets is the declining job tenure in all CEWS, i.e. the number of years employees have been with their current employer. The average job tenure for employees aged 50–54 decreased for example from 19.5 years in 1995 to 16.3 years in 2015 in Austria and from 20.4 years in 1995 to 17.7 years in 2015 in Belgium (OECD Labour Market Statistics). A shorter job tenure means higher fluidity in the labour market and might signal more flexible employment patterns with the potential of lower welfare benefits due to working career interruptions.

Regarding poverty prevention as one of the central goals of welfare states, CEWS have 14 % of the total population at risk of poverty in 2018/19, with higher values in Belgium and Germany (14.8 %) and lower in the Netherlands (13.2 %) and Austria (13.3 %) (Figure 5.11). Although reducing inequality is a further aim of most welfare states, the strong status preservation orientation in CEWS reproduces social stratification. The average Gini coefficient after social transfers in 2018/19 (27 %) did not change much compared to 1999/2000 there (Figure 5.12). Over time, Germany and Austria experienced the highest increase. The lower levels of poverty and inequality in CEWS than in other country groups are similar to Nordic countries' performances and confirm the "paradox of redistribution" (Korpi and Palme 1998): redistribution is more effective in countries with broad and egalitarian benefits involving also high-income earners rather than in countries that target low-income groups.

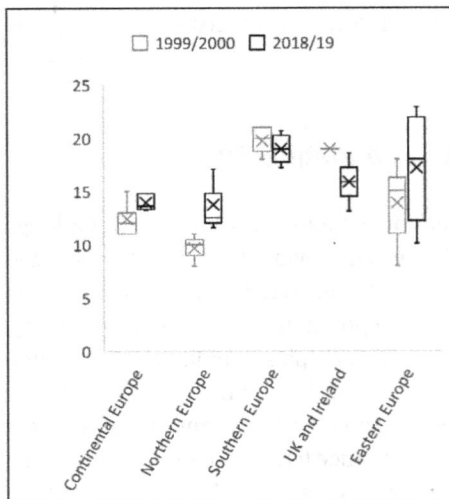

Figure 5.11: At risk of poverty rate (60 % of median equivalised income after social transfers). *Sources:* Eurostat EU-SILC and ECHP surveys [ilc_li02]. *Notes:* Continental Europe: Austria, Belgium, France, Germany and the Netherlands; Northern Europe: Denmark, Finland and Sweden; Southern Europe: Greece, Italy, Portugal and Spain; Eastern Europe: Bulgaria, Czechia, Estonia, Hungary, Latvia, Lithuania, Poland and Slovenia (the values of Czechia shown as 1999/2000 are for 2001).

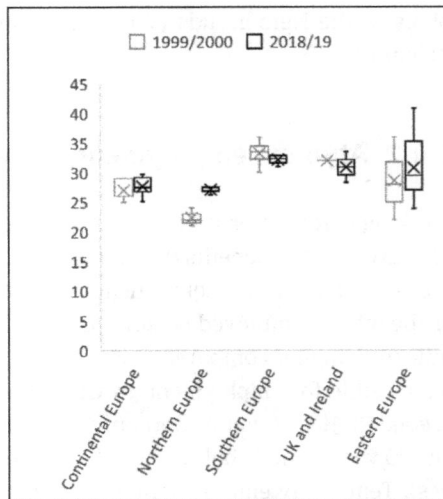

Figure 5.12: Gini coefficient after social transfer. *Sources:* Eurostat EU-SILC survey [ilc_di12]. *Notes:* see notes for Figure 5.11.

In response to more interrupted working careers, atypical employment and in order to meet old-age poverty, new means-tested minimum income schemes were introduced for those who do not qualify for benefits from pension insurance (e.g. in Germany) (Ebbinghaus, Gronwald, and Wiß 2011); contributory minimum pension benefits were increased for those with pension insurance entitlements below poverty thresholds (e.g. Austria) (Schulze and Schludi 2007); and access to public pensions for employees in arduous and hazardous jobs was improved (France).

Suffering from high structural unemployment in the 1980s and 1990s, CEWS reformed their employment policies and unemployment insurances with the aim of activating unemployed persons. Benefits for long-term unemployed have been reduced in Germany (Seeleib-Kaiser 2016), Belgium and France (Palier 2010b). While these policies contributed to an increase in employment, they promoted the dualism of labour markets and social protection with protected high-skilled core employees (insider) on the one hand and temporary and low-skilled employees with a high risk of exclusion (outsider) on the other hand (Emmenegger et al. 2012; Schwander and Häusermann 2013; Thelen 2014). According to Schwander and Häusermann

(2013), in CEWS, female and young employees are at the highest risk of atypical employment and unemployment in comparison with men and older employees. Furthermore, with the exception of France, CEWS suffer from a particularly strong gender bias.

Such labour market dualisation is likely to result in a dualisation of social protection when only labour market insiders can preserve their status undermining one of CEWS's building blocks. Recently introduced tax-financed (means-tested) minimum income schemes and increased tax-financed federal grants to social insurance schemes have therefore been developed to cover redistributive elements (e.g. for credits for times of child rearing or unemployment).

5.4.3 Gender inequalities and family policy

Significant gender inequalities in CEWS are the inheritance of the (blurring) male breadwinner model. In 2018/19, women earned on average 15.2% less than men per hour in CEWS, more than in Northern and Southern European countries, but less than in the UK, Ireland and in Eastern Europe (Figure 5.13). Among CEWS, Austria and Germany have the highest gender pay gap (19.9% and 19.2%) and Belgium a particularly low one (5.8%). Gender inequalities in the labour market often translate into gender inequalities for pensioners. Figure 5.14 reveals that CEWS have by far the largest gender pension gap (35%) and this has changed only marginally since 2006/07 (36.3%). Despite its universal basic pension scheme with quite generous benefits, the Netherlands produces the largest gap (40%), partially due to the high income share of funded occupational pensions. Austria's very generous public pension scheme, however, is only marginally better off (37%).

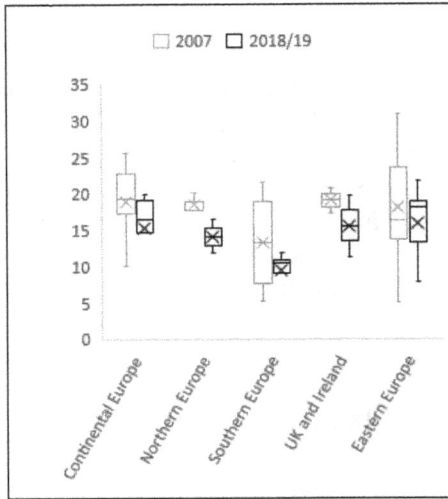

Figure 5.13: Gender pay gap (%).
Sources: Eurostat [earn_gr_gpgr2].
Notes: The gender pay gap is measured as the difference between the average gross hourly earnings of men and women expressed as a percentage of the average gross hourly earnings of men. Continental Europe: Austria, Belgium, France, Germany and the Netherlands; Northern Europe: Denmark, Finland and Sweden; Southern Europe: Greece, Italy, Portugal and Spain; Eastern Europe: Bulgaria, Czechia, Estonia, Hungary, Latvia, Lithuania, Poland, Slovenia and Slovakia.

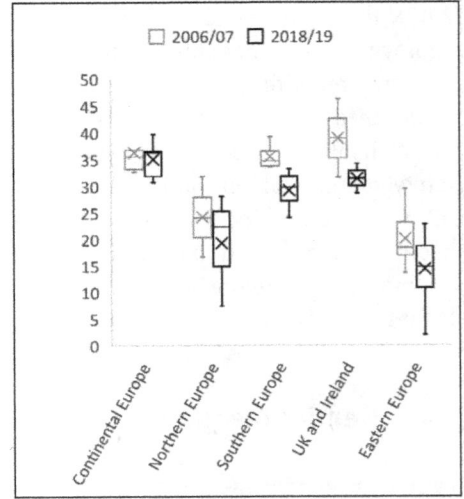

Figure 5.14: Gender pension gap.
Sources: Eurostat [ilc_pnp13].
Notes: The gender pension gap is measures as the percentage difference between the pension of men and women. For country groups, see notes for Figure 5.13.

In order to meet some of the gender inequalities, family policy has been expanding massively in most CEWS in the last two decades, weakening the male breadwinner model (Gleichen and Seeleib-Kaiser 2018). Since the 1990s, Belgium underwent a first-order change (lowest degree of change), but remained with the Christian-democratic family policy space (short to medium length of family-related leave and medium level of childcare service provision); the Netherlands moved from the liberal to the Christian-democratic space; and France remained with the social-democratic space despite a further first-order change (generous leave and comprehensive childcare arrangements) (Ferragina and Seeleib-Kaiser 2015). Austria is characterised by a second-order and Germany even by a third-order change (highest degree of change), both having moved into the social-democratic space. The introduction of earnings-related parental leave benefits with two daddy months and the entitlement to public childcare for children above one are examples of Germany's path departure from its traditional family policy (Fleckenstein and Lee 2014; Seeleib-Kaiser 2016). Austria, in contrast, still lags behind despite parental leave and childcare provision reforms.

5.4.4 Migration

The heavy inflow of refugees to Europe in 2015 provoked a rise in discussions regarding immigrants' access to welfare state benefits. Although equity-based welfare schemes such as social insurance schemes are supposed to be less prone to welfare chauvinistic appeals (Ennser-Jedenastik 2018), some CEWS provide a particularly exclusive access to welfare state benefits. Based on 25 indicators that measure to what degree several social policy programmes differentiate between native-born citizens and immigrants when granting access to welfare state benefits, no clear pattern emerges for CEWS (Koning 2021). Austria and the Netherlands are among the countries with most restrictions, Germany and Belgium have medium-high levels of immigrant exclusion, and France is the most inclusive among CEWS. Across social policy fields, means-tested social assistance programmes are more vulnerable to nativism than insurance-based benefits (Ennser-Jedenastik 2018).

At the same time, EU migration, mainly for employment reasons, did not cause significant reform discussions recently, thanks to the extensive EU regime for social security coordination regarding employment mobility and the transferability of social rights.

5.4.5 The COVID-19 pandemic

Other factors might also play a role within the current debate on welfare states. Due to the COVID-19 pandemic, self-employed, young people, low-skilled and people in atypical employment suffered from a decline in or loss of income and dismissals, especially in manufacturing, the hospitality sector, and arts and culture (Cantillon, Seeleib-Kaiser, and Veen 2021). Furthermore, lockdowns and the closure of schools and childcare institutions challenged the reconciliation of work and family life for parents, in particular working mothers.

Drawing on the experience from the 2008 financial crisis, social insurance schemes have been used as automatic stabilisers or buffers for otherwise negative social and economic consequences (Cantillon, Seeleib-Kaiser, and Veen 2021; Seemann et al. 2021). Austria, Belgium, France and Germany extended their short-time work schemes (temporary unemployment scheme in Belgium) to subsidise firms and their employees. In support of families, Austria, Belgium and Germany granted additional parental leave benefits to working parents whose children could not attend school or childcare (Koslowski et al. 2021). The Netherlands, as the only CEWS, established a new system outside of the existing social insurance scheme and made use of targeted benefits (e.g. social assistance for self-employed) and wage subsidies. Although the COVID-19 pandemic has not (yet) altered the major institutions and social policies of CEWS, it might open a window of opportunity for a partial recalibration of welfare states.

5.5 Conclusion

The building blocks of CEWS such as the dominating role of social insurance schemes and employment-related social rights are still intact. However, retrenchment in public pension schemes and for long-term unemployed and the expansion in funded market-based welfare (e.g. occupational pensions) make it increasingly difficult for labour market outsiders and partially even the middle class to achieve one of CEWS' aim, namely status maintenance in times without employment. Furthermore, the central role and power of trade unions as part of the social partnership is crumbling outside the self-administered social insurance schemes which makes it increasingly difficult to negotiate advantageous working conditions and wages as well as to exert a voice in political decision-making processes. The male breadwinner model as the dominating family ideal has been partially replaced by the dual breadwinner model (at least one full-time and one part-time earner) thanks to the promotion of female labour force participation and work/family reconciliation (childcare and parental leave policies). Furthermore, people outside employment profit from more non-contributory univer-salistic benefits.

Despite major challenges such as ageing, less stable labour markets, financial and economic crises as well as the COVID-19 pandemic, viewed as a whole, CEWS still have much in common and are to certain degrees still different from the other welfare states. However, recent reforms containing both liberal and social-democratic elements might indicate (slow) endogenous changes with the long-term potential to undermine the character of CEWS.

References

Anderson, Karen M. 2011. "Netherlands: Adapting a Multipillar Pension System to Demographic and Economic Change," In *The Varieties of Pension Governance: Pension Privatization in Europe*, edited by Bernhard Ebbinghaus, 292–317. Oxford: Oxford University Press.

Bonoli, Giuliano. 1997. "Classifying Welfare States: A Two-Dimension Approach." *Journal of Social Policy* 26 (03), 351–372.

Cantillon, Bea, Martin Seeleib-Kaiser, and Romke van der Veen. 2021. "The COVID-19 Crisis and Policy Responses by Continental European Welfare States." *Social Policy & Administration* 55 (2), 326–338.

Castles, Francis G., and Deborah Mitchell. 1993. "Worlds of Welfare and Families of Nations." In *Families of Nations: Patterns of Public Policy in Western Democracies*, edited by Francis G. Castles, 93–128. Aldershot: Dartmouth Publishing Company.

Clegg, Daniel. 2019. "Central European Welfare States." In *Routledge Handbook of the Welfare State*, edited by Bent Greve, 137–147. London: Routledge.

Ebbinghaus, Bernhard. 2010. "Reforming Bismarckian Corporatism: The Changing Role of Social Partnership in Continental Europe." In *A Long Goodbye to Bismarck?: The Politics of Welfare Reform in Continental Europe*, edited by Bruno Palier, 255–278. Amsterdam: Amsterdam University Press.

Ebbinghaus, Bernhard (ed.) 2011. *The Varieties of Pension Governance: Pensional Privatization in Europe*. Oxford: Oxford University Press.

Ebbinghaus, Bernhard, Mareike Gronwald, and Tobias Wiß. 2011. "Germany: Departing from Bismarckian Public Pensions." In *The Varieties of Pension Governance: Pension Privatization in Europe*, edited by Bernhard Ebbinghaus, 119–150. Oxford: Oxford University Press.

Emmenegger, Patrick, Silja Häusermann, Bruno Palier, and Martin Seeleib-Kaiser (eds.) 2012. *The Age of Dualization: The Changing Face of Inequality in Deindustrializing Societies*. Oxford: Oxford University Press.

Ennser-Jedenastik, Laurenz. 2018. "Welfare Chauvinism in Populist Radical Right Platforms: The Role of Redistributive Justice Principles." *Social Policy & Administration* 52 (1), 293–314.

Esping-Andersen, Gøsta. 1990. *The Three Worlds of Welfare Capitalism*. Princeton, NJ: Princeton University Press.

Estevez-Abe, Margarita, Torben Iversen, and David Soskice. 2001. "Social Protection and the Formation of Skills: A Reinterpretation of the Welfare State." In *Varieties of Capitalism: The Institutional Foundations of Comparative Advantage*, edited by Peter A. Hall and David Soskice, 145–183. New York: Oxford University Press.

EVS. 2015. European Values Study Longitudinal Data File 1981-2008 (EVS 1981-2008). *GESIS Data Archive*, Cologne. ZA4804 Data File Version 3.0.0, doi:10.4232/1.12253.

EVS/WVS. 2021. *Joint EVS/WVS 2017-2021 Dataset (Joint EVS/WVS). GESIS Data Archive, Cologne. ZA7505 Data File Version 1.1.0, doi:10.4232/1.13670.*

Ferragina, Emanuele, and Martin Seeleib-Kaiser. 2015. "Determinants of a Silent (R)Evolution: Understanding the Expansion of Family Policy in Rich OECD Countries." *Social Politics: International Studies in Gender, State & Society* 22 (1), 1–37.

Ferrera, Maurizio. 1996. "The 'Southern Model' of Welfare in Social Europe.' *Journal of European Social Policy* 6 (1), 17–37.

Fleckenstein, Timo, and Soohyun Christine Lee. 2014. "The Politics of Postindustrial Social Policy: Family Policy Reforms in Britain, Germany, South Korea, and Sweden," *Comparative Political Studies* 47 (4), 601–630.

Flora, Peter, and Arnold Joseph Heidenheimer. 1981. *The Development of Welfare States in Europe and America*. New Brunswick, NJ: Transaction Publishers.

Gingrich, Jane, and Silja Häusermann. 2015. "The Decline of the Working-Class Vote, the Reconfiguration of the Welfare Support Coalition and Consequences for the Welfare State." *Journal of European Social Policy* 25 (1), 50–75.

Gleichen, Rosa Daiger von, and Martin Seeleib-Kaiser. 2018. "Family Policies and the Weakening of the Male-Breadwinner Model." In *Handbook on Gender and Social Policy*, edited by Sheila Shaver, 153–178. Cheltenham: Edward Elgar.

Gonalons-Pons, Pilar, and Markus Gangl. 2021. "Marriage and Masculinity: Male-Breadwinner Culture, Unemployment, and Separation Risk in 29 Countries." *American Sociological Review* 86 (3), 465–502.

Hall, Peter A., and David Soskice (eds.) 2001. *Varieties of Capitalism: The Institutional Foundations of Comparative Advantage*. Oxford: Oxford University Press.

Hennock, E. P. 2007. *The Origin of the Welfare State in England and Germany, 1850–1914: Social Policies Compared*. Cambridge: Cambridge University Press.

Hinrichs, Karl. 2021. "Recent Pension Reforms in Europe: More Challenges, New Directions. An Overview." *Social Policy & Administration* 55 (3), 409–422.

Huber, Evelyne, and John D. Stephens. 2001. *Development and Crisis of the Welfare State: Parties and Policies in Global Markets*. Chicago: University of Chicago Press.

Iversen, Torben. 2005. *Capitalism, Democracy, and Welfare*. Cambridge: Cambridge University Press.

Kersbergen, Kees van. 1995. *Social Capitalism: A Study of Christian Democracy and the Welfare State*. London: Routledge.

Kersbergen, Kees van, and Philip Manow (eds.) 2009. *Religion, Class Coalitions, and Welfare States*. Cambridge Studies in Social Theory, Religion and Politics. Cambridge: Cambridge University Press.

Koning, Edward A. 2021. "Accommodation and New Hurdles: The Increasing Importance of Politics for Immigrants' Access to Social Programmes in Western Democracies." *Social Policy & Administration* 55 (5), 815–832.

Korpi, Walter. 1983. *The Democratic Class Struggle*. London and Boston: Routledge.

Korpi, Walter, and Joakim Palme. 1998. "The Paradox of Redistribution and Strategies of Equality: Welfare State Institutions, Inequality, and Poverty in the Western Countries." *American Sociological Review* 63 (5), 661–687.

Koslowski, Alison, Sonja Blum, Ivana Dobrotić, Gayle Kaufman, and Peter Moss. 2021. *International Review of Leave Policies and Research 2021*. DOI: 10.18445/20210817-144100-0. Available at: http://www.leavenetwork.org/lp_and_r_reports (accessed 7 October 2021).

Leibfried, Stephan. 1992. "Towards a European Welfare State? On Integrating Poverty Regimes into the European Community." In *Social Policy in a Changing Europe*, edited by Zsuzsa Ferge and Jon Eivind Kolberg, 245–279. Frankfurt a. M: Campus.

Lewis, Jane. 1992. "Gender and the Development of Welfare Regimes." *Journal of European Social Policy* 2 (3), 159–173.

Lohmann, Henning, and Hannah Zagel. 2016. "Family Policy in Comparative Perspective: The Concepts and Measurement of Familization and Defamilization." *Journal of European Social Policy* 26 (1), 48–65.

Nelson, Kenneth, Daniel Fredriksson, Tomas Korpi, Walter Korpi, Joakim Palme, and Ola Sjöberg. 2020. "The Social Policy Indicators (SPIN) Database." *International Journal of Social Welfare* 29 (3), 285–289.

OECD and AIAS. 2021. *Institutional Characteristics of Trade Unions, Wage Setting, State Intervention and Social Pacts*. Paris: OECD.

Palier, Bruno (ed.) 2010a. *A Long Goodbye to Bismarck? The Politics of Welfare Reforms in Continental Europe*. Amsterdam: Amsterdam University Press.

Palier, Bruno. 2010b. "Continental Western Europe." In *Oxford Handbook of the Welfare State*, edited by Francis G. Castles, Stephan Leibfried, Jane Lewis, Herbert Obinger, and Christopher Pierson, 601–615. Oxford: Oxford University Press.

Pierson, Paul. 2001. "Post-Industrial Pressures on the Mature Welfare State." In *The New Politics of the Welfare State*, edited by Paul Pierson, 80–104. New York: Oxford University Press.

Schröder, Martin. 2009. "Integrating Welfare and Production Typologies: How Refinements of the Varieties of Capitalism Approach Call for a Combination of Welfare Typologies." *Journal of Social Policy* 38 (1), 19–43.

Schulze, Isabelle, and Martin Schludi. 2007. "Austria: From Electoral Cartels to Competitive Coalition-Building.'" In *The Handbook of West European Pension Politics*, edited by Ellen M. Immergut, Karen M. Anderson, and Isabelle Schulze, 555–604. Oxford: Oxford University Press.

Schwander, Hanna, and Silja Häusermann. 2013. "Who Is In and Who Is Out? A Risk-Based Conceptualization of Insiders and Outsiders." *Journal of European Social Policy* 23 (3), 248–269.

Seeleib-Kaiser, Martin. 2016. "The End of the Conservative German Welfare State Model." *Social Policy & Administration* 50 (2), 219–240.

Seemann, Anika, Ulrich Becker, Linxin He, Eva Maria Hohnerlein, and Nikola Wilman. 2021. "Protecting Livelihoods in the COVID-19 Crisis: A Comparative Analysis of European Labour Market and Social Policies." *Global Social Policy*, 21 (3), 550–568.

Thelen, Kathleen. 2014. *Varieties of Liberalization and the New Politics of Social Solidarity*. Cambridge Studies in Comparative Politics. Cambridge: Cambridge University Press.

Wilensky, Harold L. 1975. *The Welfare State and Equality: Structural and Ideological Roots of Public Expenditures*. Berkeley/Los Angeles/London: University of California Press.

Wiß, Tobias. 2019. "Reinforcement of Pension Financialisation as a Response to Financial Crises in Germany, the Netherlands and the United Kingdom." *Journal of European Public Policy* 26 (4), 501–520.

Wiß, Tobias, and Bent Greve. 2020. "A Comparison of the Interplay of Public and Occupational Work–Family Policies in Austria, Denmark, Italy and the United Kingdom." *Journal of Comparative Policy Analysis: Research and Practice* 22 (5), 440–457.

Wittgenstein Centre for Demography and Global Human Capital. 2018. *Wittgenstein Centre Data Explorer Version 2.0 (Beta)*. Available at: http://www.wittgensteincentre.org/dataexplorer.

Elke Heins and Fiona Dukelow

6 Liberal welfare states

Abstract: This chapter discusses contemporary challenges for liberal welfare states. We first describe the key features of the liberal welfare regime from an ideal-type perspective. Then we discuss central developments in liberal welfare states. This overview is mainly based on aggregate data covering a variety of specific social policy areas as well as data on social expenditure, poverty and inequality. Third, we analyse the extent to which liberal welfare states are prepared to cope with challenges including fiscal pressures due to demographic change, migration, the digitalisation of the labour market, climate change and the COVID-19 pandemic. We conclude by commenting on the questions these challenges raise for liberal welfare states in a post-pandemic context and the likelihood of any policy learning from the pandemic being realised.

Keywords: Australia, automation, Canada, climate change, Covid-19, inequality, migration, New Zealand, United Kingdom, United States

6.1 Introduction

The liberal regime type typically comprises welfare states in English-speaking (or "Anglo-Saxon") countries per the classic typology of Esping-Andersen (1990) and subsequent welfare state typologies. In our analysis we focus on Australia, Canada, New Zealand, the United Kingdom (UK) and the United States (US) over the last ten years.[1] We present aggregate social expenditure data but also cover a broad range of specific policy areas to highlight the key trends across liberal welfare regimes.

While most of the typical liberal welfare regime features remain dominant, and have even become more prominent recently, e.g. regarding the privatisation of healthcare, the retrenchment of public pension systems or the harshness of the benefit system, there are also notable differences among the five countries, indicating that not only regime type but also politics matter. The COVID-19 crisis has laid bare the particular weaknesses and required a much greater state intervention than the liberal regime would usually allow. These came at great cost due to the absence of good social

---

1 Ireland is excluded as it represents a hybrid model (Dukelow and Heins 2017) although we acknowledge that every real empirical case only approximates a theoretical ideal type. The literature sometimes distinguishes Australia and New Zealand as a distinct "Antipodean" regime cluster or a "wage-earners' welfare state" (Castles and Mitchell 1993). We subsume both countries under the general liberal welfare regime type.

https://doi.org/10.1515/9783110721768-006

protection and social investment policies. It remains to be seen if any policy innovations will lead to longer term changes in the liberal welfare model.

We first describe the key features of the liberal welfare regime from an ideal-type perspective. Then we discuss central developments in liberal welfare states. This overview is mainly based on aggregate data covering a variety of specific social policy areas as well as data on social expenditure, poverty and inequality. Third, we analyse the extent to which liberal welfare states are prepared to cope with challenges including fiscal pressures due to demographic change, migration, the digitalisation of the labour market, climate change and the COVID-19 pandemic. We conclude by suggesting potential responses to the current challenges of liberal welfare states and the likelihood of their implementation.

6.2 The liberal ideal type

The core ideological feature of the liberal welfare regime is the value placed on individual freedom and self-reliance, emphasising the primacy of market relations that allows for the expression of individual choice regarding welfare. This is coupled with a non-interventionist approach to labour market regulation. Though there are incidences of universalism in liberal welfare states such as National Health Services or basic pensions, benefit levels are low and associated with relatively modest entitlement rules. Flat rate benefits and means testing are also typical, and both policy instruments encourage market provision of social protection, indicating low levels of decommodification (Esping-Andersen 1990). A dualism thus arises between a residual welfare state targeted at the poor and the working class, while the middle classes rely more on market provision, including health insurance and pension schemes. Therefore, welfare receipt is usually highly stigmatising, leading to a perceived distinction between those who pay and those who benefit from welfare – supporting a "welfare myth of them and us" (Hills 2014). Correspondingly, the portrayal of welfare in the media is highly negative and loaded with stereotypes (Albrekt Larsen and Engel Dejgaard 2013) and support for public welfare is low (Albrekt Larsen 2008). Welfare receipt is ascribed to laziness and other individual behaviour. "Welfare dependency" rather than structural causes of poverty and inequality is seen as the main problem and there is a strong preoccupancy with benefit fraud (Baumberg Geiger 2018).

Relatively low levels of public social expenditure are matched by low levels of taxation. Yet liberal welfare states also display a preference for fiscal welfare, or welfare via the tax system, as a means of encouraging private provision. This use of fiscal welfare also gives rise to a potentially larger "hidden welfare state" (Howard 1999) than in other welfare regimes, which in contradiction to the above-mentioned welfare myth primarily benefits the middle classes (Hills 2014).

In line with "liberal work-ethic norms" (Esping-Andersen 1990, 26) other characteristics of the liberal regime include a tendency towards a punitive, "work first" approach to activation. Since the 1990s, the established principle of means-tested benefits was supplemented with the principle of conditionality – benefits in return for demonstrated work-focused activities coupled with the use of sanctions. Not only are those in receipt of out-of-work benefits targeted, but also sometimes even those in work (Dwyer and Wright 2014).

Liberal welfare states have also been pioneers of recommodification and introducing policies, e.g. tax credits and in-work benefits, that aim at "making work pay" (Clegg 2015). As conditionality extends to in-work benefits, and the policy thrust moves from incentives to coercion, a trend of "coercive commodification" may be noted in some liberal welfare states (Dukelow and Kennett 2018).

If we extend the state–market nexus to include the family and specifically gender and care relations, traditionally liberal welfare states lacked explicit family policies and have relatively low levels of family benefits and services (Korpi 2000). Consequently, there is a greater tendency to treat all adults as non-gendered "adult workers" than elsewhere. The recent shift towards social investment is also rather weakly embedded in liberal welfare states with a tendency to expand investment in early childhood care and education via the market (White 2012).

The liberal welfare regime is closely related to the liberal market economy model of the "Varieties of Capitalism" approach (Hall and Soskice 2001). Liberal market economies are characterised by a competitive-market model for firms to secure access to finance, technology, skills and labour. Short-term profitability and share prices primarily determine how capital market decisions are made. Industrial relations in liberal market economies are similarly competitive, leading to flexible labour markets with weak employment protection legislation and general labour market insecurity. Trade unions are weak and wage bargaining is decentralised (Hall 2015). As employment in manufacturing declined steadily from the 1950s, the response to the so-called "trilemma of the service economy" (Iversen and Wren 1998) was inequality and a high incidence of low-waged work (Gallie 2007), as the growth in service sector employment was concentrated in low-paid services that offered few productivity gains (Esping-Andersen 1999). An open approach to labour migration is also found in this context. However, employment protection and access to social rights are typically restricted (Ruhs 2018).

6.3 Recent developments in liberal welfare regimes

Here we present recent trends in liberal welfare states based on aggregate OECD data. Selecting core themes discussed above and concentrating on areas where particularly notable trends have occurred, we examine whether key liberal welfare features are still prevalent. We include OECD averages where available.

In line with theoretical expectations, public social expenditure in the liberal welfare regime countries is below the OECD average of around 20 % of GDP apart from the

UK where this share is higher.[2] However, social expenditure as a percentage of GDP has been declining in the UK since 2010 due to a harsh austerity programme implemented by the Conservative government following the global financial crisis. With under 17 % of GDP, expenditure is lowest in Australia according to the most recently available data (Figure 6.1). As Starke et al. (2014) and McManus (2018) have argued, in the absence of automatic stabilisers, partisan politics mattered to explain the divergence in responses to the global financial and economic crisis. While centre-left governments maintained spending levels throughout the crisis years, centre-right governments opted for welfare retrenchment.

A reverse picture emerges if we look at private social expenditure where all liberal welfare states, apart from New Zealand, are above the OECD average. While the share of private social spending as a percentage of GDP has been slightly declining across the OECD since 2016, in the liberal welfare states private expenditure has even been slightly increasing in recent years. The US is a stark outlier, with a 40 % private share of total social spending (Figure 6.2). The dominance of market solutions and private responsibility for social risks is thus confirmed for the last decade.

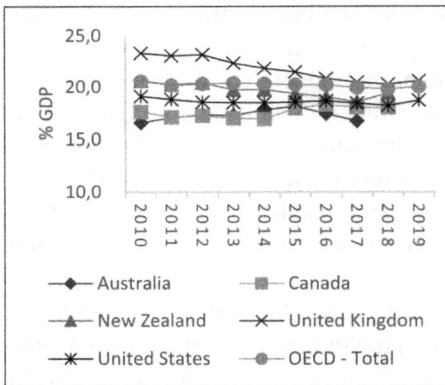

Figure 6.1: Public expenditure – total
Source: OECD SOCX Database.
Accessed 11 April 2021.

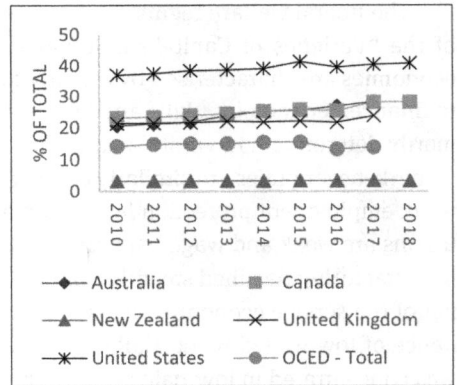

Figure 6.2: Private share of social expenditure

This emphasis on private responsibility is particularly notable regarding healthcare where again the US is a stark outlier. While around 45 % of healthcare spending in the US is by private means – reflecting the absence of a universal public healthcare

---

2 Using fixed level of spending rather than GDP indicates similar trends. 2015 prices (PPP, in US Dollars) shows that Australia and Canada each spent around $7000 in 2010 per head and approximately $8000 in 2017, New Zealand $7000, the UK approximately $9000 and the US approximately $10,000 in both years. This puts the US in a slightly more generous light than using GDP, but the degree of change over time across the countries is similar under both measures.

system – all other countries included here have a tax-financed public healthcare system. Nevertheless, due to prescription charges and the exclusion of major services, the share of private spending on healthcare (around 20%) is also relatively high in Australia and Canada (OECD, n.d.). In the US, tax expenditure related to health insurance is the largest element of its "hidden welfare state" (Tax Policy Center 2020).

A similar picture of low public and high private funding emerges when we look at pensions, often the largest single item of public spending (OECD 2019). All liberal welfare states are spending less on public pensions than the OECD average (Figure 6.3). In Australia, Canada and New Zealand this can partially be explained by favourable demographics as discussed later. However, another explanation is the strong emphasis placed on private provision for old age (Figure 6.4).

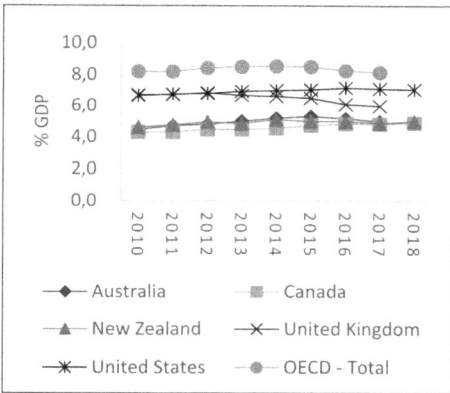

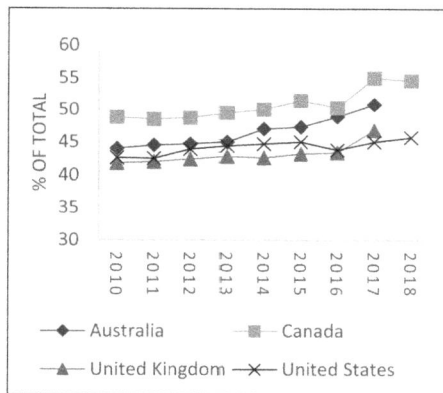

Figure 6.3: Public expenditure on old age and survivors pensions
Source: OECD SOCX Database.
Accessed 11 April 2021.

Figure 6.4: Private share of old age expenditure

The first tier of basic pensions is sometimes means-tested in liberal welfare states (as in Australia) while the second tier of mandatory earnings-related pensions is often private (as in Australia and the UK). New Zealand is an outlier as it has no mandatory second-tier pension. Canada, New Zealand, the UK and the US also have significant coverage of voluntary pensions (OECD 2019). Private pension expenditure is the area where the "hidden welfare state" and fiscal welfare plays a rather large role. Canada, Australia and the UK spend particularly large amounts on tax expenditures on private pensions (1.9, 1.7 and 1.2 per cent of GDP respectively in 2015) in contrast to the OECD average of 0.6% of GDP (OECD 2019).

This trend is also explained by the move towards financialisation that liberal welfare states underwent since the 1980s, which accompanied the rolling back of the Keynesian welfare state (Mackenzie and Louth 2020). In this new model, economic growth relies on private financial markets rather than fiscal policy to maintain consumer demand (Berry 2015).

A final policy area to illustrate the liberal regime empirically is active labour market policy (ALMP). Again, all five countries are below the OECD average regarding ALMP expenditure (Figure 6.5). This is reflected in a policy emphasis on "work-first" type activation and use of private providers paid by results which channel people towards accepting low-wage work (McKnight et al. 2016).

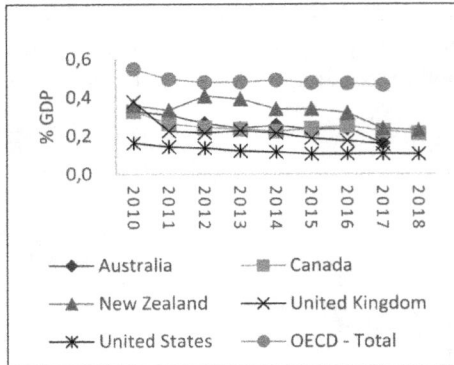

Figure 6.5: Active labour market programmes expenditure
Source: OECD SOCX Database. Accessed 11 April 2021.

The low spending levels on average across policy areas and the work first approach to activation unsurprisingly leads to detrimental social outcomes. Poverty levels (Figure 6.6) are high and so is inequality in terms of the Gini co-efficient where all countries maintained a co-efficient between 30 and 40 throughout the decade (OECD 2021a). Relatedly, low pay is widespread (Figure 6.7). Across many of these indicators, levels are highest in the US and Canada. There are strong correlations between extensive in-work benefit (tax credit) systems and the incidence of low-paid employment, particularly in the UK and the US. Welfare expenditure in liberal welfare states in this sense may tend to increase the viability of low-paid jobs (McKnight et al. 2016) and double as a form of corporate welfare. In New Zealand, in contrast, the incidence of low pay declined notably since 2017 after minimum wage rates were increased more substantially than previously.[3]

---

3 See minimum wage rates at https://www.employment.govt.nz/hours-and-wages/pay/minimum-wage/previous-rates/#:~:text=The%20training%20minimum%20wage%20was%20introduced%20in%20June%202003 (accessed 10 May 2021).

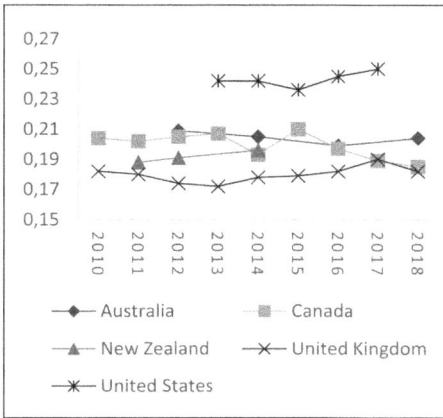

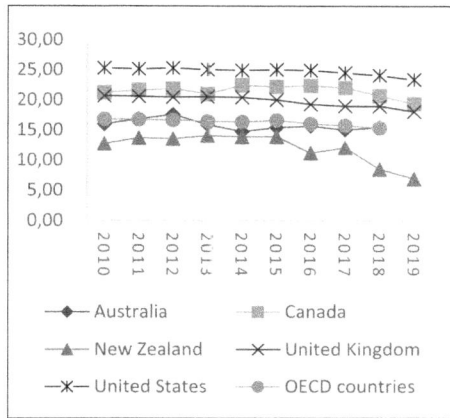

Figure 6.6: Poverty rate
Source: OECD 2021b (Fig. 6.6); OECD.Stat.
(Fig. 6.7). Accessed 28 April 2021.

Figure 6.7: Low pay incidence

6.4 Demographic challenges and migration

The liberal welfare states discussed here face the demographic challenges of population ageing and population decline typical of advanced economies, but less acutely. Part of the reason for this deviation is their openness to migration which is halting population decline and contributing to population diversity. There are also some variations, with population growth slowing more rapidly in the UK and the US than in Australia, Canada and New Zealand.

Population ageing is influenced by both falling fertility and increased life expectancy. Recent change follows steep falls in fertility rates since the 1970s, and these have continued to fall over the last decade. All five countries are now well below the 2.1 children per woman to maintain a stable population (OECD 2021c). However, excepting Canada, the majority are in a slightly better position than the OECD average. Life expectancy has improved across the countries from an average of 80.58 years in 2010 to 81.32 years in 2018, but only barely in the US (OECD 2021d).

Consequently, each country is challenged by a decline in its working age population as a proportion of total population. The working age population averaged at 67.2% for the five countries in 2010, falling to an average of 65.3% in 2018, with Canada and the UK posting the largest falls, and New Zealand remaining the most stable (OECD 2021e). Again, however, the countries are in a comparatively favourable position. The old age dependency ratio for all five countries is lower than the OECD average and is predicted to remain below the OECD average (OECD 2019).

Pensions have come under pressure given this set of demographic challenges. Bridgen (2019) finds that liberal welfare states responded to issues of financial sustainability relatively early and implemented significant pension retrenchment in the 1980s, which set the path for continued cost containment subsequently. The legacy of the turn to neoliberal ideas and retrenchment policies across all five countries is therefore still significant. While there have been aspects of resilience and even expansion of public pension provision in liberal welfare states more recently (Bridgen 2019; Béland and Waddan 2019), this is in the context of the aforementioned minimal nature of public pension provision and the strong push towards private provision.

Given the trend of increasing life expectancy, many countries in the OECD took the opportunity to increase retirement ages in response to the fiscal pressures following the 2008 economic crisis. The UK accelerated plans to raise the pension age to 67 by 2028 with a further rise to 68 by 2046. It has also managed to eliminate the lower pension age for women earlier than initially planned, and moved the second-tier public pension to a flat rate model (OECD 2019). The US is also on track to retrench its pension provision by raising the retirement age from 66 to 67, under plans instituted in the 1980s. Despite the weak power resources of labour in liberal welfare regimes, plans to retrench have not been as successful in Australia. Although the pension age here is rising from 65 to 67 by 2023 and the lower pension age for women was eliminated, further plans to increase the retirement age to 70 by 2035 have been abandoned after a backlash that centred on the feasibility of people in manual jobs to continue working until 70. The retirement age remains at 65 years in Canada, where unionisation is comparatively high, following the reversal of a decision to increase it to 67 by 2029.

All five countries have comparatively high levels of migration which have somewhat eased their demographic challenges. Australia has the largest migrant population, also globally (30 % of total population in 2019), while the lowest shares of the five are registered by the US and the UK (15.4 % and 14.1 % respectively in 2019). On balance, all five countries are "receptive" rather than "restrictive" countries, however, there has been much change in the last decade with a more restrictive climate emerging in the US and the UK.

Migration policy is also seeing relatively frequent recalibration, especially in Australia, New Zealand and Canada which operate a points-based system, a system also being adopted by the UK post-Brexit. While the thrust of migration policy is relatively liberal and "employer friendly', and this is beneficial for addressing labour market shortages and easing demographic and fiscal pressures, this is set against the dilemma of threats to social solidarity and social stability (Schultz et al. 2021). The trade-off this creates has morphed into heightened welfare chauvinism, particularly in the US and the UK. Liberal welfare states tend towards "market inclusion" (Kymlicka 2015) meaning that access to social rights are restricted and self-reliance is promoted. This is typified by the US "public charge rule" that effectively denies legal immigrants permanent residency if they were in receipt of welfare or health assistance over a specified period. Similarly, the UK applies a "no recourse to public funds" condition to temporary immigrants.

Consequent challenges of market inclusion generate the risk of poor socio-economic outcomes for migrants. Successful integration requires extending welfare to newcomers which comes at the risk of loss of solidarity, especially amongst native-born working class welfare recipients (Kymlicka 2015). For example, part of the success of the New Zealand First Party is its ability to attract the support of Māori voters and thus mobilise one minority group against another (Gethin 2021). While the reasons behind the UK's leaving the EU are complex, a politics of insecurity over immigration and the depiction of migrants as a threat was central to the right-wing populist message promoted by the UK Independence Party and the Conservative Party. Similar themes were central to Trump's presidency which relayed constant anti-immigrant messages whilst also fomenting divisions amongst the US's racially diverse and multi-ethnic population (Béland 2020).

6.5 Climate change and digital transformation

Australia, Canada, the US and, to a lesser extent, the UK are all exporters of fossil fuels and still heavily reliant on non-renewable energy consumption despite ambitious targets to reduce greenhouse gas emissions by 2030 and 2050 respectively. Reliance on fossil fuel extraction and energy-intensive industry not only heightens opposition to carbon reduction (Christoff and Eckersley 2011) but any "greening" of the economy will also have to address significant job losses in an important sector. Social, economic and ecological injustices are closely interlinked with vulnerable communities often being affected the most by the effects of climate change such as flooding. Yet these groups are the least responsible for causing them and have the fewest resources to cope with them and the mitigation policies put in place to deal with them, leading to "triple injustices" (Gough 2013). Achieving a "just transition" to a carbon neutral economy is a particular challenge for liberal welfare states given the high levels of social inequality and poverty and the emphasis that is placed on market solutions when addressing social problems.

Liberal welfare states' overall low spending levels are not providing a sufficient social protection "buffer" (Hemerijck 2014) against loss of income, for example due to redundancies resulting from the transition to a carbon-neutral economy or automation. A similar lack of ALMP spending (Figure 6.5) provides insufficient social investment to prepare their populations for the threats of climate change and digitalisation.

There is a rapidly growing literature on the connection between social policies and environmental policies or building the "eco-social state". The liberal welfare regimes typically have both lower social policy effort due to their basic safety net model and weaker environmental regulation due to their liberal market economy model and are thus not well-positioned to address the intersection of social and environmental policies (Koch and Fritz 2014). Christoff and Eckersley (2011) found proportional representation and corporatist systems that include business and labour were important for reducing greenhouse gas emissions. In contrast, the majority voting system typical of Anglo-Saxon democracies leads to a low presence (and often even absence) of Green parties in parliament and governments. The pluralist system of interest representation and general weakness of trade unions also favours business over environmental and social concerns.

New Zealand is a clear outlier within the liberal welfare regime cluster in this respect, possibly partly due to a legacy of early green politics (Gethin 2021). The country boasts a large share of renewable energy sources and is one of the most sustainable countries in terms of energy generation (MBIE 2020). This is in line with the ambition to build a "wellbeing economy'. New Zealand is internationally hailed as having introduced the first wellbeing budget, i.e. budget decisions are not primarily based on economic growth but a more holistic assessment of wellbeing, including a range of ecological, social and economic outcomes. The economy and the environment are not seen as requiring a trade-off but sustainability, wellbeing and resilience are considered together.

Similar to climate change, the transition to a digital economy has far-reaching impacts on social protection systems. On the one hand, the changes in production systems resulting from automation, online-based forms of work and spread of digital technologies create the need for welfare state adaption, e.g. to address new social risks emerging from digital exclusion or the lack of ICT skills. Since liberal market economies typically lack encompassing industrial strategies and leave investment and R&D decisions as well as skills development to individual employers and the market, liberal welfare regimes are prone to creating digital inequalities with little compensation prospects for the losers of this technological shift. Furthermore, platform workers who are typically exposed to hyper-flexible and precarious forms of work require the regulation of employment and social protection rights. For instance, digitalisation enables new ways of work organisation that could lead to a growing number of "labour-on-demand" types such as casual labour, short-term or zero-hours contracts, the latter having gained notoriety particularly in the UK, although these are not limited to a digitalised work environment. The emerging gaps in social protection and employment rights for platform workers are already an issue in highly regulated welfare states and will be even more difficult to overcome in a generally flexible and insecure employment policy environment that regards protective measures as an inhibition to the free working of the market.

On the other hand, use of digital technologies and mechanisms such as using algorithms to determine benefit eligibility have an impact on service users and benefit recipients. In the UK algorithms are used to determine eligibility for and calculate monthly rates of the main working-age benefit (Universal Credit) and to detect fraud (Booth 2019). Statistical choices based on patterns extracted from historical data may disadvantage certain groups protected by anti-discrimination laws (Desiere and Struyven 2021). Critics worry that these systems automate and propagate existing social inequalities (Eubanks 2018). Racial inequalities are deeply rooted in all countries under consideration here, due to their specific colonial histories. The technical design of benefit automation might include racial biases and thus reproduce harms and injustices without proper accountability. The reliance of liberal welfare states on sanctions and means-testing might similarly produce harsh decisions that will be difficult to redress if executed by an impersonal bot.

6.6 The impact of COVID-19

The liberal welfare dogma of self-sufficiency was seriously put into question when COVID-19 struck. It appears that liberal welfare states were less well equipped to address the crisis and the poor response to the first wave of the pandemic led to high incidence and mortality rates in the US and the UK in particular (Greener 2021). However, that result did not extend to Australia and New Zealand whose experiences of the pandemic have been markedly different, at least in the early waves, and there may have been a geographical and "island" effect at play here (Helliwell et al. 2021).

In general, we saw the temporary suspension of some of the principles of liberal welfare provision during the crisis. The pandemic required an extensive emergency response from liberal welfare states as it exposed gaps and weaknesses in its social provision. In contrast, countries that typically have high levels of social protection expenditure could make use of automatic stabilisers (e.g. in the form of unemployment insurance) and spent comparatively less on emergency funding than the liberal welfare states (IMF 2021). Additional spending has thus been markedly higher in the liberal welfare states compared to the Nordic and many other welfare states in Europe (IMF 2021).

With regard to public spending on employment and unemployment protection, we see active responses across the five countries for workers who became unemployed "through no fault of their own', in other words, not violating the liberal work ethic. Recognition of the hardships faced by people already unemployed or in poverty, in precarious work or living in low-income families also garnered some support but this has been much more uneven and limited. The US fared the worst in terms of the severity of the pandemic and the less than coherent response by the Trump administration. Unemployment insurance benefits were raised by $600 per week, undermining "the work first" mantra as it meant that two-thirds of recipients earned more in the first months of the pandemic than when they were working (*The Economist* 2021), revealing the existing realities of low pay. However, in practice it meant adding extra patches to an already patchy safety net system of unemployment insurance (Moffitt and Zilak 2020). Inadequate short-term working/job retention supports and extremely limited family supports remained problematic. The Biden administration continues the trend of emergency stimulus spending. However, a potentially path-breaking policy move in a country with limited modes of child and family support is the commitment to introduce a quasi-universal child benefit for which only the wealthiest will not qualify.

The experience of the pandemic in Canada and the nature of the response also exposed the limits of its system, however its emergency provisions are judged to be more comprehensive than in the US (Béland et al. 2021a). Interestingly, it seems that concerns about benefit fraud, usually so dominant in liberal welfare states, were paused for a while as priority was put on payment speed to smooth consumption and lessen the economic contraction.

The UK put much of its effort into the creation of a new, temporary job retention scheme, paying 80 % of usual wages. For the unemployed, the value of Universal Credit was increased by £20 a week, until Autumn 2021. Some of the conditionalities attached to out-of-work benefit receipt were cut to broaden eligibility and the claims process was also simplified. The Universal Credit rate increase was not an ungenerous sum by previous UK standards, but nonetheless demonstrates very disparate treatment of retained workers versus those who had lost their jobs or were already unemployed (Hick and Murphy 2021).

Australia and New Zealand also turned to "emergency Keynesianism'. In New Zealand's case, its wellbeing economy approach and consequent focus on health indicators appears influential. Both countries instituted job retention supports and relatively generous payments for those who lost their jobs because of the pandemic, which have now ceased. A legacy of the pandemic is the commitment to permanently increase working-age benefits in both countries. However, the adequacy of this increase is questionable. In New Zealand Humpage and Moore (2021) find that it has only a negligible difference to making ends meet for people in poverty.

While this might read like a litany of generous improvements to liberal welfare states, for the most part, their temporary, emergency nature must be stressed. As Béland et al. (2021b) remind us, they are examples of "politics for markets'. The responses do not represent a fundamental transformation of the precepts of the liberal welfare regime, but are an effort to shore up economies until they can return to "business as usual'.

6.7 Conclusions

Like other Western countries, liberal welfare states currently face several challenges, including the transition to a carbon-neutral and digitalised economy, migration and demographic ageing (although the latter is less of a problem compared to other OECD countries). The weaknesses of their market-driven and individualised model of welfare were laid bare by the COVID-19 pandemic such as the insufficient basic safety nets, high levels of social inequalities and lack of social investment policies. While various measures were implemented in response to the pandemic, it is unlikely that these will lead to any more enduring and fundamental policy changes given the long trajectory of public welfare retrenchment. Core questions remain about the post-pandemic response and how states will deal with higher levels of public debt and whether that means moving into retrenchment mode for liberal welfare states. There are also questions about long-term scars of the pandemic related to unemployment and work disruption and how they will be addressed, especially if strict "work first" and punitive activation programmes make a comeback.

Noteworthy is the case of New Zealand, an outlier in many respects; the trend towards the privatisation of healthcare and pensions was not followed and at least rhetorically the creation of a "wellbeing economy" is promoted. While there are still significant social problems, e.g. the high poverty rates (Figure 6.6), the country represents a successful model of reducing the economic and social costs of the pandemic by prioritising health and wellbeing. It remains doubtful that this model will be replicated by the other liberal welfare states, given the structural weakness of unions as well as left and green parties that would support an equal consideration of economic, social and environmental sustainability.

The past decade has also shown, however, that there is no uniform liberal welfare model as there are important differences between countries and within countries over time. This has been most clearly demonstrated in the case of the US where the idiosyncrasy of the Trump Administration led to some extreme policy decisions – such as drastic tax cuts on the one hand and a reversal of the liberal migration model on the other hand. In turn, the first policy announcements of the Biden Presidency have the potential for some path-breaking developments. There clearly are opportunities for policy learning from the pandemic; whether these will be taken, remains an open question.

References

Albrekt Larsen, Christian. 2008. "The Institutional Logic of Welfare Attitudes: How Welfare Regimes Influence Public Support." *Comparative Political Studies* 41 (2), 145–169.

Albrekt Larsen, Christian, and Thomas Engel Dejgaard. 2013. "The Institutional Logic of Images of the Poor and Welfare Recipients: A Comparative Study of British, Swedish and Danish Newspapers." *Journal of European Social Policy* 23 (3), 287–299.

Baumberg Geiger, Ben. 2018. "'Benefit 'Myths'? The Accuracy and Inaccuracy of Public Beliefs about the Benefits System." *Social Policy & Administration* 52 (5), 998–1018.

Béland, Daniel. 2020. "Right-Wing Populism and the Politics of Insecurity: How President Trump Frames Migrants as Collective Threats." *Political Studies Review* 18 (2), 162–177.

Béland, Daniel, and Alex Waddan. 2019. "Unidentical Twins: Recent Social Policy Developments in Canada and the United States." *Journal of International and Comparative Social Policy* 35 (1), 1–4.

Béland, Daniel, Shannon Dinan, Philip Rocco, and Alex Waddan. 2021a. "Social Policy Responses to COVID-19 in Canada and the United States: Explaining Policy Variations Between Two Liberal Welfare State Regimes." *Social Policy and Administration* 55 (2), 280–294.

Béland, Daniel, Bea Cantillon, Rod Hick, and Amílcar Moreira. 2021b. "Social Policy in the Face of a Global Pandemic: Policy Responses to the COVID-19 Crisis." *Social Policy and Administration* 55 (2), 249–260.

Berry, Craig. 2015. "Citizenship in a Financialised Society: Financial Inclusion and the State Before and After the Crash." *Policy and Politics* 43 (4), 509–525.

Booth, Robert. 2019. "Computer Says No: The People Trapped in Universal Credit's 'Black Hole'." *The Guardian*, 14 October. https://www.theguardian.com/society/2019/oct/14/computer-says-no-the-people-trapped-in-universal-credits-black-hole.

Bridgen, Paul. 2019. "The Retrenchment of Public Pension Provision in the Liberal World of Welfare During the Age of Austerity—And Its Unexpected Reversal, 1980–2017." *Social Policy and Administration* 53 (1), 16–33.

Castles, Francis G., and Deborah. Mitchell. 1993. "Worlds of Welfare and Families of Nations." In *Families of Nations: Patterns of Public Policy in Western Democracies*, edited by Francis G. Castles, 93–128. Aldershot: Dartmouth.

Christoff, Peter, and Robyn Eckersley. 2011. "Comparing State Responses." In *The Oxford Handbook of Climate Change and Society*, edited by John S. Dryzek, Richard B. Norgaard, and David Schlosberg, 431–448. Oxford: Oxford University Press.

Clegg, Daniel. 2015. "The Demise of Tax Credits." *Political Quarterly* 86 (4), 493–499.

Desiere, Sam, and Ludo Struyven. 2021. "Using Artificial Intelligence to Classify Jobseekers: The Accuracy-Equity Trade-off." *Journal of Social Policy* 50 (2), 367–385.

Dukelow, Fiona, and Elke Heins. 2017. "The Anglo-Saxon Welfare States: Still Europe's Outlier – or Trendsetter?". In *Handbook of European Social Policy*, edited by Patricia Kennett and Noemi Lendvai-Bainton, 230–247. Cheltenham: Edward Elgar.

Dukelow, Fiona and Patricia Kennett. 2018. "Discipline, Debt and Coercive Commodification: Post-Crisis Neoliberalism and the Welfare State in Ireland, the UK and the USA." *Critical Social Policy* 38 (3), 482–504.

Dwyer, Peter, and Sharon Wright. 2014. "Universal Credit, Ubiquitous Conditionality and its Implications for Social Citizenship." *Journal of Poverty and Social Justice* 22 (1), 27–35.

Esping-Andersen, Gøsta. 1990. *The Three Worlds of Welfare Capitalism*. Princeton, NJ: Princeton University Press.

Esping-Andersen, Gøsta. 1999. *Social Foundations of Postindustrial Economies*. Oxford: Oxford University Press.

Eubanks, Virginia. 2018. *Automating Inequality: How High-Tech Tools Profile, Police, and Punish the Poor*. New York, NY: St. Martin's Press.

Gallie, Duncan. 2007. "The Quality of Work Life in Comparative Perspective." In *Employment Regimes and the Quality of Work*, edited by Duncan Gallie, 205–232. Oxford: Oxford University Press.

Gethin, Amory. 2021. *Political Cleavages, Class Structures and the Politics of Old and New Minorities in Australia, Canada, and New Zealand 1963-2019*, World Inequality Lab Working Paper No. 2021/5 https://wid.world/document/political-cleavages-class-structures-and-the-politics-of-old-and-new-minorities-in-australia-canada-and-new-zealand-1963-2019-world-inequality-lab-wp-2021-05/ (accessed 1 May 2021).

Gough, Ian. 2013. "Climate Change, Social Policy and Global Governance." *Journal of International and Comparative Social Policy* 29 (3), 185–203.

Greener, Ian. 2021. "Comparing Country Risk and Response to COVID-19 in the First 6 Months across 25 Organisation for Economic Co-operation and Development Countries Using Qualitative Comparative Analysis." *Journal of International and Comparative Social Policy* 37 (3), 211–225.

Hall, Peter A. 2015. "The Changing Role of the State in Liberal Market Economies." In *The Oxford Handbook of Transformations of the State*, edited by Stephan Leibfried, Evelyne Huber, Matthew Lange, Jonah D. Levy and John D. Stephens, 426–444. Oxford: Oxford University Press.

Hall, Peter A., and David Soskice. 2000. *Varieties of Capitalism: The Institutional Basis of Competitive Advantage*. Oxford: Oxford University Press.

Helliwell, John, Richard Layard, Jeffrey Sachs, and Jan-Emmanuel De Neve (eds.). 2021. *World Happiness Report 2021*. New York: Sustainable Development Solutions Network.

Hemerijck, Anton. 2014. "Social Investment 'Stocks', 'Flows' and 'Buffers'." *Politiche Sociali* 1 (1), 9–26.

Hick, Rod, and Mary P. Murphy. 2021. "Common Shock, Different Paths? Comparing Social Policy Responses to COVID-19 in the UK and Ireland." *Social Policy and Administration* 55 (2), 312–325.

Hills, John. 2014. *Good Times, Bad Times: The Welfare Myth of Them and Us*. Bristol: Policy Press.

Howard, Christopher. 1999. *The Hidden Welfare State: Tax Expenditures and Social Policy*, Princeton, NJ: Princeton University Press.

Humpage, Louise, and Charlotte Moore. 2021. *Income Support in the Wake of Covid-19: Interviews*, Auckland: University of Auckland and CPAG. https://www.cpag.org.nz/assets/Covid-19%2520 INTERVIEW%2520report%2520FINAL%252012%2520April%25202021.docx%2520%25281% 2529.pdf (accessed 9 May 2021).

IMF. 2021. Database of Fiscal Policy Responses to COVID-19, July 2021 https://www.imf.org/en/ Topics/imf-and-covid19/Fiscal-Policies-Database-in-Response-to-COVID-19 (accessed 21 August 2021).

Iversen, Torben, and Anne Wren. 1998. "Equality, Employment, and Budgetary Restraint: The Trilemma of the Service Economy." *World Politics* 50 (4), 507–546.

Koch, Max, and Martin Fritz. 2014. "Building the Eco-Social State: Do Welfare Regimes Matter?" *Journal of Social Policy* 43 (4), 679–703.

Korpi, Walter. 2000. "Faces of Inequality: Gender, Class, and Patterns of Inequalities in Different Types of Welfare States." *Social Politics: International Studies in Gender, State & Society* 7 (2), 127–191.

Kymlicka, Will. 2015. "Solidarity in Diverse Societies: Beyond Neoliberal Multiculturalism and Welfare Chauvinism." *Comparative Migration Studies* 3 (17), 1–9.

Mackenzie, Catherine, and Jonathon Louth. 2020. "The Neoliberal Production of Deserving and Undeserving Poor: A Critique of the Australian Experience of Microfinance." *Social Policy and Society* 19 (1), 19–35.

McKnight, Abigail, Kitty Stewart, Sam Mohun Himmelweit, and Marco Palillo. 2016. *Low Pay and In-Work Poverty: Preventative Measures and Preventative Approaches*. Brussels: European Commission, Directorate-General for Employment, Social Affairs and Inclusion.

McManus, Ian P. 2018. "Political Parties as Drivers of Post-Crisis Social Spending in Liberal Welfare States." *Comparative European Politics* 16 (5), 843–870.

Ministry of Business, Innovation & Employment (MBIE). 2020. *Energy in New Zealand 2020*. https://www.mbie.govt.nz/dmsdocument/11679-energy-in-new-zealand-2020 (accessed 22 April 2021).

Moffitt, Robert, and James Ziliak. 2020. "COVID 19 and the US Safety Net." *Fiscal Studies* 41 (3), 515–548.

OECD. n.d. Social Expenditure Database. https://www.oecd.org/social/expenditure.htm.

OECD. 2019. Pensions at a Glance 2019: OECD and G20 Indicators. Paris: OECD Publishing. https://doi.org/10.1787/b6d3dcfc-en.

OECD. 2021a. "Income Inequality" (indicator). https://doi.org/10.1787/459aa7f1-en (accessed 15 April 2021).

OECD. 2021b. "Poverty Rate" (indicator). https://doi.org/10.1787/0fe1315d-en (accessed 15 April 2021).

OECD. 2021c. "Fertility Rates" (indicator). https://doi.org/10.1787/8272fb01-en (accessed 3 May 2021).

OECD. 2021d. "Life Expectancy at Birth" (indicator). https://doi.org/10.1787/27e0fc9d-en (accessed 3 May 2021).

OECD. 2021e. "Working Age Population" (indicator). https://doi.org/10.1787/d339918b-en (accessed 3 May 2021).

Ruhs, Martin. 2018. "Labor Immigration Policies in High-Income Countries: Variations Across Political Regimes and Varieties of Capitalism." *Journal of Legal Studies* 47 (S1), 89–127.

Schultz, Caroline, Philipp Lutz, and Stephan Simon. 2021. "Explaining the Immigration Policy Mix: Countries' Relative Openness to Asylum and Labour Migration." *European Journal of Political Research* 60 (4), 763–784.

Starke, Peter, Alexandra Kaasch, and Franca van Hooren. 2014. "Political Parties and Social Policy Responses to Global Economic Crises: Constrained Partisanship in Mature Welfare States." *Journal of Social Policy* 43 (2), 225–246.

Tax Policy Center. 2020. *Briefing Book*. https://www.taxpolicycenter.org/briefing-book/what-are-largest-tax-expenditures (accessed 4 May 2021).

The Economist. 2021. "Covid-19 has Transformed the Welfare State. Which Changes Will Endure?" 6 March 2021. https://www.economist.com/briefing/2021/03/06/covid-19-has-transformed-the-welfare-state-which-changes-will-endure (accessed 15 April 2021).

White, Linda. 2012. "Must We All Be Paradigmatic? Social Investment Policies and Liberal Welfare States." *Canadian Journal of Political Science* 45 (3), 657–683.

Marcello Natili and Matteo Jessoula

7 The Southern European welfare model

Abstract: A growing corpus of literature has analysed the main features, modes of functioning as well as the logics of institutional reproduction and change of welfare (and welfare state) arrangements in the four countries clustered in the Southern European model of welfare (Greece, Italy, Portugal and Spain). The chapter reviews such literature identifying three main phases of welfare state development in the last three decades: early-1990s–2007; the global crisis and Great Recession 2008–2014; a post-crisis period 2015–2019 – characterised by substantially different social challenges, policy responses and underpinning political dynamics. In doing so, it shows that SE welfare states deeply transformed in the last three decades, and yet maintained some core features that still differentiate them from the rest of European countries, as adopted reforms have only partially addressed its main weaknesses. Against such backdrop, the article outlines the main challenges for existing welfare arrangements in Southern Europe which mostly relate to: i) the need to fully develop welfare *services* in key policy fields such as childcare, labour market policies, long-term care; ii) reduce labour market segmentation and welfare dualism(s); iii) reconcile both pensions and healthcare sustainability with adequacy, and especially equity; iv) possible changes in welfare financing in order to effectively pursue these goals.

Keywords: Southern Europe, welfare reforms, familialism, segmentation, welfare adequacy, equity

7.1 Introduction

Since the mid-1990s, the idea that four Southern European (SE) countries constituted a separate cluster in the universe of welfare states, characterised by distinct social policy traits and a specific allocation of responsibilities between the state, the market, the family and intermediary associations, has gained prominence.

Ferrera's seminal article (1996), in particular, outlined the main common traits in SE countries' welfare state architectures and welfare regime configurations as well. Originally, they all undertook the Bismarckian path, with the aim to protect – mainly on a contributory basis – male breadwinner workers and their families from the typical risks of industrial societies. This also implied relying (implicitly or explicitly) on a family model based on a sharp gendered division of roles. During the Golden Age, SE welfare states expanded in accordance with the Bismarckian imprint until the late 1970s (Italy) and mid-1980s (Greece, Portugal and Spain), when they were hybridised with the transition towards universalistic national healthcare systems financed through general revenues (Ferrera 1996; Guillen 2002): a major – and admittedly

https://doi.org/10.1515/9783110721768-007

rather unusual – "path-shift" in welfare state history which made these countries intrinsically different from Conservative-corporatist welfare regimes. Importantly, SE welfare states also displayed a peculiar allocation of resources across the various welfare state sectors that Ferrera (1996) captured through the notion of "*functional distortion*" – admittedly more pronounced in Italy and Greece when the SE model was outlined analytically – with high-cost single-pillar pension systems (i.e. public and mostly pay-as-you-go), in contrast with rudimentary family and social assistance policies in all the four countries (Table 7.1). The lack of a minimum income scheme and underdeveloped social services (for children, families and frail elderlies) were particularly at odds with welfare state arrangements in the other three worlds of welfare capitalism – Socialdemocratic (Nordic), Conservative-corporatist (Continental) and Liberal (Anglo-Saxon).

These peculiar institutional properties had two relevant consequences: on the one side, in interaction with particularly segmented labour markets, they resulted in highly stratified welfare states, almost regressive in their distributive incidence and with limited effectiveness in poverty reduction. Indeed, SE welfare regimes were traditionally the harbinger of comparatively high levels of destitution, even in periods of economic growth (Saraceno, Benassi, and Morlicchio 2020). On the other, households traditionally had a key role in welfare provision: in fact, Saraceno (1994) called such welfare regime "familialistic by default" to emphasise the lack of alternatives to the provision of care by the family – better, by women in a strongly gender biased society and labour market. By contrast, reliance on the private welfare provision remained limited until the 1990s.

Importantly, still in the 1990s, the four Southern European welfare states presented two additional features: a level of social expenditure sensibly lower than the European average – especially in terms of per capita expenditure; some within group variation, with the Italian welfare state more developed than the other three countries' (Figure 7.1).

The institutional traits of both welfare states and welfare regimes in Southern Europe were the result of a peculiar development path characterising the countries along the Mediterranean rim: late modernisation, with delayed industrialisation and the persistence of traditional social relationships and cultural values, as well as long periods of authoritarian right-wing dictatorships in the course of the twentieth century. A delayed process of economic modernisation, and a chronic shortage of "good jobs" – particularly evident in some geographical areas – contributed to the outcomes mentioned above. Furthermore, it also shaped one of the core features of the Mediterranean social model: still during the 1970s and 1980s, in SE many of the poor were working, employed in the peripheral (agriculture, construction, etc.) and/or irregular economic sectors, characterised by very high job instability, performance-based low wages, and facing severe difficulties in accessing contributory social protection schemes (Ferreira 2000; Ferrera 2010). Beyond comparatively high poverty levels, SE welfare arrangements – in particular the key role of (extended) family as welfare and income provider for its members – penalised women's autonomy and employment opportunities, thus contributing to low levels of female employment, with the exception of Portugal (Trifiletti 1999).

In the last three decades, however, the four Southern European countries faced four challenges of considerable magnitude. Firstly, they had to face *structural transformations* such as population ageing and the shift from an industrial to a predominantly service economy: these are typically slow-moving processes, but they took an *accelerated pace* in Southern Europe, thus putting stronger pressure on existing welfare state arrangements and governments as well. Secondly, the advent of globalisation and neoliberalism, which occurred in combination with the deepening of the European integration process, prompted robust pressures on peripheral-Mediterranean countries, especially during the global economic and sovereign debt shock of 2008–2012. Thirdly, cultural and social modernisation substantially affected family relationships and the traditional division of labour as well – with major differences between the Iberian countries and Italy/Greece though (Marí-Klose and Moreno-Fuentes 2013). Finally, fourth, domestic political and especially party systems transformed due to the changing relevance of traditional cleavages, the emergence of new lines of conflict, novel socio-political mobilisation strategies and especially the legitimacy crisis that invested Southern European political elites since the 2008 global shock (Hutter, Kriesi, and Vidal 2018).

Whereas it is beyond the scope of this chapter to interpret policy developments in light of underpinning political dynamics in the four countries, this contribution has two main goals. First, to assess whether – and in case to what extent – such challenges have prompted a *transformation* of the *key traits – and distortions – of the SE model* mentioned above, in particular along the following analytical dimensions: i) ensuring pension system sustainability, while guaranteeing adequacy; ii) overcoming traditional weaknesses in family, social assistance (anti-poverty) and (in some cases also) unemployment benefits; iii) fully develop welfare services in key policy fields such as childcare, labour market policies, and long-term care. Second, to identify the *main challenges* that remain to be addressed in the field of social protection as result of either/both welfare reforms or/and structural transformations – with particular reference to radically changing labour market conditions due to increased flexibilisation – and the emergence of the COVID crisis.

The chapter is organised as follows. The second section illustrates welfare state main developments in SE in three different phases: the period of catching up and convergence with the rest of Europe (1990–2007), the period of austerity driven retrenchment reforms (2008–2014), and the pre-COVID phase (2015–2020), characterised by the timid return to social protection expansions. The third section assesses this trajectory by outlining the peculiarities that still characterise SE welfare states as well as the main challenges ahead.

7.2 Converging with Europe or drifting apart? Welfare Reform trajectories in Southern Europe since the 1990s

7.2.1 Catching up and convergence: 1990–2007

Following the full consolidation of democratic regimes in the 1980s, in the subsequent two decades Greece, Portugal and Spain underwent a fast process of welfare state expansion with the aim to catch up with EU-15 standards. Compared to public social protection expenditure increase in Western European countries in the period 1995–2008 (+64.4 %), SE figures are remarkable: the growth was slightly higher in Italy (+75 %), much higher in Spain (+94.4 %) and Portugal (+101.6 %), and especially in Greece (+129.3 %). This convergent trend lasted until the 2008 global crisis: as consequence, in 2010, social protection expenditure as percentage of GDP reached the EU-15 average in Greece, it was above average in Italy and below, but not too distant, in Spain and Portugal. Nevertheless, considering per capita expenditure in purchasing power standards (PPS, see Figure 7.1), the situation was partly different: in 2008, per capita expenditure was around the EU-15 average in Italy, below by 22 % in Greece and Spain and by 27.8 % in Portugal.

Moreover, in this period, the four SE countries only partly overcame their traditional backwardness in terms of employment levels and adequate supply of jobs compared to most other European countries. Although employment rates increased significantly in all SE countries since the mid-1990s, only in Portugal and Spain were they around the EU-15 average in 2008 (IT 58.6 %; EL 61.4 %; ES 64.5 %; PT 68 % versus EU-15 67 %). Two mutually reinforcing factors contribute to explaining this outcome: first, the comparatively high levels of female employment in Portugal and its spectacular growth in Spain (+23.7 p.p. between 1995 and 2018), in contrast with limited progress in Italy and Greece; second, labour market deregulation "at the margin" (Jessoula, Graziano, and Madama 2010) – i.e. mostly concerning the newly (young) employed – and the shift to increasingly flexible employment arrangements, particularly evident in the Spanish case. Importantly, however, labour market reforms also resulted in a growing number of low-wage, precarious workers in the formal economy, besides those in the traditionally insecure informal economy. Consequently, labour market segmentation remained high in all SE countries. Relevant to this regard, Portugal and Spain were already more successful in rationalising and making their unemployment benefit systems more inclusive in this first phase (Ferrera 2010).

Efforts to modernise the social protection system did not manage, however, to substantially affect the "functional" distortion of SE welfare states, which remained significant especially in Italy and Greece. In 2010, the expenditure for old age and survivor pensions as a percentage of total social protection expenditure was still above the EU average in all the four SE countries: 55.7 % in Greece, 58.5 % in Italy, 48.9 % in

Portugal, 39.5% in Spain versus an EU-15 average of 39.2%. This despite the retrenchment reforms adopted since the 1990s, which were particularly radical in Italy – that
both launched transition towards a multipillar architecture and changed the functioning of the first public pillar by introducing a Notional Defined Contribution system
(Jessoula 2009, 2018) – and Spain, where parametric reforms were adopted in 1997,
2002 and 2006 (Chuliá 2007). Since most measures were negotiated between governments and unions, their impact on pension expenditure was planned for the long run
in order to protect the key interests of older workers and core trade union members.

In the field of social assistance anti-poverty benefits, the Iberian countries especially underwent important changes between 1990 and 2008. Portugal was the first
Southern European country to introduce a pilot anti-poverty scheme in 1996 (Capucha
et al. 2005). In Spain, in the short period between 1988 and 1995, all *Comunidades
Autonomas* introduced regional MIS which – despite significant weaknesses and variation in generosity, inclusiveness and governance – covered the entire country (Arriba
and Moreno 2005). The story was different in Italy and Greece. In the former, the centre-left coalition launched a pilot national MIS in 1998, which was soon discontinued by
the new centre-right cabinet (2002). Although some regions introduced similar programmes in the following years, this did not lead to a diffusion of regional MIS – as in the
Spanish case – since these programmes were often rapidly repealed by centre-right regional administrations (Natili 2019). In Greece, no significant reform passed in this policy field, which thus remained significantly underdeveloped (Matsaganis 2020).

Turning to *family policies* – considering both cash transfers and care services – a similar picture emerges, with only Iberian countries – above all Spain – introducing
some key expansionary reforms. In Spain, in the early 2000s the Aznar government introduced child benefits, which were significantly enhanced in terms of generosity with
the following Zapatero government. Furthermore, in the mid-2000s, both Portugal and
Spain introduced ambitious comprehensive reforms of their long-term care system
with the aim of reaching "EU standards" – though several implementation problems
soon emerged in Spain (Arlotti and Aguilar-Hendrickson 2018). In the field of early
childhood education and care services (ECEC) for children aged 0–3 years – which are
essential to fight inequality, ensure social mobility and foster social investment as
well – coverage improved in all Southern countries, but the increase was limited in
Italy and Greece, where coverage rates remained among the lowest in the EU, whereas
Spain and Portugal made major improvements and reached above EU average levels
(European Commission 2018a). Overall, between 1995 and 2003, per capita expenditure in family policies in purchasing power standards (PPS) increased significantly in
Spain (+525%), less but still remarkably in Portugal (125.7%) and Italy (+121.5%) while
remaining de facto constant in Greece (Figure 7.3). In spite of improvements, it is worth
noting that expenditure in PPS per inhabitant remained far from the EU-15 average also
in the regional "big spender" Spain (339.69 vs 630.56).

Consistently, looking at the traditional "cash transfer-bias" of SE welfare states,
the gap with the rest of the European countries remained pronounced and expendi-

ture on in-kind benefits remained well below the EU-15 average (Figure 7.6). In 2008, in Portugal, total per capita expenditure in PPS for *in-kind* benefits considering all different welfare functions was 55.4% of the total expenditure in the same area in the EU-15 – and such share was only slightly higher in Greece (59.2%), Italy (73.7%) and Spain (75%).

To sum up, reforms in Spain and to a lesser extent in Portugal showed some degree of functional "recalibration", whereas the latter was less substantial in Italy and even slower and more limited in Greece (León and Pavolini 2014; Natili and Jessoula 2019; Petmesidou 2019). Overall, some key traits of SE welfare states persisted, in particular heavy reliance on contributory programmes especially in the high spending pension sector, labour market hyper segmentation and under-investment in family and anti-poverty policies.

7.2.2 The Great Recession and austerity driven reforms, 2008–2014

The triple challenge constituted by the financial (2008), economic (2009–2014) and sovereign debt (2010–2012) crises hit harder along the Southern European rim than in the other parts of Europe, thereby halting the process of welfare state expansion and partial recalibration outlined above.

Between 2008 and 2015, the unemployment rate increased by 9.8 p.p. on average in Southern Europe, compared to a 2.2 p.p. growth in the EU-27; similarly, the at-risk of poverty rate anchored at a fixed moment in time (2005) increased on average by 1.8 p.p. in the EU, compared to +2.3 p.p. in Portugal, +4.9 p.p. in Italy, +7 p.p. in Spain. In the same period, it skyrocketed in Greece (+ 23.5 p.p.). Against such backdrop, one might have expected an above average increase of social expenditure in SE as result of the automatic stabilisation function of the welfare state and related anticyclical effects: however, things went dramatically different and SE social policy expenditure drifted apart from the rest of EU countries (although remaining higher than in Baltic countries and Ireland).

Even though each country was exposed to different external pressures and had to face challenges of different magnitude, all the four SE countries took similar directions, introducing severe austerity reforms leading to drastic and "fast forward" welfare state retrenchment (Pavolini et al. 2015), which by and large affected all social policy fields and were prompted by powerful external pressures – due to either reinforced EU's governance mechanisms and/or structural adjustment programmes imposed by the so-called Trojka. The latter, in particular, imposed harsh welfare and labour market reforms in three out of the four SE countries – dramatically Greece but also Portugal, and Spain to a more limited extent – through hard and formal conditionality mechanisms, whereas the Italian reforms were prompted by explicit pressure and informal conditionality by the European Commission and the European Central

Bank (Sacchi 2015; Theodoropoulou 2015). Indeed, despite recession and slow economic growth between 2008 and 2015, social policy expenditure per capita in PPS increased by 24 percentage points in the EU-15, whereas it decreased by 4.7 p.p. in Greece, and increased by only 10.4 p.p. in Italy, 16 p.p. in Spain and 18.6 p.p. in Portugal (Figure 7.1). The overall outcome is that the gap in per-capita social protection expenditure between the average EU-15 figure and the four SE countries has grown after 30 years of convergence, reaching dramatic peaks in Portugal and Greece – which in 2015 spent around 60 % of the EU-15 average on a per capita basis. Remarkably, also Italy has become a country with a per capita expenditure quite below the EU-15 average (−11.9 p.p., cf. Guillén et al. 2022).

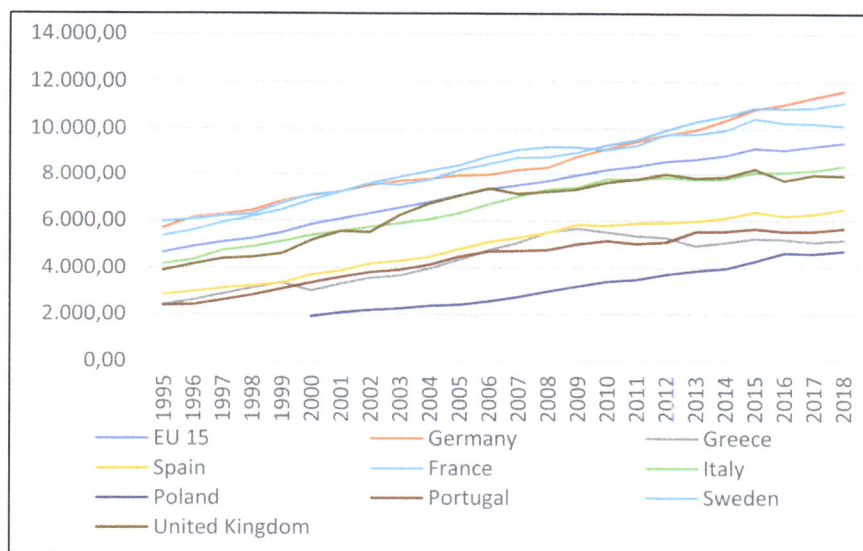

Figure 7.1: Total social protection expenditure, per capita in PPS.

Austerity measures affected all welfare state sectors, regardless of their degree of modernisation and institutionalisation: those protecting against "old" social risks (pensions and health care primarily) and against the "new social risks" as well. As argued by the Guillen et al. (2022), in health care the cuts have been draconian in Southern Europe: per capita expenditure in PPS grew between 2010 and 2015 by almost 23 % in EU-15, while remaining practically stable in Portugal, Italy and Spain and dropping by 39 % (!) in Greece (Figure 7.2). The gap in per capita public health care expenditure has thus reached dramatic peaks in Greece – where each citizen received in 2015 the equivalent of around 10 % of what an average Western European received in terms of health care expenditure – Portugal (51 %), but also Spain (65 %) and Italy (69 %), which are all far away from the rest of Western Europe.

In the field of pensions, external pressures by the European Commission, the European Central Bank, and in some cases also by the Trojka pushed governments to adopt unprecedented retrenchment measures between 2009 and 2013, mostly aimed to cut expenditure in the short–medium term. In fact, differently from reforms passed in the previous two decades, pensioners' and older workers' core interests were also touched through a variety of measures: the reduction of indexation mechanisms in Italy, Portugal and Spain, and even substantial cuts of real benefits in Greece affected retirees, whereas older and younger workers were affected by the increase of pensionable ages, tighter eligibility conditions for early retirement, introduction of "sustainability factors" for benefit calculation (Spain) or mechanisms for automatic adjustment of pensionable ages to changes in life expectancy (so called "linking" in Greece and Italy).[1] As a result, currently, both Italy (both men and women) and Portugal (women only) have exit ages from the labour market among the highest in the EU (European Commission 2021a).

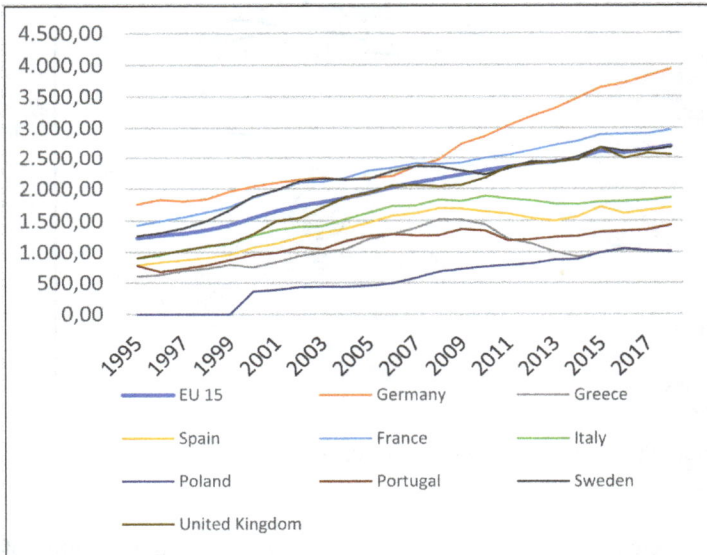

Figure 7.2: Healthcare expenditure, per capita in PPS.

---

[1] See the detailed country analysis in Volume 2 of the Pension Adequacy reports by the European Commission (2015, 2018b, 2021a)

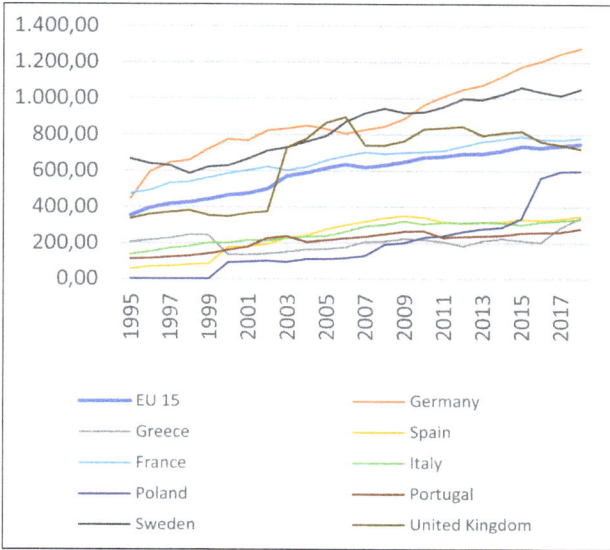

Figure 7.3: Family expenditure, per capita in PPS.

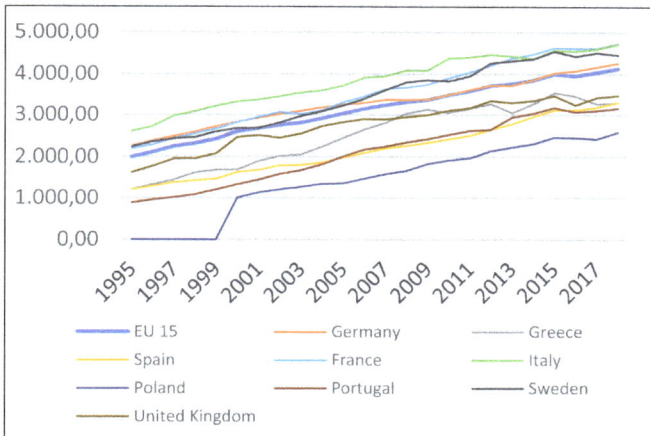

Figure 7.4: Old age and survivors, per capita in PPS.

Draconian retrenchment in health and pensions was not balanced, however, by adequate investment in social assistance and family policies (Natili and Jessoula 2019). Rather, governments also introduced significant cuts in these already underfinanced policy fields, particularly significant in the two Iberian countries that had made some steps forward in the previous decades. Indeed, in Portugal, notwithstanding the magnitude of the crisis and rapidly increasing poverty rates, expenditure on minimum income was significantly reduced along with cuts in benefit generosity and population coverage (Pereirinha et al. 2020). In Spain, family cash benefits and child services were drastically retrenched (Léon and Pavolini 2014). As to regional anti-poverty minimum income schemes, despite significant expansion, territorial differentiation and poor coordination persisted, as well as coverage gaps and inequalities in the protection of the most vulnerable (Natili 2019; Aguilar-Hendrickson and Arriba 2020). Similarly, in Italy, between 2009 and 2013 the resources allocated to the various funds for social services and childcare were repeatedly and radically cut, and only narrow initiatives were launched in the anti-poverty field both at the national and regional level (Léon and Pavolini 2014; Natili and Jessoula 2019). Overall, whereas per capita expenditure in PPS on family policies increased in the EU-15 (+16.5 %), it remained stable or even slightly decreased in SE countries, thus further widening the already existent gap (Figure 7.3).

In addition to welfare state retrenchment, since the onset of the Eurozone crisis, SE countries became the target of strong exogenous pressure to further deregulate the labour market, in particular through the relaxation of dismissal rules for workers on open-ended contracts and weakened national collective bargaining (Bulfone and Tassinari 2021). Overall, in the four countries more flexibility affecting core workers – i.e. insiders – was also introduced, leading to downward levelling of protection between permanent and temporary workers and increased across the board job insecurity (Moreira et al. 2015). This did not result, however, in reduced labour market segmentation, which actually remained pervasive since new types of low quality "cheap" atypical contracts spread in all Mediterranean countries, and the social condition of many solo-self employed critically deteriorated – thus bringing the latter group closer to precarious and vulnerable labour market outsiders. In Italy only, these de-regulating reforms were accompanied by compensatory measures through strengthening unemployment protection (Picot and Tassinari 2017) – which had previously been very limited also with respect to SE standards (Jessoula, Graziano, and Madama 2010). The level of unemployment insurance benefits was instead significantly reduced in Iberic countries, and most extensively in Greece. In the latter country, measures aimed to broaden access and coverage did not offset the severe cuts in contributory unemployment insurance (Matsaganis 2018). Overall, the income maintenance system of SE got closer to European standards in terms of *inclusiveness*, while generally reducing generosity and income security in unemployment.

7.2.3 After the storm: return to growth and welfare state expansion … but lost contact with the rest of the EU

After 2014, when the economy recovered in most SE countries, the region entered in a new phase characterised by efforts to combine strengthened social protection with fiscal rigour (Moury, De Giorgi, and Barros 2020). In Italy, Portugal and with some delay also in Spain, social expenditure in PPS began to rise moderately – while it continued to decline slightly in Greece (Figure 7.1). Such recovery did not allow, however, to catch up with the rest of Europe. Rather, both output and outcome indicators show clear signs of increasing polarisation in Europe, with Southern countries losing ground vis à vis the rest of the EU.

The bulk of structural labour market and social protection reforms remained in place (Guillen et al. 2022), although SE governments started to compensate reduced security on the labour market with social benefits. In particular, in this period, we notice a veritable path-breaking change in the anti-poverty model of SE countries. After decades of social and political neglect that made Greece and Italy the only European countries without an anti-poverty minimum income safety net in place in the 2010s, in the latter country a national, non-contributory, means-tested Minimum Income Scheme (MIS) – called Inclusion Income (REI) – was introduced in 2018, then replaced by a much more robust scheme in 2019 – the so-called Citizenship Income (RdC) (Jessoula and Natili 2020). Similarly, in Greece, the social assistance sector was finally strengthened, with the introduction of a non-categorical means-tested child benefit in 2013 and the subsequent, nationwide launch of a guaranteed minimum income programme in 2017, both marking significant progress towards a less parochial and more effective system of social protection (Matsaganis 2020). Also in Portugal, the new left-wing government reversed minimum income reforms introduced during the Eurozone crisis, thus restoring the protective capacity of the Portuguese social safety net (Pereirinha et al. 2020). Finally, in Spain, in the midst of the COVID-19 pandemic crisis, the Minimum Living Income was introduced, which is a new national social safety net complementing regional minimum income schemes.[2]

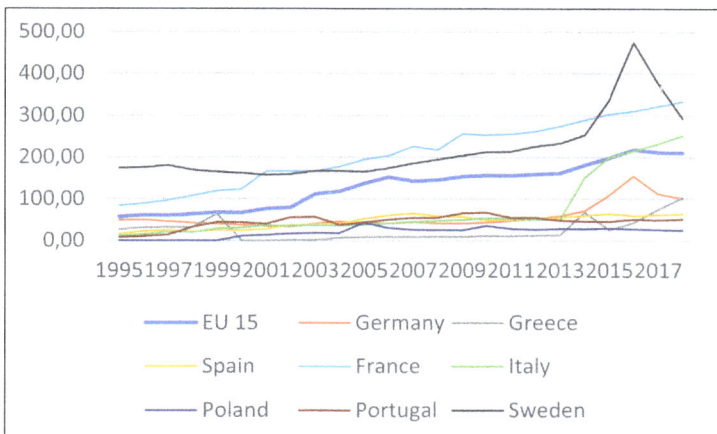

Figure 7.5: Social exclusion expenditure, per capita in PPS.

---

2 See Raitano et al. (2021) for a recent comparative analysis of MIS developments in Europe.

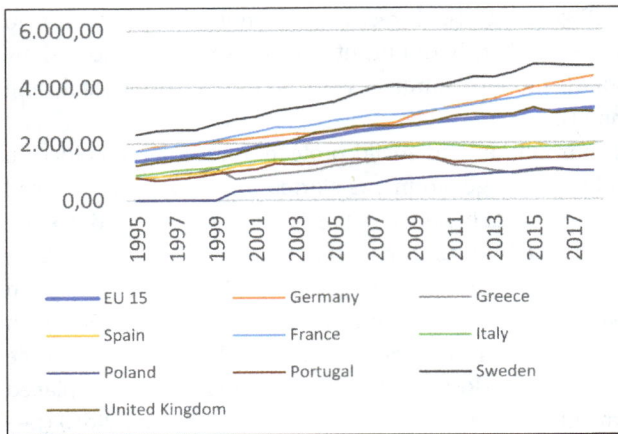

Figure 7.6: Benefits in-kind expenditure, per capita in PPS.

Such a clearly visible expansionary trend in minimum income protection was not accompanied by substantial investment in enabling social services to target new social risks. Such services remained poorly developed in Greece and Italy – with the latter making some step forward only in the provision of an integrated system of service provision for the poor. In the critical field of ECEC services for children below 3 years, coverage remains very modest in Greece (20.5 %) and Italy (28.6 % in 2019), far from the Barcelona target of 33 %, set already two decades ago, and lower than in Spain (45.8 %) and Portugal (47.5 %). Similarly, per capita expenditure in PPS for "in kind" benefits for family/children was in 2018 still incomparably lower in Greece (20.1 pps), Italy (56.4 pps) and Portugal (89.8) than in the EU 27 (263.3), with Spain performing comparatively better though being still below the EU average (199.7 pps). Also public long-term care systems remained comparatively underdeveloped: as outlined in the recent *2021 Long Term Care Report* by the EU Commission (2021b) LTC expenditure remains below the EU-27 average in all the four SE countries.

7.3 Three decades of welfare reforms: assessment and challenges ahead

To sum up, SE welfare states deeply transformed in the last three decades, and yet maintained some core features that still differentiate them from the rest of European countries.

In particular, as result of the severe cuts of the last decade, social policy expenditure per capita remains well below the European average (Figure 7.1) and, above all, it is moving further and further away from the continent's engines. Even Italy, the "big spender" among Mediterranean countries, in 2018 devoted 28 % less resources to its welfare system than Germany, a gap that has almost tripled in less than a decade. Austerity driven reforms, beyond slowing down recalibration attempts in Spain and Portugal, have been so severe to push back by decades the Greek social protection system, putting some of its key functional goals at risk (Guillén et al. 2022).

Against such backdrop, following the analytical dimensions traced in the introductory paragraph, we can draw four main conclusions. First, the functional distortion traditionally characterising SE countries – i.e. the unbalanced allocation of resources favouring pensions vis à vis social assistance and family policies – has limitedly reduced in Italy – mainly due strong retrenchment in the field of pensions for two decades – but is has possibly increased in the other three countries (Table 7.1). However, the very recent introduction of robust minimum income schemes in all Mediterranean countries and (possible) future savings resulting from harsh pension reforms may bring, in the near future, the distribution of expenditure among these welfare functions closer to the European average.

Second, the labour market remains as fragmented as ever but, compared to the past, it has become increasingly difficult to find traces of "strongly guaranteed" workers, as job security declined for all types of workers – including insiders – while the austerity reforms of the last decade generally reduced the "peaks" of generosity characterising unemployment (and pensions) benefits for certain categories of workers, in Italy and Greece in particular. Furthermore, although the welfare state has become generally more inclusive, large numbers of precarious workers and citizens still struggle in being entitled to meagre benefits to avoid falling into severe poverty.

Table 7.1: Social expenditure by function as % total social expenditure, 1980–2015

Function	Year	EU-15	Greece	Italy	Portugal	Spain
Old age and Survivors	1980	39.5 %	52.6 %	51.4 %	37.8 %	40.7 %
	1990	39.5 %	60.4 %	56.1 %	39.1 %	41.0 %
	2000	39.8 %	57.3 %	60.8 %	41.7 %	44.4 %
	2010	39.3 %	55.7 %	58.5 %	48.9 %	39.5 %
	2015	41.5 %	65.2 %	57.9 %	55.3 %	47.0 %
Health	1980	26.0 %	31.9 %	29.4 %	30.7 %	26.5 %
	1990	23.6 %	20.9 %	25.7 %	28.8 %	24.9 %
	2000	24.6 %	25.1 %	23.1 %	31.3 %	25.0 %
	2010	26.8 %	25.9 %	24.8 %	27.7 %	27.3 %
	2015	26.3 %	18.3 %	22.7 %	24.4 %	26.4 %

Table 7.1: (continued)

Function	Year	EU-15	Greece	Italy	Portugal	Spain
Family	1980	10.5 %	3.0 %	5.7 %	6.5 %	3.1 %
	1990	9.4 %	4.1 %	3.9 %	5.5 %	1.6 %
	2000	9.8 %	4.6 %	4.9 %	5.2 %	4.8 %
	2010	9.8 %	4.0 %	4.8 %	5.6 %	5.7 %
	2015	9.4 %	4.1 %	6.6 %	4.9 %	5.0 %
Housing and social assistance	1980	2.6 %	0.6 %	0.0 %	0.4 %	0.3 %
	1990	3.1 %	3.3 %	0.1 %	0.3 %	0.9 %
	2000	3.4 %	0.3 %	0.6 %	1.3 %	1.5 %
	2010	3.7 %	0.2 %	0.8 %	1.2 %	1.6 %
	2015	4.0 %	0.4 %	0.8 %	0.7 %	1.3 %
Invalidity	1980	17.0 %	9.7 %	10.3 %	21.8 %	15.6 %
	1990	15.0 %	7.6 %	10.6 %	20.2 %	11.6 %
	2000	13.1 %	8.0 %	6.6 %	13.9 %	12.0 %
	2010	11.2 %	7.3 %	6.8 %	8.9 %	10.1 %
	2015	11.0 %	7.3 %	6.8 %	8.3 %	9.7 %

Source: Guillén et al. 2022

Third, concerning the traditional cash transfer bias, monetary transfers play an even bigger role today than in the past (Guillén et al. 2022). In the last three decades, the gap with the Nordic and Continental countries in providing services and investing in skills widened rather than reduced (Figure 7.6), and Southern welfare states chronically perform worse both in terms of financing of social investment-oriented programmes and in terms of human capital and social outcomes (Ronchi 2018).

Finally, fourth, the universal health-care systems – which had contributed to an upgrading of the allocative and distributive efficiency of social expenditure in these countries (Bambra 2005) – were severely affected by fifteen years of cost containment reforms, while the growing importance of private actors in this field risks exacerbating stratification and especially inequality, which has substantially increased in SE in the last decade.

Thus, even prior to the outbreak of the COVID-19 pandemic crisis, the main challenges for existing welfare arrangements in Southern Europe mostly relate to: i) the need to fully develop welfare *services* in key policy fields such as childcare, labour market policies, long-term care; ii) reduce labour market segmentation and welfare dualism(s); iii) reconcile both pensions and healthcare sustainability with adequacy, and especially equity; iv) possible changes in welfare financing in order to effectively pursue these goals.

An investment in social services should indeed constitute a key priority, because it also contributes to enhance female participation in the labour market – still significantly below EU27 average in all SE countries with the relevant exception of Portugal – by reducing, on the one hand, the burden of "family" care traditionally carried by women and to stimulate greater participation in the labour market; on the other, by strengthening an economic sector in which women's employment is traditionally high. Such investment in capacitating and enabling services may also contribute to improve the situation of the youth, another group significantly penalised by existing welfare arrangements in Southern Europe (Chevalier 2016), as revealed by comparatively high youth unemployment and NEET rates (Karamessini et al. 2019).

Both in the *pension* and the *healthcare* sectors, the harsh cost containment reforms should be reconciled with social and political sustainability. In the former sector, carefully designed measures should aim to reduce the regressive effects of particularly high pensionable and (at least in Italy and Portugal) *effective* retirement ages as well: pension systems should thus be re-designed in order to ensure adequate pensions, at acceptable retirement ages, for the large share of workers with disadvantaged, interrupted careers (Hinrichs and Jessoula 2012). As for healthcare, increased resources are needed primarily to tackle "unmet needs" due to costs, which critically reduce the universality of the system in three out of the four countries (Greece above all, but also Italy and Portugal). Most, if not all, the policy measures necessary to address the current challenges outlined here require increased reliance on general revenues as the source of welfare state financing: distributional conflicts around social policy *financing* are likely to become a key issue in welfare state politics in the next years and decades

The COVID-19 pandemic broke out in this already difficult context. While it is too soon to assess its long-term consequences, it seems undeniable that it will have an impact on the challenges just mentioned. To cushion the social impact of the pandemic, which hit particularly hard Mediterranean economies, governments had to enlarge existing income support measures and introduce new, extraordinary, social transfers (Moreira et al. 2021). This may further intensify the "cash transfer bias" typical of SE countries and exacerbate existing differences with Northern and Continental countries. Also, such responses guaranteed varying degrees of social protection to different labour market categories, possibly widening existing inequalities.

At the same time, the EU's Recovery and Resilience Facility might represent a unique opportunity for SE countries to push reforms forward and strengthen protection especially in the fields of social services and healthcare.

References

Aguilar-Hendrickson, Manuel and Ana Arriba González de Durana. 2020. "Out of the Wilderness? The Coming Back of the Debate on Minimum Income in Spain and the Great Recession." *Social Policy & Administration* 54 (4), 556–573.

Arlotti, Marco, and Manuel Aguilar-Hendrickson. 2018. "The Vicious Layering of Multilevel Governance in Southern Europe: The Case of Elderly Care in Italy and Spain." *Social Policy & Administration* 52 (3), 646–661.

Arriba, Ana, and Luis Moreno. 2005. "Spain – Poverty, Social Exclusion, and Safety Nets." in *Welfare State Reform in Southern Europe: Fighting Poverty and Social Exclusion in Italy, Spain, Portugal and Greece*, edited by Maurizio Ferrera, pp. 110–162. London: Routledge.

Bambra, Clare. 2005. "Cash Versus Services: 'Worlds of Welfare' and the Decommodification of Cash Benefits and Health Care Services." *Journal of Social Policy* 34 (2), 195–213.

Bulfone, Fabio, and Arianna Tassinari. 2021. "Under Pressure. Economic Constraints, Electoral Politics and Labour Market Reforms in Southern Europe in the Decade of the Great Recession." *European Journal of Political Research*, 60 (3), 509–538.

Capucha, Luis, Teresa Bomba, Rita Fernandes, and Gisela Matos. 2005. "Portugal—A Virtuous Path towards Minimum Income?" In *Welfare State Reform in Southern Europe: Fighting Poverty and Social Exclusion in Italy, Spain, Portugal and Greece*, edited by Maurizio Ferrera, 163–209. London: Routledge.

Chevalier Tom. 2016. "Varieties of Youth Welfare Citizenship: Towards a Two-Dimension Typology." *Journal of European Social Policy* 26 (1), 3–19.

Chuliá, Elisa. 2007. "Spain: Between Majority Rule and Incrementalism." In *The Handbook of West European Pension Politics*, edited by Ellen M. Immergut, Karen M. Anderson, and Isabelle Schulze, 499–554. Oxford. Oxford University Press.

EU Commission 2015. *The 2015 Pension Adequacy Report*. Brussels, EU Commission.

EU Commission. 2018a. *Barcelona Objectives*. Report from the Commission to the European Parliament, the Council, the European Economic and Social Committee and the Committee of the Regions, Brussels, EU Commission.

EU Commission. 2018b. *The 2018 Pension Adequacy Report*. Brussels, EU Commission.

EU Commission. 2021a. *2021 Pension Adequacy Report*. Brussels, EU Commission.

EU Commission. 2021b. *2021 Long Term Care Report*, Brussels, EU Commission.

Ferreira, L. V. 2000. *A pobreza em Portugal na década de 80*. Lisbon: Conselho Económico e Social.

Ferrera, Maurizio. 1996. "The Southern Model of Welfare in Social Europe." *Journal of European Social Policy* 6 (1), 17–37.

Ferrera, Maurizio. 2010. "The South European Countries." In *The Oxford Handbook of the Welfare State*, edited by Francis G. Castel, Stephan Leibfried, Jane Lewis, Herbert Obinger, and Christopher Pierson, 616–629. Oxford: Oxford University Press.

Guillen, A. M. 2002. "The Politics of Universalisation: Establishing National Health Services in Southern Europe." *West European Politics* 25 (4), 49–68.

Guillén, Ana M., Matteo Jessoula, Manos Matsaganis, Rui Branco and Emmanuele Pavolini. 2022. "Southern Welfare Systems in Transition." In *Mediterranean Capitalism Revisited. One Model, Different Trajectories*, edited by Luigi Burroni, Emmanuele Pavolini, and Marino Regini. Ithaca, NY and London: Cornell University Press.

Hinrichs, Karl, and Matteo Jessoula (eds.) 2012. *Labour Market Flexibility and Pension Reforms. Flexible Today, Secure Tomorrow?* Basingstoke: Palgrave Macmillan.

Hutter, Swen, Hanspeter Kriesi, and Guillem Vidal. 2018. "Old Versus New Politics: The Political Spaces in Southern Europe in Times of Crises." *Party Politics* 24 (1), 10–22.

Jessoula, Matteo. 2009. *La politica pensionistica*. Bologna: Il Mulino.

Jessoula, Matteo. 2018. "Pension Multi-Pillarisation in Italy: Actors, 'Institutional Gates' and the 'New Politics' of Funded Pensions." *Transfer: European Review of Labour and Research* 24 (1), 73–89.

Jessoula, Matteo, and Marcello Natili. 2020. "Explaining Italian 'Exceptionalism' and its End: Minimum Income from Neglect to Hyper-Politicization." *Social Policy & Administration* 54 (4), 599–613.

Jessoula, Matteo, Paolo R. Graziano, and Ilaria Madama. 2010. "'Selective Flexicurity' in Segmented Labour Markets: The Case of Italian Mid-Siders." *Journal of Social Policy* 39 (4), 561–583.

Karamessini, Maria, Maria Symeonaki, Dimitris Parsanoglou, and Glykeria Stamatopoulou. 2019. "Mapping Early Job Insecurity Impacts of the Crisis in Europe." In *Youth Unemployment and Job Insecurity in Europe*, edited by Bjørn Hvinden, Christer Hyggen, Mi Ah Schoyen, and Tomáš Sirovátka, 24–44. Cheltenham: Edward Elgar Publishing.

León, Margarita, and Emmanuele Pavolini. 2014. "'Social Investment' or Back to 'Familism': The Impact of the Economic Crisis on Family and Care Policies in Italy and Spain." *South European Society and Politics* 19 (3), 353–369.

Marí-Klose, Pau, and Francisco Moreno-Fuentes. 2013. "The Southern European Welfare Model in the Post-Industrial Order." *European Societies* 15 (4), 475–492.

Matsaganis, Manos. 2018. "Income Support Policies and Labour Market Reform Under Austerity in Greece." In *Labour Market Policies in the Era of Pervasive Austerity: A European Perspective*, edited by Sotiria Theodoropoulou, 43–67. Bristol: Policy Press.

Matsaganis, Manos. 2020. "Safety Nets in (the) Crisis: The Case of Greece in the 2010s." *Social Policy & Administration* 54 (4), 587–598.

Moreira, Amilcar, Àngel Alonso-Domínguez, Cátia Antunes, Maria Karamessini, Michele Raitano, and Miguel Glatzer. 2015. "Austerity-Driven Labour Market Reforms in Southern Europe: Eroding the Security of Labour Market Insiders." *European Journal of Social Security* 17 (2), 202–225.

Moury, Catherine, Elisabetta De Giorgi, and Pedro Pita Barros. 2020. "How to Combine Public Spending with Fiscal Rigour? 'Austerity by Stealth' in Post-Bailout Portugal (2015–2019)." *South European Society and Politics* 25 (2), 151–178.

Natili, Marcello. 2019. *The Politics of Minimum Income. Explaining Path Departure and Policy Reversals in the Age of Austerity*. London: Palgrave Macmillan.

Natili, Marcello, and Matteo Jessoula. 2019. "Children Against Parents? The Politics of Intergenerational Recalibration in Southern Europe." *Social Policy & Administration* 53 (3), 343–356.

Pavolini, Emmanuele, Margarita León, Ana M. Guillén, and Ugo Ascoli. 2015. "From Austerity to Permanent Strain? The EU and Welfare State Reform in Italy and Spain." *Comparative European Politics* 13 (1), 56–76.

Pereirinha, José A., Francisco Branco, Elvira Pereira, and Maria I. Amaro. 2020. "The Guaranteed Minimum Income in Portugal: A Universal Safety Net Under Political and Financial Pressure." *Social Policy & Administration* 54 (4), 574–586.

Petmesidou, Maria. 2019. "Southern Europe." In *Routledge Handbook of the Welfare State*, edited by Bent Greve, 183–192. Second edition. London: Routledge. https://doi.org/10.4324/9781315207049

Picot, Georg, and Arianna Tassinari. 2017. "All of One Kind? Labour Market Reforms Under Austerity in Italy and Spain." *Socio-Economic Review* 15 (2), 461–482.

Raitano, Michele, Giovanni Gallo, Matteo Jessoula, and Costanza Pagnini. 2021. *Fighting Poverty and Social Exclusion*. Publication for the Committee on Employment and Social Affairs, Policy Department for Economic, Scientific and Quality of Life Policies, European Parliament, Luxembourg.

Ronchi, Stefano. 2018. "Which Roads (If Any) to Social Investment? The Recalibration of EU Welfare States at the Crisis Crossroads (2000–2014)." *Journal of Social Policy* 47 (3), 459–478.

Sacchi, Stefano. 2015. "Conditionality by Other Means: EU Involvement in Italy's Structural Reforms in the Sovereign Debt Crisis." *Comparative European Politics* 13 (1), 77–92.

Saraceno, Chiara. 1994. "The Ambivalent Familism of the Italian Welfare State." *Social Politics: International Studies in Gender, State & Society* 1 (1), 60–82.

Saraceno, Chiara, David Benassi, and Enrica Morlicchio. 2020. *Poverty in Italy. Features and Drivers in a European Perspective*. Bristol: Policy Press.

Theodoropoulou, Sotiria. 2015. "National Social and Labour Market Policy Reforms in the Shadow of EU Bail-Out Conditionality: The Cases of Greece and Portugal." *Comparative European Politics* 13 (1), 29–55.

Trifiletti, Rossana. 1999. "Southern European Welfare Regimes and the Worsening Position of Women." *Journal of European Social Policy* 9 (1), 49–64.

Maša Filipovič Hrast and Ivana Dobrotić

8 Eastern European welfare states

Abstract: The transformations in Eastern Europe have been multiple and extensive, and for several decades, the region has often been depicted as "in transition", marked by uncertainty and in a permanent state of emergency. Initially, the transition from a socialist to a democratic and capitalist regime was principally discussed through economic and political lenses. Still, it also entailed a transition of social welfare structures, gender relations and other transformations. This chapter briefly describes the breadth of these transformations, revealing the main similarities and differences in welfare state development in Eastern European countries and showing how the region has evolved and become more diverse over the last three decades. It shows the creation of varied hybrid welfare systems in the region, stemming from both diverse starting points and diverse development pathways. It specifically discusses the transformations related to sociodemographic pressures, care and gender equality issues.

Keywords: Eastern Europe, welfare state, transition, sociodemographic pressures, gender equality, hybrid welfare systems

8.1 Introduction

It is challenging to talk about Eastern European welfare states using a common regime terminology. Already the region is not clearly defined, while the characteristics of the welfare states vary. However, what the region does have in common is the legacy of socialism, which helped to develop the welfare state and also had wider socioeconomic and cultural implications. The discussion of welfare state developments in the region is frequently limited to the Central Eastern countries in Europe, where the Visegrád countries (Czechia, Hungary, Poland, Slovakia) and Baltic countries (Lithuania, Latvia, Estonia) often form specific clusters. South-East Europe rarely forms part of the "Eastern group" in this framework. Besides, the discussion is often limited to countries in the region that are members of the European Union (EU). In this chapter, we start from a broader geographical perspective and briefly discuss the main developments in both Central- and South-Eastern Europe (i.e. the Baltics, Visegrád countries, Bulgaria, Romania and the countries of former Yugoslavia). Yet, we do not extend the discussion to countries of the former Soviet Union that also border this region.

The transformations in Eastern Europe have been multiple and extensive, while for several decades the region has often been depicted as "in transition", marked by uncertainty (Lendvai and Stubbs 2015) and "reputed immaturity" (Kuitto 2016, 1). Initially, the transition from a socialist to a democratic and capitalist regime was principally discussed through economic and political lenses. Still, it also entailed "a transi-

https://doi.org/10.1515/9783110721768-008

tion of social welfare structures and of households and of the gender relations and assumptions within both" (Pascall and Kwak 2005, 1). This chapter will briefly describe the breadth of the latter transformations, revealing the biggest similarities and differences in welfare state development in Eastern European countries (EECs) and showing how the region has evolved and become more diverse over the last three decades.

8.2 Common features and divergent developments

EECs share the institutional legacy of the "state socialist welfare state", which is the main reason they are linked together within a common "regime". Exploring the specifics of the EECs' "regime", Mishra (2013) noted that state socialist countries developed functional alternatives to the institutions typical of Western welfare states (e.g. well-developed and broadly encompassing social insurance programmes and social assistance programmes), capable of performing similar functions of providing economic security and maintaining living standards. These "alternative welfare systems" primarily concerned guaranteed employment and consumer price subsidies that could develop because these countries remained relatively isolated from the global economy and were implemented along with a range of universal services, especially in education or healthcare. The state's chief role in all areas linked to social security (education, care, employment, social assistance) was basically the same in state socialist countries, albeit with variations in EECs' development levels and their welfare institutions.

In all these countries, the transition from a socialist to a democratic and capitalist regime meant abandoning some of the previous social protection forms, most notably "full" employment, leading to mass unemployment and economic insecurity (Deacon 2000; Mishra 2013). The transition brought an end to the sense of security, weakened workers' rights and increased poverty, particularly among certain groups like the elderly or ethnic minorities (Deacon 2000; Ferge 2008). Globalisation and economic liberalisation – also promoted by international agencies (e.g. International Monetary Fund – IMF, World Bank – WB) – put pressure on EECs' welfare states to change, often in the direction of the Western systems of welfare provision (Deacon, Hulse, and Stubbs 1997; Mishra 2013). Some authors labelled these early reforms as "shock therapy", arguing that many post-socialist countries were choosing a neoliberal path (Ferge 2001, 2008; Bohle and Greskovits 2007; Kolarič, Kopač, and Rakar 2009). The privatisation of welfare programmes – supported by international financial institutions like the IMF and WB – was indeed a significant development trend, evident in pension system reforms in many countries (e.g. the introduction of multi-pillar systems, Deacon 2000; Mishra 2013). Changes were also made to the organisation of social services and assets, and responsibilities in fields like education or healthcare by shifting responsibilities from state budgets to independent social funds and private insurance markets and increasing private provision, means-testing and targeted benefits (Kuitto 2016). The goals were to strengthen individual and decrease public responsibility, therefore establishing a "leaner state ... and a diminished welfare state" (Ferge 2008, 150). Still, the reforms described were also coupled with a continuation of the past welfare provision models and building upon them.

The complex transformation process eventually created "hybrid" welfare regimes combining characteristics of different welfare systems and dominated by elements of the conservative-corporatist welfare state (cf. Deacon 2000; Kovács 2002; Hacker 2009). Despite many differences within the region, there is a consensus on basic similarities in the welfare state development linked to generally shared historical institutional settings (Deacon 2000; Inglot 2008; Stambolieva 2016). The specificity of such historical development – which mainly sought to add new elements to already existing policies – has often led to the emerging welfare models in the EECs being described as "hybrid systems" built on pre-communist elements like Bismarckian social insurance, communist elements such as universalism, and post-communist elements linked to market-based schemes (Cerami 2006; Kuitto 2016). Common features of their welfare states are seen in elements like the dominance of contribution-based systems, lower levels of social expenditure (Figure 8.1; Table 8.1), often lower levels of rights' scope, and still a heavy reliance on a familialism in addressing care needs (Kuitto 2016; Stambolieva 2016). In that sense, we can still see some things in common; however, the variations within this cluster are large, and subclusters of "hybrid" regimes have been established.

The significant variations within the Eastern European cluster are associated with different legacy and socioeconomic conditions, the transition's deep complexity that in some cases was coupled with wars and concurrent processes of state- and nation-building, and variegated Europeanisation (cf. Deacon 2000; Lendvai and Stubbs 2015; Stubbs and Zrinščak 2019). Countries already diverged on certain policy elements during socialism (e.g. Yugoslav countries did not introduce extended childcare leave, while some developed an institutional structure in the area of unemployment and social assistance; Dobrotić 2020; Dobrotić and Stropnik 2020), which intensified in the post-1990 period when they have retained their past systems' characteristics to varying degrees and gradually developed divergent models. For example, some scholars argue that the Baltic states adopted a more neoliberal system with a more radical break from the past, trading social welfare for industrial upgrading. In contrast, the Visegrád countries have developed towards a more embedded neoliberal type with a less radical change and by sheltering workers and businesses from extreme hardships, and Slovenia a more neocorporatist regime with very gradual changes, maintaining strong links to the state and the universal public services and further developing social security systems of the conservative-corporativist type (see Bohle and Greskovits 2007; Kolarič, Kopač, and Rakar 2009). In the former Yugoslav countries, within two decades after the federal state's disintegration, the extremes of the well-developed welfare system in Slovenia and the residual welfare system in North Macedonia could be observed, with a conservative paternalistic system in Serbia lying between these two extremes (Stambolieva 2016). Differences between countries, yet also within countries, are even more pronounced when the focus is placed on the characteristics of specific systems like family policy or eldercare (cf. Szelewa and Polakowski 2008; Österle 2010). Thus, it is no surprise that analyses of EECs and attempts to distinguish regime patterns often result in a mixed picture, with some countries forming a common cluster and others joining specific clusters together with Western European countries in different ways (Kuitto 2012).

The challenges and pressures the EECs have faced over the last decade are similar to the challenges for Western European countries, ranging from economic pressures of market restructuring and globalisation through to sociodemographic pressures, as discussed in more detail later. Pressures also came from external actors (e.g. IMF, WB, EU) and, sometimes, anti-gender movements (e.g. Vučković Juroš, Dobrotić, and Flego 2020) and "populist, nationalist and paternalist backlashes" (Lendvai-Bainton 2020, 263). Several of these issues have been exacerbated by the Great Recession starting in 2008, which affected EECs in different ways. Some countries, like the Baltic tigers, have been particularly affected, and many countries have had to curb their public spending (Lendvai and Stubbs 2015). While certain countries have made gradual changes to the welfare state (e.g. Slovenia), the general trend of retrenchment remains a strong pattern in many (cf. Lendvai-Bainton 2020; Stubbs and Zrinščak 2019), with particular countries experiencing drastic retrenchments (e.g. Hungary). The austerity reforms have also been combined with some expansions, indicating a range of responses (cf. Lendvai-Bainton 2020; Blum and Kuhlmann 2020). These expansionary trends are mainly linked to the development of social policies addressing "new" social risks. For example, after the discontinuity of investments in care infrastructure in many countries, the recent decade saw a reversed trend and growing support for policies supporting the work-care balance (Borosh, Kuhlmann, and Blum 2016; Dobrotić 2020).

Accordingly, policy responses in EECs in the last decade have entailed continuous adaptive processes (Blum and Kuhlmann 2020). While sharing some commonalities, such as social expenditure lower than the EU average, there are significant variations in social expenditures within the EECs, ranging from low (e.g. Latvia, Romania) to higher (e.g. Slovenia, Croatia) (Figure 8.1). Specific expenditure functions also reveal considerable differences. For example, expenditure on unemployment ranges from 0.79 % in North Macedonia to 4.54 % in Lithuania, which is diametrical to the unemployment level in these two countries (cf. Table 8.1 and Figure 8.1) and shows variations in their system's development and generosity. The region is often depicted as in "permanent transition that is marked with strong volatility and uncertainty" (Lendvai and Stubbs 2015, 451) in relation to economic performance as well as political stability and reform implementation, while the global crisis which started in 2008 revealed the deficiencies of the neoliberal policy orthodoxy (Stambolieva 2016). Like most European countries, EECs' welfare states have seen considerable sociodemographic changes and are under constant financial pressure due to the increasing healthcare needs of the ageing population and pension expenditures, as well as often high unemployment rates together with the context of lower economic performance, as also evident in GDP per capita below the EU-27 average (see Table 8.2). All of this calls for new reforms and adjustments. There is tremendous pressure to adjust the pension and healthcare systems, which account for a major share of social expenditure in all welfare states (Table 8.1), as well as a need to develop various support systems in the areas of long-term care and childcare. We turn to these considerable challenges in the next sections.

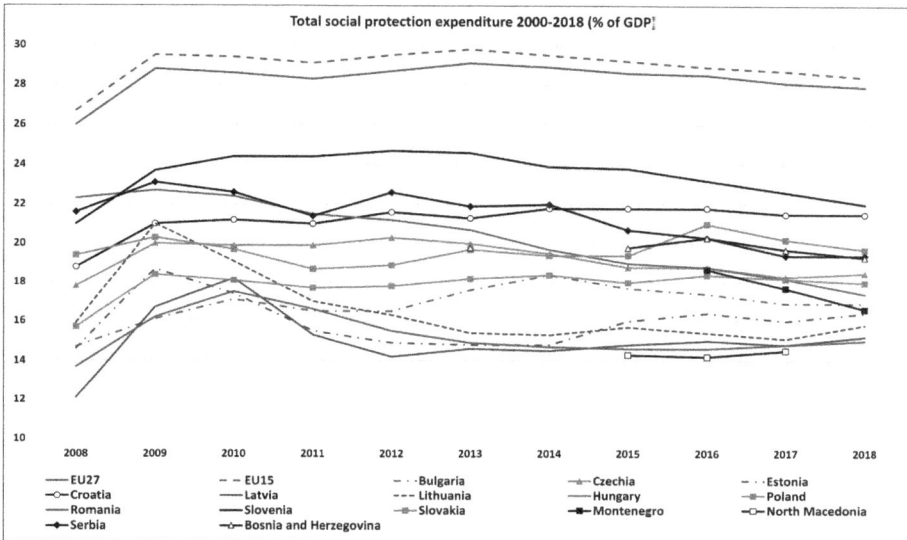

Figure 8.1: Total social protection expenditure in EECs 2000–2018 (% of GDP).
Source: Eurostat 2021.

Table 8.1: Social expenditure by function (% of total benefits, 2018).

	Health care	Disa-bility	Old age	Survi-vors	Family/ Children	Unem-ployment	Housing	Social exclusion
EU-27	29.25	7.64	40.27	6.17	8.32	4.66	1.42	2.27
Czechia	33.37	6.23	43.57	3.12	9.24	2.47	1.00	1.01
Slovakia	32.83	8.50	40.67	4.96	8.82	2.75	0.30	1.16
Hungary	28.12	5.56	44.58	5.07	11.84	1.69	2.65	0.50
Poland	22.03	6.82	47.42	8.78	13.04	1.22	0.16	0.53
Estonia	29.86	11.36	40.32	0.31	14.42	2.90	0.39	0.44
Latvia	27.39	8.71	46.33	1.24	10.85	4.42	0.39	0.68
Lithuania	30.40	8.96	41.25	2.36	10.31	4.54	0.43	1.76

Table 8.1: (continued)

	Health care	Disa- bility	Old age	Survi- vors	Family/ Children	Unem- ployment	Housing	Social exclusion
Bulgaria	29.63	7.29	43.01	5.31	10.38	3.09	0.00	1.30
Romania	28.90	6.34	49.03	4.34	10.22	0.36	0.08	0.72
Slovenia	33.76	4.65	41.73	5.78	8.37	2.34	0.11	3.26
Croatia	33.62	10.27	34.02	8.52	9.04	2.87	0.08	1.58
Montenegro	29.59	8.52	39.87	12.04	4.24	3.21	0.00	2.53
North Macedonia*	29.48	9.97	40.45	11.60	6.34	0.79	0.00	1.36
Serbia	27.04	5.53	45.54	9.33	6.46	2.97	0.08	3.06
Bosnia and Herzegovina	29.29	11.50	34.18	16.67	4.45	2.61	0.05	1.24

* 2017 data
Source: Eurostat 2021

8.3 Present and future challenges

As noted, the transition from socialism to a market economy and democracy has seen EECs further diverge in welfare state development. As briefly described below, socioeconomic difficulties and inequalities have been exacerbated by the Great Recession, which was particularly strong in the region. They are likely to be further aggravated by the current COVID-19 pandemic. Besides, sociodemographic developments have led to additional pressure and calls for changes in pension and care systems, posing a specific challenge to gender equality.

8.3.1 Economic pressures, social policy developments and inequalities

Economic hardship forms a critical background that has limited the development of welfare systems in many countries. GDP fell dramatically at the start of the transition period, thereby increasing inequalities and insecurities, (long-term) unemployment, and poverty (Kuitto 2016). Although economic growth was re-established, EECs have been lagging behind the EU average. There have also been huge differences among the EECs due to various factors like varying fiscal and monetary policies, modalities and paces of the privatisation of public enterprises and structural reforms, including those concerning the labour market and social policies, as well as international organisations' influence (cf. Nesporova 2002; Lendvai-Bainton 2020). Their starting points also differed, with Visegrád countries having much better initial socioeconomic conditions than, for example, the Baltics or Bulgaria and Romania (Lendvai-Bainton 2020). Moreover, economic and social developments were further disrupted in those former Yugoslav countries faced with the effects of the wars of the Yugoslav succession (Dobrotić and Obradović 2020; Stubbs and Zrinščak 2019).

Economic pressures in the region are closely linked to the very low social expenditures, leaving extremely limited space for new initiatives and continuing the practice of strong social expenditure concentration in "old" systems like pensions and healthcare (cf. Table 8.1; Lendvai- Bainton 2020; Stubbs and Zrinščak 2019). The already low social expenditures, particularly when compared to EU-15 (Figure 8.1), are under constant pressure, face demands for reduction and are in direct conflict with the growing pressures of social needs (e.g. due to high poverty among specific population groups; the ageing population) and new social groups seeking comprehensive social rights (e.g. war veterans in some former Yugoslav countries). Lendvai-Bainton (2020, 269) also notes that after "a decade of Europeanisation of welfare" in then-new EU member states (those joining the EU in the 2000s), the pressure to place social expenditures "under control" became even stronger with the Great Recession, especially since "soft governance has lost its significance and coercive, fiscal-based, governance tools started to dominate the EU framework" (Lendvai-Bainton 2020, 265).[1] The crisis created a new opportunity to deregulate the labour market and led to calls for "fiscal discipline" and cost-containment in different social policy areas, thereby weakening various social rights (e.g. decrease in benefits defined by collective agreements such as holidays/annual leave/travel allowances; decrease in unemployment and social benefits' level as well as increasing the conditionality of access to rights; increase in out-of-pocket treatment costs in healthcare, and longer waiting lists in hospitals) (cf. Blum and Kuhlmann 2020; Dobrotić 2020; Lendvai-Bainton 2020; Stoilova and Krasteva 2020). It also strengthened the workfare paradigm, taking an extreme form in Hungary, which has begun to rely heavily on public work schemes of a "punitive, ethnically selective (targeting Roma and other ethnic minorities) ... [form and] should anybody refuse to participate, this would mean losing all their eligible benefits altogether" (Lendvai-Bainton 2020, 277). Finally, in certain countries (e.g. Bosnia-Herzegovina, Croatia, Poland, Serbia), EU funds have become an important resource used to "patch" the welfare state's weakened ability to respond to the growing social pressures. This has paved the way for the increased "projectisation" of social services, that is, financing services on a short-term project basis, and the exposure of service users

---

1 In other words, with the Great Recession the EU strengthened the existing fiscal policy instruments and implemented new ones, reinforcing their surveillance and coercion dimensions while the instruments designed to coordinate social policy were weakened (de la Porte and Heins 2014).

Table 8.2: Socioeconomic indicators.

Country	GDP per capita in PPS (2019)	Minimum wage in euro (2015)	Average net wage in euro (2015)	At-risk-of poverty rate total (2019)	At-risk-of poverty rate 0–18 (2019)	At-risk-of poverty rate 65+ (2019)	Severe material deprivation rate (2019)	Gini coefficient (2019)	Employment rate total 20–64	Employment rate 20–64 females	Total unemployment rate	Temporary employees (% of total employees)
EU-27	31,200	–	–	16.5	18.5	16.1	5.4	30.2	73.1	67.3	6.7	11.9
Czechia	28,900	331.71	750.73	10.1	11.2	16.6	2.7	24.0	80.3	72.7	2.0	6.3
Slovakia	21,900	380.00	683.41	11.9	19.0	8.7	7.9	22.8	73.4	66.9	5.8	6.5
Hungary	22,800	332.76	558.63	12.3	11.5	11.1	8.7	28.0	75.3	67.6	3.4	5.8
Poland	22,700	409.53	689.67	15.4	13.4	17.4	3.6	28.5	73.0	65.3	3.3	17.1
Estonia	26,100	390.00	886.54	21.7	17.2	43.7	3.3	30.5	80.2	76.3	4.4	2.4
Latvia	21,500	360.00	567.88	22.9	14.5	47.9	7.8	35.2	77.4	75.5	6.3	2.6
Lithuania	26,000	300.00	554.32	20.6	22.7	31.6	9.4	35.4	78.2	77.4	6.3	1.1
Bulgaria	16,500	184.07	361.60	22.6	27.5	34.6	19.9	40.8	75.0	70.7	4.2	3.8
Romania	21,700	217.50	426.59	23.8	30.8	25.1	14.5	34.8	70.9	61.3	3.9	1.1
Slovenia	27,700	790.73	1,005.20	12.0	10.5	18.6	2.6	23.9	76.4	72.9	4.5	10.9
Croatia	20,300	395.61	684.20	18.3	17.1	30.1	7.2	29.2	66.7	61.5	6.6	15.5
Montenegro	15,700	288.05	480*	24.5	33.7	15.1	12.0	34.1	60.8	54.2	15.2	26.1
North Macedonia	11,800	213.72	368.81*	21.6	27.8	14.8	30.4	30.7	59.2	48.4	17.3	13.2
Serbia	12,700	235.04	377.21*	23.2	28.9	21.1	14.6	33.3	65.2	58.2	10.5	17.0

* Data obtained via national statistical offices and calculated based on a different methodology

Source: Eurostat 2021

to the risk of being left without any services during periods between projects since the state has not been obliged to ensure their sustainability (cf. Dobrotić and Zrinščak 2022; Stubbs and Zrinščak 2019).

All of these processes have brought asymmetric social rights and redistribution patterns into the region (Stubbs and Zrinščak 2015; Lendvai and Stubbs 2015), high levels of income poverty, material deprivation and social polarisation. There are considerable differences in living standards between the EECs and the EU-15, also among the EECs themselves, with Slovenia, Slovakia, Czechia and Hungary having lower poverty rates, unemployment rates and lower inequalities (see Table 8.2). In many countries, the welfare state's weakened capacity and the general lack of political will to address the changing structure of social risks have been coupled with fragile and increasingly precarious labour markets and insufficient employment opportunities. Social polarisations are also evident within the countries, with divisions being found across various dimensions like gender, age, class, ethnicity or territory (cf. Dobrotić and Obradović 2020; Lendvai-Bainton 2020; Stubbs and Zrinščak 2019). As a result, social contracts and social solidarities are also being questioned and are on the decline (Lendvai and Stubbs 2015).

8.4 Sociodemographic pressures and social policy developments

Dropping birth rates and strong growth of the old-age dependency ratio are pronounced in EECs and exceed the average of Western European countries (Kuitto 2016). The reforms linked to population ageing in EECs have largely focused on making their pension systems more sustainable, which have tended to be guided by neoliberal ideas (Blum and Kuhlmann 2020). The region has been marked by a common trend in the direction of introducing structural reforms and private pension pillars (a move towards multi-pillar pension systems) where international actors like the WB have been directly involved (Hinrichs and Lynch 2010; Mishra 2013), with several countries introducing compulsory, supplementarily-funded pillars. However, the Great Recession and the added risks in financial markets brought pension privatisation reversals. Namely, many countries in the region either shifted to voluntary participation in private pillars or even abolished this pillar (Wang, Williamson, and Cansoy 2016; Hinrichs 2021). As Borosh et al. (2016) noted, general retrenchment trends are particularly notable in the area of pensions, seen in an increase in the retirement age, the decreasing level of pensions, stricter eligibility criteria for disability pensions and reduced access to early retirement (e.g. in Slovenia, Serbia, Poland, Hungary, Romania, Croatia, Estonia, Lithuania, Latvia, North Macedonia). Pension system reforms have generally negatively affected older people's position and reduced the poverty alleviation function of state pensions, which has had the most adverse effect on women and those on lower incomes (Grech 2015). It is also evident in the high poverty rates among older people in many countries, although, once again, there is significant variation among them (Table 8.2).

Another important aspect of demographic ageing is the rising need for care and thus the pressure on welfare states to develop long-term care policies. In this respect, EECs all make lower investments in long-term care than the Nordic and Central Western European countries (OECD 2020). In the literature on care regimes, EECs typically belong to implicit familialism or familialism by default in relation to care for older people (see Leitner 2003; Saraceno and Keck 2010). Such a regime is characterised by poorly developed long-term care policies – either in an institutional or homecare setting – and reliance on the family care provision for older people, with little support from the state. EECs have less institutional care available, as well as fragmented and limited availability of community-based social services (Österle 2010). Further, over the last two decades, eldercare capacities' expansion has often relied on private providers entering the system (Hlebec and Rakar 2017; Dobrotić and Zrinščak 2022), potentially leading to greater inequalities in access to eldercare. Extensive reliance on familialist care can be linked to gender inequalities because care is often provided by female family members. People in the Eastern European region also strongly support the family care of older people and see it as the best option (Österle and Rothgang 2010). The weak availability of public care services is crucial for understanding the gender gap in informal care (Da Roit, Hoogenboom, and Weicht 2015). This makes issues of gender equality very relevant to the region. In many countries, they have further deteriorated also due to the weakened investments in childcare policies, as discussed in the next section.

8.5 Gender equality and changes in social policies

EECs share a socialist legacy of a relatively strong focus on policies aimed at facilitating women's employment and providing, at the time, more state support for families than in Western Europe (e.g. Pascall and Kwak 2005). Still, some gender issues – particularly those related to the private sphere (e.g. domestic violence, LGBT rights, the unequal division of care work) – were never part of socialist gender equality agendas (Havelková 2010; Dobrotić, Matković, and Zrinščak 2013). While the transition has been a critical breaking point, it is hard to discuss EECs' gender regimes while relying on a "dichotomy between 'state socialism' and 'capitalism'" (Haney 2002, 6). The region and EECs exhibited internal variations already during socialism, which only intensified with the mixed experiences of both the transition and Europeanisation processes.

The legitimisation of gender equality policy has been challenging in all EECs, especially in countries where gender topics became strongly associated with a negative image of the socialist past, anti-feminist discourses or demographic downfall and discourses about a "dying nation" (Gerber 2010; Dobrotić, Matković, and Zrinščak 2013). However, concrete policy measures seeking to assign women with primarily a reproductive and caring function (e.g. the introduction of prolonged childcare/parental leave instead of investing in nurseries) were more a characteristic of the Visegrád and Baltic countries that also kept higher investments in the function of families/children (Table 8.1)[2] than the countries of former Yugoslavia. More precisely, while the Visegrád and Baltic countries introduced prolonged childcare leave paid at a low flat-rate level, the same was not the case in the former Yugoslav countries, which mostly retained the moderate but well-paid leave (Dobrotić and Stropnik 2020). In the latter countries, the position of women in the public sphere has weakened more due to broader changes in the economy and labour markets (e.g. growing precarisation, wage stagnation), coupled with state-/nation-building processes that have tended to prioritise nation and ethnicity discourses and lacked any genuine interest in gender equality (cf. Dobrotić, Matković, and Zrinščak 2013; Dobrotić and Obradović 2020; Stubbs and Zrinščak 2019). This is reflected in leave policy development, which has remained mother-centred. Individual fathers' entitlements have slowly been introduced only in countries that had to align with the EU's parental leave directives, with just a few countries having more extensive fathers-only leave (Slovenia, Romania; Dobrotić and Stropnik 2020). Moreover, post-1990s investments in early childhood education and care (ECEC) were weak (particularly for under-3s) in all countries except Slovenia. Only in the recent decade can more visible investments in care infrastructure be noticed; however, countries are still lagging behind other parts of Europe in ECEC attendance rates (Eurydice 2019).

The EU has become an important legitimising force for legislative and institutional changes in gender equality, even regarding non-binding issues (e.g. domestic violence, LGBT rights). Still, there has been strong resistance to implementing the EU's gender equality agenda, heavily mediated through a range of country-specific circumstances (e.g. neo-liberal and conservative actors; the church; weak capacity of the women's movement; nationalism). The result is declarative adherence to the protection of gender equality rights and a clear gap between legislative compliance and the actual practices, which was never questioned in the negotiation process and even less so later (cf. Havelková 2010; Gerber 2010; Dobrotić, Matković, and Zrinščak 2013; Lendvai-Bainton 2020). With the Great Recession and already mentioned weakening of soft EU governance, as well as the rise of anti-gender movements and right-wing populism, calls to reject these policies have become louder in some countries (e.g. the term gender was banned in Poland and erased from government documents in Hungary where gender mainstreaming has been replaced by family mainstreaming; the

---

2 Spending for families/children varies across countries and exceeds the EU average in the Visegrád and Baltic countries (Table 8.1), with most funds going into cash benefits and tax breaks for families with children (OECD 2021).

ban on gender studies in Hungary; the constitutional ban of same-sex marriage in Croatia; the abortion ban in Poland) (cf. Lendvai-Bainton 2020; Vučković Juroš, Dobrotić, and Flego 2020; Szelewa 2020). Further, in the post-recession period, the EU has prioritised economic reforms even more than before, including employment-centred gender equality policies, which have been too narrow to bring about substantial change and improvements. Therefore, as indicated by the Gender Equality Index, EECs perform poorly on many gender equality indicators and are placed below the EU average (EIGE 2020).

8.6 Conclusion

In the last few decades, EECs' welfare states have faced profound transformations related to the privatisation of welfare and the transfer of responsibilities from the state to other welfare actors, often accompanied by a weakening of social rights and a strengthening of the workfare paradigm. The region is typically described as being in permanent transition – a permanent emergency or crisis state (Inglot 2008; Lendvai and Stubbs 2015). If we locate these changes in a broader context, we could say that continuous and profound structural changes have also been characteristic of Western welfare states, which are referred to as landscapes in motion denoted by cost-containment, retrenchment, restructuring and expansion (Taylor Gooby, Leeruth, and Chung 2017, Blum and Kuhlmann 2020). Still, the latter changes have been less abrupt and more moderate in their character. Despite periods of high economic growth in certain countries (e.g. the Baltics, Slovenia, Czech Republic) and strengthening of the economy over the 30 years, economic hardship, as also seen in lower GDP in PPP than the EU average in 2019 (see Table 8.2), is one of the key factors that has limited the development of the EECs' welfare systems and has been linked to historical factors, unfavourable sociodemographic conditions like population ageing and labour market developments and, in particular countries (e.g. former Yugoslav), the lack of political commitment to implement wide-ranging reforms. This has all made the region ill-equipped to follow the fast pace of change and to (re)develop their welfare systems and often led to social polarisations and the growing vulnerability of certain groups in society.

Significant differences within the region existed before the transition process to a democratic and capitalist regime commenced and, in some cases, have been even further accentuated. This growing divergence needs further unpacking, especially to better understand underexplored areas (e.g. former Yugoslav countries) and the implications for welfare state development held by certain trends like the anti-gender movements and right-wing populism that have been on the rise in the region (e.g. Hungary, Poland). In general, it is difficult to describe the region as having common regime characteristics and several subgroups seem to be forming within EECs, establishing several sub-regimes (see Stambolieva 2016).

The additional pressure created by the COVID-19 pandemic will have a significant effect on the socioeconomic situation in the region. For instance, it has put considerable pressure on the already struggling healthcare systems, characterised by limited access to healthcare, increasing privatisation, poor coordination, and the problem of "under the table" payments (see Stoilova and Krasteva 2020; Tausz 2020). This means the region continues to face major challenges regarding welfare system development and will most likely see more "transitions" and changes jeopardising a range of social rights. Due to the described ageing and social and healthcare challenges, as well as gender equality issues in the region, on top of securing the sustainability of healthcare and pension systems, policies that focus on affordable care services of good quality, the work-life balance in general together with active labour market and poverty prevention policies are critical future focus areas for policy development in the region.

Funding: Maša Filipovič Hrast acknowledges the funding from the Slovene Research Agency (contract number P5-0200, J5-2559).

References

Blum, S., and J. Kuhlmann. 2020. "Landscapes in Motion: Welfare System Reform in 28 European Countries." In *Routledge Handbook of European Welfare Systems*, edited by S. Blum, J. Kuhlmann, and K. Schubert, 577–591. 2nd ed. London and New York: Routledge.

Bohle, D., and B. Greskovits. 2007. "Neoliberalism, Embedded Neoliberalism and Neocorporatism: Towards Transnational Capitalism in Central Eastern Europe." *West European Politics* 30 (3), 433–466.

Borosh, N., J. Kuhlmann, and S. Blum. 2016. "Opening Up Opportunities and Risks? Retrenchment, Activation and Targeting as Main Trends of Recent Welfare State Reforms Across Europe." In *Challenges to European Welfare Systems*, edited by K. Schubert, 769–793. Cham [etc.]: Springer.

Cerami, A. 2006. *Social Policy in Central and Eastern Europe*. Berlin: LIT Verlag.

De la Porte, C., and E. Heins. 2014. "Game Change in EU Social Policy: Towards More European Integration." In *The Eurozone Crisis and the Transformation of EU Governance*, edited by M. J. Rodrigues and E. Xiarchogiannopoulou, 157–170. Farnham: Ashgate.

Da Roit, B., M. Hoogenboom, and B. Weicht. 2015. "The Gender Informal Care Gap." *European Societies* 17 (2), 199–218.

Deacon, B. 2000. "Eastern European Welfare States: The Impact of the Politics of Globalization." *Journal of European Social Policy* 10 (2), 146–161.

Deacon, B., M. Hulse, and P. Stubbs. 1997. *Global Social Policy: International Organisations and the Future of Welfare*. London: Sage.

Dobrotić, I. 2020. "The Croatian Welfare System: A Lack of Coherent Policy Paradigm Followed by Inconsistent Reforms?" In *Routledge Handbook of European Social Systems*, edited by S. Blum, J. Kuhlmann, and K. Schubert, 237–255. London: Routledge.

Dobrotić, I., T. Matković, and S. Zrinščak. 2013. "Gender Equality Policies and Practices in Croatia: The Interplay of Transition and Late Europeanization." *Social Policy & Administration* 47 (2), 218–240.

Dobrotić, I., and N. Obradović. 2020. "Exclusionary Side of (Women's) Social Citizenship in South Eastern Europe: Childcare Policies Development in Bosnia-Herzegovina and Gender, Social and Territorial Inequalities." *Southeast European and Black Sea Studies* 20 (3), 411–430.

Dobrotić, I., and N. Stropnik. 2020. "Gender Equality and Parenting-Related Leaves in 21 Former Socialist Countries." *International Journal of Sociology & Social Policy* 40 (5/6), 495–514.

Dobrotić, I., and S. Zrinščak. (forthcoming 2022). "(Active) Ageing, Gender and Social Policy Reforms: The Case of Pension and Eldercare Reforms in Croatia." In *Well-Being and Extended Working Life: A Gender Perspective*, edited by T. Addabbo, P. Carney, A. Leime, J. Spijker, and S. Zrinščak. London: Routledge.

EIGE. 2020. *Gender Equality Index*. https://eige.europa.eu/gender-equality-index/compare-countries.

Eurydice. 2019. *Key Data on Early Childhood Education and Care in Europe*. https://op.europa.eu/en/publication-detail/-/publication/5816a817-b72a-11e9-9d01-01aa75ed71a1/language-en/format-PDF/source-102611557.

Eurostat. 2021. *Economy and Finance, Population and Social Conditions Database*. https://ec.europa.eu/eurostat/web/main/data/database

Ferge, Z. 2001. "Welfare and 'Ill-Fare' Systems in Central-Eastern Europe." In *Globalization and European Welfare States. Challenges and Change*, edited by R. Sykes, B. Palier, and P. M. Prior, 127–152. Basingstoke and New York: Palgrave.

Ferge, Z. 2008. "Is There a Specific East Central European Culture." In *Culture and Welfare State: Values and Social Policy in Comparative Perspective*, edited by W. van Oorschot, M. Opielka, and B. Pfau-Effinger, 141–161. Cheltenham: Edward Elgar.

Gerber, A. 2010. "The Letter Versus the Spirit: Barriers to Meaningful Implementation of Gender Equality Policy in Poland." *Women's Studies International Forum* 33 (1), 30–37.

Grech, A. 2015. "Evaluating the Possible Impact of Pension Reforms on Elderly Poverty in Europe." *Social Policy & Administration* 49 (1), 68–87.

Hacker, B. 2009. "Hybridization Instead of Clustering: Transformation Processes of Welfare Policies in Central and Eastern Europe." *Social Policy & Administration* 43 (2), 152–169.

Haney, L. 2002. *Inventing the Needy: Gender and the Politics of Welfare in Hungary*. Berkeley, CA: University of California Press.

Havelková, B. 2010. "The Legal Notion of Gender Equality in the Czech Republic." *Women's Studies International Forum* 33 (1), 21–29.

Hinrichs, K. 2021. "Recent Pension Reforms in Europe: More Challenges, New Directions. An Overview." *Social Policy & Administration* 55 (3), 409–422.

Hinrichs, K., and J. F. Lynch. 2010. "Old Age Pensions." In *The Oxford Handbook of the Welfare State*, edited by F. G. Castles, S. Leibfried, J. Lewis, H. Obinger, and C. Pierson, 353–366. Oxford: Oxford University Press.

Hlebec, V., and T. Rakar. 2017. "Aging Policies in Slovenia: Before and After 'Austerity'." In *Selected Contemporary Challenges of Ageing Policy*, edited by Ł. Tomczyk and A. Klimczuk, 27–52. Krakow: Uniwersytet Pedagogiczny w Krakowie.

Inglot, T. 2008. *Welfare States in East Central Europe 1919–2004*. Cambridge: Cambridge University Press.

Kolarič, Z., A. Kopač, and T. Rakar. 2009. "The Slovene Welfare System: Gradual Reform Instead of Shock Treatment." In *The Handbook of European Welfare Systems* edited by K. Schubert, S. Hegelich, and U. Bazant, 444–461. New York: Routledge.

Kovács, J. M. 2002. "Approaching the EU and Reaching the US? Rival Narratives on Transforming Welfare Regimes in East-Central Europe." In *The Enlarged European Union. Diversity and Adaptation*, edited by P. Mair and J. Zielonka, 175–204. London: Frank Cass.

Kuitto, K. 2012. "More Than Just Money: Patterns of Disaggregated Welfare Expenditure in the Enlarged Europe." *Journal of European Social Policy* 19 (5), 348–314.

Kuitto, K. 2016. *Post-Communist Welfare States in European Context.* Cheltenham: Edward Elgar.

Leitner, S. 2003. "Varieties of Familialism: The Caring Function of the Family in Comparative Perspective." *European Societies* 5 (4), 353–375.

Lendvai, N., and P. Stubbs. 2015. "Europeanization, Welfare and Variegated Austerity Capitalisms – Hungary and Croatia." *Social Policy & Administration* 49 (4), 445–465.

Lendvai-Bainton, N. 2020. "Diversified Convergence: Uneven Welfare Trajectories in Central and Eastern Europe." In *Social Policy, Poverty, and Inequality in Central and Eastern Europe and the Former Soviet Union. Agency and Institutions in Flux*, edited by S. An, T. Chubarova, B. Deacon, and P. Stubbs, 263–283. Stuttgart: Ibidem-Verlag.

Mishra, R. 2013. "Globalisation and the Decline of 'Social Protection by Other Means': The Transformation of the Welfare Regimes in Australia, Japan and Eastern Europe." In *A Handbook of Comparative Social Policy*, edited by P. Kennett, 46–68. Cheltenham: Edward Elgar Publishing.

Nesporova, A. 2002. *Why Unemployment Remains So High in Central and Eastern Europe.* Employment paper 2002/43. https://www.ilo.org/employment/Whatwedo/Publications/WCMS_142377/lang-en/index.htm

OECD. 2020. OECDstat. *Health Statistics.* Available from OECDstat web site: https://stats.oecd.org/Index.aspx?ThemeTreeId=9#

OECD. 2021. *OECD Family Database.* https://www.oecd.org/els/family/database.htm

Österle, A. 2010. "Long-term Care in Central and South-Eastern Europe: Challenges and Perspectives in Addressing a 'New' Social Risk." *Social Policy & Administration* 44 (4), 461–480.

Österle, A., and H. Rothgang. 2010. "Long Term Care." In *The Oxford Handbook of the Welfare State*, edited by F. G. Castles, S. Leibfried, J. Lewis, H. Obinger, and C. Pierson, 378–390. Oxford: Oxford University Press.

Pascall, G., and A. Kwak. 2005. *Gender Regimes in Transition in Central and Eastern Europe.* Bristol: Policy Press.

Saraceno, C., and W. Keck. 2010. "Can We Identify Intergenerational Policy Regimes in Europe?" *European Societies* 12 (5), 675–696.

Stambolieva, M. 2016. *Welfare State Transformation in the Yugoslav Successor States.* London: Routledge.

Stoilova, R., and V. Krasteva. 2020. "The Bulgarian Welfare System: Reforms and Their Effects on Inequalities and Vulnerable Groups Between 1997 and 2018." In *Routledge Handbook of European Social Systems*, edited by S. Blum, J. Kuhlmann, and K. Schubert, 56–72. Abingdon: Routledge.

Stubbs, P., and S. Zrinščak. 2015. "Citizenship and Social Welfare in Croatia: Clientelism and the Limits of 'Europeanization'." *European Politics and Society* 16 (3), 395–410.

Stubbs, P., and S. Zrinščak. 2019. "Reforming Welfare Assemblages in Semi-Peripheral Spaces: Understanding 'Drivers of Inertia' in Bosnia-Herzegovina, Croatia and Serbia." In *Social Policy, Poverty, and Inequality in Central and Eastern Europe and the Former Soviet Union. Agency and Institutions in Flux*, edited by S. An, T. Chubarova, B. Deacon, and P. Stubbs, 285–305. Stuttgart: Ibidem-Verlag.

Szelewa, D. 2020. "Recurring Ideas: Searching for the Roots of Right-Wing Populism in Eastern Europe." *European Journal of Cultural Studies* 23 (6), 989–997.

Szelewa, D., and M. P. Polakowski. 2008. "Who Cares? Changing Patterns of Childcare in Central and Eastern Europe." *Journal of European Social Policy* 18 (2), 115–131.

Tausz, K. 2020. "Pathway to a Punitive Workfare Wystem: Hungary." In *Routledge Handbook of European Social Systems*, edited by S. Blum, J. Kuhlmann, and K. Schubert, 256–275. London: Routledge.

Taylor Gooby, P., B. Leeruth, and H. Chung. (2017) *After Austerity: Welfare State Transformation in Europe After the Great Recession*. New York: Oxford University Press.

Vučković Juroš, T., I. Dobrotić, and S. Flego. 2020. "The Rise of the Anti-Gender Movement in Croatia and the 2013 Marriage Referendum." *Europe-Asia Studies* 72 (9), 1523–1553.

Wang, X., J. B. Williamson, and M. Cansoy. 2016. "Developing Countries and Systemic Pension Reforms: Reflections on Some Emerging Problems." *International Social Security Review* 69 (2), 85–106.

Bingqin Li

9 In search of a suitable path for welfare system development in China

Abstract: As a late comer to the world of welfare states, China faces numerous choices as it tries to establish a comprehensive welfare system. Is it possible for China to copy from the West directly and avoid all the costs associated with development? What should it prioritise and who should have a say? Should the state solve social problems directly and at which level? Should the government wait for or incentivise the market to solve social problems? These choices ran through all the different stages of the social policy reforms. There have been debates even if the proposed solutions had been successful in other countries. The resulting social policies can reveal a process of China gaining better self-understanding which came with a growing sense of identity. This chapter reviews the social policy changes of China over time and examines their relation to the national development agenda and the strategies adopted in each period. It also reviews the underlying debates of each period as the social policies travelled through the path from accommodating economic transition, to maintaining social harmony and more recently to serving domestic and international political interests. The concluding section summarises the lessons that can be learnt from this process.

Keywords: China, welfare state, social policy, policy review

9.1 Introduction

There have been heated debates in China throughout the reform era on which route welfare reforms should take. The debates have several perspectives:

- Should China learn from the West and avoid the human, societal and environmental costs of economic development or should it develop according to its own needs and constraints at its own pace?
- How policy changes and services should be funded, delivered and governed? Should it be the national level government or the local level governments that design the policies and take up the responsibilities?
- Should the state solve the problems directly, wait for the market to come up with better solutions, or incentivise the market players to get involved in social provision?

These debates ran through all the different stages of the social policy reforms. The different views regardless of how successful they had been in other countries had to face reality in China. To some extent, the resulting reform policies show the process of

https://doi.org/10.1515/9783110721768-009

gaining better self-awareness which came with a growing sense of identity in social policy. This chapter reviews the social policy changes of China over time and examines their relation to the national development agenda and the strategies adopted in each period. It also reviews the underlying debates of each period as the social policies travelled through the path from accommodating economic transition, to maintaining social harmony and more recently to serving domestic and international political interests. The concluding section summarises the lessons that can be learnt from this process.

9.2 Launching the reform to accommodate the transition (1978–1991)

In the late 1970s when China launched the economic reform. Several key issues were under heated debate. The dominant philosophy of China's economic transition from the 1980s to the early 2000s had been neoliberal thinking. It was introduced to pull China out of the dysfunctional Central Planning system, through embracing decentralisation, market competition and private ownership, and through opening up to the world (Howell 1993). Conservative voices stressed that China was still a socialist country led by the Communist Party and it should not give up the Communist aspiration (O'Brien 1990; Sullivan 1988). The opposition stressed that free market principles were "value neutral" and are universally applicable (Pei 2009; Zha 1996). The value neutrality argument was challenged later (H. F. Chen 2013). Deng Xiaoping's "black cat and white cat" statement put a stop to the obsession in ideological debates: putting "politics in command" (zhengzhi guashuai) was dismissed as counterproductive and divisive.

Deciding to reform was not sufficient, another question was how aggressive the reform should be. There were concerns that the Chinese people would not be able to cope with the shock of radical reform (H. Wang 1994). In 1978, China already had a population of 975.23 million people, more than one-fifth of the world population (4.281 billion) (Pannell and Welch 1980). Taking a longer timeframe to examine all the changes introduced by the Communist Party of China (CPC) since 1949, "eagerness for quick success" (jiyu qiucheng) had been considered a major problem in the country's development. The impatience and hasty moves adopted to catch up with other countries through industrialisation in the late 1950s had directly resulted in neglect in agricultural production which led to three years of famine (Chan 2001; Schoenhals 2008). Despite the support of international experts, the Chinese reformers remained cautious (Liew 1995). The economic and political turmoil that followed the shock therapy in East Europe reminded the Chinese that radical transition could have devastating effects (Weber 2021). In this sense, the decision to adopt gradual reform is a compromise which transcended the division between the Left and the Right.

With the reform strategy decided, social policy reform followed the steps of economic reforms. Initially, the welfare state that was associated with the Central Planning system was dismantled. In the *housing* sector, repeated efforts to privatise urban housing commenced in the early 1980s. The state first started selling new houses to urban residents without much success. It also tried out different local housing reform models to encourage people to move out of the public housing sector (Shaw 1997). The key measures that led to successful housing privatisation included a) increasing the rent of public rental housing so that public rental housing would be less attractive; b) selling housing usage rights and later ownership of the public houses to existing tenants at discounted rates (B. Li 2017). Several *healthcare* reforms took place in the 1980s in urban areas. Instead of the state covering all healthcare costs of urban employees, employers got a fixed amount of healthcare funding from the government for each employee and had to reserve a matching percentage. If an employee spent less than the fixed amount, they could keep the rest. If they spent more than this fixed amount, they had to pay in advance and claimed the money back afterwards from the employers' reserved fund (Huang 2015). However, the rural cooperative healthcare system collapsed, as the ability of rural collectives to pool funds for healthcare fell to nothing because of the collapse of rural communes (Liu et al. 1995). A "beacon school" system was established to enhance competition in *education*. According to this system, primary and secondary schools as well as high schools were to train and select talented students for university education. Students were selected strictly according to their exam results. Following the same principle, investing more in rural education was considered to be inefficient as rural areas had lower population density. There had been great efforts to merge schools in this period.

On the whole, social policy reform was an important precondition for liberalising state enterprises. As a result, in the 1990s, the reform accelerated.

9.3 Maintaining social harmony (1992–2010)

The official discussion on maintaining social harmony only started in 2004. However, the efforts to sustain social stability began much earlier. The 1989 Student Movement rang an alarm bell that growing economic uncertainty – unemployment and inflation, social inequality and corruption – could ignite public resentment which would result in political demands (Sun 1991; Swartz 2011). Deng Xiaoping's speech in 1992 in Shenzhen reassured that the country would not retrack and the focus should be on continued economic development (S. Zhao 1993). Different from the earlier reforms aiming to dismantle the social welfare system, the social policy reforms in this period shifted to developing a new social protection system that would support the economic reform and maintain social stability. Or more accurately, even though pursuing economic growth was still a goal, the lack of social stability was recognised to be a barrier to sustained growth. Without a peaceful environment and shared sense of community, the past growth outcomes could be wasted and the path towards sustained growth could be blocked (Han 2008). In this sense, social stability became a goal in its own right. The Chinese government used a range of policy instruments to maintain social stability: 1. to maintain economic growth so that everyone had opportunities to benefit from it (Knight 2014); 2. To make sure that those who had not yet benefited from the economic growth believed that they would have such opportunities in the future (Wu and Li 2013); 3. when people were indeed unhappy, to avoid dissatisfaction turning into collective actions by addressing the loudest voices (Fu 2017; Qi 2014); 4. when there were collective actions, to address the needs of the people and punish the organisers (Biddulph 2014; D. Liu 2019).

In the social policy sector, the most straightforward solutions for maintaining social harmony could be to deliver socially justified outcomes so that people would not be unhappy. Clearly, making everyone happy would be a mission impossible even with the support of sustained high speed economic growth. This is particularly difficult for a country where the majority of the population suffered from poverty and policy makers had to manage with very limited resources at per capita level, even with high economic growth (Qian 2017). Therefore, alternative strategies were introduced and matched with corresponding policies to achieve economic goals and maintain social stability.

The first strategy was to help people manage social risks. This was achieved through a series of social insurance systems which aimed to establish forced savings for people to pay for necessities or cover emergency needs in the future. The social insurance schemes included housing (housing provident fund, 1992), pension (urban employee pension insurance, 1993; resident pension insurance, 2003), healthcare (urban employee basic medical insurance, 1998; resident basic medical insurance; 2009), industrial accidents (work injury insurance, 2008), unemployment (unemployment insurance, 2008), childbirth (maternity insurance, 2008). The years in the brackets show when the insurance first emerged. The insurance schemes were later rolled out after local pilots and continued improving over the years. For a long time, the social insurance schemes were segregated. They were gradually integrated and simplified into two main sub-systems: an employment based social insurance with higher contribution and entitlement and a residence based social insurance with lower contribution and entitlement (Gao, Yang, and Li 2012; B. Li 2014; Park, Wu, and Du 2012). On the whole, the employee insurances were jointly contributed to by employees and employers, the resident insurances were contributed to by individuals only. There were rural social insurances for pension (1992) and healthcare (1996). Rural social insurance was contributed to by the farmers themselves or collectively by villages. The funding was also managed separately from urban social insurance. Unlike the urban social insurance schemes, rural social insurances were highly localised.

The second strategy was to compensate the people who lost out during the reforms. The compensation took place in several sectors. First, the marketisation reform resulted in tens of thousands of laid off workers aged in their 40s and 50s, who had difficulties finding new opportunities in the new economy. In urban areas, a minimum income guarantee (Dibao) was introduced for people without income and living in difficult conditions (Gustafsson and Quheng 2011). The beneficiaries could also receive other subsidies for fee-based social services, such as healthcare and education (L. Zhao, Guo, and Shao 2017). Second, as industries and services started to grow fast, land demand grew as a result. The real estate development was supported by the housing and land reform started in the late 1990s. Local governments increasingly relied on revenues from leasing land to businesses. Cities expanded to the peri-urban areas and city centres kept getting regenerated. These resulted in land and property losses in both urban and rural areas. Cash compensation, relocation, employment arrangement and social insurance schemes were granted to the people affected to calm them down. These were in the form of compensation packages (Cao et al. 2018; Ghatak and Mookherjee 2014).

The third strategy was to offer protection for people trapped in poverty. This was mostly done via redistribution at the central government level, entailing direct cash transfers to the poor regions and poor people. However, for many years, poverty reduction was criticised for mis-targeting and generating perverse incentives for the poorer regions (X. Li and Remenyi 2004).

The fourth strategy was to strengthen the role of communities. This strategy was designed to serve several purposes. It would be easier to identify unsatisfied needs or sources of resentment early on. Community based solutions had the potential to enhance the responsiveness of the local authorities and improve people's sense of participation. The result is, however, mixed (Heberer and Göbel 2011). This approach had been hailed for improving social participation of older people, including many people who had to quit their jobs because of the reform. Communities became a space for them to escape social isolation and find meaning in life (Song 2006; Tong-jie 2015). For the younger population, there were mixed results. Engagement depended on who initiated the activities (Tian et al. 2021).

These policy strategies show that social policies that try to maintain social stability and the policies that aim to improve human wellbeing and social inequality are different, although the two types of policies may overlap with each other. The policy makers focusing on maintaining social stability may not accept that social wellbeing can be improved by social policy. It is widely held among Chinese policy makers even to this day that economic development is the answer to improving human wellbeing. Social policy can be used to reduce social anxiety and discontent. Obviously, economic development can also achieve the same goal, but in a society that is going through rapid economic growth and restructuring, anxiety and discontent can emerge and sustain as a result of a sense of social injustice. Social policy is used to keep the anxiety and resentment at bay. To some extent, maintaining social stability does not have to address the issues of the neediest. It only needs to do the minimum to keep social discontent at a controllable level. This strategy can be observed from the outcomes of social policy in this period. Poverty and social inequality were sustained, despite the social policy changes (Gong and Li 2013). As a result of actively addressing the needs of people with the loudest voices, urban formal employees including civil servants, urban retired older people, in particular those retired from public sectors, migrant workers and farmers who had lost their land all saw solid improvements in their social protection packages and services. In contrast, people with less strong voices such as people with disabilities, rural left behind older people and children received little attention (Q. Wang and Timonen 2021; Ziong 2012). There were also observations that the style of community governance was very different for urban communities that have a high proportion of migrant population and that are mainly for urban middle class (Tomba 2009).

In this period, the debate stopped focusing on whether there should be reform or the speed of reform, but rather at which level the reform should take place, i.e., whether subnational specificity matters. This was because the finance and governance of social policy was increasingly decentralised to the municipal or prefecture levels. The central government was only responsible for setting the principles and the minimum requirements. Local governments were expected to be responsible for setting local standards, financing and implementing local social policy. This was a period when the Chinese policy makers tried hard to search for inspiration from the rest of the world and international organisations such as the World Bank, other UN agencies as well as international NGOs had been deeply involved in advising and sponsoring social development in China (T. Liu and Sun 2016). At the same time, there were also criticisms on national level policy-making that often failed to consider local circumstances. Various mechanisms were introduced to integrate local variations. These include: 1) policy pilots in which local authorities could decide how the pilots were going to be formulated in order to fit the local contexts, such as health system reform and community development; 2) allowing local counter-bargains or commitments in a range of policy commitments, such as in the field of pension, social housing, and environmental protection. The "local" can be at different levels. For most social policies and social services, municipal governments played central roles.

Whilst replicating other countries' practices were criticised, cherry picking became a dominant form of policy learning – partial adoption or adaptation of internationally established practices. For example, China decided to introduce a provident fund system following the practice of Singapore. At the same time, it was also aware that Singapore was a city state. However, China was much bigger and suffered from a rural and urban divide and regional inequality, and the labour force was highly mobile between regions. A nationwide social insurance with funding pooled at the national level would create a colossal social insurance fund which would be highly risky. The central government would not want to take on such a risk. However, when the regional authorities were to set their own contribution and entitlement rates, interregional transferability became another challenge. As a result, the calls for "top level design" and "more local autonomies" co-existed. The resulting social insurance scheme at the end of this period was a hybrid system that offered differentiated treatment to people according to their employment and Household Registration status (F. Cai 2011; Y. Cai and Cheng 2014). However, such a pragmatic approach had also been criticised for its lacking in principles and consistency (Chen 1995; Goldman and Mac-Farquhar 1999; Lai 2016; Zhu 2011).

At the end of this period, there had been growing calls for "top level design" as poor regions found themselves losing out as a result of decentralised budgeting (X. Wang 2020). The poor regions exported labour force to the wealthier regions and the workers paid taxes and social insurance contributions in the hosting cities. However, when they became older or fell ill, they returned to the home counties to receive social services. However, social insurance entitlement was not transferable between regions. Transferability was difficult as there needed to be interregional agreements. With more than 30 regions, higher level coordination or redistribution would be necessary.

9.4 Lifting the bottom (2011–now)

The central task of social welfare since 2012 had been defined as "lifting the bottom (doudi)" (Fuhua and Qin 2019). Politically, China had experienced a sharp left turn. The Chinese leadership started to see the growing political trust based on the ability of the government to coordinate and deliver ambitious social and economic programmes, such as the Millennium Development Goals (MDGs). The growing social inequality and corruption had been considered to be a threat to the authorities of the Chinese Communist Party (Dickson 2016). At the beginning of this era, China had more than 10 million people living under absolute poverty. As China's absolute poverty line (US$2.3/day) was much lower than the international standard set by the World Bank (US$5.5/day), the poverty would be much higher if using a higher poverty line. The introduction of the Sustainable Development Goals demanded a change in the mode of economic development, i.e., the single-minded pursuit of GDP growth without caring for the human and environmental costs and the tolerance of widening inequality without caring for the poor had to be changed. China had committed to eradicate absolute poverty by 2020 (10 years earlier than the UN's 2030 Agenda) (M. Liu et al. 2020) and develop a green economy (Kuhn 2018). Several key challenges were frequently discussed in Chinese official documents and the media in the late 2010s, showing that they are the main policy concerns.

- Urbanisation had contributed to reduce poverty in rural areas, but also saw the increase in urban inequality. The Household Registration System continued to limit the ability of the migrant workers to integrate into cities. The largest cities suffered from the "large city illnesses", i.e. the ability of the city to provide services and infrastructures fell behind the demand of the fast growing urban population (Hu and Chen 2015).
- China might fall into "the middle-income trap" (Aiyar et al. 2013), a term developed based on the experience of Latin America and other middle-income coun-

tries that failed to break through to become higher income countries after episodes of rapid economic growth (OECD 2014). This was diagnosed by economists to be a result of the lack of ability to innovate and upgrade the economy. As other countries started to grow, these countries lost the competitive edge against the late comers (Foxley and Stallings 2016). Before Xi came into power, international observers already predicted that the middle-income trap had become a realistic threat for China (Woo 2012).

– The rapidly ageing population posed a looming challenge that could undermine China's growth. In 2001, the people over 65 years old in China reached 90.62 million, accounting for 7.1 % of the total population. According to the 2020 population census, the number of people over 60 years old in the total population reached 18.7 %, compared to 13.3 % in the 2010 census. For the policy-makers, population ageing is not only about old age care, but also about the declining momentum for further economic development. Some scholars coined a catchy phrase to capture the nature of the problem: "growing old before becoming rich" (weifu xianlao, 未富先老).

With these challenges in the background, a series of social policy has been introduced since 2011.

9.3.1 Targeted poverty alleviation (also known as precise poverty reduction).

Since the 18th National Congress of the CPC, elimination of extreme poverty in rural areas became a top priority. Different from previous poverty alleviation strategies which targeted counties and villages, the new policies targeted individuals and households. A thorough survey to identify all the poor in rural areas and case files for them was carried out in 2014. These files were used to track the poverty status and causes of poverty. A complex information system was used to collect and integrate multiple sources of data to identify and design anti-poverty strategies and monitor progress. The dynamic tracking allowed better understanding of the needs of the poor (Zhou, Cai, and Zhong 2021), and tailor-made support measures for the registered households. The government mobilised or even pressured private businesses, public sector employees including local civil servants to donate and help rural development to create more employment opportunities (Fang, Li, and Cliff 2021). The primary goal was to help the poorest to become economically independent. Social policy played a supporting role such as improving housing through relocation and housing repair funds, skills development, healthcare, and job search. Lastly, for the people who were not employable, such as the old and the frail, would receive income transfers. Extra funds for poverty alleviation were introduced to further support the deeply impoverished areas. If we only look at the special grant for poverty alleviation, the central government contributed more than CNY510 billion (~EUR68.47 billion)[1] to support local poverty alleviation during 2013 and 2019, a net increase of CNY20 billion (~EUR2.69 billion) per year for four consecutive years since 2016. From 2018 to 2020, the county-level subsidies funds for severely poor areas had grown CNY30 billion (~EUR4.03 billion) (Dong 2019). More specific social policy includes:

- In education, improving student subsidies for accommodation and nutrition and diet in poverty-stricken areas, increasing salary subsidies for teachers specially appointed to poor regions, and supporting the strengthening of the weakest links in compulsory education.
- In health care, the central government provided subsidies for the poor to participate in basic medical insurance and to provide subsidies to eligible individuals for their private medical expenses not covered by medical insurance. From 2016 to 2019, a total of CNY89 billion (EUR11.95) was allocated for these purposes. In 2019, the medical insurance subsidy standard for urban and rural residents was increased by CNY30 (~EUR4.03) to CNY520 (~69.8) per person per year, and half of the new spending would be for insurance against critical illnesses.
- To improve drinking water safety, in the "13th Five-Year Plan" period, the central government allocated CNY22 billion (~EUR2.95 billion) through central infrastructure investment to support rural drinking water safety maintenance and improvement projects in poor areas and for poor people. In 2019–2020, the central government planned to arrange CNY6 billion (~EUR0.81 billion) on the drinking water safety issue for the severely poor regions.

9.3.2 Urbanisation

Hukou (household registration) had frequently been criticised for being a discriminatory mechanism that made it difficult for rural to urban migrants to be truly urbanised (Melander and Pelikanova 2013). The new policy introduced in July 2014 set up a single national resident registration (*jumin hukou*) system for both rural and urban populations. The new reform maintains the principle of population control. The Chinese government advised cities with more than five million people to be cautious about further expansion and required the largest cities to tightly control migration. The reform severed the link between hukou and welfare entitlement. The idea was to provide long-term residents with equal access to social services and welfare. But, ultimately, access to urban social services depends on the resources and political will of local governments. In practice, cities that were either unwilling or unable to invest more in social services could use the flexible settlement criteria to set up alternative barriers for entry

---

1 In this paper, CNY1 = EUR0.13 or USD0.16, rate quoted by Google Finance, 7 October 2021.

to replace the older hukou barrier. The largest cities, such as Shanghai and Beijing, had made it even more difficult for migrants to settle down permanently than before. Several medium-sized cities also introduced policies to favour highly skilled migrants.

9.3.3 Talent attraction

If one can argue that the past economic growth was built on local governments' ability to attract investments and cheap labour to achieve economic upgrading, "human resources", i.e. talents with good education, skills and track records of successful entrepreneurship become a new edge for regional competition. Social policies, such as subsidised housing and special arrangement for settlement, were used to attract talents from other parts of the country or from abroad (Shen and Li 2020).

9.3.4 Old age care and health

A long-term care insurance was piloted in different cities to improve old age care affordability for the older people who suffer from functional losses (Y. Zhang and Yu 2019). The government also started to encourage NGOs and private businesses to enter the care sector, in particular community-based care. Healthcare infrastructure and services in urban communities have been significantly improved (B. Li, Qian, and Yang 2021). Healthy ageing was also set as a key priority in the national political agenda for health (Ye et al. 2021). Nine fields of healthy ageing were included in the plan, including health promotion and education, public health service, medical service, integrated medical and aged care services, medical insurance system, Traditional Chinese Medicine, health industry, supportive environment, and professional workforce.

9.3.5 Family planning

The lasting and controversial One Child Policy was finally replaced by a Two Child Policy in 2015 and a Three Child Policy in 2021. There had been growing social investment in subsidised childcare and paternity leave for working families (Qing Wang and Lin 2019). To support childbirth, there have been policies to grant longer paternity and fraternity leave. There have also been efforts to increase community-based childcare and aggressive suppression in after school coaching. The logic behind these policies is that research finds that young parents do not want to produce more babies because they are concerned with the childcare costs and the financial and time costs for educating children (J. Zhang 2020).

When Xi Jinping first came into power, he made a speech saying that a key feature of Chinese social policy in the past was that policies passively responded to social issues, hinting that he would take a more proactive approach. The policy changes since clearly showed much stronger government leadership. The "advantages" of the state as a leader, coordinator and manager of social policy have been recognised and advocated, even more so since the outbreak of COVID-19. On the one hand, the government assumed less responsibilities for direct delivery of social services and actively encouraged non-government actors to take on service roles that used to be taken by the government. A growing practice was that the state "created" the field and introduce the rules and let private providers and NGOs to play the games. Some of these actors worked in partnership with the local governments (Deng 2021).

An interesting phenomenon is the growing impact of an international development agenda on Chinese social policy. Internationally, the Xi's regime faced greater challenges than usual, especially after COVID-19 outbreak. There had been a growing desire to gain international recognition. In the policy fields which had a delivery deadline, such as poverty reduction, COVID-19 responses, physical and ICT infrastructures, the government was in the driver's seat and set clear performance targets. Whereas in the less prioritised fields such as healthcare affordability and community participation, the government efforts were not so successful. In the early stage at the end of MDGs, China was praised by the World Bank and other developing agencies as a successful case for delivering the MDGs (Ravallion 2011). Despite that many unsolved social issues remained and the achievement measured by the indicators set by the MDGs was clear (Liang et al. 2019). The Chinese government was increasingly viewed as a government that had a strong political will to achieve social development and could mobilise resources to deliver what it had promised to do (Asadullah and Savoia 2018; S. Wang 2013; Y. Wang et al. 2016). The international reaction to China's poverty reduction shows that keeping in line with the Global Development Agendas would make China or even the world see how China had performed in comparison to other countries. To some extent, delivering internationally decided development agendas would give the Chinese ruling party the legitimacy to stay in power. This could be observed from the fact that Xi was keen to outperform his predecessors by delivering the Sustainable Development Goals (SDGs) which were introduced not long before Xi came into power. SDGs introduced a much more comprehensive set of targets and goals that posed a much more difficult task to achieve. Given that these types of complex policy tasks would need sustained and dedicated intersectoral actions, it would require a well-coordinated government to deliver the outcomes in a limited time frame. The Chinese government with its authoritarian system has been skilful in conducting "whole government and whole society" style policy campaigns. Among the seventeen goals, poverty reduction was a favoured policy task in the social policy domain. The growing significance of trying to make good impressions internationally means that the Chinese government was increasingly confident in its ability to deliver the outcomes when it made the commitment.

9.5 Conclusion

Throughout China's social welfare reform, there have been conflicting views on various aspects of the reform. After decades of trial and error, the resulting social welfare system is funded by social insurances for the majority and by government funds for the poorest people. There is incremental coverage (including population and types of services) and multiple subsystems co-exist (by social groups, locations and regions). In this welfare system, the central government is the agenda setter but encouraged localised policy implementation and pilots. In most policy fields, the state set the field and let private providers and NGOs play, sometimes in partnership with the state. Policy inspirations often came from abroad but increasingly from inside China. Regardless of the where they are from, good practices will be adapted to fit local contexts. This process repeats at all levels of social welfare system development.

There are some possible complications with the current strategies. If the intention is to use external pressure to overcome domestic resistance to reforms, the government unavoidably faces the question of who informs these international agendas and whether the mode of delivery has the support of the people. If the intention is to outperform other countries by all means, the efforts will be difficult to sustain in the long run.

References

Aiyar, M. S., M. R. A. Duval, M. D. Puy, M. Y. Wu, and M. L. Zhang. 2013. *Growth Slowdowns and the Middle-Income Trap*. International Monetary Fund Working Paper 13/71.

Asadullah, M. N., and A. Savoia. 2018. "Poverty Reduction During 1990–2013: Did *Millennium* Development Goals Adoption and State Capacity Matter?" *World Development* 105, 70–82.

Biddulph, S. 2014. "Management of Stability in Labour Relations." In *The Politics of Law and Stability in China*, edited by S. Trevaskes, E. Nesossi, F. Sapio and S. Biddulph, 21–41. Cheltenham: Edward Elgar.

Cai, F. 2011. "Hukou System Reform and Unification of Rural–Urban Social Welfare." *China & World Economy* 19 (3), 33–48.

Cai, Y., and Y. Cheng. 2014. "Pension Reform in China: Challenges and Opportunities." *Journal of Economic Surveys* 28 (4), 636–651.

Cao, Y., M. Dallimer, L. C. Stringer, Z. Bai, and Y. L. Siu. 2018. "Land Expropriation Compensation Among Multiple Stakeholders in a Mining Area: Explaining 'Skeleton House' Compensation." *Land Use Policy* 74, 97–110.

Chan, A. L. 2001. *Mao's Crusade: Politics and Policy Implementation in China's Great Leap Forward*. Oxford: Oxford University Press.

Chen, F. 1995. *Economic Transition and Political Legitimacy in Post-Mao China: Ideology and Reform*. Albany, NY: SUNY Press.

Chen, H. F. 2018. "Friends, Not Enemies: The Globalization and Indigenization of Chinese Sociology." In *Chinese Sociology: State-Building and the Institutionalization of Globally Circulated Knowledge*, by H. F. Chen, 107–132. London: Palgrave Macmillan.

Deng, P. 2021. *Evaluating the Application of Public-Private Partnership (PPP) Funding Models in Public Nursing Institutions in Hubei Province, China*. Paper presented at the 6th International Conference on Financial Innovation and Economic Development (ICFIED 2021).

Dickson, B. J. 2016. "The Survival Strategy of the Chinese Communist Party." *The Washington Quarterly* 39 (4), 27–44.

Dong, B. 2019. "The Central Government Makes Every Effort to Guarantee the Poverty Alleviation Funds." *Economics Daily (Jingji Ribao)*. Retrieved from http://www.gov.cn/xinwen/2019-07/18/content_5410741.htm

Fang, L., B. Li, and T. Cliff. 2021. "Emergent Political Norms in Local State–Private Enterprise Relations during China's Big Push for Poverty Reduction." *American Behavioral Scientist* 66 (2), 213–231.

Foxley, A., and B. Stallings. 2016. *Innovation and Inclusion in Latin America : Strategies to Avoid the Middle Income Trap*. New York: Palgrave Macmillan.

Fu, D. 2017. "Disguised Collective Action in China." *Comparative Political Studies* 50 (4), 499–527.

Fuhua, Z., and G. Qin. 2019. "Strengthening Coordination between Rural and Urban Dibao: Evidence and Implications." *China: An International Journal* 17 (1), 96–108.

Gao, Q., S. Yang, and S. Li. 2012. :Labor Contracts and Social Insurance Participation Among Migrant Workers in China." *China Economic Review* 23 (4), 1195–1205.

Ghatak, M., and D. Mookherjee. 2014. "Land Acquisition for Industrialization and Compensation of Displaced Farmers." *Journal of Development Economics* 110, 303–312.

Goldman, M., and R. MacFarquhar (eds.) 1999. *The Paradox of China's Post-Mao Reforms*: Cambridge, MA: Harvard University Press.

Gong, S., and B. Li. 2013. *Inequality in China: A Case Study*. Beijing: Save the Children.

Gustafsson, B. A., and D. Quheng. 2011. "Di Bao Receipt and Its Importance for Combating Poverty in Urban China." *Poverty & Public Policy* 3 (1), 1–32.

Han, A. G. 2008. "Building a Harmonious Society and Achieving Individual Harmony." *Journal of Chinese Political Science* 13 (2), 143–164.

Heberer, T., and C. Göbel. 2011. *The Politics of Community Building in Urban China*. London: Routledge.

Howell, J. 1993. *China Opens Its Doors: The Politics of Economic Transition*. Boulder, CO: Lynne Rienner Publishers.

Hu, B., and C. Chen. 2015. "New Urbanisation under Globalisation and the Social Implications in China." *Asia & the Pacific Policy Studies* 2 (1), 34–43.

Huang, Y. 2015. *Governing Health in Contemporary China*. London and New York: Routledge.

Knight, J. 2014. "Economic Causes and Cures of Social Instability in China." *China & World Economy* 22 (2), 5–21.

Kuhn, B. M. 2018. "China's Commitment to the Sustainable Development Goals: An Analysis of Push and Pull Factors and Implementation Challenges." *Chinese Political Science Review* 3 (4), 359–388.

Lai, H. 2016. *China's Governance Model: Flexibility and Durability of Pragmatic Authoritarianism*. London and New York: Routledge.

Li, B. 2014. "Social Pension Unification in an Urbanising China: Paths and Constraints." *Public Administration and Development* 34 (4), 281–293.

Li, B. 2017. "Housing Welfare Policies in Urban China." In *Handbook of Welfare in China*, edited by B. Carrillo, J. Hood, and P. Kadetz, 123–143. Cheltenham: Edward Elgar Publishing.

Li, B., J. Qian, and S. Yang. 2021. "The Mindset: Tackling the Challenges of the Old Age Care in Communities in China." *China: An International Journal* 19 (3), 148–167.

Liang, J., X. Li, C. Kang, Y. Wang, X. R. Kulikoff, M. M. Coates, … H. Wang. 2019. "Maternal Mortality Ratios in 2852 Chinese Counties, 1996–2015, and Achievement of Millennium Development

Goal 5 in China: A Subnational Analysis of the Global Burden of Disease Study 2016." *The Lancet* 393 (10168), 241–252.

Li, X., and J. Remenyi. 2004. "Towards Sustainable Village Poverty Reduction: The Development of the County Poverty Alleviation Planning (CPAP) Approach." In *Community Participation in China: Issues and Processes for Capacity* Building, edited by J. Plummer and J. G. Taylor, 269–306. London: Routledge.

Liew, L. H. 1995. "Gradualism in China's Economic Reform and the Role for a Strong Central State." *Journal of Economic Issues* 29 (3), 883–895.

Liu, D. 2019. "Punish the Dissidents: The Selective Implementation of Stability Preservation in China." *Journal of Contemporary China* 28 (119), 795–812.

Liu, M., X. Feng, S. Wang, and H. Qiu. 2020. "China's Poverty Alleviation over the Last 40 Years: Successes and Challenges." *Australian Journal of Agricultural and Resource Economics* 64 (1), 209–228.

Liu, T., and L. Sun. 2016. "Urban Social Assistance in China: Transnational Diffusion and National Interpretation." *Journal of Current Chinese Affairs* 45 (2), 29–51.

Liu, Y., W. C. Hsiao, Q. Li, X. Liu, and M. Ren. 1995. "Transformation of China's Rural Health Care Financing." *Social Science & Medicine* 41 (8), 1085–1093.

Melander, A., and K. Pelikanova. 2013. "Reform of the Hukou System: A Litmus Test of the New Leadership." *ECFIN Economic Brief* 26, 1–16.

O'Brien, K. J. 1990. "Is China's National People's Congress a 'Conservative' Legislature?" Asian Survey 30 (8), 782–794.

OECD. 2014. *Economic Outlook for Southeast Asia, China and India 2014: Beyond the Middle-Income Trap*. https://www.oecd-ilibrary.org/development/economic-outlook-for-southeast-asia-china-and-india-2014_saeo-2014-en

Pannell, C. W., and R. Welch. 1980. "Recent Growth and Structural Change in Chinese Cities. *Urban geography* 1 (1), 68–80.

Park, A., Y. Wu, and Y. Du. 2012. *Informal Employment in Urban China: Measurement and Implications*. Washington, DC: World Bank.

Pei, M. 2009. *From Reform to Revolution: The Demise of Communism in China and the Soviet Union*. Cambridge, MA: Harvard University Press.

Qi, D. 2014. "Chinese Society: Social Stability and Social Governance." *East Asian Policy* 6 (01), 55–62.

Qian, Y. 2017. *How Reform Worked in China: The Transition from Plan to Market*. Cambridge, MA: MIT Press.

Ravallion, M. 2011. "A Comparative Perspective on Poverty Reduction in Brazil, China, and India." *The World Bank Research Observer* 26 (1), 71–104.

Schoenhals, M. 2008. "The Global War on Terrorism as Meta-Narrative: An Alternative Reading of Recent Chinese History." *Sungkyun Journal of East Asian Studies* 8 (2), 179–201.

Shaw, V. N. 1997. "Urban Housing Reform in China." *Habitat International* 21 (2), 199–212.

Shen, Y., and B. Li. 2020. "Policy Coordination in the Talent War to Achieve Economic Upgrading: The Case of Four Chinese Cities." *Policy Studies*, 1–21. https://doi.org/10.1080/01442872.2020.1738368

Song, L. 2006. "The Old People's Social Participation and Their Self-harmony [J]." *Journal of Nanjing College for Population Programme Management* 2.

Sullivan, L. R. 1988. "Assault on the Reforms: Conservative Criticism of Political and Economic Liberalization in China, 1985–86." *China Quarterly* 114, 198–222.

Sun, Y. 1991. "The Chinese Protests of 1989: The Issue of Corruption." *Asian Survey* 31 (8), 762–782.

Swartz, D. 2011. "Jasmine in the Middle Kingdom: Autopsy of China's (Failed) Revolution." *America Enterprise Institute for Public Policy Research* 1, 1–5.

Tian, S., R. He, C. Huang, Q. Feng, and F. Jiang. 2021. "A SCI Analysis Model: Research on Influencing Factors of Local E-Government Responsiveness in China." *Discrete Dynamics in Nature and Society, 2021.* doi: https://doi.org/10.1155/2021/6654354

Tomba, L. 2009. "Of Quality, Harmony, and Community: Civilization and the Middle Class in Urban China." *Positions: East Asia Cultures Critique* 17 (3), 591–616.

Tong-jie, L. 2015. "An Investigation into Elderly Human Resources Development Based on the Perspective of Social Participation." *Journal of Langfang Teachers University (Social Sciences Edition).*

Wang, H. 1994. *The Gradual Revolution: China's Economic Reform Movement.* Piscataway, NJ: Transaction Publishers.

Wang, Q., and M. Lin. 2019. "Work–Family Policy and Female Entrepreneurship: Evidence from China's Subsidized Child Care Program." *China Economic Review* 54 (C), 256–270.

Wang, Q., and V. Timonen. 2021. "Retirement Pathways and Pension Inequality in China: A Grounded Theory Study." *International Journal of Sociology and Social Policy* 41 (13/14), 96–111.

Wang, S. 2013. "Reducing Poverty Through Agricultural Development in China." *IDS Bulletin* 44 (5–6), 55–62.

Wang, X. 2020. "Permits, Points, and Permanent Household Registration: Recalibrating Hukou Policy under 'Top-Level Design'." *Journal of Current Chinese Affairs* 49 (3), 269–290.

Wang, Y., X. Li, M. Zhou, S. Luo, J. Liang, C. A. Liddell, … H. Wang. 2016. "Under-5 Mortality in 2851 Chinese Counties, 1996–2012: A Subnational Assessment of Achieving MDG 4 Goals in China." *The Lancet* 387 (10015), 273–283.

Weber, I. M. 2021. *How China Escaped Shock Therapy: The Market Reform Debate.* London and New York: Routledge.

Woo, W. T. 2012. "China Meets the Middle-Income Trap: The Large Potholes in the Road to Catching-Up." *Journal of Chinese Economic and Business Studies* 10 (4), 313–336.

Wu, X., and J. Li. 2013. *Economic Growth, Income Inequality and Subjective Well-Being: Evidence from China.* Population Studies Center Research Report.

Xiong, Y. 2012. "Social Inequality and Inclusive Growth in China: The Significance of Social Policy in a New Era." *Journal of Poverty and Social Justice* 20 (3), 277–290.

Ye, P., Y. Jin, Y. Er, L. Duan, A. Palagyi, L. Fang, B. Li, R. Ivers, L. Keay, and M. Tian. 2021. "A Scoping Review of National Policies for Healthy Ageing in Mainland China from 2016 to 2020." *The Lancet Regional Health-Western Pacific*, 100168.

Zha, D. 1996. "Black Cat, White Cat: An Inside View of Reform and Revolution in China." *China Review International* 3 (1), 118–119.

Zhang, J. 2020. "Influence of Parenting Costs on Second-Child Fertility Anxiety Among Adults of Childbearing Age in China: The Moderating Role of Gender." *SAGE Open* 10 (2), https://doi.org/10.1177/2158244020920657

Zhang, Y., and X. Yu. 2019. "Evaluation of Long-Term Care Insurance Policy in Chinese Pilot Cities." *International Journal of Environmental Research and Public Health* 16 (20), 3826.

Zhao, L., Y. Guo, and T. Shao. 2017. "Can the Minimum Living Standard Guarantee Scheme Enable the Poor to Escape the Poverty Trap in Rural China?" *International Journal of Social Welfare* 26 (4), 314–328.

Zhao, S. 1993. "Deng Xiaoping's Southern Tour: Elite Politics in Post-Tiananmen China." *Asian Survey* 33 (8), 739–756.

Zhou, D., K. Cai, and S. Zhong. 2021. "A Statistical Measurement of Poverty Reduction Effectiveness: Using China as an Example." *Social Indicators Research* 153 (1), 39–64.

Zhu, Y. 2011. "'Performance Legitimacy' and China's Political Adaptation Strategy. *Journal of Chinese Political Science* 16 (2), 123–140.

Ijin Hong
10 East Asia: welfare determinants and issues in the post-developmentalism era

Abstract: With the partial exception of Japan, many economies in East Asia, including China, South Korea, Singapore, Hong Kong and Taiwan, spend less on welfare than elsewhere in advanced welfare states. Is this area dominated by a logic of "small welfare state", as previous literature suggests? This chapter engages with the developmentalism/productivism literature and compares official statistics to discuss how the situation has evolved as of recent. It is found that welfare systems in East Asia do display several similarities, such as a comparatively lower social expenditure, a strong statism, efficient healthcare systems, and common structural challenges due to demographic ageing and conflictual family values that cause low fertility. Yet, a different colonial legacy reflects in the composition of social expenditure, in that Japan, South Korea and Taiwan spend considerably on social protection and health, whereas Singapore and Hong Kong are heavily tilted towards housing and community services, with incentives to individual compulsory savings. In this chapter, it is suggested that the importance of the political determinants of welfare development are an important topic for current and future research, especially regarding the "social protection" cases of Japan, South Korea, and Taiwan, where the logic of electoral competition and the social policy legacy are comparatively stronger.

Keywords: East Asia, developmentalism, social expenditure, social security, provident funds, demographic ageing, universal healthcare, familialism, welfare politics

10.1 Introduction: two paths of welfare development in East Asia

What initially sparked interest towards East Asia in political economy and social policy literature of the 1980s–1990s was the phenomenal speed of industrialisation and economic growth that characterised this area (World Bank 1993), prompting pundits to wonder whether Asian countries had a secret in their combination of economic growth and small welfare commitments (Jacobs 2000). And indeed, these newly emerging political economies had a fair share of common traits, but they also had differences as well, making it hard to view an East Asian welfare regime as a category on its own (Walker and Wong 2005; Goodman, Kwon, and White 1998). Consequently, the regions formerly under Japanese colonialisation (Japan, South Korea, Taiwan) and the ex-British colonies bloc (Singapore and Hong Kong) are commonly understood as belonging to two different patterns that eventually shaped their welfare commitments in a clearly path-dependent way (Holliday 2000; Peng and Wong 2010; Chang and Ku

https://doi.org/10.1515/9783110721768-010

2013; Hong 2017; London 2018). Quite interestingly, with the partial exception of Japan, all the East Asian area, including China, South Korea, Singapore, and the regions of Hong Kong and Taiwan, keeps spending less on welfare than elsewhere in advanced capitalistic countries – what Yang (2017) labels "small welfare state". Yet, their colonial legacy reflects in the composition of their social expenditure, in that Japan, South Korea and Taiwan spend considerably on social protection and health, whereas Singapore and Hong Kong are heavily tilted towards housing and community services, with incentives to individual compulsory savings (ADB 2021; OECD SOCX 2019).

In this chapter, I focus on the "social protection" cases of Japan, South Korea, and Taiwan, and the "provident fund" city-economies of Singapore and Hong Kong. These five political economies are often observed together due to their similar timing and levels of economic development (with labels such as "newly industrialised economies" or "tiger economies") (Holliday 2000; Peng & Wong 2010; Hwang 2020; Chen and Shi 2021) (for the case of China, readers may refer to the dedicated chapter from Bingqin Li in the present volume). The labels "social protection" and "provident savings" are here used with the sole aim of highlighting their main social policy approaches, in the hopes of improving conceptual clarity.

Just by looking at levels of *social expenditure*, it is quite evident that all these economies devote a considerable portion of their national accounts to social expenditure, hence they are not so residual as they used to (Figure 10.1 and Table 10.1). Yet, the composition of social expenditure for these cases differs considerably.

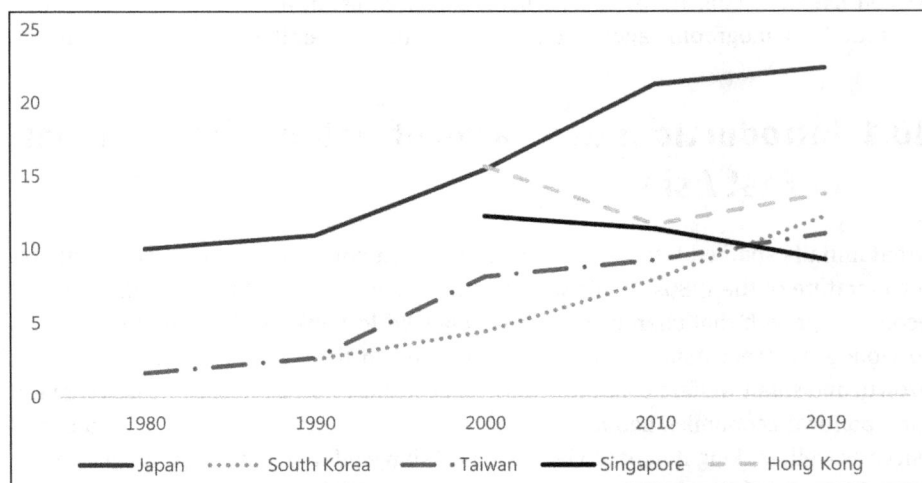

Figure 10.1: Social expenditure as % of GDP in East Asia (1980–2019).

Table 10.1: Social expenditure as % of GDP in East Asia (1980–2019).

Unit: % of GDP

	1980	1990	2000	2010	2019
Japan	10.0	10.9	15.4	21.2	22.3 (2017)
South Korea	–	2.5	4.4	7.9	12.2
Taiwan	1.6	2.6	8.1	9.2	11
Singapore	–	–	12.23	11.35	9.23
Hong Kong	–	–	15.63	11.66	13.71 (2018)

Source: OECD SOCX (2019), DGBAS (2019), ADB (2021).
Note: Taiwan followed the IMF standard for measuring social expenditure, but since 2000 it abided to the OECD standard. Therefore, data pre-2000 and post-2000 are not perfectly comparable. Data for Hong Kong and Singapore in the 2000s are taken by ADB (2021), combining health, social protection, and housing expenditures (Karim, Eikemo, and Bambra, 2010).

The two city economies ("provident fund") tend to rely on a social security system of individual compulsory savings with low redistribution, due to their reliance on the labour market and a mentality of strong budgetary self-reliance that give a stronger say to business owners and financial tycoons. Singapore's Central Provident Fund (CPF) (est. 1955), in particular, includes a series of welfare measures such as retirement, housing, health and education (Yeh, Cheng, and Shi 2021). In comparison, Hong Kong splits its health system and its pension scheme into, respectively, a tax-financed programme inspired by the British NHS, and the Mandatory Provident Fund (MPF) (est. 2010), which is privately managed and still insufficien in providing protection in old age (Yeh, Cheng, and Shi 2021; Hwang 2020).

In contrast, Japan, Korea and Taiwan adopted a social security approach focused on Bismarckian social insurances – a policy learning by-product, from when imperial Japan sent its functionaries to Germany in the twentieth century to learn about social insurance systems as part of its aggressive "catch up" industrialisation policy meant to modernise the Empire and raise its productivity in the shortest time possible (Chang and Ku 2013).

This chapter aims to utilise this dichotomy to have a fresh look at discussions about the East Asian "productivist welfare capitalism" (PWC) from the 2000s, and to assess whether concepts utilised then are still relevant to this day. In order to do so, I will summarise the main tenets of developmentalism and productivism in the next section. This will be followed by the presentation of important socio-economic indicators and an overview of relevant policy issues and reforms meant to understand main similarities and differences amonst the cases here considered. The chapter will conclude with some recommendations for future research.

10.2 Developmentalist and productivist welfare systems

Early English-language studies published in the 1980–1990s mostly paid attention to East Asian political economies due to their transition from relative underdevelopment to industrialised status (Johnson 1982; Cumings 1984; Vogel 1991; Dore 2000). This literature has highlighted the common developmentalist logic of these welfare state "laggards" that subordinated redistributive concerns and social policies to an economic growth-first mentality, taking inspiration from the tumultuous early economic growth of Japan (Kwon 2005). In a 1997 article, Gøsta Esping-Andersen paid attention to the pioneering case of Japan, which, along with Korea, was regarded as a possible "hybrid" welfare regime, halfway between the conservative corporatist model of continental Europe, and the liberal model typical of Anglo-Saxon countries (Esping-Andersen 1997). Following the same concern of locating East Asian economies in the welfare modelling business, Holliday reelaborated developmentalism studies, and proposed to integrate the famous classification of the three regimes of Esping-Andersen welfare with a fourth model, labelled "Productivist Welfare Capitalism" (PWC) (Holliday 2000). Covering the cases of Japan, South Korea, Taiwan, Hong Kong and Singapore, PWC was further divided in three parts: a more universalist subgroup for the first three economies, an extremely market-oriented case represented by Hong Kong, and Singapore, falling in between. Holliday (2000) claimed that common traits between these five economies could be summarised broadly as a strong intervention of the state in the economy, and a democratic deficit that prevented the working classes from influencing social policies, unlike the strategies of "class coalitions" found elsewhere in Europe (Esping-Andersen 1990; Pierson 2007). As further studies emerged in the 2000s, uncertainty on whether the East Asian productivist model is useful started to emerge.

Scholars expressed concern that conceptual clarity was lacking (Choi 2007), and criteria for inclusion to this fourth type were judged to be based on "[...] miscellaneous and unsystematic features that result in an incoherent and selective interpretation" (Kim 2008, 112).

A problematic aspect of this early literature was the belief that all newly industrialised economies were following the pioneering growth model of Japan (Esping-Andersen 1997; Amable 2003; Schröder 2009). Amable (2003), for example, suggested to reelaborate the VoC classification with an enlarged typology of five models of capitalism, distinguishing, within the block of CME countries, an Asian-type capitalism characterised by long-term economic strategy, de facto employment protection, and a weak social protection system, typically Japanese traits (Amable 2003, 107). At first, it looked as if the first phase of developmentalism of the 1960s and 1970s could have followed a similar path for many newly industrialised economies, and social policies continued to be instrumental to economic growth also when democratisation trends surfaced in South Korea and Taiwan (1980–1990s). However, after the Asian economic crisis of 1997 and the ensuing post-industrialism phase, these welfare systems started to follow their own distinctive paths (Hudson and Hwang 2013; Peng and Wong 2008). Since then, scholarly opinions and views varied widely, and there are still debates on whether welfare systems in this geographic area are still residual and productivist (Aspalter 2006; Holliday 2000, 2005; Hwang 2012; Yang 2017), or whether welfare expansion is taking place (Kim 2008; Hong 2014). Several single case studies, often in edited publications, have been published during the 2000s, so that welfare modelling discourses have been discussed less frequently in the following years (Walker and Wong 2005; White et al. 1998; Ramesh 2004; Tang 2000; Haggard and Kaufman 2008; Kwon 1998; Lin 1991; Ahn and Lee 2012).

Nonetheless, enumerating early observations on how economies afferent to the "productivist welfare capitalism" (PWC) can still be useful in understanding how they evolved afterwards. Here, I present a list of ten standards that have appeared throughout scholarly discussions in the 2000s. They have been described as follows (Hong 2014, 2017):

1) Policy priority accorded to *economic development* above all else (Lee and Ku 2007; Walker and Wong 2005; Tang 2000; Holliday 2000; Ramesh 2004; Takegawa 2009)

2) Social policies aimed at ensuring the *reproduction of a healthy and efficient workforce,* such as education and public health (Gough 2001)

3) A *top-down approach* in the distribution of social rights, with a preference for loyal state collaborators, such as *public employees and the military* (Holliday 2000; Tang 2000; Walker and Wong 2005; Kwon 1998; Ku and Finer 2007; Peng and Wong 2010)

4) A negligible role of the labour movement, both as a labour party and of union organisation (Wong 2004; Caraway 2009; Peng and Wong 2010; Fleckenstein and Lee 2017)

5) Different colonial legacies (the UK for the city-states of Singapore and Hong Kong, and Japan for Taiwan and South Korea) (Walker and Wong 2005; Hort and Kuhnle 2000; Gough 2001)

6) Low public spending on social protection, with a broad involvement required of families and the private sector in the welfare mix (Jacobs 2000; Gough 2001; Lee and Ku 2007; Walker and Wong 2005; Aspalter 2006; Tang 2000; Yang 2017; Kim 2020)

7) A subsidiary/regulatory role of the state in welfare and more care responsibilities for the family, based on Confucian values (Jones 1993; Goodman, Kwon, and White 1998; Kwon 1998; Walker and Wong 2005; Ku and Finer 2007), and inadequate public commitment to care services for the children and the elderly (Walker and Wong 2005).

For the sake of a fuller discussion, three commonly cited structural criteria are here added.

1) A relatively young population structure
2) Low levels of wealth inequality and
3) Low levels of (youth) unemployment (Jacobs 2000; Aspalter 2019).

Over time, many of these assumptions have lost interpretive value. To begin with, the productivist rationale of "economic growth first" is no longer the main policy priority, and more attention is paid to social issues and redistribution. More crucially, East Asian regions no longer enjoy the benefits of a young demographic distribution structure, and are troubled by one of the most rapid population ageing trends in the world. The next section provides some empirical evidence for this.

10.3 Similarities and differences in the "social protection" and the "provident fund" types

10.3.1 Similarities

Newly Industrialisd Economies in East Asia have all experienced a compressed process of economic growth and modernisation over the past decades, Japan being a forerunner. They generally share in common low levels of social expenditure in comparison to other advanced capitalisms (the "small welfare state" approach) (Yang 2017, 2020). Besides that, common features in this geographical region are mostly structural (demographic ageing, deindustrialisation, health outcomes) and cultural (declining fertility rates due to less marriages).

Despite obvious differences in terms of the size of the population and of the economy (i.e. GDP per capita), the five East Asian economies here considered are all affected by a process of deindustrialisation and tertiarisation of their industries (Cousins 2005; Lee 2016) (Table 10.2). This has had consequences on their labour market structure. To cite an example, the proportion of non-regular workers in Japan, which was only about 20 % in the early 1990s, has increased to nearly 40 % since the mid-2010s (Kim 2020); but generally speaking, increasing working poverty and job precariousness are common traits of these economies following the 1997 Asian economic crisis (Peng and Wong 2010; Lee 2016; Teo 2018). Economic growth rates, once close to two-digits, have now slowed down considerably, and income inequality is especially high in Singapore and Hong Kong. With a polarising labour market, younger generations have been prompted to become more competitive, and this has resulted in over-educated new entrants to the labour market (the case of Korea is quite extreme with a generational gap of 25 % between youth aged 25–34 and middle-aged people of 55–64 years old) (Table 10.2). The biggest issue is, though, the rapid demographic ageing process, for which Japan is, once again, a forerunner. Elderly people over 65 years old as a percentage of the population are on the rise in most of the industrialised world, however the slope of East Asian regions is particularly pronounced in comparison to the OECD average (Figure 10.2).

Unit: %

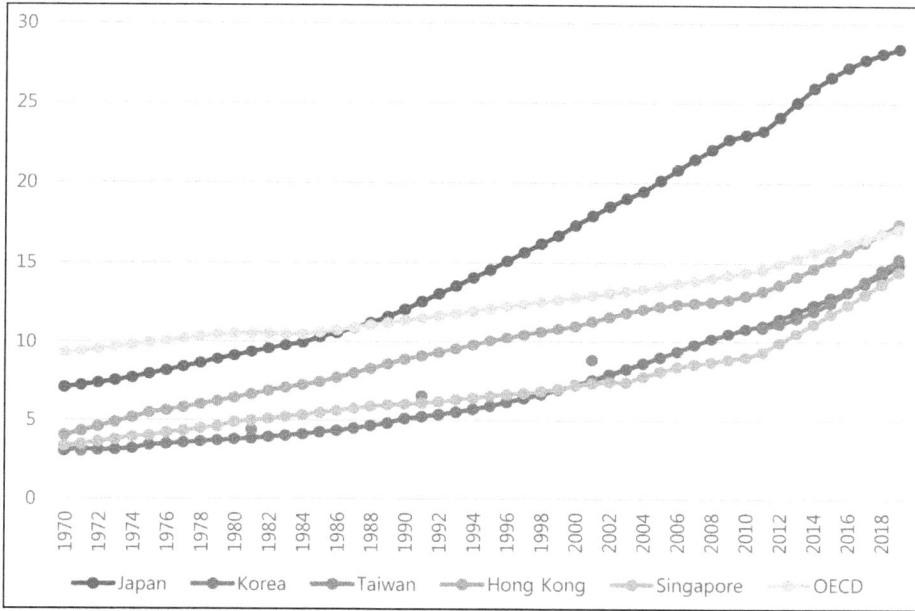

Figure 10.2: Elderly people above 65 years of age as % of the population (1970–2018).
Sources: OECD data (various years); knoema; ROC (various years)

Table 10.2: Main indicators of socio-economic development in East Asia (2019, pre-Covid).

	Japan	South Korea	Taiwan	Singapore	Hong Kong
Population size	125,210,000[1]	51,779,203[2]	23,580,000[3]	5,638,676	7,507,400
Political system	Parliamentary democracy	Presidential democracy	Semi-presidential democracy	Parliamentary democracy	Special Administrative Region (SAR) of P.R. China
GDP per capita (current $)[4]	40,113	31,489	25,941	59,797	46,323

---

1 https://www.stat.go.jp/english/
2 Korea Statistics: http://kostat.go.kr/portal/eng/index.action
3 https://eng.stat.gov.tw/mp.asp?mp=5
4 https://data.worldbank.org/indicator/NY.GDP.PCAP.CD?locations=HK

Tableau 10.2: (continued)

	Japan	South Korea	Taiwan	Singapore	Hong Kong
Economic growth rate	0.5	2.039	3.33	1.345	−1.68
Gini coefficient	0.334 (2018)	0.345 (2018)[5]	0.339[6]	0.452	0.473 (2016)[7]
Educational attainment, completed tertiary education (at least bachelor or equivalent, 25+)	61.5 % (25–34 y.o.) 44.5 % (55–63 y.o.)	69.8 % (25–34 y.o.) 25.1 % (55–64 y.o.)	46.5 % (above 15 y.o.)[8]	58.45 % (above 25 y.o., 2020)	30.6 % (above 15 y.o., 2016)[9]
Life expectancy at birth[10] Female Male	87.7 81.6 (2020)	86.3 80.3	84.23 77.69[11]	86 81	88 82
Infant mortality rate (per 1,000 births)	2	3	3.8[12]	2	1.26[13]
Total fertility rate[14]	1.4	0.9	1.05[15]	1.1	1.1
Share of births outside marriage (% of all births)[16]	2.3 % (2018)	2.3 %	3.8 %[17]	2 %	8 %
Crude marriage rate (no. of marriages per 1,000 people)	4.8	4.7	5.16	5.2	5.9
Unemployment rate[18]	2.4	3.75	3.7[19]	3.1	2.93

5 OECD 2021, Income inequality (indicator). doi: 10.1787/459aa7f1-en (Accessed on 24 May 2021)

6 https://www.statista.com/statistics/922574/taiwan-gini-index/

7 https://www.censtatd.gov.hk/en/EIndexbySubject.html?pcode=D5321605&scode=459#section3

8 https://www.taiwan.gov.tw/content_9.php

9 https://www.bycensus2016.gov.hk/data/16bc-summary-results.pdf#page=63

10 OECD data KR JP

11 https://eng.stat.gov.tw/public/data/dgbas03/bs2/yearbook_eng/y006.pdf

12 https://eng.stat.gov.tw/public/data/dgbas03/bs2/yearbook_eng/Yearbook2019.pdf

13 https://www.macrotrends.net/countries/HKG/hong-kong/infant-mortality-rate'> Hong Kong Infant Mortality Rate 1950-2021. www.macrotrends.net. Retrieved 24 May 2021.

14 Data WB

15 https://www.singstat.gov.sg/-/media/files/news/press080022021a.pdf

16 https://stats.oecd.org/index.aspx?queryid=68249

17 Nikkei Asia 2021.

18 Data WB

19 https://eng.dgbas.gov.tw/ct.asp?xItem=37336&ctNode=2046&mp=2

Not all common indicators are necessarily negative, though. All of these East Asian economies have successfully achieved a redistributive and universal health system (although out-of-pocket payments remain high in Singapore, Korea and Taiwan) (Ramesh and Holliday 2001; Ramesh 2008; Hwang 2020). As a result, life expectancy at birth and infant mortality rates reach the top of health outcome standards in the world (Table 10.2; also see section 10.4 of this chapter).

East Asian economies also share common cultural assumptions about marriage as a *sine qua non* to form a family. With the partial exception of Hong Kong at 8 %, most of the cases under consideration present abysmally low levels of childbirth outside the wedlock (2–3 %), which demonstrates how non-traditional forms of family are still frowned upon, with consequences to the overall crude marriage rate, which has been halved since the 1990s, when it was still around 10 marriages every 1,000 people (Table 10.2).

10.3.2 Differences

The most relevant differences in our sample are, as previously mentioned, a different colonial past and different social policy strategies, which are more tilted towards comprehensive social protection for South Korea, Taiwan and Japan, and towards provident fund-based compulsory savings in Hong Kong and Singapore. Two other important differences merit attention: the democratic transition (and what it entails in terms of different political coalitions and the prospects for welfare reform); and institutional policy legacies.

In terms of democracy, Singapore and Hong Kong are not regarded as very strong, according to several international agencies (e.g. Transparency International, World Bank DPI). Even though Singapore has universal suffrage and holds elections regularly, its dominant political party (PAP) has never been replaced as the government by progressive opposition parties since the founding of the city-state in 1959. The chief executive of Hong Kong is elected according to an Election Committee appointed by representatives of various sectors, which account for only 6 % of the electorate.

In contrast, the "social protection" oriented group has taken a turn to democratisation. With Japan being a forerunner, Korea and Taiwan adopted a system of electoral democracy after 1987 only, following a time of heated civil protests. Political competition in these democratic systems emerged as an important welfare determinant much later in the 2000s, when progressive opposition parties rose to power (the DP in Japan between 2009 and 2012; progressive governments in South Korea in 1998–2008 and 2017–2021; DPP-led legislatures in Taiwn during 2000–2003 and 2016–2021). This can be considered an important factor behind rising welfare expenditure levels (Kwon 1997; Lee and Ku 2007; Hong 2014; Yang 2017; Fleckenstein and Lee 2017). While labour movements have not been particularly relevant in determining welfare expansion in East Asia (Caraway 2009; Hong 2014), political coalitions advocating welfare

reforms, and public opinion, are becoming increasingly important in democratic social protection-oriented East Asian welfare systems (Kim 2008; Yeh, Cheng, and Shi
2021; Kim 2020; Hong et al. 2022).

Finally, a few words can be said on institutional legacies. A typical example could
be the societalisation of social care, for children and the elderly. While South Korea
and Japan have both adopted a long-term care insurance system, following their tradition of relying on social insurance, Hong Kong and Singaporean families make large
use of their governments' migration policies which encourage the work of migrant
care workers from neighbour developing countries, hence encouraging the provision
of cheap domestic care from the private market (Peng 2018; Teo 2018).

10.4 Welfare reforms and the new challenges of COVID-19

10.4.1 Welfare reforms amidst challenges

The past five decades have been a time of tumultuous change for the East Asian
economies here considered. As an era of economic growth took off for this region, social science researchers in the 1980s were engaged in hotly debated discussions on
what were the factors that determined the coexistence of high economic growth, low
unemployment, high social stability, residual social security, and low tax burden, all
the while Western capitalistic economies were still struggling in the aftermath of the
oil crisis of the mid-1970s (Vogel 1979). However, since the 2000s (and even earlier for
Japan) East Asian economies have transitioned into post-industrial societies, and this
winning, "secret" combination has lost most of its appeal. East Asia thus entered the
era of demographic ageing, and slower economic growth, unemployment and precarious work, economic stagnation, low fertility rates, skyrocketing housing prices, have
all become part of the public debates on welfare development, unveiling the need to
cater to the needs of the vulnerable in society (women, elderly, youth, disabled, migrants), who had been previously overlooked during the years of developmentalist
economic growth.

Since this is a group of welfare laggards, several structural weaknesses remain in
their social security system, for both "social protection" and "provident fund" paths.

As income protection for the elderly is yet in its developing stage, recent reforms
have pushed in several directions, with retrenchment reforms in Japan and Korea lowering wage replacement rates of public pensions to 40–45 % in the 1990s–2000s (Park
and Osawa 2013), expansion reforms such as the new pension legislation in Taiwan in
2008 with generous replacement rates, or the Korean universal basic pension introduced in 2007, and modified with the introduction of a means test in 2014, meant to
compensate for the fall in the purchasing power of pensioners; there is also the case of

Hong Kong, were pension provisions remain inadequate (Hwang 2012; Yeh, Cheng, and Shi 2020). Since most of the social security entitlements in East Asia are tied to employment, investing in workers' employability through active labour market policies such as training, employment services, and direct job creation has been an important policy strategy for these governments, especially in times of economic crisis (Kim and Shi 2020; Teo 2018). Even so, due to the mounting precarisation of the labour market for young labour market entrants, additional measures such as increasing the minimum wage and providing targeted youth allowances have been part of the government and local government agenda in South Korea during the centre-left Moon administration (2017–2021) (Kwon and Hong 2019).

Certainly one of the most successful policy fields in East Asia is health policy, where quality, cost efficiency, and health outcomes score relatively well in global rankings, and where universal coverage has been attained in all of the considered economies. On the one hand, the "social protection" approach is evident in Japan's social insurance model based on a multi-payer system, and Korea and Taiwan's National Health Insurance (NHI) with a single-payer system. On the other hand, Hong Kong and Singapore rely, respectively, on a heavily subsidised, non-compulsory health insurance (Yin and He 2018), and on a mandatory savings account (Medisave), which also subsidises health providers (Hwang 2020).

Finally, it is noteworthy to highlight ongoing developments in the field of social care, with a range of different solutions used by each economy: the introduction of LTCI in Japan (2000) and in Korea (2008) signal an important step in the direction of socialisation of care, as well as publicly subsidised universal childcare facilities (2013), which represent a formidable investment from the Korean government in meeting the care needs of mothers (Hong and Lee 2021). The Taiwanese support to working women is also visible through a generous parental leave of up to a year with a reimbursement equal to 60 % of the previous pay extendable for another year without salary (Tsai 2012), the introduction of a new childcare scheme in 2019, and the introduction of the Ten-year Long-Term Care Plan 2.0 (2017), with the inauguration of the present progressive DPP government (2016) (Yeh 2020). In contrast, Singapore supports work family reconciliation through tax reliefs for married women, the Baby Bonus (a cash subsidy and a co-savings account under the child's name, to be kept until 12 years of age), and the HOPE (Home Ownership Plus Education) programme of housing grants and subsidies for the low-income, with incentives when irreversible sterilisation is undergone after two children have already been born (Teo 2018). As for Hong Kong, the government has had a tradition of funding, regulating, and controlling service eligibility via a centralised system that guarantess low copayments, and a pilot programme allowing use of a voucher (the "money follows the older person" funding scheme) has recently been introduced to tackle rising care needs in the city (Lum et al. 2020).

10.4.2 New challenges and COVID-19

As it often happens, reality transcends imagination, and even more complex tasks are looming in contemporary societies. With the raging of the worst pandemic of the century, namely COVID-19 originated from the city of Wuhan in January 2020, all the political economies here considered somehow resorted to a path-dependent legacy of strong public intervention, by virtually shutting down national boundaries and implementing a series of policies to test and track infected people in the swiftest way possible. This resulted in a very favourable yearly assessment made by Bloomberg in terms of health efficiency, with the result that formerly underdeveloped East Asian regions are now all included in the top 10 of the most virtuous economies, with Singapore ranking first, followed by Hong, Taiwan, South Korea, and Japan following behind (10th in ranking). Admittedly, these economies have been constantly improving their ranking positions, with Hong Kong ranking first in 2016 as well. It is also worth noting that the Bloomberg index efficiency score is very simplified and normally takes in account very broad indicators such as life expectancy and absolute health expenditures, which do not take into account food and health habits. Nevertheless, for a region that is still considered stingy in welfare expenditures in comparison with other advanced capitalist economies, this is still a remarkable result.

Table 10.3: Most efficient healthcare systems in the COVID-19 era.

Rank	Change	Economy	Score	Life expectancy	Health % GDP	Cost per capita	COVID-19 mortality	Counts – new cases	GDP 1Y%	Rank
1	+1	**SIN**	67.79	83.15	4.4	$2,619	4.96	246.67	−6.00	2
2	−1	**HK**	64.89	84.93	6.2	$2,849	14.94	265.71	−7.47	1
3	+12	**TW**	51.69	80.69	6.6	$1,550	0.29	8.65	+0.05	15
4	+2	**KR**	50.79	82.63	7.6	$2,283	10.63	338.68	−1.88	6
5	−2	**ISR**	46.44	82.80	7.4	$3,145	335.72	26,349.82	−5.89	3
6	+1	**IRE**	45.22	82.26	7.2	$4,977	425.07	9,140.75	−3.00	7
7	+3	**AUS**	41.74	82.75	9.2	$5,332	35.61	86.67	−4.16	10
8	+10	**NZ**	40.21	81.86	9.2	$3,937	5.18	66.57	−6.07	18
9	+5	**THA**	38.79	76.93	3.7	$247	0.86	9.38	−7.15	14
10	−2	**JP**	38.02	84.21	10.9	$4,169	18.30	725.09	−5.27	8

Source: https://www.bloomberg.com/news/articles/2020-12-18/asia-trounces-u-s-in-health-efficiency-index-amid-pandemic (Accessed 17 May 2021)

Another notable result is represented by East Asian region rankings in PISA OECD assessments, which measure 15-year-old pupils' school performance on mathematics, science and reading. Despite the many criticisms, PISA tests were first started in

2000, and implemented every three years since. Hong Kong, Singapore and South Korea have constantly shown top results in this ranking. Of course, caution is needed as there are limits of data representativeness (some nations tend to push forward the most brilliant students, and not average ones), but this attention to quality indicators and investments in education show how much this region is pushing towards developing its human capital, and probably a need for legitimisation has resulted in the constant need to show positive policy outcomes to the public (as the recent public health emergency of COVID-19 attests). As a result, heated discussions on policy change and innovation are characterising the development of social policies in this area of the world.

10.5 Conclusion

Welfare systems in East Asia have outgrown the productivist model they were originally acknowledged for, and they are keen in tackling a series of societal issues by actively learning from the policy experience of Europe, the United States, and the like. We may grossly divide the five economies here considered in an inclusive, expansive "social protection type" (Japan, South Korea, Taiwan), and the more targeted, market-oriented, "provident fund" (Singapore and Hong Kong).

Referring to the discussions from the developmentalism/productivism literature, we may assert that, the economy-first productivist approach is not so obvious, or at least it does not result in welfare dumping (point 1); nevertheless, these political economies do focus on employability and workforce, as income protection schemes are still somewhat immature, and overall social spending levels are quite small in comparison to advanced capitalistic systems (point 6). Generally speaking, research investigating the politics of welfare in East Asia is still at an early stage; this is also due to the scarce relevance of labour movements (point 4). Structural challenges, however, are important across all the observed cases. The pre-existing demographic advantage of a young population is now lost (point 8), and the state keeps exerting a subsidiary role by heavily relying on private market competition and regulation for health and social care services; nevertheless, the state is investing considerably in child- and/or elderly care, with the creation of *ad hoc* programmes (point 6). The build-up of universal and redistributive medical systems, despite the high out-of-pocket payments, has guaranteed optimal efficiency in health policy and longer life expectancy (point 2), but limited opportunities for good jobs for highly educated young labour market entrants are creating labour shortages and unemployment at the same time (Japan being a partial exception in this respect) (point 10). As familialistic values are slow to change, young people of marriageable age might choose to forego marriage at all (point 7).

Low fertility and demographic ageing are certainly amongst the biggest challenges that East Asia is facing, and several solutions are packaged by an increasingly dynamic and international epistemic policy community, active in universities, think tanks and policymaking communities. Future research should take note of this increasing complexity and analyse welfare systems in East Asia based on both structural (new politics of welfare, deindustrialisation: structure of the labour markets, systems of production, skill acquisition and distribution of risks) and political determinants of welfare development (e.g. political partisanship and its meanings, public opinion and civil society, political coalitions, local governments, female politicians, political ideology, etc.). A political analysis is especially relevant for the "social protection" oriented cases of Japan, South Korea and Taiwan, since the logic of electoral competition and a heavier social policy legacy pushes them to expand welfare more. Future studies covering East Asia are set on a bright and dynamic path of exciting discoveries for comparative social policy research, with plentiful discussions and implications to be drawn (Hort and Kuhnle 2000; Kim 2008; Estévez-Abe and Kim 2014; Lee 2016; Abrahamson 2017; Fleckenstein and Lee 2017; Peng 2018; Kwon and Hong 2019; Chen and Shi 2020; Yeh, Cheng, and Shi 2020; Kim 2020; Kwon 2020).

References

Abrahamson, Peter. 2017. "East Asian Welfare Regime: Obsolete Ideal-Type or Diversified Reality." *Journal of Asian Public Policy* 10 (1), 90–103.

Ahn, Sang-Hoon, and Sophia Seung-yoon Lee. 2012. "Explaining K orean Welfare State Development with New Empirical Data and Methods." *Asian Social Work and Policy Review* 6 (2), 67–85.

Amable, Bruno. 2003. *The Diversity of Modern Capitalism*. Oxford: Oxford University Press.

An, Mi Young, and Ito Peng. 2016. "Diverging Paths? A Comparative Look at Childcare Policies in Japan, South Korea and Taiwan." *Social Policy & Administration* 50 (5), 540–558.

Asian Development Bank (ADB). 2021. https://data.adb.org/

Aspalter, Christian. 2006. "The East Asian Welfare Model." *International Journal of Social Welfare* 15 (4), 290–301.

Aspalter, Christian. 2019. "Welfare Regime Analysis: 30 Years in the Making." *International Social Work* 62 (1), 76–88.

Caraway, Teri L. 2009. "Labor Rights in East Asia: Progress or Regress?." *Journal of East Asian Studies* 9 (2), 153–186.

Chang, Yu-fang, and Yuen-wen Ku. 2013. "Social Policy and its Implications to Structural Shifts: A Comparison between Taiwan and Korea in the Colonial Era." In *Handbook on East Asian Social Policy*, edited by Misa Izuhara, 65–85. Cheltenham: Edward Elgar.

Chen, Hsiu-Hui, and Shih-Jiunn Shi. 2021. "Changing Dynamics of Social Policy in Democracy: Comparing Pension and Health Reforms in Taiwan." *Journal of Asian Public Policy* 14 (1), 30–44.

Choi, Young Jun. 2007. *Coming to a Standstill: A New Theoretical Idea of East Asian Welfare Regimes*. Barnett Papers in Social Research 3. Oxford: Department of Social Policy and Social Work.

Chon, Yongho. 2019. "The Effects of Marketization of Long-Term Care Services for Older Adults in Korea." *Journal of Social Service Research* 45 (4), 507–519.

Cousins, Mel. 2005. *European Welfare States: Comparative Perspectives*. London: Sage.

Cumings, Bruce. 1984. "The Origins and Development of the Northeast Asian Political Economy: In-dustrial Sectors, Product Cycles, and Political Consequences." *International Organization* 38 (1), 1–40.

DGBAS. 2019. Statistical Yearbook of the Republic of China 2019. https://eng.dgbas.gov.tw/public/data/dgbas03/bs2/yearbook_eng/Yearbook2019.pdf.

Dore, Ronald Philip. 2000. *Stock Market Capitalism: Welfare Capitalism: Japan and Germany versus the Anglo-Saxons.* Oxford: Oxford University Press.

Economist. 2012. "Asia's Next Revolution." 8 September. https://www.economist.com/leaders/2012/09/08/asias-next-revolution

Esping-Andersen, Gøsta. 1990. *The Three Worlds of Welfare Capitalism.* Princeton, NJ: Princeton University Press.

Esping-Andersen, Gøsta. 1997. "Hybrid or Unique? The Japanese Welfare State between Europe and America." *Journal of European Social Policy* 7 (3), 179–189.

Estévez-Abe, Margarita, and Yeong-Soon Kim. 2014. "Presidents, Prime Ministers and Politics of Care – Why Korea Expanded Childcare Much More than Japan." *Social Policy & Administration* 48 (6), 666–685.

Estevez-Abe, Margarita, Jae-Jin Yang, and Young Jun Choi. 2016. "Beyond Familialism: Recalibrating Family, State and Market in Southern Europe and East Asia." *Journal of European Social Policy* 26 (4), 301–313.

Fleckenstein, Timo, and Soohyun Christine Lee. 2017. "Democratization, Post-Industrialization, and East Asian Welfare Capitalism: The Politics of Welfare State Reform in Japan, South Korea, and Taiwan." *Journal of International and Comparative Social Policy* 33 (1), 36–54.

Goodman, Roger, Huck-Ju Kwon, and Gordon White. 1998. *The East Asian Welfare Model: Welfare Orientalism and the State.* London: Routledge.

Gough, Ian. 2001. "Globalization and Regional Welfare Regimes: The East Asian Case." *Global Social Policy* 1 (2), 163–189.

Haggard, Stephan. 2004, "Institutions and Growth in East Asia." *Studies in Comparative International Development* 38 (4), –81.

Haggard, Stephan, and Robert Kaufman. 2008. *Democracy, Development and Welfare States: Latin America, East Asia, and Eastern Europe.* Princeton, NJ: Princeton University Press.

Hamilton, Gary G., and Nicole Woolsey Biggart. 1988. "Market, Culture, and Authority: A Comparative Analysis of Management and Organization in the Far East." *American Journal of Sociology* 94, S52–S94.

HK Statistical Yearbook. https://www.yearbook.gov.hk/2019/en/

Holliday, Ian. 2000. "Productivist Welfare Capitalism: Social Policy in East Asia." *Political Studies* 48 (4), 706–723.

Holliday, Ian. 2005. "East Asian Social Policy in the Wake of the Financial Crisis: Farewell to Productivism?" *Policy & Politics* 33 (1), 145–162.

Hong, Ijin. 2014. "Trends and Determinants of Social Expenditure in Korea, Japan and Taiwan." *Social Policy & Administration* 48 (6), 647–665.

Hong, Ijin. 2017. "I sistemi di welfare in Asia tra produttivismo e diritti sociali." *Stato e Mercato* 2, 311–338.

Hong, Ijin. 2018. "Immigration and the Boundaries of Social Citizenship in East Asia: Theoretical Considerations in a Comparative Perspective." *OMNES: The Journal of Multicultural Society* 8 (2), 37–66.

Hong, Ijin, and Jieun Lee. 2021. "Does Social Investment Make the Labour Market 'Flow'? Family Policies and Institutional Complementarities in Italy, Spain, Japan and South Korea." In *Welfare Reform and Social Investment Policy in Europe and East Asia*, edited by Young Jun Choi, Timo Fleckenstein and Soohyun Christine Lee, 129–166. Bristol: Policy Press.

Hong, Ijin, Chung-Yang Yeh, Jieun Lee, and Jen-Der Lue. 2022. "Public Opinion on Social investment in the Developmental States." In *The World Politics of Social Investment (Volume II): The Politics of Varying Social Investment Strategies*, edited by Julian L. Garritzmann, Silja Häusermann, and Bruno Palier. Oxford and New York: Oxford University Press.

Hort, Sven Olsson, and Stein Kuhnle. 2000. "The Coming of East and South-East Asian Welfare States." *Journal of European Social Policy* 10 (2), 162–184.

Hudson, John, and Gyu-Jin Hwang. 2013. "Pathways of Welfare State Development in East Asia." In *Handbook on East Asian Social Policy*, edited by Misa Izuhara, 15–40. Cheltenham: Edward Elgar Publishing.

Hwang, Gyu-Jin. 2012. "Explaining Welfare State Adaptation in East Asia: The Cases of Japan, Korea and Taiwan." *Asian Journal of Social Science* 40 (2), 174–202.

Hwang, Gyu-Jin. 2020. "The Political Economy of Welfare in Singapore: Explaining Continuity and Change." *Policy Studies* 41 (1), 63–79.

Izuhara, Misa (ed.) 2013. *Handbook on East Asian Social Policy*. Cheltenham: Edward Elgar Publishing.

Jacobs, David. 2000. "Low Public Expenditures on Social Welfare: Do East Asian Countries Have a Secret?" *International Journal of Social Welfare* 9 (1), 2–16.

Johnson, Chalmers. 1982. *MITI and the Japanese Miracle: The Growth of Industrial Policy, 1925–1975*. Redwood City, CA: Stanford University Press.

Jones, Catherine. 1990. "Hong Kong, Singapore, South Korea and Taiwan: Oikonomic Welfare States." *Government and Opposition* 25 (4), 446–462.

Jones, Catherine. 1993. "The Pacific Challenge: Confucian Welfare States." In *New Perspectives on the Welfare State in Europe*, edited by Catherine Jones. London and New York: Routledge, 1993

Karim, Syahirah Abdul, Terje A. Eikemo, and Clare Bambra. 2010. "Welfare State Regimes and Population Health: Integrating the East Asian Welfare States." *Health Policy* 94 (1), 45–53.

Kim, Dokyun. 2020. "The Development of Functional Equivalents to the Welfare State in Post-War Japan and South Korea." In *The Small Welfare State: Rethinking Welfare in the US, Japan, and South Korea*, edited by Jae-Jin Yang, 163–189. Cheltenham: Edward Elgar Publishing.

Kim, Mason M. S. 2015. *Comparative Welfare Capitalism in East Asia: Productivist Models of Social Policy*. London: Palgrave Macmillan.

Kim, So Young. 2010. "Do Asian Values Exist? Empirical Tests of the Four Dimensions of Asian Values." *Journal of East Asian Studies* 10 (2), 315–344.

Kim, Sung-won. 2020. "Weak Social Security but Strong Employment Security in the Japanese Welfare State." In *The Small Welfare State: Rethinking Welfare in the US, Japan, and South Korea*, edited by Jae-Jin Yang, 190–210. Cheltenham: Edward Elgar Publishing.

Kim, Won-Sub, and Shih-Jiunn Shi. 2020. "East Asian Approaches of Activation: The Politics of Labor Market Policies in South Korea and Taiwan." *Policy and Society* 39 (2), 226–246.

Kim, Yeon-Myung. 2008. "Beyond East Asian Welfare Productivism in South Korea." *Policy & Politics* 36 (1), 109–125.

Kim, Yun Young, and Young Jun Choi. 2020. "Does Social Protection Crowd Out Social Investment?." *Policy and Society* 39 (2), 208–225.

Korea Statistics. http://kostat.go.kr/portal/eng/index.action

Ku, Yeun-wen, and Catherine Jones Finer. 2007. "Developments in East Asian Welfare Studies." *Social Policy & Administration* 41 (2), 115–131.

Kwon, Huck-Ju. 1997. "Beyond European Welfare Regimes: Comparative Perspectives on East Asian Welfare Systems." *Journal of Social Policy* 26 (4), 467–484.

Kwon, Huck-Ju. 1998. *The Welfare State in Korea: The Politics of Legitimization*. London: Palgrave Macmillan.

Kwon, Huck-Ju. 2005. "Transforming the Developmental Welfare State in East Asia." *Development and Change* 36 (3), 477–497.

Kwon, Soon-Mee. 2020. "Why Welfare State Building is of Secondary Importance to Leftists in Japan and South Korea". In *The Small Welfare State: Rethinking Welfare in the US, Japan, and South Korea*, edited by Jae-Jin Yang, 140–162. Cheltenham: Edward Elga-.

Kwon, Soon-Mee, and Ijin Hong. 2019. "Is South Korea as Leftist as It Gets? Labour Market Policy Reforms under the Moon Presidency." *The Political Quarterly* 90 (1), 81–88.

Lee, Siu-Yau, and Kee-Lee Chou. 2016. "Trends in Elderly Poverty in Hong Kong: A Decomposition Analysis." *Social Indicators Research* 129 (2), 551–564.

Lee, Sophia Seung-Yoon. 2016. "Institutional Legacy of State Corporatism in De-Industrial Labour Markets: A Comparative Study of Japan, South Korea and Taiwan." *Socio-Economic Review* 14 (1), 73–95.

Lee, Sung-Hee. 2017. "The Socialization of Childcare and a Missed Opportunity Through Path Dependence: The Case of South Korea." *Social Politics: International Studies in Gender, State & Society* 24 (2), 132–153.

Lee, Yih-Jiunn, and Yeun-wen Ku. 2007. "East Asian Welfare Regimes: Testing the Hypothesis of the Developmental Welfare State." *Social Policy & Administration* 41 (2), 197–212.

Lin, Wan-I. 1991. "The Structural Determinants of Welfare Effort in Post-War Taiwan." *International Social Work* 34 (2), 171–190.

Lin, Ka, and Chack-kie Wong. 2013. "Social Policy and Social Order in East Asia: An Evolutionary View.: *Asia Pacific Journal of Social Work and Development* 23 (4), 270–284.

Lin, Yi-Yin, and Chin-Shan Huang. 2016. "Aging in Taiwan: Building a Society for Active Aging and Aging in Place." *The Gerontologist* 56 (2), 176–183.

London, Jonathan D. 2018. "Developmental Welfare States?: Korea and Taiwan, Hong Kong and Singapore." In *Welfare and Inequality in Marketizing East Asia*, by Jonathan D. London, 223–267. London: Palgrave Macmillan.

Lum, Terry, Cheng Shi, Gloria Wong, and Kayla Wong. 2020. "COVID-19 and Long-Term Care Policy for Older People in Hong Kong." *Journal of Aging & Social Policy* 32 (4–5), 373–379.

Midgley, James, and Kwong-leung Tang. 2001. "Introduction: Social Policy, Economic Growth and Developmental Welfare." *International Journal of Social Welfare* 10 (4), 244–252.

Miura, Mari. 2012. *Welfare Through Work: Conservative Ideas, Partisan Dynamics, and Social Protection in Japan*. Ithaca, NY: Cornell University Press.

Mok, Ka Ho. 2007. "Questing for Internationalization of Universities in Asia: Critical Reflections." *Journal of Studies in International Education* 11 (3–4), 433–454.

Mok, Ka Ho. 2013. "After the Regional and Global Financial Crises: Social Development Challenges and Social Policy Responses in Hong Kong and Macau." In *Handbook on East Asian Social Policy*, edited by Misa Izuhara, 129–149. Cheltenham: Edward Elgar.

Nikkei Asia. 2021. "Taiwan's Falling Birthrate 'Threatens its Economic Security'." https://asia.nikkei.com/Life-Arts/Life/Taiwan-s-falling-birthrate-threatens-its-economic-security2

Ng, Irene Y. H. 2013. "Social Welfare in Singapore: Rediscovering Poverty, Reshaping Policy." *Asia Pacific Journal of Social Work and Development* 23 (1), 35–47.

OECD SOCX. 2019. https://www.oecd.org/social/expenditure.htm

Park, Sung Ho, and Kimiko Osawa. 2013. "The Politics of Welfare Reform in Japan and Korea, 1990s–2000s: The Ratchet Mechanism and the Sustainability of Reform." In *APSA 2013 Annual Meeting Paper, American Political Science Association 2013 Annual Meeting*.

Peng, Ito. 2018. "Shaping and Reshaping Care and Migration in East and Southeast Asia." *Critical Sociology* 44 (7–8), 1117–1132.

Peng, Ito, and Joseph Wong. 2008. "Institutions and Institutional Purpose: Continuity and Change in East Asian Social Policy." *Politics & Society* 36 (1), 61–88.

Peng, Ito, and Joseph Wong. 2010. "East Asia". In *The Oxford Handbook of the Welfare State*, edited by Francis G. Castles, Stephan Leibfried, Jane Lewis, Herbert Obinger, and Christopher Pierson, 656–671. Oxford: Oxford University Press.

Pierson, Christopher. 2007. *Beyond the Welfare State? The New Political Economy of Welfare* (3rd ed.). Cambridge: Polity Press.

Powell, Martin, and Ki-tae Kim. 2014. "The 'Chameleon' Korean Welfare Regime." *Social Policy & Administration* 48 (6), 626–646.

Ramesh, Mishra. 2004. *Social Policy in East and Southeast Asia: Education, Health, Housing and Income Maintenance*. London: Routledge.

Ramesh, M. 2008. "Reasserting the Role of the State in the Healthcare Sector: Lessons from Asia." *Policy and Society* 27 (2), 129–136.

Ramesh, Mishra, and Ian Holliday. 2001. "The Health Care Miracle in East and Southeast Asia: Activist State Provision in Hong Kong, Malaysia and Singapore." *Journal of Social Policy* 30 (4), 637–651.

Republic of China (Taiwan). National Statistics. https://eng.stat.gov.tw/mp.asp?mp=5

Saunders, Peter, and Vera Mun-yu Tang. 2019. "Adult and Child Deprivation in Hong Kong." *Social Policy & Administration* 53 (6), 820–834.

Schröder, Martin. 2009. "Integrating Welfare and Production Typologies: How Refinements of the Varieties of Capitalism Approach Call for a Combination of Welfare Typologies." *Journal of Social Policy* 38 (1), 19–43.

Seeleib-Kaiser, Martin, and Tuukka Toivonen. 2011. "Between Reforms and Birth Rates: Germany, Japan, and Family Policy Discourse." *Social Politics* 18 (3), 331–360.

Singapore Department of Statistics. 2019. *Yearbook of Statistics Singapore 2019*. https://www.singstat.gov.sg/-/media/files/publications/reference/yearbook_2019/yos2019.pdf

Statistics Korea. http://kostat.go.kr/portal/eng/index.action

Storz, Cornelia, Bruno Amable, Steven Casper, and Sebastien Lechevalier. 2013. "Bringing Asia into the Comparative Capitalism Perspective." *Socio-Economic Review* 11 (2), 217–232.

Takegawa, Shogo. 2005. "Japan's Welfare-State Regime: Welfare Politics, Provider and Regulator." *Development and Society* 34 (2), 169–190.

Takegawa, Shogo. 2009. "International Circumstances as Factors in Building a Welfare State: Welfare Regimes in Europe, Japan and Korea." *International Journal of Japanese Sociology* 18 (1), 79–96.

Tang, Kwong-Leung. 2000. *Social Welfare Development in East Asia*. London: Palgrave Macmillan.

Teo, Youyenn. 2018. "Whose Family Matters? Work–Care–Migration Regimes and Class Inequalities in Singapore." Critical Sociology 44 (7–8), 1133–1146.

Tsai, Pei-Yuen. 2012. "The Transformation of Leave Policies for Work–Family Balance in Taiwan." *Asian Women* 28 (2), 27–54.

Vogel, Ezra F. 1979. *Japan as No. 1: Lessons for America*. Tokyo: Charles E. Tuttle Co.

Vogel, Ezra F. 1991. *The Four Little Dragons: The Spread of Industrialization in East Asia*. Vol. 3. Cambridge, MA: Harvard University Press.

Walker, Alan, and Chack-kie Wong (eds.) 2005. *East Asian Welfare Regimes in Transition: From Confucianism to Globalisation*. Bristol: Policy Press.

Wong, Joseph. 2004. "The Adaptive Developmental State in East Asia." *Journal of East Asian Studies* 4 (3), 345–362.

World Bank (WB). *Database of Political Institutions (DPI)*. https://datacatalog.worldbank.org/search/dataset/0039819/Database-of-Political-Institutions (various years)

World Bank (WB). *World Development Indicators*. Washington, DC: World Bank (various years). https://databank.worldbank.org/source/world-development-indicators

World Bank. 1993. *The East Asian Miracle*. New York: Oxford University Press.

Yang, Jae-jin. 2017. *The Political Economy of the Small Welfare State in South Korea*. Cambridge: Cambridge University Press.

Yang, Jae-jin (ed.) 2020. *The Small Welfare State: Rethinking Welfare in the US, Japan, and South Korea*. Cheltenham: Edward Elgar.

Yeh, Chung-Yang, Hyunwook Cheng, and Shih-Jiunn Shi. 2020. "Public–Private Pension Mixes in East Asia: Institutional Diversity and Policy Implications for Old-Age Security." *Ageing & Society* 40 (3), 604–625.

Yeh, Ming-Jui. 2020. "Long-Term Care System in Taiwan: The 2017 Major Reform and its Challenges." *Ageing & Society* 40 (6), 1334–1351.

Yi, Ilcheong, Hyuk-Sang Sohn, and Taekyoon Kim. 2015. "Linking State Intervention and Health Equity Differently: The Universalization of Health Care in South Korea and Taiwan." *Korea Observer* 46 (3), 517–549.

Yin, Jason Dean-Chen, and Alex Jingwei He. 2018. "Health Insurance Reforms in Singapore and Hong Kong: How the Two Ageing Asian Tigers Respond to Health Financing Challenges?" *Health Policy* 122 (7), 693–697.

Yu, Sam Wai Kam, Liam Foster, Ruby Chui Man Chau, and Yuk Pun Yu. 2021. "Defamilisation / Familisation Measures and Pensions in Hong Kong and Taiwan." *Journal of Aging & Social Policy* 33 (2), 161–176.

Part III **Issues and challenges**

Philipp Trein

11 Health policy in a comparative perspective

Abstract: The regulation, financing and provision of health services is one of the main tasks for contemporary welfare states. There is a great amount of scholarship that deals with different aspects of health policymaking. This chapter introduces the reader to this literature in three steps. Firstly, it defines the scope of health policy by distinguishing health care policies, which aim at curing diseases, from public health policies that focus on preventing the outbreak of sickness. Secondly, the chapter presents different typologies of health care systems and discusses how they have evolved over time and how various countries differ regarding their expenditure for health. After that, the paper explores whether the type of health care system has consequences for the capacity of the country to put into place preventative health policies. Thirdly, the chapter introduces readers to the topic of health inequalities and elaborates some of the most recent findings from this literature.

Keywords: Health care, public health, prevention, health insurance, health expenditure, health inequalities

11.1 Introduction

The provision of health care for the sick and the protection of the population from health hazards is an important policy challenge and a major issue of concern for decisionmakers. Health and health policy have for a long time been a central welfare state issue. In developed democracies, policymakers have historically faced the challenge to create comprehensive health policies that include a variety of policy measures, such as financing health care services, regulating medicines but also providing vaccines and food safety regulations. More recently, policymakers have begun to face additional policy challenges related to health, such as rising health care costs due to fiscal pressures and new technologies that improve treatments. Furthermore, decisionmakers are confronted with rising cases of non-communicable diseases due to lifestyle habits and ageing populations as well as new infectious diseases, such as pandemics.

Against this backdrop, this chapter has two goals. Firstly, it aims to introduce the reader to the field of health policy and provides an overview of different policies that are part of this policy field. Secondly, the chapter intends to give an overview of how different countries provide health care and deal with some of the problems that go beyond the medical dimension of health policy, notably health inequalities.

Therefore, the chapter poses three related research questions. The next section asks how we can distinguish different elements of health policy, pointing notably to the distinction between health policy understood as public health on the one hand, as

https://doi.org/10.1515/9783110721768-011

well as health care on the other. The section demonstrates how public health can be defined as disease prevention and needs to be distinguished from health care, which focuses primarily on disease treatment. Section three poses the question how health systems are different and similar between countries, how they have evolved over time, and how health systems organise health policies, focusing on the financing of health care services as well as the ability to protect the entire population from health hazards. The fourth section of the chapter analyses how health inequalities as well as inequalities in access to health care have persisted in different countries and to what extent policymakers in various health systems have succeeded in dealing with these problems.

11.2 Different health policies

Which elements are part of health policy and how can we organise and compare different health policies? This section proposes a comparative analysis of different health policies, in distinguishing public policies that provide health care services for the sick from measures that aim at protecting those individuals, groups and the population from health hazards. Typically, scholars broadly define health policy as the regulation, financing and provision of services that aim at curing those who suffer from disease and preventing the healthy from getting sick (Blank, Burau, and Kuhlmann 2017; Böhm et al. 2013; Trein 2018). Health policy is different from other types of welfare policy, such as pensions and unemployment insurance, because an important part entails the provision of services and not only transfer payments. This implies that traditionally health policy comprises not only of the financing but also of the regulation and organisation of all kinds of health services (Barr 2020). As a consequence, health professions and industrial-scientific interest groups and firms that are relevant to health service provision have an important political influence in health policy (Immergut 1992; Rothgang et al. 2010).

Table 11.1: Health policy according to timing of intervention and target

	Illness-focused	Health-hazard-focused
Individual-focus	Medical treatments for individuals (e.g., pharmaceutical intervention, operations)	Services and treatments related to early diagnosis (e.g., cancer screening, counselling regarding health behaviour)
Population-focus	Treatment of groups or populations (e.g., measles, influenza, COVID-19)	Regulations of health protection (e.g., food safety, occupational safety, regulations to contain infections), vaccination, mass diagnosis

Note: based on Trein 2017, 749.

To describe different aspects of health policy, I use a simple two by two table that combines the level of the policy's target group with the timing of the health policy intervention in relation to disease progress. Specifically, I distinguish whether health policies focus rather on individuals, or if they tend to address a population or sub-group of the population at the same time. Furthermore, I separate whether health policies mainly address the moment once a disease is present, i.e., can be diagnosed clinically, or whether health policy action mainly addresses health hazards (Trein 2017, 2018).

Table 11.1 shows how this distinction offers the possibility of comparing different health policy interventions. Firstly, there are health policies that address medically diagnosed sickness and focus only on the individual level. Such policies regulate medicines, diagnosis techniques and skills, finance health care services, for example through health insurance, and organise the provision of services. Secondly, health policies focus on the individual level only, but address health hazards, i.e., the moment prior to the arrival of a disease. These are health policies that regulate, finance and provide preventive diagnostic services, for example screening regarding non-communicable diseases and health counselling. Thirdly, there are health policies that focus on the treatment once a sickness is medically diagnosed but extend this to the level of groups or populations. Examples for these types of health policies are measures dealing with the coordinated treatment of groups suffering from the same disease, such as COVID-19. Fourth, Table 11.1 distinguishes health policies that focus on health hazards at the population level. On the one hand, these are policies aiming at preventing the spread of a highly infectious disease through testing and vaccination, such as in the case of the COVID-19 virus. On the other hand, these are regulatory public health policies, for example food and occupational safety regulations or tobacco control policies, such as smoking bans. These policies extend beyond the policies that are at the core of health care policy.

These different types of health policies overlap considerably between institutions and organisations of health policies. Especially the first three types of health policies are often integrated in one law, such as the national health insurance laws, as well as in the same organisations and practitioners who are responsible for service provision, such as hospital or medical practices of independent doctors (Blank, Burau, and Kuhlmann 2017). Other policies, such as health regulations and policies to counteract the pandemic are more decoupled from health policies that are at the core of the health system and are part of health regulations (Bell, Salmon, and McNaughton 2011). In recent years policymakers have begun to propose health policies that integrate different aspects of health policies into other policies, such as those related to employment, environmental protection and transportation, which aims at combining as many of the fields mentioned in Table 11.1 as possible (Kickbusch and Buckett 2010).

The various elements of health policy differ according to their budgetary importance. In normal times, governments spend the largest part of their budget on health for services aiming at the cure of sick individuals and only a very small part on the preventative efforts (Trein 2018, 66). Expenditures in other fields of social policy, such as education, unemployment insurance and social assistance also have health impacts as they contribute to preventing sickness (Mackenbach 2019). Different health policies also vary concerning the political feedback effects (i.e., electoral rewards, support by interest groups), they produce for politicians. Health care policies that pay and provide cure for sicknesses, for example through extending health care coverage, are likely to create political support by politicians and interest groups (Hacker 2019; Jacobs, Mettler, and Zhu 2021). Contrariwise, it is much more difficult to create political support amongst the population and interest groups for preventative health policies. The reason for this is that public health and prevention address problems which individuals do not yet experience, and therefore are unlikely to prioritise in elections. At the same time, these policies often produce negative effects for influential interest groups, such as the tobacco or food industry, and these actors oppose public health policy through lobbying or in courts (Cairney and Denny 2020; Gailmard and Patty 2019; Healy and Malhotra 2009).

11.3 Health expenditure and health protection in different health care systems

An important part of research on health policy is the distinction of different health care systems. In most rich countries, governments have developed policies aiming at the development of universal health care services, which cover (in principle) the entire population. Nevertheless, there are important differences between countries regarding how to achieve such universality. In order to take into account the diversity in health policy, authors have put forward various comparative analyses of how countries regulate, finance and organise the provision of health care (Böhm et al. 2013; Reibling, Ariaans, and Wendt 2019; Rothgang et al. 2010; Saltmann, Busse, and Figueira 2004; Wendt, Frisina, and Rothgang 2009). An important insight from this research is that health care systems do not overlap particularly well with different welfare state systems, notably the distinction between liberal and small welfare states on the one hand, and continental European and Nordic welfare states on the other. Specifically, countries with a rather liberal welfare state (Emmenegger et al. 2015), such as Australia, Canada, and the UK have a largely publicly financed comprehensive health care system (Bambra 2005; Rothgang et al. 2010).

11.3.1 Diversity of health system typologies

In the following, the chapter contrasts two recently published typologies of health care systems that reveal the complexity that students and researcher face in the analysis of health systems. One typology by Böhm et al. (2013) distinguishes four groups of health care systems, according to how three dimensions – a) regulation, b) financing, and c) provision – of health care are coordinated, based on the governance literature (Benz 2004). Notably, each dimension can either be governed by the state, by interest groups, or by the market. The first group of health care systems are *National Health Service* systems where the state dominates the regulation, financing and provision of health care (e.g., Denmark, Finland, Sweden, Norway, Portugal, Spain, UK). The second group of countries are a *National Health Insurance* type and combine state regulation and financing with largely private provision (e.g., Australia, Canada, Ireland, New Zealand, Italy). The third group are countries representing *Social Health Insurance* systems, in which interest groups (peak associations) have an important degree of autonomy regarding the regulation and financing of health care whereas service provision is private (e.g., Austria, Germany, Luxembourg, Switzerland). The fourth group is called *Etatist Social Health Insurance* systems that combine state control of regulation, interest group control of financing and private provision (e.g., Belgium, Estonia, France, Czech Republic, Hungary, Netherlands, Poland, Slovakia, Israel, Japan, Korea). The U. S. is an outlier in this typology where private actors have a dominant role in health care governance and provision (Böhm et al. 2013, 263).

Table 11.2: Two typologies of health systems

Theoretically driven typology (Böhm et al. 2013)		Empirically driven typology (Reibling, Ariaans, and Wendt 2019)	
System type	Countries	System type	Countries
National Health Service	Denmark, Finland, Sweden, Norway, Portugal, Spain, UK	*Supply-and choice oriented public systems*	Australia, Austria, Belgium, Czech Republic, Germany, France, Ireland, Luxembourg
National Health Insurance	Australia, Canada, Ireland, New Zealand, Italy	*Performance- and primary-care oriented public systems*	Finland, Japan, South Korea, Norway, New Zealand, Portugal, Sweden
National Health Insurance	Austria, Germany, Luxembourg, Switzerland	*Regulation-oriented public systems*	Canada, Denmark, Spain, Italy, Netherlands, UK
Etatist Social Health Insurance	Belgium, Estonia, France, Czech Republic, Hungary, Netherlands, Poland, Slovakia, Israel, Japan, Korea	*Low-supply and low performance mixed systems*	Estonia, Hungary, Poland, Slovakia
Private Health System	U. S.	*Supply- and performance-oriented private systems*	Switzerland, U. S.

Another and more recently published typology uses an empirical approach to classify health care systems. Therein, the authors combine information on the supply of health care services (practitioners and expenditure), public–private mix, access regulation, primary care orientation, and performance (alcohol and tobacco consumption). In using cluster analysis, the authors visualise five clusters of health care systems that can be separated into two pairs respectively, as well as a fifth cluster that is not connected to the other two systems. The first cluster is named *Supply-and choice oriented public systems* amongst which are countries such as Australia, Austria and Germany. The second cluster, which is closely connected to the first one, is named *Performance- and primary-care oriented public systems* (e.g., Finland, Japan, New Zealand, and Portugal). A third cluster of countries is more distant from the first two and is entitled *Regulation-oriented public systems*. Notably, Canada, Denmark, Italy and the UK are part of this group. The fourth cluster, closely connected to the third one, is named *Low-supply and low performance mixed systems* (e.g., Estonia, Hungary and Poland). Finally, Switzerland and the U. S. are combined in a cluster named *Supply- and performance-oriented private systems* and are disconnected from the other four clusters (Reibling, Ariaans, and Wendt 2019, 615–617).

The important point to retain is that the literature on comparative health systems has a tradition of separating different health systems with quite different results (Table 11.2). The main reason for this divergence is that scholars have either taken a deductive approach that is theory-driven and based on different modes of governance, such as hierarchy (state), networks (interest groups) and markets (Böhm et al. 2013). Other researchers have used a much more empirically driven approach, which comes to a considerably different result regarding the separation of health care systems (Reibling, Ariaans, and Wendt 2019). Both health system typologies reveal important insights for the understanding of health care policy. On the one hand, they show how the internal governance logic of health systems works. On the other, the empirical approach builds on the policy outputs and outcomes that these health systems produce.

11.3.2 Similarities between countries in their development over time

Another strand in the literature on health policy and health care focuses on temporal dynamics in health and the changes in health systems over time. Such reforms were also part of health policy, notably the health care sector. For example, in many countries policymakers reformed hospital payment systems to make the delivery of health care more efficient. Notably, governments began to introduce Diagnosis Related Groups (DRGs), Disease Staging and Patient Management Categories. These are classification systems aiming at making the health care sector more cost-efficient by changing the billing structure for hospitals. Despite the differences between their health care systems, countries around the world adopted these management tools in their health care sector (Gilardi, Füglister, and Luyet 2009). These reforms are part of a general dynamic that aimed at increasing the role of market elements within health care financing and provision. In the UK, a variety of different NHS (National Health Service) reforms increased the role of market elements within national health policy (Greener 2002). Up to now, the impact of marketisation reforms in the health care sector probably have not been very well researched. A recent paper systematically analysed the usage of market instruments in hospitals in Madrid and showed that the cost-effectiveness of these types of reforms is limited (Alonso, Clifton, and Díaz-Fuentes 2015).

Another type of reform in the health care sector during the last three decades entails the decentralisation of health services to lower levels of government. The rationale behind this decision was to get the organisation of services closer to citizens and to take into account that regional governments are better placed for the organisation of services and the adaption of needs to local situations (Costa-Font and Greer 2016). For example, in Italy, regional governments received important competences in the organisation and financing of health care, in order to make health policy more cost efficient (Terlizzi 2019). In addition to decentralisation and the usage of market elements in health care governance, austerity was a third element of health care reform, especially in some European countries. Notably, in the wake of the global financial and economic crisis after 2007 many European governments aimed at reducing public expenditure, which also touched health policy, for example in Greece and Italy but also in the UK (McKee et al. 2012).

To illustrate some of these dynamics, I will now turn to a descriptive analysis of health expenditure against the background of the discussed insights from the literature. Therefore, I compare the relationship of the mean health expenditure per capita and mean out-of-pocket expenditure per capita in different OECD countries from 2000–2009 and 2010–2019. The data are in USD and weighed for purchasing power parity. First, the results suggest that there are differences in the patterns of expenditure between different countries that correspond only partially to the above discussed patterns of health care governance. Only Switzerland and the U. S. are clear outliers. Secondly, the comparison of the two decades indicates that health expenditure augmented considerably, but this increase varies between countries. Some Southern and Eastern European countries augmented their health expenditure at a much lower level compared to other countries in the sample. Furthermore, out-of-pocket health expenditure augmented, i.e., the share of health care cost that private households must cover themselves and that is not taken on by health insurance (Figure 11.1). Although these figures need to be interpreted in the context of a growing economy, they outline a common trend towards an increase in health expenditure as well as a growing share of health cost that needs to be covered by private households. This is a problem especially for low-income households, which tend to avoid investing in medical examinations if they have to cover them out of their own pocket (Agarwal, Mazurenko, and Menachemi 2017). The chapter further points to this problem below in the section on inequalities related to health outcomes and access to health care.

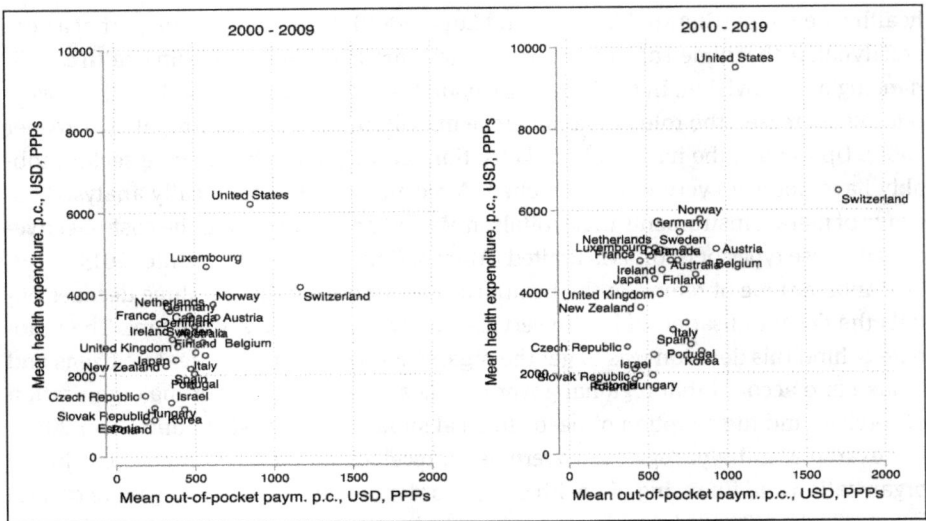

Figure 11.1: Health expenditure and out-of-pocket payments in OECD countries

This data suggests that there are some important elements of convergence between different health systems across developed democracies towards more marketisation and an increasing investment into health care services. Nevertheless, another dynamic of convergence also goes towards an increase in health care coverage through publicly regulated health insurance programmes. In 1996, Switzerland introduced a national health insurance law that extended coverage to all inhabitants, as regionally and locally organised health insurance models did not work anymore (Uhlmann and Braun 2011). In 2010, the U. S. Congress approved a national health insurance law that offered the possibility of obtaining health care coverage for those that could not afford health insurance (Affordable Care Act) (Rosenbaum 2011).

11.3.3 Do health care systems affect the capacity to make preventative policy?

In this section, the chapter turns to the analysis of preventative and protective health policy. The above-discussed comparisons of health systems do not take into account the capacity to make preventative health policies, although some of the texts account for tobacco consumption as a measure of health system performance (Reibling, Ariaans, and Wendt 2019). Nevertheless, different strands of literature have shown that there are differences between countries regarding their capacity to put into place health policies that prevent health hazards and that include non-medical policies.

This finding can be illustrated using the example of tobacco control policy. Researchers and international organisations have compared how different countries vary in their adoption of measures aiming at the prevention of non-communicable diseases, for example through tobacco control policy (Anderson, Becher, and Winkler 2016; Studlar, Christensen, and Sitasari 2011). In this context, scholars have also assessed which factors explain why countries adopt measures such as tobacco control policy. For example, researchers have held that corporatist institutions tend to explain a delay in the implementation of tobacco control policy as interest groups and firms, such the tobacco industry have more influence on public policy (Cairney, Studlar, and Mamudu 2011). Another explanation points out that if governments finance their health care systems through taxes, they will implement preventative health policies, for example tobacco control, as this will reduce the health care cost they have to cover through taxes (Trein 2017). Nevertheless, more research needs to be done to determine what explains the capacity of different countries to put into place preventative health policies.

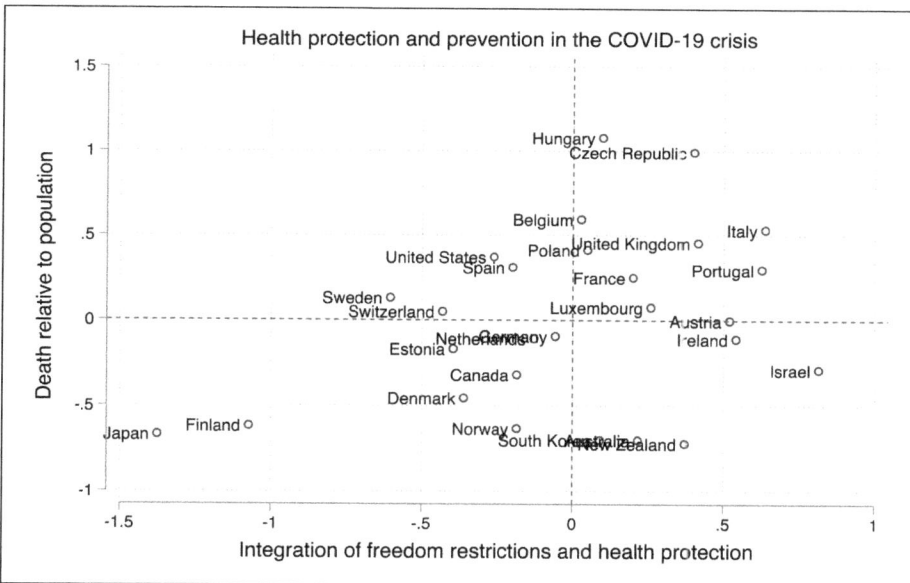

Figure 11.2: Variations in public health policy

The COVID-19 pandemic has brought to the fore the question of how and why countries differ in their capacity to put into place policies that aim at addressing an infectious disease at the population level. This instance is different from the problem of non-communicable diseases because governments face the challenges of combatting an epidemic. The arrival of COVID-19 and its massive impact on societies has sparked many research efforts, which also cover the capacity of countries to respond to the pandemic by "locking down" societies as well as the capacity of governments to create measures that protect the population, for example through testing and vaccination measures. The *COVID-19 Government Response Tracker* provides an index that combines the capacity of governments to restrict individuals' freedoms, for example through school closures or curfews with measures that protect the population on a rather voluntary basis, such as testing, contact tracing and vaccination (Hale et al. 2021).

To analyse this data, I combine the maximum value of the government containment index in the period of measurement (12/2019–05/2021) with the number of reported deaths related to COVID-19. To simplify the interpretation of the variables, I standardised them around their mean (Figure 11.2). The results show that there are important differences between countries. Some countries, such as Austria, Hungary, Italy, Israel and New Zealand managed to achieve a high level of integration between measures that severely restrict individual liberties with health protection measures. Other countries, such as Sweden, Switzerland, Japan or Finland did not pursue a high intensity response that integrated different types of public health policies. Importantly, there is a considerable variance regarding the impact of the pandemic between the countries that display a high response capacity. For example, New Zealand shows a high degree of integration between health protection and restrictions of freedom combined with little impact of the pandemic whereas the Czech Republic and Hungary have also high level of integration between different policy measures but in combination with a high level of crisis impact. When it comes to dealing with public health challenges, such as pandemic, not only the response capacity matters to achieve better health outcomes but also the timing, i.e., the ability to respond quickly (Oliu-Barton et al. 2021). Furthermore, different types of health care systems and worlds of welfare capitalism do not seem to be clearly correlated with the response capacity and outcomes related to public health (Figure 11.2).

11.4 Health inequalities and inequalities to health care access

The third research question that is important in relation to health policy in different countries relates to health inequalities as well as inequalities in access to health care services. For example, scholars have asked the question how different countries perform concerning the combat between health inequalities and if there is a difference between health systems regarding their ability to address health inequalities. Health inequalities are an important topic as they link health care back to other dimensions of welfare state research, such as pension and unemployment policy.

There is burgeoning literature that analyses health inequalities and the differences between countries, for example differences in health status and behaviour according to income and education (Bambra 2019). Researchers have pointed out that there is a paradox of public health. Although there is increasing investment in welfare state and health care policies, health inequalities have persisted throughout developed democracies (Bambra and Eikemo 2009; Lynch 2020; Mackenbach 2019). Notably, the literature has shown that socio-economic inequalities in mortality are a universal and substantial element of modern societies. In the European context, such inequalities are smaller in poorer Southern European countries but larger in wealthier Northern European countries. Furthermore, socioeconomic inequalities in mortality are widening and do not respond to policies that aim at reducing these goals. Lifestyle factors play an important role to explain these health inequalities. Oftentimes, the robustness of an individual's socioeconomic position is a fundamental cause for the mortality risk compared to other groups (Mackenbach 2019). Contrariwise, higher expenditure for health care reduces mortality across European countries. Thereby the gap in mortality rates between different education cohorts becomes smaller the more a country spends on (public) health care plans (Mackenbach et al. 2017, 1116).

In a recently published book, Julia Lynch assesses the question why health inequalities persist in different welfare states. Therefore, she conducted a comparative analysis of the politics of health inequalities in Finland, France and the UK. Lynch argues that despite their differences in terms of the welfare state, in none of these countries have decisionmakers acted to fundamentally address the causes of health inequalities. Rather than using more traditional options of statecraft, such as taxation, redistribution and labour market regulation, decisionmakers medicalised health inequalities, i.e., government policy documents essentially frame action against health inequalities through the professional lens of primary care and health promotion. Such a policy frame avoids addressing some of the more substantial causes, which would entail pushing back against neoliberal ideas of a small state with a limited redistribution capacity (Lynch 2017, 2020).

These persistent inequalities in health outcomes are mirrored by equally persisting inequalities in access to health care. It is well known that in the United States access to health care differs between poor and rich parts of the population. Poorer groups, amongst them often African Americans, remain in many cases excluded from health care services, even after the federal government extended coverage in the wake of the Affordable Care Act (Dickman, Himmelstein, and Woolhandler 2017). In Europe, there are considerable differences between countries regarding access to health care services. A recent report that compares expert reports from 35 countries points to the following key findings: (1) There are large differences between countries in Europe concerning how much they spend for health care services. (2) Countries with underfunded health care systems also have a bad performance regarding equality in access to health care. (3) In some countries, a substantive part of the population (up to 20 percent) has no public health care coverage. (4) High and increasing out-of-pocket payments are a cause for concern in many countries. (5) Inequalities in access are not linked to the model of the health care system. (6) Shortage of health care personnel is a problem in many European countries. (7) Waiting lists for treatments are a major problem in many European countries. (8) Experts warn that voluntary and occupational health insurance might increase inequalities in access to health care. (9) Disadvantaged groups, such as those with lower income as well as ethnic minorities, often face inequalities regarding access to healthcare (Baeten et al. 2018).

11.5 Conclusion

This chapter has analysed health policy in advanced democracies by taking a broad and comparative perspective. In a first step, the chapter has distinguished different realms of health policy by pointing out that health policy entails measures aiming at healing sick individuals but also policies to prevent diseases at the population level. In a second step, the chapter has demonstrated how researchers have distinguished different health systems, how health systems have evolved, and how they are linked to policy outputs. Specifically, the second section shows that researchers have conceived comparative analyses of health systems by either taking a deductive or an inductive approach, with quite different results. Then the second section also discusses how different health systems have evolved and how health expenditure has developed in different countries. Eventually, the second section of the chapter has pointed out how countries differ in their ability to respond to a pandemic. The third section of the chapter has drawn attention to health inequalities as well inequalities in access to health care. The chapter holds that researchers have found health inequalities to be persisting across countries and different institutions of health governance. Furthermore, the chapter has demonstrated that recent scholarship found that different governments have not addressed the fundamental causes of health inequalities as well as access to inequalities in health care.

Overall, this chapter introduces different themes in health policy. Furthermore, the text offers readers information on important frontiers for research in health policy. Notably, these are questions related to the evolution of the private share in health expenditure as well as the persistence of health inequalities in different developed democracies.

References

Agarwal, Rajender, Olena Mazurenko, and Nir Menachemi. 2017. "High-Deductible Health Plans Reduce Health Care Cost And Utilization, Including Use Of Needed Preventive Services." *Health Affairs* 36 (10), 1762–1768.

Alonso, José M., Judith Clifton, and Daniel Díaz-Fuentes. 2015. "The Impact of New Public Management on Efficiency: An Analysis of Madrid's Hospitals." *Health Policy* 119 (3), 333–340.

Anderson, Carrie L., Heiko Becher, and Volker Winkler. 2016. "Tobacco Control Progress in Low and Middle Income Countries in Comparison to High Income Countries." *International Journal of Environmental Research and Public Health* 13 (10), 1039.

Baeten, Rita, Slavina Spasova, Bart Vanhercke, and Stéphanie Coster. 2018. *Inequalities in Access to Healthcare: A Study of National Policies*. Brussels: European Commission. https://data.europa. eu/doi/10.2767/371408 (Accessed 13 October 2021).

Bambra, Clare. 2005. "Cash Versus Services: 'Worlds of Welfare' and the Decommodification of Cash Benefits and Health Care Services." *Journal of Social Policy* 34 (2), 195–213.

Bambra, Clare. 2019. "Governing Health Inequalities." In *The Governance Report*, edited by Hertie School, 51–66. Oxford: Oxford University Press.

Bambra, C., and T. A. Eikemo. 2009. "Welfare State Regimes, Unemployment and Health: A Comparative Study of the Relationship between Unemployment and Self-Reported Health in 23 European Countries." *Journal of Epidemiology & Community Health* 63 (2), 92–98.

Barr, Nicholas. 2020. *Economics of the Welfare State*. Oxford: Oxford University Press.

Bell, Kirsten, Amy Salmon, and Darlene McNaughton. 2011. "Alcohol, Tobacco, Obesity and the New Public Health." *Critical Public Health* 21 (1), 1–8.

Benz, Arthur. 2004. "Governance – Modebegriff oder nützliches sozialwissenschaftliches Konzept?" In *Governance – Regieren in komplexen Regelsystemen: Eine Einführung*, edited by Arthur Benz, 11–28. Wiesbaden: VS Verlag für Sozialwissenschaften.

Blank, Robert, Viola Burau, and Ellen Kuhlmann. 2017. *Comparative Health Policy*. London: Palgrave Macmillan.

Böhm, Katharina, Achim Schmid, Ralf Götze, Claudia Landwehr, and Heinz Rothgang. 2013. "Five Types of OECD Healthcare Systems: Empirical Results of a Deductive Classification." *Health Policy* 113 (3), 258–269.

Cairney, Paul, and Emily St Denny. 2020. *Why Isn't Government Policy More Preventive?* Oxford: Oxford University Press.

Cairney, Paul, Donley Studlar, and Hadi M. Mamudu. 2011. *Global Tobacco Control: Power, Policy, Governance and Transfer*. Houndsmills, Basingstoke: Palgrave Macmillan.

Costa-Font, Joan, and Scott Greer (eds.) 2016. *Federalism and Decentralization in European Health and Social Care*. Houndsmills, Basingstoke: Palgrave.

Dickman, Samuel L., David U. Himmelstein, and Steffie Woolhandler. 2017. "Inequality and the Health-Care System in the USA." *The Lancet* 389 (10077), 1431–1441.

Emmenegger, Patrick, Jon Kvist, Paul Marx, and Klaus Petersen. 2015. "Three Worlds of Welfare Capitalism: The Making of a Classic." *Journal of European Social Policy* 25 (1), 3–13.

Gailmard, Sean, and John W. Patty. 2019. "Preventing Prevention." *American Journal of Political Science* 63 (2), 342–352.

Gilardi, Fabrizio, Katharina Füglister, and Stéphane Luyet. 2009. "Learning From Others: The Diffusion of Hospital Financing Reforms in OECD Countries." *Comparative Political Studies* 42 (4), 549–573.

Greener, Ian. 2002. "Understanding NHS Reform: The Policy-Transfer, Social Learning, and Path-Dependency Perspectives." *Governance* 15 (2), 161–183.

Hacker, Jacob S. 2019. "Medicare Expansion as a Path as Well as a Destination: Achieving Universal Insurance through a New Politics of Medicare." *The ANNALS of the American Academy of Political and Social Science* 685 (1), 135–153.

Hale, Thomas, Noam Angrist, Rafael Goldszmidt, Beatriz Kira, Anna Petherick, Toby Phillips, Samuel Webster, Emily Cameron-Blake, Laura Hallas, Saptarshi Majumdar, and Helen Tatlow. 2021. "A Global Panel Database of Pandemic Policies (Oxford COVID-19 Government Response Tracker)." *Nature Human Behaviour* 5 (4), 529–538.

Healy, Andrew, and Neil Malhotra. 2009. "Myopic Voters and Natural Disaster Policy." *American Political Science Review* 103 (3), 387–406.

Immergut, Ellen M. 1992. *Health Politics: Interests and Institutions in Western Europe*. Cambridge: Cambridge University Press.

Jacobs, Lawrence R., Suzanne Mettler, and Ling Zhu. 2021. "The Pathways of Policy Feedback: How Health Reform Influences Political Efficacy and Participation." *Policy Studies Journal*. https://onlinelibrary.wiley.com/doi/abs/10.1111/psj.12424 (Accessed 6 April 2021).

Kickbusch, Ilona, and Kevin Buckett. 2010. *Implementing Health in All Policies: Adelaide 2010*. Adelaide: Government of South Australia.

Lynch, Julia. 2017. "Reframing Inequality? The Health Inequalities Turn as a Dangerous Frame Shift." *Journal of Public Health* 39 (4), 653–660.

Lynch, Julia. 2020. *Regimes of Inequality: The Political Economy of Health and Wealth*. Cambridge: Cambridge University Press.

Mackenbach, Johan P., Yannan Hu, Barbara Artnik, Matthias Bopp, Giuseppe Costa, Ramune Kalediene, Pekka Martikainen, Gwenn Menvielle, Bjørn H. Strand, Bogdan Wojtyniak, and Wilma J. Nusselder. 2017. "Trends in Inequalities in Mortality Amenable to Health Care in 17 European Countries." *Health Affairs* 36 (6), 1110–1118.

Mackenbach, Johan P. 2019. *Health Inequalities: Persistence and Change in Modern Welfare States*. Oxford and New York: Oxford University Press.

McKee, Martin, Marina Karanikolos, Paul Belcher, and David Stuckler. 2012. "Austerity: A Failed Experiment on the People of Europe." *Clinical Medicine* 12 (4), 346–350.

Oliu-Barton, Miquel, Bary S. R. Pradelski, Philippe Aghion, Patrick Artus, Ilona Kickbusch, Jeffrey V. Lazarus, Devi Sridhar, and Samantha Vanderslott. 2021. "SARS-CoV-2 Elimination, Not Mitigation, Creates Best Outcomes for Health, the Economy, and Civil Liberties." *The Lancet* 397 (10291), 2234–2236.

Reibling, Nadine, Mareike Ariaans, and Claus Wendt. 2019. "Worlds of Healthcare: A Healthcare System Typology of OECD Countries." *Health Policy* 123 (7), 611–620.

Rosenbaum, Sara. 2011. "The Patient Protection and Affordable Care Act: Implications for Public Health Policy and Practice." *Public Health Reports* 126 (1), 130–135.

Rothgang, Heinz, Mirella Cacace, Lorraine Frisina, Simone Grimmeisen, Achim Schmid, and Claus Wendt. 2010. *The State and Healthcare: Comparing OECD Countries*. Houndsmills, Basingstoke: Palgrave Macmillan.

Saltmann, Richard, Reinhard Busse, and Josep Figueira (eds.) 2004. *Social Health Insurance Systems in Western Europe*. New York: Open University Press.

Studlar, Donley T., Kyle Christensen, and Arnita Sitasari. 2011. "Tobacco Control in the EU-15: The Role of Member States and the European Union." *Journal of European Public Policy* 18 (5), 728–745.

Terlizzi, Andrea. 2019. "Health System Decentralization and Recentralization in Italy: Ideas, Discourse, and Institutions." *Social Policy & Administration* 53 (7), 974–988.

Trein, Philipp. 2017. "Coevolution of Policy Sectors: A Comparative Analysis of Healthcare and Public Health." *Public Administration* 95 (3), 744–758.

Trein, Philipp. 2018. *Healthy or Sick? Coevolution of Health Care and Public Health in a Comparative Perspective*. Cambridge: Cambridge University Press.

Uhlmann, Björn, and Dietmar Braun. 2011. *Die schweizerische Krankenversicherungspolitik zwischen Veränderung und Stillstand*. Chur: Rüegger.

Wendt, Claus, Lorraine Frisina, and Heinz Rothgang. 2009. "Healthcare System Types: A Conceptual Framework for Comparison." *Social Policy & Administration* 43 (1), 70–90.

Amílcar Moreira and Daniel Béland

12 COVID-19 and the welfare state: impacts, mechanisms, and responses

Abstract: After emerging at the start of 2020, the COVID-19 pandemic has swept the globe prompting a previously unseen level of damage in modern times – be it in terms of lives lost or of the destruction of economic value. The chapter aims to provide an overview of the existing evidence on how the pandemic has affected the most economically advanced nations, the policy response put in place, and how the interaction between these two has shaped the impact of the COVID-19 pandemic on their economies, labour markets, and the financial situation of individuals/households.

Keywords: COVID-19, containment strategies, economic shock, labour market, fiscal response, social policy, income distribution

12.1 Introduction

In 2003, the outbreak of severe acute respiratory syndrome (SARS) raised alarm bells in the international community concerning the possibility of the emergence of a global pandemic (see LeDuc and Barry 2004). Luckily, those fears did not materialise. Alarms were raised again in 2013, with the outbreak of the Ebola epidemic in Western Africa (CDC 2021). Again, the spread of the virus was successfully contained, and a global pandemic was averted. At the end of 2019, the first cases of COVID-19 were identified in China. On March 11, 2020, the World Health Organization (WHO) declared that, given its alarming levels of spread and severity, COVID-19 should be treated as a global pandemic (WHO 2020). This time, the threat of a massive global pandemic did materialise.

The health, social, and economic upheaval caused by the COVID-19 pandemic is enormous, having even superseded the socio-economic impact of the 2008 Financial Crisis (see Moreira and Hick 2021). The pandemic also prompted a very strong response by public authorities, both to contain the spread of the virus and to mitigate its economic impact (see Béland et al. 2021). Matching the scale of its socio-economic impact, the pandemic also stimulated an unprecedented effort by the academic community to study on the causes, consequences, and response to COVID-19. This translated into numerous studies, cross-national surveys, policy-trackers,[1]

---

[1] For a comprehensive list of the numerous surveys and policy-trackers developed in recent months see the 'Oxford Supertracker' (Daly et al. 2020).

https://doi.org/10.1515/9783110721768-012

and even dedicated publications such as the *COVID Economics* open access journal.[2]

The present chapter aims to provide a stocktake of the evidence that has been accumulated thus far on how the pandemic has affected economically advanced countries, the policy responses they put in place, and how the interaction between these two has shaped the impact of the COVID-19 pandemic on their economies, labour markets, and the financial situation of individuals/households.

With this in mind, the chapter is structured as follows. We first look at the variations in the incidence and severity of the pandemic both across countries and across specific social groups. Then, we discuss the mechanisms by which COVID-19 has impacted on the economies of the most advanced nations. Subsequently, we look at cross-national differences in the policy response to COVID-19 in two critical areas: the efforts to contain the spread of the virus, and the efforts to shield the economy from the negative effects of the pandemic. Building on this, we examine the evidence on how the pandemic has impacted economic activities, the labour markets, and the financial situation of the individuals/families. We conclude with a discussion of the future potential avenues for research on this topic.

12.2 The COVID-19 pandemic in OECD countries

By the time that it was officially classified as a pandemic (March 11, 2020), COVID-19 had already expanded from China to other countries in East-Asia and to Europe and was days away from reaching North America (Moreira and Hick 2021). In Europe at least, the first wave of the pandemic was finally put under control by the end of May. A second wave of the COVID-19 pandemic emerged at the beginning of October 2020. Yet, by the end of the year, as the number of cases was beginning to subside, the emergence of the significantly more contagious and lethal Alpha variant prompted the rise of a third and larger wave of infections and deaths (Turner et al. 2021).

---

2 https://cepr.org/content/covid-economics-vetted-and-real-time-papers.

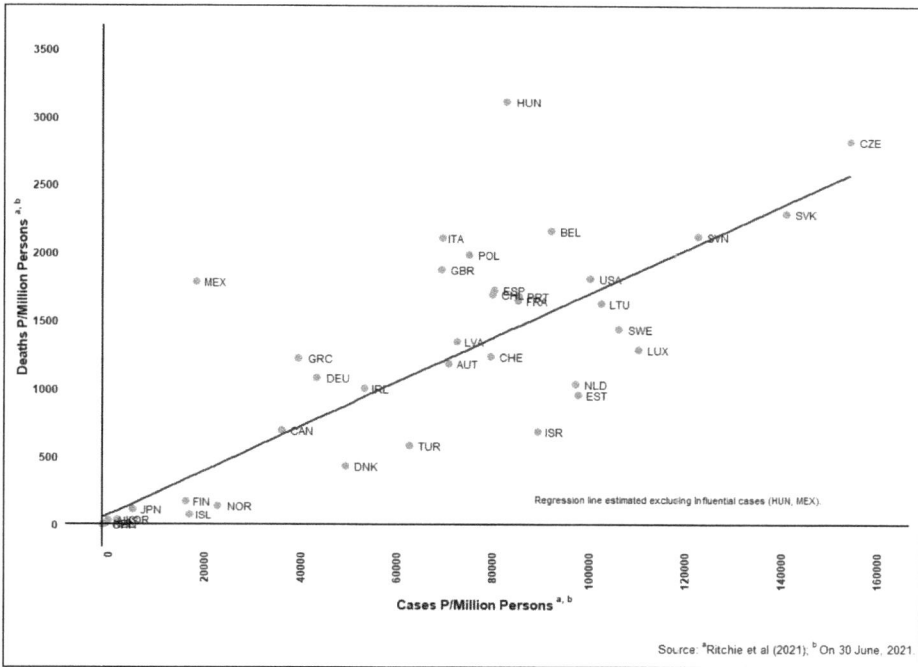

Figure 12.1: Incidence and Severity of COVID-19.

In Figure 12.1, we use the (cumulative) number of COVID-19 infections and the (cumulative) number of COVID-related deaths to chart differences in the incidence and severity of the pandemic across economically advanced countries. As can be seen, up to the end of June 2021, Czechia and Slovenia had been the most hard-hit countries. At the other end, China, Japan, Korea, Australia, New Zealand, Norway, and Finland had been the least affected by the pandemic. Although in general the number of deaths was positively correlated with the number of cases, there were some exceptions. For instance, in Hungry and Mexico the number of deaths was significantly higher than in other countries with comparable levels of COVID-19 cases. At the other end of the scale, Denmark, Turkey, Israel, Estonia, and the Netherlands witnessed a comparably lower rate of COVID deaths.

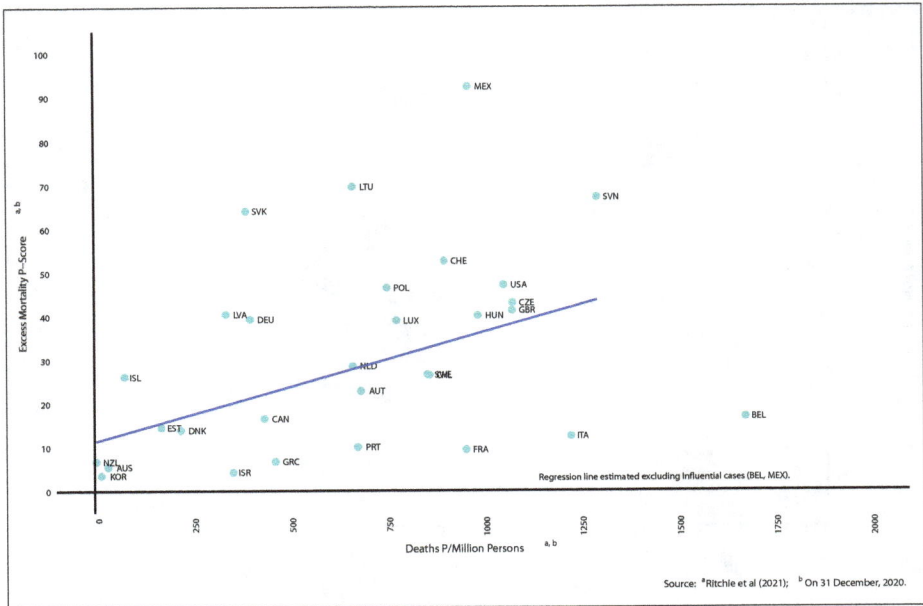

Figure 12.2: Total COVID-19 Deaths, per Million vs. Excess Mortality.

In the sense that it is able to capture the indirect health effects of the pandemic – namely deaths caused by delayed or foregone treatments caused by the overloading of healthcare systems – excess mortality provides us with an important indicator of the full-range of health-related impacts of the COVID-19 pandemic (Morgan et al. 2020). Using the P-Score (for all ages) (Giattino et al. 2022) as a proxy, Figure 12.2 shows that COVID-19 related deaths explain but a small part of the total variation in excess mortality in 2020. Not only that, Figure 12.2 suggests that, in countries like Belgium, Italy and France, the high number of COVID-19 related deaths was compensated by a reduction in other fatalities. In contrast, excess mortality in México, Lithuania, Slovenia and Slovakia was significantly higher than in countries with comparable levels of COVID-19 deaths.[3]

Although proper comparative evidence on these matters is not yet available, Bambra et al (2020) provide comprehensive evidence that suggests there were significant inequalities in the risk of exposure to the virus, and in the severity of the infections. Thus, workers in more elementary occupations (builders, cleaners, carers, etc.) and working in certain sectors (agriculture or the care and leisure industry) seemed to face

---

3 Besides significant differences in excess mortality across 29 advanced economies, Islam et al. (2021) find that controlling for age differences, in 2020, excess mortality rates were much higher for men than for women.

a higher risk of COVID-19 related death than other workers. Inequalities across ethic lines were also particularly visible, with individuals from ethnic minorities displaying higher risks of infection, hospitalisation, and death. In fact, Bambra et al (2020) go on to argue that these inequalities reflected, and exacerbated, previously recorded inequalities in both economic status and the prevalence of chronic conditions, a situation pointing to the social determinants of health. In that sense, for deprived communities, COVID-19 was experienced as a syndemic.

12.3 A pandemic shock to the economy

As the pandemic spread across countries, economists and international organisations turned their focus to understanding how the pandemic would impact the economies of affected countries (see European Commission 2020; Eichenbaum, Rebelo, and Trabandt 2020).[4]

The research on this topic is structured along two key issues. The first concerns whether the pandemic (and the adoption of lockdown measures) would lead either to a reduction in the labour used to produce goods (i.e., aggregate supply shock) or to a reduction in demand (i.e. aggregate demand shock) (see Auray and Eyquem 2020 and Brinca, Duarte, and Faria-e-Castro 2020).[5]

The second issue concerns whether the economic impact of the pandemic is the product of the restrictions (work-place closures, travel restrictions, etc.) put in place to contain the spread of the virus (see section 12.4.1), or if this is driven instead by the (voluntary) reduction of social activities prompted by the fear of infection.[6]

Looking through the literature, we do find evidence that the adoption of non-pharmaceutical interventions (NPIs) to curb the spread of the pandemic was successful in reducing mobility (see Mendolia, Stavrunova, and Yerokhin 2021: Santamaria et al. 2020), particularly in high income countries (Maloney and Taskin 2020; Pincombe, Reese, and Dolan 2021). They have also led to a reduction in daily activities (Connolly et al. 2021). Not only that, Deb et al. (2020) find that the confinement measures introduced in 57 countries in response to the first outbreaks of COVID-19 accounted for an estimated (month-on-month) 15% drop in industrial production. Dreger and Gros (2020) also find a negative correlation between industrial production and the strictness of confinement measures in Europe.

---

4 For a tentative systematisation of the mechanisms identified in the early literature, see Moreira and Hick (2021).

5 For a simulation of the potential impact of the COVID-19 pandemic on the demand and supply sides see Del Rio-Chanona et al. 2020.

6 Although this is not covered in detail here, another important part of this debate is whether the adoption less restrictive confinement measures will not hurt the economy in the medium/long-term (see Bodenstein, Corsetti, and Guerrieri 2020).

However, there is evidence to suggest that the impact of confinement measures on mobility might be smaller than initially anticipated. Maloney and Taskin (2020) and the IMF (2020) suggest that, in high income countries, voluntary self-confinement was more important than NPIs at explaining reductions in mobility. By pointing that mobility in Europe increased well before the lift of lockdown measures, Chen et al. (2020) further stress the idea that compliance needs to be taken into consideration when assessing the impact of confinement measures on mobility.[7]

Furthermore, there is also evidence that the impact of confinement policies on economic activities might be smaller than previously thought. Using restaurant reservations and theatre revenues as indicators of economic activity in the US and Sweden (respectively), Maloney and Taskin (2020) argue that drops in economic activity predated the adoption of confinement measures. Chen et al. (2020) show that, for Europe, the positive correlation between the stringency of confinement policies and energy consumption only held for the first weeks of the pandemic. In fact, according to the authors, economic activity started to increase before the lift of confinement measures.

12.4 The policy response to the COVID-19 pandemic

As Moreira and Hick (2021) show, across economically advanced countries, the COVID-19 pandemic prompted a rapid and very comprehensive response from policymakers. In this section, we focus on two areas that are more significant to understand differences in the socio-economic impact of the pandemic: the measures to contain the spread of the virus, and the measures to shield the economy from the effects of the pandemic.

12.4.1 Containing the spread of the pandemic

Upon the outset the COVID-19 pandemic, countries put in place a range of policies to break transmission chains through contact-tracing systems (Quilty et al. 2021) and to contain the spread of the virus through non-pharmaceutical interventions (travel bans, imposing restrictions on public gatherings and public events, stay-at-home orders, and restrictions on internal movement) aimed at reducing the possibility of transmission (OECD 2020a).

---

7 For a discussion of the factors influencing the effectiveness of confinement policies see Castex, Dechter, and Lorca 2020.

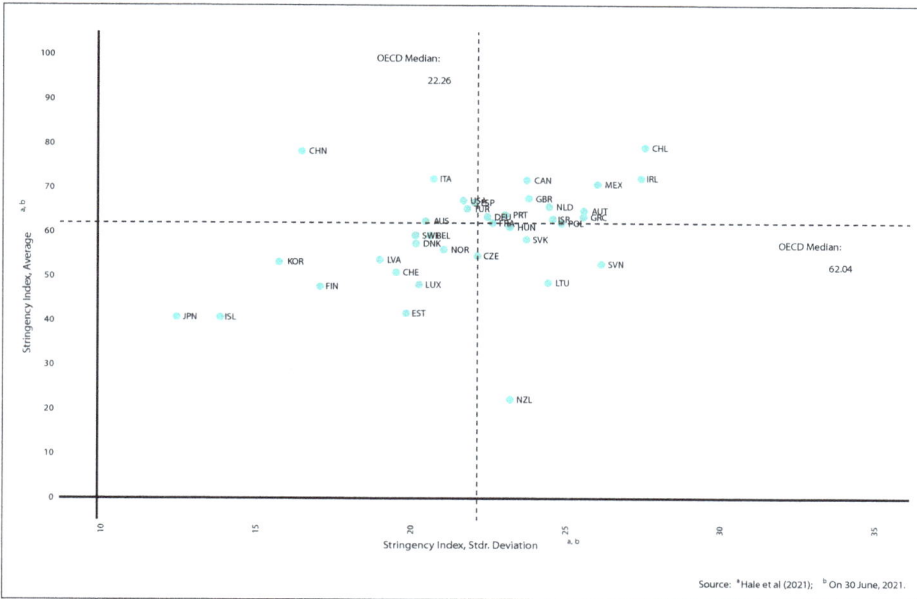

Figure 12.3: Stringency of COVID-19 Containment Policies.

Perhaps reflecting the importance given to non-pharmaceutical interventions in explaining the impact of the pandemic on economic activities, a significant share of the literature tries to map differences in the use of such interventions. Put forward by Hale et al. (2021), the COVID-19 Stringency Index has become a popular benchmark to compare cross-national differences in the strictness of these measures (see OECD 2020b; Fuller et al. 2020; König and Winkler, 2021).[8]

In Figure 12.3, we use the COVID-19 Stringency Index to capture cross-national differences in the stringency of containment measures in OECD (Organisation for Economic Co-operation and Development) countries – and how this has varied over time – as captured by the standard deviation of the this indicator during the period under analysis. As can be seen, with some notable exceptions (New Zealand, Japan and Iceland), there are no significant differences in containment strategies pursued in most OECD member states, both with regard to the (overall) strictness of the measures adopted and their degree of variation over time. This seems to suggest that, as the various waves of COVID-19 hit, countries have mimicked (if not coordinated) containment efforts between each other.

An alternative, and perhaps more fruitful, literature stream on this topic seeks to understand how the contact-tracing and containment measures are combined to pursue different strategies to deal with the COVID-19 pandemic. Countries are compared by reference to three ideal-typical strategies:

---

8 For an alternative approach see Gros, Ounnas, and Yeung 2021.

– The mitigation strategy, epitomised by Sweden, aims to generate community (herd) immunity by allowing the controlled infection of people, while minimising the associated morbidity and mortality burden of the virus and the impact on the economy, the educational system, and the response capacity of the healthcare system. This strategy is implemented through risk-tailored strategies to protect seniors against the risk of contagion, and on recommendations – rather than restrictive measures – about social distancing (see Kayı and Sakarya 2020; Baral et al. 2021).

– The elimination/suppression strategy, best exemplified by New Zealand, aims at quickly stopping the reproduction of the virus while reducing the incidence of COVID cases to zero. This goal is achieved through the extensive use of track-and-trace to contain transmission chains as well as a systematic and (rapidly) scalable response, starting with travel restrictions, moving quickly to measure to enforce social distancing all the way to mandatory (and fully universal) stay-at-home orders (see Jefferies et al. 2020; Lu et al. 2021).

– The containment ('flattening the curve') strategy, which is the most popular strategy, involves containing the spread of the virus (ideally bellow a basic reproduction number (Ro) of 1) with the aim of protecting the response capacity of hospitals and, in particular, of intensive care units. While making use of a similar range of tools, this type of approach relies less on contact-tracing than the elimination strategy (see Kayı and Sakarya, 2020; Lu et al. 2021).

Later on, as vaccines finally became available, large-scale vaccination schemes were implemented to foster community immunity (Turner et al. 2021).

12.4.2 Shielding the economy from the effects of the pandemic

Acknowledging the potential detrimental impacts of the pandemic on their economies, governments put forward a series of policies to mitigate these effects. This involved both adjustments to macro-economic policy and the leveraging of fiscal policy to support firms and households (see Bemelech and Tzur-Ilan 2020). In the remainder of this section, we focus on the use of the fiscal policies to minimise the impact of the pandemic.

As can be seen in Table 12.1, this leveraging of fiscal policies involved two sets of measures to help firms and households deal with the direct impact of the pandemic: budgetary measures to support individuals/households infected by COVID-19 and/or subsidise firms so that they can keep their workers; and liquidity measures to improve the liquidity (and financial resilience) of firms and households.[9]

---

[9] A number of international organisations such as the OECD (2021c), IMF (2021), or Eurofound 2021a have put together policy-trackers that monitor the policies introduced during this period. For a more

Table 12.1: Fiscal Response to COVID-19[a, b]

	Budgetary Measures	Liquidity Measures
Expenditure Side	– Wage subsidies – Paid Sick and Family Leave – Enhancement or extension of unemployment benefits – Front loading of planned social expenditure	– Government loans to business and households – Equity injections – Guarantees on business loans – Advancement of refunds for firms
Revenue Side	– Cuts to Value-Added-Tax – Cuts to social security contributions	– Expanding loss carry-back rules – Postponing social security contributions – Reducing advance tax payments

Notes:

[a] Based on IMF 2021; Haroutunian, Osterloh, and Sławińska 2021; and Moreira and Hick 2021.

[b] Although they directly impact on the government fiscal balance, increases in spending that are not meant to deal with the impact of COVID-19 on jobs and incomes (such as healthcare or education) are not included here.

The first attempts at mapping these type of meayres pointed to important variations in their size and composition in the initial fiscal response to the COVID-19 pandemic (Benmelech and Tzur-Ilan 2020; Siddik 2020; Moreira and Hick 2021; Li and Liang 2021; Chen et al. 2021). However, as they were based on data from the fiscal packages announced at the start of the pandemic, these studies only capture differences in the planned response and not in the policies as effectively implemented.

---

systematic approach at comparing the initial policy response to COVID-19, see Béland et al. (2021) and Moreira and Hick (2021).

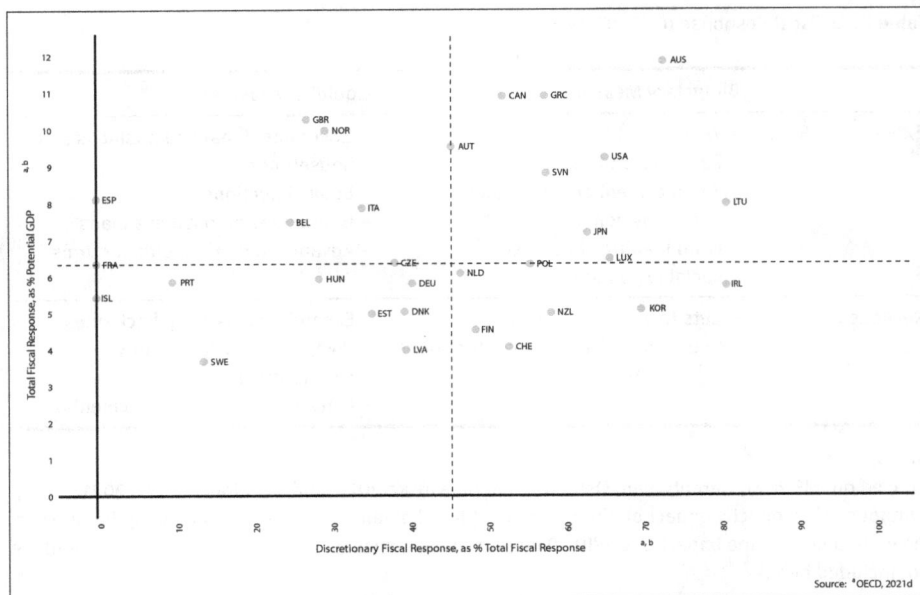

Figure 12.4: Discretionary Fiscal Response to COVID-19.

A more adequate approach for comparing the fiscal response to the COVID-19 is to look at the changes in the government fiscal balance (see Cameron 2012; Raess and Pontusson 2015).[10] In the event of a contraction of GDP, the overall fiscal balance is expected to depreciate as a result of a) policies enacted by governments to counteract the impact of crisis (i.e., the discretionary fiscal response); b) the automatic response prompted by a set of rules/institutions (i.e., automatic stabilisers) in the tax system and the welfare system, which help stabilise variations in the business cycle;[11] and, finally, c) changes in the value of interest payments (Fedelino, Ivanova, and Horton 2009).

---

10 Admittedly, this type of approach fails to capture important dimensions of the fiscal response to COVID-19, namely the impact of measures to strengthen the liquidity of firms and households and the frontloading spending, that that are not reflected in the general government primary balance.

11 The size of the automatic response is determined by the design of these institutions. Progressive tax systems have a stronger stabilising effect than flat-tax systems. Unemployment benefits with less stringent entitlement conditions will also have a stronger stabilising effect (Fedelino, Ivanova, and Horton 2009).

In Figure 12.4, we depict cross-national differences in the size[12] and composition[13] of the fiscal response to COVID-19 in 2020. As can be seen, the fiscal response to COVID-19 was quite substantive – with the median response valued at 6.3% of potential GDP. The total fiscal response was particularly strong in Australia, Greece, Canada and the UK – where it exceeded 10% of potential GDP. At the other extreme of the fiscal scale, Sweden, Latvia, Czechia, Finland, Slovakia and Estonia put forward a fiscal response worth only between 4 and 5% of potential GDP.

Moreover, we identify four distinct fiscal approaches in dealing with the economic impact of COVID-19. The first approach, which is best illustrated by Australia, involves a large fiscal response fundamentally driven by discretionary policies put in place in response to the pandemic. The second approach, epitomised by Great Britain and Norway, consists in a large fiscal response that is fundamentally driven by automatic stabilisers in the tax and benefit system. A third approach, exemplified by Sweden, involves a limited fiscal response to COVID-19 mostly driven by the effect of automatic stabilisers. A fourth (even if less well-defined) approach, consists in a moderate/low fiscal response, but that relies more on discretionary policies than in other countries with a comparable aggregate fiscal response. This approach is best exemplified by Ireland and Korea.

12.5 The role of the welfare state in the response to the pandemic

As the previous section makes clear, cross-national differences in the size of the fiscal response to COVID-19 and in the importance given to automatic stabilisers intercept the dividing lines between the traditional models of social protection in advanced economies (Esping-Andersen 1990; Bonoli 1997; Arts and Gelissen 2002). This, of course, raises questions as to how countries have used social policies to respond to the COVID-19 pandemic and to what degree differences in the response to the pandemic reflect differences in the prevailing model of social protection.

Looking at the existing literature on this, the first feature that stands out is that social policies were used not only as means to protect citizens from the sudden and ne-

---

12 With the view to capture differences in the total fiscal response (vertical axis), we look at the year-on-year change in the primary fiscal balance, which corresponds to change in the overall fiscal balance, subtracted by the variation in interest payments, as a percentage of potential GDP (Raess and Pontusson 2015).

13 With the view to capture differences in the composition of the fiscal response to COVID-19, we look at discretionary fiscal response (horizontal axis), measured as the year-on-year change in the cyclically-adjusted primary balance, as percentage of potential GDP, as a share of the total fiscal response (see Raess and Pontusson 2015).

gative economic impact of the pandemic, but also as means to sustain non-pharmaceutical interventions to stop the spread of the virus (see Moreira and Hick, 2021).[14]
This involved the adoption of measures to expand existing sickness benefits to cover
COVID-related infections and the enactment of schemes to support families who are
required to provide care for children subsequent to the closure of schools and childcare facilities (see Baptista et al. 2021).

The other notable feature is that job-retention schemes,[15] rather than unemployment benefits, were at the forefront of the social policy response to the COVID-19 pandemic (Baptista et al. 2021; Moreira and Hick, 2021). As evidenced by the recent OECD
Employment Outlook (OECD 2021a), a number of countries introduced temporary
wage subsidy schemes to help companies to retain workers in the face of the steep
economic contraction prompted by the pandemic. Not only that, access to this type of
scheme has been made easier and the payments have been made more generous.

Parallel to efforts to retain employees, developed nations have sought to strength-
en the safety-nets for those in a more precarious position in the labour market. Access
to unemployment benefits was facilitated, and their duration was extended (Baptista
et al. 2021). Eligibility rules to social assistance were also relaxed, and the generosity
and duration of payments was increased in a number of countries (Baptista et al.
2021; Moreira and Hick 2021). Moreover, a number of countries have introduced targeted, temporary, schemes to provide income protection to the self-employed (Baptista et al. 2021).

The final noticeable feature concerns the focus given to housing policies in the
fight against COVID-19 (see Moreira and Hick 2021). A significant number of advanced
economies introduced temporary schemes to support tenants and mortgage holders,
including bans on evictions or pay deferrals. A number of countries have also introduced measures to provide temporary housing solutions for homeless (Baptista et al.
2021).

As the previous paragraphs show, there are important commonalities in how
more developed nations have responded to the economic fallout of the COVID-19 pandemic. Does this mean that the response to the economic fallout of COVID-19 is fundamentally shaped by the depth and specificity of the crisis (see Section 12.3)? Or that,
however similar in nature and objective, these measures are implemented in a way
that reflects the institutional legacies of the prevailing models of social protection?

Although it does not provide definite answers, a special issue of *Social Policy &
Administration* – co-edited by Béland et al. (2021) provides a set of important insights

---

14 Looking at evidence from the US, Warner and Zhang (2021) show that having stronger safety-nets
allowed policymakers to pursue more stringent containment strategies, namely anticipating the introduction of stay-at-home orders – and delaying the lifting of these measures.
15 For a comprehensive overview of the use of wage subsidies/ furlough/short time schemes in the response to the COVID-19 pandemic see Konle-Seidl (2020), OECD (2020b), and Ebbinghaus and Lenher
(2022). On the effectiveness of these schemes, see IMF (2021) and OECD (2021a).

on this matter. For instance, Greve et al. (2021) suggest that, despite differences in the epidemiological approach adopted to contain the pandemic, the policy response to COVID-19 in the Nordic regime[16] was largely path-dependent. In contrast, the social policy response in Liberal countries,[17] involving the introduction of job retention schemes and substantive increases in welfare payments, signifies a visible (even if temporary) departure from the prevailing principles that organise social protection (Hick and Murphy 2021).

There is also evidence of important path-dependencies in shaping the response to COVID-19, but that reflect long-term processes of intra-group divergence. Looking at developments in the Continental Regime, Cantillon et al. (2021) show that differences in the policy response between Belgium and Germany and the Netherlands reflect the fact that the last two have moved in a liberal direction in recent years. Looking at the East Asian Regime, Soon et al. (2021) show that unlike China and Taiwan, Japan and Korea have put a greater emphasis on support to childcare and those in precarious employment – which reflects the shift towards the social investment paradigm in these two countries.

12.5.1 Assessing the impact of the COVID-19 pandemic

On economic output

Unfortunately, the literature on the factors that explain such large differences in the economic impact of the COVID-19 pandemic remains scarce (but see Deb et al. 2020; Sapir 2020; König and Winkler 2021; Pitterle and Niermann 2021). Moreover, some studies (Sapir 2020; Pitterle and Niermann 2021) only look at the factors that influence downward revisions of GDP in 2020. Still, the existing evidence does provide important insights into the factors that might explain differences in the economic impact of the COVID-19 pandemic.

Based on a large sample of 156 (developed, developing, and transition) countries, and controlling for a variety of other factors – stringency of containment measures, size of the fiscal response, quality of governance, and degree of (macro)economic vulnerability – Pitterle and Niermann (2021) find that countries with a higher number of COVID-19 deaths (per 100.000 people) saw larger drops in GDP growth. However, looking at the effective changes in GDP in the first three quarters of 2020 in 42 advanced economies, König and Winkler (2021) do not confirm this. In fact, their analysis suggests that the impact of the mortality rate on GDP was only visible during the

---

16 Greve et al. (2021) cover policy developments in Denmark, Sweden, Finland, and Norway.
17 Hick and Murphy (2021) cover policy developments in the UK and Ireland.

second quarter of 2020, once most of the countries had introduced fairly strict confinement policies, and disappeared in the third quarter of the same year.

As evident in Figure 12.5, the COVID-19 pandemic affected the economies of OECD member states in a very diverse way. The UK, Mexico, and Southern European countries were hit particularly hard, registering GDP drops between minus 8% and minus 11%, compared to the previous year. In contrast, Norway, New Zealand, Korea and Lithuania were relatively spared, with GDP drops under 2%. Although it has not produced an outright recession, the pandemic also trimmed annual growth in China (from 6% to 2.3%) and Ireland (from 5.9% to 2.5%). The only exception to this was Turkey, who saw a small GDP increase (from 0.9% to 1.8%) in 2020 (OECD 2021b).

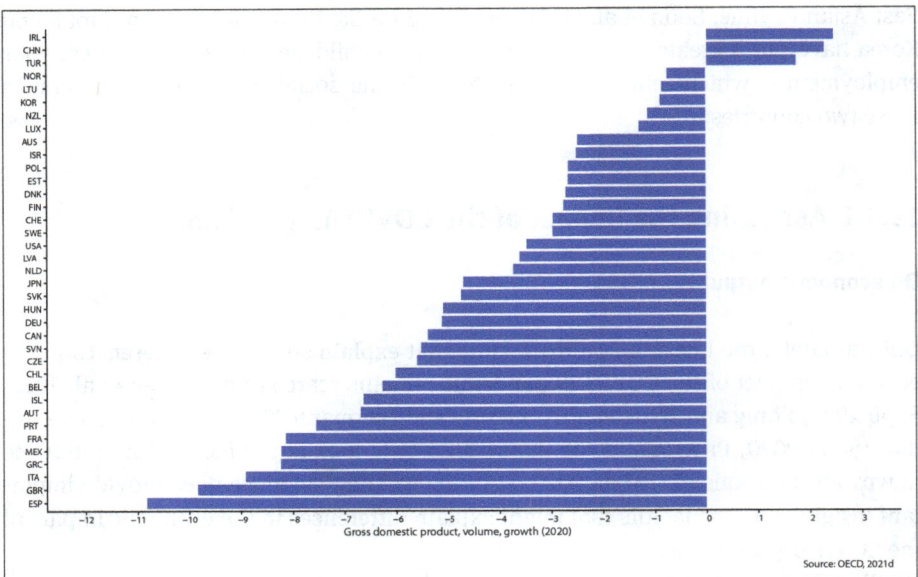

Figure 12.5: GDP Growth Rates in OECD countries, 2020.

Using the share of tourism as a portion of GDP as a measure of the structural vulnerability of the economy facing the pandemic, Sapir (2020) and Pitterle and Niermann (2021) find that countries that relied more on tourism saw larger downward revisions in GDP growth. This finding is further confirmed by König and Winkler (2021), who show that the importance of tourism in a country's economy is among the most important predictors of the cross-national differences in the pandemic's economic impact.

Consistent with the evidence that suggests that the size of the fiscal response helped to mitigate the economic impact of previous pandemics (see Ma, Rogers, and Zhou 2020), Deb et al. (2020) find that the negative effect of containment measures on economic activity (as measured by nitrogen dioxide emissions) proved stronger in countries with a smaller fiscal response. Pitterle and Niermann (2021) also find that, controlling for confounding variables, countries with larger fiscal stimulus witnessed smaller downward revisions of GDP growth. However, these results are sensitive to the choice of estimation strategy (see Pitterle and Niermann 2021).

Finally, Sapir (2020) as well as König and Winkler (2020) suggest that the quality of institutions strongly mediated the economic impact of the COVID-19 pandemic. Thus, controlling for other factors, countries that with better governance infrastructures witnessed smaller downward revisions of GDP/drops in GDP.

On the labour market

Looking at the changes in total employment alone (see Figure 12.6), it could be reasonably argued that the impact of the pandemic on labour markets was fairly weak – namely if taking into consideration the sharp drops in economic output. Thus, most countries experienced a reduction in total employment of ranging between 1% and 2%. The exceptions were Mexico, the US, and Spain, which experienced large reductions in total employment of 7.3%, 5.5% and 4.2%, respectively.

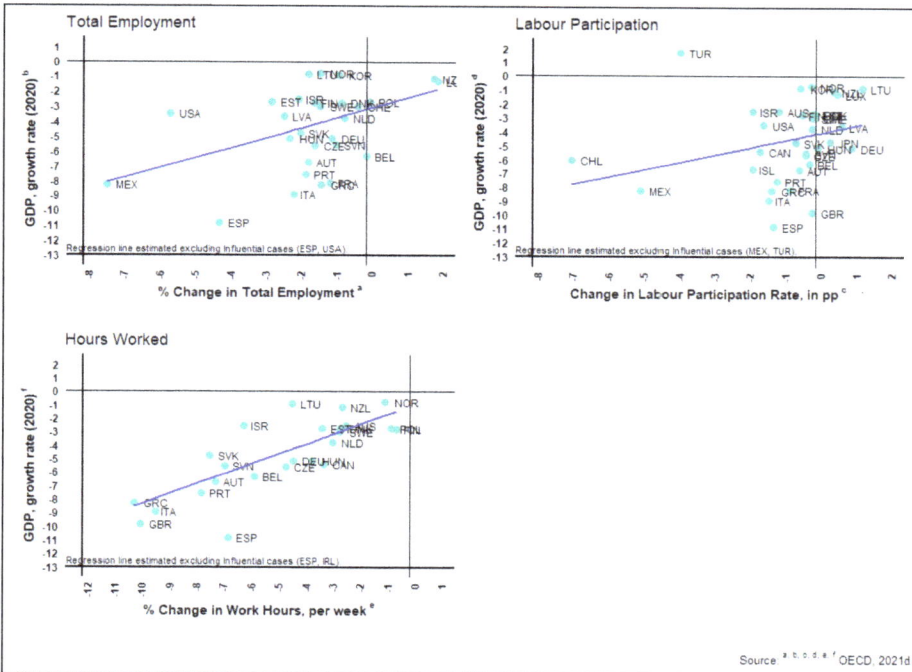

Figure 12.6: Key Labour Market Outcomes of COVID-19.

As it captures both the destruction of jobs and the reduction in the number of hours worked prompted by the combined effect of workplace closures and furlough schemes, the change in the number of hours worked is perhaps a better indicator of how COVID-19 impacted labour market dynamics in economically advanced countries. As can be seen in Figure 12.6, the reduction in hours worked was very much in line with the drop in economic output. Thus, countries whose economies were significantly more impacted by the pandemic – such as the UK, Greece, and Italy – were also the countries with the steepest reductions in the number of hours worked (by 10%, 9.9% and 9%, respectively). In contrast, countries like Finland, Poland and Norway, whose economies have been the least affected by the pandemic, only reported marginal losses (under 1%) in the number of hours worked.

The comprehensive use of furlough/short-time schemes in the economic response to the COVID-19 pandemic helps explain why the reduction in hours worked did not translate into a substantive increase in unemployment (see Figure 12.6).[18] This is particularly evident in the evolution of unemployment in the US and Canada, which chose not to use these types of schemes in their response to the pandemic (see OECD 2021b).

However, this is not the whole story. As can be seen in Figure 12.6, labour market participation rates declined in a number of OECD countries. According to an OECD Employment Outlook (2021a), this decline reflects a variety of situations: a) persons who, having lost their job, stopped looking for work (due to the limitations imposed by the pandemic) and have thus been classified as inactive; b) people (namely, women) who were forced to stay at home to provide care to their children (or dependent adults); and c) young people who left the education system and struggled to find a job in a tight labour market.

Importantly, the existing evidence points to important variations in how job losses and working hour reductions were distributed within the labour market, both across groups and over time. Evidence of the European Labour Force Survey suggests that "contact-intensive" sectors – such as accommodation, the travel industry, and the food and beverages industry – saw the largest reductions in the number of jobs and of hours worked (per week) in 2020 (Eurofound 2021b).[19] There is also evidence suggesting that job losses were particularly frequent among younger workers (ILO 2021). People in non-standard employment and women were particularly affected by the initial shock of the COVID crisis, but this effect decreased over time (OECD 2021b).

---

18 In fact, the OECD Employment Outlook (2021a) suggests that two-thirds of the decline in hours in OECD countries relate to the use of furlough/short-time schemes.
19 In contrast, more knowledge-intensive sectors such as the telecommunications and information industry where productive activities can be more easily transferred from of the workplace actually registered an increase in total employment (Eurofound 2021b).

On the financial situation of households

Having looked at the impact of COVID-19 on economic output and on labour markets, we now turn to how the pandemic impacted on the financial situation of households. Although data on this topic remains scarce – especially concerning changes in household's disposable income (see Figure 12.7) – the existing evidence does seem to suggest that the impact of the pandemic on household finances largely depends on whether the employment situation of one of the members household has been affected.

Households that were not directly affected by the pandemic benefited from a double dividend. First, they saw their earnings from work increase (see Figure 12.7). Second, as the result of the forced contraction in spending prompted by the pandemic, they were able to accumulate important savings (see Figure 12.7, top right). In fact, as can be seen in Figure 12.7, even countries that were heavily affected by the pandemic such as Italy, Portugal, and Canada saw very significant increases in household savings.

By contrast, the households directly affected by the pandemic saw their financial situation significantly disrupted. Looking at the immediate impact of the crisis (April 2020) in four European countries, Cantó et al. (2021) point to significant drops in households' original income (i.e., income before transfers and taxes) – ranging from 16 % in Spain to 26 % in Italy. The same study also suggests that, with the exception of Italy, the impact of the pandemic was significantly regressive, with lower income groups reporting larger drops in original income.

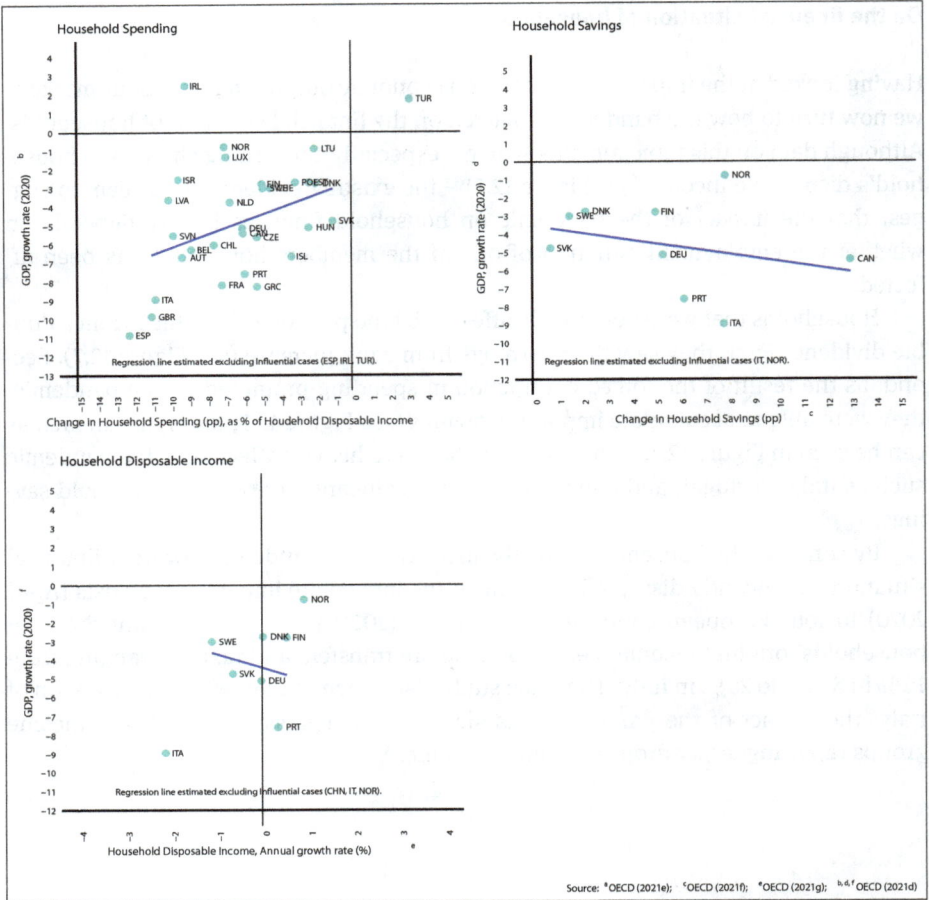

Figure 12.7: Impact of COVID-19 on Household Finances.

Although the body of literature on the distributional effects of the fiscal response to COVID-19 has been growing,[20] the comparative evidence (Almeida et al. 2021; Cantó et al. 2021) on this topic remains scarce. Not only that, the difference in the methodologies adopted make the findings of existing studies difficult to compare.[21]

---

20 For country-based assessments of the distributional effects of policy-responses to COVID-19, see Li et al. (2020) on Australia; Marchal et al. (2021) on Belgium; Bruckmeier et al. (2021) on Germany; Figari and Fiorio (2020) on Italy; O'Donoghue et al. (2020) and Beirne et al. (2020) on Ireland; Bronka, Collado, and Richiardi (2020), and Brewer and Tasseva (2020) on the UK.

21 Almeida et al (2021) provide a comprehensive study of the distributive impact of discretionary fiscal response to the pandemic in EU member states. Yet, their analysis focuses on the impact of fiscal policies on the families directly affected by the pandemic. Cantó et al (2021) offer a more systematic ap-

Still, the existing evidence does suggest that that the fiscal policies put in place during this period strong moderating effect. A counterfactual analysis carried out by Almeida et al. (2021) covering all European Union (EU) member states suggests that (on average) the adoption of discretionary measures during the first year of the pandemic reduced the drop in household disposable income from 9.3 % to 4.3 %. According to Cantó et al. (2021), if the effect of automatic stabilisers is accounted for, the moderator effect of the fiscal response to COVID-19 proved even stronger than that suggested by Almeida et al. (2021).

The fiscal response to COVID-19 not only reduced the impact of the pandemic on households' disposable income, but it also helped to reduce its regressive nature. According to Almeida et al. (2021), the discretionary fiscal measures introduced during 2020 prompted a more homogenous drop in disposable income across income deciles – ranging from 6.2 % for the lowest income decile to 3.8 % in the top income decile. Focusing solely on directly affected families, Cantó et al. (2021) point to a very strong moderating effect, which allows for the full reversion of the regressive effects of the pandemic on the distribution of incomes.[22]

The combination between increased earnings and savings and the strong moderating effect of the fiscal policies enacted during this period to assist those directly affected by the pandemic may help explain why the (overall) disposable income of families did not fall in line with the drop in economic output. In fact, in a number of countries, disposable income actually increased in 2020 (see Figure 12.7, bottom).

12.6 Conclusion

As mentioned at the start of this chapter, the COVID-19 pandemic has prompted an unprecedented surge in data collection and analysis in all relevant fields of scientific knowledge. In the previous sections, we have charted the established knowledge about the health and economic impacts of the pandemic and the policy responses to it. Although much knowledge has been gained, further research on this topic will be required, in part to inform future policy responses to COVID-19 and other pandemics.

---

proach, which covers the impact of both discretionary fiscal policies and automatic stabilisers. However, they only cover a restricted number of countries (Italy, Spain, Belgium, and the UK) and the policies introduced in the first two months of the pandemic crisis.

22 In this regard, Canto et al. (2021) provide important insight as to how the combination between automatic stabilisers (unemployment benefits, means-tested benefits and tax/social security contributions) and discretionary measures (notably, earning compensation schemes to employees and self-employed) help explain differences in the moderating effect of the fiscal response on the economic impact of the pandemic.

To a certain degree, the future research on this topic will be influenced by how the pandemic is likely to evolve and by how fast the economies of economically advanced countries will recover. As the 2021 OECD Economic Outlook (2021b) points out, this will depend on the progress made in the deployment of vaccines, and on their efficacy in the face of COVID-19 variants. If vaccine production is not sufficient to contain the spread of the virus, and/or if the new variants emerge for which the current vaccines do not provide sufficient protection, it might be necessary to reintroduce confinement measures, a situation that would surely dampen economic recovery. More specifically, the limited availability of vaccines in many low-income countries is a global challenge that could make it difficult to actually end the pandemic (Padma 2021).

Other than continue to monitor the dynamics of the pandemic and the pace of economic recovery, future research will certainly have to look at what are the likely long-term effects of the pandemic. An obvious topic of interest concerns the impact of what has been dubbed 'Long-COVID' – a condition whereby the symptoms associated with COVID-19 persist for more than 12 weeks (see Sykes et al. 2021). Besides adding to our knowledge about the risk-factors associated with this condition, future research should look at the policies that are being put in place to protect the jobs and incomes of individuals/households affected by this condition.

Further research should also focus on the long-term effects of the socio-economic shocks imposed by the pandemic. Simulations produced by the World Bank (Azevedo et al. 2020) and Hanushek and Woessmann (2020) suggest that the school closures of 2020 could lead to important short-term learning losses among school-aged children and also drops in their life-time incomes. Even though comparative evidence on this is not yet available, country-based case studies seem to confirm this early prediction (see Engzell, Frey, and Verhagen 2021). With this in mind, further research should also seek to generate new evidence about the impact of school closures on learning losses, but also on the recovery strategies adopted by different countries to mitigate those losses (see Azevedo et al. 2020).

In line with the accumulated evidence of the long-term impacts of both unemployment in the early stage of one's career (Schmillen and Umkehrer 2017) and entering the labour market during a recession (Kahn 2010), more research will also be needed on how the COVID recession hit young workers/labour market entrants.

Finally, further research is necessary on the distributional impacts of the pandemic, both within countries (Sayed and Peng 2021) and at the global level (Deaton 2021). In particular, given that women were particularly affected by the pandemic (more represented in high-exposure professions/sectors and forced to take on more care work during school closures), more research should study how the pandemic helped to reshape the gap between men and women in the labour market – both in the short and in the long-term.

References

Almeida, V., S. Barrios, M. Christl, S. De Poli, A. Tumino, and W. van der Weilen. 2021. "The Impact of COVID-19 on Households' Income in the EU." *Journal of Economic Inequality*, 19, 413–431.

Arts, W., and J. Gelissen. 2002. "Three Worlds of Welfare Capitalism or More?" *Journal of European Social Policy* 12 (2), 137–158.

Auray, S., and A. Eyquem. 2020. "The Macroeconomic Effects of Lockdown Policies." *Journal of Public Economics* 190 (6), 104260. DOI: 10.1016/j.jpubeco.2020.104260

Azevedo, J. P., A. Hasan, D. Goldemberg, S. A. Iqbal, and K. Geven. 2020. *Simulating the Potential Impacts of COVID-19 School Closures on Schooling and Learning Outcomes: A Set of Global Estimates*. Policy Research Working Paper 9284. https://elibrary.worldbank.org/doi/abs/10.1596/1813-9450-9284

Bambra, C., R. Riordan, J. Ford, and F. Matthews. 2020. "The COVID-19 Pandemic and Health Inequalities." *Journal of Epidemiology and Community Health* 74 (11), 964–968.

Baptista, I., E. Marlier, S. Spasova, R. Peña-Casas, B. Fronteddu, D. Ghailani, S. Sabato, and P. Regazzoni. 2021. *Social Protection and Inclusion Policy Responses to the COVID-19 Crisis. An Analysis of Policies in 35 Countries*. https://data.europa.eu/doi/10.2767/10153

Baral, S., R. Chandler, R. Prieto, S. Gupta, S. Mishra, and M. Kulldorff. 2021. "Leveraging Epidemiological Principles to Evaluate Sweden's COVID-19 Response." *Annals of Epidemiology* 54, 21–26.

Beirne, K., K. Doorley, M. Regan, B. Roantree, and D. Tuda. 2020. *The Potential Costs and Distributional Effect of COVID-19 Related Unemployment in Ireland*. EUROMOD Working Paper 05/20, Institute for Social and Economic Research, University of Essex, Essex, UK.

Béland, D., B. Cantillon, R. Hick, and A. Moreira. 2021. "Social Policy in the Face of a Global Pandemic: Policy Responses to the COVID-19 Crisis." *Social Policy & Administration* 55 (2), 249–260.

Benmelech, E., and N. Tzur-Ilan. 2020. *The Determinants of Fiscal and Monetary Policies During the Covid-19 Crisis*, NBER Working Paper 27461. Cambridge, MA: National Bureau of Economic Research.

Bodenstein, M., G. Corsetti, and L. Guerrieri. 2020. *Social Distancing and Supply Disruptions in a Pandemic*, Finance and Economics Discussion Series 2020-031. Washington: Board of Governors of the Federal Reserve System. https://doi.org/10.17016/FEDS.2020.031.

Bonoli, G. 1997. "Classifying Welfare States: A Two-Dimension Approach." *Journal of Social Policy* 26 (3), 351–372.

Brewer, M. and I. Tasseva. 2020. *Did the UK Policy Response to COVID-19 Protect Household Incomes?* EUROMOD Working Paper 12/20, Institute for Social and Economic Research, University of Essex, UK.

Brinca, P., J. B. Duarte, and M. Faria-e-Castro. 2020. "Measuring Sectoral Supply and Demand Shocks during COVID-19." *Covid Economics* 20. London: CEPR Press.

Bronka, P., D. Collado, and M. Richiardi. 2020. "The COVID-19 Crisis Response Helps the Poor: The Distributional and Budgetary Consequences of the UK Lockdown." *COVID Economics* 26, 79–106.

Bruckmeier, K., A. Peichl, M. Popp, J. Wiemers, and T. Wollmershauser, 2021. "Distributional Effects of Macroeconomic Shocks in Real-Time: A Novel Method Applied to the Covid-19 Crisis in Germany." *Journal of Economic Inequality* 19, 499–481.

Cameron, D. 2012. "European Fiscal Responses to the Great Recession." In *Coping with Crisis*, edited by N. Bermeo and J. Pontusson, 91–129. New York: Russell Sage Foundation Press.

Cantillon, B., M. Seeleib-Kaiser, and R. van der Veen. 2021. "The COVID-19 Crisis and Policy Responses by Continental European Welfare States." *Social Policy & Administration* 55 (2), 326–338.

Cantó, O., F. Figari, C. V. Fiorio, S. Kuypers, S. Marchal, M. Romaguera-de-la-Cruz, I. V. Tasseva, and G. Verbist. 2021. *Welfare Resilience at the Onset of the COVID-19 Pandemic in a Selection of Eur-*

opean Countries: Impact on Public Finance and Household Incomes. *Review of Income and Wealth.* https://doi.org/10.1111/roiw.12530

Castex, G., E. Dechter, and M. Lorca. 2021. "COVID-19: The Impact of Social Distancing Policies, Cross-Country Analysis." *Economics of Disasters and Climate Change* 5, 135–159.

CDC. 2021. *2014–2016 Ebola Outbreak in West Africa.* https://www.cdc.gov/vhf/ebola/history/2014-2016-outbreak/index.html

Chen, C., Y. Shi, P. Zhang. And C. Ding. 2021. "A Cross-Country Comparison of Fiscal Policy Responses to the COVID-19 Global Pandemic." *Journal of Comparative Policy Analysis: Research and Practice* 23 (2), 262–273.

Chen, S., D. Igan, N. Pierri, and A. Presbitero. 2020. *Tracking the Economic Impact of COVID-19 and Mitigation Policies in Europe and the United States,* IMF Working Papers, Issue 125

Connolly, F. F., J. Olofsson, G. Malmberg, and M. Stattin. 2021. *Adjustment of Daily Activities to Restrictions and Reported Spread of the COVID-19 Pandemic Cross Europe.* SHARE Working Paper Series 62-2021. DOI: 10.17617/2.3292885.

Daly, M., B. Ebbinghaus, L. Lehner, M. Naczyk, and T. Vlandas. 2020. *Oxford Supertracker: The Global Directory for COVID Policy Trackers and Surveys,* Department of Social Policy and Intervention. https://supertracker.spi.ox.ac.uk

Deaton, A. 2021. *COVID-19 and Global Income Inequality,* NBER Working Paper 28392. http://www.nber.org/papers/w28392

Deb, P, D Furceri, J Ostry and N Tawk (2022), "The Effects of Containment Measures on the COVID-19 Pandemic", Covid Economics: Vetted and Real-Time Papers 19: 53–86.

Del Rio-Chanona, M., P. Mealy, A. Pichler, F. Lafond, and J. Farmer. 2020. "Supply and Demand Shocks in the COVID-19 Pandemic: An Industry and Occupation Perspective." *Oxford Review of Economic Policy* 36, Issue Supplement 1, S94–S137.

Dreger, C., and D. Gros. 2020. "Social Distancing Requirements and the Determinants of the COVID-19 Recession and Recovery in Europe." *Inter Economics* 55 (6), 365–371.

Ebbinghaus, B., and L. Lehner. 2022. "Cui Bono – Business or Labour? Job Retention Policies During the Covid-19 Pandemic in Europe." *Transfer* 27 (1) (forthcoming Feb. 2022).

Eichenbaum, M., S. Rebelo, and M. Trabandt. 2020. *The Macroeconomics of Epidemics,* NBER Working Papers 26882. Cambridge, MA: National Bureau of Economic Research.

Engzell, P., A. Frey, and M. Verhagen. 2021. "Learning Loss Due to School Closures During the COVID-19 Pandemic." *PNAS* 118 (17), 1–7. https://doi.org/10.1073/pnas.2022376118

Esping-Andersen, G. 1990. *The Three Worlds of Welfare Capitalism.* Princeton, NJ: Princeton University Press.

Eurofound. 2021a. *COVID-19 EU PolicyWatch.* https://www.eurofound.europa.eu/data/covid-19-eu-policywatch

Eurofound. 2021b. *Living and Working in Europe 2020.* Luxembourg: Publications Office of the European Union.

European Commission. 2020. *European Economic Forecast. Spring 2020.* Brussels, Belgium: Directorate-General For Economic and Financial Affairs.

Fedelino, A., A. Ivanova, and M. Horton. 2009. *Computing Cyclically-Adjusted Balances and Automatic Stabilizers.* IMF Technical Notes and Manuals No. 2009/05. https://www.imf.org/external/pubs/cat/longres.aspx?sk=23394.0

Figari, F. and C. V. Fiorio. 2020. *Welfare Resilience in the Immediate Aftermath of the COVID-19 Outbreak in Italy.* EUROMOD Working Paper 06/20, Institute for Social and Economic Research, University of Essex, Essex, UK.

Fuller, J., A. Hakim, K. Victory, K. Date, M. Lynch, B. Dahl, and O. Henao. 2020. "Mitigation Policies and COVID-19–Associated Mortality — 37 European Countries, January 23–June 30." *Morbidity and Mortality Weekly Report* 70 (2), 58–62.

Furceri, D., Loungani, P., Ostry, J. D. and Pizzuto, P.: Will COVID-19 affect inequality? Evidence from Past Pandemics, COVID Economics, 12, 138–157, *Centre for Economic Policy Research (CEPR)* (2020)

Giattino, C., H. Ritchie, M. Roser, E. Ortiz-Ospina, and J. Hasell. 2022. *Excess Mortality During the Coronavirus Pandemic (COVID-19).* https://ourworldindata.org/excess-mortality-covid

Greve, B., P. Blomquist, B. Hvinden, and M. van Gerven. 2021."Nordic Welfare States—Still Standing or Changed by the COVID-19 Crisis?" *Social Policy & Administration* 55 (2), 295–311.

Gros, D., A. Ounnas, and T. Y.-C. Yeung. 2021. "A New Stringency Index For Europe." *Covid Economics* 66, 115–137.

Hale, T., N. Angrist, R. Goldszmidt, B. Kira, A. Petherick, T. Phillips, S. Webster, E. Cameron-Blake, L. Hallas, S. Majumdar, and H. Tatlow. 2021. "A Global Panel Database of Pandemic Policies (Oxford COVID-19 Government Response Tracker)." *Nature Human Behaviour* 5, 529–538.

Hanushek, E., and L. Woessmann. 2020. *The Economic Impacts of Learning Losses.* OECD Education Working Paper No. 225. https://doi.org/10.1787/21908d74-en.

Haroutunian, S., S. Osterloh, and K. Sławińska. 2021. "The Initial Fiscal Policy Responses of Euro Area Countries to the COVID-19 Crisis." *ECB Economic Bulletin* 1, 80–100.

Hick, R., and M. P. Murphy "Common Shock, Different Paths? Comparing Social Policy Responses to COVID-19 in the UK and Ireland." *Social Policy & Adminstration* 55 (2), 312–325.

ILO. 2021. *ILO Monitor: COVID-19 and the World of Work. Seventh edition.* Updated estimates and analysis. https://www.ilo.org/global/topics/coronavirus/impacts-and-responses/WCMS_767028/lang–en/index.htm

IMF. 2020. *World Economic Outlook, October 2020: A Long and Difficult Ascent.* Washington, DC: International Monetary Fund. https://www.imf.org/en/Publications/WEO/Issues/2020/09/30/world-economic-outlook-october-2020

IMF. 2021. *COVID-19 Policy Tracker.* https://www.imf.org/en/Topics/imf-and-covid19/Policy-Responses-to-COVID-19

Islam, N., V. Shkolnikov, R. Acosta, I. Klimkin, I. Kawachi, R. Irizarry, G. Alicandro, K. Khunti, T. Yates, D. Jdanov, M. White, S. Lewington, and B. Lacey. 2021. "Excess Deaths Associated with Covid-19 Pandemic in 2020: Age and Sex Disaggregated Time Series Analysis in 29 High Income Countries." *British Medical Journal* 373:n1137. http://dx.doi.org/10.1136/bmj.n1137

Jefferies, J., N. French, C. Gilkison, G. Graham, V. Hope, J. Marshall, C. McElnay, A. McNeill, P. Muellner, S. Paine, N. Prasad, J. Scott, J. Sherwood, L. Yang, and P. Priest. 2020. "COVID-19 in New Zealand and the Impact of the National Response: A Descriptive Epidemiological Study." *The Lancet Public Health* 5 (11), e612–e623. https://doi.org/10.1016/S2468-2667(20)30225-5.

Kahn, L. 2010. "The Long-Term Labor Market Consequences of Graduating from College in a Bad Economy." *Labour Economics* 17 (2), 303–316.

Kayı, İ., and S. Sakarya. 2020. "Policy Analysis of Suppression and Mitigation Strategies in the Management of an Outbreak Through the Example of COVID-19 Pandemic." *Infectious Diseases and Clinical Microbiology* 2 (1), 30–41.

Konle-Seidl, R. 2020. *Short-time Work in Europe: Rescue in the Current COVID-19 Crisis?* IAB Research Report 4/2020. http://doku.iab.de/forschungsbericht/2020/fb0420_en.pdf

König, M., and A. Winkler. 2021. "COVID-19: Lockdowns, Fatality Rates and GDP Growth." *Intereconomics* 56 (1), 32–39.

LeDuc, James W., and M. Anita Barry. 2004. "SARS, the First Pandemic of the 21st Century." *Emerging Infectious Diseases* 10 (11), e26. https://dx.doi.org/10.3201%2Feid1011.040797_02

Li, J., Y. Vidyattama, H. La Anh, R. Miranti, and D. M. Sologon. 2020. *The Impact of COVID-19 and Policy Responses on Australian Income Distribution and Poverty.* Ideas RePEc Working Paper No. 2009.04037.

Li, S.-K., and X. Liang. 2021. "Determinants of the Fiscal Support of Governments in Response to the COVID-19 Pandemic." *Frontiers in Public Health* 8, 1–5.

Lu, G., O. Razum, A. Jahn, Y. Zhang, B. Sutton, D. Sridhar, K. Ariyoshi, L. von Seidlein, and O. Müller. 2021. "COVID-19 in Germany and China: Mitigation versus Elimination Strategy." *Global Health Action* 14 (1). https://doi.org/10.1080/16549716.2021.1875601

Ma, C., J. Rogers, and S. Zhou. 2020. *Modern Pandemics: Recession and Recovery.* International Finance Discussion Papers 1295. Washington: Board of Governors of the Federal Reserve System. https://doi.org/10.17016/IFDP.2020.1295.

Maloney, W., and T. Taskin. 2020. *Determinants of Social Distancing and Economic Activity during COVID-19: A Global View.* Policy Research Working Paper No. 9242. World Bank, Washington, DC. https://openknowledge.worldbank.org/handle/10986/33754.

Marchal, S., J. Vanderkelen, B. Cantillon, K. Decancq, A. Decoster, S. Kuypers, I. Marx, J. Spinnewijn, W. Van Lancker, L. Van Meensel, and G. Verbist. 2021. *The Distributional Impact of the COVID-19 Shock on Household Incomes in Belgium.* COVIVAT Working Paper 2.

Mendolia, S., O. Stavrunova, and O. Yerokhin. 2021. "Determinants of the Community Mobility during the COVID-19 Epidemic: The Role of Government Regulations and Information.: *Journal of Economic Behavior & Organization* 184, 199–231.

Moreira, A., and R. Hick. 2021. "COVID-19, The Great Recession and Social Policy: Is This Time Different?" *Social Policy & Administration*, 55 (2), 261–279.

Morgan, D., J. Ino, G. Di Paolantonio, and F. Murtin. 2020. *Excess Mortality: Measuring the Direct and Indirect Impact of COVID-19.* OECD Health Working Paper 122. https://doi.org/10.1787/c5dc0c50-en.

O'Donoghue, C., D. M. Sologon, I. Kyzyma, and J. McHale. 2020. "Modelling the Distributional Impact of the COVID-19 Crisis." *Fiscal Studies* 41 (2), 321–336.

OECD. 2020a. "Walking the Tightrope: Avoiding a Lockdown while Containing the Virus." *OECD Policy Responses to Coronavirus (COVID-19).* Paris: OECD Publishing. https://doi.org/10.1787/1b912d4a-en.

OECD. 2020b. "Evaluating the Initial Impact of COVID-19 Containment Measures on Economic Activity." *OECD Policy Responses to Coronavirus (COVID-19).* Paris: OECD Publishing. https://oecd.org/coronavirus/policy-responses/evaluating-the-initial-impact-of-covid-19-containment-measures-on-economic-activity-b1f6b68b/#section-d1e38

OECD. 2021a. *OECD Employment Outlook 2021: Navigating the COVID-19 Crisis and Recovery.* Paris: OECD Publishing. https://doi.org/10.1787/5a700c4b-en.

OECD. 2021b. *OECD Economic Outlook. Interim Report March 2021.* Paris: OECD. https://www.oecd.org/economic-outlook/march-2021/#press-conference

OECD. 2021c. *OECD COVID-19 Policy Tracker.* https://oecd.github.io/OECD-covid-action-map/

OECD. 2021d. *Economic Outlook No 109 – May 2021.* https://stats.oecd.org/

OECD. 2021e. *Household Spending (Indicator).* https://doi.org/10.1787/b5f46047-enhttps://data.oecd.org/hha/household-spending.htm#indicator-chart

OECD. 2021f. *Household Savings (Indicator).* https://doi.org/10.1787/cfc6f499-en https://data.oecd.org/hha/household-savings.htm#indicator-chart

OECD. 2021g. *Household Disposable Income (Indicator).* https://doi.org/10.1787/dd50eddd-en https://data.oecd.org/hha/household-disposable-income.htm#indicator-chart

Padma, T. V. 2021. *"COVID Vaccines to Reach Poorest Countries in 2023—Despite Recent Pledges."* https://www.nature.com/articles/d41586-021-01762-w

Pincombe, M., V. Reese, and C. Dolan. 2021. "The Effectiveness of National-Level Containment and Closure Policies across Income Levels during the COVID-19 Pandemic: An Analysis of 113 Countries." *Health Policy Planning* 36 (7), 1152–1162.

Pitterle, I., and L. Niermann. 2021. *The COVID-19 Crisis: What Explains Cross-Country Differences in the Pandemic's Short-Term Economic Impact?* DESA Working Paper No. 174. https://www.un.org/en/desa/covid-19-crisis-what-explains-cross-country-differences-pandemic%E2%80%99s-short-term-economic-impact

Pontusson, J., and D. Raess. 2012. "How (and Why) is This Time Different? The Politics of Economic Crisis in Western Europe and the United States." *Annual Review of Political Science* 15, 13–33.

Quilty, B., S. Clifford, J. Hellewell, T. Russell, A. Kucharski, S. Flasche, and W. Edmunds, et al. 2021. "Quarantine and Testing Strategies in Contact Tracing for SARS-CoV-2: A Modelling Study." *The Lancet Public Health* 6 (3), e175–e183. https://doi.org/10.1016/S2468-2667(20)30308-X.

Raess, D., and J. Pontusson. 2015. "The Politics of Fiscal Policy during Economic Downturns, 1981–2010." *European Journal of Political Research* 54, 1–22.

Ritchie, H., E. Mathieu, L. Rodés-Guirao, C. Appel, C. Giattino, E. Ortiz-Ospina, J. Hasell, B. Macdonald, D. Beltekian, and M. Roser. 2021. *Coronavirus Pandemic (COVID-19)*. https://ourworldindata.org/coronavirus

Santamaria, C., F. Sermi, S. Spyratos, S. Iacus, A. Annunziato, D. Tarchi, and M. Vespe. 2020. "Measuring the Impact of COVID-19 Confinement Measures on Human Mobility using Mobile Positioning Data. A European Regional Analysis." *Safety Science* 132, 104925. https://doi.org/10.1016/j.ssci.2020.104925.

Sapir, A. 2020. *Why Has COVID-19 Hit Different European Union Economies so Differently?* Policy Contribution 2020/18, Bruegel. https://www.bruegel.org/2020/09/why-has-covid-19-hit-different-european-union-economies-so-differently/

Sayed, A., and B. Peng. 2021. "Pandemics and Income Inequality: A Historical Review." *SN Business & Economics* 1 (54), 1–17. https://doi.org/10.1007/s43546-021-00059-4

Schmillen, A., and M. Umkehrer. 2017. "The Scars of Youth: Effects of Early-Career Unemployment on Future Unemployment Experience." *International Labour Review* 156 (3–4), 465–494.

Siddik, N. 2020. "Economic Stimulus for COVID-19 Pandemic and its Determinants: Evidence from Cross-Country Analysis." *Heliyon* 6 (12), 1–10. https://doi.org/10.1016/j.heliyon.2020.e05634.

Soon, S., C. C. Chou, and S.-J. Shi. 2021. "Withstanding the Plague: Institutional Resilience of the East Asian Welfare State." *Social Policy & Adminstration* 55 (2), 374–387.

Sykes, D., L. Holdsworth, N. Jawad, P. Gunasekera, A. Morice, and M. Crooks. 2021. "Post-COVID-19 Symptom Burden: What is Long-COVID and How Should We Manage It?" *Lung* 199, 113–119. https://doi.org/10.1007/s00408-021-00423-z

Turner, D., B. Égert, Y. Guillemette, and J. Botev. 2021. *The Tortoise and the Hare: The Race Between Vaccine Rollout and New COVID Variants*. OECD Economics Department Working Papers No. 1672. https://www.oecd-ilibrary.org/economics/the-tortoise-and-the-hare-the-race-between-vaccine-rollout-and-new-covid-variants_4098409d-en

Warner, M., and X. Zhang. 2021. "Social Safety Nets and COVID-19 Stay Home Orders across US States: A Comparative Policy Analysis." *Journal of Comparative Policy Analysis: Research and Practice* 23 (2), 176–190.

WHO. 2020. *WHO Timeline – COVID-19*. https://www.who.int/news/item/27-04-2020-who-timeline—covid-19

Fabrizio Antenucci, Luigi Salvati and Pasquale Tridico

13 Through the COVID-19 pandemic: perspectives for the welfare state

Abstract: The COVID-19 pandemic has put a strain on governments' ability to support the economy. Intervention was necessary to sustain families and businesses afflicted by the economic crisis. Welfare policies highlighted the differences among countries reflecting their welfare models. The decades before the pandemic had been characterised in most european economies by austerity and liberalisation policies. Among the consequences of these policies, in many countries access to welfare measures has become increasingly category-based – in some cases it happened alongside with a retrenchment of the welfare state – rather than universal. In this chapter, we reconstruct the stages of the reduction in welfare spending by the countries of the EU. We also discuss the reasons why a reversal of these policy would be desirable. In particular, we show that the pandemic has highlighted the problems of welfare systems most subject to spending cuts, which have had great difficulty in providing for the needs of workers left outside the social safety net. In the case study taken into consideration, that of Italy, it is shown that it is more difficult to guarantee the social rights of all citizens with a category-based welfare system, despite the measures undertaken by the government.

Keywords: welfare policies, COVID-19, social spending, universal welfare, Italy

13.1 Introduction

The advent of a pandemic disrupts people's lives and at the same time puts pressure on the resilience of social institutions. Focusing on the economic dimension, the strength of the impact depends not only on the violence of the pandemic, but also on the safety net a country has adopted for its citizens. In other words, it depends on the welfare regime adopted in a country or group of countries. The dramatic nature of the COVID-19 pandemic has highlighted the diversity of welfare models and the ability to cope with it in different countries. Obviously, the COVID-19 pandemic struck in different ways and at different times among countries, and this is something that must be considered when making comparisons. And yet, despite these differences, we have had a demonstration of what the limits of national welfares can be but, at the same time, governments have had an opportunity to design new income support policies that substantially changed the welfare model. However, these measures of a temporary nature will most likely be removed as soon as "normality" resumes. The aim of this chapter is to show, within the European Union, that traditional welfare states need to change their shape. Indeed, before the pandemic broke out, even the most successful

https://doi.org/10.1515/9783110721768-013

European welfare states were still category-based and linked to old job schemes, characterized by principles such as means-testing, social insurance and very strict conditionality. Within the emergency, the welfare systems proved inadequate, in different degrees, to withstand the impact of the pandemic and far-reaching measures were needed to prevent a large share of the population from being attracted into the vortex of poverty. In several countries, governments had to discuss which measures to take, which groups to protect and the extent of economic support. This has led to delays in intervention and insufficient support. Obviously, a dramatic and totally unexpected situation such as the COVID-19 pandemic would have found any welfare state unprepared. Yet, a universal welfare model would have worked better. Adopting a welfare system based on a universalistic principle, with appropriate conditionality linked to income, would not only serve to deal with emergency situations, such as the COVID-19 pandemic, but also to cure the pathologies of our economic systems that have become increasingly widespread in recent years: inequality and poverty (even in-work poverty).

To deal with the topic, the chapter is organised as follows. In section 13.2 we explore the literature about welfare models highlighting across the European Union a tightening of the conditionalities for entitlement to welfare policies which, therefore, become even more category based. In section 13.3 we discuss why it would be necessary to reverse this trend not only during the pandemic period, but as a lasting solution. In section 13.4 we focus on the Italian case by highlighting the types of policies that were implemented during the pandemic. The extraordinary measures demonstrate the effort to guarantee protection to as many citizens as possible but also the inadequacy of a welfare system anchored to old principles. Section 13.5 concludes.

13.2 The evolution of the welfare state and its anchorage to a category-based system

The vast literature on welfare regimes has outlined the differences among countries also highlighting the changes that have taken place over the years, starting from the pioneering contribution *Three Worlds of Welfare Capitalism* (Esping-Andersen 1990) which identified three models: i) market-oriented in Anglo-Saxon countries, where the state plays a residual role; ii) the family-oriented "corporative model" in continental Europe, where the state and employers play a supporting role; iii) state-oriented for the Scandinavians, with universal protections and services. Yet, in recent decades, there has been a noticeable shift in the welfare regimes towards the liberalist paradigm of the Anglo-Saxon countries. In fact, even the Scandinavian model has undergone several transformations (Kvist and Greve 2011) that have limited the universality of welfare, making it more constrained and conditional (Jensen and van Kersbergen 2017; Taylor-Gooby et al. 2017). The neo-liberal reforms in Denmark make it the most obvious case of how the universality of welfare has slowly been transformed into conditionality (Trenz and Grasso 2018), yet something similar has also happened in Sweden since 1990 (Blomqvist and Palme 2020). In more general terms, the last thirty years have witnessed a more stringent conditionality of welfare policies in most countries or, in other words, a new conception of welfare – the so-called new welfarism – considered to better adapt to the changed economic and social conditions marked by post-Fordism. In some cases, increased conditionality has coincided with a retrenchment of the welfare state that was seen as a logical and necessary consequence of globalisation (Taylor-Gooby 1997). Yet, although there has been a profound change in economic and social conditions, other welfare trajectories would have been pursuable if only they had been recognised (Hay 1998).

One of the main explanations for the retrenchment of the welfare state was the concern for its fiscal sustainability, which was threatened by globalisation – especially by financialisation and technical progress leading to increased unemployment of unskilled workers – and by an ageing population. Both would have led to increased spending on unemployment benefits and pensions, respectively, and reduced revenues due to a lower share of employed people in the population. A branch of the recent literature considers the economic policy paradigm of the last twenty years as a direct expression of the so-called "Washington consensus", with reference to the processes of globalisation and financialisation (Palley 2012; Galbraith 2012; Arestis, Charles, and Fontana 2013; Stockhammer 2015), within which new institutional forms based on labour market flexibility have been implemented (Tridico 2012), the latter understood as less rigidity in the practices of hiring and firing workers (Storm and Naastepad 2012). More generally, those who oppose a "generous" welfare state do so because of arguments that understand the expansion of social security as an obstacle to competitiveness and economic growth due to increasing labour costs or reduced work incentives.

However, the arguments concerning the relationship between social spending and growth are rather conflicting. On the one hand, in the framework of the so-called "efficiency thesis", Blackmon (2006) argues that globalisation has linked the downsizing of the welfare state to the achievement of greater competitiveness. On the other hand, other economists argue that increasing social spending does not induce better economic performance (Alesina and Perotti 1994) and that reducing the size of government can foster higher incomes and competitiveness (Mitchell 2005). Moreover, embracing the so-called "compensation thesis", some scholars have endorsed the view that social spending has contributed to, rather than inhibited, economic growth (Rodrik 1998; Lindert 2004; Furceri and Zdzienicka 2012; Tridico and Paternesi Meloni 2018). As experienced by Scandinavian economies (see among others Bergh 2014), from the 1990s to the 2008–2009 crisis, challenges and threats of globalisation and financialisation in terms of growth, inequality and competitiveness could be better addressed by increasing public social spending, rather than reducing welfare. This means that the sustainability of a universal welfare would certainly be favoured if such a policy was associated with higher economic growth and lower inequality.

Although, in most European countries, spending on basic welfare such as retirement pensions and health care has not declined since the turn of the millennium (Greve 2020), changes in the production system – and consequently changes in the labour market – have made the welfare state less effective. This is because, among other things, the welfare state itself has become more and more targeted to specific categories (Borosch, Kuhlmann, and Blum 2016). This was probably one of the causes of the growth of private welfare (Hyde, Dixon, and Drover 2003), at company level, as is typical of Anglo-Saxon countries, even in countries where there was a universal welfare (Svallfors and Tyllström 2017). There has been a shift from welfare to a new neoliberal paradigm, i.e., workfare (Jessop 2018). When the welfare state makes way to private welfare, whether provided by firms or not, this means that the citizen must have an income which, in most cases, coincides with having a job. However, the labour market itself has undergone radical transformations in recent decades. In fact, flexibility has become in many cases precariousness, and with economic stagnation this has often translated into unemployment or underemployment, as witnessed by the growing – but far from being new (Klein and Rones 1989) – phenomenon of the working poor in the advanced economies of the European Union (Andress and Lohmann 2008; Pradella 2015).

13.3 The great challenge: a new beginning of universal welfare

The paradigm of welfare policies within the European Union has been progressively changing, moving more and more towards means-tested programmes with well-defined targets – a feature that was distinctive of liberal Anglo-Saxon welfare states – that has now found its social legitimacy (Van Oorschot and Roosma 2017). Yet, the COVID-19 pandemic has shown how welfare policies in most countries are mainly oriented towards categories of workers belonging to the past and have therefore proved to be totally inadequate, leaving many new types of workers outside the safety net. The emergency meant that governments did not have time to think about redesigning the welfare intervention scheme. In fact, with the aim of reaching as many citizens as possible, governments allocated extraordinary measures to reach those categories that were previously cut off from the welfare. In 2020 the International Labour Organization estimated that from the start of the epidemic more than 1,600 social-protection policies have been activated (ILO 2021, 68). The International Monetary Fund estimates that in 2020, average overall fiscal deficit as a percentage of GDP was 11.7 % for advanced economies (an increase of about 9 percentage points with respect to the value of 2019, 2.9 %), in order to support health care systems, households, and firms (IMF 2021). Not surprisingly, the states with the lowest welfare levels were the ones that had to increase spending the most.

At the origin of the ineffectiveness of welfare models is the great change that has taken place in the labour market over the last thirty years. The most evident aspect is the fragmentation of contract types, with a strong use of part-time or fixed-term contracts and a significant increase in self-employed workers. These types of workers are less likely to have a safety net because the welfare system in European countries is mainly based on the old concept of a Fordist society, based on stable and secure employment through permanent contracts. In this respect, a comparison among three of the main European economies – France, Germany and Italy – reveals a heterogeneous picture (Figure 13.1) before the COVID-19 pandemic broke out. In fact, although there is a common trend of increase in the share of workers with fixed-term contracts, its growth occurs with very different intensities. In Germany the trend has been reversed since 2011 and we are witnessing a decrease in the proportion of workers with fixed-term contracts, which is returning to the levels of 2003: in that year, fixed-term workers accounted for 8.2 %, while in 2019 it stood at 9.0 %. In contrast, in 2011, the pace of growth increased in France and Italy. In Italy the share of fixed-term workers has almost doubled over the timespan: it was 6.9 % in 2003 and reached 13.1 % in 2019, far outstripping France (10.1 % in 2003 and 13.0 % in 2019).

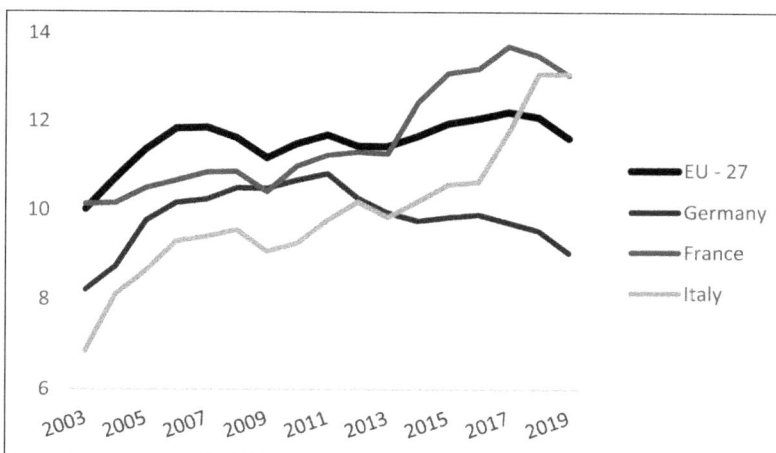

Figure 13.1: Share of temporary workers over total workers.
Source: Eurostat LFS Database

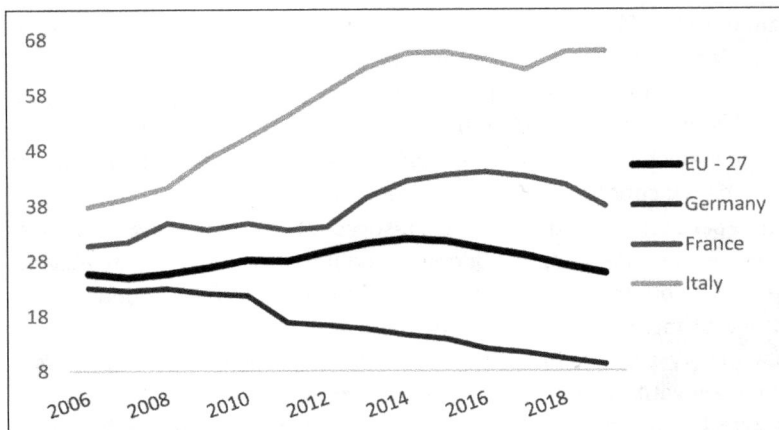

Figure 13.2: Share of involuntary part-time workers over part-time workers.
Source: Eurostat LFS Database

The fragmentation of the labour market in Europe is also reflected in another aspect, namely the increase in part-time contracts. In this respect, it is important to emphasise that this trend is not always the result of the employee's choice. In Italy most workers with part-time contracts would have preferred a full-time job (Figure 13.2). Indeed, in Italy the share of involuntary part-time workers has risen from 37.8 % in 2006 to 65.8 % in 2019. From 2008 to 2019, the labour market in Italy has been deeply marked by the advent of the crisis. In ten years, the composition of employment has been disrupted. Those employed part-time – because they could not find a full-time job – grew by 1,560,000, from 5.8 % to 12.3 %, while those employed full-time lost almost 680,000, falling from 85.7 % to 81 % (CNEL 2019, 36). This explains the rapid growth of involuntary part-time workers. The opposite trend can be observed in Germany over the same period, where the share of involuntary part-time was 23.1 % in 2006 and fell to 9.2 % in 2019.

Underlining the greater fragmentation of the Italian labour market is the share of self-employed workers, much higher than the EU27 average, as well as France and Germany. Although slightly lower than in the past, the share of self-employed workers in Italy in 2019 is 20.4 % (Figure 13.3).

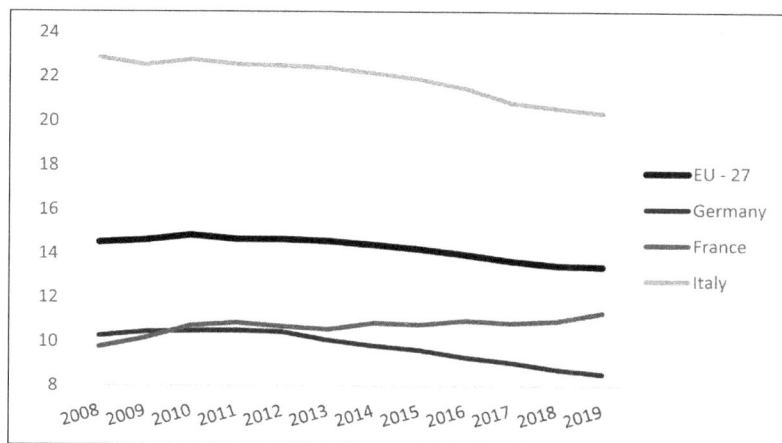

Figure 13.3: Share of self-employment over total workers.
Source: Eurostat LFS Database

The increased use of temporary and part-time contracts fostered a sadly known phenomenon within the European Union, namely in-work poverty. Although the increasing risk of in-work poverty is a common trend throughout the European Union, in Italy the situation is more alarming (Figure 13.4). In fact, in 2005 the percentage of Italian workers at risk of poverty was very close to the EU27 average. However, in 2019 in Italy the same percentage reached 11.8 % – while the EU27 average stood at 9 % – much higher than France (7.4 %) and Germany (8.0 %). The ever-increasing diffusion of the phenomenon of in-work poverty calls into question the rules governing the negotiation of working conditions. On the one hand, in recent years a "corporatisation" of bargaining has taken place: bargaining at national and/or sector level co-exist with decentralised bargaining at the firm level, in many cases weakening the bargaining power of workers. Furthermore, there is no effective regulation of trade union representation at the national level. This has favoured the formation (mushrooming) of small unrepresentative unions, with the effect of an increasingly widespread proliferation of so-called pirate contracts. On the other hand, Italy suffers from the lack of a law on the minimum wage. In recent years, several bills have been introduced into the Parliament, but none of them have reached the stage of final approval.

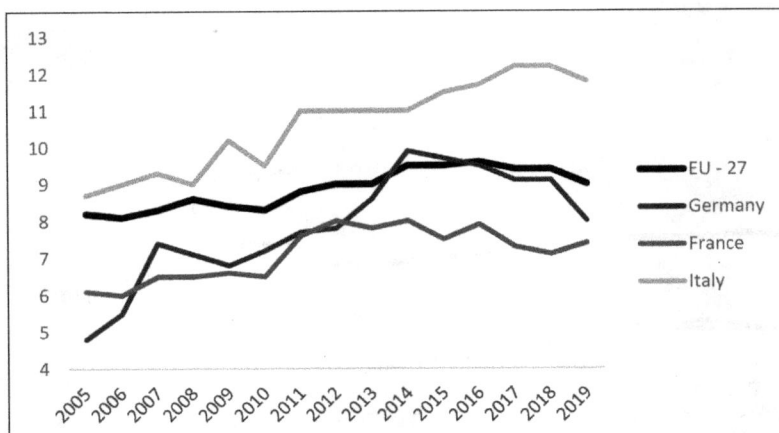

Figure 13.4: Percentage of workers at risk of poverty.
Source: Eurostat LFS Database

The picture suggests that the greater flexibility achieved has exposed workers to a greater risk of poverty. It is therefore necessary to improve labour market conditions in the European Union, especially in Italy. However, the labour market must co-exist with a welfare model that is able to provide citizens with adequate assistance both in terms of active labour policies and income support. In this last aspect, the European Union is lagging far behind if we think, for example, of the assistance it provides during the period of unemployment. Significant is the figure for short-term unemployment, an event that can be predicted when adopting a production model in which labour is flexible. Yet, in 2019 only a third of the workers, 36.7 %, who find themselves unemployed for 1–2 months receive assistance or benefits within the EU27 (Table 13.1). This is worse than in 2002, when 39.2 % of these unemployed received assistance or benefits. In Italy, although the situation has improved significantly since the early 2000s – in 2002 only 2.8 % of the unemployed received benefits/assistance, while in 2019 they reached 24.7 % – the share of those who receive benefits or assistance when unemployed are far from the European average, and it is incomparable with countries such as Germany[1] (in 2019, 60.2 %).

---

[1] However, after the Hartz IV reform in Germany the generosity (in terms of remuneration and duration of coverage) of unemployment benefits, in particular long-term unemployment benefits, and social assistance were reduced, and this is shown by a general lowering of the share of workers receiving unemployment benefits or social assistance.

Table 13.1: Unemployment share receiving benefits/social assistance by duration: 1–2 months.

	2011	2012	2013	2014	2015	2016	2017	2018	2019
EU27	39	38.4	36.2	35.1	34.2	33.8	34.6	36.1	36.7
Germany	84.5	81.5	80.4	66.2	65.1	63.1	59.2	55.9	60.2
France	42.5	45.5	39.8	40.7	40	39.6	45.5	43.8	42
Italy	13	11.8	15.1	15.7	16.5	16.8	17.6	n.a.	24.7

Source: Eurostat LFS Database

Table 13.2: Unemployment share receiving benefits/social assistance by duration: 12+ months.

	2011	2012	2013	2014	2015	2016	2017	2018	2019
EU27	28.5	25	23.4	22.8	22.9	21.8	22.9	23.7	24.8
Germany	86	86.4	86.6	79.8	79.9	77	77.1	77.7	76.4
France	34.1	34.7	36.6	36.7	40.4	36.5	38.4	37.6	36.1
Italy	1.8	1.7	1.9	1.9	2	2.6	3.5	n.a.	9.1

Source: Eurostat LFS Database

The main difference between Italy and Germany is that the percentage of unemployed workers covered by welfare has an opposite trend according to the duration of unemployment. In Italy, in fact, the percentage of workers receiving assistance/benefits decreases as the number of months of unemployment increases. Conversely, in Germany the percentage of workers receiving assistance/benefits increases as the number of months of unemployment increases. In fact, in Italy in 2019 the percentage of workers receiving assistance/benefits is only 9.1 % for those unemployed for more than a year, while in Germany the 76.4 % workers received benefits or assistance (Table 13.2). Probably, in Italy the percentage is very low despite the introduction in 2016 of an unemployment benefit scheme for employees that involuntarily lose their job (NASpI) because, as we have seen, there is a high percentage of self-employed workers who are not covered by welfare policies. However, in Italy the share is significantly higher than in previous years, thanks to the introduction of a measure of universal character such as the so-called Citizenship income (*Reddito di cittadinanza*).

Yet, the situation is still very worrying also because in Italy long-term unemployment accounts for more than half of the total unemployed (Table 13.3). In fact, in Italy there are many more long-term unemployed than short- or very short-term unemployed. This is a well-known picture that outlines how unemployment in Italy is mainly structural, while frictional unemployment is very small. The scenario that emerged before the outbreak of the COVID-19 pandemic was therefore far from reassuring, especially in Italy. When such a shock occurred, with the interruption of many work activities, many citizens found themselves without a lifeline.

Table 13.3: Unemployment share by duration: 12 months or over.

	2011	2012	2013	2014	2015	2016	2017	2018	2019
EU-27	36.6	38.3	41.0	43.4	43.2	42.3	40.9	39.5	36.9
Germany	41.2	38.8	38.0	37.8	37.3	34.3	35.2	35.3	32.7
France	34.9	34.4	35.0	38.1	38.5	39.9	39.9	37.2	35.5
Italy	46.7	47.7	51.1	54.7	53.6	53.0	53.4	53.6	51.8

Source: authors' elaboration from Eurostat LFS Database

The lack of a universal welfare in a country where the labour market is highly fragmented exposes citizens to a higher risk of poverty. There is therefore a need, now more than ever, to reverse course: welfare can no longer be seen as something that must be limited to a few categories, subject to means-tests and stringent conditionalities. The COVID-19 pandemic has not undermined the country's social stability, it has only revealed its fragile nature. In the next section we will describe the extraordinary measures taken in Italy to deal with this situation.

13.4 During the COVID-19 pandemic in Italy: the extraordinary measures

The pandemic crisis has led the Italian government to experiment with new ways of providing welfare benefits (Table 13.4 summarises all forms of intervention implemented in 2020, updated to 10 October 2020). As will be seen from the brief illustration that follows, although simplified procedures have been developed – aimed at reaching the largest number of workers exposed to the consequences of the economic crisis – little has been done to overcome the principle of a category-based distribution of the benefits. The outbreak of the pandemic revealed how the Italian welfare system was fragmented and how many categories were without protection as regards the coverage of income support instruments in periods of slowdown in economic activity. The wage integration schemes envisaged in normal times, in fact, were intended only for certain sectors and for firms that meet the criterion of a minimum size of the workforce. For these reasons, it was necessary to identify single categories of workers not covered by any form of economic support. For each of these broad categories, specific income support provisions were then introduced.

Table 13.4: COVID-19 provisions 2020.

Provision	N.	Unit of analysis	
600-euro allowances (12 categories)	5,387	applications	thousands
600-euro allowances (12 categories)	4,140	beneficiaries	
Extension of parental leave	319	applicants	
Baby-sitting voucher	1,303	applications	
Baby-sitting voucher	830	applicants	
Leave for caregivers	223	beneficiaries	
CIG: authorised hours	3,058	authorised hours	millions
Ordinary (CIGO)	1,476	authorised hours	
Solidarity funds	988	authorised hours	
CIGD	594	authorised hours	
CIG: direct payment	*3,418*	beneficiaries	
CIGO	942	beneficiaries	
Solidarity funds	1,024	beneficiaries	
CIGD	1,453	beneficiaries	
CIG: balance with monthly social contributions	3,097	benefic aries	thousands
CIG: monthly allowances – direct payment	12,019	allowances	
CIG: balance with monthly social contributions	8,114	allowances	
Emergency income (REM)	600	beneficiary households	
Domestic workers allowance	212	beneficiaries	
Domestic workers allowance	275	applications	
RDC/PDC	1,424	Paid households 2020	

Source: INPS, https://www.inps.it/news/misure-covid-19-i-dati-al-10-ottobre-2020

One of the main instruments of state intervention was that of the so-called "bonuses". Different categories of self-employed workers, such as freelancers, artisans and shop-keepers, but also collaborators, seasonal employees (especially in the tourism sector), agricultural workers with fixed-term contracts, entertainment sector workers, have been granted allowances of different amounts. These categories, in fact, were not protected through ordinary income support instruments. The distribution of the bonuses followed a very simplified procedure, aimed at quickly reaching the workers most in need of economic aid. Nonetheless, these interventions did not change the fact that the Italian welfare system is still profoundly category based. In other words, it was not an intervention oriented towards new forms of universal welfare.

The pandemic emergency also made it necessary to intervene in support of working parents who were facing the consequences of the closure of schools. These workers, in fact, needed to stay at home to look after their children. Consequently, paid leave was established for employees in the private sector, for members of the so-called *Gestione separata* (i.e., the pension fund, managed by INPS (the Italian Institute for Social Security), intended, among others, for freelancers without a social security fund, collaborators, door-to-door salespeople, research fellows, PhD students with scholarships, local administrators, etc.) and for other categories of self-employed workers. Alternatively, the same subjects were offered a voucher for the purchase of baby-sitting services. Paid leave was also granted to employees in the public sector. For employees of the health sector, belonging to certain categories the baby-sitting bonus was granted for a higher amount. It was also necessary to intervene in support of disabled workers in serious or non-self-sufficient situations, as well as of relatives of subjects of the same conditions, increasing the number of days of paid leave destined for them.

However, the main tool to support workers and firms was that of layoff schemes. In this regard, it was necessary to change the legislation because firms and workers, that were not normally covered by the protection of wage supplements, could obtain this type of income support.[2] In addition, it was necessary to allow for the provision of this kind of support also to workers for whom the duration limits provided for by the legislation had already been exceeded. The main part of the wage support is the so-called *Cassa Integrazione Guadagni*. The latter is divided into *Cassa Integrazione Guadagni Ordinaria* (CIGO), *Cassa Integrazione Guadagni Straordinaria* (CIGS) and *Cassa Integrazione Guadagni in Deroga* (CIGD). The CIGO is aimed at non-construction industrial firms, as well as industrial and artisan companies in the construction sector, that suspend or reduce the firms' activity due to temporary and transient reasons. The CIGS can be requested for corporate restructuring, reorganisation, and conversion, for crises of particular social importance.[3] The CIGD is aimed at workers of companies excluded from other schemes or to companies that have made use of the ordinary tools up to reaching the duration limits. It is granted in cases in which some sectors are in a serious employment crisis. Finally, there are the so-called "solidarity funds", which provide support for workers in sectors where the legislation on wage sup-

---

2 For instance, the business sector of the firm was not among those covered by the legislation or the firm's size, regarding the number of employed people, was too small.

3 In 2019, the CIGS was intended for companies with, on average, more than 15 employees in the semester preceding the request for intervention; the companies were those of the industrial and construction sectors, of the related crafts (i.e. with a single client receiving CIGS), of the canteen and catering services of the related industries, of agricultural cooperatives; and also commercial companies with more than 200 employees (in transitional regime also with a number of employees from 51 to 200), newspaper publishing companies for which the limit of 15 employees is not applied shipping and transport companies in the tertiary sector and travel agencies and tourism with more than 50 employees.

plementation cannot be applied. INPS has registered, in 2020, the authorisation of over 4 billion hours of salary supplements, for a total of over 19 billion euros. Of these, just under 3 billion hours constituted CIG interventions (CIGO+CIGS+CIGD, see Figure 13.5). To give an idea of the magnitude of the intervention that was necessary to support the economic system, it is useful to observe that in the worst year from 1980 to today, 2010, *just* about 1.2 billion hours of CIG were authorised. In 2019, the last year before the crisis, the total number of authorised CIG hours was approximately 260 million hours. As for solidarity funds, more than 1.3 billion hours were authorised in 2020, compared to just under 17 million in 2019.

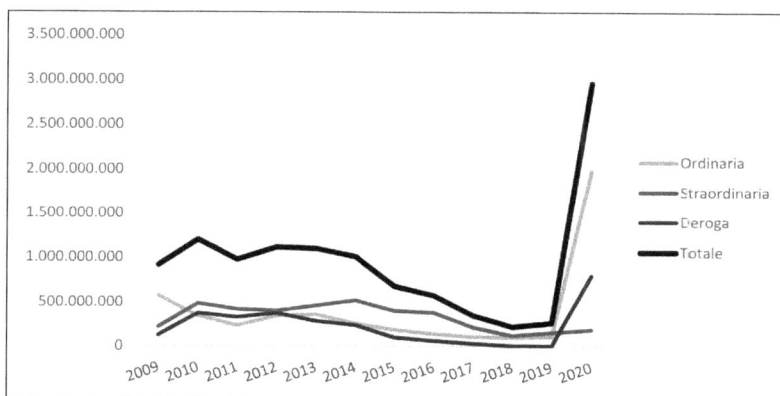

Figure 13.5: Wage subsidies – authorised CIG hours.
Source: "Cassa integrazione guadagni e fondi di solidarietà – Ore autorizzate", Osservatori Statistici INPS

One of the provisions established following the COVID-19 pandemic, i.e., the so-called "Reddito di emergenza" ("emergency income"), stands out from the others as it is not based on the criteria of belonging to a specific production sector, ownership of a specific type of employment contract or type of social security registration. The provision made it possible to provide a special support to income to households in possession, at the time of the application, of a series of residence, income and wealth requirements. The thresholds of income and wealth and the generosity of the benefit vary according to the number of members of the household and in the case of the presence in the same household of at least one component in a condition of serious disability or non-self-sufficiency. However, this measure also suffered from some important limitations. In particular, it was characterized by the same problem of Citizenship Income (*Reddito di cittadinanza*, or RdC), in the sense that it tends to disadvantage very large families. In fact, the value of the benefit was equal to 400 euros multiplied by the relative parameter of the equivalence scale of the RdC, up to a maximum of 2 (or 2.1 in the case in which in the family unit there are members in conditions of severe disability or non-self-sufficiency). The parameter of the equivalence scale is equal to 1 for the first member of the household and is increased by 0.4 for each additional member over the age of 18 and by 0.2 for each additional member of a minor age.

Among the provisions already provided before the start of the pandemic crisis, the RdC – called Citizenship Pension (*Pensione di Cittadinanza* or PdC) in some cases[4] – certainly deserves a mention. Although not, an emergency provision, it played a fundamental role in mitigating the consequences of the economic crisis, especially in the southern regions of Italy. RdC is a benefit in support of low-income individuals and households, established in April 2019 to contrast poverty, inequality and social exclusion. The measure also has the objective of promoting the right to information, education, training, and culture through policies aimed at providing economic support and social integration to those at risk of marginalisation in society and in the labour market. Thus, this instrument is also considered an active labour policy, since, for some beneficiaries, participation in training courses and a commitment to accept certain job offers are required.

RdC has brought good results both from the point of view of the reduction of inequality, and from the point of view of the reduction of poverty. As for inequality, the ratio of the equivalent income of the 20 % of the population with the highest incomes to the 20 % with the lowest incomes (quintile ratio) has decreased from 6.4 to 5.9 (Figure 13.6).

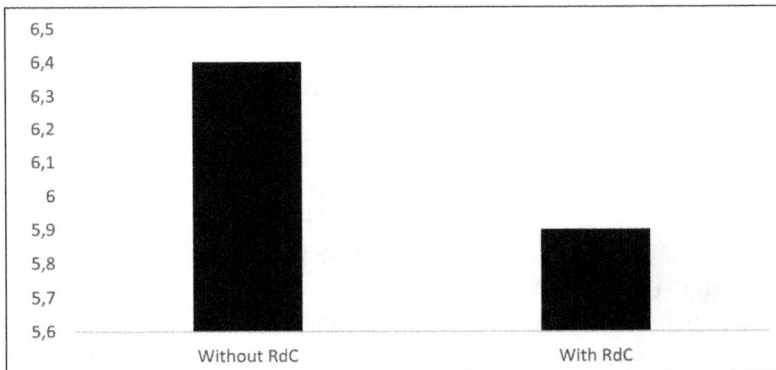

Figure 13.6: The reduction of inequality with RdC.
Source: INPS 2020

Furthermore, RdC has led to a reduction of 0.7 points in the Gini index of concentration of equivalent disposable income (Table 13.5). As regards poverty (Table 13.6), with RdC there has been both a reduction in the incidence of poverty (the percentage of the popu-

---

4 PdC is intended for families in which all members have reached the age of 67 (to be adjusted based on changes in life expectancy). PdC can also be granted in cases where the member or members of the family unit aged 67 or over cohabit exclusively with one or more people in a condition of serious disability or non-self-sufficiency, under the age of 67 years.

lation that has an income that places it below the poverty threshold) and in the intensity of poverty (the percentage difference between the income of individuals below the threshold and the poverty threshold itself). The 2020 INPS annual report, which reports data updated to 8 September 2020, underlines that the number of beneficiary households with at least one payment is 1,304,259, with 3,080,667 individuals involved. The average monthly amount per household is 524 euros. The largest part of the beneficiaries is found in the southern regions, with 802,588 beneficiaries (households) – equal to 61.5 % of the total beneficiaries – and over 2 million people involved.

Table 13.5: Gini coefficient with and without RdC

Gross equivalent income (before taxes and benefits)	39.2 %
Disposable income without RdC	33.9 %
Disposable income with RdC	33.2 %

Source: INPS 2020

Table 13.6: Poverty with and without RdC

	Without RdC	With RdC
Headcount Ratio	14.9 %	14.2 %
Poverty Gap Ratio	39.2 %	33.4 %

Source: INPS 2020

Finally, it should be noted that the government, in order to counter the spread of the COVID-19 pandemic, decided the closure of several production sectors.[5] In these sectors, many workers were forced to stay at home. This resulted, for many of them, in a suspension of income. A measure that affected workers employed in the affected sectors regardless of their income level. Figure 13.7a shows a projection of what would have been the loss of income resulting from the suspension of work in the sectors affected by the decree. This estimate was made by comparing the equivalent disposable household income received in the same timespan before the pandemic occurred. As can be seen, in all five quintiles of the distribution there would have been a loss of income of between 35 and 45 per cent. Thanks to the welfare policies implemented between March and May 2020, it was possible to intervene in income distribution to the benefit of the lowest quintile of workers. In fact, these workers even saw their income

---

5 The sectors are those identified by the Decree of the President of the Council of Ministers (DPCM) of 10 April 2020.

increase thanks to the welfare measures discussed in this section (Figure 13.7b). In general, there is a much smaller reduction in income for all workers than would have occurred in the absence of the specific measures taken.

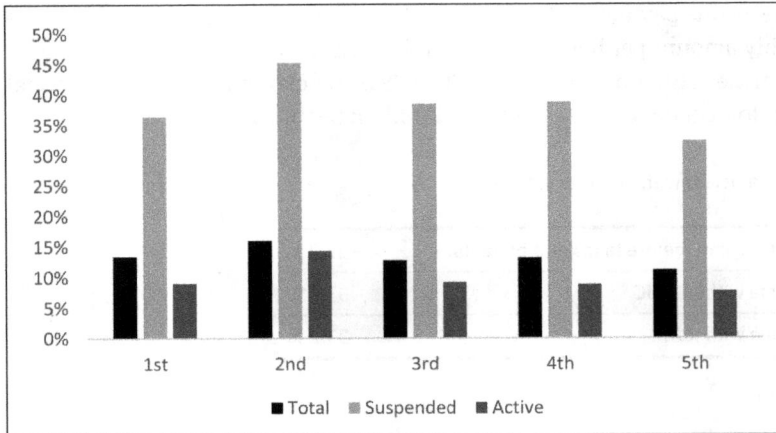

Figure 13.7a: Percentage of lost income – no measures scenario.
Source: Direzione Studi e Ricerche economico fiscali, Ministero dell'Economia e delle Finanze

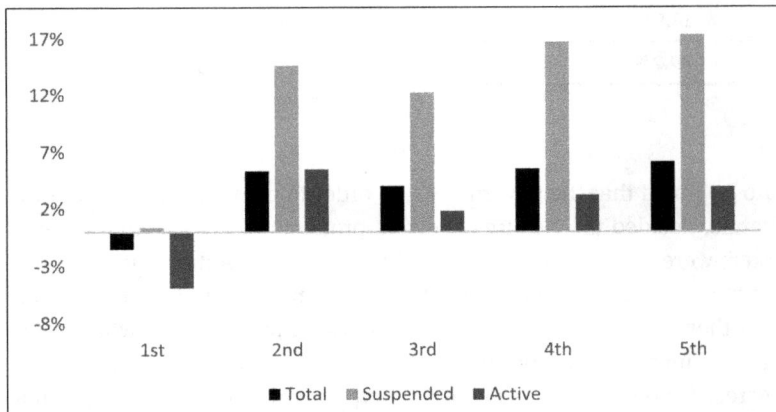

Figure 13.7b: Percentage of lost income – scenario with implemented policies.
Source: Direzione Studi e Ricerche economico fiscali, Ministero dell'Economia e delle Finanze

The RdC, due to its universality, proved to be the most effective tool during the pandemic. Nonetheless, the pandemic has shown some of the aspects in which RdC can be improved to effectively provide coverage as a universal welfare tool. It was in fact necessary, as we have seen, to create the Emergency Income (REM), a specific tool for the support of households and individuals who, despite being in poverty, could not access

RdC due to lack of one or more requirements (for example, for the requirements of residence, movable and real estate assets, possession of vehicles and boats), not required or less stringent for the REM. The extraordinary measures that have been adopted in Italy, as in many other countries, demonstrate the need to design a new welfare paradigm that will make its implementation faster and more streamlined, especially at times when it is necessary to intervene promptly and effectively. It is therefore necessary to think primarily about forms of income support that are accessible to all those citizens, who temporarily or permanently find themselves without the means necessary to live a decent life, regardless of their employment status or types of contracts. With appropriate conditionalities linked to household income, a safety net provided by welfare policies must be guaranteed to the widest possible segment of the population. In other words, the first lesson we have learned from the pandemic is that we need to adopt a welfare system that runs counter to the past, i.e., a welfare without categories and conditionalities. We need universal welfare not only to overcome economic crises or health pandemics, but to cure the ills that were already present and continuing to grow unabated in our societies before the COVID-19 pandemic broke out. We must put a stop to economic inequality and poverty. The European Union must guarantee, as it expressly states in its intentions, a decent life for all European citizens.

13.5 Conclusion

In this chapter we have addressed a topic that is crucial now, namely the need to move welfare towards a universal approach, not anchored to category-based policies, able to provide assistance for people in difficulties. This would be a radical change, a real U-turn from the last decades in which we have seen a downsizing of welfare and its transformation towards more and more specific categories. The pandemic had a considerable impact from the health point of view, of course, but also from the socio-economic point of view. Governments intervened, as is well known, with closures of economic activities and restrictions on freedom of movement, as a preventive measure, first in certain areas, and then throughout the whole national territories. The two dimensions (health and socio-economic) are closely linked, since in the sectors left open (so-called essential sectors) there were more COVID-19 cases and more deaths. The pandemic also affected the perception of the role of the state in the economy. Indeed, the COVID-19 emergency has brought the state back to the centre of the country's economic life. After decades of liberalisation of the labour market, austerity and progressive reduction of the role of the public sector, the crisis has shown how necessary state intervention is to ensure the well-being of citizens. The State intervened both through public spending, in particular with income support instruments, and through forms of labour market regulation, e.g., the freeze of dismissals, aimed at preventing the crisis from turning into a socio-economic crisis of enormous proportions over an extended period of time.

Looking at Italy, the list of measures adopted shows how much effort is needed to deal with unexpected crisis situations in such a fragmented labour market and in the absence of a universal welfare system. A fragmentation that, besides creating unequal rights and protections, reduces the capacity of the welfare system to adapt to the changing needs of workers and firms. The welfare state needs to be modernised. As it is, it was born under a different social organisation, to protect against risks different from the ones prevailing today. A new welfare state should provide enough flexibility not to discourage work too much but must also be ready to take over during crises.

Extraordinary measures were taken in all countries. Europe that had to recover after the Second World War chose to build a welfare model that would provide a safety net for its citizens, protecting them from poverty and guaranteeing them public services that improved their lives while reducing economic inequalities. Europe today faces a similar challenge. It is a matter of seizing the opportunity to build a universal welfare system that provides governments with a fast and effective instrument capable of intervening whenever necessary. This experience has shown that the more a country has a category-based welfare system, the more it is forced to take extraordinary measures that take time to implement and which, however, are not able to provide the same coverage for all citizens. It is therefore not even a question of keeping the measures implemented during the pandemic, but precisely of designing tools that are able to go beyond the category-based approach. The pandemic will hopefully one day be behind us. The task of guaranteeing people a dignified life remains ahead of us.

References

Alesina, A., and R. Perotti. 1994. *The Welfare State and Competitiveness (No. w4810)*. Cambridge, MA: National Bureau of Economic Research.

Andress, H. J., and H. Lohmann (eds.) 2008. *The Working Poor in Europe: Employment, Poverty and Globalisation*. Cheltenham: Edward Elgar Publishing.

Arestis, P., A. Charles, and G. Fontana. 2013. "Financialization, the Great Recession, and the Stratification of the US Labor Market." *Feminist Economics* 19 (3), 152–180.

Bergh, A. 2014. "What are the Policy Lessons from Sweden? On the Rise, Fall and Revival of a Capitalist Welfare State." *New Political Economy* 19 (5), 662–694.

Blackmon, P. 2006. "The State: Back in the Center of the Globalization Debate." *International Studies Review* 8 (1), 116–119.

Blomqvist, P., and J. Palme. 2020. "Universalism in Welfare Policy: The Swedish Case Beyond 1990." *Social Inclusion* 8 (1), 114–123.

Borosch, N., J. Kuhlmann, and S. Blum. 2016. "Opening Up Opportunities and Risks? Retrenchment, Activation and Targeting as Main Trends of Recent Welfare State Reforms Across Europe." In *Challenges to European Welfare Systems*, edited by K. Schubert, P. de Villota, and J. Kuhlmann, 769–791. Cham: Springer.

CNEL. 2019. *XXI rapporto mercato del lavoro e contrattazione collettiva*. https://www.cnel.it/Comunicazione-e-Stampa/Notizie/ArtMID/694/ArticleID/966/LUCI-E-OMBRE-DEL-MERCATO-DEL-LAVORO-NEL-XXI-RAPPORTO-CNEL.

Esping-Andersen, G. 1990. *The Three Worlds of Welfare Capitalism*. Princeton, NJ: Princeton University Press.

Furceri, D., and A. Zdzienicka. 2012. "The Effects of Social Spending on Economic Activity: Empirical Evidence from a Panel of OECD Countries." *Fiscal Studies* 33 (1), 129–152.

Galbraith, J. K. 2012. *Inequality and Instability: A Study of the World Economy Just Before the Great Crisis*. Oxford: Oxford University Press.

Greve, B. 2020. *Austerity, Retrenchment and the Welfare State: Truth or Fiction?* Cheltenham: Edward Elgar Publishing.

Hay, C. 1998. "Globalisation, Welfare Retrenchment and 'The Logic of No Alternative': Why Second-Best Won't Do." *Journal of Social Policy* 27 (4), 525–532.

Hyde, M., J. Dixon, and G. Drover. 2003. "Welfare Retrenchment or Collective Responsibility? The Privatisation of Public Pensions in Western Europe." *Social Policy and Society* 2 (3), 189–197.

ILO. 2021. *World Social Protection Report 2020–22: Social Protection at the Crossroads – In Pursuit of a Better Future*. https://www.ilo.org/global/publications/books/WCMS_817572/lang-en/index.htm.

IMF. 2021. *Fiscal Monitor. A Fair Shot. April 2021*. https://www.imf.org/en/Publications/FM/Issues/2021/03/29/fiscal-monitor-april-2021.

INPS. 2020. *XIX Rapporto annuale – Tra emergenza e rilancio*. https://www.inps.it/docallegatiNP/Mig/Allegati/XIX_Rapporto_INPS_31_10_2020_compressed.pdf

Jensen, C., and K. van Kersbergen. 2017. "Goldilocks' Frankenstein Monster: The Rise, Political Entrenchment and Transformation of the Scandinavian Welfare States." In *The Routledge Handbook of Scandinavian Politics*, edited by P. Nedergaard and A. Wivel, 69–79. London and New York: Routledge.

Jessop, B. 2018. "Neoliberalism and Workfare: Schumpeterian or Ricardian." In *SAGE Handbook of Neoliberalism*, edited by D. Cahill, M. Cooper, M. Konings, and D. Primrose, 347–358.

Klein, B. W., and P. L. Rones. 1989. "A Profile of the Working Poor." *Monthly Labor Review* 112, 3–13.

Kvist, J., and B. Greve. 2011. "Has the Nordic Welfare Model been Transformed?" *Social Policy & Administration* 45 (2), 146–160.

Lindert, P. H. 2004. *Growing Public: Social Spending and Economic Growth Since the Eighteenth Century*. Cambridge: Cambridge University Press.

Mitchell, D. J. 2005. "The Impact of Government Spending on Economic Growth." *The Heritage Foundation* 1813, 1–18.

Palley, T. I. 2012. *From Financial Crisis to Stagnation: The Destruction of Shared Prosperity and the Role of Economics*. Cambridge: Cambridge University Press.

Pradella, L. 2015. "The Working Poor in Western Europe: Labour, Poverty and Global Capitalism." *Comparative European Politics* 13 (5), 596–613.

Rodrik, D. 1998. "Why Do More Open Economies Have Bigger Governments?" *Journal of Political Economy* 106 (5), 997–1032.

Stockhammer, E. 2015. "Rising Inequality as a Cause of the Present Crisis." *Cambridge Journal of Economics* 39 (3), 935–958.

Storm, S., and C. W. M. Naastepad. 2012. *Macroeconomics Beyond the NAIRU*. Cambridge, MA: Harward University Press.

Svallfors, S., and A. Tyllström. 2017. *Lobbying for Profits: Private Companies and the Privatization of the Welfare State in Sweden*. Stockholm: Institute for Futures Studies, Working Paper 1, 1–30.

Taylor-Gooby, P. 1997. "In Defence of Second-Best Theory: State, Class and Capital in Social Policy. *Journal of Social Policy* 26 (2), 171–192.

Taylor-Gooby, P., B. Leruth, and H. Chung (eds.) 2017. *After Austerity: Welfare State Transformation in Europe After the Great Recession*. Oxford: Oxford University Press.

Trenz, H. J., and M. Grasso. 2018. "Toward a New Conditionality of Welfare? Reconsidering Solidarity in the Danish Welfare State." In Solidarity in Europe: Citizens' Responses in Times of Crisis, edited by C. Lahusen and M. Grasso, 19–41. Cham: Palgrave Macmillan.

Tridico, P. 2012. "Financial Crisis and Global Imbalances: Its Labour Market Origins and the Aftermath." *Cambridge Journal of Economics* 36 (1), 17–42.

Tridico, P., and W. Paternesi Meloni. 2018. "Economic Growth, Welfare Models and Inequality in the Context of Globalisation." *The Economic and Labour Relations Review* 29 (1), 118–139.

Van Oorschot, W., and F. Roosma. 2017. "The Social Legitimacy of Targeted Welfare and Welfare Deservingness." In *The Social Legitimacy of Targeted Welfare: Attitudes on Welfare Deservingness*, edited by W. van Oorschot, F. Roosma, B. Meuleman, and R. Reeskens, 3–35. Cheltenham: Edward Elgar Publishing.

Alexandra Lopes and Virginija Poškutė
14 Long-Term Care in ageing societies

Abstract: Although Long-Term Care (LTC) has taken the lead in many debates about the challenges faced by the contemporary Welfare States in fast ageing populations, at present, only a few EU countries provide comprehensive social protection to cover the need for care in old age. The demand for LTC for older people, however, is growing and is expected to increase in the coming years, despite any optimistic forecasts about gains in healthy years in old age. Mirroring historical paths of institutional development, as well as cultural norms and social roles different stakeholders are assigned when defining responsibilities, the institutional landscape one finds across Europe is varied and often fragmented.This chapter discusses the recent trends in the development of LTC for older people across Europe looking at both demand and supply side dynamics. It looks at the opportunities as well as the limitations of different paths of policy design and welfare state development in tackling the main elements of pressure that shape recent trends and challenges in policy development in the field of LTC: growing demand for formal care provision; demand for higher levels of quality in service provision; centrality of the person-centered care model and ageing in place.

Keywords: Long-Term Care, ageing, formal care, care workforce, welfare state, informal care, quality of care, dependency, social protection

14.1 Introduction

There has been a widespread consensus about the importance of Long-Term Care (LTC) in ageing societies (Colombo et al. 2011). The belief that as people age and live more years increases the likelihood of them needing some help for activities of daily living and assistance with personal care has been at the core of many calls for expansion and improvement of existing care provisions (Rodrigues, Huber, and Lamura 2012). One could say it is an old story that has been around in policy discourses for quite a long time. Recent times, however, have been revealing about how little has changed over the years and about how the gaps and weaknesses of existing LTC systems still endure, with terrible consequences to those requiring assistance. The recent public-health emergency due to the COVID-19 pandemic has been, for many, an eye-opener. It has brought to surface the structural problems that LTC systems have been facing since their inception, despite the diversity of arrangements one finds worldwide and even in those countries traditionally known to have the more advanced systems in place (Rostgard 2020). Ill-prepared to deal with the impacts of the pandemic among the older and frailer citizens, governments across Europe have witnessed rising numbers of infections and deaths among those living in institutional care facilities

https://doi.org/10.1515/9783110721768-014

(Comas-Herrera et al. 2020). Lock-downs and restrictions in home-help services as a mechanism to stop the spread of the transmission of the virus were put in place, leaving many deprived of their usual support mechanisms and with little to no room to replace them. If one thing all agree in the aftermath of the pandemic, things cannot go back to what they were before.

Old challenges, especially those related to affordability, equity in access, and coverage, remain unchanged and are not tackled appropriately. But new challenges have gained momentum and are likely to take the front page of policy debates in the coming years: securing efficient arrangements that safeguard fundamental rights and freedoms; promoting models of care provision that are person-centred and offer the necessary flexibility to accommodate freedom of choice and autonomy; deinstitutionalising and promoting ageing in the community.

In this chapter, the authors wish to address the current state of affairs of LTC to older persons across Europe. The chapter will start with a general outline of the landscape of LTC models in place, focusing on their historical paths of development and the specifics of their arrangements in tackling their older citizens' needs. The authors move then to the discussion of some contemporary trends in LTC that cut across all national systems, albeit with different impacts and implications, and summarise the challenges that LTC systems will have to face in the coming decades.

14.2 LTC in Europe: a fragmented and unchanged landscape

European countries are ageing rapidly. Increasing numbers of people living longer implicate that there will be more older[1] people at risk of suffering mental and physical frailty and needing either formal or informal care (Rodrigues, Huber, and Lamura 2012).

Arrangements for Long-Term Care of older persons vary a lot among European countries (Greve 2017a). A wide variety of available formal and informal arrangements in Europe, on one hand, can be explained by cultural traditions and different perceptions about family and state responsibilities towards older persons and their care. On the other hand, Long-Term Care of older persons in some countries is a relatively recent "social risk" that still lacks full embodiment in national legislation. Historically, in many European countries, care of older family members was secured by their families (Ranci and Pavolini 2013). However, increasing numbers of older people and much longer life expectancy, coupled with changing family arrangements (less extended families, fewer children, higher divorce rates, more single people, increasing

---

1 Older people here are considered those who are aged 65 and over.

migration, etc.) have been putting under pressure those traditional arrangements (Pickard 2015). Family networks are often not there anymore. Thus in many European countries, especially in Eastern, Central, and Southern Europe where most of the care at an older age is still provided informally, via family networks, LTC has been gaining more attention in national legislation. Slowly these countries have been converging around the need to advance on formal LTC to prevent situations when an older person is left without necessary support when needed. They are, however, in a relative state of infancy when it comes to their LTC systems. In Scandinavian and some Western countries, on the other hand, care is much more formalised, and there is a variety of institutional arrangements available for those needing care.

Furthermore, there is no uniform definition of LTC across European countries – each country defines Long-Term Care according to their national laws. A person might be recognised as needing care in one country, but not necessarily in another country. Legal regulations concerning LTC of older persons in European nations are widely dispersed among social security, health care, and social assistance laws. Long-Term Care is often approached as a mix of different services and benefits, funded through various sources and organised at different levels (national and local). Long-Term Care in this chapter refers to the organisation and delivery of a broad range of services and assistance to people with a reduced degree of functional capacity, physical or cognitive, and who are consequently dependent for an extended period on help with basic activities of daily living (ADL).[2]

Legal requirements to be considered as needing care at older age stipulate costs of public LTC. Benefits and services to be granted to older people are directly related to the assessment rules and criteria of different capabilities in daily life (ADL). The type and extent of benefits and services offered to older persons needing LTC in turn very much relate to available financial resources and social policy priorities in a country. As most needs have to be dealt with individually through personal aid and support, LTC services are quite costly for national budgets as they are labour intensive. One of the common trends that countries have been following, including those with more mature LTC systems, is the allocation of care according to the severity of the dependency. Rationing care delivery based on needs assessment and prioritising the most severe cases is a policy path that one finds across Europe. It indeed contains the expansion of formal care arrangements and respective pressures on funding. Thus, slower legitimation of LTC in some countries can probably also be explained by reluctance to increase necessary financial resources significantly. As the available data indicates, despite increasing demand for LTC and ongoing public debates about the necessity to broaden service availability, the percentage of GDP devoted for LTC did not change significantly during the last decade (refer to Figures 14.1 and 14.2) (Eurostat; OECD 2019).

---

2 Definition used in Horizon2020 project SPRINT (https://cordis.europa.eu/project/id/649565). Deliverable 2.2.

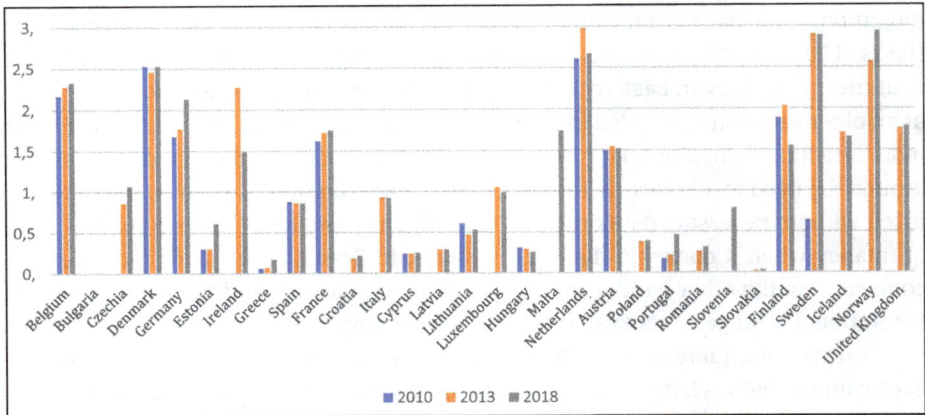

Figure 14.1: Long-Term Care (health) expenditure as % of GDP in selected European countries.
Source: Eurostat

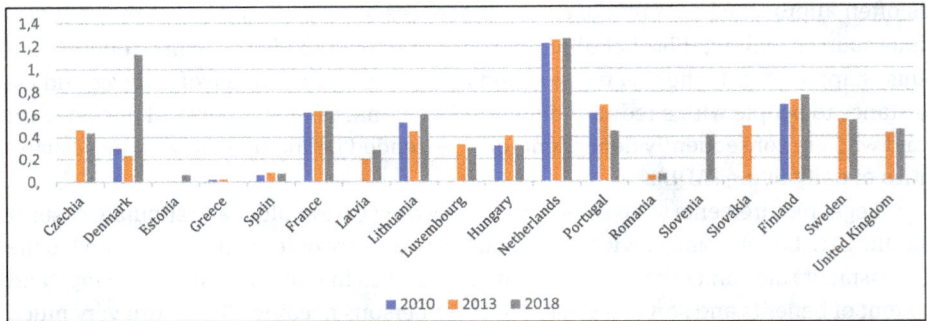

Figure 14.2: Long-Term Care (social) expenditure as % of GDP in selected European countries.
Source: Eurostat

As LTC benefits and services are related to various needs of older people – assistance with daily life routines, health care, social and psychological services – a broad range of stakeholders are usually involved in organising and delivering the care. Very often, only well-coordinated efforts of policymakers, regulators, and providers at the national level together with care planners, organisers, and providers at the local level, often coming from public, private, and non-governmental sectors, can satisfy rapidly the increasing demand for care and ensure system efficiency (Poškutė, Kazlauskaitė, and Matonytė 2021). In some of the countries, when responsibilities are widely dispersed among such a large number of LTC stakeholders, care is quite fragmented as each stakeholder deals only with a particular issue within LTC. There are various initiatives among European countries, some more formalised than others, to introduce integrated health and social services together for older people, as often they overlap or complement each other. Integration of the services may increase the quality and efficiency of the care and improve access to it. However, the quality of coordination between LTC and other services only in Austria, Belgium, Denmark, Finland, Latvia and Sweden was indicated as "rather good", while in most of the European countries (Bulgaria, Czech Republic, England, Estonia, France, Germany, Italy, Lithuania, The Netherlands, Poland, Slovakia, Slovenia, and Spain) provision of the care is indicated as fragmented and often posing a challenge for a (prospective) care recipient (Kraus et al. 2010; EC 2016). Hungary and Romania are listed as "very poor" in terms of the coordination and posing regular or severe challenges for (prospective) care recipients (EC 2016, 206).

LTC systems in Europe can be clustered in relation to formal versus informal care arrangements, the financing mode (national budget, social security, private out-of-pocket, or private insurance) and the levels of spending (please refer to Table 14.1 and Table 14.2.) (EC 2016). However, even the most generous, affordable, and accessible European LTC systems, as Denmark, The Netherlands, and Sweden, require private cost-sharing, which differs depending on type of delivered service and institutions where services are provided. Cost-sharing for the services might take several forms: individuals may be required to contribute if the costs for the LTC services exceed publicly financed services, flat-rate cost sharing might be applied as a percentage of LTC costs or cost-sharing depends on care recipient's income and/or assets owned. Private insurance for Long-Term Care is still of limited availability in Europe.

Table 14.1: Typology of Long-Term Care systems in Europe.

Cluster/type	Countries
Formal care-oriented provision, accessible and affordable, generous.	Denmark, The Netherlands, Sweden
Formal care of medium accessibility. Some informal care orientation in the provision.	Belgium, Czech Republic, Germany, Slovakia, Luxembourg
Formal care of medium to low accessibility. Medium informal care orientation in the provision.	Austria, England, Finland, France, Slovenia, Spain, Ireland
Low formal care accessibility. Strong informal care orientation in provision.	Hungary, Italy, Greece, Poland, Portugal
Rather low formal care accessibility. Almost exclusive informal care orientation in provision.	Bulgaria, Cyprus, Estonia, Lithuania, Latvia, Malta, Romania, Croatia

Source: EC 2016, 173. Copyright says: © European Union, 2016 Reproduction is authorised provided the source is acknowledged.

Despite the welfare state model, in all European countries (even those with well-developed state support and care of older persons) the informal sector[3] plays an impor-

---

3 Informal carers – those who provide help to older family members, friends, and people in their social network, living inside or outside of their household. Informal care usually is provided at the home of the care recipient and is typically free of charge.

tant or even central role in the care provided. The number of informal caregivers is estimated to be at least twice as big as the formal care providers, even in the countries with a well-developed supply of formal LTC (EU 2014). However, it is challenging to provide comprehensive estimations of numbers of informal carers as in some countries with strong familial networks, carers might not report as such when questioned. As some studies indicate, about two-thirds of informal carers are women aged 50 and over caring for a parent or a spouse (Colombo et al. 2011; OECD 2019).

Lack of formal LTC services for older people causes problems not only for people needing care but also for their family members. Most older people in need of care prefer staying in their own private environment and receive care at home over institutional care. It is estimated that around 70 % of LTC users receive services at home (Colombo et al. 2011). When supply of formal care services (for example, help with daily living activities) at home is limited, most of LTC services come informally from relatives or family members (refer to Figure 14.3). Informal care not only allows older people to have the psychological comfort of being at home but also helps to increase the financial sustainability of LTC systems (as it is most often provided voluntarily without payments). However, such a situation can significantly impact the carers themselves – their possibilities to balance work and life, professional careers, physical and mental health, and well-being. There are various attempts to evaluate these impacts (Bouget, Spasova, and Vanhercke 2016; Spasova et al. 2018; Colombo et al. 2011), however the information on the effects is quite fragmented as there is lack of available data for the analysis and clear methodology on how to evaluate the impact of informal care on various aspects of the carer's life as well as its input into the sustainability of LTC systems and the economy as a whole.

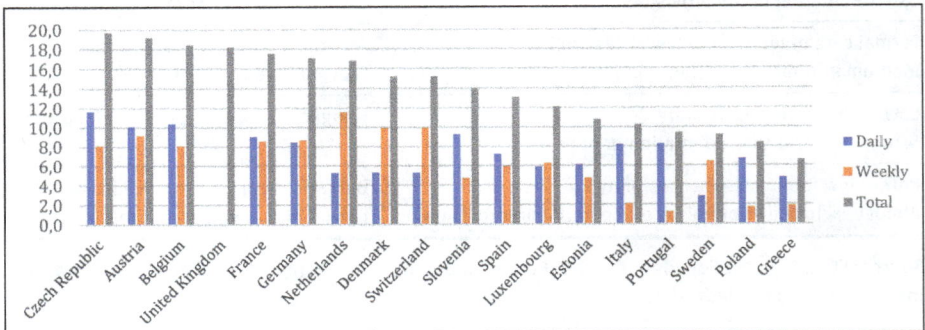

Figure 14.3: Population aged 50 and over reporting to be informal carers in selected European countries, %, 2017 (or nearest year).
Source: OECD 2019.

There is increasing interest and involvement of non-public institutions (private sector and NGOs) to provide services for older people in most European countries. Marketisation of LTC can be observed in all European countries, despite variation in welfare state models. However, compensation for the services via such organisations varies a lot within Europe. In some Scandinavian and Western European countries private sector is included as a "partner" in public care programmes trying to satisfy the increasing demand for the services and shortage of public services. These services often are at least partially if not fully compensated from the public budget. However, in other countries with reliance mostly on informal care (such as Southern, Central and Eastern Europe) private sector and NGOs try to fill the gap in the formal LTC system. As the services are costly and often reimbursed only partially or not at all, only a limited part of the population can afford to use them in these countries.

The labour force traditionally employed in the formal LTC sector is primarily female, not very young in age and typically with low qualifications when compared to the labour force in the health care sector. Estimates for the OECD countries suggested that around 90 % of LTC workers are women, with a median age of 45 plus. In the majority of countries, their qualifications are low (OECD 2020). Wages are generally low, contributing to the low attractiveness and high rotation of the job. OECD estimates point to the average hourly pay of around 9 euros to LTC workers, although this number comes with high variation across countries. In countries such as Portugal or Estonia, LTC workers in charge of personal care have their wages set at the national minimum wage level (OECD 2020).

Rotation of workers is another classic feature of the labour force in LTC. This is not only the result of low pay and the general low status of care professions, but also a direct result of the demanding, often hazardous working conditions. Care workers often work in shifts, which creates unique challenges for work–life balance. They carry out demanding tasks, both physically and mentally. Despite their low qualifications and the often absent training to do the job, these workers are asked to perform tasks that are complex and for which they often lack any specific training (Schulz 2013). This not only puts additional pressure on workers but also impacts the quality of care they provide (Nunes and Cerqueira 2020).

As jobs in this sector are often characterised by low salaries, part or short time contracts and low social recognition, this does not encourage younger people to choose a carer's professional career. Furthermore, differences in living standards between European countries encourage carers' migration from countries with lower average salaries to wealthier countries to provide care services formally or informally as the shortage of care employees is faced everywhere.

It is in this fragmented and persistent context that yesterday's call for better, more affordable, sustainable and equitable LTC remains today's call and most likely tomorrow's call. In the next section of the paper the authors offer an overview of some of the most pressing contemporary challenges that LTC across Europe will have to face.

14.3 LTC across Europe: challenges and opportunities

Long-Term Care of older people faces significant challenges in all European countries. Satisfaction of the rapidly growing demand for LTC is challenged by a shortage of carers, both formal and informal. As the availability of informal carers is decreasing because of changing family patterns, demand for formal care services is likely to increase further. If the current average ratio of 5 LTC workers for every 100 people aged 65 and older is kept in OECD countries, the number of workers in the sector will have to increase by 13.5 million by 2040 (OECD 2020). As for European countries, it is forecasted that future employment growth in health and social care sectors will increase by 10.1 % from 2020 to 2030 in the EU (Cedefop database[4]).

Another issue that LTC systems around Europe face is the improvement of the governance and coordination of provision of various services from health, social care, or LTC sectors. Improved coordination would increase administrative efficiency as well as help advance LTC financing arrangements. Labour intensive and more individualised LTC services are costly for public budgets (refer to Figure 14.4). As demand for these services is rapidly increasing, it is expected that public LTC expenditure in the EU will increase from 1.6 % to 2.7 % of GDP, which implies coming pressure on public finances (European Commission 2016). Without an indication of LTC of older people as a special social risk and without prioritising it in national social policies, there might be challenges for public budgets.

As most European countries encourage home care, support for informal carers has to be either introduced or advanced. There are attempts in several countries to introduce carers' leave or benefits in cash and in kind that help carers to balance their work and care obligations. Labour market flexibility is also of importance, allowing carers to stay in employment. So far, only Denmark, Finland, and Sweden within the EU have developed mature support schemes for informal carers (Bouget, Spasova, and Vanhercke 2016).

Better access and a higher quality of services is likely to be the expectation for LTC in the very near future. As self-care and staying at home is desired by most older people, more assistive devices facilitating self-care and preventive measures will have to be introduced. Personalised approaches and investment in ICT allowing to better source information, manage, and coordinate care services seem inevitable as well.

In this section of the chapter the authors revise some contemporary debates about the way forward for LTC and look at examples of policy developments that countries across Europe experience while trying to embody those principles.

---

4 https://skillspanorama.cedefop.europa.eu/en/dashboard/future-employment-growth?year=2020-2030&country=EU27_2020#2.

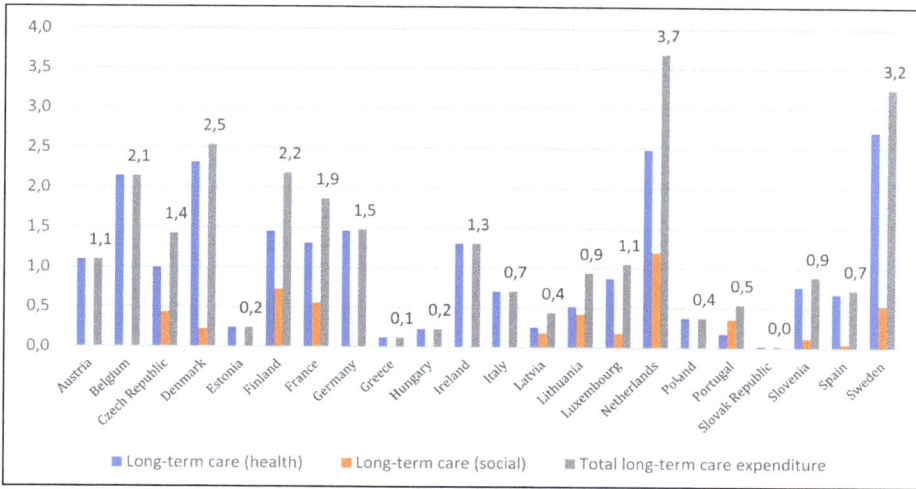

Figure 14.4: Long-Term Care expenditure (health and social components) by government and compulsory insurance schemes, as a share of GDP, 2017 (or nearest year).
Source: OECD 2019.

14.3.1 Tackling supply: how to increase the number and the retention of LTC workers? What is the place for informal care?

Within the diversity of LTC arrangements found across Europe, there is one trend that seems to be cutting across all countries – the increase in the number of older people takes place faster than the increase in the number of workers engaged in LTC. Although a case could be made for it not being necessary that the two should walk in parallel, considering increased life expectancy and particularly increases in years of good health, it is a statement that would only hold for a very few countries. For example, in Sweden the marked decrease in the ratio of staff/old persons is not a cause for concern if one looks at the high levels of LTC workers and that Sweden is one of the countries with the highest life expectancy free of disease.

The same, however, cannot be said for countries such as Portugal or Hungary, still in their infancy with regard to the LTC labour force and where accelerated ageing of the population is likely to aggravate existing gaps in LTC provision. Figure 14.5 below shows, for a handful of countries, the variation found across Europe in this respect. The data concerns the ratio of personal carers[5] to older people. The lines, in all

---

5 Personal care workers (caregivers) include formal workers providing LTC services at home or in institutions (other than hospitals) and who are not qualified or certified as nurses. As per the definition in the ISCO-08 classification (5322 for Home-based personal care workers and 5321 for Personal care assistants), personal care workers are defined as people providing routine personal care, such as bath-

scenarios represented by the selected countries, show a downward trend in the number of personal carers per older population.

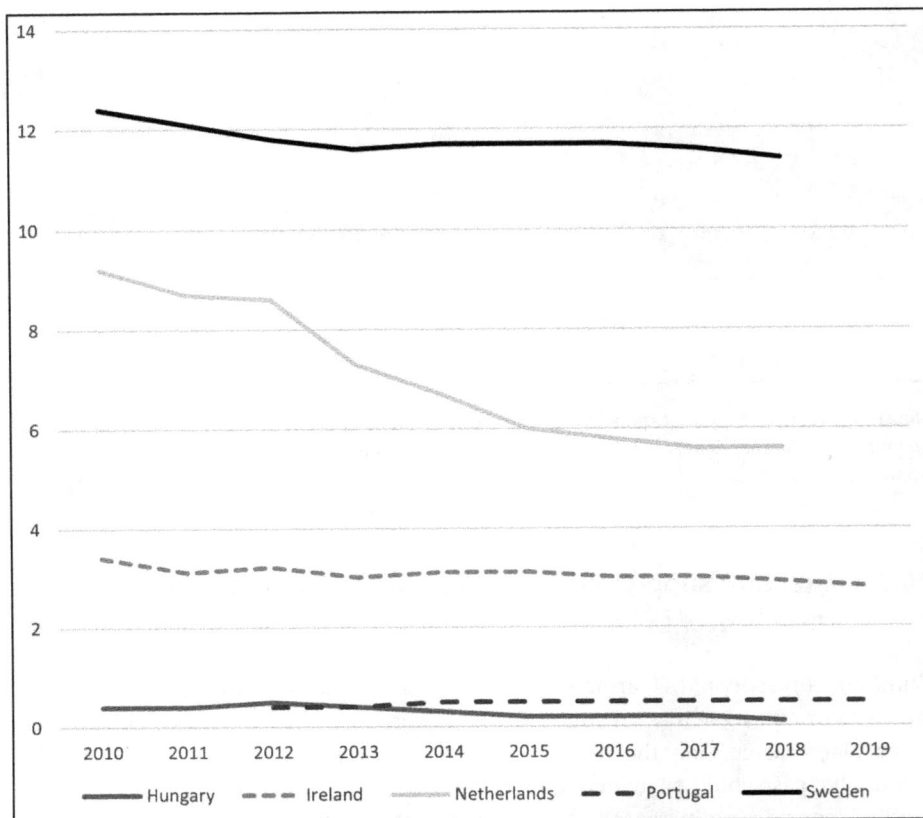

Figure 14.5: Personal carers per 100 population aged 65 years old and over (2010–2019).
Source: OECD Health Statistics 2018, https://doi.org/10.1787/health-data-en

There is a growing consensus that in many countries across Europe the need to expand the number of LTC workers will be a sizeable challenge. For instance, studies show the number of LTC workers will decrease in Germany and Poland and stagnate in the Netherlands, while demand for LTC services will increase in the coming decades (Geerts 2011). Recently, a report commissioned by the Ministry of Social Security in France estimated that over 150,000 full-time equivalent workers will be needed by

---

ing, dressing, or grooming, to persons who are in need of such care due to effects of ageing, illness, injury, or other physical or mental conditions, in private homes and or in institutions (other than hospitals) (Source: OECD Health Statistics 2021, Definitions, Sources and Methods, https://www.oecd.org/els/health-systems/Table-of-Content-Metadata-OECD-Health-Statistics-2021.pdf.)

2030 (Libault 2019). There are countries where the situation is even more complex as in some Eastern and Central European countries (for example, Poland, Romania, and Slovakia). The stock of LTC workers in these countries represents less than half the OECD average, according to the latest estimates, and no signs of change are foreseen (OECD 2020). In Southern Europe, countries such as Portugal and Italy are under severe pressure by insufficient numbers of formal workers.

Countries are at different stages of development and institutionalisation of their LTC systems, as discussed in the previous section, and therefore the challenge of increasing the number of LTC workers will certainly be addressed in different ways. There are, however, some aspects that seem to cut across all countries. Those aspects are related to some of the intrinsic characteristics of care professions, historically associated with females and to gendered notions of caring, with low to no entrance requirements in terms of skills or training, typically paying low or very low salaries. All these characteristics explain the low social status of care professions, which, together with the hard working conditions and the health risks they pose, make them unattractive. Estimates about the turnover of workers in the LTC sector in OECD countries suggest that, on average, workers do not stay in their jobs for more than two years (OECD 2020). Work hours in LTC tend to be hard, as it is the type of work that often involves working in shifts, which makes the work–life balance a challenge. Work-related injuries and mental health conditions are more prevalent among these workers than in other sectors. This is due to the physically demanding tasks they have to perform, especially when providing personal care, and the combined effect of inadequate training and low use of assistive technology.

Based on these considerations, the challenge ahead is more complex than just opening new posts. It seems to be about being able to attract workers to those posts, which demands increasing the profile of care professions. On the other hand, it will be about improving working conditions to increase retention rates. Some countries have been relying heavily on migrant care workers to feed the demand for care workers. Although they may offer an immediate solution for the shortage of workers in a given country, massive flows of migrant care workers leave care gaps in their countries of origin, therefore, increasing the global pressure on LTC. Additionally, their willingness to endure hard working conditions, often working more and longer hours than nationals, does not necessarily mean they will stay for longer in the job or that they will constitute a long-term reserve of workers (Sowa-Kofta et al. 2019).

National LTC systems will have to find ways to make the job more attractive if they wish to achieve relevant changes in their stock of LTC workers. There is more than one path available, and some countries across Europe have already started taking some steps in that direction.

One approach involves attempts to raise the social status of care professions, namely with planned campaigns that try to raise awareness about LTC among the general public attracting younger people to the sector or target those already in care professions aiming to increase retention rates. The UK has launched the Proud to Care initiative that includes outreach activities to help the population understand better what care work entails.[6] The same approach has been followed in Belgium (Flanders) and France, with campaigns promoting the positive aspects of caring and values-based recruitment (OECD 2020). Other initiatives promote social recognition of care professionals, such as the Caregiver of the Year Award patronised by the Czech Republic Ministry of Labour and Social Affairs.

Another approach is found in countries such as Norway or the Netherlands, where campaigns such as the Job Winner (Norway) and We Have Something For You (Netherlands) target unemployed people and offer them job opportunities in LTC. These are campaigns that are typically opened to the general labour force as LTC is a sector primarily employing low-skilled employees. Some countries have implemented specific programmes to integrate long-term unemployed individuals in the labour market and often pool them into the LTC sector. Such is the case of Portugal, although with results that often involve a significant mismatch between skills and expectations of the worker and the work actually offered.

Some countries have been pursuing a more traditional approach and trying to increase recruitment in the traditional segments of the workforce associated with LTC. This involves, on one hand, strengthening the ties between those providing the training and those looking for workers. This often translates into internship opportunities and additional training experiences, in view of attracting young students to the LTC sector. Germany has been developing such initiatives. On the other hand, some countries have actively pursued efforts to bring back to LTC those who left. Estonia, for example, has implemented the Nurse Back to Health Care Programme. Germany, on the other hand, launched the initiative Concerted Action on Nursing to promote retraining into the profession (OECD 2020).

A fourth line of action targets overcoming gendered representations of LTC and attracting male workers to care professions. Some documented initiatives can be found in Norway, with its Men in Health Recruitment Programme, or in the United Kingdom with its Men Into Care Programme. Some more subtle initiatives can be found in other countries, where the imagery of LTC is being reshaped. A couple of years ago, in France, The Caisse Nationale de Solidarité Pour l'Autonomie (CNSA) has released a TV campaign to inform older people and their relatives about how to tackle needs for LTC. In the campaign, male characters were used as care providers working in institutional care facilities.[7]

Although merits can be seen in all the different initiatives found across Europe, a significant shift in the number of LTC workers is unlikely to occur if working conditions, including wages, are not improved. However, improving working conditions

---

6 https://www.proudtocarenorthlondon.org.uk/
7 https://www.pour-les-personnes-agees.gouv.fr/videotheque/e3466be2-d8b4-4d0c-8d95-c95d84e6 d924

may mean, in many cases, an increase in the need for workers. Improving work sche-dules and managing the replacement of absent workers without overburdening those at work are needed to increase job satisfaction and retention of workers but cannot be implemented without increasing the number of workers.

Improving training and skills of LTC workers, especially those engaged in perso-nal care, is also a promising path to improve working conditions and increase chances of workers retention, as workers will be better prepared to deal with aspects of work that often end up being severe sources of stress and illness due to lack of preparation on the worker's side. However, and once more, this is a line of action that will have likely side effects, namely in terms of wages, as better qualifications go hand in hand with the increase of wages.

An essential element to consider in the equation of the stock of LTC workers con-cerns the role of informal, unpaid carers. They are too often absent from macroeco-nomic projections, as they tend to be regarded by mainstream economics as free, un-limited, and self-replacing resources that are independent from the market. Recent events in pandemic times have been enough to convince even the most sceptical that it might not be an entirely accurate vision.

When addressing needs for LTC workers, one must consider the invisible care work that has been secured over the years by families, especially in some countries where these constitute the lion's share of care provision. Economic policies across Europe have emphasised fiscal sustainability associated with integration in the labour market, which puts a lot of pressure on the available reserves of informal carers. Poli-cies to promote gender equality are mostly focused on integrating more women into the labour market, which further decreases the availability of informal carers. Jug-gling these two parameters is the challenge, and countries across Europe are slowly understanding that there is a significant social return from policies targeting support to informal carers. Initiatives to formalise the status of informal carers have spread across Europe, with most countries already including in their LTC systems some provi-sions concerning informal carers, even if minimal. Table 14.2 below displays the cur-rent state of affairs across EU countries in the specific area of policies/benefits target-ing informal carers of older dependent persons.

Table 14.2: Current policies/benefits targeting informal carers of dependent older people and projections of LTC for 2030 as % of GDP with and without any shift in demand for formal care (marks signal existing provisions in the national legislation).

Country	(1)	(2)	(3)	(4)	(5)	(6)	(7)	(8)	(9)	(10)
Austria	●			●	●	●		●	2.3	2.9
Belgium		●		●		●		●	2.6	3.0
Bulgaria		●				●	●		0.5	0.7
Croatia									1.0	1.4

Table 14.2: (continued)

Country	(1)	(2)	(3)	(4)	(5)	(6)	(7)	(8)	(9)	(10)
Cyprus									0.4	0.4
Czech Republic	●	●	●				●	●	1.8	2.3
Denmark		●	●	●		●		●	3.3	4.0
Estonia		●				●		●	1.0	1.2
Finland	●	●	●	●	●			●	3.0	3.4
France	●		●	●		●	●		1.9	2.4
Germany	●		●	●		●	●		1.7	2.5
Greece						●			0.1	0.1
Hungary		●	●				●	●	0.8	1.0
Ireland		●	●	●			●	●	1.7	2.1
Italy	●					●		●	2.0	2.4
Latvia	●	●							0.5	0.7
Lithuania	●			●					1.3	1.5
Luxembourg	●		●	●	●	●		●	1.6	1.9
Malta	●			●		●			1.3	1.4
Poland				●					0.7	1.1
Portugal	●		●	●		●		●	0.7	1.9
Romania									0.4	0.5
Slovakia		●	●	●		●			1.1	1.6
Slovenia	●	●							1.1	1.5
Spain	●	●		●		●		●	1.2	1.4
Sweden	●	●	●	●	●	●		●	3.8	4.6
The Netherlands		●	●	●	●			●	4.4	5.2

Dimensions of analysis:
(1) Carer's allowance paid directly to person requiring care
(2) Carer's allowance paid directly to informal carer
(3) Possibility of carer's training
(4) Possibility of respite care for carer's rest
(5) Health and well-being inspections/visits
(6) Possibility of paid care leave from work
(7) Possibility of unpaid care leave from work
(8) Guarantee of social and health insurance
(9) Long-Term Care public expenditure projected for 2030: constant scenario at 2016 (% of GDP)

(10) Long-Term Care public expenditure projected for 2030 with estimates of 1 % yearly increase in number of older people using formal care (% GDP)
Source: Own classification using information available at MISSOC (Mutual Information System on Social Protection) (https://www.missoc.org/) and information compiled by Eurocarers in the Country profile Reports (https://eurocarers.org/country-profiles/).

With very few exceptions, most countries have moved to include in their LTC provisions some care allowance in cash (columns 1 and 2). In some countries, it is the care recipient that gets the care allowance. In others, the allowance is paid directly to the informal carer. In others there is a combination of both. In any case, there is a widespread acknowledgment that some exchange of money must be involved in informal caregiving, if not to fully pay the costs of care, at least to minimise the loss of income of those who have to forfeit paid work to care for a relative. Care allowances in cash vary quite a lot in generosity, mirroring both the strength of the national economies and the maturity of their welfare state arrangements. They also vary in terms of entitlement/eligibility principles, ranging from a universal flat-rate approach to a variety of conditional access based on income (of care recipient and/or carer) and based on the level of need of the recipient.

Benefits in kind for informal carers are less developed, and there are still many countries where provisions are totally absent or very scarce (columns 3 and 4). This is particularly so when we focus on the provision of mechanisms of support targeting the carer's well-being regularly, where only 5 out of 27 countries have some specific tools in place (column 5).

Adjustments in labour legislation to account for the conciliation of work-care are still underdeveloped across most European countries (columns 6, 7, and 8). Even in those where we find some dispositions concerning the possibility of paid and/or unpaid leave to care for older dependent relatives, typically they come with a lot of conditions that need to be met for eligibility and are often very limited in the duration of the leave. As a result, existing provisions tend to be very narrow in scope and do not facilitate the participation and/or the return of carers to the regular labour market.

The specific effect of shifting care from informal provision to formal provision illustrates the variety of arrangements countries have in place but overall offers evidence for the economic interest of supporting informal carers (columns 9 and 10). Projections for the needs of formal LTC workers are often run on somewhat optimistic terms in what concerns the changes in the available stock of informal carers. Supporting the latter is of critical consequence for the former.

14.3.2 Tackling quality: how to enforce guidelines and quality control mechanisms to assure the quality of care?

Policy discussions about LTC, even in countries with less developed systems, have long gone beyond just quantitative issues of access and coverage to include quality, effectiveness, and responsiveness issues. There is, in fact, a broad consensus about securing that care provided to those who need it, is care of good quality that safeguards human rights and enables individuals to live their lives as much as possible as they prefer, defending their autonomy and freedom of choice.

The acknowledgment of such a principle has led to many calls for improving quality and quality control mechanisms in LTC, even from those typically more focused on issues of financial sustainability and fiscal balances. In 2013 the OECD partnered with the European Commission to launch the joint report to improve and monitor quality in LTC (OECD/European Union 2013). The report offers a general overview of existing quality monitoring trends and mechanisms in LTC across Europe. It shows that solutions are quite different across countries, but the topic still falls far short of the stated political ambition in the vast majority.

The available evidence signals different paths and points to the complexity of the topic especially considering the number of stakeholders involved in LTC (Lopes and Dias 2018; Greve 2017b). In some countries, there are variations across regions and municipalities and there are even reports of a "post code lottery" of LTC to account for territorial variations inside the same country (Zigante and King 2018). There are variations in what quality means, across countries and across stakeholders and how to measure it (Poškutė, Kazlauskaitė, and Matonytė 2021). The challenge ahead may be precisely harmonising criteria and developing structures to monitor and enforce quality standards. For example, among the 27 EU countries, only five have explicit LTC quality guidelines (Denmark, Finland, Ireland, Italy and The Netherlands).

Looking at developments across Europe, countries will soon need to tackle some aspects if to answer effectively to calls for quality improvement and quality enforcement. We briefly outline some of those aspects in the following paragraphs. Overall, the challenges ahead can be summarised into two main lines of action: one, more focused on processes, must tackle responsiveness and coordination of LTC systems – LTC arrangements must respond adequately to the needs of those who need care, meeting their preferences and expectations and addressing their needs and life circumstances from a holistic perspective; the other, more focused on outcomes, must tackle safeguarding and the promotion of quality of life – LTC arrangements must offer safe solutions to meet needs while creating opportunities for individuals to enjoy life in a fulfilling manner, safeguarding their fundamental rights and freedoms.

The first aspect that is still not fully developed across national LTC systems concerns the classic approach to quality based on setting regulatory standards. This involves licensing, accreditation, and the definition of minimum standards that LTC providers need to meet if allowed to operate. Across Europe, and when looking at formal LTC provision, especially in institutional care facilities, one can find some regulatory frameworks. This is particularly so in the licensing of institutions. The same, however, cannot be said in respect of home care services, where few rules exist and where monitoring mechanisms are much less developed (Tarricone and Tsouros 2008). This is certainly an aspect to consider, particularly taking into account the pressure to prioritise care in the community arrangements and ageing in place approaches to LTC. The same goes for informal care provision. There is significant variation across Europe in what concerns the degree of formalisation of informal care. In the countries that rely more on this type of care, we find less developed, or even absent, regulations focusing on the quality of care. There are, in all countries, general dispositions that extend to informal care settings and focus on abuse prevention. Still, the quality of care in daily life and assessments of both carers and recipients of care is absent in most countries.

A second aspect that the sector will need to tackle concerns the training and qualification of staff working in LTC. There is ample evidence in the literature about the importance of staff safeguarding quality of care. Training of workforce dominated by individuals with low or very low qualifications is of critical importance. Training, however, cannot focus exclusively on technical skills to perform the task but must also include aspects of person-centred care and rights and freedoms. However, improving the qualifications of the workforce will likely need to be accompanied by enhancements in working conditions and better salary conditions. This is likely to put additional pressure on costs.

A third aspect we would like to address concerns setting guidelines. There are not many countries across Europe that have implemented national guidelines for the LTC sector. The importance of having such guidelines is that they set standards that normalise care. They set objectives against which practices and achievements can be assessed. Once these guidelines are set, a series of other processes can be triggered, namely establishing rankings based on achievements, awards distinguishing promising practices, financial incentives, among other mechanisms of distinction and stimulus to improvement.

A fourth and last aspect in regard to quality of care concerns disseminating information and overall transparency in the sector. It is still challenging for citizens to make decisions about how to meet their needs for care in some countries as information is scarce and often dispersed (Kraus et al. 2010; Poškutė, Kazlauskaitė, and Matonytė 2021). This is detrimental not only for easy access but hampers significantly the exercise of choice.

14.4 From institutions to community: how to reconcile ageing in place and freedom of choice with traditions of institutional care in LTC provision?

There is a wide consensus, built over the years, about the preferred path of LTC development to tackle needs of those requiring care – that path is the one of ageing in place. From the European Commission to the World Health Organization, from the OECD to the World Bank, all seem to speak with one voice on this particular issue – home-based help and community-based arrangements are the best as they combine the potential to secure good quality of life in old age while offering the most affordable arrangements from a financial costs perspective.

The European pillar of social rights stresses the right to affordable Long-Term Care services of good quality, particularly home-based care and community-based services, and joins a broader call for the development of community-based LTC solutions. However, these calls have had a shy translation in the development of the sector, especially in countries taking their first steps into formal LTC over the last two decades. Institutional care is still one of the preferred arrangements and is still expanding across many parts of Europe. Even in countries where it has been experiencing some decline, estimates suggest it may be pressured to expand once again in the near future (Alders and Schutz 2019).

There is not a specific history of the evolution of home care services in Europe, but rather many and varied histories, as service provision for older people is part of broader welfare state development that, as we know, has followed different paths across countries. Home help services are relatively developed in some systems, especially in the Nordic countries or in the UK, less in others, especially in Southern and Eastern European countries. In some places, they are organised at the local, municipal level. In others, they are managed centrally. Scope of care also varies, namely concerning the boundaries between health services and social/personal care services. Home-help has relied historically on informal carers, and countries differ as well on the level of support they grant to these carers.

One aspect of LTC provision that often goes unaccounted for in policy analysis is normative dispositions concerning old age. National arrangements in matters of social provision embody cultural traditions and normative dispositions that gather broad consensus among the respective populations. One cannot expect to understand one without considering the other. And here, the variation across Europe is also substantial.

Despite the variety found across Europe, there are some fundamental aspects that gather consensus across borders. The preference stated by most older people about not leaving their homes if the need for care comes their way is probably the number one consensus. Much literature discusses findings from international surveys on expectations and preferences about LTC, and results systematically seem to point in the direction of staying in one's home being the preferred solution (Lehnert et al. 2019).

To meet these preferences, LTC systems will need to find ways to reconcile some fundamental aspects of care provision and reimagine models of organisation, placing ageing in place at the centre of the equation. The challenges ahead are several.

Firstly, home-based care, understood as the best way to secure person-centred care, will require changes in cultures of care, largely subdued by a dominant culture of institutionalisation, where block-treatment and standardisation tend to be the rule. Flexibility to tailor care to the needs and preferences of each individual is certainly easier to achieve in a home setting but does not automatically happen just with the shift in the location of the care delivery. Care provision involves interactions between many professionals, the recipient of care, his/her relatives and friends, and these interactions are often challenging. Training of staff, support to informal carers and relatives of the recipient of care will be fundamental to secure a good quality of care.

Secondly, home-based care must take stock of the recent developments in assisted living technologies. LTC systems must move forward into the incorporation of new devices and services to facilitate the organisation of home-based services, particularly for those situations that require more complex arrangements due to the complexity of the health conditions of the recipient of care. Dementia offers an excellent example of both the challenges of tackling difficult health conditions in home-based settings and the potential of technology to help deliver complex care arrangements (Klimova, Valis, and Kuca 2018).

Thirdly, there must be a major shift from assistance to reablement and rehabilitation as part of preventing and postponing the onset of dependency and need for more acute and intensive care. The entire paradigm of healthy ageing is very much focused on preventing the need for care by building environments, skills, and resources that are conducive to a longer healthy life span. Reablement is the other side of that coin and as it has been demonstrated in some countries it may be a promising approach to contain costs while promoting quality of life and independence in old age. Reablement is about developing tailored care that targets the recovery of functional abilities rather than providing care that focuses solely on securing the assistance required due to loss of abilities. This is an approach that has been embraced in a more prominent way in Denmark with the Fredericia model. Fredericia is showing signs of being very cost-effective and has been an inspiration to other countries that are considering pursuing a similar path.

Lastly, we would like to emphasise the regulatory challenges, namely implementing an effective mechanism that can successfully enforce rules and guidelines concerning quality in home-based services. Structures to monitor quality will be in high demand, and they will have to be planned taking into account the locus of care provision, a place that is hidden from the public eye, given its private nature and where traditional mechanisms employed in institutional settings may not work as effectively.

14.5 Conclusion

Challenges of Long-Term Care have already been acknowledged for a long time in Europe. However, institutionalisation of LTC did not progress along with the acknowledgment of it in many countries. There is a wide variety in LTC definitions in national laws, in interpretations, on who is considered to be a dependent person at older age needing a support from a state, on the range of services that are included in LTC provision, on LTC financing levels and arrangements in different countries.

The social right to affordable Long-Term Care services of good quality is listed among the principles of the Social Pillar in the EU. However, with such a variety in arrangements and no clear consensus how this social right has to be secured, it seems that affordable and good quality Long-Term Care remains to be a desirable objective to reach, which might take a long time for many EU countries.

Long-existing and newly emerged LTC challenges due to the COVID-19 pandemic in ensuring availability of services for older people are related to a shortage of formal and informal carers, provision of good quality services, availability of financial resources, application of a person-centred approach, flexibility of arrangements in designing care and regulation and support to home care. As rapidly increasing demand for care is not likely to be satisfied without additional financial resources from public budgets, inclusion of Long-Term Care in national policies and instruments as an important social risk to be taken care of seem to be necessary in many European countries. EU coordination of LTC policies remains limited, as it is the responsibility of the countries to reach internal political consensus on inclusion of LTC into strategic priorities within national social policies. As organisation of efficient and sustainable LTC system requires motivation and efforts of many stakeholders on multiple levels, prioritising LTC on a national level would enable and encourage movement towards affordable and good quality Long-Term Care in Europe.

References

Alders, P., and F. T. Schut. 2019. "Trends in Ageing and Ageing-In-Place and the Future Market for Institutional Care: Scenarios and Policy Implications." *Health Economics, Policy and Law* 14 (1), 82–100.

Bouget, D., S. Spasova, and B. Vanhercke. 2016. *Work–Life Balance Measures for Persons of Working Age with Dependent Relatives in Europe. A Study of National Policies*. European Social Policy Network (ESPN), Brussels: European Commission.

Colombo, F., A. Llena-Nozal, J. Mercier, and F. Tjadens. 2011. *Help Wanted? Providing and Paying for Long-Term Care*. OECD Health Policy Studies. Paris: OECD Publishing. Available at: https://read.oecd-ilibrary.org/social-issues-migration-health/help-wanted_9789264097759-en#page3

Comas-Herrera, A., J. Zalakaín, E. Lemmon, D. Henderson, C. Litwin, A. T. Hsu, A. E. Schmidt, G. Arling, F. Kruse, and J. L. Fernández. 2020. *Mortality Associated with COVID-19 in Care Homes: International Evidence*. ltccovid.org, International Long-Term Care Policy Network, CPEC-LSE. 1 February 2021.

European Commission. 2016. *Joint Report on Health Care and Long-Term Care Systems and Fiscal Sustainability*. Volume 1. Luxembourg: EU. Available at: https://ec.europa.eu/info/sites/info/files/file_import/ip037_vol1_en_2.pdf. Accessed 8 April 2021.

European Commission. Directorate-General for Economic and Financial Affairs. 2019. *Joint Report on Health Care and Long-Term Care Systems & Fiscal Sustainability: Prepared by the Commission Services (Directorate-General for Economic and Financial Affairs), and the Economic Policy Committee (Ageing Working Group). Country Documents – 2019 Update*. Institutional Paper 105. Available at: https://ec.europa.eu/info/sites/info/files/economy-finance/ip105_en.pdf. Accessed 8 April 2021.

European Union. 2014. *Adequate Social Protection for Long-term Care Needs in an Ageing Society*. Report jointly prepared by the Social Protection Committee and the European Commission. Available at: http://ec.europa.eu/social/main.jsp?catId=738&langId=en&pubId=7724.

Geerts, J. 2011. *The Long-Term Care Workforce: Description and Perspectives*. Brussels: Centre for European Policy Studies, Brussels. http://www.ancien-longtermcare.eu/sites/default/files/ENEPRIRR93_ANCIENWP3_0.pdf.

Greve, B. (ed.) (2017a). *Long-term Care for the Elderly in Europe: Development and Prospects*. London: Routledge.

Greve, B. (2017b) *The Long-Term Care Resourcing Landscape*. SPRINT project report. Available at: http://sprint-project.eu/wp-content/uploads/2015/12/SPRINT_LTC_Resourcing_Landscape.pdf, accessed 16 August 2018.

Klimova, B., M. Valis, and K. Kuca. 2018. "Exploring Assistive Technology as a Potential Beneficial Intervention Tool for People with Alzheimer's Disease – A Systematic Review." *Neuropsychiatric Disease and Treatment* 14, 3151–3158.

Kraus, M., M. Riedel, E. Mot, P. Willemé, G. Röhrling, and T. Czypionka. 2010. *A Typology of Long-Term Care Systems in Europe*. ENEPRI Research Report No. 91. Brussels: CEPS.

Lehnert, T., M. A. X. Heuchert, K. Hussain, and H. H. Koenig. 2019. "Stated Preferences for Long-Term Care: A Literature Review." *Ageing and Society* 39 (9), 1873–1913.

Libault, D. 2019. *Concertation: Grand âge et autonomie*. Paris: Ministère des Solidarités et de la Santé. https://solidarites-sante.gouv.fr/IMG/pdf/rapport_grand_age_autonomie.pdf.

Lopes, A., and I. Dias. 2018. "The Portuguese Stakeholders' Perspective on Social Investment and Quality Assessment in LTC." *Journal of International and Comparative Social Policy* 34 (2), 140–150.

Nunes, L. M., and A. F. Cerqueira. 2020. "Training Models for Formal Caregivers of Elderly Persons at Home: Studies and Gaps." In *Handbook of Research on Health Systems and Organizations for an Aging Society*, edited by C. Fonseca, M. J., D. Mendes, F. Mendes, and J. García-Alonso, 226–246. Hershey, PA: IGI Global.

OECD. 2019. *Health at a Glance 2019: OECD Indicators*. Paris: OECD Publishing. https://doi.org/10.1787/4dd50c09-en.

OECD. 2020. *Who Cares? Attracting and Retaining Care Workers for the Elderly, OECD Health Policy Studies*. Paris: OECD Publishing. https://doi.org/10.1787/92c0ef68-en.

OECD/European Union. 2013. *A Good Life in Old Age?: Monitoring and Improving Quality in Long-Term Care*. OECD Health Policy Studies. Paris: OECD Publishing, https://doi.org/10.1787/9789264194564-en.

Pickard, L. 2015. "A Growing Care Gap? The Supply of Unpaid Care for Older People by Their Adult Children in England to 2032." *Ageing & Society* 35 (1), 96–123.

Poškutė, V., R. Kazlauskaitė, and I. Matonytė. 2021. "Stakeholder Collaboration in Long-Term Care of Older People in Lithuania." *Health and Social Care in the Community* 30 (1), 193–202.

Ranci, C., and E. Pavolini (eds.) 2013. *Reforms in Long-Term Care Policies in Europe*. New York: Springer.

Rodrigues, R., M. Huber, and G. Lamura. 2012. *Facts and Figures on Healthy Ageing and Long-Term Care*. Vienna: European Centre for Social Welfare Policy and Research.

Rostgaard, T. 2020. *The COVID-19 Long-Term Care Situation in Denmark*. ltccovid.org, International Long-Term Care Policy Network, CPEC-LSE, 25 May 2020.

Schulz, E. 2013. *Employment in Health and Long-Term Care Sector in European Countries*. Supplement A to NEUJOBS working paper D12.1. September 2013. Available at: https://www.econstor.eu/bitstream/10419/128598/1/Schulz_2013_Employment-Health-Long.pdf. Accessed 11 April 2021.

Sowa-Kofta, A., R. Rodrigues, G. Lamura, A. Sopadzhiyan, R. Wittenberg, G. Bauer, and H. Rothgang. 2019. "Long-Term Care and Migrant Care Work: Addressing Workforce Shortages While Raising Questions for European Countries." *Eurohealth* 25 (4), 15–18.

Spasova, S., R. Baeten, S. Coster, D. Ghailani, R. Peña-Casas, and B. Vanhercke. 2018. *Challenges in Long-Term Care in Europe. A Study of National Policies*, European Social Policy Network (ESPN). Brussels: European Commission.

Social Protection Investment in Long-Term Care (SPRINT). HORIZON 2020 – Grant Agreement No 649565. Deliverable 2.2.

Tarricone, R., and A. D. Tsouros (eds.) 2008. *Home Care in Europe: The Solid Facts*. Copenhagen: WHO Regional Office Europe.

Zigante, V., and D. King. 2018. *Quality Assurance Practices in Long-Term Care in Europe. Emerging Evidence on Care Market Management*. Luxembourg: Publications Office of the European Union.

Athina Vlachantoni

15 Pension

Abstract: Pension reform has been on the agenda of most welfare states in the developed world for almost a century. Theories of welfare regime and pension regime typologies, developed in the 1990s and 2000s, continue to contribute a great deal to our understanding of "winners" and "losers" within changing systems of welfare protection in different countries. This chapter provides a succinct summary of pension reforms in the developed world in the last half-century or so, drawing primarily on European examples, and critically discussing the differential impact of pension reforms on different parts of the population. It first summarises the key demographic changes taking place which have been concomitant with pension reform, including population ageing and the extension of longevity. It then critically discusses socio-economic changes which have also been taking place during this time, including increasing insecurity in labour market and the rise of "working poor" individuals and households. Common patterns of pension reform in the developed world are summarised next, before identifying mechanisms within pension systems which perpetuate inequalities within the population. The chapter concludes with a critical discussion of the parameters which are necessary for achieving income adequacy and financial sustainability for pension systems in the future.

Keywords: pension reform, welfare regimes, longevity, inequalities, adequacy, sustainability

15.1 Introduction

For the best part of the nineteenth century and the beginning of the twentieth century, pension reform has been on the agenda of most welfare states in the developed world, as a result of the combined effect of demographic changes, such as increasing longevity and decreasing fertility, and socio-economic changes, such as the changing composition of labour markets (Natali 2017). Such changes have challenged pension systems, which were traditionally designed to compensate for the loss of earnings due to older age among a less heterogeneous population with a shorter average life expectancy. The policy responses, perhaps not surprisingly, have varied depending on a number of factors including the nature and scale of demographic changes, the underlying ideology permeating political decision-making in that country, as well as the constraints created by historical legacies of pension protection, the so-called path dependence of pension systems (Myles and Pierson 2001; Schmitt 2012). A key factor in the development of pension systems and their responses to challenges has been the balance between the private and public sectors, and the extent to which the "risk"

https://doi.org/10.1515/9783110721768-015

of living longer is born by the individual, the state and the private sector (Carone et al. 2016).

Within this context, the diversity of country-specific "pension regimes" is difficult to evade. Indeed, theories of welfare regime and pension regime typologies, developed in the 1990s and 2000s, continue to contribute a great deal to our understanding of "winners" and "losers" within systems of welfare protection in different countries (e.g. Esping-Andersen 1990; Lewis 1992; Bonoli 2003). A body of literature has debated the boundaries between the classic categories of Bismarckian and Beveridgean pension systems, shifting away from individuals' link to the labour market as the primary entitlement principle, and indicating the emergence of "hybrid" systems around Europe which are aimed at reforming the entitlement structures of the welfare state and relieving the pressure on public finances (e.g. Jaime-Castillo 2013). A large body of academic work has sought to categorise pension systems according to different indicators, aimed both at understanding their past and distributional effects, but also to assess their ability to withstand future socio-economic challenges (see for example Bonoli and Palier 2007). Against this background, this chapter aims at providing a succinct and by no means exhaustive, summary of pension reforms in the developed world in the last half-century or so, drawing primarily on European examples, and critically discussing the differential impact of pension reforms on different parts of the population. The rest of the chapter is structured as follows.

Section 15.2 summarises the key demographic changes taking place which have been concomitant with pension reform. Chief among the demographic changes, and one of the main triggers for the reform of pension systems, has been population ageing and the extension of longevity. Other demographic changes have also been taking place at the same time and have implications for how pension reform impacts on different population groups, such as changes in the ethnic composition of populations with increasing diversity becoming more prevalent, changes in more traditional family structures and changes in the timing of key demographic events in individuals' life courses. Section 15.3 turns to summarise socio-economic changes which have also been taking place during this time, including increasing insecurity in labour market and the rise of "working poor" individuals and households, as well as the greater combination of paid work with family life, mostly among women. Section 15.4 provides a summary of common patterns of pension reform in the developed world, notwithstanding the importance of categorising pension systems and contextualising them within so-called welfare regimes. Against the previous sections, Section 15.5 is an attempt to "take stock" of pension reforms so far, and identify mechanisms within pension systems which perpetuate inequalities within the population. The Conclusion draws the key arguments of the chapter together, and critically discusses the parameters which are necessary for achieving income adequacy for individuals in the future and financial sustainability for pension systems as a whole.

15.2 Changing demographic context

Demographic changes underpin much of policy change in contemporary welfare states, including pension reform and other policy areas (see Chapter 14 on Long-Term Care). Increasing longevity at a global level is a cause for celebration in principle (Murphy and Grundy 2003), but can also pose challenges for individuals, families, societies and policymakers alike. Research to-date has evidenced the improvement of life expectancy, especially in older ages, which can result in a greater proportion of the population relying on pensions in later life (Wiemers and Bianchi 2015). Within Europe and North America in particular, changes such as the increase in cohabitation and the postponement of fertility, partly due to the extension of education in the earlier part of the lifecourse (Stone, Berrington, and Falkingham 2014), also signal "disruption" to traditional paths to family formation and can have an effect on the start of individuals' working life with implications for their pension contributions. Changing demographic structures and behaviours are important in so far as they affect individuals' behaviours in the labour market, and by extension how they fare within modern pension systems. For example, longitudinal analysis of the SHARE dataset by Bertogg et al. (2021) shows that in the case of most European countries, providing care to one's older parents was less relevant to the decision to remain in the labour market than providing care to one's siblings, friends, neighbours or grandchildren.

A fundamental driver behind pension reforms has been the portrayal of an increasingly ageing world, using different indicators such as the ratio between the number of persons aged 65 and over per 100 people of working age (20–64), shown for the OECD average in Figure 15.1. Notwithstanding some variations between different countries, during the last half a century or so, the old-age to working-age ratio across the OECD has increased just over 50 %, reaching about 31 in 2020; and it is projected to continue increasing to reach around 58 by 2100. It is important to interpret such indicators critically, for example not all persons aged 65 and over are out of paid work, and not all persons aged 20–64 are in work; and there are significant gender differences permeating individuals' work and life courses, which will be addressed later in the chapter. Nevertheless, such stark evidence reflects a policy urgency for governments worldwide, yet pension systems affect more than one generation of individuals at any one time, and the academic literature has shown that if often takes more than one generation to reform them (see for example, Hinrichs' (2009) apt description of pension systems as "elephants on the move").

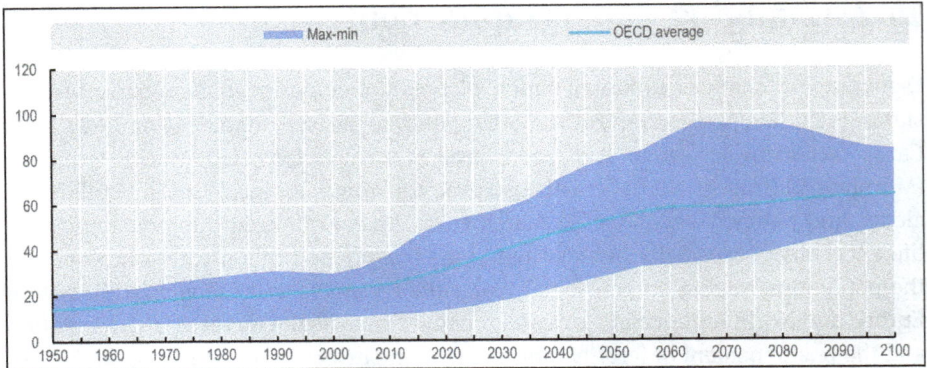

Figure 15.1: Old-age to working-age ratio, 1950–2100.
Source: OECD 2019a, figure 1.1
Note: The centre line is the OECD average old-age to working-age ratio. The shaded area indicates the range between the country with the lowest old-age to working-age ratio and the country with the highest old-age to working-age ratio. Data from the United Nations World Population Prospects: The 2019 Revision.

At the same time as the population is ageing and family structures are changing, populations in the developed world, and certainly in Europe, are becoming increasingly diverse in terms of ethnic background, owing in large part to recent waves of migration, in addition to the long-standing presence of minority ethnic communities in particular parts of Europe (Maxwell 2012) (see Chapter 16 on migration and ethnicity as challenges and opportunity). Patterns of migration have a direct bearing on the ethnic composition of labour forces, challenging the structures of benefit entitlement within pension systems and welfare systems more broadly (Wright and Clibborn 2019). On the one hand, research has shown that economic migration into European countries has eased the financial pressure on public pensions, and even contributed to the expansion of private pension systems (Han 2013). On the other hand, research has highlighted limitations with the portability of pension and other welfare rights within Europe, impacting adversely on migrants' pensions (see for example, Lafleur and Vintila 2020). For example, Bridgen and Meyer (2019) projected the post-retirement income of hypothetical EU migrants who had worked both in their origin and host countries, and showed that the large wage gap between different EU countries projected incomes below the relative poverty line for most of the migrant workers. The changing composition of populations is a fundamental component of the debate on pension reform, however such demographic changes are taking place within a socio-economic context which is also in flux.

15.3 Changing socio-economic context

The changes in the demographic composition and behaviour of the population described above have been taking place at the same time as socio-economic changes
with implications for pension protection and reform. Within the European context, the
financial market crisis of 2008 directly impacted several countries' ability to deliver
adequate pensions without major restructuring, while the impact of the recent COV-
ID-19 pandemic is yet to be fully measured (see Chapter 12 on COVID as a case). Recent
analysis notes that, although the short-term effects of the pandemic on pensions may
amount to a temporary reduction or deferral of social contributions, nevertheless the
longer-term effects could have a major impact on both the adequacy of pensions for
individuals and the financial sustainability of pension systems as a whole (Natali
2020). Indeed, the impact of the pandemic could extend far beyond the pension outcomes for particular cohorts of retirees, and into more fundamental debates about intergenerational fairness and support. Natali (2020, 4) writes that the current debate
about the impact of the pandemic "... recalls old debates regarding the intergenerational clash between younger generations in need of greater financial support and
older generations with unsustainable social (and pension) rights".

At the same time, an increase in labour market insecurity has been evidenced in
existing research for European countries, directly impacting individuals' chances of
securing an adequate pension income in retirement (Hinrichs and Jessoula 2012).
Less standard types of employment, such as zero-hour contracts, are becoming more
prevalent in the developed world, and this has implications for individuals' investment in their financial resources across the lifecourse and in later life in the form of
pensions (Koumenta and Williams 2019). Figure 15.2 shows that, for most of the 14
OECD countries for which dynamic data was available, temporary employment has
been slowly increasing over time from making up about 10 % of total employment in
the mid-1980s to about 14 % by 2017. Such a trend has implications for individuals'
pension protection throughout their lifecourse, and their income security in later life.
Lersch and Dewilde (2015) analysed data from the EU Statistics on Income and Living
Conditions between 2007 and 2011 in order to capture the impact of the global economic downturn on employment (in)security and individuals' pathways into home
ownership, and found that the adverse impact of employment insecurity on younger
individuals' transition into home ownership is significant throughout Europe, albeit
less intense in familialistic systems. Labour market insecurity is a key factor threa-
tening to ignite policy debates about "winning" and "losing" generations of workers,
and the role of the pension system in smoothing inter-generational relations in society.

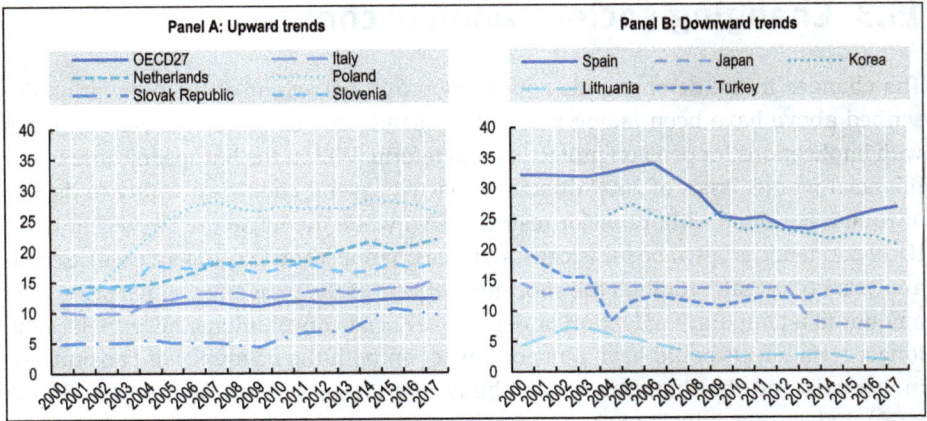

Figure 15.2: Trends in temporary employment (% of temporary employment as a share of total employment), selected OECD countries 2000–2017.
Source: OECD 2019a, figure 2.1
Note: Countries selected based on the outstanding dynamics. Data from: OECD Labour Force Statistics.

15.4 Common patterns of pension reform in the developed world

Pension systems around the world have had to contend with a rapidly shifting demographic and socio-economic landscape, and the nature of their response has been dependent not only on their basic structure which affects the policy tools available to them, but also on the relative impact of the political cycle governing what is and is not possible within a certain timeframe (Carone et al. 2016). Such response has been neither uniform nor concomitant, but it includes the combination of at least some of the following mechanisms.

Firstly, research has evidenced the profound impact of what the World Bank introduced in the early 1990s as the multi-pillar model paradigm, and the idea that the risk for living longer should be borne by more than one resource provider (World Bank 1994). This model was adopted to varying degrees and with varying degrees of success in countries with less developed pension systems, for example in Chile (Orenstein 2013), however the fundamental idea of diversifying the risk of old age and introducing multiple "policy tools" to mitigate it, echoed at a global level. This has not necessarily resulted in the replacement of the state as the key provider of pensions, however it has permitted governments to explore the extent to which funded pensions can be part of the future configuration of their pension systems. A key trend reflecting such a shift of risk has been the decline in defined-benefit pension schemes and the concomitant increase in defined-contribution pension schemes (Hinrichs 2021). Since then, the balance between the public (state) and private sector in providing pension protection for individuals has been at the heart of academic and policy debates alike (Carone et al. 2016; Bridgen and Meyer 2018; Yeh, Cheng, and Shi 2020). Figure 15.3 below shows the complexity and variance in the composition of older people's income. Of the four main sources of income that older people can draw from, it is public transfers (including earnings-related pensions and resource-tested benefits) and private occupational transfers (including pensions and severance payments) which accounted for two-thirds of the total income at the OECD level. On average, 55% of older persons' income comes from public transfers, while work accounts for about 25%, and occupational transfers and capital income make about 10% each. A key question for future research in pension protection is whether the composition of the income of future cohorts of older persons will remain stable. Another important question is whether future patterns of income composition will reflect such significant variance at the country level or whether there is divergence taking place towards the OECD average, as a result of pension policy reforms.

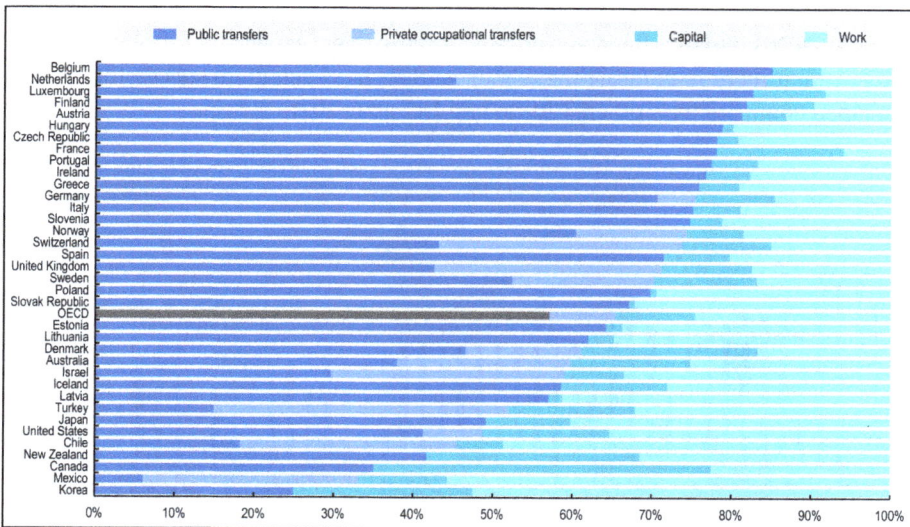

Figure 15.3: Income sources of older people 2016 or latest available year (% of total equivalised gross household income and transfers).
Source: OECD 2019a, figure 7.1.
Note: Income from work includes both earnings (employment income) and income from self-employment. Private occupational transfers include pensions, severance payments, death grants and other. Capital income includes private personal pensions and income from the returns on non-pension savings. Data from: OECD Income Distribution Database, http://www.oecd.org/social/income-distribution-database.htm (September 2019 version).

Secondly, pension systems have sought to extend individuals' working lives to take into account the average increase in life expectancy. The rise in pension eligibility ages and the introduction of flexible retirement policies have been evidenced throughout the developed world (Kuitto and Helmdag 2021), albeit not uniformly (Komp 2018). Figure 15.4 juxtaposes current and future retirement ages across OECD countries, using a man entering the labour market at age 22 with a full career as a base. As can be seen in Figure 15.4, the normal retirement age for people entering the labour market is set to increase in a number of countries (e.g. Denmark, Estonia), although a larger number of countries have not yet introduced legislation to increase this age (e.g. Canada, Austria), and a smaller number of countries have a normal retirement age still below 65 (e.g. Greece, Luxembourg).This tool has differential effects on different groups in society, for example in many countries women and men have, or used to have, different retirement ages and have quite different employment histories as women have been more likely to have interrupted and overall shorter careers, due to caring obligations. In addition, individuals from lower socio-economic strata and manual occupations tend to have a lower life expectancy and to spend fewer years in retirement (see for example Wenau, Grigoriev, and Shkolnikov 2019; Leinonen et al. 2020). Finally, the extension of working lives, especially for older workers who are entering or re-entering the labour market, has been more successful in some developed countries than others (Kuitto and Helmdag 2021).

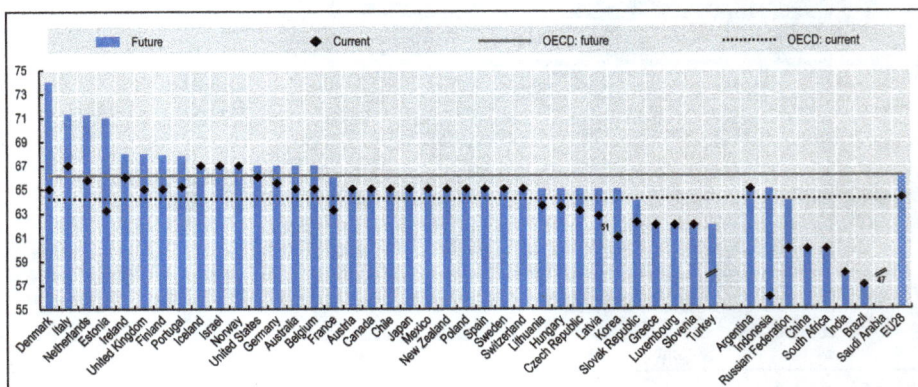

Figure 15.4: Current and future retirement ages, OECD countries (based on men entering the labour market at age 22 with a full career).
Source: OECD 2019a, figure 1.10.
Note: The normal retirement age is calculated for a man with a full career from age 22. Future refers to the year in which someone is eligible for full retirement benefits from all mandatory components, without reduction, assuming labour market entry at age 22 in 2018; this year differs by country. The current retirement age for Italy does not reflect the "quota 100" since that was introduced in 2019. In Brazil, a pension reform passed a final vote in the Senate in October 2019.

Thirdly, many pension systems have aimed to reduce the overall cost of providing pensions by amending the calculation method, and reducing the value, of the pension benefit (Hinrichs 2021). At the OECD level, pension reforms in the last half century or so have resulted in about one percentage-point decrease on average in the pension replacement rates between individuals born in 1940 and those retiring about today (those who were born around 1956). Figure 15.5 below compares the replacement rates for these two cohorts for a full-career worker born in 1996 compared to one born in 1940, and shows that in about 60 % of OECD countries the replacement rates are expected to be lower for the younger cohort compared to the older cohort; in about 30 % of countries they are expected to be higher, and in about 10 % of countries the replacement rates are expected to remain stable (OECD 2019b). At the country level, research has dissected pension reform to reveal more nuanced differences. For example, Bridgen (2019) conducted empirical analysis on six liberal pension systems between 1980 and 2017 and found that there was significant retrenchment in most welfare states after 1980, which has been reversed to some extent since the mid-1990s. Notwithstanding the differences in responses, Hinrichs writes that "in very blunt terms, the general direction of pension reforms in Europe has been to contain the *rise* of public pension spending" (emphasis in original) (Hinrichs 2021, 418). A key question then arises on whether such general direction of pension reforms has adversely affected specific parts of the population disproportionately.

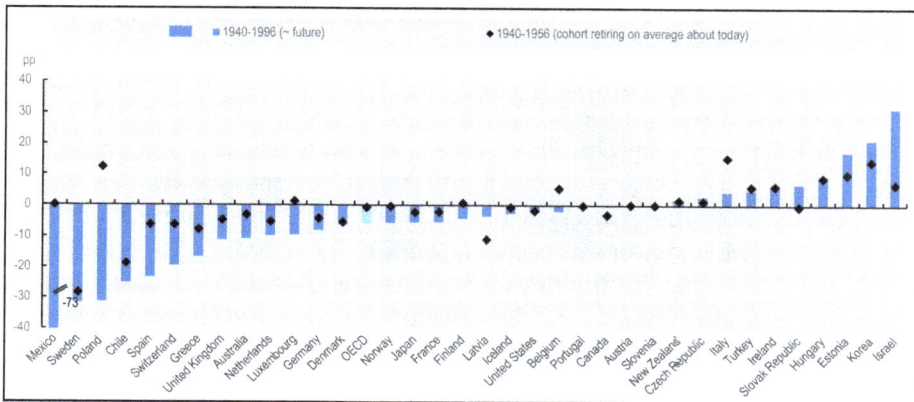

Figure 15.5: Replacement rates for current and future retirees (change in theoretical gross replacement rate 1940–1956 and 1940–1996).
Source: OECD 2019a, figure 1.17.
Note: Lithuania is not shown as data for the 1940 cohort are missing, and is not included in the OECD average. Source: OECD 2019b.

15.5 Unequal impact of pension reform

Old-age pension systems were originally created to compensate for the loss of earnings in later life of a primarily male and full-time labour force with a relatively short life expectancy, working uninterrupted and with an increasing salary. Consequently, pension protection has inherently caused inequalities between social groups, and has been a profound policy challenge vis-à-vis groups of individuals, such as women and migrants (across the lifecourse), whose work and life histories do not "fit" within a typical employment history. At the same time, the average lifecourse of individuals is changing, as a result of increasing longevity, extended periods of education at earlier stages and extended periods of retirement at later stages. Achieving the dual goal of income adequacy at the individual level and financial sustainability at the systemic level, has been a constant challenge in the context of social change.

The European Pension Adequacy Report (2021) notes that about 18.5 % (or 16.1 million) or persons aged 65 and over in the EU were at risk of poverty or social exclusion in 2019, although in some countries this percentage reached almost 50 % of the older population (EU 2021). Gender permeates the poverty risk in later life, with women over the age of 75 being particularly vulnerable; and the same report indicates that the depth of poverty among the older poor population has continued to increase (EU 2021). Recent analysis of EU-SILC data by Ebbinghaus (2021) showed that typical Bismarckian systems are better suited for addressing poverty, but can create inequalities between social groups; whereas Beveridgean systems are less able to shield individuals from poverty. Figure 15.6 below plots the at-risk-of-poverty rate (measured at 60 % median equivalised disposable income) of the working population aged under 65 (horizontal axes) against the rate for persons aged 65 and over (vertical axes), using data from the EU-SILC 2017/18 database. It indicates that in about half of European countries, relative poverty among working-age persons is higher than among older persons (those countries below the diagonal), while the opposite is true for a smaller number of European countries, while many countries are close to the diagonal indicating a similar poverty risk for working-age persons as for older persons. Within the OECD, the incomes of older persons are on average lower than those of the total population, for example in 2016, people aged 65 and over had 87 % of the income of the total population; and in 22 out of a total 36 OECD countries, public transfers provided more than half of the gross income for individuals after the age 65 (OECD 2019b).

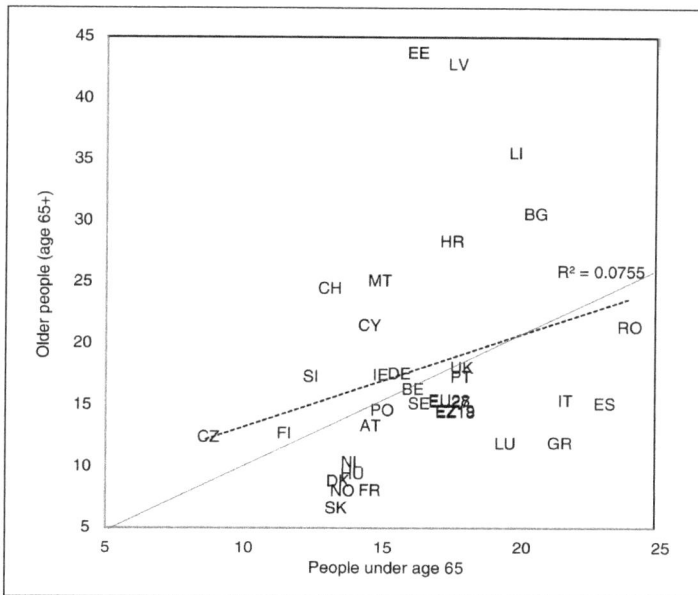

Figure 15.6: At-risk-of-poverty rate by age group in European countries.
Source: Ebbinghaus 2021, figure 1.

A significant body of work has evidenced the adverse impact of pension systems on individuals with atypical life and employment histories, often pointing to the additional complexity of taking individuals' cohort into account (see for example, Foster and Smetherham 2013; Meyer, Bridgen, and Andow 2013; Gehring 2017). Analysis of private pension schemes around the world also shows a significant disadvantage faced by women, especially belonging to older cohorts, whose family and employment histories have not resulted in pension adequacy in later life (Yabiku 2000; Foster and Heneghan 2017). Whether examining financial resources at the individual level (e.g. Sefton et al. 2011) or at the household level (e.g. Möhring 2021), research has shown the combined effect of individual characteristics and behaviours over the lifecourse on the one hand, and of the design of the pension system on the other hand, can result in a higher risk of poverty in later life.

Most pension systems of the developed world have adjusted incrementally over time to "relax" (to various degrees) the link between individuals' pension contributions and the final pension outcome, and to apply redistributive mechanisms which can compensate for deviations from the soon-to-be-extinct "normal" pattern of working life (see for example Halvorsen and Pedersen 2018 on Norway). For example, Möhring (2015) analysed the SHARE dataset to show that countries which offer unconditional basic pension schemes offer the strongest chance of mitigating low-income and interrupted periods earlier in one's working life. There are obvious gender dimensions which permeate this type of analysis, consistently evidencing that women and mothers fare better in terms of pension income in countries with pension systems which offer a strong redistributive mechanism (Stahlberg, Kruse, and Sunden 2005). The extent to which pension systems will continue to include, and enhance, such redistributive elements in their operation, will largely depend on how they are funded (e.g. through general taxation) and on whether future cohorts of working-age individuals will support them. For instance, recent analysis of the European Social Survey by Riekhoff (2021) argues that although support for so-called "pro-old" welfare policies has declined in most EU countries between 2008 and 2016, nevertheless this has not necessarily undermined the generational welfare contract.

15.6 Conclusion

Achieving income adequacy for individuals and financial sustainability for pension systems as a whole are key goals for pension systems throughout the world. Notwithstanding the nuanced differences between differently structured pension systems and their development since the nineteenth century, the research to-date notes that policymakers have been focusing more on the systems' sustainability into the future than pension outcomes at the individual level and the eradication of poverty in later life. Both principles are important for the smooth operation of pension systems, and both principles appear to be challenged to an extent in pension systems with different structures. The comparative analysis of poverty rates, writes Ebbinghaus (2021, 452), "demonstrate[s] the double-edged effect of multi-pillar pension systems, cutting in both directions: poverty and inequality in old age".

The changing demographic and socio-economic landscape will continue to place pension systems under pressure to deliver on both goals of income adequacy and financial sustainability into the future. Increased longevity, changing life courses, greater movement of individuals within and across country borders, and increasing insecurity for younger cohorts in the labour market, point to the need for greater flexibility in the way pensions are calculated and delivered. However, as gradual shifts in the risk of providing for older age have taught us, the role of the welfare state in providing the ultimate safety net and ensuring dignity for all individuals in later life, cannot be underestimated.

References

Bertogg, A., T. Nazio, and S. Strauss. 2021. "Work–Family Balance in the Second Half of Life: Caregivers' Decisions Regarding Retirement and Working Time Reduction in Europe." *Social Policy & Administration* 55 (3), 485–500.

Bonoli, G. 2003. "Two Worlds of Pension Reform in Western Europe." *Comparative Politics* 35 (4), 399–416.

Bonoli, G., and B. Palier. 2007. "When Past Reforms Open New Opportunities: Comparing Old-Age Insurance Reforms in Bismarckian Welfare Systems." *Social Policy and Administration* 41 (6), 555–573.

Bridgen, P. 2019. "The Retrenchment of Public Pension Provision in the Liberal World of Welfare During the Age of Austerity—and its Unexpected Reversal, 1980–2017." *Social Policy & Administration* 53 (1), 16–33.

Bridgen, P., and T. Meyer. 2018. "Individualisation Reversed: The Cross-Class Politics of Social Regulation in the UK's Public/Private Pension Mix." *Transfer* 24 (1), 25–41.

Bridgen, P., and T. Meyer. 2019. "Divided Citizenship: How Retirement in the Host Country Affects the Financial Status of Intra-European Union Migrants." *Ageing & Society* 39 (3), 465–487.

Carone, G., P. Eckefeldt, L. Giamboni, V. Laine, and S. Pamies Sumner. 2016. *Pension Reforms in the EU Since the Early 2000's: Achievements and Challenges Ahead*. European Economy, Discussion Paper 042 (December 2016). Luxembourg: Publications Office of the European Union.

Ebbinghaus, B. 2021. "Inequalities and Poverty Risks in Old Age Across Europe: The Double-Edged Income Effect of Pension Systems." *Social Policy & Administration* 55 (3), 440–455.

Esping-Andersen, G. 1990. *The Three Worlds of Welfare Capitalism*. Cambridge: Polity Press.

European Union. 2021. *The 2021 Pension Adequacy Report: Current and Future Income Adequacy in Old Age in the EU*. Luxembourg: Publications Office of the European Union.

Foster, L., and J. Smetherham. 2013. "Gender and Pensions: An Analysis of Factors Affecting Women's Private Pension Scheme Membership in the United Kingdom." *Journal of Aging & Social Policy* 25 (3), 197–217.

Foster, L., and M. Heneghan. 2017. "Pensions Planning in the UK: A Gendered Challenge." *Critical Social Policy* 38 (2), 345–366.

Gehring, A. 2017. "Mobile Pensioners: Retirement Migrants' Perspectives of EU Citizenship and Free Movement." *Innovation: The European Journal of Social Science Research* 32 (2), 254–269.

Halvorsen, E., and A. West Pedersen. 2018. "Closing the Gender Gap in Pensions: A Microsimulation Analysis of the Norwegian NDC Pension System." *Journal of European Social Policy* 29, 130–143.

Han, K. J. 2013. "Saving Public Pensions: Labor Migration Effects on Pension Systems in European Countries." *The Social Science Journal* 50 (2), 152–161.

Hinrichs, K. 2009. "Elephants on the Move. Patterns of Public Pension Reform in OECD Countries." *European Review* 8 (3), 353–378.

Hinrichs, K. 2021. "Recent Pension Reforms in Europe: More Challenges, New Directions. An Overview." *Social Policy & Administration* 55 (3), 409–422.

Hinrichs, K., and M. Jessoula (eds.) 2012. *Labour Market Flexibility and Pension Reforms: Flexible Today, Secure Tomorrow?* Houndmills, Basingstoke: Palgrave Macmillan.

Jaime-Castillo, A. 2013. "Public Opinion and the Reform of the Pension Systems in Europe: The Influence of Solidarity Principles." *Journal of European Social Policy* 23 (4), 390–405.

Komp, K. 2018. "Shifts in the Realized Retirement Age: Europe in Times of Pension Reform and Economic Crisis." *Journal of European Social Policy* 28 (2), 130–142.

Koumenta, M., and M. Williams. 2019. "An Anatomy of Zero-Hour Contracts in the UK." *Industrial Relations Journal* 50 (1), 20–40.

Kuitto, K., and J. Helmdag. 2021. "Extending Working Lives: How Policies Shape Retirement and Labour Market Participation of Older Workers." *Social Policy & Administration* 55 (3), 423–439.

Lafleur, J. M., and D. Vintila (eds.) 2020. *Migration and Social Protection in Europe and Beyond*, volume 1, *Comparing Access to Welfare Entitlements*. Cham: Springer.

Leinonen, T., T. Chandola, M. Laaksonen, and P. Martikainen. 2020. "Socio-Economic Differences in Retirement Timing and Participation in Post-Retirement Employment in a Context of a Flexible Pension Age." *Ageing & Society* 40 (2), 348–368.

Lersch, P. M., and C. Dewilde. 2015. "Employment Insecurity and First-Time Homeownership: Evidence from Twenty-Two European Countries." *Environment and Planning A: Economy and Space* 47 (3), 607–624.

Lewis, J. 1992. "Gender and the Development of Welfare Regimes." *Journal of European Social Policy* 2 (3), 159–173.

Maxwell, R. 2012. *Ethnic Minority Migrants in Britain and France: Integration Trade-Offs*. Cambridge: Cambridge University Press.

Meyer, T., P. Bridgen, and C. Andow. 2013. "Free Movement? The Impact of Legislation, Benefit Generosity and Wages on the Pensions of European Migrants." *Population, Space and Place* 19 (6), 714–726.

Möhring, K. 2015. "Employment Histories and Pension Incomes in Europe: A Multilevel Analysis of the Role of Institutional Factors." *European Societies* 17 (1), 3–26.

Möhring, K. 2021. "The Consequences of Non-Standard Working and Marital Biographies for Old Age Income in Europe: Contrasting the Individual and the Household Perspective." *Social Policy & Administration* 55 (3), 456–484.

Murphy, M., and E. Grundy. 2003. "Mothers with Living Children and Children with Living Mothers: The Role of Fertility and Mortality in the Period 1911–2050." *Population Trends* 112, 36–44.

Myles, J., and P. Pierson. 2001. "The Comparative Political Economy of Pension Reform." In *The New Politics of the Welfare State*, edited by P. Pierson, 305–333. Oxford: Oxford University Press.

Natali, D. (ed.) 2017. *The New Pension Mix in Europe: Recent Reforms, Their Distributional Effects and Political Dynamics*. Brussels: Peter Lang.

Natali, D. 2020. *Pensions in the Age of Covid-19: Recent Changes and Future Challenges*. Brussels: European Trade Union Institute, ETUI Policy Brief No. 13/2020.

OECD. 2019a. *Pensions at a Glance 2019: OECD and G20 Indicators*. Paris: OECD Publishing.

OECD. 2019b. *Will Future Pensioners Work for Longer and Retire on Less?* https://www.oecd.org/pensions/public-pensions/OECD-Policy-Brief-Future-Pensioners-2019.pdf

Orenstein, M. A. 2013. "Pension Privatization: Evolution of a Paradigm." *Governance* 26 (2), 259–281.

Riekhoff, A.-J. 2021. "Pension Reforms, the Generational Welfare Contract and Preferences for Pro-Old Welfare Policies in Europe." *Social Policy & Administration* 55 (3), 501–518.

Schmitt, S. 2012. "Sequences of Active Policy Dismantling? Path Dependency in Pension Reform Processes." In *Dismantling Public Policy: Preferences, Strategies, and Effects*, edited by M. W. Bauer, A. Jordan, C. Green-Pedersen, and A. Héritier, 57–80. Oxford: Oxford University Press.

Sefton, T., M. Evandrou, J. Falkingham, and A. Vlachantoni. 2011. "The Relationship Between Women's Work Histories and Incomes in Later Life in the UK, US And West Germany." *Journal of European Social Policy* 21 (1), 20–36.

Stahlberg, A.-C., A. Kruse, and A. Sunden. 2005. "Pension Design and Gender: Analyses of Developed and Developing Countries." *Gender Issues* 22, 6–45.

Stone, J., A. Berrington, and J. Falkingham. 2014. "Gender, Turning Points, and Boomerangs: Returning Home in Young Adulthood in Great Britain." *Demography* 51, 257–276.

Wenau, G., P. Grigoriev, and V. Shkolnikov. 2019. "Socioeconomic Disparities in Life Expectancy Gains Among Retired German Men, 1997–2016." *Journal of Epidemiology and Community Health* 73 (7), 605–611.

Wiemers, E. E., and S. M. Bianchi. 2015. "Competing Demands from Aging Parents and Adult Children in Two Cohorts of American Women." *Population and Development Review* 41, 127–146.

World Bank. 1994. *Averting the Old Age Crisis: Policies to Protect the Old and Promote Growth*. Oxford and New York: Published for the World Bank [by] Oxford University Press.

Wright, C. F., and S. Clibborn. 2019. "Migrant Labour and Low-Quality Work: A Persistent Relationship." *Journal of Industrial Relations* 61 (2), 157–175.

Yabiku, S. T. 2000. "Family History and Pensions: The Relationships Between Marriage, Divorce, Children, and Private Pension Coverage." *Journal of Aging Studies* 14 (3), 293–312.

Yeh, C.-Y., H. Cheng, and S.-J. Shi. 2020. "Public–Private Pension Mixes in East Asia: Institutional Diversity and Policy Implications for Old-Age Security." *Ageing & Society* 40 (3), 604–625.

Philipp Lutz and Carlo Knotz

16 The legitimacy of the welfare state in the age of migration

Abstract: Migration and its consequences for the legitimacy of the welfare state have been the subject of a number of controversial discussions over the past several decades, and remain highly salient issues today. To be legitimate, welfare states need to function well and to deliver what is expected of them ("output-legitimacy"), but they also need to do so in a way that conforms with popular sentiments ("input-legitimacy"). Migration is likely to affect both dimensions of legitimacy. This chapter reviews the existing research on the relationship between migration and the welfare state and maps how international mobility and ethnic diversity interact with contemporary welfare states. In particular, we focus on the tension between the economic and fiscal rationale for more migration and the socio-political rationale for less migration, and spell out the conflicting policy imperatives and difficult trade-offs involved. A central theme here is that welfare states often need migration to remain fiscally sustainable and to maintain their redistributive capacity, but migration may simultaneously undermine the political sustainability of inclusive welfare states. We also discuss a number of potential remedies to this tension, drawing, inter alia, on insights from research on prejudice and discrimination in social psychology.

Keywords: welfare state, immigration, legitimacy, welfare chauvinism, deservingness

16.1 Introduction

Modern welfare states institutionalised social solidarity with those affected by hardship in the context of disruptions produced by early capitalism and the formation of modern nation states (Flora and Alber 1981). At the time of nation state formation social boundaries were redrawn and the concept of social solidarity rested on the idea that national communities were ethnically and culturally homogeneous. Recent decades have seen the world experiencing growing international migration that has notably included the internationalisation of labour markets. These developments have subsequently increased both the political salience of migration and the scholarly interest in the immigration-welfare nexus.

A large body of literature suggests that there is a fundamental tension between migration and the institution of the welfare state (Alesina and Glaeser 2004; Freeman 1986). For example, the economist Milton Friedman once famously stated that "you cannot simultaneously have free *immigration* and a *welfare*

https://doi.org/10.1515/9783110721768-016

state".[1] This raises the question of whether there is a "progressive dilemma" (Goodhart 2004), whereby one cannot reconcile open borders with social solidarity.

To shed light on this debate, we propose that the challenge immigration poses to the welfare state should be understood as a two-fold relationship between welfare state institutions and international migration (cf. Jakubiak and Kaczmarczyk 2018). Applying the conceptualisation of democratic legitimacy as based on input and output legitimacy (Scharpf 1999), we contend that the legitimacy of the welfare state rests on sufficient political consent and social solidarity (input) as well as on the fiscal capacity necessary to actually deliver social protection (output). In order to preserve the stability of existing welfare state institutions in a context of significant international migration, states face the challenge of allowing economically beneficial migration without undermining public support for welfare programmes.

The remainder of this chapter discusses the empirical evidence on the tension between welfare state institutions and international migration and also provides an overview of potential mitigation strategies.

16.2 Taking stock of migration's effect on welfare state legitimacy

16.2.1 The "output" side: immigrants and the fiscal sustainability of welfare states

Migration affects the economic foundation of welfare states by altering the size and composition of a country's population. Specifically, the effect of migration on the way welfare states function can be assessed from a contributing and a receiving side. On the one hand, migration can help strengthen the economic foundation of welfare states by providing additional labour force and complementary human capital as well as by counteracting demographic imbalances such as ageing and population decline. As the societies of most established welfare states have grown older and experience low birth rates, immigration has become an important source of population growth (Malmberg 2006, 133; Parsons and Smeeding 2009, 2–3). Indeed, demographic ageing is a good predictor of the extent to which OECD countries have liberalised labour immigration over the past several decades (Lutz 2020). This liberalisation process has taken place across all types of welfare states. Continuous immigration allowed receiving countries to ease the pressure on their pension systems (Han 2013), to address domestic labour needs, to fill skill shortages, to attract additional human capital, and to

---

1 Milton Friedman in an interview at the Institute for Liberty and Policy Analysis (ISIL) 18th Annual World Libertarian Conference, 20 August 1999.

increase their economies' competitiveness and innovation capability (Hollifield 2004). As immigrants tend to be young adults well past the fiscally costly phase of their childhoods when they arrive in the destination countries, they indeed strengthen the contributory side of welfare states by expanding the absolute and relative size of the working-age population (Coleman 2008). This economic imperative has been the driving force behind the immigration policy liberalisations that took place over the past few decades. Openness to immigration continues to be crucial for countries' economic competitiveness and the strengthening of the demographic foundation of their welfare states.

The extent to which immigrants are net-contributors strongly depends on their successful integration into the labour markets of receiving countries. In many contexts, immigrants are more likely to be unemployed, and this is especially the case for low-skilled immigrants from non-Western countries (e.g., Fleischmann and Dronkers 2010; Kogan 2006; van Tubergen, Maas, and Flap 2004). Nevertheless these and other studies also show that this is not a general rule – in some countries immigrants are in fact *better* integrated into labour markets than natives. Moreover, deficits in immigrants' labour market integration have also been partially linked to host country institutions, such as labour market policies (Cohen and Kogan 2007; Kogan 2006), and, notably, to discrimination by employers (Auer et al. 2019; Zschirnt and Ruedin 2016; but see also Koopmans 2016). Immigrants' weak economic integration is thus far from inevitable and to a considerable degree not attributable to immigrants themselves.

A related concern focuses on the adverse selection of immigrants through generous welfare programmes (Borjas 1999). According to this idea of a "welfare magnet", the prospects of welfare benefits attract (low-skilled) immigrants and thereby increase the fiscal burden on receiving countries. Economists have assessed the causal effect of welfare state generosity on immigration levels and found mixed results (Agersnap, Jensen, and Kleven 2020; Giulietti et al. 2013). Overall, the scholarship suggests that the main drivers of migration are economic opportunities and family networks and not the prospect of welfare benefits (De Giorgi and Pellizzari 2009; Geis, Uebelmesser, and Werding 2013). While migration tends to fluctuate with the business cycle, its fiscal impact also depends on the degree to which immigrants serve as a buffer whereby unemployment is exported in economically bad times (Afonso 2005). Recent evidence on the fiscal impact of immigration found that immigrants are to a large extent net contributors – and in several countries including Germany, Austria, Ireland, and the United Kingdom at higher rates than natives (Boeri 2010). Analysing immigrants' contributions to the welfare state in the United Kingdom, Dustmann and Frattini (2014) find that European immigrants have a net positive and non-European immigrants have a net negative impact. Overall, studies on immigrants' fiscal impact are inconclusive, suggesting that the latter tends to be small and highly depends on both the country context and immigrants' characteristics, such as their skill-level (Boeri, Hanson, and McCormick 2002; Hanson 2009; Huang, Kaushal, and Wang 2020; OECD 2013).

In light of this, does immigration hence strengthen or undermine the economic foundation of welfare states? The existing empirical research suggests that immigrants often make important contributions to the welfare state but may under certain circumstances also have a higher welfare dependency. Migration sustains economic competitiveness and strengthens the demographic foundation of welfare states with overall limited fiscal risks for receiving countries.

16.2.2 The "input" side: immigration and political support for the welfare state

Immigration may also affect the socio-political foundations of welfare states. Of primary concern here is the increased cultural and ethnic diversity that results from immigration, which may be a threat to social solidarity – a view that is strongly influenced by the observation that ethnic and especially racial diversity may explain why both welfare state development and public support for redistribution are lagging in the United States compared to the historically more ethnically homogeneous countries in Europe (Alesina and Glaeser 2004; Gilens 1999; Luttmer 2001). In contrast, the alternative "compensation" hypothesis contends that immigration may in fact *increase* support for social protection. This hypothesis derives from the idea that economic globalisation generates increased competition and insecurities that in turn create a demand for more social protection (Rodrik 1998). As far as immigration is concerned, those who fear that they could be replaced by immigrants willing to work for lower wages are expected to become more supportive of social protection and redistribution (Burgoon, Koster, and van Egmond 2012).

The empirical evidence on the effect of immigration on public support for the welfare state is mixed. On the one hand, many studies focusing on industrialised democracies have found that immigrant inflows are indeed associated with subsequent reductions in popular support for fiscal redistribution and welfare spending (Dahlberg, Edmark, and Berg 2017; Eger 2010; Stichnoth 2012). Nevertheless, several others have demonstrated that perceptions of immigrants as an economic threat and of increased competition for jobs are actually associated with higher support for redistribution (Ervasti and Hjerm 2012; Finseraas 2008) and that immigration is in some cases linked to increased public support for the welfare state (Brady and Finnigan 2014; Burgoon, Koster, and van Egmond 2012; Gaston and Rajaguru 2013; Steele 2016). Overall, there is no strong evidence that immigration and ethnic diversity necessarily undermines welfare support, and empirical studies suggest that their effects vary across different contexts (e.g. Mau and Burkhardt 2009).

Despite the mixed evidence on the link between immigration and public support for the welfare state as a whole, the public has clear preferences on the narrower question of what social rights immigrants should have. Research on welfare deservingness perceptions (van Oorschot 2000) has repeatedly shown that there is a strong and persistent "welfare deservingness gap" between immigrants and members of the native population (Ford 2016; Reeskens and van der Meer 2019), whereby the former are seen as less deserving of social protection just by virtue of their immigration status, even if they contribute as much as their native counterparts. The literature refers to this phenomenon also as "welfare chauvinism" (Andersen and Bjørklund 1990, 212; see also Careja and Harris 2022).

This deservingness gap exists across a range of welfare benefits and services, from cash benefits like unemployment insurance (Buss 2019) all the way to critical medical care, including in the context of the COVID-19 pandemic (M. H. Larsen and Schaeffer 2021; see also Eick and Larsen 2022). Even though one could expect that there might be greater support for providing social protection to higher-skilled immigrants than to lower-skilled ones, this expectation does not seem to be borne out by the evidence (Kootstra 2016, 331). The reluctance to give immigrants access to social protection is also quite robust across countries and welfare regimes. Recent research has produced considerable experimental evidence of the "deservingness gap" across the different welfare regimes (e.g. Ford 2016; M. H. Larsen and Schaeffer 2021; O'Dell et al. 2019; Reeskens and van der Meer 2019), although some earlier studies using systematic multi-level comparisons found that welfare chauvinism is less pronounced in social democratic welfare states than in liberal and conservative ones (van der Waal, De Koster, and van Oorschot 2013). It should of course also be pointed out that there is also variation at the individual level, specifically that the desire to restrict immigrants' access to social protection is more pronounced among those who perceive immigrants as a threat to their country's economy and culture (Kros and Coenders 2019; see also Scheepers, Gijsberts, and Coenders 2002). In addition, studies have identified authoritarian personality traits, i.e., a desire for order, conformity, and obedience to established social norms (Feldman 2003), as a salient predictor of the preference to limit migrants' social rights (Crepaz 2020).

Overall, we find that immigration does not systematically undermine public support for the welfare state as a whole but rather affects the kind of welfare state that citizens want. What the public (or at least a sizeable part of it) seems to want is not so much a smaller welfare state, but a smaller welfare state *for immigrants* (see also Banting 2016; Goldschmidt 2015). This preference is also reflected in concrete policy changes. While the effect of immigration on the welfare state as a whole remains ambiguous – with some studies finding negative effects (Kalm and Lindvall 2019; Soroka et al. 2016; Tabellini 2020) and others finding no or even positive effects on welfare state generosity and spending (Brady, Beckfield, and Seeleib-Kaiser 2005; Fenwick 2019; Taylor-Gooby 2005) – the patterns become clear once we examine what reforms are introduced. For instance, evidence from several European countries suggests that welfare state cutbacks are often driven by a desire to specifically exclude immigrants (Careja et al. 2016; Slaven, Casella Colombeau, and Badenhoop 2021). Denmark in recent years has in particular introduced measures with the explicit and declared intent to limit immigrants' social rights. A prime example is a 2002 reform that lowered welfare benefits for non-EU/EFTA immigrants (Agersnap, Jensen, and Kleven 2020). In other cases, Danish reforms have targeted immigrants more indirectly, for example, by mandating stricter checks on benefit claimants living outside of the country in 2010 (Careja et al. 2016). Other countries have embarked on similar efforts: for instance, in 2016, Germany curtailed EU migrants' access to social assistance in order to deter "benefit tourism".[2] What these reforms indicate is, again, that although the welfare state generally remains resilient in the face of immigration – partly because immigrants themselves ensure its fiscal sustainability but also because the majority population remains supportive of social protection, at least for itself – immigrants' rights to social protection and the public's support for these rights are considerably more vulnerable. Still, in cases where immigrants are only indirectly the target of cutbacks, the social rights of other vulnerable groups are also at risk.

16.3 Strategies to reduce the tension between immigration and the welfare state

Contemporary welfare states seem to be stuck between a rock and a hard place: They often need immigration to remain fiscally sustainable, particularly as far as public pensions are concerned, but at the same time, the increased ethnic and cultural diversity ensuing from immigration can create political pressure for restrictions and cutbacks targeted directly or indirectly at immigrants. This poses a potential threat to the legitimacy of inclusive and universal welfare states, for immigrants and vulnerable natives alike.

This, in turn, raises the question whether effective ways of addressing these challenges that allow preserving the sustainability of welfare institutions in the age of migration do exist. How can welfare states allow for economically beneficial migration without undermining their public support? Existing research that has identified several potential moderators of immigration's effect on welfare state support and on welfare policies can provide relevant insights.

The first potential remedy for welfare chauvinism has to do with tightening eligibility requirements in order to signal that benefits are only given to those who have previously contributed to welfare systems. For example, Reeskens and van Oorschot (2012) show that the idea of giving immigrants access to welfare benefits enjoys relatively widespread popular acceptance when the potential recipients have contributed to their host societies by working and paying taxes for some time. The authors thus re-

---

2 See the 2016 reform (BGBl. I 2016, No. 65, p. 3155) and the German government's statement (https://www.bundesregierung.de/breg-de/aktuelles/sozialleistungen-fuer-eu-auslaender-346428, last accessed on 13 August 2021).

commend that governments "reconsider universal and selective social policies and bring in more elements of social insurance, with its built-in logic of equivalence between contribution and benefit" (Reeskens and van Oorschot 2012, 132–133). However, this solution would arguably face some problems in practice. Specifically, the universal nature of many social protection programmes enjoys considerable public support – such as the universal health care programmes available in many countries – and whether the public would accept or even demand the introduction of stronger contribution requirements *for all* in response to immigration remains unclear. For example, Neundorf and Cavaille (2016), in their analysis of how support for universal access to health care in the UK is affected by immigration, found that immigrant inflows reduce support only marginally, and that this effect is confined to those on the political right.

A second, more radical alternative would be to simply endorse "welfare chauvinism" and make sure that immigrants receive fewer welfare benefits than natives. The underlying idea consists in aligning the scope of the welfare state with the accepted boundaries of social solidarity (Banting 2010, 798). Simply put, excluding immigrants is expected to dissolve natives' concerns that undeserving immigrants receive benefits and create a fiscal burden on receiving countries. There are, however, limits to the feasibility of this approach in many contexts, in particular due to legal prohibitions of discrimination against at least some groups of immigrants. Within the European Union, for instance, common market rules restrict member countries' ability to exclude EU migrants from social protection as long as the latter do not impose "unreasonable burdens" on their host countries (Eigmüller 2013). Similarly, the international human rights regime imposes constraints when it comes to the treatment of humanitarian migrants (Hollifield 2004). Added to this (and more important) are also some contradicting empirical findings, including the fact that attempts at "de-racialising" US welfare politics by strengthening work requirements did not appear to enjoy much success (Soss and Schram 2007) and the aforementioned results from deservingness research, which show that even when immigrants do contribute, they continue not being seen as equally deserving. Finally, citizens' perceptions of immigrants' fiscal impact mostly do not correspond to objective realities (Blinder and Markaki 2019) and fiscal self-interests have not been found to be a reliable predictor of opposition to immigration (Hainmueller and Hopkins 2014). Therefore, shielding welfare state institutions from immigrants' (potential or imagined) fiscal risks is unlikely to shift the public's opinion about their deservingness.

A third approach consists in going in the opposite direction and in actually increasing the universality and generosity of welfare states. Here, the idea is that a generous and inclusive welfare state would allow for the expansion of the boundaries of social solidarity and would attenuate redistribution conflicts (Boräng 2015). This rationale is derived from the findings in several studies that welfare chauvinism is least pronounced in the universal regimes of Northern Europe – a pattern that stems from the fact that these regimes reduce the income differences between natives and immigrants and the extent to which these two groups have to compete for access to social protection (Crepaz and Damron 2009). However, the viability of this solution is also unclear. For one, we can question whether voters in other welfare regimes, such as the United States, would accept a social-democratic transformation of their welfare states (Brooks and Manza 2006). Second, even though welfare chauvinist attitudes might be less pronounced in the Nordic countries, they still clearly do exist and matter there (Eger 2010; C. A. Larsen 2011). After all, the very term "welfare chauvinism" originates from a study on party strategies in the Nordic countries (Andersen and Bjørklund 1990). Therefore, the strategy of attenuating concerns about immigration by making welfare institutions more generous and universal also faces severe limitations in practice.

The final strategy does not seek to adapt welfare states to the presence of prejudice, but rather to actually address and reduce prejudice and bias in the first place. Experimental research from psychology and related fields shows that the relevance of even very powerful and persistent social categories like race and the biases that result from them can indeed be reduced if not eliminated.

This can in turn be achieved in two ways (Paluck and Green 2009, 345–347). The first approach comes down to encouraging contact between different groups. The central idea here is that contact between members of different social groups – natives and immigrants – reduces prejudice and discrimination by a) providing new knowledge about the respective outgroup; b) changing behaviour toward the other group; c) generating emotional ties, notably friendships; and d) promoting the re-evaluation of one's own group and its norms and values – otherwise known as a "deprovincialisation" of attitudes (Pettigrew 1998).

The second way to reduce prejudice involves breaking or recasting social categories, which can have a strong effect both on the saliency of previously important groups and on discriminatory behaviour (see e.g., Gaertner et al. 1989; see also Hewstone, Rubin, and Willis 2002, 589–593). For example, Kurzban et al. (2001) show that even the saliency of race as a feature distinguishing social groups can be eliminated with simple visual cues (coloured shirts) and behaviour indicating allegiance to shared goals. These studies strongly suggest that anti-immigrant attitudes and xenophobia are far from hard-wired into the human brain and that inclusive integration policies can indeed reduce the emphasis people place on group differences and increase communities' inclusiveness. Moreover, recent data indicates that despite the growing proportion of immigrants in their countries and the 2015 refugee crisis, the citizens of European democracies have adopted more positive views on immigration over time (Lutz and Karstens 2021).

Naturally, deploying these strategies outside of a laboratory setting is a daunting task, to say the least, and it is also not always clear that successful experimental manipulations do actually travel to the real world (Paluck and Green 2009). Still, there is evidence that multicultural integration policies can encourage meaningful and enduring contact between members of different groups and, thus, reduce tensions (Green et al. 2020). For example, Canada has long implemented policies in place that explicitly recognise and encourage cultural diversity, prohibit discrimination, and support the integration of immigrants through comparatively liberal family reunification policies or education policies that encourage linguistic diversity, among others. At the same time, immigrants in Canada also enjoy relatively unrestricted access to social protection – all without sparking a "welfare chauvinist" backlash. While the Canadian example shows the potential of large-scale immigration, multiculturalism and redistribution forming a stable equilibrium, the extent to which this model can be applied in other countries remains an open question (Banting 2010).

Overall, we suggest that there could be a way to overcome or at least attenuate welfare chauvinism and reconcile the apparent contradiction between the fiscal need for immigration and the political reality of prejudice and discrimination. This is best achieved through inclusive integration policies aimed at fostering mutual recognition and contact between natives and immigrant groups.

16.4 Conclusion

Immigration is often seen as a threat to the legitimacy of welfare states. This contribution has illustrated that the conflict between openness to migration and a generous welfare state is not a necessary one. Yes, immigration can *conceivably* undermine the legitimacy of welfare states if citizens view immigrants' access to social protection as unjustified. But immigrants can also (and in many cases do) contribute to the functioning and fiscal sustainability of welfare states and thus ensure that welfare states continue to deliver what citizens have come to expect of them. It is also not evident that opposition to immigrants' inclusion into welfare states cannot be overcome. Given the often mixed evidence and many open questions, more research is necessary to shed light on the relationship between migration and welfare states.

The empirical evidence suggests that welfare states are not doomed in the age of migration. What is clear is that welfare states face risks both when there are too few immigrants and when there are too many of them (cf. Lutz 2020). Policymakers should be aware of the significant tensions that do exist and should carefully design policies that not only ensure the fiscal sustainability of welfare institutions but also preserve public support for social solidarity in order to maintain the legitimacy of contemporary welfare states.

References

Afonso, Alexandre. 2005. "When the Export of Social Problems is No Longer Possible: Immigration Policies and Unemployment in Switzerland." *Social Policy & Administration* 39 (6), 653–668.

Agersnap, Ole, Amalie Jensen, and Henrik Kleven. 2020. "The Welfare Magnet Hypothesis: Evidence from an Immigrant Welfare Scheme in Denmark." *American Economic Review: Insights* 2 (4), 527–542.

Alesina, Alberto, and Edward Glaeser. 2004. *Fighting Poverty in the US and Europe: A World of Difference*. Oxford: Oxford University Press.

Andersen, Jørgen Goul, and Tor Bjørklund. 1990. "Structural Changes and New Cleavages: The Progress Parties in Denmark and Norway." *Acta Sociologica* 33 (3), 195–217.

Auer, Daniel, Giuliano Bonoli, Flavia Fossati, and Fabienne Liechti. 2019. "The Matching Hierarchies
Model: Evidence from a Survey Experiment on Employers' Hiring Intent Regarding Immigrant
Applicants." *International Migration Review* 53 (1), 90–121.

Banting, Keith G. 2010. "Is There a Progressive's Dilemma in Canada? Immigration, Multiculturalism
and the Welfare State." *Canadian Journal of Political Science / Revue Canadienne de Science
Politique* 43(4),797–820.

Banting, Keith. 2016. "Migration, Diversity, and the Welfare State." In *Encyclopedia of Migration*, edited by Frank D. Bean and Susan K. Brown, 1–8. Dordrecht: Springer.

Blinder, Scott, and Yvonni Markaki. 2019. "The Effects of Immigration on Welfare Across the EU: Do
Subjective Evaluations Align with Estimations?" *REMINDER Working Paper*.

Boeri, Tito. 2010. "Immigration to the Land of Redistribution." *Economica* 77 (308), 651–687.

Boeri, Tito, Gordon Hanson, and Barry McCormick. 2002. *Immigration Policy and the Welfare System:
A Report for the Fondazione Rodolfo Debenedetti*. Oxford: Oxford University Press.

Boräng, Frida. 2015. "Large-Scale Solidarity? Effects of Welfare State Institutions on the Admission of
Forced Migrants." *European Journal of Political Research* 54 (2), 216–231.

Borjas, George J. 1999. "Immigration and Welfare Magnets." *Journal of Labor Economics* 17 (4), 607–
637.

Brady, David, Jason Beckfield, and Martin Seeleib-Kaiser. 2005. "Economic Globalization and the
Welfare State in Affluent Democracies, 1975–2001." *American Sociological Review* 70 (6), 921–
948.

Brady, David, and Ryan Finnigan. 2014. "Does Immigration Undermine Public Support for Social Policy?" *American Sociological Review* 79 (1), 17–42.

Brooks, Clem, and Jeff Manza. 2006. "Why Do Welfare States Persist?" *The Journal of Politics* 68 (4),
816–827.

Burgoon, Brian, Ferry Koster, and Marcel van Egmond. 2012. "Support for Redistribution and the
Paradox of Immigration." *Journal of European Social Policy* 22 (3), 288–304.

Buss, Christopher. 2019. "Public Opinion towards Targeted Labour Market Policies: A Vignette Study
on the Perceived Deservingness of the Unemployed." *Journal of European Social Policy* 29 (2),
228–240.

Careja, Romana, Christian Elmelund-Præstekær, Michael Baggesen Klitgaard, and Erik Gahner Larsen. 2016. "Direct and Indirect Welfare Chauvinism as Party Strategies: An Analysis of the Danish
People's Party." *Scandinavian Political Studies* 39 (4), 435–457.

Careja, Romana, and Eloisa Harris. 2022. "Thirty years of welfare chauvinism research: Findings and
challenges." *Journal of European Social Policy* 32 (2), 212–224.

Cohen, Yinon, and Irena Kogan. 2007. "Next Year in Jerusalem … or in Cologne? Labour Market Integration of Jewish Immigrants from the Former Soviet Union in Israel and Germany in the 1990s."
European Sociological Review 23 (2), 155–168.

Coleman, D. 2008. "The Demographic Effects of International Migration in Europe." *Oxford Review of
Economic Policy* 24 (3), 452–476.

Crepaz, Markus M. L. 2020. "Coveting Uniformity in a Diverse World: The Authoritarian Roots of
Welfare Chauvinism in Postmigrastion Crisis Germany." *Social Science Quarterly* 101 (4), 1255–
1270.

Crepaz, Markus M. L., and Regan Damron. 2009. "Constructing Tolerance: How the Welfare State
Shapes Attitudes About Immigrants." *Comparative Political Studies* 42 (3), 437–463.

Dahlberg, Matz, Karin Edmark, and Helene Berg. 2017. "Revisiting the Relationship between Ethnic Diversity and Preferences for Redistribution: Reply." *Scandinavian Journal of Economics* 119 (2), 288–294.

De Giorgi, Giacomo, and Michele Pellizzari. 2009. "Welfare Migration in Europe." *Labour Economics* 16 (4), 353–363.

Dustmann, Christian, and Tommaso Frattini. 2014. "The Fiscal Effects of Immigration to the UK." *The Economic Journal* 124 (580), F593–F643.

Eger, Maureen A. 2010. "Even in Sweden: The Effect of Immigration on Support for Welfare State Spending." *European Sociological Review* 26 (2), 203–217.

Eick, Gianna Maria, and Christian Albrekt Larsen. 2022. "Welfare Chauvinism across Benefits and Services." *Journal of European Social Policy* 32 (1), 19–32.

Eigmüller, Monika. 2013. "Europeanization from Below: The Influence of Individual Actors on the EU Integration of Social Policies." *Journal of European Social Policy* 23 (4), 363–375.

Ervasti, Heikki, and Mikael Hjerm. 2012. "Immigration, Trust and Support for the Welfare State." In *The Future of the Welfare State: Social Policy Attitudes and Social Capital in Europe*, edited by Heikki Ervasti, Jørgen Goul Andersen, Torben Fridberg, and Kristen Ringdal, 153–171. Cheltenham and Northampton, MA: Edward Elgar.

Feldman, Stanley. 2003. "Enforcing Social Conformity: A Theory of Authoritarianism." *Political Psychology* 24 (1), 41–74.

Fenwick, Clare. 2019. "The Political Economy of Immigration and Welfare State Effort: Evidence from Europe." *European Political Science Review* 11 (3), 357–375.

Finseraas, Henning. 2008. "Immigration and Preferences for Redistribution: An Empirical Analysis of European Survey Data." *Comparative European Politics* 6 (4), 407–431.

Fleischmann, Fenella, and Jaap Dronkers. 2010. "Unemployment among immigrants in European Labour Markets: An Analysis of Origin and Destination Effects." *Work, Employment and Society* 24 (2), 337–354.

Flora, Peter, and Jens Alber. 1981. "Modernization, Democratization, and the Development of Welfare States in Western Europe." In *The Development of Welfare States in Europe and America*, edited by Peter Flora and Arnold J. Heidenheimer, 37–80. New Brunswick, NJ and London: Transaction Books.

Ford, Robert. 2016. "Who Should We Help? An Experimental Test of Discrimination in the British Welfare State." *Political Studies* 64 (3), 630–650.

Freeman, Gary P. 1986. "Migration and the Political Economy of the Welfare State." *The Annals of the American Academy of Political and Social Science* 485 (1), 51–63.

Gaertner, Samuel L., Jeffrey Mann, Audrey Murrell, and John F. Dovidio. 1989. "Reducing Intergroup Bias: The Benefits of Recategorization." *Journal of Personality and Social Psychology* 57 (2), 239–249.

Gaston, Noel, and Gulasekaran Rajaguru. 2013. "International Migration and the Welfare State Revisited." *European Journal of Political Economy* 29, 90–101.

Geis, Wido, Silke Uebelmesser, and Martin Werding. 2013. "How Do Migrants Choose Their Destination Country? An Analysis of Institutional Determinants: Migrants' Choice of Their Destination Country." *Review of International Economics* 21 (5), 825–840.

Gilens, Martin. 1999. *Why Americans Hate Welfare: Race, Media, and the Politics of Antipoverty Policy*. Chicago and London: University of Chicago Press.

Giulietti, Corrado, Martin Guzi, Martin Kahanec, and Klaus F. Zimmermann. 2013. "Unemployment Benefits and Immigration: Evidence from the EU." *International Journal of Manpower* 34 (1), 24–38.

Goldschmidt, Tina. 2015. "Anti-Immigrant Sentiment and Majority Support for Three Types of Welfare." *European Societies* 17 (5), 620–652.

Goodhart, David. 2004. "Too Diverse?" *Prospect* 95, 30–37.

Green, Eva G. T., Emilio Paolo Visintin, Oriane Sarrasin, and Miles Hewstone. 2020. "When Integration Policies Shape the Impact of Intergroup Contact on Threat Perceptions: A Multilevel Study across 20 European Countries." *Journal of Ethnic and Migration Studies* 46 (3), 631–648.

Hainmueller, Jens, and Daniel J. Hopkins. 2014. "Public Attitudes Toward Immigration." *Annual Review of Political Science* 17, 225–249.

Han, Kyung Joon. 2013. "Saving Public Pensions: Labor Migration Effects on Pension Systems in European Countries." *The Social Science Journal* 50 (2), 152–161.

Hanson, Gordon H. 2009. "The Economic Consequences of the International Migration of Labor." *Annual Review of Economics* 1 (1), 179–208.

Hewstone, Miles, Mark Rubin, and Hazel Willis. 2002. "Intergroup Bias." *Annual Review of Psychology* 53, 575–604.

Hollifield, James F. 2004. "The Emerging Migration State." *International Migration Review* 38 (3), 885–912.

Huang, Xiaoning, Neeraj Kaushal, and Julia Shu-Huah Wang. 2020. "What Explains the Gap in Welfare Use Among Immigrants and Natives?" *Population Research and Policy Review* 40, 819–860.

Jakubiak, Igor, and Paweł Kaczmarczyk. 2018. "Migration and the Welfare State." In *The Routledge Handbook of the Politics of Migration in Europe*, edited by Agnieszka Weinar, Saskia Bonjour, and Lyubov Zhyznomirska, 374–382. London and New York: Routledge.

Kalm, Sara, and Johannes Lindvall. 2019. "Immigration Policy and the Modern Welfare State, 1880–1920." *Journal of European Social Policy* 29 (4), 463–477.

Kogan, Irena. 2006. "Labor Markets and Economic Incorporation among Recent Immigrants in Europe." *Social Forces* 85 (2), 697–721.

Koopmans, Ruud. 2016. "Does Assimilation Work? Sociocultural Determinants of Labour Market Participation of European Muslims." *Journal of Ethnic and Migration Studies* 42 (2), 197–216.

Kootstra, Anouk. 2016. "Deserving and Undeserving Welfare Claimants in Britain and the Netherlands: Examining the Role of Ethnicity and Migration Status Using a Vignette Experiment." *European Sociological Review* 32 (3), 325–338.

Kros, Mathijs, and Marcel Coenders. 2019. "Explaining Differences in Welfare Chauvinism Between and Within Individuals over Time: The Role of Subjective and Objective Economic Risk, Economic Egalitarianism, and Ethnic Threat." *European Sociological Review* 35 (6) 860–873.

Kurzban, Robert, John Tooby, and Leda Cosmides. 2001. "Can Race Be Erased? Coalitional Computation and Social Categorization." *Proceedings of the National Academy of Sciences* 98 (26), 15387–15392.

Larsen, Christian Albrekt. 2011. "Ethnic Heterogeneity and Public Support for Welfare: Is the American Experience Replicated in Britain, Sweden and Denmark?" *Scandinavian Political Studies* 34 (4), 332–353.

Larsen, Mikkel Haderup, and Merlin Schaeffer. 2021. "Healthcare Chauvinism during the COVID-19 Pandemic." *Journal of Ethnic and Migration Studies* 47 (7), 1455–1473.

Luttmer, Erzo F. P. 2001. "Group Loyalty and the Taste for Redistribution." *Journal of Political Economy* 109 (3), 500–528.

Lutz, Philipp. 2020. "Welfare States, Demographic Transition and Immigration Policies." In *The European Social Model under Pressure*, edited by Romana Careja, Patrick Emmenegger, and Nathalie Giger, 331–348. Wiesbaden: Springer VS.

Lutz, Philipp, and Felix Karstens. 2021. "External Borders and Internal Freedoms: How the Refugee Crisis Shaped the Bordering Preferences of European Citizens." *Journal of European Public Policy* 28 (3), 370–388.

Malmberg, Bo. 2006. *Global Population Ageing, Migration and European External Policies*. Stockholm: Institute for Future Studies.

Mau, Steffen, and Christoph Burkhardt. 2009. "Migration and Welfare State Solidarity in Western Europe." *Journal of European Social Policy* 19 (3), 213–229.

Neundorf, Anja, and Charlotte Cavaille. 2016. "Support for Universal and Equal Access to Health Care in Diversifying Neighborhoods." *ISER Working Paper Series* 2016–10.

O'Dell, Heather W., Benjamin J. McMichael, Suzie Lee, Jay L. Karp, R. Lawrence VanHorn, and Seth J. Karp. 2019. "Public Attitudes toward Contemporary Issues in Liver Allocation." *American Journal of Transplantation* 19 (4), 1212–1217.

OECD. 2013. "The Fiscal Impact of Immigration in OECD Countries." In *International Migration Outlook 2013*, 125–189. Paris: OECD Publishing.

van Oorschot, Wim. 2000. "Who Should Get What, and Why? On Deservingness Criteria and the Conditionality of Solidarity among the Public." *Policy & Politics* 28 (1), 33–48.

Paluck, Elizabeth Levy, and Donald P. Green. 2009. "Prejudice Reduction: What Works? A Review and Assessment of Research and Practice." *Annual Review of Psychology* 60 (1), 339–367.

Parsons, Craig A., and Timothy M. Smeeding. 2009. *Immigration and the Transformation of Europe*. Cambridge: Cambridge University Press.

Pettigrew, Thomas F. 1998. "Intergroup Contact Theory." *Annual Review of Psychology* 49 (1), 65–85.

Reeskens, Tim, and Tom van der Meer. 2019. "The Inevitable Deservingness Gap: A Study into the Insurmountable Immigrant Penalty in Perceived Welfare Deservingness." *Journal of European Social Policy* 29 (2), 166–181.

Reeskens, Tim, and Wim van Oorschot. 2012. "Disentangling the 'New Liberal Dilemma': On the Relation between General Welfare Redistribution Preferences and Welfare Chauvinism." *International Journal of Comparative Sociology* 53 (2), 120–139.

Rodrik, Dani. 1998. "Why Do More Open Economies Have Bigger Governments?" *The Journal of Political Economy* 106 (5), 997–1032.

Sassen, Saskia. 1996. *Losing Control? Sovereignty in the Age of Globalization*. New York: Columbia University Press.

Scharpf, Fritz W. 1999. *Governing in Europe: Effective and Democratic?* Oxford: Oxford University Press.

Scheepers, Peer, Mérove Gijsberts, and Marcel Coenders. 2002. "Ethnic Exclusionism in European Countries. Public Opposition to Civil Rights for Legal Migrants as a Response to Perceived Ethnic Threat." *European Sociological Review* 18 (1), 17–34.

Slaven, Mike, Sara Casella Colombeau, and Elisabeth Badenhoop. 2021. "What Drives the Immigration-Welfare Policy Link? Comparing Germany, France and the United Kingdom." *Comparative Political Studies* 54 (5), 855–888.

Soroka, Stuart N., Richard Johnston, Anthony Kevins, Keith Banting, and Will Kymlicka. 2016. "Migration and Welfare State Spending." *European Political Science Review* 8 (2), 173–194.

Soss, Joe, and Sanford F. Schram. 2007. "A Public Transformed? Welfare Reform as Policy Feedback." *The American Political Science Review* 101 (1), 111–127.

Steele, Liza G. 2016. "Ethnic Diversity and Support for Redistributive Social Policies." *Social Forces* 94 (4), 1439–1481.

Stichnoth, Holger. 2012. "Does Immigration Weaken Natives' Support for the Unemployed? Evidence from Germany." *Public Choice* 151(3–4),631–654.

Tabellini, Marco. 2020. "Gifts of the Immigrants, Woes of the Natives: Lessons from the Age of Mass Migration." *The Review of Economic Studies* 87 (1), 454–486.

Taylor-Gooby, Peter. 2005. "Is the Future American? Or, Can Left Politics Preserve European Welfare States from Erosion through Growing 'Racial' Diversity?" *Journal of Social Policy* 34 (4), 661–672.

van Tubergen, Frank, Ineke Maas, and Henk Flap. 2004. "The Economic Incorporation of Immigrants in 18 Western Societies: Origin, Destination, and Community Effects." *American Sociological Review* 69 (5), 704–727.

van der Waal, Jeroen, Willem De Koster, and Wim van Oorschot. 2013. "Three Worlds of Welfare Chauvinism? How Welfare Regimes Affect Support for Distributing Welfare to Immigrants in Europe." *Journal of Comparative Policy Analysis: Research and Practice* 15 (2), 164–181.

Zschirnt, Eva, and Didier Ruedin. 2016. "Ethnic Discrimination in Hiring Decisions: A Meta-Analysis of Correspondence Tests 1990–2015." *Journal of Ethnic and Migration Studies* 42 (7), 1115–1134.

Ron Thompson

17 Education and the welfare state: worlds of early school leaving in Europe

Abstract: This chapter examines institutional aspects of the phenomenon of early school leaving in Europe. The chapter begins by briefly reviewing the place of education in the welfare state, introducing the classification system of Esping-Andersen and outlining how it has been applied to education. The concept of stratification is then related to both institutional arrangements and access to education, including the social composition and status of a particular educational level. De-commodification is interpreted in terms of the extent to which participants in education are shielded from market forces, and the public-private mix in educational provision. The main questions of the chapter are then stated: what are the patterns of early school leaving, and how are these patterns related to educational institutions and policies in different welfare regimes? These questions are addressed using comparative policy literature and secondary data from 26 European countries. For early school leaving, the chapter constructs measures of de-commodification and stratification and investigates their relationships to broader features of welfare states, asking in particular whether countries with similar welfare regimes tend to cluster in relation to these key aspects of education. Drawing on the findings from this analysis, the chapter discusses the factors underlying high rates of early school leaving, highlighting aspects of policy that appear to offer prospects for improvement.

Keywords: early school leaving, welfare regimes, decommodification, stratification, education systems, education policy

17.1 Introduction

Education is widely considered to be a pillar of the welfare state, providing its citizens with the knowledge and competences required for employment, cultural activity and political participation. However, the relationship between the nature of welfare states and their education systems is complex: educational institutions are to some extent autonomous from other areas of the welfare state (Willemse and De Beer 2012; West and Nikolai 2013). Moreover, tensions between meritocracy and egalitarianism – particularly the role of education systems in reproducing social disadvantage – suggest that education is something of a "special case" in welfare state provision (Wilensky 1975, 3). This chapter focuses on one aspect of education that throws such tensions into sharp relief: early school leaving, and its relationship to the institutional and socioeconomic contexts of welfare regimes in Europe. In 2020 there were over three million EU citizens aged 18–24 classified as early leavers, representing around 10 % of the

https://doi.org/10.1515/9783110721768-017

age cohort, and it is well-established that there are high individual and social costs associated with early school leaving. These include lost earnings, ill health and the costs to society of welfare benefits, lost tax revenues and higher crime levels (Brunello and De Paola 2014). Increasingly, completion of upper secondary education is seen in policy terms as the minimum acceptable level of educational attainment.

The chapter reviews the place of education in the welfare state, introducing the classification system of Esping-Andersen (1990) and outlining how the key concepts of de-commodification and stratification have been applied to education. The main questions of the chapter are then stated: what are the patterns of early school leaving, and how are these patterns related to educational institutions and policies in different welfare regimes? These questions are discussed using comparative policy literature and secondary data from OECD and EU sources. The chapter constructs measures of de-commodification and stratification related to early school leaving and investigates their relationships to broader features of welfare states, asking whether countries with similar welfare regimes tend to cluster in relation to these aspects of education. Drawing on the findings from this analysis, the chapter concludes that there is considerable diversity in patterns of ESL, even between similar welfare states. Although the greatest challenges occur in Southern European and some post-socialist welfare regimes, other welfare systems – including those often idealised as social-democratic regimes – may find reductions in ESL difficult to sustain.

17.2 Welfare regimes and education regimes

The typology of welfare capitalism developed by Gøsta Esping-Andersen has been hugely influential, informing social policy studies over the last 30 years (Powell, Yörük, and Bardu 2020). Beginning from the observation that it is not how much welfare states spend or redistribute that matters, but the qualitative properties of welfare arrangements, Esping-Andersen (1990) introduces two analytical dimensions. First, social rights are conceptualised in terms of their capacity for *decommodification*, their ability to shield individuals from the market in critical arenas such as health, social security and education. Second, the welfare state is considered as a system of *stratification*: what impact do welfare arrangements have on social solidarity, and do they enhance or diminish existing differences of class or status? Esping-Andersen (1990, 23) notes that "The welfare state is not just a mechanism that intervenes in ... the structure of inequality; it is, in its own right, a system of stratification". To differing degrees, welfare states act upon and produce hierarchies of status, often creating dualisms which parallel historical distinctions between the deserving and undeserving poor. Welfare state institutions do not merely provide services or benefits: they help to position welfare recipients in the system of social relations.

Using the concepts of decommodification and stratification alongside the "welfare mix" – the interaction between state, market and family in welfare provision –

Esping-Andersen (1990, 26–27) identified three ideal-typical welfare-state regimes, from which real-life welfare states emerge in various hybrid forms. A "conservative-corporatist" regime is characterised by modest redistribution but with welfare benefits stratified according to social status; a "liberal" regime, in which state provision is also modestly redistributive but largely residual, provides a safety net for those unable to access market provision; whilst "social democratic" regimes are highly redistributive with universal and relatively generous benefits. Since the early 1990s, in response to increasing globalisation and the emergence of new and post-socialist economies, Esping-Andersen's typology has been extensively critiqued and more complex classifications have been developed. Nevertheless, the concepts of decommodification and stratification retain their analytical power, and can be valuable in understanding national education policies and their impact on educational outcomes (Alexiadou, Helgøy, and Homme 2019).

17.2.1 Decommodification and stratification in education

The development of education systems has been a lengthy and complex process, shaped by many of the same processes which have influenced the development of welfare states. Partisan politics, shifting conceptions of the state, and "path dependency" in features such as the relationship between church and state in welfare provision, have been important factors in the creation of educational as well as more general welfare institutions (Ansell 2008; Ansell and Lindvall 2013; Green 2013). It is therefore to be expected that conceptualisations of the welfare state may also be useful in an educational context, albeit with certain important differences. Indeed, a welfare regimes approach has been used by several authors to analyse the features of educational institutions and outcomes (Beblavy, Thum, and Veselkova 2011; Willemse and De Beer 2012; West and Nikolai 2013). The concepts of decommodification and stratification have also been used to classify educational systems without necessarily referring to the welfare context, for example in the study of educational inequalities by Bukodi et al. (2018). However, some care is needed in interpreting these concepts. The original formulation by Esping-Andersen (1990) related decommodification to cash benefits such as pensions rather than to service provision. Consequently, his elaboration of the concept in terms of eligibility, income replacement and range of entitlements needs to be recast in a form appropriate to education. Decommodification is normally thought of as the extent to which education is provided by the state as a public good, rather than purchased on the market (Beblavy Thum, and Veselkova 2011; Bukodi et al. 2018). The equivalent of income replacement is therefore to be found in variables such as state expenditure on relevant phases of education, the balance between public and private expenditure, and the proportion of students enrolled in public or private institutions. Who is eligible for state provision must also be considered, in terms of access to education and the duration of this support – Esping-Andersen's "exit" condition (1990, 47). In an era where *theoretical* eligibility for higher levels of education depends purely on academic requirements – if any – practical eligibility is perhaps more significant: how many students participate, and from what backgrounds. Consequently, we may express eligibility in terms of both the formal requirements for participation and the actual percentages of the population enrolled at a particular level (Willemse and De Beer 2012). Finally, the range of entitlements to education may be expressed in terms of direct and indirect support for participation, such as financial support for students and more general support to families, aimed at alleviating poverty and reducing the opportunity costs of remaining in education (for example study grants, child benefit and tax relief for parents).

Comparative studies of education systems tend to conceptualise stratification in terms of two factors: differentiation and selectivity (Bukodi et al. 2018). The meaning of stratification in Esping-Anderson's work is somewhat broader, concerning how the welfare state shapes class and status, by allocating people to different forms of benefit depending on their social standing and influencing that standing through welfare provision itself. For this reason, some authors supplement the concepts of differentiation and selectivity with additional factors such as the vocational efficacy of educational qualifications and the extent of inequalities in educational attainment (Beblavy, Thum, and Veselkova 2011; Willemse and De Beer 2012; West and Nikolai 2013). These additional factors will be used in this chapter to capture the interaction between the educational system and external stratifications such as labour-market status and socio-economic status.

Differentiation denotes the existence of separate "tracks" within a particular educational level, either through formally distinct institutional types or by different curriculum arrangements within a single institution, often through streaming or subject-specific ability grouping. Selectivity refers to organising the transition from earlier, possibly untracked educational levels into the available tracks. This may involve academic selection based on previous performance, the recommendations of teachers based on academic and non-academic criteria, or parental choice. Both tracking and selection are known to reinforce the effects of social background on educational attainment, by providing opportunities for more advantaged parents to deploy material and cultural resources both in identifying higher-status tracks and in ensuring access to these tracks, for example by purchasing private tuition. Typically, tracking is associated with specialisation in terms of general or vocational education.

17.3 Patterns of early school leaving in Europe

Lower-attaining young people are often conceptualised in policy discourse as vulnerable to unemployment and other social risks in later life; and there is ample evidence in the literature of the potential "scarring" effects of early exclusion from education and the labour market (Ralston et al. 2016; Hvinden et al. 2019). In particular, the EU average unemployment rate for 20–24-year-olds with only lower secondary education or below is currently around twice that for upper secondary graduates.[1] In order to identify those most in need, various categories of youth vulnerability have been developed since the early 1990s. As well as the concept of early school leaving (ESL), the classification "not in education, employment or training" (NEET) has become particularly widespread. The discourses associated with these categories have been extensively critiqued, revealing their dependence on precarious assumptions about the nature of post-industrial employment and the growth of a knowledge-based economy (see, for example Thompson 2011; Ross and Leathwood 2013). Indeed, some authors have argued that categories such as ESL or NEET serve mainly as a technology for surveillance and governance of young people for whom the state is unable to provide employment, and, indeed, of states and education systems themselves (Gillies and Mifsud 2016; Grimaldi and Landri 2019). Nevertheless, there is little doubt that leaving education before completing at least the upper secondary stage is a serious disadvantage, and one which systems of welfare would wish to address – although perhaps in different ways.

We adopt the definition of early school leaving used within the European Union, that early school leavers are young people aged 18–24 who have completed at most lower secondary education and are not currently in education or training. More precisely, they have completed at most ISCED 2011 level 2,[2] and have not participated in education or training within the last four weeks. However, young people may leave formal education but still retain some connection with educational activities, for example through courses aimed at re-engaging those disaffected from schooling (Simmons, Thompson, and Russell 2014). This possibility is recognised by the ELFE indicator (early leavers from formal education): the difference between the ELFE and ESL rates represents the proportion of young people in the relevant age group who have left formal education with below upper secondary attainment but are engaged in non-formal learning activities.[3] According to these definitions, early school leaving is very much a description of an end-state, relating to the activities of young people possibly several years after the events and decisions occurred which ended their involvement with education. The ESL category may therefore encompass young people who have experienced a range of processes, such as dropout before or immediately after the compulsory school leaving age, failure to complete a lower secondary qualification, and unsuccessful participation in the upper secondary stage (Gonzalez-Rodriguez, Vieira, and Vidal et al. 2019).

---

1 Unemployment rates of 27 % and 15 % respectively in Quarter 3 of 2020 (Eurostat lfsq_urgaed).
2 International Standard Classification of Education, UNESCO (2012).
3 "Non-formal education and training is defined as any institutionalised, intentional and organised/ planned learning activities outside the formal education system. In the sense used here, this excludes guided on-the-job training. Eurostat, https://ec.europa.eu/eurostat/cache/metadata/en/edat1_esms. htm.

Early school leaving rates should not be considered in isolation. Their trends over time and relationship to other societal and educational factors must also be taken into account. Table 17.1 presents, for 26 European countries, a range of variables which provide a broader context to early school leaving. These include their ESL rates (2010 and 2019; ELFE for 2019 only), alongside an ESL trend term (the gradient of the regression line for annual observations between 2010 and 2019 inclusive). Many countries in Table 17.1 show a statistically significant decline in ESL rates, with the greatest reductions occurring in countries such as Spain and Portugal where 2010 rates were the highest. In addition, Table 17.1 illustrates the gendered nature of early school leaving, by showing the odds ratio for ESL in 2019 between young men and young women. In all but the Czech Republic, males are more likely than females to be early school leavers; in some countries, notably Portugal but also including Spain, Poland and the Netherlands, this difference is considerable (odds ratio near to 2).

Table 17.1: Early school leaving and low educational attainment.

Country	Code	Aged 18–24, no upper secondary (%)		Aged 25–34, no upper secondary (%)		Early school leavers (ESL) (%)		ESL Trend	Gender odds ESL (M/F)	ELFE (%)
		2010	2019	2010	2019	2010	2019	2010–2019	2019	2019
Ireland	IE	20.8	14.1	14.2	7.4	11.9	5.1	−0.83	1.4	5.4
United Kingdom	UK	20.5	15.3	16.6	13.9	14.8	10.9	−0.50	1.35	11.6
Mean liberal		**20.7**	**14.7**	**15.4**	**10.7**	**13.4**	**8.0**	**−0.70**	**1.4**	**8.5**
SD liberal		0.2	0.6	1.2	3.3	1.5	2.9	0.20	0.0	3.1
Austria	AT	27.4	20.1	12.2	10.6	8.3	7.8	−0.10	1.62	9.4
Belgium	BE	25.6	25.9	17.9	14.8	11.1	8.4	−0.48	1.77	9
France	FR	22.5	15.2	16.3	12.6	12.7	8.2	−0.50	1.43	9.6
Germany	DE	40.9	35.2	13.3	13.2	11.8	10.3	−0.14	1.40	10.7
Luxembourg	LU	43.5	31.1	16	12.3	7.1	7.2	−0.01	1.68	7.9
Netherlands	NL	32.1	27.6	17.6	12.4	10.1	7.5	−0.30	1.80	8.6
Mean conservative		**32.0**	**25.9**	**15.6**	**12.7**	**10.2**	**8.2**	**−0.30**	**1.6**	**9.2**
SD conservative		7.8	6.6	2.1	1.2	2.0	1.0	0.20	0.2	0.9
Greece	GR	20.9	11.5	24.5	10.2	13.5	4.1	−1.10	1.56	4.2
Italy	IT	35.7	30.7	28.9	23.8	18.6	13.5	−0.57	1.40	13.9
Portugal	PT	47.3	24.6	47.5	24.8	28.3	10.6	−1.79	1.99	11.3
Spain	ES	43.7	30.9	34.7	30.2	28.2	17.3	−1.24	1.82	18.9
Mean Mediterranean		**36.9**	**24.4**	**33.9**	**22.3**	**22.2**	**11.4**	**−1.20**	**1.70**	**12.1**
SD Mediterranean		10.1	7.9	8.6	7.4	6.4	4.8	0.40	0.20	5.3

Table 17.1 (continued)

Country	Code	Aged 18–24, no upper secondary (%)		Aged 25–34, no upper secondary (%)		Early school leavers (ESL) (%)		ESL Trend	Gender odds ESL (M/F)	ELFE (%)
		2010	2019	2010	2019	2010	2019	2010–2019	2019	2019
Denmark	DK	44.5	37.9	20.8	18	11.5	9.9	−0.12	1.67	11.8
Finland	FI	31.6	27.2	9.2	8.7	10.3	7.3	−0.28	1.46	8.3
Norway	NO	43.2	34.9	17.1	16.1	17.4	9.9	−0.89	1.49	11.9
Sweden	SW	27.8	30.5	12.6	11.4	6.5	6.5	0.05	1.37	8.2
Mean Nordic		**36.8**	**32.6**	**14.9**	**13.6**	**11.4**	**8.4**	**−0.30**	**1.5**	**10.1**
SD Nordic		7.2	4.1	4.4	3.7	3.9	1.5	0.40	0.1	1.8
Bulgaria	BG	26.2	27.8	18.8	17.6	12.6	13.9	0.14	1.11	13.9
Czech Republic	CZ	24.6	28.9	5.8	7	4.9	6.7	0.22	0.97	7
Estonia	EE	30.5	29.4	13.1	11.4	11	9.3	0.00	1.96	10.9
Hungary	HU	31.9	25	13.6	12.7	10.8	11.8	0.13	1.19	12.3
Latvia	LV	33.0	39.4	16.3	9.8	12.9	8.7	−0.42	1.61	8.8
Lithuania	LT	29.5	24	11.7	5.9	7.9	4.0	−0.39	1.87	4.1
Poland	PL	24.9	26.6	6.4	6	5.4	5.2	−0.07	1.92	5.5
Romania	RO	33.0	26.2	23.9	22	19.3	15.3	−0.25	0.93	15.4
Slovak Republic	SK	23.9	28.5	5.9	9.1	4.7	8.3	0.49	1.12	8.4
Slovenia	SI	22.2	20.3	6.5	4.9	5	4.6	0	1.39	4.7
Mean post-socialist		**28.0**	**27.6**	**12.2**	**10.6**	**9.5**	**8.8**	**0.0**	**1.4**	**9.1**
SD post-socialist		3.9	4.7	5.9	5.2	4.5	3.7	0.3	0.4	3.7

Sources: Col 3–6, Eurostat [edat_lfs_9903]; Col 7–10, [edat_lfse_14]; Col 11, [edat_lfse_15].

Categories such as ESL imply a dichotomy between inclusion and exclusion, suggesting that all is well provided young people remain in education, whatever their level of attainment. However, educational marginality, in which young people continue in various forms of education or training without achieving an upper secondary qualification, can be as problematic as early leaving (Thompson 2017). This suggests that early leavers should be considered as part of a broader category: young people aged 18–24 who have not attained ISCED level 3, irrespective of whether they are currently in education or training. Table 17.1 shows the proportion of the age cohort who fall into this category, again for 2010 and 2019. There is a moderately high correlation between this proportion and the proportion counted as early leavers; the difference between these proportions indicates the success (or otherwise) of a country in retaining low-attaining young people in education. However, being in education at 18–24 does not imply successful completion of an upper secondary qualification, and Table 17.1 also shows for both years the proportion of 25–34-year-olds who have not achieved this level.

17.3.1 Early school leaving and welfare regimes

To provide an initial insight into possible relationships between early school leaving and welfare regimes, the countries in Table 17.1 are organised according to their usual classifications in terms of regime types. These include a small liberal group (Ireland and the UK); a West-Central European group of broadly conservative welfare states; a Mediterranean (more precisely, Southern European) group; and the four Nordic countries. A further group comprises ten post-socialist countries. For each regime, the mean and standard deviation of the ESL-related variables is given. Perhaps the most striking feature of this perspective is the lack of variation in ESL rates between certain regime types compared with the variation within them, particularly for the most recent data. Excluding the Southern European group, the mean 2019 ESL rate varies by less than one percentage point, whilst variation within groups can be as much as ten percentage points. However, the Southern European group itself has a mean ESL rate considerably higher than these other groups, in spite of a significant reduction since 2010.

The other variables in Table 17.1 reveal rather more variation between regime types, and some consistency within them. In all but the post-socialist group, ESL rates have fallen significantly since 2010, whilst in seven of the ten post-socialist countries these rates have either increased slightly or have been broadly stable. Except for the liberal group, non-completion rates for upper secondary for 18–24-year-olds have been in the region of 30 % in the period 2010–2019. However, non-completion for 25–34-year-olds is considerably lower for all but the Southern European group, with particularly notable reductions in the Nordic countries. These patterns suggest some differences in adult education provision for early leavers. Although ELFE rates are generally not much different to ESL, the ratio (ELFE – ELET)/ELFE, which represents the proportion of those who have left formal education who remain in some kind of informal education or training, is greatest in the Nordic and some conservative countries. In Norway, almost 21 % of the ELFE cohort in 2019 were still engaged in informal education. Finally, reflecting the familialist conceptions of the role of a male breadwinner often associated with these regime types, ESL rates appear to be more gendered (masculinised) in the conservative and Southern European groups than in the other welfare regimes.

This landscape of converging ESL rates against a background of persistent differences in related variables suggests that significant policy differences exist between welfare regime types. However, it does not answer the question of how, if at all, patterns of early school leaving correspond to the theoretical dimensions of decommodification and stratification. We therefore construct quantitative measures of these two concepts, using variables of relevance to ESL rates. Before doing so, we motivate the selection of variables by outlining some of the socioeconomic and institutional factors that have been implicated in early school leaving.

17.3.2 Factors associated with early school leaving

An extensive literature exists on the possible causes of early school leaving. A large part of this literature is concerned with individualised factors that may increase a young person's chances of leaving education before attaining an upper secondary qualification (see Gonzalez-Rodriguez, Vieira, and Vidal 2019). These include low educational expectations and poor school performance, lack of engagement with schooling (often manifested by truancy or sanctions such as exclusion from school), and experiencing bullying or victimisation (Kaye et al. 2017). Such factors point to early school leaving, particularly within the 15–19 age range, as the culmination of a lengthy process of interaction between the individual and their schools, rather than a discrete event (Santos et al. 2020). Moreover, ESL as a description applying to 18–24-year-olds suggests that these processes are affected by the nature of post-compulsory and adult education (De Witte et al. 2013). Family and social background factors are also important: having foreign-born parents, social class (Duckworth and Schoon 2012), family poverty, parental education (Chevalier et al. 2013; Lavrijsen and Nicaise 2015), and parental expectations for a young person's educational attainment (Kaye et al. 2017) have all been identified as influencing ESL risk.

Rather less attention has been paid to the impact of the socioeconomic and institutional context, including features of education systems and labour market policies (De Witte et al. 2013; Lavrijsen and Nicaise 2015; Helgøy et al. 2019; Grimaldi and Landri 2019). These macro-level factors may operate in either of two ways: by influencing the absolute level of early school leaving in a particular country, or by modifying the impact of the individualised factors discussed above. For example, educational tracking intensifies the socioeconomic gradient of early school leaving, whilst the labour-market returns of educational qualifications and the extent of vocational education influence absolute ESL rates (Lavrijsen and Nicaise 2015). Of the socioeconomic factors that have been investigated, poverty rates appear to affect both absolute ESL rates and social background inequalities in ESL. However, poverty does not appear to influence significantly the proportion of early school leavers who remain in some kind of "second chance" adult education (De Witte et al. 2013). Greater GDP, and also GDP growth, are associated with lower absolute ESL rates. Although increasing youth and adult unemployment may, on the face of it, lead to young people staying in education longer, this is not necessarily the case, and it is possible that a "discouraged student" effect may operate, in which young people question the point of obtaining qualifications if this is unlikely to stave off unemployment. Of the institutional factors, some authors argue that increasing the length of compulsory schooling reduces early school leaving, although the limited degree of variation across European countries means that the evidence for this is weak (Lavrijsen and Nicaise 2015). Grade retention practices increase ESL rates, whilst the proportion of students in selective schools and the proportion of students in vocational education have a negative impact on absolute rates (De Witte et al. 2013) but may increase the socioeconomic gradient.

17.4 Regimes of early school leaving in Europe

In this section we construct indices of decommodification and stratification using variables describing the environment in which early school leaving takes place, drawing on the previous two sections. These indices are applied to 26 European countries with two aims: firstly, to understand the extent to which countries cluster together in relation to the dimensions of decommodification and stratification; and secondly, to investigate the association between these two dimensions and early school leaving. Countries are selected on the basis of relevant data being available for all the variables used in constructing the indices. The values and data sources for these variables are presented in Tables A1 and A2.

We assume that the processes involved in early school leaving are influenced by institutional and socioeconomic conditions over a period of several years leading up to a young person being counted as a member of the ESL category (see Lavrijsen and Nicaise 2015). Furthermore, certain variables may fluctuate year-on-year, and it is therefore inappropriate to rely entirely on single-year data in constructing indices of decommodification and stratification. Where annual data is available, we therefore average variables over a five-year period as indicated in the data tables. For the purposes of comparison with 2019 ESL rates, the period 2013–2017 is chosen to correspond to a substantial proportion of the secondary and post-compulsory education experience of 18–24-year-olds, whilst being sufficiently recent to retain its contemporary relevance. To ensure an acceptable degree of concept-measure consistency (Goertz 2006), the selection of variables is guided by Table 17.2, which shows how specific measures have been derived from the general concepts of decommodification and stratification.

Table 17.2: Concept-measure correspondence for analysis of ESL regimes.

First-level concept	Second-level concepts	Indicators	Measures
De-commodification	Access and duration	Effective school-leaving age	Participation at age 18 (%)
		Utilisation of public education	Pupils in public education institutions (%)
	Standard of public provision	Public expenditure on education	Education expenditure (% of GDP)
			Per-pupil expenditure
		Staffing levels	Pupil–teacher ratio
		Average attainment	Mean reading performance at age 15
	Range of entitlements	Effective financial support to families	Child poverty rate (%)
		Financial assistance to students	Decommodification score for financial assistance entitlements
Stratification	Differentiation	Different tracks available to students, either within or between schools	Age of first tracking
			No. of tracks at age 15
			Students in vocational tracks (%)
	Selectivity	Prevalence of academic selection, either on entry or during school career	Students in academically selective schools (%)
			Students in schools with ability grouping (%)
		Strong framing of progression	Students repeating grades (%)
	Vocational specificity	Labour-market returns to education	Odds ratio for unemployment between upper and lower secondary
	Relationship to social stratification	Inequality of opportunity	Difference in PISA reading score between upper and lower SES quartiles

17.4.1 Decommodification

Eight variables relevant to early school leaving are used to construct the decommodification index (Table A1). These include some which are specific to upper secondary education and others relating to the broader school career. Public investment in education and its impact on the quality of educational provision are represented by three variables: total education expenditure on primary and secondary education as a percentage of GDP; the pupil–teacher ratio in primary and secondary education; and per-pupil expenditure in upper secondary education, expressed in purchasing power standard (PPS). Access to a complete secondary education career is represented by the proportion of 18-year-olds in education, irrespective of level. The quality of public education provision is further represented by a country's mean PISA reading score at age 15. The distribution of financial resources available to families is represented by the child poverty rate, defined in terms of 60 % of median income after social transfers. The range of financial support to students in upper secondary education is represented by the rules governing eligibility rather than by expenditure per se (cf. Esping-Andersen 1990, 47). The coding system summarised in Table A3 is used to allocate a decommodification score based on entitlements to child benefit, tax relief, study grants, and other forms of support such as free school meals and subsidised travel. The final variable indicates the balance between public and private utilisation of education: the percentage of students in private institutions at primary and secondary levels. Each of these variables is standardised to a mean of 0 and standard deviation 1, taking into account its directionality – for example, a lower poverty rate implies greater decommodification. The decommodification index is then the average of the eight standardised variables.

17.4.2 Stratification

Eight variables are used in constructing the index of stratification (Table A2). Three are concerned with tracking: the age at which tracking decisions are first made; the number of tracks available to 15-year-olds; and the percentage of students in vocational tracks. A fourth variable indicates the labour market returns of upper secondary education: the odds ratio for 20–24-year-olds of being unemployed compared with young people having only lower secondary education or below. Two further variables correspond to selectivity: the percentage of 15-year-olds in schools where academic performance is always taken into account in admissions; and the percentage of students in schools which use ability grouping for some or all subjects. The strength of vertical stratification is indicated by the percentage of students who have experienced grade retention at least once. Finally, the relationship between stratification in school performance and broader stratifications in society is represented by the difference in Pisa reading scores at age 15 between the upper and lower quartiles of socioeconomic status. The stratification index is then calculated in a similar procedure to that for de-commodification.

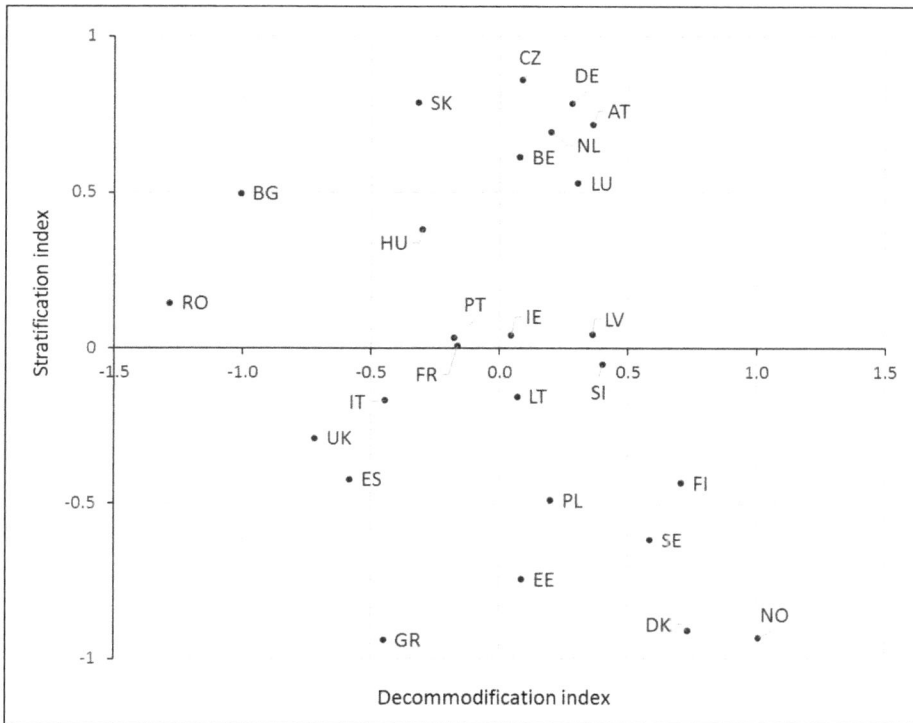

Figure 17.1: Clustering of countries according to the indices of decommodification and stratification.

17.4.3 Analysis of ESL regimes

The indices for all 26 countries are plotted in Figure 17.1, with decommodification along the horizontal axis and stratification along the vertical axis. Although some broad associations according to these dimensions can be seen immediately, we use hierarchical cluster analysis to refine the groupings. This method attempts to maximise the similarity of cases (countries) within each cluster, so that in terms of the variables included items in each cluster are similar to others in the cluster and dissimilar to those in other clusters. In the analysis, Ward's method is used, applying squared Euclidean distance as the measure of similarity. The results are displayed in the dendrogram of Figure 17.2, which shows (reading from left to right) how clusters are combined at each stage until only a single cluster remains. Table 17.3 summarises the membership of these clusters.

Table 17.3: Clustering of 26 European countries according to indices of decommodification and stratification.

Country	Decommodification	Stratification	Country	Decommodification	Stratification
Denmark	0.733	−0.910	France	−0.166	0.008
Finland	0.708	−0.435	Ireland	0.044	0.042
Norway	1.008	−0.931	Latvia	0.361	0.046
Sweden	0.587	−0.617	Lithuania	0.069	−0.155
Mean	**0.759**	**−0.723**	Portugal	−0.178	0.035
			Slovenia	0.400	−0.052
Austria	0.362	0.718	**Mean**	**0.088**	**−0.013**
Belgium	0.078	0.614			
Czech Republic	0.088	0.863	Estonia	0.088	−0.745
Germany	0.281	0.786	Poland	0.198	−0.490
Hungary	−0.301	0.383	**Mean**	**0.143**	**−0.617**
Netherlands	0.199	0.696			
Luxembourg	0.303	0.529	Bulgaria	−1.008	0.498
Slovakia	−0.319	0.789	Romania	−1.285	0.146
Mean	**0.086**	**0.672**	**Mean**	**−1.146**	**0.322**
Italy	−0.445	−0.166	Greece	−0.450	−0.937
Spain	−0.583	−0.423			
UK	−0.720	−0.290			
Mean	**−0.582**	**−0.293**			

The most distinctive groupings emerging from the analysis are the Nordic countries and a broadly conservative cluster, containing countries traditionally thought of as conservative welfare states alongside the Czech and Slovak Republics. Both of these clusters conform to what might be expected from Esping-Andersen's classification: the Nordic countries have high levels of decommodification alongside low stratification (Finland and Sweden less so), whilst the conservative group is highly stratified with average levels of decommodification. The educational regimes of the remaining countries show a rather looser connection with their respective welfare regimes. States normally considered to be conservative, such as France, Italy and Portugal, are split between two clusters, together with the liberal countries Ireland and the UK. Cluster 3, of which France and Ireland are both members, has near-average levels of decommodification and stratification (Latvia and Slovenia are slightly more decommodified than other members of this cluster). Cluster 4 contains Spain, Italy and the UK: all three are below average in both measures. The final two clusters differ markedly in both decommodification and stratification. Poland and Estonia are as unstratified as the Nordic countries but with average or slightly below-average levels of decommodification, whilst Bulgaria and Romania have above-average stratification and low decommodification. Greece is best thought of as an isolated case.

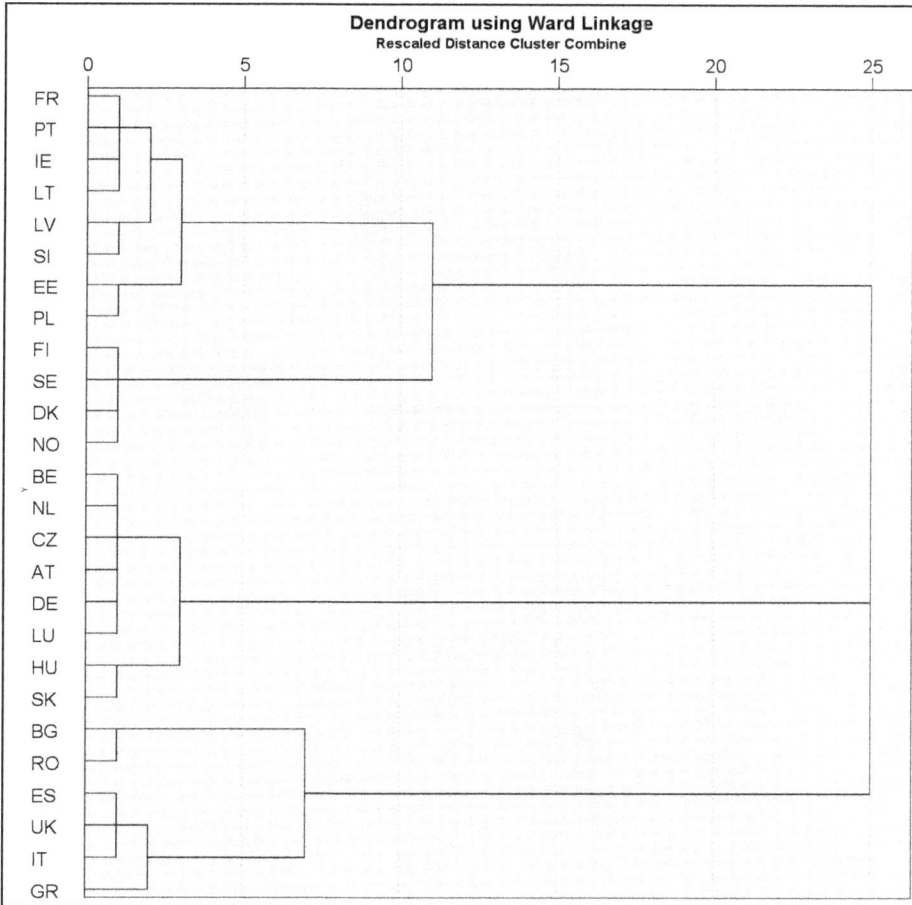

Figure 17.2: Dendrogram showing the results of hierarchical cluster analysis on indices of decommodification and stratification.

We turn now to the relationship between early school leaving rates, decommodification and stratification. Figure 17.3 shows the relationship between ESL rates in 2019 as the dependent variable and decommodification, whilst Figure 17.4 does the same for stratification. Figure 17.3 indicates some correlation between ESL rates and decommodification; however, Figure 17.4 suggests that ESL rates are largely independent of stratification.

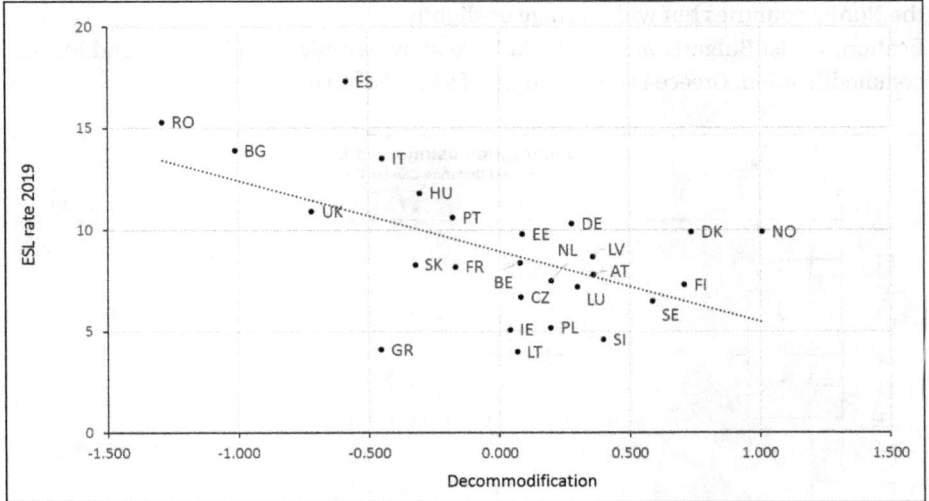

Figure 17.3: Association between ESL rates and the decommodification index.

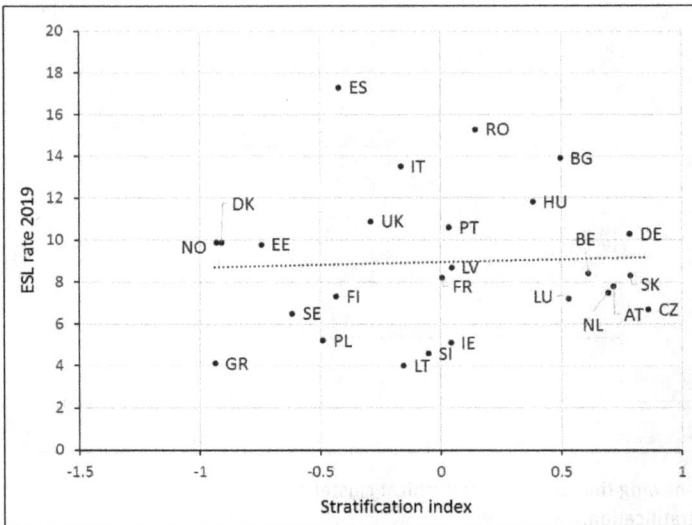

Figure 17.4: Association between ESL rates and the stratification index.

The visual impressions obtained from the figures are confirmed by a multiple regression analysis, the results of which are shown in Table 17.4. The regression model with decommodification as the independent variable accounts for a little over one-quarter of the variance in early school leaving rates; the regression coefficient is significant at the 1% level. However, adding stratification as a second independent variable does not improve the model, reducing the proportion of variance accounted for. The regression coefficient for stratification is not statistically significant.

Table 17.4: Results of regressing ESL rates on the indices of decommocification and stratification.

Variable	Model 1 regression coefficient	Model 2 regression coefficient
Decommodification	−3.455***	−3.556***
Stratification		−0.442
R^2	0.298	0.269
R^2 adjusted	0.303	0.243

17.5 Discussion and conclusion

Three main findings emerge from the analyses in this chapter. Firstly, there is no straightforward correspondence between early school leaving and welfare regimes; variation in ESL rates is often larger within regime types than between them. Nevertheless, certain regularities can be observed, such as the reduction and convergence of ESL rates since 2010, the higher rates in most Mediterranean welfare states than elsewhere, and the marked increases in upper secondary completion between younger and older age groups in the Nordic and some conservative welfare states. Secondly, it is possible to interpret Esping-Andersen's (1990) organising concepts of decommodification and stratification in the context of ESL (or more broadly, upper secondary education) to produce recognisable clusters of "ESL regimes', albeit ones that differ from the general welfare state typologies. Finally, whilst there is a statistically significant association between decommodification and absolute ESL rates, this accounts for only one-quarter of the variance in rates. Stratification appears to have little effect on absolute ESL rates, at least with the relatively small number of observations available here. However, this does not imply that stratification has no impact on early school leaving: other evidence suggests that it may increase *relative* rates according to social background (Lavrijsen and Nicaise 2015).

The diversity of ESL environments emerging from these findings is perhaps less surprising given the significant policy differences both within and between regime types. One of the key features of policy design in this area is the variation between countries and even individual policy initiatives in two dimensions: perception of the problem and approaches to tackling it. The ESL "problem" has been framed along a continuum ranging from a focus on individual deficits to an appreciation of the changing structural, economic and political context within which young people must work and learn. Approaches to solving this problem have variously emphasised empowerment, activation, compensation and prevention (Parreira do Amaral and Zelinka 2019). For young people still in education, this has involved different emphases between generalised approaches affecting all students and more targeted initiatives aimed at preventing dropout amongst specific "at-risk" groups. For example, Sweden has taken a largely generalised approach involving reforms to the organisation and structure of upper secondary education, whilst in Norway a mixture of targeted and generalised approaches has been used (Helgøy et al. 2019). In Italy, Grimaldi and Landri (2019) describe a process of "reculturing" as European policies on ESL have become entangled with opposing elitist and welfarist legacies in the education system. For those who have already left education, particularly the NEET category, active labour market policies have been increasingly prevalent. Although there is some evidence that such policies can have a significant impact in the longer term, particularly for low-skilled individuals, their short-term benefits are often negligble (Card et al. 2018). Impacts also tend to be sensitive to labour-market conditions and the particular target groups involved, increasing the dispersion between countries of their effects on early school leaving.

The clustering of countries described here supports the analyses of other authors, particularly Willemse and De Beer (2012) who found a similar picture of partial correspondence between welfare and educational regimes in the context of higher education. However, the present analysis differs from theirs in including post-socialist countries which are highly diverse in relation to the variables used to construct the indices of decommodification and stratification. The resulting distribution of these states across all but the Nordic cluster may perhaps be understood in terms of different varieties of the "hybridisation" between conservative, liberal and social democratic regimes that has developed in these countries according to their historical and cultural associations. Thus path dependency, in which Bismarckian, status-dependent policies were only partially overwritten during communist rule and re-emerged in the 1990s, has competed to differing degrees with the penetration of market-based economic reforms (Saxonberg and Sirovatka 2019).

There is little robust evidence that ESL rates have converged downwards as a result of the EU policy focus on early school leaving, in spite of around 8 billion Euros of ESF funding allocated to this priority during 2014–2020 (Donlevy et al. 2020). However, it is likely that it has had some effect, and increased attention to the issue, alongside improving economic conditions since 2010, may have helped to retain more young people in education. The question then arises, what will be the future direction of change, and how might further reductions be achieved? Target-driven policy can have the unfortunate side-effect of diverting attention from less acute, but more fundamental problems. The findings of this chapter suggest that reductions in ESL rates alone may be difficult to sustain whilst the population of young people who have not completed upper secondary education remains large, as it does in most Southern European and some post-socialist countries. Retaining young people in education is not enough in itself: they must achieve as well as participate. The chapter also suggests that reforming the structure of education systems, which typically affects stratification, is unlikely to reduce absolute ESL rates, although such reforms may be important for equality of opportunity. Greater decommodification, through increased education spending, improvements in the quality of general education, reductions in poverty, and greater universality in financial assistance to students, offers more prospect of preventing early school leaving. However, such reforms are likely to entail considerable "dead-weight" costs, by involving students who would have stayed in education anyway. They also perhaps fit less well with the dominant individualised emphasis on the perception of the ESL problem.

References

Alexiadou, N., I. Helgøy, and A. Homme. 2019. "Lost in Transition: Policies to Reduce Early School Leaving and Encourage Further Studying in Europe. *Comparative Education* 55 (3), 297–307.

Ansell, B. 2008. "University Challenges: Explaining Institutional Change in Higher Education." *World Politics* 60 (2), 189–230.

Ansell, B., and J. Lindvall. 2013. "The Political Origins of Primary Education Systems: Ideology, Institutions, and Interdenominational Conflict in an Era of Nation-Building." *American Political Science Review* 107 (3), 505–522.

Beblavy, M., A.-E. Thum, and M. Veselkova. 2011. "Education Policy and Welfare Regimes in OECD Countries." *CEPS Working Document No. 357*. Brussels: Centre for European Policy Studies.

Brunello, G., and M. De Paola. 2014. "The Costs of Early School Leaving in Europe." *IZA Journal of Labour Policy* 3 (22), 1–31.

Bukodi, E., F. Eibl, S. Buchholz, S. Marzadro, A. Minello, S. Wahler, H.-P. Blossfeld, R. Erikson, and A. Schizzerotto. 2018. "Linking the Macro to the Micro: A Multidimensional Approach to Educational Inequalities in Four European Countries." *European Societies* 20 (1), 26–64.

Card, D., J. Kluve, and A. Weber. 2018. "What Works? A Meta-Analysis of Recent Active Labor Market Program Evaluations." *Journal of the European Economic Association* 16 (3), 894–931.

Chevalier, A., C. Harmon, V. O'Sullivan, and I. Walker. 2013. "The Impact of Parental Income and Education on the Schooling of their Children." *IZA Journal of Labor Economics* 2 (1), 1–22.

De Witte, K., I. Nicaise, J. Lavrijsen, G. Van Landeghem, C. Lamote, and J. Van Damme. 2013. "The Impact of Institutional Context, Education and Labour Market Policies on Early School Leaving: A Comparative Analysis of EU Countries." *European Journal of Education* 48 (3), 331–345.

Donlevy, V., J. Sennett, M. Georgallis, and A. Ciffolilli. 2020. *Study for the Evaluation of ESF Support to Education and Training (Thematic Objective 10)*. Luxembourg: Publications Office of the European Union.

Duckworth, K., and I. Schoon. 2012. "Beating the Odds: Exploring the Impact of Social Risk on Young People's School-To-Work Transitions During Recession in the UK." *National Institute Economic Review* 222, 38–51.

Esping-Andersen, G. 1990. *The Three Worlds of Welfare Capitalism*. Oxford: Polity Press.

European Commission/EACEA/Eurydice 2018. *The Structure of the European Education Systems 2018/ 19: Schematic Diagrams*. Eurydice Facts and Figures. Luxembourg: Publications Office of the European Union.

Gillies, D., and D. Mifsud. 2016. "Policy in Transition: The Emergence of Tackling Early School Leaving (ESL as EU Policy Priority." *Journal of Education Policy* 31 (6), 819–832.

Green, A. 2013. *Education and State Formation*. 2nd ed. Basingstoke: Palgrave Macmillan.

Grimaldi, E., and P. Landri. 2019. "Tackling Early School Leaving and the Governing of Educational Transitions in Italy." *Comparative Education* 55 (3), 386–403.

González-Rodríguez, D., M.-J. Vieira, and J. Vidal. 2019. "Factors That Influence Early School Leaving: A Comprehensive Model." *Educational Research* 61 (2), 214–230.

Helgøy, I., A. Homme, L. Lundahl, and L. Rönnberg. 2019. "Combating Low Completion Rates in Nordic Welfare States: Policy Design in Norway and Sweden." *Comparative Education* 55 (3), 308–325.

Hvinden, B., C. Hyggen, M.-A. Schoyen, and T. Sirovatka. 2019. *Youth Unemployment and Job Insecurity in Europe*. Cheltenham: Edward Elgar.

Kaye, N., A. D'Angelo, L. Ryan, and M. Lőrinc. 2017. "Early School Leaving: Risk and Protective Factors." *RESL.eu Publications* 4, 1–59.

Lavrijsen, J., and I. Nicaise. 2015. "Social Inequalities in Early School Leaving: The Role of Educational Institutions and the Socioeconomic Context." *European Education* 47 (4), 295–310.

Parreira do Amaral, M., and J. Zelinka. 2019. "Lifelong Learning Policies Shaping the Life Courses of Young Adults. An Interpretative Analysis of Orientations, Objectives and Solutions." *Comparative Education* 55 (3), 404–421.

Powell, M., E. Yörük, and Bardu. 2020. "Thirty Years of *The Three Worlds of Welfare Capitalism*: A Review of Reviews." *Social Policy & Administration* 54 (1), 60–87.

Ralston, K., Z. Feng, D. Everington, and C. Dibben. 2016. "Do Young People Not in Education, Employment or Training Experience Long-Term Occupational Scarring?" *Contemporary Social Science* 11 (2–3), 203–221.

Ross, A., and D. Leathwood. 2013. "Problematising Early School Leaving." *European Journal of Education* 48 (3), 405–418.

Santos, S., C. Nada, E. Macedo, and H. Araújo. 2020. "What Do Young Adults' Educational Experiences Tell Us About Early School Leaving Processes?" *European Educational Research Journal* 19 (5), 463–481.

Saxonberg, S., and T. Sirovatka. 2019. "Central and Eastern Europe." In *Routledge Handbook of the Welfare State*, edited by B. Greve, 300–313. 2nd ed. London: Routledge.

Simmons, R., R. Thompson, and L. Russell. 2014. *Education, Work and Social Change: Young People and Marginalization in Post-Industrial Britain*. Basingstoke: Palgrave Macmillan.

Thompson, R. 2011. "Individualisation and Social Exclusion: The Case of Young People Not in Education, Employment or Training." *Oxford Review of Education* 37 (6), 785–802.

Thompson, R. 2017. "Opportunity Structures and Educational Marginality: The Post-16 Transitions of Young People Outside Education and Employment." *Oxford Review of Education* 43 (6), 749–766.

West, A., and R. Nikolai. 2013. "Welfare Regimes and Education Regimes: Equality of Opportunity and Expenditure in the EU (and US)." *Journal of Social Policy* 42 (3), 469–493.

Wilensky, H. 1975. *The Welfare State and Equality: Structural and Ideological Roots of Public Expenditure*. Berkeley, CA: University of California Press.

Willemse, N., and P. De Beer. 2012. "Three Worlds of Educational Welfare States? A Comparative Study of Higher Education Systems across Welfare States." *Journal of European Social Policy* 22 (2), 105–117.

Appendix

Table A1: Indicators of decommodification.

Code	Expenditure on primary and second-ary educa-tion, (% GDP, 2013–2017)	Pupil-teacher ratio primary and secondary (2013–2017)	Per pupil expenditure in upper second-ary education (000s PPS, 2013–2017)	Students in education at age 18 (% of age group, 2013–2017)	Mean read-ing score age 15, PISA 2015	Child poverty rate 2013–2017 (%)	Financial assistance score for upper secondary	Pupils in private institutions 2013–2017 (%)
AT	3.11	10.0	11.51	73.8	485	18.0	9.50	8.8
BE	4.26	10.8	10.22	88.9	499	18.0	4.00	56.9
BG	2.36	13.8	2.84	81.8	432	29.3	2.63	3.1
CZ	2.48	13.7	5.50	89.5	487	13.3	8.00	6.4
DK	4.36	12.0	9.86	86.3	500	9.6	8.00	14.8
EE	2.66	12.7	4.80	87.7	519	18.6	5.75	4.6
FI	3.95	13.2	6.59	95.1	526	9.9	6.69	9.4
FR	3.52	15.2	9.46	77.7	499	18.4	4.25	21.1
DE	2.66	13.8	9.13	82.8	509	15.0	9.00	8.0
GR	2.63	8.8	4.58	73.3	467	26.3	4.00	5.0
HU	2.49	11.1	5.02	80.4	470	21.2	8.00	19.9
IE	2.96	15.3	8.25	88.8	521	18.1	2.00	0.6
IT	2.75	11.7	6.37	79.6	485	26.0	1.50	6.3
LV	3.10	10.0	5.23	92.3	488	21.6	9.00	2.4
LT	3.53	8.2	3.99	94.6	472	26.1	3.25	2.6
LU	2.76	9.6	14.73	71.1	481	22.4	10.75	15.1
NL	3.42	16.9	8.49	88.2	503	13.9	6.00	3.7
NO	3.67	10.1	13.04	90.0	513	11.7	8.00	5.2
PL	2.98	10.6	4.48	94.3	506	20.6	5.50	8.2
PT	3.65	11.1	6.19	81.0	498	23.6	1.75	14.9
RO	1.64	14.4	2.68	72.5	434	36.3	5.75	1.1
SK	2.58	14.0	4.78	82.6	453	20.1	9.50	9.7
SI	3.17	12.1	5.53	92.8	505	13.7	6.25	2.0
ES	2.72	12.4	6.42	79.9	496	25.1	4.00	29.9
SE	3.90	12.9	9.96	96.3	500	18.5	8.00	13.6
UK	4.00	17.4	6.92	65.3	498	19.7	5.25	48.2

Sources: Col 2, Eurostat [educ_uoe_fine06]; Col 3, Eurostat [educ_uoe_perp04]; Col 4, Eurostat [educ_uoe_fine09]; [edat_lfs_9903]; Col 5, Eurostat [educ_uoe_enra05]; Col 6, Pisa 2015 Table I.4.3; Col 7, [ilc_li02]; Col 8, Eurydice and Table A3; Col 9, Eurostat [educ_uoe_enra01].

Table A2: Indicators of stratification.

Code	Age of first tracking	Number of tracks at age 15	Students in vocational tracks 2013–2017 (%)	Unemployment odds age 20–24 (LS/US) 2013–2017	Students in academically selective schools (%)	Students in schools with ability grouping (%)	Reading performance (top–bottom SES quartile)	Grade repetition 2015 (%)
AT	10	4	69.4	3.39	73.7	10.7	93	15.2
BE	14	4	59.3	2.86	19.6	40.2	109	34.0
BG	11	3	52.2	2.92	81	32.2	102	8.3
CZ	11	5	73.1	4.38	52.3	20.5	105	4.8
DK	16	1	41.5	1.65	5.1	23.4	78	3.4
FI	16	2	70.9	2.23	3.3	31.8	79	3.0
FR	15	3	41.5	2.59	25.7	16.4	107	22.1
DE	10	5	46.8	3.52	40.5	27.6	113	18.1
EE	16	1	36.8	1.43	25.4	33.6	87	4.0
GR	15	2	30.6	1.12	2.8	9.7	84	5.0
HU	10	3	23.8	2.58	87.0	29.4	113	9.5
IE	12	2	35.7	3.51	13.2	92.8	75	7.2
IT	14	4	56.5	1.42	44.2	13.8	75	15.1
LV	13	4	39.1	2.00	25.2	19.1	121	5.0
LT	11	3	27.1	2.74	20.2	42.9	89	2.5
LU	12	4	60.7	1.88	54.9	64.3	72	30.9
NL	12	4	67.6	2.00	66.7	68.4	88	20.1
NO	16	1	50.6	*1.95	4.9	13.1	73	0.0
PL	15	1	50.2	2.01	17.1	33.4	90	5.3
PT	10	3	43.7	1.41	6.8	11.8	95	31.2
RO	15	4	57.2	0.72	80.3	54.2	80	17.4
SK	11	4	68.8	3.86	56.6	35.7	106	6.5
SI	15	3	68.3	3.28	24.5	35	80	1.9
ES	15	2	34.7	1.50	2.7	38.4	*79	31.3
SE	16	1	39.9	3.53	1.9	16	89	4.0
UK	16	1	45.4	2.45	18.2	98.5	80	2.8

Sources: Col 2, Eurydice (2018); Col 3, Pisa 2018 Figure V.3.2; Col 4, Eurostat [educ_uoe_enrs05]; Col 5, Eurostat [lfsa_urgaed]; Col 6, Pisa 2018 Table V.B1.3.4; Col 7, Pisa 2018 Table V.B1.3.7; Col 8, Pisa 2018 Table II.B1.2.5; Col 9, Pisa 2018 Table V.B1.2.9.
Note: Ireland (IE) vocational track percentage is for 2018 only.

Table A3: Coding system for the decommodification score for financial assistance to students and their families.

Eligibility		Duration		Performance criterion (study grants only)	
Not available	0	Ends at 16	0	Dependent on performance	0.75
Fully means tested	1	Ends between 16 and 18	1	Universal	1
Partly means tested	1.5	Ends between 19 and 21	1.5		
Universal	2	Ends between 23 and 25 or above	2		

The forms of support included are: child benefit, tax relief, study grants, and subsidies for travel, meals or equipment. Each of these forms is scored by multiplying the eligibility value by the duration value. In the case of study grants the result is further multiplied by the performance criterion value. The individual scores are then added together, with tax relief weighted by 0.5 because of its restriction to families with taxable income. The result is the decommodification score for financial assistance shown in Table A1. The sources for the eligibility rules are the Eurydice National Education Systems database https://eacea.ec.europa.eu/national-policies/eurydice/national-description_enand the Employment, Social Affairs and Inclusion database of the European Union, https://ec.europa.eu/social/main.jsp?catId=858&langId=en

Bent Greve

18 Economic inequality – a growing issue?

Abstract: The focus of this chapter is the rising inequality that is seen as a key challenge for many welfare states and must be expected to continue in the years to come. A number of different issues can contribute to inequality. The focus here is mainly on more affluent welfare states, and the degree and change in economic inequality is central. How to measure the degree of inequality methodically is shown, while also providing a brief overview of the development of inequality in the European welfare states. The consequences of inequality are examined, including whether they are due to political decisions or changes of, for example, a demographic nature. Lastly, the possible instruments welfare states may have to influence the degree of inequality are discussed.

Keywords: inequality, measurement, economic inequality, role of welfare states, policy instruments, affluent countries

18.1 Introduction

There has been rising economic inequality in many countries over the last 10–15 years, even though inequality and poverty globally have declined. Thus the world overall has become more equal, whereas there has been growing inequality in the US and Europe (Milanovic 2016). This partly reflects the development and economic growth in large countries such as China and India, where many have been lifted out of poverty, thereby affecting overall global inequality (Chuliang, Shi, and Sicular 2018). Rising inequality is seen as a key challenge for many welfare states and must be expected to continue in the coming years. In this chapter, economic inequality will be central, and thus a number of other societal degrees of inequality will not be looked at (for a perspective on this see Greve 2021), for example, related to health (for this see Bambra 2016). There has in recent years been an abundance of books and articles related to inequality, so the literature in this chapter only includes a limited number of examples (however see also Stiglitz 2012; T. Atkinson 2015; Alvaredo et al. 2017, 2018; as well as Greve 2021). The chapter will further not look into whether there is formal equality, equality of opportunity, etc. (see instead Fitzpatrick 2011).

A number of different issues can cause inequality and measuring differing inequalities poses different challenges. In this chapter, since the focus is mainly on more affluent welfare states, the degree and change in economic inequality will be central. How to measure the degree of inequality methodically will be the focus in section 18.2. At the same time, it provides a brief overview of the development of inequality in European welfare states. The focus of section 18.3 discusses what the

https://doi.org/10.1515/9783110721768-018

consequences of inequality are, including whether they are due to political decisions or changes, for example, of a demographic nature. Section 18.4 then looks, albeit briefly, at what possible instruments welfare states may have to influence the degree of inequality. Again, the focus will be on the degree of economic inequality. Finally, section 18.5 summarises the knowledge and conclusions of the chapter.

18.2 Methodological issues and recent trends

There are a number of factors that can have an impact on the degree of inequality, and there is also a wide range of methodological issues related to measuring the degree of inequality. The quality of data can also affect the measurement of inequality, i.e. because they can come from different sources.

There are a number of elements to consider when measuring the degree of inequality in a society. These elements include, at least, the following: inequality of what, between whom, which sources are used and by which measure (Hasell, Morelli, and Roser 2019). By choosing to focus on economic inequality means that a number of other types of inequalities are not included in this analysis (Aaberge and Brandolini 2015; Alkire et al. 2015; Chakravarty and Lugo 2019; and Greve 2021 can direct the reader to a larger number of references to other books and articles.)

The first problem is how inequality should be measured. There are many and very different methods for measuring the level of inequality. Here the two most commonly used methods will be used. This is linked to a discussion on the income of the richest percentage, which, although it does not say anything about overall economic distribution, is an indicator of a special degree of economic inequality, which in recent years has been seen as a clear indicator of how skewed economic distribution is.

The data problem is large because not all countries have registers with solid data available to assess differences in income, and although there may be some data from tax registers, these do not have to be accurate or include all incomes, such as those associated with activities in the hidden economy. It can also reflect the fact that there may be a difference across countries about what income is taxable, and what is not. Reliability of statistics is thus an important issue. In addition, the calculation of income does not necessarily include all capital income (for example, return on owning one's own home) and thus actual wealth may be different. It will have an impact on the level of economic conditions for different groups with apparently similar income distribution, for example between students and pensioners. This also illustrates that there may be a difference in income as a result of individual behaviour over a number of years (for example, the choice between consumption and savings), so figures for a single year do not necessarily reflect a difference in life-time income. Whether a society intervenes and supports those on a low income might also depend on the length of time the person has a low income. Statistically, for example, a newly started self-employed person will often have a low and perhaps even negative income but might in the next few years have a good and solid level of income and consumption possibilities.

In addition, there will be a difference in whether the economic distribution is looked at before and after society's intervention in the distribution, for example as a result of taxes and duties and income transfers.

There is also the problem of whether or not to look at and compare income for individuals or for households. What speaks for the individual is an assessment that the individual must have the opportunity to live his or her life as he or she wishes, but at the same time in many countries there is a difference between participation in the labour market and wages between men and women. Therefore, looking at a household could give a different picture of what the distribution looks like, and although it presupposes an equal distribution in a household, this may not be certain (Daly 2018). When measuring, in order to avoid differences in family size, attempts are made to correct for this by using equivalent income scales. This also reflects that more people living under the same roof is cheaper per person than one person living alone.

The most commonly used measure of inequality is the Gini-coefficient. This was proposed as early as 1912 (Ou-Yang 2019), but has ever since been seen as a sensible measure. It has generally been found to be a useful measure of the degree of inequality in a society, with a value between 0 and 1, and the closer to zero the more even the distribution is. It has been shown that even in income distributions where the average income is different, social welfare will be higher in the distributions closest to the 45 degree line in a Lorenz curve (Shorrocks 1983). Using data over a longer time-spell is especially informative as change from one year to another might be influenced by sudden shocks, such as on the labour market. Thus, often a longer time perspective is needed in order to get a view on what is actually going on and to be able to argue for whether or not there is a change in the degree of inequality.

The criticism of the GINI coefficient has been that there is not sufficient focus on where in the distribution changes are. It is different if you look at the income of the richest 20 % compared to the poorest 20 %. This is called 80/20 measurement, and the higher the number is, the more unequal the economic distribution.

Similarly, in recent years, especially in continuation of Piketty's book (Piketty 2014), there has been an increased focus on the income of the richest 1 %, as this is seen as a clearer trend of how skewed economic distribution is at present. The world inequality database,[1] has a large amount of data on different ways of measuring inequality as well as a number of analyses. The data here does not include the richest 1 % in its distribution as it is a narrower approach to economic inequality.

Table 18.1 shows the overall development of inequality in EU countries since 2010.

---

[1] https://wid.world/, accessed 23 June 2021.

Table 18.1: Gini-coefficient of equivalised disposable income in EU since 2010

	2010	2011	2012	2013	2014	2015	2016	2017	2018	2019
Average	29.7	29.7	29.7	30.0	30.4	30.4	30.2	30.0	29.8	29.8
Standard deviation	3.7	3.5	3.5	3.7	3.7	4.2	3.8	4.0	4.2	4.0
Coefficient of variation	8.1	8.5	8.5	8.1	8.1	7.3	8.0	7.4	7.0	7.4

Source: Eurostat, ild_di12, accessed 24 June 2021
Note: This is EU28 including the UK.

Overall, the development does not on average indicate a growing level of inequality within the EU since 2010, but does conceal different types of development within countries. This can be witnessed by the fact that the coefficient of variation has gone down implying that the differences among the countries have been reduced, and in order for that to happen there will have to have been either higher reductions or increased levels in some of the countries.

The variation in the development across the different EU countries since 2010 is shown in Table 18.2.

Table 18.2: Change in GINI-coefficient from 2010 to 2019 in EU-countries

	Change 2010–2019
Slovakia	−3.1
Poland	−2.6
Croatia	−2.4
Ireland	−2.4
Greece	−1.9
Portugal	−1.8
Lithuania	−1.6
Belgium	−1.5
Czechia	−0.9
Estonia	−0.8
Austria	−0.8
Latvia	−0.7
France	−0.6
Malta	−0.6

Table 18.2 (continued)

	Change 2010–2019
Spain	−0.5
Slovenia	0.1
Germany	0.4
Denmark	0.6
United Kingdom	0.6
Finland	0.8
Cyprus	1
Italy	1.1
Romania	1.3
Netherlands	1.3
Sweden	2.1
Hungary	3.9
Luxembourg	4.4
Bulgaria	7.6

Source: see Table 18.1
Note: A minus implies increased degree of equality.

It is thus a very diverse picture with a very strong increase in inequality in Bulgaria, Hungary and Luxembourg, and with a decline in Slovakia, Croatia and Poland. It is also notable that all three Nordic countries have an increase in the degree of inequality implying that different welfare states have fewer variations than they used to have.

The picture is the same when presenting the 80/20 ratio and its development as shown in Figure 18.1.

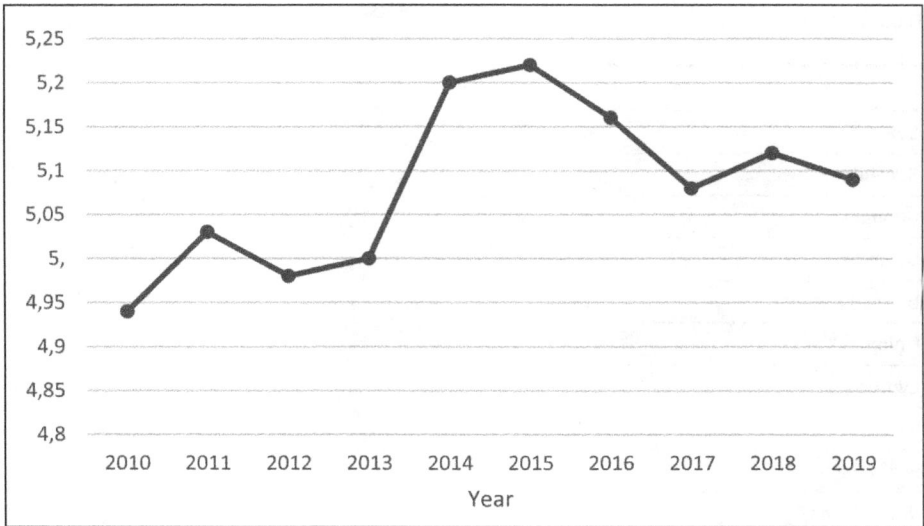

Figure 18.1: Income quintile share ratio (S80/S20) (2010–2019) for EU28.
Source: EUROSTAT data, TESSI180, accessed 2 October 2021.

The level of the 80/20 is highest in Bulgaria and lowest in Slovakia. The development to a large degree follows the development in the level of inequality measured by the GINI-coefficient as presented above.

Naturally, the changes do not inform us about why there has been these changes, for example whether it is due to political decisions changing different types of instruments (see below section 18.4), or to the population ageing and other demographic changes. This change in inequality might be related to a change in age structure, labour market participation and types of cohabitation (such as rich with rich, poor with poor) (Aaberge et al. 2018; Søgaard 2018; Pareliussen and Robling 2018; see also Förster and Tóth 2015 for a more elaborate discussion on the impact of demographic changes). Or, as also argued by Cohen and Ladaique (2018, 39), "Demographic and societal change – more single and single-parent households, more people with a partner in the same earnings group – also played a role for increasing inequality, but much less than sometimes assumed." This will not be included in the analysis below which focuses on the more classical ways of looking into consequences and reasons for inequality.

18.3 Consequences of inequality

It may be difficult to demonstrate a direct causation between the levels of economic inequality, but on the other hand there seem to be clear connections between the degree of inequality and social cohesion. As pointed out, now a number of years ago, economic inequality is important for and has consequences on, for example, crime, children's upbringing, obesity, health, etc. (Wilkinson and Pickett 2009; 2018), because high levels of economic inequality are often connected to high levels of poverty (see Chapter 19 as well as a number of chapters in Greve 2020b).

A high degree of inequality can also have negative consequences for the economic growth of a country (Cingano 2014; Berg and Ostry 2011), including creating a smaller degree of development in human capital. The OECD has thus (albeit for the time between 1990 and 2010) estimated that for OECD-countries the increase in inequality has reduced accumulated growth by 4.7 %, and impacted on human-capital (OECD 2015). In addition, because a higher degree of inequality also has an impact on confidence, it can make economic activity more expensive than it would otherwise be. This is despite the fact that there does not seem to be a clear connection between the level of inequality and GDP per capita. This is witnessed by the fact that in most Eastern European countries there is a lower degree of inequality than in the Nordic countries, even though the Nordic welfare states are generally richer than the countries of Eastern Europe. Similarly, the higher degree of economic inequality in liberal welfare states cannot be explained by a lower level of GDP, but must to a greater extent be assumed to be rooted in differences in ideological perceptions and understanding of what is an acceptable level of inequality and what creates different degrees of inequality.

At the same time there is no indication that economic growth in itself will reduce inequality. If countries get richer this is not in itself a guarantee that societies will become more equal. There will still be a need for using the possible instruments available in order to reduce the level of inequality, not only in order to reduce yearly inequalities, but also over the life cycle given we are in different positions at different times of the life cycle. This indicates that the welfare state is also a piggy-bank, for example the welfare state helps with the distribution of resources of the life-cycle (Barr 2001). Thus, the next section discusses what instruments the welfare states has at its disposal.

18.4 Welfare states instruments

Welfare states have several options to use to cope with inequality if they so wish. To know what to do we need to know what the possible reasons and arguments for a change in the level of inequality are. The following is a summary of possible explanations of causes for change in inequality and not indicating direction of change:
1. "Structural macroeconomic sectoral changes
2. Globalisation and technology change
3. Labour market and other relevant institutions
4. Politics and political processes
5. Tax/transfer schemes
6. Demographic and other microstructural changes" (Förster and Tóth 2015, 1799).

Here the focus will mainly be on issues 2, 3 and 5 as they are the ones where states possibly have the strongest role in order to influence the level of inequality. The role of the welfare states will be touched upon as they are important in the redistribution of wealth from rich to poor not only over the life-course, but also each year.

Looking into points 2 and 3 the issue is whether states might have an opportunity to contribute to the fact that most people of working age have the opportunity to get and keep a job even in volatile labour markets. This is also true because there are significant and constant changes on the way new technology impacts on labour markets (see Chapter 20), and also as a result of growing international global competition (Ravallion 2018; Bourguignon 2017). The risk is that more people end up in very precarious jobs (Kreshpaj et al. 2020), with low wages and periods of unemployment. It increases economic inequality while creating a greater social division in societies and is thus an indicator of less social cohesion.

Income transfers play a role, point 5, in which welfare states reduce the degree of economic inequality as a consequence of market forces, and is also the reason for and a tool used to indicate the role of the state by showing the GINI-coefficient before and after transfers. Access to services also has a role to play but is often not included in the analysis due to data issues. In addition, an individual's access to services cannot easily be changed to other types of consumption, and services may only be available when a certain condition occurs, such as being sick. Naturally, whether, for example, health care is free of charge or with limited user charges has an impact on the risk of living in poverty. This is not to neglect the importance of the structure and delivery of welfare services on the living standard of individuals, it is more to reflect upon that for example including a change in income transfers can influence the degree of inequality in both an upward and downward direction.

The classical way to reduce economic inequality is to choose a taxation structure, cf. point 5, so that there is progressive income and capital taxation, as overall this would point towards the fact that those with a higher income pay more in tax both absolutely and relatively. It is further the case that progressive taxation not only influences after tax inequality, but also pre-tax inequality by reducing the incentives for high-income earners to demand higher wages (Alvaredo et al. 2018). The authors also argue in favour of progressive taxation on wealth and inheritances. Higher levels of duties on goods mainly used by high income earners can also influence the degree of inequality, implying a need to be aware that not all kinds of duties will reduce inequality, but in fact some have a risk of increasing it given the higher relative burden on low-income earners. Reducing tax evasion as well as tax-avoidance and broadening the tax base are additional options including reducing the options of using tax havens (Zucman 2015), as this implies a higher tax-revenue making it possible either to increase transfers or decrease other taxes and duties.

To illustrate the points made above, a number of empirical studies showing the impact of using tax/duties and transfers will be presented. It has been estimated that after the financial crisis (in the years 2012–2013) the combined effect of taxes and transfers was a reduction in economic inequality, measured by the Gini-coefficient of 31%, with two-thirds from transfers and one-third from taxes (Caminada et al. 2019a). Another study also indicated that since the financial crisis there has been an increase in fiscal redistribution (Caminada et al. 2019b).

To indicate the magnitude, Figure 18.2 shows the different levels of inequality as measured by the GINI-coefficient for European countries as well as OECD average and the US.

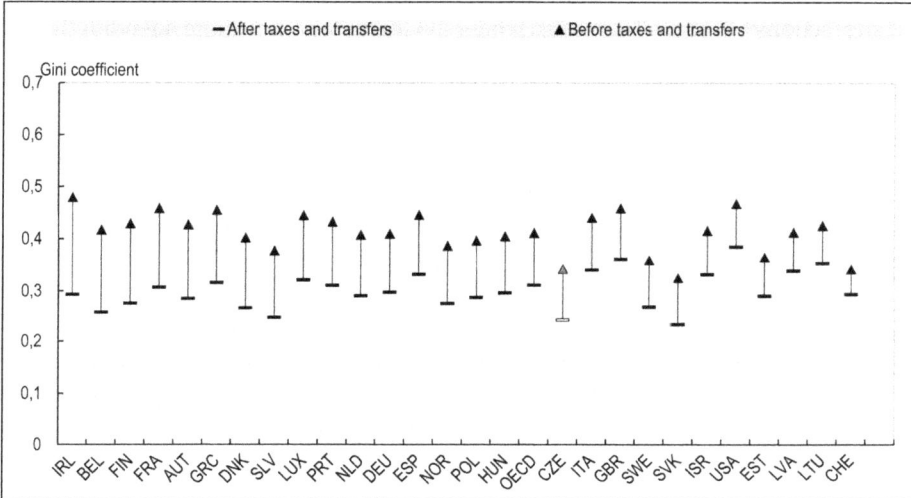

Figure 18.2: Differences in household income inequality pre and post-tax and government transfers, 2018.
Source: OECD, *Government at a Glance 2021*, figure 13.7, accessed 9 July 2021
Note: Countries are ranked from those with largest to lowest impact on the GINI-coefficient.

As can be witnessed from Figure 18.2, in all countries taxes and transfers have a strong role to play in the degree of inequality without a clear pattern across welfare regimes.

Naturally, this might change over the years. An analysis indicates that the Scandinavian countries have been more able to reduce inequality, for example, after the financial crisis (Amate-Fortes, Guarnido-Rueda, and Molina-Morales 2017), thereby also showing that policy matters, albeit as indicated by Table 18.2 there has been an increase in the level of inequality in the Nordic welfare states over a longer time perspective. The role of transfers and taxes does not need to be uniform across welfare states, as, for example, changes in Eastern Europe from 2007 to 2014 given the tendency to have flatter income taxes in some countries, whereas in Western Europe the combined change in tax-benefit systems increased equality (Bussolo et al. 2019). This study showed development from 2007 to 2014, and, data in Table 18.2 show a pattern of differences among countries in both Eastern and Western Europe since then. Another study, using data from 1995 to 2010, showed that there, at least historically, has been a stronger impact on redistribution in Northern and Western Europe, thus implying an impact of variation in redistribution across welfare state regimes (Kyriacou, Muinelo-Gallo, and Roca-Sagalés 2017). However, it has also been argued that welfare states have done too little in relation to the consequences of increasing globalisation and thereby the increase in inequality (Fadda and Tridico 2018), or even that several welfare states have been eroded due to a variety of austerity policies (Konzelmann et al. 2018). It is albeit very difficult to find support for this in macro data on welfare states spending (Greve 2020a), however naturally there might be an impact on different subsections of the welfare states where the legitimacy of welfare spending is less strong.

18.5 Concluding remarks

The chapter argues that the GINI-coefficient is a useful instrument to measure and understand the development in economic inequality.

Using the GINI as a benchmark, on average there has been a standstill in the degree of inequality in EU countries. This masks strong variations among countries with some having an increase in the degree of inequality while others have reduced their level. This has implied that the variation across countries has been reduced indicating a convergence, albeit limited, in the degree of inequality within EU member states since 2019.

Overall, there is negative consequence for societies, development of increase in inequality being a reason for the need to be aware of how to cope with this.

The data on the changes in levels of inequality do not inform on the causes of these changes, but indicate that if there is willingness to do something about inequality this is possible, and, the chapter has also indicted a number of available instruments that can be used to do so.

References

Aaberge, R., C. André, A. Boschini, L. Calmfors, K. Gunnarsson, M. Hermansen, A. Langørgen, P. Lindgren, C. Orsetta, and J. Pareliussen. 2018. *Increasing Income Inequality in the Nordics. Nordic Economic Policy Review 2018.* TemaNord 2018:519. Copenhagen: Nordic Economic Council. https://doi.org/10.6027/TN2018-519.

Aaberge, Rolf, and Andrea Brandolini. 2015. "Multidimensional Poverty and Inequality." In *Handbook of Income Distribution*, edited by A. B. Atkinson and F. Bourguignon, vol. 2A, 141–216. Amsterdam: Elsevier.

Alkire, Sabina, José Manuel Roche, Paola Ballon, James Foster, Maria Emma Santos, and Suman Seth. 2015. *Multidimensional Poverty Measurement and Analysis.* New York: Oxford University Press.

Alvaredo, Facundo, Lucas Chancel, Thomas Piketty, Emmanuel Saez, and Gabriel Zucman. 2017. "Global Inequality Dynamics: New Findings from WID. World." *American Economic Review* 107 (5), 404–409.

Alvaredo, Facundo, Lucas Chancel, Thomas Piketty, Emmanuel Saez, and Gabriel Zucman. 2018. *World Inequality Report 2018*. Cambridge, MA: Belknap Press.

Amate-Fortes, Ignacio, Almudena Guarnido-Rueda, and Agustin Molina-Morales. 2017. "Crisis and Inequality in the European Union." *European Review* 25 (3), 438–452.

Atkinson, Tony. 2015. "What Can Be Done about Inequality?" *Juncture*. https://doi.org/10.1111/j.2050-5876.2015.00834.x.

Bambra, C. 2016. *Health Divides – Where You Live Can Kill You*. Bristol: Policy Press.

Barr, N. 2001. *The Welfare State as a Piggy Bank. Information, Risk, Uncertainty, and the Role of the State*. Oxford: Oxford University Press.

Berg, Andrew G., and Jonathan D. Ostry. 2011. *Inequality and Unsustainable Growth: Two Sides of the Same Coin?* IMF Staff Discussion Note 11/08. Washington, D. C.: International Monetary Fund.

Bourguignon, François. 2017. *The Globalization of Inequality*. Princeton, NJ: Princeton University Press.

Bussolo, Maurizio, Carla Krolage, Mattia Makovec, Andreas Peichl, Marc Stockli, Ivan Torre, and Christian Wittneben. 2019. "Vertical and Horizontal Redistribution: The Cases of Western and Eastern Europe." EM 1/19. EUROMOD Working Paper Series. Colchester: Institute for Social and Economic Research.

Caminada, Koen, Kees Goudswaard, Chen Wang, and Jinxian Wang. 2019a. "Income Inequality and Fiscal Redistribution in 31 Countries After the Crisis." *Comparative Economic Studies* 61 (1), 119–148.

Caminada, Koen, Kees Goudswaard, Chen Wang, and Jinxian Wang. 2019b. "Has the Redistributive Effect of Social Transfers and Taxes Changed over Time across Countries?" *International Social Security Review* 72 (1), 3–31.

Chakravarty, Satya R., and Maria Ana Lugo. 2019. "Multidimensional Indicators of Inequality and Poverty." In *Poverty, Social Exclusion and Stochastic Dominance*, edited by Satya R. Chakravarty, 223–259. Singapore: Springer.

Chuliang, Luo, Li Shi, and Terry Sicular. 2018. "The Long-Term Evolution of Income Inequality and Poverty in China." WIDER Working Paper 2018/153. Helsinki: UNU-WIDER.

Cingano, Federico. 2014. "Trends in Income Inequality and Its Impact on Economic Growth." *OECD Social, Employment and Migration Working Papers*, No. 163, OECD Publishing. https://doi.org/10.1787/5jxrjncwxv6j-en.

Cohen, Guillaume, and Maxime Ladaique. 2018. "Drivers of Growing Income Inequalities in OECD and European Countries." In *Reducing Inequalities: A Challenge for the European Union?*, edited by Renato Miguel Carmo, Cédric Rio, and Márton Medgyesi, 31–43. Cham: Springer International Publishing.

Daly, Mary. 2018. "Towards a Theorization of the Relationship between Poverty and Family." *Social Policy & Administration* 52 (3): 565–77.

Fadda, Sebastiano, and Pasquale Tridico. 2018. *Inequality and Uneven Development in the Post-Crisis World*. London and New York: Routledge.

Fitzpatrick, Tony. 2011. *Welfare Theory: An Introduction to the Theoretical Debates in Social Policy*. Basingstoke: Macmillan International Higher Education.

Förster, Michael F., and István György Tóth. 2015. "Cross-Country Evidence of the Multiple Causes of Inequality Changes in the OECD Area." In *Handbook of Income Distribution*, edited by Anthony B. Atkinson and François B. T. Bourguignon, 2, 1729–1843. Amsterdam: Elsevier.

Greve, B. 2020a. *Austerity, Retrenchment and the Welfare State. Truth of Fiction?* Cheltenham: Edward Elgar.

Greve, B. 2020b. *Routledge International Handbook of Poverty*. Routledge International Handbook of Poverty. London and New York: Routledge.

Greve, B. 2021. *Multidimensional Inequalities. International Perspectives Across Welfare States*. Berlin: De Gruyter.

Hasell, Joe, Salvatore Morelli, and Max Roser. 2019. "Recent Trends in Income Inequality." In *Reducing Social Inequalities in Cancer: Evidence and Priorities for Research*, edited by S. Vaccarella, J. Lortet-Tieulent, R. Saracci, D. I. Conway, K. Straif, and C. P. Wild. 205–227. Lyon: International Agency for Research on Cancer.

Konzelmann, Suzanne J., Simon Deakin, Marc Fovargue-Davies, and Frank Wilkinson. 2018. *Labour, Finance and Inequality: The Insecurity Cycle in British Public Policy*. London and New York: Routledge.

Kreshpaj, Bertina, Cecilia Orellana, Bo Burström, Letitia Davis, Tomas Hemmingsson, Gun Johansson, Katarina Kjellberg, Johanna Jonsson, David H. Wegman, and Theo Bodin. 2020. "What is Precarious Employment? A Systematic Review of Definitions and Operationalizations from Quantitative and Qualitative Studies." *Scandinavian Journal of Work, Environment & Health* 46 (3), 235–247.

Kyriacou, Andreas P., Leonel Muinelo-Gallo, and Oriol Roca-Sagalés. 2017. "Redistributive Efficiency in 28 Developed Economies." *Journal of European Social Policy* 28 (4), 370–385.

Milanovic, Branko. 2016. *Global Inequality: A New Approach for the Age of Globalization*. Cambridge, MA: Harvard University Press.

OECD. 2015. *In It Together: Why Less Inequality Benefits All*. Paris: OECD Publishing.

Ou-Yang, Kui. 2019. "Lexical Measures of Social Inequality: From Pigou-Dalton to Hammond." *Review of Income and Wealth* 65 (3), 657–674.

Pareliussen, Jon, and Per Olof Robling. 2018. "Demographic Change and Inequality Trends in the Nordic Countries." In *Nordic Economic Policy Review 2018*, edited by R. Aaberge et al., 136–166. Copenhagen: Nordic Economic Council.

Piketty, Thomas. 2014. *Capital in the Twenty-First Century*. London: Harvard University Press.

Ravallion, Martin. 2018. "Inequality and Globalization: A Review Essay." *Journal of Economic Literature* 56 (2), 620–642.

Shorrocks, Anthony F. 1983. "Ranking Income Distributions." *Economica* 50 (197), 3–17.

Søgaard, Jakob Egholt. 2018. "Top Incomes in Scandinavia–Recent Developments and the Role of Capital Income." In *Nordic Economic Policy Review 2018*, edited by R. Aaberge et al., 66–94. Copenhagen: Nordic Economic Council.

Stiglitz, Joseph E. 2012. *The Price of Inequality: How Today's Divided Society Endangers Our Future*. New York: WW Norton & Company.

Wilkinson, R., and K. Pickett. 2009. *The Spirit Level – Why Equality Is Better for Everyone*. London: Allen Lane.

Wilkinson, R., and K. Pickett. 2018. *The Inner Level. How More Equal Societies Reduce Stress, Restore Sanity and Improve Everyone's Well-Being*. S. Ives: Allen Lane.

Zucman, Gabriel. 2015. *The Hidden Wealth of Nations: The Scourge of Tax Havens*. Chicago: University of Chicago Press.

M. Azhar Hussain

19 Poverty in the five welfare regimes of Europe

Abstract: Relative poverty within Europe is explored, making a distinction between five types of welfare regimes: Nordic, Central European, Liberal, Southern-European and Post-Socialist. A household is defined as poor if its equivalised disposable income is below 60 % of the national contemporary median income. The level of poverty is stable over time, which justifies looking at all three investigated years (2009, 2014 and 2019) together. Seven events (poverty determinants/risk factors) are analysed, including demographic and labour market factors. There are remarkable poverty risk differences between population sub-groups delimited by the seven determinants. Generally, in the Nordic and the Southern-European welfare states risk factors are less detrimental compared to particularly the Liberal welfare states. The largest excess poverty risk for female led households compared to male led is found in the Southern-European regime (5 % points). Similarly, the largest excess risks for respectively singles, low education families, students, the unemployed, permanently disabled, and pensioners, are respectively in the Southern-European (8 % points), Post-Socialist (16 % points), Nordic (11 % points), Liberal (26 % points), Continental (19 % points) and Liberal welfare (3 % points) regime. Identifying different avenues to reduce poverty, counter-factual simulations show which regimes have the largest potential of poverty reduction by closing the seven investigated poverty gaps. The poverty reduction potential is smallest in the Nordic welfare regime (6 % points) and largest in the Liberal regime (12 % points), reflecting the fact that the Nordic regime already has low inequality.

Keywords: European welfare regimes, EU-SILC microdata, income poverty, risk factors, demographics, education, labour market, linear probability model, counter-factual simulations

19.1 Introduction

Poverty in an absolute sense has practically been eliminated in European countries given the high income levels. Thus, the vast majority can afford basic necessities of life in terms of nutrition, clothing and shelter (as well as heath and education). In affluent European societies the focus is thus more on issues beyond basic necessities and more related to living standards compared to the norm of a country. This calls for a focus on relative poverty, and unless otherwise mentioned, the applied poverty concept here is the relative poverty concept to be operationalised below. This is not to say that absolute poverty is eradicated or that it is no more an issue. Poverty has many determi-

https://doi.org/10.1515/9783110721768-019

nants including individual level characteristics and factors at the macro level, and some of the main ones comprise educational level (productivity), household composition, health, labour market success, macroeconomic conditions as well as structural changes taking place in the economy. Government policy in terms of taxation and social benefits (as well as public services) are also expected to affect poverty via its effect on income distribution. Thus, the goal of this chapter is to quantify how the choice of welfare regime by a country's population affects the risk of poverty in European nations during 2009–2019 based on microdata from the EU-SILC database. Five regimes are in focus: Nordic, Central European, Liberal, Southern-European, and Post-Socialist. The next section briefly reviews the literature on the concept of poverty and poverty in welfare regimes in Europe. Section 19.3 presents evidence on poverty in welfare regimes for sub-populations whose characteristics are particularly associated with economic (and social) hardship. Section 19.4 highlights poverty risks associated with different lifecycle, social and other events and individual characteristics, taking different controls into account, and also discusses possible remedies. The final section concludes.

19.2 Literature review

Poverty is defined as either being absolute or being relative (Foster 1998; Greve 2021), while for some purposes subjective poverty would be a relevant concept as well. Absolute poverty means that a person is not able to afford the very basic goods in life. This includes, water, food, and non-food items, including clothing and housing (Arndt et al. 2016a; Arndt, Mahrt, and Tarp 2016b; Hussain 2021). The absolute poverty line is thus defined as the income necessary to buy these items, and depends on the composition of the household (gender, age and physical activity), e.g., the calories required, which for simplicity are assumed to depend on age. Absolute poverty lines are primarily used in developing countries, but in some adjusted form also exist in developed nations, including for instance in the United States (Census Bureau 2021). The UN has a broader definition of poverty (UN 1996).

Poverty in developed nations is usually measured by applying a relative approach (Saltkjel and Malmberg-Heimonen 2021), e.g. meaning the relative poverty line shifts according to the income level of the country rather than simply with inflation. The relative poverty approach is also applied here since we are only looking at European nations which are generally considered to have eliminated absolute poverty to a large extent. In the relative approach, we need disposable household income, an equivalence scale, and the median equivalised disposable income of the country. Disposable income is the sum of all market and non-market incomes minus all income taxes and mandatory contributions. This is measured at the household level. Economies of scale and differential consumption requirements depending on age, means that instead of using per capital household disposable income we divide household income by adult equivalents defined as (OECD modified scale): Equivalence Scale = 1 + (#Adults aged 14+ years) × 0.5 + (#Children aged 0–13 years) × 0.3. Other equivalence scales also exist (Hagenaars, de Vos, and Zaidi 1994), but here the Eurostat/OECD standard is followed. Once the household disposable income is divided by the household equivalence scale the result will be the equivalised disposable income of each household member. Next using individual equivalised incomes, the median income of the country can be calculated. The poverty line is then taken to be a percentage of this median. In Eurostat and here, 60 % of median income is used, while for instance OECD uses half median income. The American poverty line is around 40 % of the national median. As is standard in international comparisons, the whole population is included in the poverty calculations, which then also means that students are included. Students are characterised by high poverty rates, but this is often a transitory phenomenon since they are expected to have high earnings after graduation. Including or excluding students can thus have significant effects on poverty rates.

There will not be a deeper discussion of welfare state regime theory since that is covered in Chapters 4–8 investigating respectively the Nordic, Continental, Liberal, Southern-Europe, and Post-Socialist welfare states. So here, broadly the Esping-Andersen (1990) welfare state typology is followed, but of course with later extensions (Greve 2018; Kangas, Palme, and Kainu 2020; chapters 4–8) since the fall of the Berlin Wall saw former socialist countries beginning to become welfare states in a more western sense.

To the author's knowledge, only one study (Whelan and Maître 2010) systematically pursues a welfare regime approach to prosperity in Europe. They have a social class approach to poverty, social exclusion and multidimensional deprivation. They find that levels of economic vulnerability vary across welfare regimes in line with the comprehensiveness and generosity of the regimes, e.g. vulnerability increase comparing the social democratic to the corporatist to the liberal to the southern European and finally Post-Socialist regimes. The study looks at 26 countries using one of the earliest waves of the EU-SILC dataset, while in this chapter we have much more recent data and furthermore include 31 countries in the analyses. Vandecasteele (2010) looks at four countries representing different European welfare state models, and finds that the poverty trajectories after partnership dissolution are different across countries, such that Denmark shows the smallest long-term poverty risk, while Germany and the United Kingdom have the largest long-term poverty group. For the United Kingdom the residual welfare state is used as an explanation and for Germany it is identified as mainly a female problem (lone mothers). Regarding poverty trajectories after leaving the parental home, it is found that the poverty risk is negligible in Spain, while young Danes are particularly vulnerable to experiencing a short-term poverty risk after leaving home. The study has a focus on poverty duration applying panel-data from older survey data (ECHP) and excludes eastern European welfare states and it is not at the welfare regime level, while the focus in this chapter is on more recent data and including almost all welfare states in Europe applying a regime approach.

19.3 Poverty levels

19.3.1 Welfare state typology and variable definitions

Based on the literature review above, the 31 European nations included in this study are classified into the five welfare regimes as shown in Table 19.1. Some of the classifications are debatable, for instance regarding the Post-Socialist cluster, which could possibly be subdivided.

Table 19.1: Welfare regime typology

Welfare regime	list countries alphabetically
Nordic	Denmark, Finland, Iceland, Norway, Sweden
Continental	Austria, Belgium, Switzerland, Germany, France, Luxembourg, Netherlands
Liberal	Ireland, United Kingdom
Southern-European	Cyprus, Greece, Spain, Italy, Portugal
Post-Socialist	Bulgaria, Czechia, Estonia, Croatia, Hungary, Lithuania, Latvia, Poland, Romania, Serbia, Slovenia, Slovakia

The specific definition of the dependent variable poverty, and the seven dependent "event" variables as well as age and weights to get representativeness are presented in Table 19.2. Social assistance "event" would also be relevant as a separate risk but is not handled here due to unavailability of relevant data.

Table 19.2: Variable definitions regarding the dependent variable (poor), independent variables, and population weights.

Arena	Variable	Variable is 1 if below fulfilled, otherwise it is 0
Poverty	Poor	Equivalised disposable HH income is below 60 % of contemporaneous national equivalised income. Income is usually from the previous year
Male/female HH composition	Only males	Only males among 16+ years in the HH
	Only females	Only females among 16+ years old in the HH
	Males and females	Both males and females among 16+ years old in the HH
Parental HH composition	Single parent	Household size is at least 2 and at least one person is 0–17 years and one person is unmarried ("Marital status")

Table 19.2 (continued)

Arena	Variable	Variable is 1 if below fulfilled, otherwise it is 0
Educational attainment	Low education	At least one person in the household has pre-primary, primary or lower secondary education ("Highest ISCED level attained")
Educational status	Student	At least one person in the HH is either pupil, student, in further training, or gaining unpaid work experience ("Self-defined current economic status")
Labour market status	Unemployed	At least one person is unemployed ("Self-defined current economic status")
Health status	Permanently disabled	At least one person is permanently disabled or/and unfit to work ("Self-defined current economic status")
Retirement status	Pensioner	At least one person is in retirement or in early retirement or has given up business ("Self-defined current economic status")
Age	Age	Average age of all 16+ old persons in the HH
	Age squared / 100	See age
Representativeness	Weight	Household weight multiplied by the household size ("Household cross-sectional weight"). These are population weights.

Source: Own construction based on the EU-SILC database and the data documentation in EC (2019).

19.3.2 Sample size

The analyses in this and the next section are carried out using the EU-SILC database covering 2009, 2014, and 2019. A total of 1,873,020 respondents from 31 countries are included. The database does contain 32 countries, but Malta is excluded here since own calculations of the poverty rates for Malta far from matched the Eurostat published figures for 2019. The exclusion should not affect the results much since Malta has a small population compared to the size of its welfare regime. Data did not exist for four countries in specific years and those years were therefore represented by a nearby year. For Croatia 2009 is represented by 2010, for Iceland and UK 2019 is represented by 2018, and for Serbia 2009 is represented by 2013. Again, this is perhaps not a big problem for the analyses because structural phenomena such as poverty rates and its determinants are likely to be rather stable from one year to the next (see also the discussion below about temporal development in poverty in all the included countries).

From Table 19.3 it is seen that the average sample size is 20,140 respondents, with a minimum of 8,545 (Iceland 2009) and a maximum of 51,196 (Italy 2009). The very high sample sizes are an advantage in terms of the hypotheses testing happening later. Data cleaning details are presented in Table A1 in the Appendix.

Table 19.3: Sample sizes and poverty rates 2009–2019

	Sample size				Poverty rate %			
	2009	**2014**	**2019**	**Total**	**2009**	**2014**	**2019**	**Total**
DK	15,025	14,075	12,038	41,138	13.1	12.1	12.5	12.6
FI	25,157	27,142	23,164	75,463	13.9	12.8	11.6	12.8
IS	8,545	8,841	8,652	26,038	10.1	7.9	8.8	8.9
NO	13,855	18,419	14,715	46,989	11.8	10.9	12.7	11.8
SE	18,441	14,026	13,461	45,928	14.6	15.6	17.1	15.8
Nordic	**81,023**	**82,503**	**72,030**	**235,556**	**14.3**	**14.8**	**14.4**	**14.5**
AT	13,604	12,982	12,357	38,943	14.5	14.0	13.3	13.9
BE	14,721	14,346	15,516	44,583	14.6	15.5	14.8	15.0
CH	17,561	15,651	16,662	49,874	15.6	13.8	16.0	15.1
DE	28,368	26,499	23,925	78,792	15.9	16.7	15.1	15.9
FR	25,611	26,787	26,484	78,882	12.9	13.3	13.6	13.3
LU	11,406	9,982	10,520	31,908	14.9	16.4	17.5	16.3
NL	23,687	24,494	29,899	78,080	11.2	11.6	13.2	12.0
Continental	**134,958**	**130,741**	**135,363**	**401,062**	**17.4**	**16.8**	**18.2**	**17.5**
EI	12,641	14,228	10,809	37,678	15.1	17.0	13.4	15.2
UK	19,380	22,474	38,705	80,559	17.6	16.8	18.6	17.7
Liberal	**32,021**	**36,702**	**49,514**	**118,237**	**19.2**	**20.6**	**19.8**	**19.9**
CY	9,283	12,027	10,974	32,284	15.9	14.4	14.7	15.0
EL	18,035	20,995	39,803	78,833	20.1	22.1	17.9	20.0
ES	36,865	31,622	39,852	108,339	20.2	22.2	20.7	21.0
IT	51,196	47,136	43,400	141,732	18.4	19.4	20.1	19.3
PT	13,013	17,221	33,081	63,315	18.2	19.5	17.2	18.3
Southern-European	**128,392**	**129,001**	**167,110**	**424,503**	**17.7**	**18.5**	**17.3**	**17.8**
BG	15,047	12,184	17,012	44,243	21.9	21.8	22.6	22.1

Table 19.3 (continued)

	Sample size				Poverty rate %			
	2009	2014	2019	Total	2009	2014	2019	Total
CZ	23,302	18,210	19,150	60,662	8.6	9.7	10.1	9.5
EE	13,542	15,051	15,126	43,719	19.7	21.8	21.7	21.1
HR	9,863	14,039	19,569	43,471	20.6	19.4	18.3	19.4
HU	25,053	22,708	15,141	62,902	12.4	15.0	12.3	13.2
LT	12,852	11,898	11,360	36,110	20.3	19.1	20.6	20.0
LV	14,403	14,054	11,394	39,851	26.4	21.2	22.9	23.5
PL	38,541	36,127	50,788	125,456	17.1	17.0	15.4	16.5
RO	18,703	17,393	16,791	52,887	22.5	25.1	23.8	23.8
RS	20,069	19,094	16,170	55,333	24.5	25.0	23.2	24.2
SI	29,576	27,697	25,253	82,526	11.4	14.5	11.9	12.6
SK	16,137	15,711	14,654	46,502	11.0	12.6	11.9	11.8
Post-Socialist	237,088	224,166	232,408	693,662	13.3	14.0	0.0	9.1
Total	613,482	603,113	656,425	1,873,020	16.3	16.6	16.2	16.4

Source: Own calculations based on the EU-SILC database.
Notes: The totals for poverty rates are unweighted averages.

19.3.3 Poverty rates for whole populations

As mentioned in the previous section, the poverty rates are estimated using equivalised household disposable income and the 60 % of national median equivalised income (poverty line) in a given year. This resulted in the poverty rates (officially denoted "at risk of poverty" by Eurostat) in Table 19.3. These poverty rates very closely resemble the published Eurostat poverty rates. Thus, the average discrepancy is only 0.03 % points, and the biggest underestimation is −0.2 % points (Spain 2009) and the biggest overestimation is 0.4 % points (Germany, Greece and Romania in 2009), which might be due to different versions of the EU-SILC databases used. Out of 93 (31 countries in 3 years each) poverty rates, there is 0 % points discrepancy in 73 cases, in another 10 cases the discrepancy is only 0.1 % points.

Poverty rates across welfare regimes to some extent follows the expected pattern with the most generous welfare regime, the Nordic model, having the lowest poverty rate at 13.6 %, followed by the Continental welfare regime at 14.5 %, while the Liberal regime have a poverty risk of 17.5 % and the Southern-Europe regime has 19.9 %. The Post-Socialist welfare regime could perhaps be expected to have the highest poverty rate since income levels are lower, but is actually down at 17.8 % (in line with relatively low inequality levels), which is above the average, but below the Southern-European regime and close to the Liberal model. This ranking of welfare regimes is robust over the eleven-year time period under consideration. Although, the poverty rate in the Post-Socialist regime is below the Southern-Europe regime, the latter still have a lower income level since the poverty measure is relative to the country's income level.

Poverty levels across the countries show a remarkable degree of persistence although the years from 2009 to 2019 were characterised by rather large changes in the economy, including the financial crises at the beginning of the period. This is in line with multidimensional analyses of welfare in EU countries before, during and after the Great Recession (Hussain, Siersbæk, and Østerdal 2020). The average of maximum poverty rate change across the 31 countries is 2.1 % points, with the lowest change being 0.7 % point (France) and the largest change being 5.2 % points (Latvia).

Based only on the poverty risks, the heterogeneity within welfare regimes is not excessive. The lowest coefficient of variation (CV) is seen for Liberal, Continental and Southern welfare regimes (CV between 0.08 and 0.11). Even though the Nordic countries are considered rather homogenous, their CV is nevertheless 0.18. The highest CV is for the Post-Socialist model with CV=0.28. It is thus difficult to disqualify the welfare regime typology in Table 19.1 when we only consider variation in intra-regime poverty rates.

Not surprisingly, the temporal variation in poverty rates in welfare regimes is even lower than for the different individual countries. The average maximum change in regime poverty rates is 1 % point, with the maximum observed for Liberal and Southern clusters (1.4 % points) and the lowest maximum change observed in the Continental regime (0.5 % points). This poverty rate stability over the observed analyses period justifies in the following aggregating the three analyses years 2009, 2014, and 2019.

19.3.4 Poverty rates for central sub-populations

In Table 19.4, the poverty rates are displayed for different main risks that modern welfare states are supposed to mitigate through the tax-benefit system and other policies, particularly labour market policy.

Gender equality is an important goal in European welfare states and also a stated goal at the supra-national EU level. The problem in this context is that the gender wage gap in European nations (Hedija 2017) is still a persistent problem in even mature welfare states. When all 16+ years old in a household are females, the poverty rate is 28.7 % for the individuals belonging to those households in the Nordic welfare regime (Table 19.4). In contrast, the poverty rate is 26.0 % if all 16+ years olds are males. This represents a gender poverty gap of nearly 3 % points to the disadvantage of women. The Post-Socialist countries have a gender gap of the same magnitude. This gender gap is much higher in the Southern-Europe cluster with 8 % points.

Table 19.4: Poverty rates in sub-populations by welfare regime. 2009, 2014 and 2019 aggregated. %

	Nordic	Continental	Liberal	Southern-European	Post-Socialist	Total
Male/female HH composition:						
Only males	26.0	23.7	23.9	20.6	25.6	23.5
Only females	28.7	27.3	29.4	28.5	28.2	28.1
Males and females	8.2	10.9	14.8	18.7	16.2	14.5
Parental HH composition:						
Others	13.4	13.6	15.9	19.0	16.8	16.0
Single parent	14.9	21.2	27.1	32.9	30.4	25.0
Educational attainment:						
Others	11.5	11.8	13.6	11.8	10.9	11.8
Low education	17.0	19.7	24.0	24.0	28.2	23.3
Educational status:						
Others	10.8	13.7	16.1	19.2	17.3	16.0
Student in HH	24.6	18.6	25.1	23.1	20.0	21.2
Labour market status:						
Others	12.1	12.4	15.5	15.2	14.5	13.9
Unemployed	31.0	37.0	41.6	37.0	36.0	36.9
Health status:						
Others	13.4	13.7	16.2	19.7	17.3	16.2
Permanently disabled	17.0	31.6	34.1	24.4	25.7	28.2
Retirement status:						
Others	13.7	14.8	16.6	22.4	19.1	17.7
Pensioner	13.4	13.7	20.7	13.7	15.7	14.9
Total	13.6	14.5	17.5	19.9	17.8	16.9

Source: See Table 19.3.

Single parents traditionally represent a group with particular challenges and often consists of a single female head living with her children. Work incentives are sometimes small for this group (Regan, Keane, and Walsh 2018) because their combined effective marginal tax rates are high, sometimes even exceeding 100 %, since social benefits in the form of child and housing related benefits etc. are phased out with higher income. In the Nordic welfare model, these single parents nevertheless only have a marginally higher poverty risk (14.9 %) than others (13.4 %), e.g. an excess risk of around 2 % points. This excess risk is 14 % points in Southern and Post-Socialist regimes, and around 10 % points in the remaining regimes.

Low education can be a disadvantage since it can transform into low wages, jobs with higher health risks as well as higher unemployment rates (the reverse might also be of some importance). Together, this can result in lower income and thus a higher poverty risk. Indeed, this is exactly what is observed across welfare regimes but to a very varying degree such that the poverty gap is increasing according to the welfare regime generosity (the order of welfare regimes in the table). Thus, the poverty rate more than doubles for low education people from nearly 11 % to 28 %, e.g. an excess poverty risk of 17 % points in the Post-Socialist regime. This excess risk is much lower in the other welfare regimes, particularly in the Nordic one where the disadvantage is down at 6 % points.

While Nordic countries fare comparatively well for people with low education, there is almost the reverse relationship between welfare state generosity and students' excess poverty risk. In the Nordic welfare regime, one-quarter of individuals in households with student(s) are poor, while around one-tenth of individuals without student (s) in the household are poor, which represents an excess poverty risk of 14 % points for students. This excess risk is only 3–4 % points in the Southern and Post-Socialist clusters. While this is a serious enough gap between students and non-students in the Nordic regime, it probably reflects the fact that young people in this cluster tend to move out of their parent's house rather earlier (Aassve, Arpino, and Fargas 2013; Eurostat 2021), which means the economies of scale evident from the equivalence scale definition above will often not exist to the same degree as for students living with their parents.

Unemployment is both detrimental to income as well as to social exclusion and subjective well-being. Although it usually affects a smaller fraction of the workforce in any given year, quite a large fraction will have experienced it during their labour market career. The poverty rate among unemployed people in the Nordic regime is 31 % (19 % points excess poverty), while in the Liberal regime the poverty rate is 42 % (26 % excess poverty). Nordic Southern and Post-Socialist welfare models are the most successful in protecting unemployed people from poverty (compared to others), while the Liberal and Continental models are doing somewhat less well. The similarity across all welfare states is that unemployed people's excess poverty is the biggest among the risks presented in Table 19.4.

Disability's effect on the poverty rate very much follows the pattern seen for unemployment though with a much lower poverty gap. In the Nordic welfare regime cluster, 17 % of individuals in households with a permanently disabled person (aged

16+) are poor, while 13 % of individuals without a permanently disabled person are poor, which represents an excess poverty rate of 4 % points. In the Southern and Post-Socialist models, the poverty gaps are also low (5–8 % points), while they are very large in the Liberal and Continental models (18 % points).

Households with retired persons have the lowest poverty risk in the Nordic cluster (13.4 %) and the highest risk in the Liberal cluster (21 %). Although the Nordic case has an excess poverty gap to the advantage of pensioner households, this same gap is much higher in magnitude in Southern-Europe (–9 % points), and also negative in Continental and Post-Socialist regimes. The Liberal regime is the only one with a positive, albeit small, excess poverty for pensioners (4 % points). In general, it seems that retired persons are generally faring well in terms of poverty.

To conclude from the descriptive analyses, we see that the Nordic welfare model outperforms all the other welfare models regarding five out of the seven presented risks. The exceptions are pensioners and students, where nevertheless, for the former, the Nordic cluster at least has the lowest poverty rate (but not the lowest poverty gap), and for the latter, the Nordic cluster do not have the highest poverty rate (but the highest poverty gap). The picture is even more mixed when we want to identify the welfare model at the other end of the spectrum, but applying a simple counting approach, the Liberal model more often than others has the highest poverty gap. Indeed, averaging the poverty gaps for the seven risks in Table 19.4, the Nordic cluster ends up with 6.6 % points and the Liberal cluster ends up with 12 % points. The degree to which any differences between welfare regimes is significant is the topic scrutinised in the next section.

19.5 Net effects of social events on poverty

19.5.1 Linear probability regression models

Important differences between the five welfare states' mitigation ability were presented in the previous section. A more technical approach is required to decide whether the welfare state differences are mere coincidences or robust structural differences taking the statistical uncertainty into account. To proceed, a linear probability regression model is applied, although a logit approach would be theoretically more appropriate given the dichotomous nature of the dependent variable (poverty), which is a 0/1 state at the individual level, e.g. 0 for non-poor and 1 for poor. The ordinary least squares (OLS) approach is nevertheless applied since it is easier to interpret. The known heteroscedasticity problem introduced when applying OLS to a binary 0/1 outcome is remedied by producing robust standard errors of estimated regression parameters (Wooldridge 2020). Logit regressions are available from the author upon request.

The total sample size in the regressions is 760,797 households. This number differs from the much higher number of 1,873,020 in Table 19.3 since that is the number of individuals (respondents). All right-hand side variables are at the household level usually concerning household members aged 16+ years. The explanatory power of the different models is between 9.8 % and 16.3 %, which is not at all surprising given that the observations are at the household level (microdata). It is more important to note that almost all estimated parameters are significant at lower than the 0.001 significance level.

Table 19.5: Linear probability regression models for poverty in five European welfare regimes. 2009–2019 covering 31 countries. % points

	Nordic	Continental	Liberal	Southern-European	Post-Socialist	Total
Only females	2.311**	1.924***	3.141**	5.278***	1.268**	2.541***
Males and females	−17.24***	−14.59***	−8.950***	−6.215***	−12.09***	−12.17***
Single parent	−0.899	4.054***	6.785***	8.437***	7.640***	5.080***
Low education	2.523***	7.283***	7.015***	12.52***	16.40***	9.995***
Student in HH	10.71***	3.066***	7.625***	1.374**	−2.889***	2.402***
Unemployed	19.38***	23.46***	25.72***	20.38***	20.40***	22.14***
Permanently disabled	8.763***	18.51***	16.74***	3.480***	8.120***	11.67***
Pensioner	0.929	2.288***	3.423***	−7.657***	−7.019***	−2.689***
Age	−2.620***	−1.493***	−1.577***	−1.577***	−1.149***	−1.609***
Age squared/100	2.432***	1.329***	1.539***	1.448***	1.150***	1.511***
Sample size, N	94972	175743	50186	172799	267097	760797
R^2	0.163	0.111	0.104	0.098	0.126	0.107

* $p<0.05$, ** $p<0.01$, *** $p<0.001$.
Source: See Table 19.3.
Notes: "Only females" and "Males and females" refers the gender composition. All variables refer to the situation of 16+ years olds in the household level. The number of observations is much smaller here than in Table 19.3 since the regressions in this table are at the household level while the figures in Table 19.5 represents individual respondents. All variables are dichotomous (0/1), except (average) age and age squared. Two-year dummies and 30 country dummies are also included but estimates are not shown here, but they are available from the author upon request.

Compared to Table 19.4, some significant changes appear regarding the order of welfare regimes with respect to successfulness in mitigating the seven investigated risks.

The female poverty gap is the lowest in the Post-Socialist regime (1.3 % points), but generally low also in the Continental and Nordic regimes (1.9 and 2.3 % points). Single parents now have no poverty gap to other household compositions in the Nordic cluster, but the Southern-European cluster still have a rather large excess poverty among single parents (8.4 % points). Effects of low education has a ranking according to the generosity of welfare states, but with lower magnitude than in Table 19.4. For the remaining risks we see almost the same pattern as in Table 19.4, but generally with lower magnitudes.

The changes (from Table 19.4 to Table 19.5), albeit small, in parameters representing the excess poverty due to a given risk factor do not in the end alter the ranking of welfare regimes, with the Nordic regime again at the top and the Liberal again at the bottom regarding ability to mitigate risks. But, the difference between the Nordic, Southern-European and Post-Socialist when taking the average of excess poverty rates (Figure 19.1) are practically zero (6.25, 6.26 and 6.27 % points), which leads to the surprising conclusion that generally speaking the seven risks taken together have the same effect on poverty change in all three welfare regimes, e.g. the old much richer Nordic and Southern European welfare states are not better in handling the risks than the less affluent Post-Socialist welfare states. Not to mention that the also rich Continental (average excess poverty of 8.66 % points) and Liberal (10.06 % points) welfare states fare even worse than the Post-Socialist welfare states in mitigating risks.

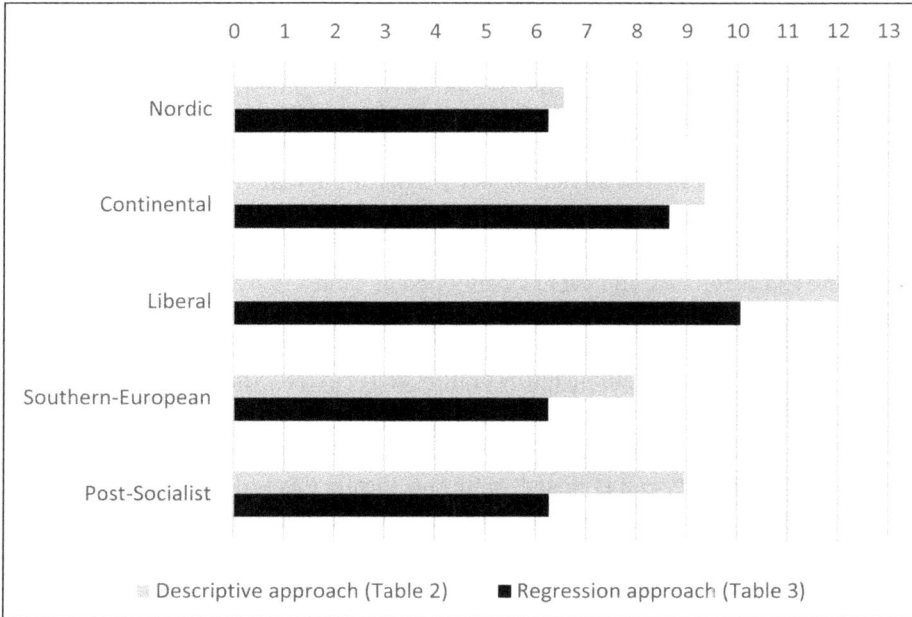

Figure 19.1: Average excess poverty rates for the seven risk factors in Tables 19.4 and 19.5 in five welfare regimes. % points.

Whether this ranking of welfare regimes is robust to an eventual macro-economic convergence (Durlauf and Johnson 1995; Galor 2011) of the 31 economies needs to be seen. Specifically, one would expect that the Post-Socialist welfare regimes will come closer to the income levels of the other richer welfare clusters. And the question is whether high persistent growth for some years/decades will lead to increased inequality within Post-Socialist countries such that poverty gaps due to different risk will increase and perhaps be harder to close, e.g. welfare state mitigation becomes more difficult.

In the analyses above the welfare regime is used as the decisive factor (mitigation ability of the welfare state). To what extent active welfare state policies are driving the mitigation effort or whether other structural factors, including demographic and cultural, are at play, is debatable. One example is the high excess poverty rate among Nordic households with students. In a sense this has less to do with public policy than with cultural norms, where the Nordic youth is willing to trade (short-term) consumption possibilities for independence from the parental household.

19.5.2 Counter-factual simulations

In all five welfare states there is continuous discussion and negotiation about the adequacy of the welfare state, including whether the government is involved enough (Greve and Hussain 2021) in altering the income distribution, or, whether it is too much involved with claimed adverse effects on taxation and labour supply.

There are many possible strategies to reduce inequality and poverty. Some require increased public spending and therefore increased tax revenue (or higher public deficits). Other strategies could involve changing the culture around working regardless of work incentives as well as increased focus on assuring that every child receives enough further education to succeed on the labour market as well as in other arenas. Regardless, one ultimate goal could be to assure that people's risk of poverty is independent of the characteristics and events mentioned in Tables 19.4 and 19.5. Therefore, in this sub-section, it is estimated what effects closing the poverty gaps in Table 19.5 would have for overall regime poverty rates. The simulations are of the ceteris paribus type since changes in the poverty line (or other effects as a consequence of closing the different poverty gaps) are not taken into account.

In Table 19.6, counter-factual simulations are carried out, where for each event we assume that the poverty gap is closed. More specifically this is done by assuming that the right-hand side variable of interest is set to 0, e.g. unemployed are assumed to be not unemployed, and permanently disabled are assumed not to be permanently disabled. The effects of being able to close a poverty gap depends on the estimated parameters in Table 19.5 as well as on the prevalence of a given event, e.g. the percentage of the workforce being unemployed.

Table 19.6: Counter-factual poverty rates when poverty gaps are closed in a given welfare regime. 2009–2019.

	Nordic		Continental		Liberal	
	CF poverty rate, %	Reduction, % points	CF poverty rate, %	Reduction, % points	CF poverty rate, %	Reduction, % points
Only females	13.3	0.4	14.2	0.3	17.1	0.4
Single parent	13.8	−0.2	14.0	0.5	16.5	1.0
Low education	12.6	1.0	12.0	2.5	14.9	2.6
Student	11.4	2.2	14.0	0.5	16.3	1.2
Unemployed	12.1	1.5	12.5	2.0	15.5	2.0
Permanently disabled	13.1	0.5	13.7	0.8	16.3	1.2
Pensioner	13.4	0.2	13.9	0.6	16.8	0.7
Total	8.0	5.6	7.2	7.3	8.3	9.2
Actual poverty rate	13.6		14.5		17.5	

	Southern-European		Post-Socialist		All regimes	
	CF poverty rate, %	Reduction, % points	CF poverty rate, %	Reduction, % points	CF poverty rate, %	Reduction, % points
Only females	19.3	0.6	17.7	0.1	16.6	0.3
Single parent	19.3	0.6	17.3	0.6	16.4	0.5
Low education	11.6	8.3	11.2	6.6	12.5	4.4
Student	19.6	0.3	18.4	−0.6	16.5	0.4
Unemployed	15.5	4.4	14.7	3.1	14.0	2.9
Permanently disabled	19.7	0.2	17.3	0.6	16.3	0.6
Pensioner	22.1	-2.2	20.4	−2.6	17.7	-0.8
Total	7.9	12.0	10.0	7.9	8.4	8.5
Actual poverty rate	19.9		17.8		16.9	

Source: See Table 19.3.
Notes: "CF poverty rate" is the counter-factual poverty rate simulated using estimated parameters in Table 19.5 and setting the variable in the row to 0. "Change" is the counter-factual poverty rate minus the "Actual poverty rate" in the past row.

Closing the gender poverty gap or the single parent poverty gap or the disability poverty gap only has minor effects on the aggregate poverty rate (reduction between – 0.2 and 1.2 % points), which is due to either a low estimated parameter in Table 19.5 (gender) or low prevalence (lone parent) as is indicated in Table 19.A2. Closing the education poverty gap has a higher effect (reduction of 1–8.3 % points) both due to generally higher estimated parameters and higher prevalence. In spite of high estimated parameters there is only a smaller effect of closing the unemployment poverty gap (reduction of 1.5–4.4 % points) due to the small prevalence. Closing the pensioner poverty gap, decreases poverty rates slightly in the Nordic, Continental and Liberal regimes, while there is a significant increase in poverty in Southern and Post-Socialist regimes since negative parameters were estimated for the latter two regimes. Although, the effects of closing different poverty gaps can seem small, like for the unemployment gap in the Nordic countries, which reduces the poverty rate with 1.5 % points, it must be remembered it still means lifting almost 400,000 people out of poverty (the Nordic regime population is around 26 million on average during 2009–2019). Similarly, closing the same poverty gap in Southern-Europe reaching 4.4 % points means a staggering more than 5.5 million fewer people in poverty (there are about 128 million inhabitants in the welfare cluster).

Due to the linear nature of the regressions, the poverty reduction arising when simultaneously closing all seven poverty gaps is the addition of the contributions from each poverty gap. Thus, in the Nordic case the total poverty reduction achieved would be 5.7 % points (from an actual level of 13.6 % to a counter-factual level of 8 %), which represents a reduction of nearly 1.5 million poor people. In the Southern-Europe case, the poverty reduction is huge at 12 % points, representing more than 15 million fewer people in poverty. The distribution of simulated poverty rates for all five regimes without and with poverty gaps closed are shown in Figure 19.2 for illustrative purposes.

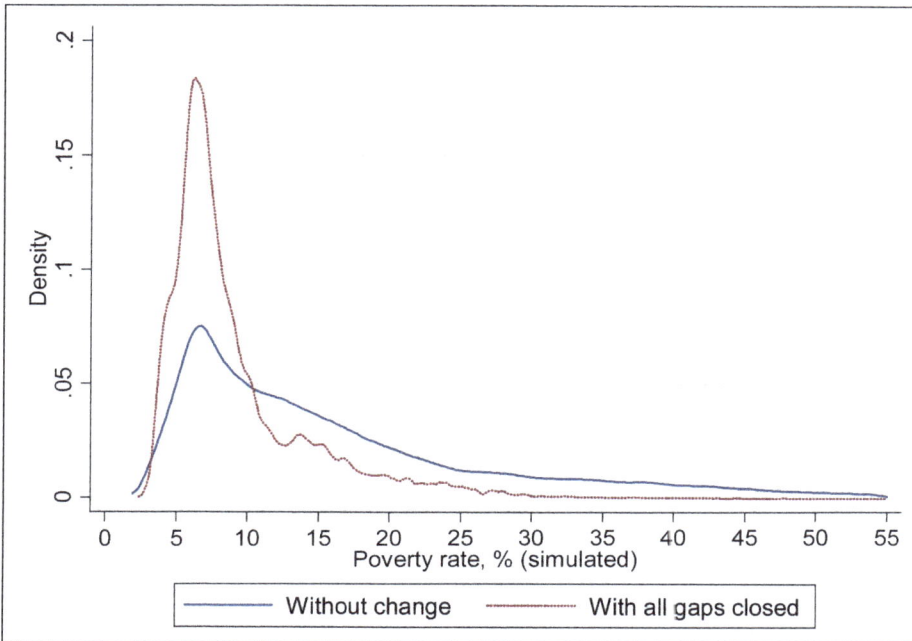

Figure 19.2: Distribution of simulated poverty rates before and after closing poverty gaps. All five regimes. %.
Source: See Table 19.3.
Notes: The logit model was used to simulate poverty rates. The distributions have been truncated at 55 % for expositional reasons (leaving out 1.4 % of observations). Half of the original sample was used to reduce estimation time, but still the statistical uncertainty is very low because of the high number of observations.

Above, the simulations assumed that poverty gaps were closed somehow. In practice, it is less clear how to close the sometimes huge poverty gaps observed within the seven dimensions.

The gender poverty gap for singles is likely a result of the gender wage gap on the labour market. A continued focus on equal pay for equal job could therefore lead to a reduced gender poverty gap. At the same time closing the gender wage gap might be insufficient since an unequal distribution of male and female employment across sectors and industries might still produce significant differences in male and female average wages.

The huge gap between couples and singles is hard to do anything about since it is primarily a consequence of utilisation of economies of scale that inevitably arises when a household consists of two persons instead of one person. Thus, no policy instrument is available, or rather desirable, in this case.

The single parent issue is a recurring topic in modern welfare states and a product of welfare states where high combined marginal tax rates effectively keeps particularly lone mothers with low education trapped in poverty since accepting job offers meanings phasing out of various social benefits and increased income taxes, which lowers employment incentives. If the skills/education of these poverty trapped persons can be increased, translating into higher productivity, the employment incentive can be increased and the poverty risk can be reduced.

Low educational attainment as a poverty risk factor can possibly be mitigated by focusing on active labour market policies aiming at reducing the unemployment risk, including practical training, and more smoothly working labour markets. The remedy for unemployed individuals could be of a similar type.

Higher poverty risk for students is not much of a focus area since this group of people will usually end up in the upper end of the income distribution. Nevertheless, access to loans for this group of people might be a way out of poverty, particularly if they are liquidity constrained.

The poverty risk gap for people with disabilities could be partially closed by introducing job subsidies such that the person earns a decent wage without being an economic risk for private enterprises. Of course this might affect the government budget balance, but on the other hand the job subsidy might be self-financed to some degree as other social benefits might be reduced (housing allowance, disability pension, etc.).

Old age poverty can be reduced by assuring people themselves save for retirement during periods of employment, e.g. pensioners do not solely rely on public pension benefits, which cannot be too high, particularly in the foreseeable future, where demographic shifts are implying an ageing population in almost all western economies.

19.6 Conclusion

With around 0.75 million households representing nearly 2 million respondents from the representative EU-SILC database, poverty variations caused by different life events across five European welfare state regimes is analysed. The level of poverty follows the generosity of welfare states such that lowest poverty is seen in the Nordic cluster, followed by the Continental model and the Liberal model, but the Southern-European cluster has the highest poverty rate, while the Post-Socialist cluster has the second highest poverty rate. A relative poverty approach at the national level is used, so although poverty rates are lower in the Post-Socialist regime, Southern-Europe still has higher income levels than in the Post-Socialist regime.

At first sight, the Nordic model clearly is better at mitigating the seven investigated risks, while the Liberal model fares less well. Further scrutiny applying a regression approach reveals that Nordic, Southern-European and Post-Socialist clusters in fact practically have the same level of success (on average) in mitigating risk.

Different measures are available to reduce or eliminate the excess poverty experienced due to the seven risks. Using simulations, the potential in terms of poverty reduction applying different policy and other measures is quantified. In some regimes poverty can be cut in less than half. Closing all seven poverty gaps in the five regimes could lift 46 million people out of relative poverty.

References

Aassve, A., B. Arpino, and T. Fargas. 2013. "Age Norms on Leaving Home: Multilevel Evidence from the European Social Survey." *Environment and Planning A: Economy and Space* 45 (2), 383–401.

Arndt, C., U. R. Beck, M. A. Hussain, K. Mahrt, K. Simler, and F. Tarp. 2016a. "User Guide to Poverty Line Estimation Analytical Software-PLEASe." In *Measuring Poverty and Wellbeing in Developing Countries*, edited by C. Arndt and F. Tarp, 305–324. Oxford: Oxford University Press.

Arndt, C., K. Mahrt, and F. Tarp. 2016b. "Absolute Poverty Lines." In *Measuring Poverty and Wellbeing in Developing Countries*, edited by C. Arndt and F. Tarp, 10–23. Oxford: Oxford University Press.

Census Bureau. 2021. *How the Census Bureau Measures Poverty*. United States Census Bureau. https://www.census.gov/topics/income-poverty/poverty/guidance/poverty-measures.html. Accessed 8 May 2021.

Durlauf, S. N., and P. A. Johnson. 1995. "Multiple Regimes and Cross-Country Growth Behavior." *Journal of Applied Econometrics* 10 (4), 365–384.

EC. 2019. *Methodological Guidelines and Description of EU-SILC Target Variables*. 2019 operation (Version January 2019. DocSILC065 (2019 operation). European Commission, Eurostat, Directorate F: Social Statistics, Unit F-4: Quality of life.

Esping-Andersen, G. 1990. *The Three Worlds of Welfare Capitalism*. Princeton, NJ: Princeton University Press.

Eurostat. 2021. https://ec.europa.eu/eurostat/databrowser/view/YTH_DEMO_030__custom_926 270/default/table?lang=en. Accessed 9 May 2021.

Foster, J. E. 1998. "Absolute versus Relative Poverty." *The American Economic Review* 88 (2), 335–341. Papers and Proceedings of the Hundred and Tenth Annual Meeting of the American Economic Association (May 1998), American Economic Association.

Galor, O. 2011. *Unified Growth Theory*. Princeton, NJ: Princeton University Press.

Greve, B. 2018. *Routledge Handbook of the Welfare State*. London: Routledge.

Greve, B. 2021. *Routledge International Handbook of Poverty*. London and New York: Routledge.

Greve, B., and M. A. Hussain. 2021. "Support for Governmental Income Redistribution in Nordic Countries." *European Review* 2021, 1–19. https://doi.org/10.1017/S1062798721000089.

Hagenaars, A., K. de Vos, and M. A. Zaidi. 1994. *Poverty Statistics in the Late 1980s: Research Based on Micro-Data*. Luxembourg: Office for Official Publications of the European Communities.

Hedija, V. 2017. "Sector-Specific Gender Pay Gap: Evidence from the European Union Countries." *Economic Research-Ekonomska Istraživanja* 30 (1), 1804–1819.

Hussain, M. A. 2021. "Absolute Poverty." In *Routledge International Handbook of Poverty*, edited by B. Greve, 11–23. London and New York: Routledge.

Hussain, M. A., N. Siersbæk, and L. P. Østerdal. 2020. "Multidimensional Welfare Comparisons of EU Member States Before, During, and After the Financial Crisis: A Dominance Approach." *Social Choice and Welfare* 55 (4), 645–686.

Kangas, O., J. Palme, and M. Kainu. 2020. "Welfare State Entry and Exit over the Life Course: Employment and the Sustainability of the Welfare State in Different Worlds of Welfare." In *Shaping and Re-Shaping the Boundaries of Working Life*, edited by N. F. Savinetti, and A.-J. Riekhoff, 29–40. Tampere: Tampere University Press.

Regan, M., C. Keane, and J. R. Walsh. 2018. *Lone-Parent Incomes and Work Incentives*. Budget Perspectives 2019, Paper 1. Dublin: The Economic and Social Research Institute. https://doi.org/10.26504/bp201901.

Saltkjel, T., and I. Malmberg-Heimone. 2021. "Absolute or Relative? Definitions and the Different Understandings of Poverty." In *Routledge International Handbook of Poverty*, edited by B. Greve, 24–32. London and New York: Routledge.

UN. 1996. *Report of the World Summit for Social Development*. Copenhagen, 6–12 March 1995. A/CONF. 166/9. New York: United Nations.

Vandecasteele, L. 2010. "Poverty Trajectories after Risky Life Course Events in Different European Welfare Regimes." *European Societies* 12 (2), 257–278.

Whelan, C. T., and B. Maître. 2010. "Welfare Regime and Social Class Variation in Poverty and Economic Vulnerability in Europe: An Analysis of EU-SILC." *Journal of European Social Policy* 20 (4), 316–332.

Wooldridge, J. M. 2020. *Introductory Econometrics. A Modern Approach*. 7th ed. Andover: Cengage.

Appendix

Table 19.A1: Data cleaning issues and remedies.

Data cleaning issues and remedies
– Due to missing or zero household weight values, 51 observations are excluded from the analyses. 4 observations are from Croatia (3 from 2014 and 1 from 2019), 17 are from Hungary (2014), and the remaining 30 are from Luxembourg (2019). Given the large sample size, this exclusion is not assumed to affect the analyses in any significant way.
– 68 respondents from Bulgaria, 9 from Iceland, 2 from Norway, and 156 from Romania belongs to households with apparently no adult present (16+ years aged person). For these household (members) the average age of the 16+ years is set to 16 years (the variable Age). Alternatively, these 235 respondents could have been excluded from the analyses. Either way, this is not believed to affect the conclusions of the analyses since this age imputation represent only a tiny fraction of regime sample sizes.

Table 19.A2: Summary statistics for data used in regressions. 2009–2019. 31 countries. Unweighted. N=760,797 observations (households).

	Mean	Std.Dev.	Minimum	Maximum
Dependent variable:				
Poverty (percent)	17.07	37.63	0	100
Independent variables:				
Only females	0.2115	0.4084	0	1
Males and females	0.6729	0.4691	0	1
Single parent	0.0729	0.2599	0	1
Low education	0.4380	0.4961	0	1

Table 19.A2 (continued)

	Mean	Std.Dev.	Minimum	Maximum
Student in HH	0.1327	0.3392	0	1
Unemployed	0.1071	0.3092	0	1
Permanently disabled	0.0543	0.2265	0	1
Pensioner	0.4016	0.4902	0	1
Age	52.04	16.40	16	81
Age squared/100	29.8	17.6	2.560	65.61
Year	2014.3	4.12	2009	2019
Country	16.4	8.65	1	31

Source: See Table 19.3.

Notes: See Table 19.5. The year variable is transformed into two dummies, and the country variable is transformed into 30 dummies.

Bent Greve

20 Employment and unemployment

Abstract: The chapter first describes what a labour market is, the types of unemployment and welfare states' policies with regard hereto. This includes what we know about Active Labour Market Policy (ALMP), including its effectiveness as well as compensation for those who are unemployed. The expected development in jobs specifically related to new technology is shown. Whether welfare states are prepared for these changes as a result of the more general changes in the labour market is analysed, including also the specific challenges arising from the tendency for stronger social pressures, among other things, to be caused as a result of the new platforms related to the labour market. Based on these discussions, the chapter considers what the future holds for jobs, including what opportunities there are for inclusive employment and whether there is a need to change the distribution of work, as well as the role of social policies mainly related to income transfers and training.

Keywords: unemployment, employment, labour market, technology, active labour market policy, future jobs, social policy

20.1 Introduction

Work has always been central for mankind. This chapter focuses on employment, unemployment, and related issues, especially with regard to the role of welfare states.

Historically, there have been discussions about whether or not there would continue to be work for everyone. The fear of technology's impact on social development, including that jobs would disappear, goes back to the Roman Empire during the reign of Vespasian (Frey 2019). Later examples include Gutenberg's printing press, spinning machines in England, and so on. Anxiety about the impact of new technology on the number of jobs has also always been with us.

A core question to be answered in this chapter is, therefore, whether we will have even more significant changes in the number of jobs than earlier, often referred to as the Fourth Industrial Revolution (Global Affairs 2017; Schwab 2016). Further, if this is the case, how welfare states and social policy might help in ensuring that these changes will not cause an increased split between insiders and outsiders in the labour market, thereby creating stronger dualisation in societies.

The chapter is structured so that section 20.2 describes what a labour market is, the types of unemployment and welfare states' policies with regard hereto. This includes what we know about Active Labour Market Policy (ALMP), including its effectiveness as well as compensation for those who are unemployed. Section 20.3 then gives a brief description of the expected development in jobs specifically related to

https://doi.org/10.1515/9783110721768-020

new technology. Next, in section 20.4, we discuss how and whether welfare states are prepared for these changes as a result of the more general changes in the labour market, whereas section 20.5 looks more closely at the specific challenges arising from the tendency for stronger social pressures, among other things, to be caused as a result of the new platforms related to the labour market (Schwellnus et al. 2019). Based on these discussions, section 20.6 considers what the future holds for jobs, including what opportunities there are for inclusive employment and whether there is a need to change the distribution of work, as well as the role of social policies mainly related to income transfers and training. Section 20.7 will conclude the chapter with some final remarks about the future challenges for labour market development and policies.

20.2 What is a labour market?

Given the scope of this chapter, the description of the labour market is necessarily brief. A labour market is, basically, a place for buying and selling labour. In contrast to the market for consumer goods, it is individual persons who supply work and companies that buy work. A self-employed person provides work as an individual; however, in principle, this is the same. Recent years have seen new types of employment, such as working via a platform, which might entail physical work (such as delivering goods and/or services) or digital work (such as consultancy, IT).

There are often a number of labour markets (based upon education or geography, for example). However, there are many variations and exceptions in relation to the normal commodity market, including that wages can be set by the state (minimum wages), through collective agreements and/or through individual negotiations, which can vary from country to country. Wages vary depending on the level of education, so they are typically higher for the highly educated than for groups without education. Income from work can vary depending on the extent of the work, but also the risk of becoming unemployed varies.

The structures of the labour markets also depend on the country, region and development, including how high the employment and unemployment rates are. Unemployment can be influenced by economic conditions, but can also be seasonal, geographical or related to the types of jobs. In recent years, and this is one of the areas that the chapter looks at in particular, the technological explanation of changes as to who has a job and the development of unemployment is also an important aspect.

The security of having a job, or returning to work if unemployed, depends – as with the level of unemployment benefit – on the welfare state the individual lives in, including the ALMPs in individual countries and their effectiveness. For questions about security and unemployment, see for example data from organisations such as the ILO and the OECD. One way of comparing countries has been to look at what forms the interplay between flexibility and security take (see for example on flexi-curity, Bekker and Mailand 2019; Bekker 2018; Tros and Wilthagen 2013). Welfare states influence a large number of elements in the labour markets through legislation. For EU countries there are a number of directives (for example on equal pay, safety and health, working hours) that are important, just as there are often a number of agreements between the social partners in addition to pay in relation to working hours, holidays, education, etc. Welfare states also have a role in relation to the overall level of education, which has an impact on the extent of employment, which is outside the scope of this chapter. In addition, the chapter does not look at differences in employment and unemployment across countries, see instead data from Eurostat or the OECD.

There are various explanations for the level of unemployment. Supply-side economics argues that if wages adjust and people are willing to work at the existing wage rate then in the long-run there will be full employment, as those who are unemployed are thus voluntarily unemployed. This is in contrast to the Keynesian approach that it is the total demand for labour influenced by cyclical development as well as possible state intervention that is crucial, so that the level of unemployment is also dependent on the demand for labour and not only willingness to work for the ongoing wage rate in the labour market. This is not central here, but it explains the variations in the understanding of unemployment from being voluntary to the impact of the business cycle, as well as the above-mentioned points.

As mentioned earlier, ALMP might be part of supporting people to have a job. Still, it can have different rationales (Bonoli 2010), which, however, are not the focus here. The central point, instead, is whether ALMP is effective or not, and if so, which parts of ALMP are effective. In relation to this, the explanation is that if there are increased difficulties in getting supply and demand to match, especially as a result of new technology, then it will be the ALMP, which in particular must be assumed to contribute to the reduction of the problems. The OECD splits labour market policy into the following eight elements:

1. Public employment services and administration
2. Training
3. Employment incentives
4. Sheltered and supported employment and rehabilitation
5. Direct job creation
6. Start-up incentives
7. Out-of-work income maintenance and support
8. Early retirement.[1]

The first six are the active and the last two are the passive parts of the employment policy.

---

1 http://www.oecd.org/els/emp/ALMPdata-Scope-and-Comparability.pdf, accessed 21 November 2021.

Overall, based upon a number of studies the knowledge is that employment incentives in private companies and increasing human capital by investing in training and education (especially in times of low economic activity) are the most effective (Card, Kluve, and Weber 2018; Nordlund and Greve 2019; Vooren et al. 2016; Caliendo and Schmidl 2016).

In order to receive unemployment benefit, there might be a condition to participate in ALMP, which is often labelled as being activated. Whereas activation in the private sector as mentioned above might be effective, activation in the public sector seems to be less effective. Despite this, the movement towards activation is sometimes argued as part of using a threat-effect in order to get people to search for jobs that are outside the scope of their qualifications and at a lower wage level, thereby having a coercive nature (Fossati 2018). Thus, there are instruments available that might have an impact on the level of unemployment.

When measured by spending, it looks like ALMP is most developed in the Nordic welfare states and some central European,[2] albeit the spending also depends on the level of unemployment. Thereby, if there is pressure on the labour markets, such as due to the business cycle, but also new technology (see more in next section), then ALMP can be a way to cope with the risk for those pressured as a consequence hereof.

ALMP does not necessarily cope with more precarious employment situations, which might still have an impact on life. Precarious employment might include employment insecurity, low income and lack of social rights and protection against unfair dismissal, albeit it is not always clearly defined in studies (Kreshpaj et al. 2020). Here the focus is mainly on the precarity stemming from new technology.

20.3 How many jobs are at risk?

There is growing knowledge about the ways in which new technology can have an impact on the labour market. They are, with variations, based on the distinction between jobs that are routine or not routine, and whether there is complementarity or substitution possibilities, as outlined in a classic article (Autor, Levy, and Murnane 2003). Differences in calculations of the impacts include an assessment of how many jobs are at high risk and which jobs can be automated. However, the scope may depend on whether an approach is based on tasks or types of jobs. Overall, it is seemingly routine based jobs that are disappearing, in line with a long historical development of changes to jobs in agriculture and industry. Naturally, there is variation in the estimation of the number of jobs disappearing (Nedelkoska and Quintini 2018; PWC 2017, 2018).

---

2 http://www.oecd.org/employment/activation.htm, accessed 11 August 2021.

The uncertainty of the calculations of changes in the number of jobs lies partly in whether the companies actually adopt new technology and at what speed they do so. What is more, it is at least uncertain how many new jobs are created, including what types of jobs can and will be created in a world where the speed at which IT can take over job functions is growing and, as a consequence, what qualifications are needed.

In addition, there are differences in the existing analysis of whether parts of jobs or entire jobs can and will be automated. Regardless of the choice of method, any projection will have the risk of underestimating as well as overestimating the scope of this, as knowledge about the development of new technology, its implementation and new types of jobs will be difficult to predict.

Figure 20.1 shows an assessment for a number of OECD countries of the number of jobs that are at either high risk or very high risk.

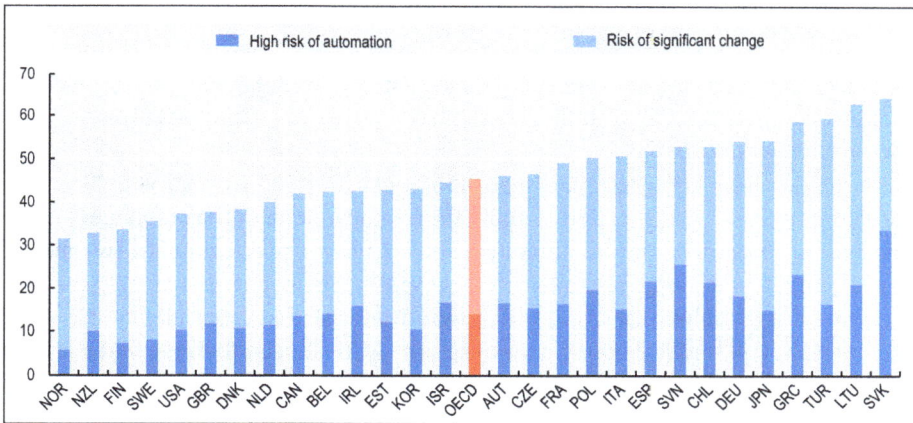

Figure 20.1: Jobs at risk of automation in OECD countries.
Source: Figure 2.6 OECD, Employment Outlook, 2019.
Note: Jobs are at high risk of automation if the likelihood of being automated is at least 70 %. Jobs at risk of significant change are those with the likelihood of being automated estimated at between 50 % and 70 %.

Figure 20.1 shows that the biggest changes will happen in those countries where changes away from more traditional industrial production have, so far only to a limited extent, taken place, and in these countries, more than 60 % of current jobs are at high risk due to new technology. Across the OECD area, close to every other job is at risk, which, however, cannot directly be transferred into the knowledge about the number of jobs that will be gone. This is because changes in technology might influence the level of employment in two ways – a displacement effect and a productivity effect. The displacing effect means that jobs are reduced as tasks are being automated, whereas the productivity effect is due to an increase in demand for other goods related to new types of production (Chiacchio, Petropoulos, and Pichler 2018; Acemoglu and

Restrepo 2017a). It is the case that if the increase in productivity gains are, at least partly, implying lower prices, this will then also raise demand for other goods as there will be some resources left with which to buy other goods and services. As a French study showed, this can then imply higher demand for labour (Antonin et al. 2020). The overall impact can, however, be difficult to estimate.

As another example, it has been shown that one additional robot per thousand workers is estimated to reduce the employment rate by 0.16 % to 0.20 percentage points. This is based on a study in six European countries, albeit with data not later than 2007 (Chiacchio, Petropoulos, and Pichler 2018). Thus, the situation might have increased substantially since then, and it might be that the transition is faster than ever before.

Studies do not agree upon which impact is the strongest. Thus, for example, one study argues that despite a strong displacement effect, the increase in demand has implied net employment growth, but also that it is critical whether there is a flow back of money to ensure demand (by, for example, unemployment benefit). The number of new jobs might thus vary between different local areas, implying that even if new jobs are created at the societal level, there can be strong regional variations (Gregory, Salomons, and Zierahn 2019).

Overall, there is knowledge that many jobs and many job functions will disappear in the coming years. The uncertainty about the consequences for the number of job vacancies is mainly due to the variation in expectations for the creation of new types of jobs, as well as the implementation time. Overall, this means that many jobs will change over the coming years, and with a significant risk that especially people without education will find it more difficult to get into work or keep their job in the labour market, even though there might also be an impact on a number of current jobs needing a high level of education.

This is in line with the fact that historically classic manual jobs that could be automated or outsourced have experienced this more than other jobs. There has gradually been a greater focus on it also being possible that at least part of the functions of a number of jobs for those with higher education (low, medium or high) will be automated. Overall, this increases the risk of a greater degree of dualisation in the labour market (Yoon and Chung 2016; Rueda 2014; Chung 2016). Such a development will contribute to more fragmented societies and the risks associated herewith.

The extent of fragmentation depends on the number of jobs created, as indicated above, and the assessment thereof is different (Acemoglu and Restrepo 2017b; Ford 2015). It also means that there can be a bright as well as dark side of development (Greve 2017). The bright side is where many new jobs are created so that the risk of increased unemployment is limited. The dark side is when many people become unemployed and thus the dualisation and difference between insiders and outsiders in the labour market grows. It can also affect quality of life, as being unemployed has a negative impact on quality of life (Helliwell and Huang 2014), as does being concerned about losing one's job (Chung 2016; De Neve, Krekel, and Ward 2018). Furthermore, automation might also imply a fear among those having routine jobs that their social position will be in decline (Im and Komp-Leukkunen 2021). However, this applies regardless of the fact that there will be a number of people in the labour market whose current skills do not match the need for the new types of jobs. Therefore, there will, as a minimum, be a transitional period where many people become unemployed and where some through, for example, upskilling of qualifications will have a better opportunity to return to the labour market, whereas for others it may mean that the probability of getting a job again is very limited. This indicates the need for a high quality and effective ALMP. The length of working time can also have an impact, see more in section 20.6.

In addition, it is not given that the new jobs will have the same quality in terms of wages and working conditions as the jobs that disappear, which is returned to in section 20.5 in relation to the platform economy. One risk is that the lack of increase in wages for the middle income groups and lack of social integration might result in what has been labelled "deaths of despair" (Case and Deaton 2015, 2020). The next section discusses whether welfare states are ready and prepared for the dramatic changes ahead.

20.4 Are welfare states prepared?

The question is whether welfare states are prepared to cope with the changes in the labour market. This includes the ability to finance welfare, as a possible lower employment rate might reduce state income from taxation. The financing of welfare states is not only due to technological change under pressure, but also as a result of globalisation and the risk that large companies will not pay taxes on their activities, which in turn increases the pressure on the welfare state (Cournède, Fournier, and Hoeller 2018). More broadly, this can be reflected at the international level by the ambition to ensure a common framework for paying taxes within the EU, the Common-Consolidated-Corporate-Tax-Base (CCCTB),[3] the aim being to ensure a more consistent tax on the international companies within the EU. There is also ongoing work among 135 countries to put an end to Base Erosion and Profit Shifting (BEPS) by multinational enterprises which is estimated to imply a loss of corporation tax revenue of between 4 % and 10 %.[4] This also includes debates on how to tax based upon location, for example, a tax on the turnover of a company's activities, and how to use transfer-pricing rules.

Naturally, part of the way in which welfare states can be financed depends also on economic growth (McKinsey&Company 2017). However, the distribution of growth is

---

3 See https://ec.europa.eu/taxation_customs/business/company-tax/ccmmon-consolidated-corpora te-tax-base-ccctb_en, accessed 11 August 2021.
4 See https://www.oecd.org/tax/beps/, accessed 11 August 2021.

an important parameter, as well as what form the growth takes, and also the debates on environmental issues.

In some countries, there is the risk that the difference in taxation between the employed and self-employed implies a risk of tax-arbitrage, and thereby lower tax revenue. This is especially the case where part of the overall financing is due to social security contributions paid by the employer for the employed, given there is not the same responsibility to do that for the self-employed (Milanez and Bratta 2019). Thus, increases in solo-self-employed people as a result of increased platform work not only influence job-insecurity, but also state economic insecurity.

Welfare state spending might be more difficult to finance, which can then be detrimental for societal development. As a result, "smart machines can mean long-term misery for all" (Benzell et al. 2015, 20), despite the fact that new technology might imply cheaper products, but still with the need for change in the distribution of income (Peralta-Alva and Roitman 2018). It is often overlooked that income transfers are a form of automatic stabiliser in economic policy (Stiglitz and Rosengaard 2015), and therefore if they cannot be financed then there will be a risk of a negative spiral as the overall demand for goods as a result of new technology will go down. This is the case without income transfers from the welfare states, as those without work do not have the opportunity to buy goods and services. In addition, if redistribution contributes to productivity gains from automation benefiting all generations, then it can contribute to better living conditions for many rather than just a few (Sachs, Benzell, and LaGarda 2015). Thus, the distribution of change in economic development and its impact will be influenced by how the gains are distributed. In a way, this is a classical issue in welfare states' development.

The structure and function of industrial relations can also have an impact, as countries with stronger traditions for co-operation on the labour market might better be able to find solutions acceptable for both workers and companies, but also be better able to cope with people in more precarious positions (Shin and Ylä-Anttila 2018).

Overall, welfare states with stronger automatic stabilisers, high levels of education and good industrial relations systems, and which have been through the transition from classical industrial production towards the services economy are better prepared.

20.5 The platform economy and its impact on labour markets

In recent years, there has been a growth in what is termed the sharing and/or platform economy, etc. Here, the term platform economy is preferred as it indicates that the work is either mediated or directly done via a platform, whereas the sharing economy may include the joint use of a number of goods and services without a profit motive.

This is also because, for example, Uber is not a sharing economy, but shares people's money alone (Sundararajan 2016). Platforms enable the employment of labour worldwide in a variety of areas, but not all areas (Pearson 2015). This has helped to make working conditions more insecure in a number of areas, among other things due to the fact that it is more difficult to organise those active on the platforms into trade-unions, but also that it increases the risk for more non-standard employment (Eichorst and Marx 2015).

The platform economy contributes to the assessment of the development in the number of self-employed persons being less accurate than before, as a number of platforms and similar types of jobs are based on the fact that the individual "owns" his business, although, in reality, it is reminiscent of employment, as well as raising new social security issues (Palier 2019; Behrendt, Nguyen, and Rani 2019; Sundararajan 2016). Furthermore, one can no longer use the development in the number of self-employed persons as an indicator of innovation and new approaches as many of those own-account workers, in reality, are employed and not self-employed. At the same time, the development of solo self-employed can be a way of assessing the impact on the labour market of the new technology as rapid increase here is an indicator of an increase in the gig-economy, but also a blurring of the data on the total level of employment.

In addition to the risk of losing one's job, there are also a number of other problems associated with the application of new technology to the labour markets. It is about the interface between employment and self-employment, where, for example, platform work entails the risk of not being covered by social security schemes, as well as safety and health (Greve 2017), and it can contribute to downward pressure on the quality of work. This can have consequences when online work leads to: "workers usually be denied the right to paid sick leave leads to increased illness morbidity. Working while sick can increase the risk of injury" (Garben 2019, 99), and there is further no guarantee of the use of the individual's qualifications, nor of ensuring the necessary continuing education and up-skilling. It seems that there is a link between welfare regimes and coverage for self-employed workers (Spasova et al. 2019), as more encompassing welfare states also cover platform workers better. This is because, in most welfare states the self-employed are not covered by any welfare benefits, as well as being outside the scope of ALMP. As platform work is often done by "own account workers", combined with the fact that those working on platforms seem to be under-employed (Codagnone, Abadie, and Biagi 2016), this increases the precariousness. The volatility of income when trying to earn on the platform might imply, in societies with less strong social safety nets, fewer automatic stabilisers from the public-sector economy. Part of this also reflects that workers on the platforms can come from all around the world, using a global workforce (Pearson 2015). In many countries, these new kind of jobs also increase the probability that some will do this on a self-employed basis.

In 2016, own-account workers were estimated to be around 10 % of the workforce, and may even have a positive impact on overall employment, but a negative one for employees (Schwellnus et al. 2019). The consequences of platform work although difficult to estimate, are confirmed in another study on the impact of Uber in the US that showed more work was done by taxi-driving, including more self-employed, but also lower hourly wages for hired drivers (Berger, Chen, and Frey 2018).

Lastly, a risk is that income tax from these activities will be reduced if the income level is lower than at the existing labour market, together with the difficulty in taxing the platforms (Blix and Bustos 2020).

20.6 The future of labour market policy

The discussion of the consequences of changes in the labour market often do not seem to involve the fact that, for at least the past 150 years, people have actually used part of the increasing wealth to reduce working time, whether it be hours per day, days per week or more holidays. Thus, in 1870, the working hours across a number of Western countries per week were 64.3, which for men in 2000 was 40.1 and for women 36.3. On average, the annual number of working hours halved and the number of holidays almost tripled (Huberman and Minns 2007). Obviously, part of the benefit of new technology is to bring about better working conditions for some, given that heavy physical work will be reduced as these monotonous types of jobs are some of the first it has been possible to change. So, amidst the strong issue of losers and winners from the changes, there is a group of workers with the possibility of having better working conditions in the future than today.

In a continuation of the historical development, one possibility to cope with the increased risk of inequality on the labour market, and the risk that a growing proportion will be outside the labour market for shorter or longer time-spells, would be to continue to reduce the total working time, so that the existing work is shared between several people. This could be through longer vacations, shorter daily working hours, or a four-day working week rather than a five-day week, as is typical in developed welfare states.

The way in which this would have an impact on the number of people having a job might not be the same in all types of jobs. This is also due to the fact that before the discussion of sharing the number of working hours has gained momentum, a number of companies have already tried to change the work-schedule towards a four-day week, often being closed on Fridays, but also with other variations. It is often argued that a lower number of working hours has not implied a need for more employed people (Pang 2020). This partly reflects the fact that most of the companies making reductions have a number of creative people (marketing, chefs, advertising, IT) and less with face-to-face type of work, such as day-care or elderly care. Still, it implies a paradox that one of the historical ways to ensure that with fewer jobs available, the sharing of working hours was a way to help more people to have a job, might not be available in all sectors. Albeit, it seems that in personal services this should still be an option, so that one might reduce the risk of more split societies as the consequences of increasing levels of unemployment would imply.

Sharing jobs can also include, instead of a continuous increase in the age of retirement, that a larger part of welfare gains is taken out by making it possible to retire and have more life-years outside the labour market, but also that reducing working hours, for example, by working part-time, might make it possible for some to continue longer on the labour market instead of retiring.

Not only job security, but also income security is important. It has thus further been argued that as a consequence of technological changes there is a need for increasing unemployment benefits as well as more ALMP, etc. (Chiacchio, Petropoulos, and Pichler 2018). For a number of reasons, already only a limited number of the unemployed receive unemployment benefits (OECD 2018), including having been unemployed for a long-time, not having worked enough to qualify for benefits, or having paid into an unemployment insurance fund. The coverage of the self-employed is also very rare in welfare states. The reasons vary, but there is also a need to look into how to ensure a living standard for those in very precarious positions on the labour market.

ALMP can continue to help ensure that the necessary competences in order to get a job are available (see section 20.2). This is because – especially on platforms, but also due to the risk of free-riding from companies – given this important task is not solved by the market, it will need intervention by the state. Thereby, ALMP becomes an even more important social policy instrument given the expected rapid transitions on the labour markets. In this context, new ways to ensure effectiveness might be the use of profiling of the unemployed (see Desiere, Langenbucher, and Struyven 2019). However, this might not necessarily help, for example, those platform workers who have qualifications, but there is a lack of demand for their services and who have a high level of job-insecurity.

In order to reduce both the lack of demand (which might cost jobs) and also the degree of social cohesion, it will be important that welfare states' ability to redistribute is retained, including relatively generous benefits when unemployed; without this, rising inequalities and reduced social cohesion will take place. As a consequence, given the possible negative impact on societies' development, it also becomes important to ensure that it is possible to continue to finance the welfare states.

Thereby, that it is not only the number of jobs and how they are distributed that is important for the future development, but also the change in, and the continuity of, the welfare systems to support and help those who, for different reasons, have difficulties in achieving an income and the ability to enter and stay on the labour market during their working lives.

20.7 Some concluding remarks

Undoubtedly, significant changes are on the way in labour markets. These changes will affect many people. Particularly disadvantaged are the unskilled, but also people who are highly specialised in an area that is being automated have a high probability of both losing their jobs and having difficulty re-entering the job market. Whether or not new jobs are created, there will be a transition period, with many being outside the labour market and some never entering it again.

This challenges welfare states in two ways. One is the ability to fund welfare states and welfare services, the other is to ensure some degree of equality between those who have work and those who do not. The risk is a development towards even more fragmented societies with the possible negative impact this will have on social cohesion. The fragmentation can also be increased if social security systems do not adapt towards and ensure the coverage of "own-account" workers, as in many systems they do not have access to coverage of even the historical social risks. Effective and high quality ALMP is also important.

Lastly, there is the question of how the labour market will develop in the years to come. It can be about understanding what work is, but also about continuing the historical evolution of working fewer years and hours in the labour market. It may be too much of a change to move directly to a four-day working week, but this might over time be an option, as well as longer vacations. It may vary from region to region, and from country to country. However, given that robots and AI will be able to take on a large number of jobs and functions, there will be a need to gradually reduce working hours in the coming years if society is not to experience an increased divide between what have historically been called insiders and outsiders.

To sum-up, if one wants to improve the situation on the labour markets and the financing of welfare states, then:
– effective ALMP is important
– new ways to bring security to own-account workers should be implemented
– it should be ensured that platforms pay taxes.

References

Acemoglu, Daron, and Pascual Restrepo. 2017a. "Robots and Jobs: Evidence from US Labor Markets." *SSRN*. https://doi.org/10.2139/ssrn.2940245.

Acemoglu, Daron, and Pascual Restrepo. 2017b. "Secular Stagnation? The Effect of Aging on Economic Growth in the Age of Automation." *American Economic Review* 107 (5), 174–179.

Antonin, Céline, Simon Bunel, Xavier Jaravel, and Philippe Aghion. 2020. "What Are the Labor and Product Market Effects of Automation? New Evidence from France." CEPR Discussion Paper DP14443. Paris.

Autor, David H., Frank Levy, and Richard J. Murnane. 2003. "The Skill Content of Recent Technological Change: An Empirical Exploration." *The Quarterly Journal of Economics* 118 (4), 1279–1333.

Behrendt, Christina, Quynh Anh Nguyen, and Uma Rani. 2019. "Social Protection Systems and the Future of Work: Ensuring Social Security for Digital Platform Workers." *International Social Security Review* 72 (3), 17–41.

Bekker, Sonja. 2018. "Flexicurity in the European Semester: Still a Relevant Policy Concept?" *Journal of European Public Policy* 25 (2), 175–192.

Bekker, S. and M. Mailand. 2019. "The European Flexicurity Concept and the Dutch and Danish Flexicurity Models: How Have They Managed the Great Recession?" *Social Policy & Administration* 53 (1), 142–155.

Benzell, Seth G., Laurence J. Kotlikoff, Guillermo LaGarda, and Jeffrey D. Sachs. 2015. "Robots Are Us: Some Economics of Human Replacement." Cambridge, MA: National Bureau of Economic Research.

Berger, Thor, Chinchih Chen, and Carl Benedikt Frey. 2018. "Drivers of Disruption? Estimating the Uber Effect." *European Economic Review* 110, 197–210.

Blix, Mårten, and Emil Bustos. 2020. "Money for Nothin' – Digitalization and Fluid Tax Bases." IFN Working Paper No. 1316. Stockholm: Research Institute of Industrial Economics.

Bonoli, Giuliano. 2010. "The Political Economy of Active Labor-Market Policy." *Politics & Society* 38 (4), 435–457.

Caliendo, Marco, and Ricarda Schmidl. 2016. "Youth Unemployment and Active Labor Market Policies in Europe." IZA Journal of Labor Policy 5. https://doi.org/10.1186/s40173-016-0057-x.

Card, David, Jochen Kluve, and Andrea Weber. 2018. "What Works? A Meta Analysis of Recent Active Labor Market Program Evaluations." *Journal of the European Economic Association* 16 (3), 894–931.

Case, A., and A. Deaton. 2015. "Rising Morbidity and Mortality in Midlife among White Non-Hispanic Americans in the 21st Century." *Proceedings of the National Academy of Sciences* 112 (49), 15078–15083.

Case, Anne, and Angus Deaton. 2020. *Deaths of Despair and the Future of Capitalism*. Princeton, NJ: Princeton University Press.

Chiacchio, Francesco, Georgios Petropoulos, and David Pichler. 2018. "The Impact of Industrial Robots on EU Employment and Wages: A Local Labour Market Approach." 2. Bruegel Working Paper. https://www.bruegel.org/wp-content/uploads/2018/04/Working-Paper-AB_25042018.pdf

Chung, Heejung. 2016. "Dualization and Subjective Employment Insecurity: Explaining the Subjective Employment Insecurity Divide between Permanent and Temporary Workers across 23 European Countries." *Economic and Industrial Democracy* 40 (3), 700–729.

Codagnone, C., F. Abadie, and F. Biagi. 2016. "The Future of Work in the 'Sharing Economy'. Market Efficiency and Equitable Opportunities or Unfair Precarisation?" Brussels: Publications Office of the European Union.

Cournède, Boris, Jean-Marc Fournier, and Peter Hoeller. 2018. "Public Finance Structure and Inclusive Growth," no. 25. https://doi.org/10.1787/e99683b5-en.

Desiere, Sam, Kristine Langenbucher, and Ludo Struyven. 2019. "Statistical Profiling in Public Employment Services." OECD Social, Migration and Employment Papers, no. 224. https://doi.org/10.1787/b5e5f16e-en.

Eichorst, W., and P. Marx. (eds). 2015. *Non-Standard Employment in Post-Industrial Labour Markets. An Occupational Perspective*. Cheltenham: Edward Elgar.

Ford, Martin. 2015. *The Rise of the Robots: Technology and the Threat of Mass Unemployment*. London: Oneworld Publications.

Fossati, Flavia. 2018. "Who Wants Demanding Active Labour Market Policies? Public Attitudes towards Policies That Put Pressure on the Unemployed." *Journal of Social Policy* 47 (1), 77–97.

Frey, Carl Benedikt. 2019. *The Technology Trap: Capital, Labor, and Power in the Age of Automation*. Princeton, NJ: Princeton University Press. Kindle edition.

Garben, Sacha. 2019. "The Regulatory Challenge of Occupational Safety and Health in the Online Platform Economy." *International Social Security Review* 72 (3), 95–112.

Global Affairs. 2017. "The Fourth Industrial Revolution." https://doi.org/10.17226/24699.

Gregory, Terry, Anna Salomons, and Ulrich Zierahn. 2019. "Racing With or Against the Machine? Evidence from Europe." IZA DP No. 12063. https://docs.iza.org/dp12063.pdf.

Greve, B. 2017. *Technology and the Future of Work. The Impact on Labour Markets and Welfare States.* Cheltenham: Edward Elgar.

Helliwell, John F., and Haifang Huang. 2014. "New Measures of the Costs of Unemployment: Evidence from the Subjective Well-being of 3.3 Million Americans." *Economic Inquiry* 52 (4), 1485–1502.

Huberman, Michael, and Chris Minns. 2007. "The Times They Are Not Changin': Days and Hours of Work in Old and New Worlds, 1870–2000." *Explorations in Economic History* 44 (4), 538–567.

Im, Zhen Jie, and Kathrin Komp-Leukkunen. 2021. "Automation and Public Support for Workfare." *Journal of European Social Policy* 31 (4), 457–472.

Kreshpaj, Bertina, Cecilia Orellana, Bo Burström, Letitia Davis, Tomas Hemmingsson, Gun Johansson, Katarina Kjellberg, Johanna Jonsson, David H Wegman, and Theo Bodin. 2020. "What Is Precarious Employment? A Systematic Review of Definitions and Operationalizations from Quantitative and Qualitative Studies." *Scandinavian Journal of Work, Environment & Health* 46 (3), 235–247.

McKinsey&Company. 2017. "Shaping the Future of Work in Europe's Digital Front-Runners." https://www.mckinsey.com/~/media/mckinsey/featured%20insights/europe/shaping%20the%20future%20of%20work%20in%20europes%20nine%20digital%20front%20runner%20countries/shaping-the-future-of-work-in-europes-digital-front-runners.ashx

Milanez, Anna, and Barbara Bratta. 2019. "Taxation and the Future of Work: How Tax Systems Influence Choice of Employment Form." OECD Taxation Working Papers. Paris: OECD. https://doi.org/10.1787/20f7164a-en.

Nedelkoska, Ljubica, and Glenda Quintini, G. 2018. "Automation, Skills Use and Training." OECD, Social, Employment and Migration Working Papers 202. Paris: OECD. https://doi.org/10.1787/2e2f4eea-en.

Neve, Jan-Emmanuel De, Christian Krekel, and George Ward. 2018. "Work and Well-Being: A Global Perspective." *Global Happiness Policy Report*, 74–128.

Nordlund, Madelene, and Bent Greve. 2019. "Focus on Active Labour Market Policies." In *The Routledge Handbook of the Welfare State*, edited by Bent Greve, 2nd ed., 366–377. London and New York: Routledge.

OECD. 2018. *Employment Outlook, 2018.* Paris: OECD.

Palier, Bruno. 2019. "Work, Social Protection and the Middle Classes: What Future in the Digital Age?" *International Social Security Review* 72 (3), 113–133.

Pang, Alex Soojung-Kim. 2020. *Shorter: How Working Less Will Revolutionise the Way Your Company Gets Things Done.* London: Penguin Books.

Pearson, T. 2015. *The End of Jobs. Money, Meaning and Freedom without the 9 to 5.* Austin, TX: Lioncrest Publishing.

Peralta-Alva, A., and A. Roitman. 2018. "Technology and the Future of Work." WP/18/207. IMF Working Paper.

PWC. 2017. "Will Robots Steal Our Jobs? The Potential Impact of Automation." https://www.pwc.co.uk/economic-services/ukeo/pwcukeo-section-4-automation-march-2017-v2.pdf.

PWC. 2018. "Will Robots Really Steal Our Jobs? An International Analysis of the Potential Long Term Impact of Automation." 2018. https://www.pwc.co.uk/economic-services/assets/international-impact-of-automation-feb-2018.pdf.

Rueda, David. 2014. "Dualization, Crisis and the Welfare State." *Socio-Economic Review* 12 (2), 381–407.

Sachs, J., Z. Benzell, and G. LaGarda, G. 2015. "Robots: Curse or Blessing? A Basic Framework." 21091. *NBER Working Paper Series*. Cambridge, MA: National Bureau of Economic Research.

Schwab, K. 2016. *The Fourth Industrial Revolution. Davos*: World Economic Forum.

Schwellnus, Cyrille, Assaf Geva, Mathilde Pak, and Rafael Veiel. 2019. "Gig Economy Platforms: Boon or Bane?" OECD Economics Department Working Papers 1550. Paris: OECD.

Shin, Young-Kyu, and Tuomas Ylä-Anttila. 2018. "New Social Risk Groups, Industrial Relations Regimes and Union Membership." *Journal of European Social Policy* 23 (3), 242–254.

Spasova, Slavina, Denis Bouget, Dalila Ghailani, and Bart Vanhercke. 2019. "Self-Employment and Social Protection: Understanding Variations between Welfare Regimes." *Journal of Poverty and Social Justice* 27 (2), 157–175.

Stiglitz, J., and J. Rosengaard. 2015. *Economics of the Public Sector*. 4th ed. London: W. W. Norton & Company.

Sundararajan, Arun. 2016. *The Sharing Economy: The End of Employment and the Rise of Crowd-Based Capitalism*. Cambridge, MA: MIT Press.

Tros, Frank, and Ton Wilthagen. 2013. "Flexicurity: Concepts, Practices, and Outcomes." In *The Routledge Handbook of the Welfare State*, edited by B. Greve, 1st ed., 125–135. London and New York: Routledge.

Vooren, Melvin, Carla Haelermanst, Wim Groot, and Henriëtte Maassen van den Brink. 2016. "The Effectiveness Of Active Labour Market Policies: A Systematic Meta-Analysis." *Journal of Economic Survey*, 33 (1), 125–149.

Yoon, Y. and H. Chung. 2016. "New Forms of Dualization? Labour Market Segmentation Patterns in the UK from the Late 90s Until the Post-Crisis in the Late 2000s." *Social Indicator Research* 128, 609–631.

Paul Bridgen and Mi Ah Schoyen

21 Sustainability

Abstract: Consideration of sustainability in the comparative welfare state literature over recent decades has mainly focused on economic and demographic parameters. This chapter draws on an emerging literature which suggests an ecological dimension, especially the global climate crisis, must be brought into these discussions. This literature includes efforts to conceptualise eco-social states, political economies that aspire to reconcile social and ecological considerations, and theoretical work on transitions to such arrangements.

The chapter delineates three approaches to sustainability and their policy recommendations for a transition to future low-carbon welfare states – ecological modernisation or green growth, the Green New Deal or egalitarian growth, and post-growth approaches. In the context of these three approaches, it reviews the literature on transitions to an eco-social state, focusing particularly on whether some types of welfare state are better placed than others to achieve this.

The chapter finishes by briefly outlining the future research agenda. It suggests that most important in this respect are: (i) the need for theoretical innovations to develop new models of sustainable institutional arrangements; and (ii) the development of a better theoretical and empirical understanding of how countries or governments can manage eco-social state transitions.

Keywords: sustainable welfare, ecological modernisation, eco-social policy, post-growth, Green New Deal, environmental crisis

21.1 Introduction

In the abundant scholarship on welfare state restructuring of the past thirty years or so, questions about the future *sustainability* of welfare states have mainly focused on economic and demographic parameters. Concerns over tight budget constraints due to international competition, government debt, budget deficits and population ageing have dominated policy discourses and predictions about welfare state futures. This chapter adopts a different perspective on sustainability. We draw on the emerging literature suggesting an ecological dimension, especially the global climate crisis, must be brought into discussions about contemporary threats to mature welfare states; that conceptualising and promoting eco-social states is necessary, i.e. states that aspire to reconcile social and ecological considerations within a political economy that treats equally economic, social and ecological objectives. If we look beyond traditional welfare state research, this conceptualisation of sustainability – conceived as a continuous interplay between the ecological, social and economic spheres – is quite conventional.

https://doi.org/10.1515/9783110721768-021

There are several reasons why environmental threats, and most pressingly climate change, are relevant to welfare states. First, climate change is widely accepted as one of the greatest policy challenges of the twenty-first century. European Commission President Ursula van der Leyen's State of the Union Address in September 2020 exemplifies the central position climate change already takes on global and European political agendas. She emphasised: "There is no more urgent need for acceleration than when it comes to the future of our fragile planet. While much of the world's activity froze during lockdowns and shutdowns, the planet continued to get dangerously hotter" (Van der Leyen 2020). The authoritative Intergovernmental Panel on Climate Change (IPCC) has repeatedly illustrated the potentially wide-ranging implications of global warming for the planet and populations across the world (e.g. IPCC 2014; 2019; 2021). In some locations, climate change has already had negative consequences for food security, ecosystems and biodiversity and is linked to more frequent episodes of extreme weather events such as heavy rainfalls, floods, and heatwaves. These natural events affect humans and societies. Prolonged extreme heat adversely affects public health and reduce people's work capacity. Violent rainfalls and floods are associated with damages to people's housing or livelihoods. In sum, global warming generates new social risks which the welfare state should address. More fundamentally, the challenges raised by climate change also encourage a re-consideration of the parameters, purpose and targets of welfare states. In a world more aware of limitations in the availability or usability of natural resources, the concept of sustainability extends transnationally and inter-generationally the scope of consideration of welfare needs.

Second, the urgency of the need to slow down global warming means governments, especially in the Global North, are under pressure to restructure their production and employment systems. Opinions differ on the required scale of this restructuring, but ultimately consumption patterns may also be affected. A low-carbon economic and societal transformation is likely to place greater demands on social protection systems, public employment services, social regulation and public investments in education and building infrastructure. Workers whose jobs are affected, will need income maintenance and other forms of support – for instance, via public employment services and the education system – to find alternative career paths. Citizens will face increasing expectations to switch from fossil to renewable energy sources, for instance in domestic heating. Social interventions will be required to ensure the costs of such transitions do not fall on those least able to bear the cost, particularly given their smaller carbon footprint. In the literature this relationship is sometimes referred to as a "double injustice" (e.g. Gough 2019).

Third, simultaneously, governments in advanced democracies still face the challenge of "balancing pressures on public spending" (Taylor-Gooby 2011, 11). Ecologically-driven restructuring may thus reduce the budgetary scope for public spending on social protection and other areas of (costly) state welfare. Governments will want to direct an increasing share of economic resources towards policy initiatives capable of nudging societies in a low-carbon direction, currently endorsed by the European Parliament and the Council.[1]

For comparative welfare state research, the implications of adopting this more holistic and, in practical terms, more demanding perspective on welfare state sustainability are considerable. We need theoretical innovation to develop new models of sustainable institutional arrangements. Moreover, we need a better understanding of how governments can manage the transition to eco-social states offering social protection within planetary resource boundaries, independent of carbon-intensive forms of economic growth. In this regard, there is still much conceptual and not least empirical groundwork to do. For instance, are some types of welfare regimes or political economies advantaged because of favourable institutional conditions or policy legacies?

Against this background, the aim of the chapter is threefold. First, it introduces literature we consider most relevant to discussions of welfare state sustainability. It will take a political economy perspective, outlining three main approaches to sustainability and their policy recommendations for a transition to future low-carbon welfare states. The main distinctions are between ecological modernisation (EM) or green growth, the Green New Deal (or egalitarian growth), and post-growth approaches. Secondly, in the context of these three approaches we consider the literature on transitions to an eco-social state. Finally, we briefly outline the future research agenda on eco-social or sustainable welfare states.

21.2 Three political economy approaches to sustainable welfare

A wide-ranging consensus now exists that the seriousness of the threats posed by climate change compels a significant transformation in social and economic practices at a global level. With Joe Biden's election in the United States, the last, significant outpost of climate change denial in the Global North was removed. Biden approved his country's re-engagement with the Paris Agreement and in April 2021 committed the US to halve GHG emissions by 2030 (based on 2002 emission levels) using some of a $2 trillion infrastructure plan to boost investment in clean energy (Khan et al. 2021). Similarly, the European Commission announced in March 2020 a "European Green Deal", which committed the Union to reducing emissions by at least 55 % over the decade, against 1990 levels (Khan et al. 2021). The United Nations, in the meantime, has re-committed its members to urgent action to meet its longstanding Sustainable

---

1 See Commission website on the Clean Energy for all Europeans package: https://ec.europa.eu/energy/topics/energy-strategy/clean-energy-all-europeans_en (accessed 26 April 2021).

Development Goals (SDG). Many nations have committed themselves to targets for achieving net zero[2] GHG emissions, most by 2050, others sooner (United Nations 2015).

Yet, notwithstanding this consensus, disagreement is still widespread about what action should entail – how fundamental a transformation is required particularly in the existing social and economic practices of the Global North. For example, while the United States' recent plan focused on private sector-led technological solutions, the EU plan envisaged a stronger role for the state and broader changes in citizens' way of life (Khan et al 2021). The pace of the transition is also frequently debated and contested. Two illustrative examples in this regard are the long-standing debate about the phasing out of coal as part of Germany's energy transition (*Energiewende*) (Litz 2019) and the question of future oil production in Norway (Froggatt et al. 2020). Outside government, among other political actors and academics, policymakers' commitments are more fundamentally questioned, particularly whether there is a full appreciation of the transformative change necessary to control global temperature rise below the 1.5 degree centigrade increase since pre-industrial times (IPCC 2014).

These disagreements in the Global North can be delineated based on three general approaches: EM or green growth; the Green New Deal (GND); and Post- or de-growth. While there are some important crossovers particularly between the first two approaches, significant differences exist between them with respect to the scale of social and economic change required to prevent dangerous climate change, the state's role in facilitating this change and how centrally they embed social policy concerns in their frameworks. Each approach differs, in short, with respect to their understanding of sustainability and the type of eco-social state, if any, required to embed this concept in public policy. In what follows, we detail the implications of these differences for welfare state development over coming decades.

21.2.1 Ecological modernisation as green growth

EM is the mainstream position on sustainability closest to the approach pursued by most Global North governments. The approach does not question market-based capitalist principles and the desirability of growth but proposes economic restructuring in line with environmental standards (Dryzek 2013; Hayden 2014). To address climate change, growth in economic output (or GDP) has to be decoupled from carbon emissions and resource use (Koch 2018). This process of decoupling demands considerable technological progress in a relatively short amount of time (Smulders, Toman, and Withagen 2014). An expansion of green economic sectors would bring environmental

---

2 Net zero has been interpreted differently between nations, but is generally understood as a goal of reducing carbon (GHG) emission as low as possible with any continuing emissions captured or offset.

benefits, while also creating employment opportunities ("green jobs"), thereby weakening or even fully removing the strong correlation between growth and emissions. Such mechanisms would balance environmental and economic concerns enabling a future where economic growth remains the primary goal of policymakers. Indeed, according to the influential UK Stern Review (Stern 2007), the central motivation for addressing global warming is to prevent the long-term economic damage it would otherwise wreak (OECD 2011; European Commission 2019).

Jänicke (2008, 558), who identified EM discourses in German political debates already in the 1980s, highlights the belief "in the possibility of ecological-economic 'win-win' solutions, achieved, above all, through cost reduction and competition for innovation". Crucial is the role attributed to technological progress incentivised by public policy. Three objectives are central: increased efficiency in resource usage; technological innovations; and the commercial opportunities created by environmental challenges, such as the development of renewable energy. The last of these particularly ensures continued opportunities for capital accumulation despite restrictions in some emission-heavy markets (Barry and Paterson 2004).

EM proponents generally accept state intervention will increase: the required change is now too great and urgent to be left entirely to markets. However, the state's role should be limited to correcting market failures within a predominantly liberal market economic framework. This means widespread use of market-based instruments, such as tradeable permits and eco-taxes, to shift corporate and individual behaviours away from environmental "bads" towards those involving lower GHG emissions (Stern 2007). The UK Treasury's Stern Review, on which many subsequent EM reports (e.g., OECD 2011) and policy proposals have been based, envisaged three types of policy initiatives:

1. Carbon pricing – justified economically because environment degradation is an externality of market exchanges, i.e. GHG emitters do not fully bear the costs of their actions.
2. Technology policy (e.g. R&D incentives) designed to promote low-carbon, high-efficiency technologies needed for deep emissions cuts.
3. Regulation, information and financing policies to remove barriers to eco-friendly behavioural change by consumers (Stern 2007, 308–309).

EM's commitment to existing economic goals and limited, market-based state interventions, means climate change is not regarded as posing fundamental problems for Global North welfare states. Actions to reduce climate change are largely consistent with the type of competition state green growth proponents favour. Indeed, increased efficiency might in the longer term raise growth levels (ETC 2020) while shifts from labour-based to environmental taxation could raise employment levels (NAO 2021). It is accepted that the introduction of carbon taxes and GHG reduction will create distributive challenges (Stern 2007), but only very limited attention has been given to addressing them. Generally favoured are limited labour market interventions to encourage re-training and improve skills, and targeted forms of financial compensation to the most-affected groups (OECD 2011, 26).

21.2.2 The Green New Deal – egalitarian growth

Since its development in the early 1990s, critiques of the EM approach have focused on three main aspects. First, critics have argued the EM approach underestimates the scale of the climate crisis and is excessively optimistic about the likely speed of technological innovation. Secondly, the EM approach downplays the extent to which climate change is an inherent product of capitalism, particularly in its neo-liberal form. Thirdly, EM fails to sufficiently embed considerations of social justice. Two main alternative approaches to EM currently compete with it and each other in the literature – the GND (or egalitarian growth) and Post- or de-growth. This section considers the first of these.

The GND originated in work by the New Economics Foundation (2008) and the UN Environmental Programme (Barbier 2010) in the late noughties as a response to post-financial crisis austerity, proposing as an alternative a kind of green Keynesianism focused on green investment and job creation. Variants of the GND have since been adopted, at least discursively, by a range of political actors across countries of the Global North, including left Democrats in the US (116th Congress 1st Session 2019). The "new deal" label thus deliberately harks back to the ambitious programme of public economic and social intervention pursued after the Great Depression in the 1930s.

Notwithstanding criticism of EM, the GND shares some basic assumptions. Most importantly, while strongly critical of neo-liberalism, the GND does not demand fundamental economic and social change: capitalism requires reform not abolition; growth remains possible, both in the Global North and South. Similar to the EM approach, the GND thus views technological change, particularly a rapid move towards "clean energy", as the primary means for addressing global warming (Pollin 2019). The aim is not to restrict global economic expansion, suggests Pollin (2019), one of the leading proponents of a GND, but to focus it on green investments designed to facilitate an absolute decoupling of output growth and GHG emissions.

Where the GND approach differs most from EM is its scepticism towards market-based interventions alone to facilitate necessary changes, a concern encouraged by the slow pace of reforms since the early 1990s and mounting IPCC evidence (2021) climate change is advancing more rapidly than expected. In this context, the GND approach suggests greater public action both at a national and international level. Thus, for example, Pollin calls for "a worldwide program" to raise energy-efficiency standards and expand clean renewable energy supply amounting to 1.5–2% of global GDP per year designed to reduce global CO_2 emissions by 40% relative to today within 20 years.

The GND approach also incorporates a much stronger concern for social justice. Job creation is centre stage. Thus Pollin's work on a range of locations suggests significant increases in job creation wherever green investment takes place (2019, 315). Gough, similarly, points to Germany's success using investment and interest rate subsidies since 2006 in creating 900,000 jobs in retrofitting homes and public buildings (2017, 143). This greater faith in the state's role is also reflected in proposals for more extensive and elaborate compensation schemes than suggested by EM. Thus, to support workers displaced by the shift away from fossil fuels or affected by carbon pricing, Pollin suggests a threefold approach: 1) income, retraining, and relocation support for workers facing retrenchments; 2) pension guarantees for workers in the affected industries; and 3) transition programmes for fossil-fuel dependent communities. The German "coal compromise" did much of this. The Commission on Growth, Structural Change and Employment recommended the full closure of all German coal fired power plants by 2038 in return for substantial structural investments in the affected coal mining regions. It also paid careful attention to ensuring a just transition for affected workers (Commission on Growth, Structural Change and Employment 2019).

Gough goes further, outlining a more fully worked through scheme embedding social policy in the GND (2017). He proposes new "proactive" and "integrated" forms of "eco-social" policy as opposed to the "reactive and countervailing" EM approaches. He regards the latter as problematic because of targeting difficulties and expense (2017, 139). Much better are policies within which both environmental and social objectives are fully and simultaneously embedded. This generally involves targeting GHG emission reductions on higher income groups by, for example, distinguishing between necessitous and non-necessitous/luxury goods. Thus, for example, a large-scale publicly financed or subsidised domestic energy efficiency programmes, targeting those in fuel poverty (Gough 2017, 141–142), would be a way of significantly reducing a major source of GHG emissions, while protecting those who spend the greatest proportion of their income on domestic energy (Büchs, Bardsley, and Duwe 2011; Gough 2017, 152–153). In a similar vein, a "smart" consumption tax could be levied on high-carbon, non-necessitous items, such as frequent flying; and personal carbon allowances, could be introduced allocating to each adult citizen the same amount of annual emissions. More generally, Gough (2017, 162–163) proposes an increase in tax-financed social consumption, particularly in the utility sector as a means to redistributive provision according to need, reduce private consumption and increase energy efficiency.

21.2.3 Post-growth

The strongest criticism of EM comes from commentators who argue only fundamental institutional change to modern capitalism is sufficient given the scale of emerging environmental challenges (e.g. Jackson 2017; Koch 2013; Victor 2008). Successful action to prevent dangerous climate change requires, it is suggested, a paradigmatic shift in public policy goals in the Global North (Hall 1993): at the very least policy must become indifferent to whether growth occurs. For discussions about the future of welfare states a particularly relevant variant of the post-growth perspective is that of "sustainable welfare", developed most consistently in the works of Max Koch (2013; 2018; Koch et al. 2016; Koch and Mont 2016). Central, is a normative argument for a much more equal global distribution of resources. In short, sustainable welfare "[...] is oriented towards satisfying human needs within ecological limits, from an intergenerational and global perspective" (Koch et al. 2016, 704).

The post-growth orientation is based particularly on scepticism about the plausibility of EM's central claim, that rising GHG emissions can be absolutely decoupled from economic growth. Post-growth scholars highlight that, despite economists' optimistic modelling, almost no countries have yet achieved absolute decoupling, particularly when trade-related emissions (i.e. those produced in other countries as part of the manufacture of imported goods) are accounted for (Schor and Jorgenson 2019; Knight and Schor 2014; Cohen et al. 2017; Jackson 2017). EM's and the GND's focus on technological innovation is important, but will simply not be enough (Gough 2017, 172).

One consequence of this more radical approach is a focus on general consumption levels: they will need to significantly decline in the Global North so that any future growth and GHG emissions are focused globally where they are most needed (Gough 2017, 146–49; Jackson 2017: 202). The Global North would operate some form of "steady state" economy under which a constant aggregate throughput of resources would occur at a level to ensure long-term sustainability (Daly 1996). Some sectoral growth might occur and the private sector could continue to play a role but the size of the public sector would substantially increase. Only the state, suggests Jackson (2017: 222), can ensure the longer term, less productive types of investment essential for sustainability.

The consequences of this type of fundamental economic transformation for social policy would be substantial. The post-war Keynesian welfare state was after all built on a growth assumption both as a means of financing its expansion, through rising tax revenues, and as a facilitator of redistribution acceptable to the middle classes. Büchs (2021a) argues for such a transformation but nevertheless outlines clearly the scale of contemporary European welfare states' growth dependencies. For instance, labour market policy often focuses on the enhancement of human capital and workers' productivity and employees tend to pay pension contributions hoping to maintain more or less their purchasing power when they withdraw from the labour market. Maintaining large public pension systems in the face of population ageing, it is agreed, would pose a particular challenge.

Post-growth scholars suggest policy would have to be concertedly need-focused to cope with such circumstances (Gough 2017, 38–63). A minimum and maximum level of income would be set (Daly 2007) and wealth ownership more broadly distributed, through for example social dividends on capital formation (Gough 2017, 180–181). Some post-growth advocates propose a Universal Basic Income, a regular rights-based benefit or even Universal Basic Services, i.e., unconditional public services to meet universally basic needs (Büchs 2021b). Others question such universal and expensive expansions of the central state's financial role (Gough 2017, 184–186), with some favouring radically decentralised needs-based state provision incorporating "co-production" (Ostrom 1996) and communal involvement.

Consideration has also been given to reduced working time as a means to reduce growth, lower income and thus consumption while, at the same time, improving work/life balances with potential wellbeing benefits (Schor 1991; Victor and Jackson 2013) – a classic eco-social synergy. However, such a policy faces considerable distributive challenges. Compulsory restrictions, for example, would hit hardest those in low wage jobs reliant on long hours (Gough 2017, 190).

The scale of these changes inevitably raises questions of political feasibility (Gough 2017, 208). The post-growth literature has succeeded in clearly delineating the ecological and normative challenges generated by the current economic order without yet identifying policy levers that make a transformative transition a practical proposition. In terms of imagined welfare state futures, moreover, there is a conceptual and practical tension between calls for a large, active state directing long-term public investment and universal needs and rights-based welfare programmes, on the one hand, and a decentralised, local level (welfare) state favouring citizen participation, on the other.

Table 21.1: Summary of core arguments in the three approaches[3]

	The scale of social and economic change	Role of the state	Role of social policy
Economic modernisation	– Win-win situation, as green growth will solve the ecological crisis – Technological progress important premise – Market-based capitalist structures not questioned – Economic growth desirable, but must follow environmental standards	– Limited: correct market failures and incentivise technological progress (through tradable permits, taxation), support commercial opportunities (e.g. in renewable energy)	– "Reactive" approach: transition entails some distributive challenges for compensating the losers (targeted support, retraining)

---

3 We are grateful to Maria Petmesidou for suggesting this concise way of synthesising our arguments.

Table 21.1 (continued)

	The scale of social and economic change	Role of the state	Role of social policy
Green (New) Deal	– Critical of neo-liberal growth models – Capitalism requires reform not abolition – Substantial technological change necessary and possible	– Active and facilitating role (e.g., via green investments) – Promote programmes for raising energy efficiency worldwide	– "Proactive" and "integrated" forms of "eco-social" policy (e.g., extensive compensation schemes to offset costs for vulnerable groups)
Post-growth	– Fundamental systemic changes in Global North political economies – Decoupling at the speed needed for averting environmental degradation not possible	– Paradigmatic shift in public policy goals (extensive intervention by the eco-social state) – Promote well-being in a "steady-state" economy	– Reconfiguration of social policy/welfare states – Needs-based policy (e.g., Universal Basic Income, Universal Social Services)

21.3 Towards an eco-social state

The three preceding sections have thus shown that broadening discussions about welfare state sustainability to include an ecological dimension implies on some readings fundamental changes in the way welfare states operate. EM has the least implications. In contrast, the GND and much more so post-growth perspectives demand a paradigmatic shift (Hall 1993). Some type of eco-social state would maximise citizens' welfare but rest on less optimistic assumptions about the compatibility between existing production and consumption patterns in the Global North and the satisfaction of transnational and intergenerational needs within planetary limits. To a lesser or greater extent, an innovative and synergistic approach to eco-social policy development, would be required under which "simultaneously and explicitly ... [policies] pursue both equity/justice and sustainability/sufficiency goals" (Gough 2017, 197). Reliance on downstream, offsetting economic compensations would decline in favour of upstream efforts, involving bureaucratic coordination, shifts in state/market relationships and cost redistribution (Gough 2019, 146–147; see also Golubchikov and Deda 2012).

This transformational imperative directs attention to institutional arrangements likely to facilitate or obstruct such developments. Attention has focused particularly on the institutional context provided by existing deeply entrenched welfare institutions (Gough et al. 2008), with welfare capitalist regime theory used as an analytical framework (Dryzek et al. 2003; Esping-Andersen 1990; Hall and Soskice 2001). Such regimes constitute highly complex, self-reinforcing institutional configurations, determined over time by the balance of economic, political and social forces. Social democratic, conservative, liberal – and perhaps Southern European – worlds of welfare, it is suggested, will respond distinctively to external challenges (Pierson 2001).

Using such frameworks, Dryzek reached the "provisional conclusion" that in response to the external challenge of climate change, social democratic coordinated capitalism is most suited to managing environmental/social policy interaction in a way that "mainstream[s] ... both environmental and equality concerns" (Gough et al. 2008, 330). Institutionally, strong, inclusive and integrated corporatist welfare states mean bureaucratic capacity and interest intermediation processes are sufficient to manage environmental/social policy coordination without exacerbating existing inequities (Dryzek et al. 2003; Gough 2016; 2017). Eco-social synergies are aided by the greater egalitarian commitment, at least historically, of social democratic welfare states with levels of inequality comparatively lower (Halvorsen, Hvinden, and Schoyen 2016). Citizens are accustomed to and to some degree accept taxes and levies directed at specific behaviour, for example, sugar consumption or car driving (see Umit and Schaffer 2020). Proportional electoral systems, ensuring greater Green Party representation (Carter 2013), aid the general adoption of EM discourses. Thus more expected are thoroughgoing eco-social approaches, upstream interventions to enhance policy coordination, correct market inequalities and redistribute costs. Where conservative welfare states share such social democratic features, similar eco-social developments would be expected.

Liberal welfare capitalism, in contrast, is expected to be less conducive to eco-social policy development (Bridgen 2021). Its strong liberal ideological and institutional legacies mean the state is smaller and less coordinated (Hall and Soskice 2001, 13); there has been a preference for market and voluntary solutions (Esping-Andersen 1990, 42), a faith strongly reinforced by the rise of neo-liberalism. The integration of different policy objectives is thus more difficult, particularly given carbon-producing energy companies are strongly placed to resist unwanted social interventions (Dryzek et al. 2003; Geels 2014). Green business will be weaker (Bridgen 2021). Politically, first-past-the-post electoral systems weaken the incentives for mainstream political parties to integrate environmental issues fully into their agendas (Carter 2013). Even an EM approach makes limited headway. Eco-social policy is expected at best to involve the incremental, uncoordinated and upstream interventions (Gough 2013).

Theoretical and empirical scrutiny of such conclusions is embryonic. Theoretically, arguments rest (implicitly) on more rigid regime models, which emphasise entrenched obstacles to change rather than more recent dynamic theories of institutional change (e.g. Streeck and Thelen 2005, 26). Empirically, early tests of eco-social policy development are mainly quantitative and tend not to operationalise eco-social policy in a way designed to highlight policy synergies (e.g. Koch and Fritz 2014; Jakobsson, Muttarak, and Schoyen 2017). Results are mixed. Koch and Fritz's study is mainly one of policy succession rather than policy synergies i.e. whether countries with comprehensive welfare states result in institutional conditions that are more favourable to stringent environmental legislation and regulation. Perhaps for this reason they find few connections between welfare regimes, environmental outcomes and attitudes (Koch and Fritz 2014). Zimmermann and Graziano (2020), more concertedly explore connections between states' environmental and social outcomes in the context of broader regime features. They find some support for Dryzek's conclusions in that the "best existing eco-social states" (in terms of outcomes) are found in their cluster of mainly Nordic countries, a result primarily explained, they suggest, by the influence of union density. However, overall, the picture is mixed, with economic factors (e.g. GDP levels), rather than social ones, more clearly related to environmental performance.

Thus, overall, while these studies are useful and suggestive, they are not designed appropriately to test Dryzek's predicted causal dynamics. Such a test requires in-depth qualitative institutional analyses (Hall 2003) to trace the impact of pre-existing policy legacies on subsequent eco-social policy development, with the latter operationalised explicitly in relation to policy synergies. Only Bridgen's (2021) case study of the domestic energy efficiency in the liberal UK has so far adopted this type of approach. He finds that in this policy area, liberal capitalism's institutional and ideational constraints have, as expected, inhibited eco-social synergies, but that innovative political agents (i.e. policy entrepreneurs) operating in more fluid institutional contexts than envisaged by rigid forms of regime theory have been able to generate a more dynamic eco-social policy process than regime-centred predications suggest.

21.4 Conclusion

In the abundant scholarship on welfare state restructuring of the past thirty years or so, questions of sustainability have mainly been discussed on the basis of economic and demographic parameters. In this chapter we adopted a different perspective on sustainability, drawing instead on the emerging literature that suggests that the ecological dimension and especially the global climate crisis have to be brought into the discussion of challenges to mature welfare states. As has been seen much of this literature argues that rather than traditional welfare states we now need to move towards eco-social states, i.e. political economic systems that give at least as much weight to social and ecological priorities as economic ones.

Against this background, the chapter took a political economy perspective, to outline the three main approaches to sustainability and detail the policies recommended in the transition to future low-carbon welfare states. Here the main distinctions were between EM, the GND, and post-growth approaches. Debates between these perspectives, both between policymakers and governments, and between scholars, are intense and ongoing. In the final section, we summarised the literature on transitions to an eco-social state.

It is clear from the above that the implications of adopting a more holistic and, in practical terms, more demanding perspective on welfare state sustainability are considerable. Work has started on this task but much more is required. Most important in this respect are theoretical innovations to develop new models of sustainable institutional arrangements and the development of a better understanding of how countries or governments can manage the transition to a kind of eco-social state. EM currently dominates given its general support from the most powerful global actors. Its critics have, so far, succeeded better in identifying flaws than fashioning a coherent alternative. With notable exceptions (Gough 2017), the GND remains more a slogan than a fully worked-through framework for action, capable of being applied flexibly in different national contexts. Post-growth perspectives, on the other hand, while attractive for their attention to intergenerational and global justice and the ability to move beyond the Western and European-centredness common in mainstream welfare state literature, are still quite far away from articulating convincing political solutions. We still know far too little about the institutional conditions and policy legacies more or less conducive to more radical systemic changes to modern capitalist political economies. In short, there is still much conceptual and not least empirical groundwork to do.

References

116th Congress 1st Session. 2019. *H. RES. 109 – Recognizing the Duty of the Federal Government to Create a Green New Deal*. 116th Congress (2019–2020). https://www.congress.gov/bill/116th-congress/house-resolution/109/text.

Barbier, Edward B. 2010. *A Global Green New Deal: Rethinking the Economic Recovery*. Cambridge: Cambridge University Press.

Barry, John, and Matthew Paterson. 2004. "Globalisation, Ecological Modernisation and New Labour." *Political Studies* 52 (4), 767–784.

Bridgen, Paul. 2021. *"Eco-Social Policy Development in Liberal Capitalism: Obstacles and Opportunities in the UK's Efforts to Equitably Improve Domestic Energy Efficiency, 1992–2015."* Forthcoming.

Büchs, Milena. 2021a. "Sustainable Welfare: Independence between Growth and Welfare Has to Go Both Ways." *Global Social Policy* 21 (2), 323–327.

Büchs, Milena. 2021b. "Sustainable Welfare: How Do Universal Basic Income and Universal Basic Services Compare?' *Ecological Economics* 189 (November), 107152. https://doi.org/10.1016/j.ecolecon.2021.107152.

Büchs, Milena, Nicholas Bardsley, and Sebastian Duwe. 2011. "Who Bears the Brunt? Distributional Effects of Climate Change Mitigation Policies." *Critical Social Policy* 31 (2), 285–307.

Carter, Neil. 2013. "Greening the Mainstream: Party Politics and the Environment." *Environmental Politics* 22 (1), 73–94.

Cohen, Gail, João Tovar Jalles, Prakash Loungani, and Ricard Marto. 2017. "Emissions and Growth: Trends and Cycles in a Globalized World." *IMF Working Paper* 17 (191), 1–56.

Commission on Growth, Structural Change and Employment. 2019. *Final Report*. Berlin: Federal Ministry for Economic Affairs and Energy (BMWi). https://www.bmwi.de/Redaktion/EN/Publikationen/commission-on-growth-structural-change-and-employment.pdf?__blob=publicationFile&v=3.

Daly, Herman E. 1996. *Beyond Growth: The Economics of Sustainable Development*. Boston, MA: Beacon Press.

Daly, Herman E. 2007. *Ecological Economics and Sustainable Development, Selected Essays of Herman Daly*. Cheltenham, UK: Edward Elgar Publishing.

Dryzek, John. 2013. *The Politics of the Earth. Environmetal Discourses*. 3rd ed. Oxford: Oxford University Press.

Dryzek, John, David Downes, Christian Hunold, Hans-Kristian Hernes, and David Schlosberg. 2003. *Green States and Social Movements: Environmentalism in the United States, United Kingdom, Germany, and Norway*. New York: Oxford University Press.

Esping-Andersen, Gøsta. 1990. *The Three Worlds of Welfare Capitalism*. Cambridge: Polity Press.

ETC. 2020. *Making Mission Possible. Delivering a Net-Zero Economy*. Energy Transitions Committee. https://www.energy-transitions.org/wp-content/uploads/2020/09/Making-Mission-Possible-Full-Report.pdf.

European Commission. 2019. "The European Green Deal." COM(2019) 640 final. Communication from the Commission to the European Parliament, the European Council, the Council, the European Economic and Social Committee and the Committee of the Regions. Brussels: European Commission. https://eur-lex.europa.eu/resource.html?uri=cellar:b828d165-1c22-11ea-8c1f-01aa75ed71a1.0002.02/DOC_1&format=PDF.

Froggatt, Antony, Paul Stevens, Siân Bradley, Germana Canzi, and Amanda Burton. 2020. *Expert Perspectives on Norway's Energy Future*. London: Royal Institute of International Affairs. https://www.chathamhouse.org/sites/default/files/2020-06-29-expert-perspectives-norway-oil-froggatt-et-al_0.pdf.

Geels, Frank W. 2014. "Regime Resistance against Low-Carbon Transitions: Introducing Politics and Power into the Multi-Level Perspective." *Theory, Culture & Society* 31 (5), 21–40.

Golubchikov, Oleg, and Paola Deda. 2012. "Governance, Technology, and Equity: An Integrated Policy Framework for Energy Efficient Housing." *Modeling Transport (Energy) Demand and Policies* 41 (February), 733–741.

Gough, Ian. 2013. "Carbon Mitigation Policies, Distributional Dilemmas and Social Policies." *Journal of Social Policy* 42 (2), 191–213.

Gough, Ian. 2016. "Welfare States and Environmental States: A Comparative Analysis." *Environmental Politics* 25 (1), 24–47.

Gough, Ian. 2017. *Heat, Greed and Human Need Climate Change, Capitalism and Sustainable Wellbeing*. Cheltenham, UK and Northampton, MA: Edward Elgar.

Gough, Ian. 2019. "Necessities and Luxuries: How to Combine Redistribution with Sustainable Consumption." In *What Next for Sustainable Development?*, edited by James Meadowcroft, David Banister, Erling Holden, Oluf Langhelle, Kristin Linnerud, and Geoffrey Gilpin, 138–158. Cheltenham: Edward Elgar Publishing.

Gough, Ian, Ian Meadowcroft, John Dryzek, Jürgen Gerhards, Holger Lengfeld, Anil Markandya, and Ramon Ortiz. 2008. "JESP Symposium: Climate Change and Social Policy." *Journal of European Social Policy* 18 (4), 325–344.

Hall, Peter A. 1993. "Policy Paradigms, Social Learning, and the State: The Case of Economic Policy-making in Britain." *Comparative Politics* 25 (3), 275–296.

Hall, Peter A. 2003. "Aligning Ontology and Methodology in Comparative Research." In *Comparative Historical Analysis in the Social Sciences*, edited by James Mahoney and Dietrich Rueschemeyer, 373–406. Cambridge and New York: Cambridge University Press.

Hall, Peter A, and David Soskice. 2001. *Varieties of Capitalism: The Institutional Foundations of Comparative Advantage*. Oxford: Oxford University Press.

Halvorsen, Rune, Bjørn Hvinden, and Mi Ah Schoyen. 2016. "The Nordic Welfare Model in the Twenty-First Century: The Bumble-Bee Still Flies!' *Social Policy and Society* 15 (1), 57–73.

Hayden, A. 2014. *When Green Growth Is Not Enough: Climate Change, Ecological Modernization, and Sufficiency*. Montreal and Kingston: McGill-Queen's University Press.

IPCC. 2014. *Climate Change 2014: Synthesis Report. Contribution of Working Groups I, II and III to the Fifth Assessment Report of the Intergovernmental Panel on Climate Change*. Geneva, Switzerland: IPCC.

IPCC. 2019. *Climate Change and Land: An IPCC Special Report on Climate Change, Desertification, Land Degradation, Sustainable Land Management, Food Security, and Greenhouse Gas Fluxes in Terrestrial Ecosystems*. https://www.ipcc.ch/site/assets/uploads/sites/4/2020/08/200730-IPCCJ7230-SRCCL-Complete-BOOK-HRES.pdf.

IPCC. 2021. *Climate Change 2021: The Physical Science Basis. Contribution of Working Group I to the Sixth Assessment Report of the Intergovernmental Panel on Climate Change*. [Edited by Masson-Delmotte, V., P. Zhai, A. Pirani, S. L. Connors, C. Péan, S. Berger, N. Caud, Y. Chen, L. Goldfarb, M. I. Gomis, M. Huang, K. Leitzell, E. Lonnoy, J. B. R. Matthews, T. K. Maycock, T. Waterfield, O. Yelekçi, R. Yu, and B. Zhou]. Cambridge: Cambridge University Press. In Press.

Jackson, Tim. 2017. *Prosperity without Growth. Foundations for the Economy of Tomorrow?* 2nd ed. London and New York: Routledge.

Jakobsson, Niklas, Raya Muttarak, and Mi Ah Schoyen. 2017. "Dividing the Pie in the Eco-Social State: Exploring the Relationship between Public Support for Environmental and Welfare Policies." *Environment and Planning C: Politics and Space* 36 (2), 313–339.

Jänicke, Martin. 2008. "Ecological Modernisation: New Perspectives." *Journal of Cleaner Production* 16 (5), 557–565.

Khan, Mehreen, Leslie Hook, Victor Mallet, and Katrina Manson. 2021. "New US Climate Strategy Opens up Old Faultlines with Europe Biden's Environmental Comeback Only Masks Divergent Approaches between the Two Economic Powerhouses." *Financial Times*, 23 April 2021.

Knight, Kyle W., and Juliet Schor. 2014. "Economic Growth and Climate Change: A Cross-National Analysis of Territorial and Consumption-Based Carbon Emissions in High-Income Countries." *Sustainability* 6 (6), 3722–3731.

Koch, Max. 2013. "Welfare after Growth: Theoretical Discussion and Policy Implications." *International Journal of Social Quality* 3 (1), 4–20.

Koch, Max. 2018. "Sustainable Welfare, Degrowth and Eco-Social Policies in Europe." In *Social Policy in the European Union: State of Play 2018. Nineteenth Annual Report*, edited by Bart Vanhercke, Dalila Ghailani, and Sebastiano Sabato, 35–50. https://www.etui.org/sites/default/files/Chapter%202_9.pdf.

Koch, Max, and Martin Fritz. 2014. "Building the Eco-Social State: Do Welfare Regimes Matter?' *Journal of Social Policy* 43 (4), 679–703.

Koch, Max, Anne Therese Gullberg, Mi Ah Schoyen, and Bjorn Hvinden. 2016. "Sustainable Welfare in the EU: Promoting Synergies between Climate and Social Policies." *Critical Social Policy* 36 (4), 704–715.

Koch, Max, and Oksana Mont (eds.) 2016. *Sustainability and the Political Economy of Welfare*. New York: Routledge.

Litz, Philipp. 2019. "Germany's Long Goodbye from Coal." In *Towards a Just Transition: Coal, Cars and the World of Work*, edited by Béla Galgóczi, 57–80. Brussels: European Trade Union Institute.

NAO. 2021. *Environmental Tax Measures*. London: National Audit Office. https://www.nao.org.uk/wp-content/uploads/2021/02/Environmental-Tax-Measures.pdf.

OECD. 2011. *Towards Green Growth*. Paris: OECD Publishing. https://doi.org/10.1787/978926411 1318-en.

Ostrom, Elinor. 1996. "Crossing the Great Divide: Coproduction, Synergy, and Development." *World Development* 24 (6), 1073–1087.

Pierson, Paul (ed.) 2001. *The New Politics of the Welfare State*. Oxford: Oxford University Press.

Pollin, Robert. 2019. "Advancing a Viable Global Climate Stabilization Project: Degrowth versus the Green New Deal." *Review of Radical Political Economics* 51 (2), 311–319.

Schor, Juliet. 1991. *The Overworked American: The Unexpected Decline of Leisure*. [New York, N.Y.]: Basic Books.

Schor, Juliet, and Andrew K. Jorgenson. 2019. "Is It Too Late for Growth?' *Review of Radical Political Economics* 51 (2), 320–329.

Smulders, Sjak, Michael Toman, and Cees Withagen. 2014. "Growth Theory and "Green Growth"." *Oxford Review of Economic Policy* 30 (3), 423–446.

Stern, Nicholas. 2007. *The Economics of Climate Change. The Stern Review*. Cambridge: Cambridge University Press.

Streeck, Wolfgang, and Kathleen Thelen. 2005. "Institutional Change in Advanced Political Economies." In *Beyond Continuity: Institutional Change in Advanced Political Economies*, edited by Wolfgang Streeck and Kathleen Thelen, 1–39. Oxford: Oxford University Press.

Taylor-Gooby, Peter. 2011. "Squaring the Public Policy Circle: Managing a Mismatch between Demands and Resources." *New Paradigms in Public Policy*. London: British Academy. http://www.britac.ac.uk/policy/Squaring_the_public_policy_circle.cfm.

Umit, Resul, and Lena Maria Schaffer. 2020. "Attitudes towards Carbon Taxes across Europe: The Role of Perceived Uncertainty and Self-Interest." *Energy Policy* 140 (May): 111385. https://doi.org/10.1016/j.enpol.2020.111385.

United Nations. 2015. *Transforming Our World: The 2030 Agenda for Sustainable Development*. Resolution Adopted by the General Assembly on 25 September 2015 (A/RES/70/1). https://www.un.org/ga/search/view_doc.asp?symbol=A/RES/70/1&Lang=E.

Van der Leyen, Ursula. 2020. "State of the Union Address." Delivered to the European Parliament Plenary presented at the European Parliament Plenary, Brussels, 16 September 2020. https://ec.europa.eu/commission/presscorner/detail/ov/SPEECH_20_1655.

Victor, Peter. 2008. *Managing Without Growth: Slower by Design, Not Disaster*. Cheltenham, UK: Edward Elgar Publishing.

Victor, Peter, and Tim Jackson. 2013. *Green Economy at Community Scale*. Metcalf Foundation. https://metcalffoundation.com/wp-content/uploads/2013/10/GreenEconomy.pdf.

Zimmermann, Katharina, and Paolo Grazioni. 2020. "Mapping Different Worlds of Eco-Welfare States." *Sustainability* 12 (5), 1–20.

Gregor Fitzi
22 Populism

Abstract: The keyword provides an historical introduction to the topic of populism and to the difficulties of its scientific definition. By reconstructing the meaning of the concept in the state of art it describes the specific political morphology of populism since the financial and economic crisis of 2007/08. This introduces us to the possible explanation of the societal backdrop of populism, which concerns the transformation of welfare state systems under the pressure of neoliberal policies in the last decades. To analyse this context, an historical sociological frame of analysis is developed that articulates in six steps. Firstly, the sociological theory of legitimation crisis in late capitalism is presented and critically reframed with reference to current societal change. Secondly, the social fragmentation risen in recent decades, especially the transformation of labour markets, is examined. Subsequently, a symptomatic of the populist mobilisation is established focusing on the relationship between its social and political factors of development. Fourthly, the keyword reconstructs the vertical and horizontal divides that populist mobilisations establish within society. Then, the consequences are assessed that populist mobilisations have on welfare state systems. Finally, the conclusions give a short outlook on the possible developments of populism in the era after the historical caesura represented by the 2020/21 pandemic.

Keywords: citizenship, neoliberalism, normative societal structuration, political entrepreneurship, populism, social legitimation, societal fragmentation, societal membership, welfare state compromise

22.1 Introduction

Populism is a phenomenon so multifaceted that research is traditionally grounded on a debate about the difficulties of defining it (Priester 2007). In historical terms, literature distinguishes between US American rural populism, the Russian movement of the so-called Narodniki, the grassroots democracy of Europe's workers' council revolutions and South American political regimes that understood themselves as a direct expression of the "people's will" (Puhle 1986). In an epoch-making conference at the *London School of Economics* in May 1967, under the direction of Ionescu and Gellner, the major experts in the field tried to give a definitive appraisal of populism (Ionescu and Gellner 1969). Unfortunately, the result of the conference was that there were several competing definitions of populism and no broad agreement was possible on the topic. About a decade later, Canovan's landmark study on populism appeared (1981). She embarked on a phenomenological approach concerned with the description of populist movements, rather than with the explanation of their possible causes. Yet,

https://doi.org/10.1515/9783110721768-022

Canovan could assess that there is a grounding distinction between two main strands of the phenomenon: agrarian populism and political populism.

In recent years a minimalist definition of populism has become established to compare widely divergent variants of the phenomenon with each other. Following the heuristic strategy of the studies on nationalist ideologies (Freeden 1996), populism is considered primarily as a "thin political ideology" with a Manichean substrate. This treats society as ultimately divided into two homogenous and antagonistic groups: "the pure people" and the "corrupt elite". The different versions of populism emanate from the particular mixture of "thin" populist ideology with elements of "thick ideologies" characterising the political culture of single countries. Grounded on this approach, Mudde developed his influential comparative research on populist radical right-wing parties in Europe (2007) and then extended it to the comparison with South and North American populism (Mudde and Rovira Kaltwasser 2012).

After the financial and economic crisis of 2007/08 – above all in Europe and the USA – populism acquired more specific characteristics that point to a wider societal unease capable of expanding the electoral potential of populist parties (Müller 2016). Different research approaches have flourished to grasp its manifold phenomenology. A main focus of research is the political morphology of populism. It entails the analysis of populism's specific political style, performance and self-dramatisation (Moffit 2016); it reconstructs the predilection of right-wing populism for stoking fears (Wodak 2015) and examines the typological differences between populism on the left and right (Priester 2012). On the other hand, the systematic evaluation of populism's meaning for the development of political systems underlines its symptomatic character for the crisis of modern parliamentary democracy (Albertazzi and McDonnell 2008; Mény and Surel 2002; Panizza 2005; Pasquino 2005; Urbinati 2014). Furthermore, wide-ranging statistical studies show trends indicating a convergence between economic crisis, fluctuation of electoral behaviour and the success of populist political parties since 2007/08 (Kriesi and Pappas 2015). Yet, the literature often addresses the issue on a strict politological level of analysis, without developing a theory of the correlated societal transformation or even without making assumptions about the social phenomena that may underlie the detected correlation of statistical evidences. In parallel to this, the sociological inquiry seems not really to gain momentum that analyses the relationship between the rise of populism in the 2010s and the societal transformation that occurred in the preceding decades under the pressure of neoliberal policies, which induced a curtailment of welfare state systems (Gidron and Bonikowski 2013).

By doing so, research somehow follows the path taken by the mainstream of societal self-interpretation that established itself after the financial and economic crisis of 2008/09. A reflection develops about the correlation of the political crisis with the return of a "great recession" similar to the 1930s (Walby 2015), yet there is still resistance to asking whether this is related to the restrictive welfare state reforms of previous decades. The predominance of this attitude is rooted in recent political history (Martel et al. 2001). Social democratic parties expected rapid economic growth and chances for redistribution from a more competitive positioning of their countries on the global economic markets. Thus, they adhered more or less explicitly to the ideological assumption that globalisation would mostly have a positive impact on societal development and adopted, or at least supported, restrictive social policies and labour market reforms, which resulted in lower wage and social security costs (Nachtwey 2009). Showing that the adoption of these policies and their socio-political consequences correlate in whatever degree with the rise of populism since the 2010s would offer it an unexpected legitimation, so that anti-populist societal self-interpretation shows greater reservation in proceeding along this line of reasoning. This reticence, however, prevents social sciences from understanding how the current societal transformation developed and to what degree it undermined the legitimacy of social security systems designated by the label of "welfare states". Since the 1990s, social divides have been growing; economic crises recur and the environmental emergency challenges the current model of economic development (Piketty 2014). The socioeconomic consequences that must be expected after the 2020/21 pandemic seem to multiply these effects. In this frame, an increasing number of worried voting citizens develop greater sensitivity for simplistic political narratives. Yet, to understand the articulation of the populist phenomenon since the 2010s, it must be analysed in the context of the overall societal transformation and legitimation crisis that occurred in the preceding decades.

In the following, a historical-sociological perspective of analysis will be developed to address the possible relationship between the change in social security systems and the rise of populist political parties. This will occur in six steps. Firstly, the sociological theory of legitimation crisis in late capitalism will be presented and critically reframed with reference to the current societal change. Secondly, the social fragmentation developed in recent decades will be examined, in particular, the transformation of labour markets. Subsequently, a symptomatic of the populist mobilisation will be established that focuses on the relationship between its social and political factors of development. Fourthly, the symptomatic will be integrated by a reconstruction of the vertical and horizontal divides that populist mobilisations try to establish within society. Then, the consequences that populist mobilisations have on welfare state systems will be assessed. Finally, the conclusions will give a short outlook on the possible future developments of populism in the era after the historical caesura represented by the 2020/21 pandemic.

22.2 The social legitimation issue

Societal self-interpretation is characterised by cycles of oblivion that also filter through to the social sciences (Connerton 2015). Since the rise of the neoliberal age in the 1980s, the awareness of the socio-political reasons that led to the development of the welfare state systems after World War II disappeared from public debate (Harvey 2005). In Europe, the traumatic experiences of dictatorship, war and genocide had showed beyond doubt the possible extent of the socio-political consequences of un-controlled economic crises and depressions (Arendt 1951). The awareness of these risks cemented the so-called "post-war consensus" about the limits of the predomi-nant economic development model and the necessity to compensate it through a "welfare state compromise" (Dutton 1994). The result was a reform process shared by both social democratic and conservative parties, which since 1945 implemented dif-ferent welfare state systems around Europe (Castles 1998; Esping-Andersen 1990). A normative conception of citizenship that includes not only civil and political, but also social rights developed in parallel and found its theoretical elaboration in Marshall's citizenship sociology (1996, first published in 1950). Yet, the post-war consensus did not survive the attacks of the neoliberal revolution (Duménil, and Lévy 2004). There-fore, it is all the more important to understand how the weakening of the welfare state systems undermined the legitimacy of the socio-political compromise that these pre-suppose.

The investigation of the topic needs an analytical framework capable of assessing the relationship between the issues of social inequality and the legitimation of socio-political systems. In this respect, a comparison with Habermas' theory of "legitimation crisis in late capitalism" (1973) allows us to grasp the specificity of the societal transfor-mation that occurred in recent decades. This is based on the presupposition that we un-derstand the historical gap between the legitimation crisis that emerged when the wel-fare state compromise still held and the crisis developing in the wake of the restrictive restructuring, which the social protection systems underwent since the 1980s. Fol-lowing Habermas, the sociological concept of "social crisis" addresses the persistent disturbance in the "systemic integration" of qualitatively differentiated societies, which has its cause in the conflict between the contradictory imperatives of economy and politics. The societal imbalance is classified as the structural expression of the un-equal distribution of the socially produced wealth, which arises from the private own-ership of the economic means of production. In the historical phase of welfare state regulation since 1945, societies proved to be capable of compensating for this systemic tension, by redistributing wealth and ensuring both economic and social development (Fourastié 1979). Yet, the welfare state systems that were constructed after World War II run in a legitimation crisis since the 1970s as their capacity decreased to correct and justify the social inequality produced by the capitalist economy.

The failure of systemic integration thus undermined the social integration of so-ciety (Lockwood 1964). Social actors experienced a growing contradiction between their formal status as citizens, who formally enjoy civil, political and social rights and the uncontrolled factual proliferation of social divides. The imbalance increased with the restrictive social policies of the neoliberal age. Following Habermas, one could ex-pect that the contradiction between social praxis and legal orders would be reab-sorbed through the capacity of complex societies to resume the process of normative structuration that generated the welfare state systems. Accordingly, a starting point for the development of the "theory of communicative action" was to show that in democratically constituted societies public opinion has the potential to deliver the critical performance necessary for normative structuration (Habermas 1984). Yet, in the course of the neoliberal revolution since the 1980s, welfare state systems were restructured in a way that acknowledged less the needs of the most disadvantaged social strata, inducing a legitimation crisis so important that communicative action did not manage to compensate it.

To the objective factors for the crisis of legitimation that invested in "administered" or "democratic capitalism", as Streeck calls it (2011), however, is added a crucial subjective factor. In the 1980s, political parties that traditionally represented the interests of working classes reoriented themselves ideologically to the conquest of the middle classes (Chadwick and Heffernan 2003). The decision was due to the strategic intent to win elections at the centre of the political spectrum. Yet, it was also accompanied by the ideological assumption that political narratives were outdated that were grounded on the issue of social divide (Giddens 1998). The political axis of social democracies shifted to the question of civil rights and fragmented into a thousand manifold claims for recognition, allowing the neoliberal emptying out of politics for equal dignity (Lukes 2007). The feeling of being left behind in difficult times of societal transformation thus spread and often sanctioned the divorce between the popular strata and social democracy, as Eribon well described for the French case (2009).

22.3 Societal fragmentation

Since the 2000s, the manifold mix of subjective and objective factors of societal transformation that characterised the neoliberal age resulted in an increased societal fragmentation. There are many different symptomatic expressions of the phenomenon that range from growing income inequality, to educational divides and to a crisis of social housing (Piketty 2014; Scanlon, Whitehead, and Fernández 2014). Yet, its most striking development is given by the transformation of labour markets, which evidence an increasing divarication between granted sectors of employment that still underlie protective legislation, and the vast prairies of wage labour that have been conceded to open exploitation. The main analytical category here is "dualisation of labour markets" (Emmenegger et al. 2014) – that is the process by which society's insiders and outsiders are increasingly treated differentially with respect to the access to workers' rights (Greve 2021, 57–75). It is thus a process that starts first informally, tolerating areas of shade beside legal working relations and develops then into an institutionalised divide between a granted and precarious workforce (Standing 2011). These changes affect countries which suffer from the global economic challenge as well as globalisation winners. At the same time, they extend not only to marginal or outdated sectors of production but also to leading sectors of large-scale industry.

An emblematic example for the dualisation of labour markets is the very successful German automotive industry (Wolf 2019). Here the overall transformation of production strategies enforced a far-reaching fragmentation of industrial relations. A constant back and forth takes place between out- and insourcing of development, production and logistics units that keeps both options permanently open. The single process sections (and the people working in them) are always "under reserve" and find themselves just temporarily in the replaceable shell into which the factory has been transformed. Uncertainty thus becomes the keynote of industrial relations. Every arrangement is under permanent evaluation and labour contracts last, in the best case, for three years. Yet, this development was not simply the result of the industrial restructuration logic. It was enabled and proactively supported by the legislation for labour market flexibilisation adopted by the Social Democrat–Green government around 2003/05 (Hegelich, Knollmann, and Kuhlmann 2011). The labour market deregulation consisted not least of various measures to liberalise temporary employment, so that from 2003 to 2010 loan labour more than doubled in Germany to almost 900,000 units. The resulting dualisation of employment conditions, thus institutionalising different treatment for equal work, is perceived by workers as a failure of the overall labour market legislation. They call for this to be reinstated (Wolf 2019, 168).

The processes of dualisation and precarisation – observed here in the ideal-typical case of the German automotive industry – characterise the development of labour markets in many different countries, even if they belong to different welfare state typologies (Böttcher 2020; Hultzsch 2019). Within the welfare state systems that were established since 1945 to alleviate the life conditions of the lowest social strata and legitimise residual social inequality, growing islands of normative exception established themselves and undermined the principle of a compensation of inequality through welfare. Democratic capitalism transformed into a new societal arrangement that does not recognise democratic control over the economy and instead employs legislation to enforce economic interests to the detriment of society's common good. The resulting social fragmentation generates legal uncertainty that is perceived as a failure of formally stated orders, so provoking what can be called the "legitimation crisis of late neoliberal capitalism". This trend reached its peak in 2007/08 when the costs for the crisis generated by the unregulated, reckless financial speculation were "socialised", compelling states to bail out financial institutions with taxpayer's money (Kotz 2015).

The systemic crisis of neoliberal capitalism was accompanied by massive material losses of real estate and private pension provisions in the middle-classes, spreading the perception that its irrationality can indiscriminately hit anyone (Palley 2013). Traditionally wealthy social strata that cannot keep pace with the technological transformation of the free professions have since to expect a worsening of their living standards (Reckwitz 2020). Diverging interests and fears thus meet an increasingly fragmented social reality and generate material and symbolic conflicts transforming societies into reservoirs of conflicting resentments. This scenario constitutes the best breeding ground for a populist mobilisation exploiting and amplifying the already existing societal legitimation crisis. Yet, these objective factors would not suffice to trigger it, as long as a crucial subjective factor does not compound things. In a socio-political reality, in which several social groups feel for different reasons that their demands go unheard, a political instance must arise that promises them a fair hearing and recognition.

22.4 Symptomatic of the populist mobilisation

Seen from a sociological viewpoint, populism at its core is neither a political ideology in Mudde's meaning (2007), nor a political style as Moffit suggests (2016), nor a symptom for the crisis of modern parliamentary democracy as the debate on this topic assumes (Albertazzi and McDonnell 2008; Mény and Surel 2002; Panizza 2005; Pasquino 2005; Urbinati 2014). Populism is rather the late output of the legitimation crisis that characterises societies with growing levels of social inequality in Habermas' sense (1973). This state of things is due to shifting welfare state guarantees accompanied by a poor level of political representation for the instances of the social strata hit by socio-economic decline. Hence, populism is the expression of a societal transformation process that takes the shape of a rising tide of social delegitimation seeking its interpreters. Like all social phenomena, it has a specific duration and can lead to serious political damages, as it brings anti-democratic and xenophobic political movements to power (Funke, Schularick, and Trebesch 2015). Yet, it can also be reabsorbed, if society develops anew a capacity of normative structuration comparable to that of the welfare state compromise after World War II and successfully decreases social inequality and exploitation, by acknowledging the demands of the most endangered social strata. The question thus arises about the typological characteristics of the political subjects who claim the right to become interpreters of the social legitimation crisis, and the precise phases and symptoms of the rising populist mobilisation.

To answer the questions, the entrepreneurial character of populist political organisations must become the subject of analysis (De Vries and Hobolt 2020; Tilly and Tarrow 2015). "Populists" do not simply thematise the societal legitimation crisis, as commentators or social scientists do; they exploit it for a specific purpose. The kind of political professional who embarks on the populist adventure has a keen sensibility for the critical side of political representation and intervenes in it with the aim of gaining as much political power as possible within the shortest time. The fight between "traditional" and "populist" politicians is thus above all a fight for the redistribution of accumulated political capital in Bourdieu's sense (1981). The populist mobilisation starts with a violent attack on the legitimately elected political representatives, stigmatising them as an "illegitimate power elite", exploiting society for their own ends. The polemic has an important semantic side. It is a question of disarticulating the collective frameworks of political language that legitimise the public institutions enforcing the existing social order. Therefore, the fight between "political correctness" and the will to openly violate it, is often a constitutive part of the attack on accumulated political capital. This manoeuvre can succeed, yet only if within society there is sufficient matter of consent that a legitimation crisis is actually taking place, as we have observed in the case of the shifting welfare state compromise. If the first move of the populist mobilisation proves successful, the fight for reciprocal delegitimation between established parties and emerging political entrepreneurs expands. In this context, the label "populist" comes first to the fore. The expression is used to counterattack the forces that do not adhere to the institutional rules regulating the political game in liberal democracies, including the principle of the governing prerogatives of parliamentary majorities. Political entrepreneurs are designated as populists, because they attack the legally elected people's representatives labelling them a "corrupt elite" and thereby seek to usurp already allocated shares of political capital.

Hence, the first phase of the populist mobilisation is characterised by the abandonment of shared codes of political communication. Political entrepreneurs break with the institutional rules of regulated democratic competition, because they know that this can deliver an increase of political capital in times of societal legitimation crisis. A new political language is born and this introduces the second phase of the populist mobilisation. Populists succeed in setting the political agenda and traditional parties often feel compelled to adopt some of their topics and slogans to compete on the market of political consensus. Yet, the impetus of populist mobilisation can also channel instances of social justice and demands for democratisation, of which populists claim to be the representatives. Whether these expectations are then met or not remains an open question. This aspect of populism, above all in its Latin American variation, is what made it sympathetic to a left-wing intellectual audience (Laclau 2005; Mouffe 2019) and spurred the development of populist movements and parties of socialist inspiration around Europe (Prentoulis 2021).

Regardless of the different talent of populist political entrepreneurs, however, an objective condition for the success of their mobilisation must exist in the background. It does not matter whether objectively grounded or not, yet the crisis of social legitimation must already have started to transform into a crisis of political representation. In this context, an important number of citizens feel, on the one hand, that their access to material or symbolic resources is not as secure as they would like it to be or are afraid that this will be the case in the future. On the other hand, they feel that their real or supposed condition of distress is not properly recognised and symbolically taken into account by the rulers. In other words, the perception grows of a lack of political recognition for social demands. If the populist mobilisation succeeds, it achieves an activation of these latent lines of conflicts, emphasising them rhetorically as the vertical fracture of society (Tilly 2016). Yet, populism always pursues the institutionalisation of a double vertical and horizontal divide that has a major impact on the restrictive restructuration of welfare state systems, not only if populist political parties come to office, yet also if they simply succeed in dictating the political agenda. This introduces the third phase of the populist mobilisation.

22.5 Vertical and horizontal populist divides

For the sake of a redistribution of political capital to their advantage, political entrepreneurs try to establish new divides within society. The societal dynamics that populism attempts to exploit, by addressing democratic elected rulers as a "corrupt elite", is that of the representation crisis in times of shifting social security. So the question arises as to the meaning of the second societal dynamics that populism tries to trigger by redefining the political concept of people's sovereignty on the basis of a pre-political narrative. In the wake of neoliberal policies since the 1980s, the legislation that granted universal access to citizenship rights has been substantially weakened. Thus, basic criteria of societal membership permitting the access to welfare state protection were called into question. Accordingly, different social strata directly experienced or at least fear social decline in a time of shifting welfare protection, so entering into a competition for their condition to be politically acknowledged (Gidron and Hall 2017).

Concomitant with the crisis of welfare state systems in the neoliberal age, increasing migration flows provoked a growing "social under-stratification" relegating the bulk of the newcomers to precarious and illegal spheres of work in a shifting labour market (Hoffmann-Nowotny 1973). Migrants were thus perceived as potential competitors that contribute to a worsening of the overall frame conditions of employment. The growing social fragmentation thus results in an increase of claims requiring political recognition and awakens fears that the already meagre welfare resources must be redistributed to a wider range of needy people. Political entrepreneurship exploits these kinds of real, yet more often perceived factors of social conflict, by overemphasising their dividing symbolic appearances and obscuring the common interests of the different groups. The political semantics is thus reorganised into symbolical, religious and cultural oppositions between "them and us" that impede the understanding of the underlying socio-economic divides, which would rather find native and migrant workforce on the same side (Marzouki, McDonnell, and Roy 2016).

The production of these new social categorisations results in populism's ideological performance *par excellence*. Coining the idea of an "honest native people", allegedly free of any internal divisions, fighting against the corrupt elite that exploits it in cahoots with its external enemies, first and foremost the migrants, becomes the core of populist mobilisation. It is a divisive conception of society that ignores the common interest of all components of the workforce in fighting against the development of dual labour markets and reproduces in practice the socio-economic divides that it pays lip service to eradicating. This worldview, which specifically characterises right-wing populism, results in the plea for a restrictive, pre-legal and pre-political redefinition of the social groups, "the people", entitled to enjoy citizenship rights and access to welfare state protection. A focus on this aspect can thus establish a criterion to distinguish between right- and left-wing populism, because the latter tends to take a position of universalistic openness concerning the access to welfare (Priester 2012).

Yet, the right-wing populist narrative concerning the necessary restrictive reform of the welfare state systems is by far the most predominant in recent political history. It identifies the rescue from the ongoing erosion of citizenship rights in their further restriction for the solely allegedly ethnical or culturally "genuine members" of the people. By these means, the crisis of the welfare state systems takes a leap forward and transforms welfare populism into welfare chauvinism (Greve 2021). The populist narrative distorts social reality and invents the myth of the "innocent and brave people" as an allegedly ethnical, social, cultural and religious uniform entity, which must supposedly be rescued from the domination of the "parasitic elite" and its "external allies". The continuous weaving of this divisive narrative thus represents the decisive subjective element that fosters the populist mobilisation. To establish their cultural hegemony populist political entrepreneurs must be able to master the demagogic skills that intercept really existing or perceived elements of social distress and transfigure ideologically the related feelings of a lack of political recognition.

22.6 Consequences for the welfare state compromise

Historically it can be observed that political democratisation and the development of welfare states systems after World War II endowed the members of national states with a full set of civil, political and social rights, so filling the gaps of previous citizenship's arrangements (Marshall 1996, 9). Moreover, an increasingly inclusive interpretation of the citizenship status allowed, to a greater or lesser extent, for access to the same rights also for groups of citizens without "full nationals" status, such as foreigners, guest workers, migrants or refugees (Aleinikoff and Klusmeyer 2000; Tomasi et al. 1992). These developments were not at all free from conflicts and rejections, as the history of several countries in Europe and the US shows. Yet, the societal arrangement around the welfare state or New Deal compromise allowed turning above all labour into a driver of social integration. Social groups of workers, migrants and minorities managed to organise collectively to claim the recognition of their common rights. The attack on the welfare state systems, conducted by the neoliberal deregulation and austerity policies from the 1980s onwards, made it instead increasingly difficult to establish a societal consensus granting inclusive access to citizenship rights (Duménil and Lévy 2004).

Full citizens today often feel that their access to material or symbolic resources is not as secure as they would like it to be (Gidron and Hall 2017). Yet, because of the ongoing societal fragmentation, they miss the necessary frame to articulate these needs, so that the longing grows for external interpreters of their not sufficiently acknowledged condition of distress. Moreover, the condition of post-Fordist labour relations frustrates the efforts for organising collective paths of action to claim the full acknowledgement of social rights (Deyo 1996). Angry, insecure and feeling left behind native blue and white collars thus face discriminated, illegal migrant workers, in which they only see competitors. New conflict lines develop that threaten the chances of a renewed normative structuration of society based on a welfare state compromise. Political entrepreneurs are very aware of the malaise concerning the failing redistribution of societal resources, so that they exploit the ongoing objective and symbolic conflicts between societal groups to propagate their narrative. By redefining the concept of the "people" in a restrictive manner, the populist mobilisation deliberately stigmatises specific social groups as competitors for material and symbolic goods.

Irrespective of the different circumstances in which populist parties and movements come into office, participate in government or fail to do so, the populist mobilisation leaves its mark, because it establishes restrictive conceptions of social closure within the legitimated political culture (Albertazzi and Mueller 2013). The effects of the populist mobilisation thus reach beyond the boundaries of the community that actively supports it, invest the centre of society and enforce the neoliberal logic of depriving growing groups of society's members of their rights. Furthermore, established political parties tend to adopt populist shibboleths to score points against their challengers during election campaigns, so that restrictive redefinitions of societal membership spread (Caiani and Graziano 2016). Conceptions of citizenship that are incompatible with a pluralistic and inclusive arrangement of society become part of the legitimate political culture and, ultimately, of the amended welfare state legislation. Thereby the populist mobilisation reaches its peak. The "cultural hegemony" (Gramsci 2014, 1638; 2010) of right-wing populist narratives intensifies the downgrading spiral of the welfare state compromise that erodes inclusive definitions of citizenship by establishing stricter criteria of social closure. The final result is thus a worsening in the legitimation crisis of complex societies, because wider social groups feel that the growing social inequalities do not find compensation.

22.7 Conclusions

The assessment of the societal backdrop of populism and its correlation with the crisis of the welfare state compromise seems to result in a pessimistic diagnosis for the ongoing transformation of complex societies. A populist cultural hegemony indeed exposes societies to major political and social risks. Yet, the underlying legitimation crisis is a societal phenomenon of intermittent character that comes and goes, so that in the long run also the populist mobilisation loses intensity. In this sense, populism constitutes a variation of charismatic authority and shares its strengths and weakness (Weber 1978, 241–245). If its overblown promises are not fulfilled, after a certain period of time its grip on the social strata seeking recognition declines. Accordingly, normative societal structuration can recover and a renewed welfare state compromise can be found. Yet, its precondition consists in the establishment of a political culture that acknowledges the need for a compensation of the imbalance in the systemic integration of complex societies through an enforced social integration (Lockwood 1964). In a way that was unimaginable in the previous four decades of neoliberal cultural hegemony, the pandemic of 2020/21 seems to have awakened anew the awareness of the issue. Active government policies to manage aggregate demand in order to address or prevent economic recessions in the Keynesian sense as well as elements of New Deal legislation appear on the horizon (Tooze 2021). The interventions on the socio-economic urgencies of societies hit by the abrupt interruption of the irrational development of global capitalism seem to have also mitigated to a certain degree the looming social legitimation crisis. At the same time, the state of exception in health due to the pandemic seems to have put a strain on populist mobilisation, which has to find a new pace to keep up with the changed societal situation (Burleigh 2021; Katsambekis and Stavrakakis 2020). Whether these developments will have an impact that strengthens welfare systems and reopens them in a universalistic and inclusive sense is, however, too early to tell. Only the next decades can show whether complex societies are capable of restarting a normative structuration process that compensates for the social and environmental consequences of the prevailing development model. If they succeed on this path, it is to be expected that their legitimation crisis will fade away and thus also its political expression, which is called populism.

References

Albertazzi, D., and D. McDonnell (eds.) 2008. *Twenty-First Century Populism: The Spectre of Western European Democracy*. Basingstoke: Palgrave Macmillan.

Albertazzi, D., and S. Mueller (eds.) 2013. "Populism and Liberal Democracy: Populists in Government in Austria, Italy, Poland and Switzerland." *Government and Opposition* 48 (3), 343–371.

Aleinikoff, T. A., D. and Klusmeyer. 2000. *From Migrants to Citizens: Membership in a Changing World*. Washington, D.C.: Carnegie Endowment for International Peace.

Arendt, H. 1951. *The Origins of Totalitarianism*. New York: Harcourt, Brace and Co.

Böttcher, M. 2020. *Der Null-Stunden-Vertrag. Arbeitszeitflexibilisierung nach deutschem und britischem Recht*. Beiträge zum Arbeitsrecht 9. Tübingen: Mohr Siebeck.

Bourdieu, P. 1981. "La représentation politique. Éléments pour une théorie du champ politique." *Actes de la recherche en sciences sociales* 36–37, 3–24.

Burleigh, M. 2021. *Populism: Before and After the Pandemic*. London: Hurst and Company.

Caiani, M., and P. Graziano. 2016. "Varieties of Populism: Insights from the Italian Case." *Italian Political Science Review/Rivista Italiana Di Scienza Politica* 46 (2), 243–267.

Canovan, M. 1981. *Populism*. New York: Harcourt Brace Jovanovich.

Castles, F. G. 1998. *Comparative Public Policy: Patterns of Post-War Transformation*. Northampton, MA: Edward Elgar Publishing.

Chadwick, A., and R. Heffernan. 2003. *The New Labour Reader*. Cambridge: Polity Press.

Connerton, P. 2015. *How Modernity Forgets*. Cambridge: Cambridge University Press.

De Vries, C. E., and S. Hobolt. 2020. *Political Entrepreneurs: The Rise of Challenger Parties in Europe*. Princeton, NJ and Oxford: Princeton University Press.

Deyo, F. C. 1996. *Social Reconstructions of the World Automobile Industry: Competition, Power, and Industrial Flexibility*. New York: St. Martin's Press.

Duménil, G., and D. Lévy. 2004. *Capital Resurgent: Roots of the Neoliberal Revolution*. Cambridge, MA: Harvard University Press.

Dutton, D. 1994. *British Politics Since 1945: The Rise and Fall of Consensus*. Oxford: Blackwell.

Emmenegger, P., S. Hausermann, B. Palier, and M. Seeleib-Kaiser. 2014. *The Age of Dualization: The Changing Face of Inequality in Deindustrializing Societies*. New York: Oxford University Press.

Eribon, D. 2009. *Retour à Reims*. Paris: Fayard.

Esping-Andersen, G. 1990. *The Three Worlds of Welfare Capitalism*. Princeton, NJ: Princeton University Press.

Fourastié, J. 1979. *Les Trente Glorieuses, ou la révolution invisible de 1946 à 1975*. Paris: Fayard.

Freeden, M. 1996. *Ideologies and Political Theory*. Oxford: Clarendon Press.

Funke, M., M. Schularick, and C. Trebesch. 2015. *Going to Extremes: Politics After Financial Crisis, 1870–2014*. Munich: CESifo.

Giddens, A. 1998. *The Third Way: The Renewal of Social Democracy*. Cambridge: Polity.

Gidron, N., and B. Bonikowski. 2013. *Varieties of Populism: Literature Review and Research Agenda*. Working Paper Series, Waterhead Center for International Affairs, Harvard University.

Gidron, N., and P. A. Hall. 2017. "The Politics of Social Status: Economic and Cultural Roots of the Populist Right." *British Journal of Sociology* 68 (S1), 57–84.

Gramsci, A. 2014. *Quaderni dal carcere*. Vol. 1. Edited by Valentino Gerratana. Torino: Einaudi.

Greve, B. 2021. *Welfare Populism and Welfare Chauvinism*. Bristol: Policy Press.

Habermas, J. 1973. *Legitimationprobleme im Spatkapitalismus*. Frankfurt/M.: Suhrkamp.

Habermas, J. 1984. *The Theory of Communicative Action*. Boston: Beacon.

Harvey, D. 2005. *Brief History of Neoliberalism*. Oxford: Oxford University Press.

Hegelich, S., D. Knollmann, and J. Kuhlmann. 2011. *Agenda 2010: Strategien, Entscheidungen, Konsequenzen*. Wiesbaden: VS Verlag für Sozialwissenschaften.

Hoffmann-Nowotny, H.-J. 1973. *Soziologie des Fremdarbeiterproblems. Eine theoretische und empirische Analyse am Beispiel der Schweiz*. Stuttgart: Enke.

Hultzsch, F. 2019. *Nullstundenverträge. Grenzen arbeitsvertraglicher Flexibilisierungsmöglichkeiten im Hinblick auf Lage und Dauer der Arbeitszeit*. Schriften zum Sozia - und Arbeitsrecht 357. Berlin: Duncker and Humblot.

Ionescu, G., and E. Gellner (eds.) 1969. *Populism: Its Meanings and National Characteristics*. London: Weidenfeld and Nicolson.

Katsambekis, G., and Y. Stavrakakis (eds.) 2020. *Populism and the Pandemic: A Collaborative Report*. POPULISMUS Interventions No. 7, 2020. Thessaloniki.

Kotz, D. M. 2015. *The Rise and Fall of Neoliberal Capitalism*. Cambridge, MA: Harvard University Press.

Kriesi, H., and T. S. Pappas (eds.) 2015. *European Populism in the Shadow of the Great Recession*. Colchester: ECPR Press.

Laclau, E. 2005. *On Populist Reason*. London: Verso.

Lockwood, D. 1964. "Social Integration and System Integration." In *Explorations in Social Change*, edited by G. K. Zollschan and W. Hirsch, 244–257. London: Routledge and Kegan Paul.

Lukes, S. 2007. "Die Politik gleicher Würde und die Politik der Anerkennung" (translation of the unpublished lecture "The Politics of Equal Dignity and the Politics of Recognition", 1993, Georg Simmel Visiting Professorship at the Humboldt University of Berlin). In *Moderne Staatsbürgerschaft*, edited by J. Mackert and H.-P. Müller, 311–322. Wiesbaden: VS.

Marshall, T. H. 1996. *Citizenship and Social Class* (1950). London: Pluto.

Martell, L., C. van den Anker, M. Browne, S. Hoopes, P. Larkin, Charles Lees, F. McGowan, and N. Stammers (eds.) 2001. *Social Democracy: Global and National Perspectives*. New York: Palgrave.

Marzouki, N., D. McDonnell, and O. Roy. 2016. *Saving the People: How Populists Hijack Religion*. London: Hurst and Company.

Mény, Y., and Y. Surel. 2002. *Democracies and the Populist Challenge*. New York: Palgrave.

Moffit, B. 2016. *The Global Rise of Populism: Performance, Political Style, and Representation*. Stanford, CA: Stanford University Press.

Mouffe, C. 2019. *For a Left Populism*. London and New York: Verso.

Mudde, C. 2007. *Populist Radical Right Parties in Europe*. Cambridge: Cambridge University Press.

Mudde, C., and C. Rovira Kaltwasser (eds.) 2012. *Populism in Europe and the Americas*. Cambridge: Cambridge University Press.

Müller, J.-W. 2016. *What is Populism?* Philadelphia, PA: University of Pennsylvania Press.

Nachtwey, O. 2009. *Marktsozialdemokratie: Die Transformation von SPD und Labour Party*. Wiesbaden: VS Verlag für Sozialwissenschaften.

Palley, T. I. 2013. *From Financial Crisis to Stagnation: The Destruction of Shared Prosperity and the Role of Economics*. New York: Cambridge University Press.

Panizza, F. 2005. *Populism and the Mirror of Democracy*. London: Verso.

Pappas, T. S. 2014. *Populism and Crisis Politics in Greece*. New York: Palgrave Macmillan.

Pasquino, G. 2005. *Populism and Democracy*. Bologna: The Johns Hopkins University Bologna Center.

Piketty, T. 2014. *Capital in the Twenty-First Century*. Cambridge, MA: Harvard University Press.

Prentoulis, M. 2021. *Left Populism in Europe: Lessons from Jeremy Corbyn to Podemos*. London: Pluto Press.

Priester, K. 2007. *Populismus. Historische und aktuelle Erscheinungsformen*. Frankfurt and New York: Campus.

Priester, K. 2012. *Rechter und linker Populismus. Annäherung an ein Chamäleon*. Frankfurt and New York: Campus.

Puhle, H. J. 1986. "Was ist Populismus?" In *Populismus und Aufklärung*, edited by H. Dubiel, 12–32. Frankfurt am Main: Suhrkamp.

Reckwitz, A. 2020. *The Society of Singularities*. Cambridge; Medford, MA: Polity.

Scanlon, K., C. M. E. Whitehead, and A. M. Fernández. 2014. *Social Housing in Europe*. Chichester: Wiley Blackwell.

Standing, G. 2011. *The Precariat*. London: Bloomsbury Academic.

Streeck, W. 2011. "The Crises of Democratic Capitalism." *New Left Review* 71, 5–29.

Taggart, P. 2000. *Populism*. Buckingham: Open University Press.

Tilly, C. 2016. *Identities, Boundaries, and Social Ties*. London: Routledge.

Tilly, C., S. G., and Tarrow. 2015. *Contentious Politics*. New York: Oxford University Press.

Tomasi, L. F., and Center for Migration Studies U. S. 1992. *Legal immigration reform in the U. S., immigration policy in a global perspective, bilateral and multilateral agreements and implications of a single European market, reforming refugee resettlement, U. S. farmworker access to health care: Proceedings of the 1991 Annual National Legal Conference on Immigration and Refugee Policy*. New York: Center for Migration Studies.

Tooze, A. 2021. *Shutdown: How COVID Shook the World's Economy*. New York: Viking.

Urbinati, N. 2014. *Democracy Disfigured: Opinion, Truth, and the People*. Cambridge, MA: Harvard University Press.

Walby, S. 2015. *Crisis*. Cambridge: Polity Press.

Weber, M. 1978. *Economy and Society*. Edited by C. Wittich and G. Roth. Berkeley, CA: University of California Press.

Wodak, R. 2015. *The Politics of Fear: What Right-Wing Populist Discourses Mean*. London: Sage.

Wolf, H. 2019. "Fragmentierte Arbeit im Postfordismus: Übersehene Wechselwirkungen zwischen betrieblicher und überbetrieblicher Rationalisierung in der Automobilindustrie." In *Blick zurück nach vorn. Sekundäranalysen zum Wandel von Arbeit nach dem Fordismus*, edited by W. Dunkel, H. Hanekop and N. Mayer-Ahuja, 135–174. International Labour Studies. Frankfurt/M: Campus Verlag.

Edward Cartwright and Anna Cartwright
23 Behavioural public policy

Abstract: Behavioural public policy can broadly be defined as public policy, using insights from behavioural economics, that aims to influence human behaviour. To introduce key ideas and illustrate the nature of behavioural public policy we begin with an example that has been widely studied across many countries, namely the wording of tax reminder letters. We summarise evidence that simple changes to the wording of tax reminder letters can positively influence repayment rates. We next discuss the methods of behavioural public policy including Nudge, MINDSPACE and the COM-B model. These methods provide a framework for identifying choice settings where behavioural insights are likely to be most relevant, and also provide a framework for identifying and evaluating possible behavioural interventions. We finish the chapter with some further examples of behavioural public policy in action, such as the Save More Tomorrow programme for retirement saving.

Keywords: Nude, MINDSPACE, COM-B, tax reminder letters, public policy, behavioural economics

23.1 Introduction

Economic theorising throughout much of the twentieth century was based on models of a rational homo-economicus who knew how to maximise his or her utility (see e.g. Bruni and Sugden 2007). The choices of homo-economicus are driven by the incentives, constraints and information that she faces. For instance, if there is a change in the tax legislation then homo-economicus would "do the calculations" (or behave as if she had done the calculations) and optimally adjust her work, leisure, consumption and saving patterns appropriately. Moreover, homo-economicus would not be influenced by anything other than her incentives, constraints and information. For instance, her choice would not depend on how the change in tax legislation was framed by the policymaker or media etc. The homo-economicus approach offers a very powerful way of making predictions on changes in government policy. The analyst can map the changes in incentives and constraints of, say, a change in the tax rate, and then predict the impact on behaviour. This approach has become dominant in economic policy modelling.

There is, though, a fundamental problem with the rational choice approach: people do not behave like homo-economicus (Thaler and Sunstein 2009). Instead, they use heuristics, or simple "rules of thumb", to make decisions that deviate in significant ways from the predictions based on homo-economicus. For instance, they struggle to understand complex tax legislation and can be influenced by innocuous changes in the

https://doi.org/10.1515/9783110721768-023

way policies are framed (Halpern 2015). This is not to say that people are "dumb", just that predictions based on homo-economicus can lead us astray. The field of behavioural economics has emerged over the last few decades to shift economics away from an over-reliance on homo-economicus (Bruni and Sugden 2007; Thaler 2015). This revolution has naturally impacted on policymaking with the birth (or re-birth) of behavioural public policy (Oliver 2013), which can be broadly defined as "means and modes of public policy aiming at influencing human behavior by using insights from behavioral economics" (Straßheim 2020, 116).

A pivotal moment in the rapid rise of behavioural public policy was the formal establishment, in 2010, of a Behavioural Insights Team or "Nudge Unit" by the UK Government, tasked with applying behavioural science to public policy. The unit, building on the seminal contribution of Thaler and Sunstein (2009), and set up with the direct input of Professor Richard Thaler, was somewhat controversial but ultimately deemed a resounding success (Halpern 2015; Halpern and Sanders 2016). Headlines boldly claimed that it had saved the UK taxpayer hundreds of millions of pounds in lost revenue through simple, essentially costless, behaviour change interventions. The success of the unit, coupled with the appeal of costless interventions at a time of austerity and spiralling government debt, spurned the establishment of similar units in other countries. Active Behavioural Insight Units or Networks now exist across the world, including in Canada, the US, Austria, Germany, Netherlands, Peru, India and Singapore. Global institutions are also very pro-active in this area. For instance, the Mind, Behavior, and Development Unit (eMBeD) at the World Bank helps teams use behaviourally informed policy to tackle global poverty and inequality (Manning et al. 2020). Similarly the OECD provides support and advice to public institutions on how to apply behavioural policy (OECD 2017, 2019).

As critics often point out, behavioural public policy long predates the publication of *Nudge* or the setting up of nudge units. There can be no denying, however, that the last 10–20 years have seen an explosion of interest in behavioural insights (Straßheim 2020). An important point to recognise is that this interest has been coupled with a more systematic use of behavioural science (Halpern 2015). Specifically, we see an increasing use of experiments and randomised control trials to evaluate and compare different policy options. This interest in "methods" is particularly important when it comes to distinguishing different ways in which behavioural science has been applied within public policy. Nudge units have grabbed headlines for novel interventions that sit aside from and complement conventional policy. Behavioural policy can, though, be applied more generally in questioning whether policy can have unintended behavioural consequences. Viewed in this way, behavioural insights apply across all of government, rather than being some kind of "add-on service" (Dolan et al. 2010).

In this chapter we will review the use of behavioural public policy, discussing methods and providing several specific applications. To introduce key ideas and illustrate the nature of behavioural public policy we begin with an example that has been widely studied across many countries, namely the wording of tax reminder letters

(Halpern 2015). We then broaden the discussion to cover the general principles of behavioural public policy.

23.1 Nudging people to pay tax

Interest in tax reminder letters was first sparked by an experiment in the UK conducted by the Behavioural Insights Team (Halpern 2015). Most people in the UK pay income tax "automatically" through their employer. There is, however, a sizeable number of people required to complete a self-assessment tax return and then make tax payments in January and July. If the payments are not made on time the tax authority (HMRC) pursues the debt, escalating from reminders to debt recovery. Two large field experiments were conducted, one in August 2011 and a second in August 2012, that varied the wording of the initial reminder letter that debtors received after missing the July payment (Hallsworth et al. 2017).

The variation in frame involved adding one or two sentences to the standard letter that HMRC would otherwise have sent. For example, one treatment in the first experiment used the following wording:

> Our records show that your Self Assessment tax payment is overdue.
> Nine out of ten people pay their tax on time.
> It is easy to pay. Please call the phone number above to pay by direct debit, credit card, or Direct Debit.
> You can also pay using the internet and telephone banking. For more information on when and how to pay, go to www.hmrc.gov.uk/payinghmrc/
> If you don't believe that this payment is overdue, please contact us on the number above.
> If you have already paid, thank you. If not, please act now.

The phrase "Nine out of ten people pay their tax on time" was inserted into the standard letter and so distinguishes this frame relative to others. Table 23.1 details the variations in frame that were used in experiments 1 and 2. It also details the number of individuals in each treatment that received a letter and the marginal effects (to be discussed shortly).

The different frames used in the experiments are motivated by a range of theories and experimental evidence in behavioural science (Halpern 2015; Hallsworth et al. 2017). For instance, in settings with social norms and conformity individuals can react positively to information on compliance, for example nine out of ten people pay their tax (e.g. Bobek, Hageman, and Kelliher 2013; Farrow, Grolleau, and Ibanez 2017). The more personalised the message, for example referring to the UK or people in your area, the more salient can be the norm (Wenzel 2005). The experiment also contrasts different motives for paying the tax from a positive societal benefit, i.e. vital public services, and avoidance of social negative cost, i.e. not losing out on vital public services, as well as material benefit, i.e. avoidance of interest charges. The experiment also allows comparison of injunctive and descriptive norms, where injunctive norms focus on what the majority think is the right thing to do and descriptive norms focus on what the majority actually do (Bicchieri 2016; Jacobson, Mortensen, and Cialdini 2011).

As one might expect, given these experiments have attracted much attention, the framing of the tax reminder letters systematically influenced the rate at which recipients subsequently paid their tax. The right-hand column in Table 23.1 details the estimated marginal effect on payments within 23 days, relative to the control letter. These effects are from logistic regressions that control for demographics and the size of debt (Hallsworth et al. 2017). The baseline level of repayment in experiment 1 was 35.8 % and that in experiment 2 was 33.6 %. So, in interpretation the rate of repayment within 23 days in 2011 was 35.8 % with the standard letter and 5.1 % higher with the minority norm frame. In 2012 it was 33.6 % with the standard letter and 4.5 % higher with the minority descriptive norm frame. Note that as the tax authorities escalate their pursuit of the debt, and as more debtors pay, the effects of the initial reminder letter naturally taper out. What we are seeing, therefore, is an acceleration of payments with people paying earlier.

The headline result from the 2011 experiment is that the minority norm frame led to a particularly pronounced increase in repayment. Crucially that effect is replicated in 2012 giving a good deal of confidence in the result. Pointing out that the debtor is "currently in the very small minority of people who have not paid us yet" seems, therefore, to make a positive difference. This ultimately reduces the need for the tax authorities to pursue debt. There are now a sizeable number of studies exploring related issues. For instance, Haynes et al. (2013) find that text messages, particularly if they address the recipient by name can significantly increase the rate of paying outstanding court fines. Similarly, Dwenger et al. (2016) study tax compliance in Germany and the benefits of simplifying the message and highlighting deterrence or reward. Moreover, the approach has been applied across many different countries, including Guatemala (Kettle et al. 2016) and Poland (Hernandez et al. 2017). Crucially, such studies have shown that the framing makes a difference in countries where compliance is much lower than the UK. For instance, in Guatemala, the frame that "nine out of ten people pay their tax on time" had to be adapted to reflect that only around 6 out of 10 pay on time. Even so, social norm framing made a significant positive difference.

Table 23.1: Details of tax letter experiment including number of observations per frame/treatment and the marginal effect on compliance within 23 days. * indicates statistically significant at p = 0.01 level. Data from Hallsworth et al. (2017)

Frame	Text	Number	Effect
Experiment 1 (2011)			
Control	Standard tax letter wording	17,038	–
Basic norm	Nine out of ten people pay their tax on time.	17,026	1.3 %
Country norm	Nine out of ten people in the UK pay their tax on time.	16,926	2.1 % *
Minority norm	Nine out of ten people in the UK pay their tax on time. You are currently in the very small minority of people who have not paid us yet.	16,515	5.1 % *
Gain framed public services	Paying tax means we all gain from vital public services like the NHS, roads, and schools.	16,807	1.6 % *
Loss-framed public services	Not paying tax means we all lose out on vital public services like the NHS, roads and schools	17,159	1.5 % *
Experiment 2 (2012)			
Control	Standard tax letter wording	8,558	–
General descriptive norm	The great majority of people in the UK pay their tax on time.	8,300	1.5 %
Local descriptive norm	The great majority of people in your local area pay their tax on time.	8,403	2.3 % *
Debt descriptive norm	Most people with a debt like yours have paid it by now.	8,643	3.6 % *
Local and debt descriptive norm	The great majority of people in your local area pay their tax on time. Most people with a debt like yours have paid it by now.	8,643	5.4 % *
Minority status	You are currently in the very small minority of people who have not paid us yet.	8,587	5.2 % *
Minority descriptive norm	Nine out of ten people in the UK pay their tax on time. You are currently in the very small minority of people who have not paid us yet.	8,731	4.5 % *

Table 23.1 (continued)

Frame	Text	Number	Effect
Moral duty	Everyone in the UK should pay their tax on time.	8,507	2.2 % *
General injunctive norm	The great majority of people agree that everyone in the UK should pay their tax on time.	8,595	0.5 %
Fraction injunctive norm	Nine out of ten people agree that everyone in the UK should pay their tax on time.	8,490	1.6 %
Percentage injunctive norm	88 % of people agree that everyone in the UK should pay their tax on time.	8,428	2.9 % *
Injunctive and descriptive norm	Nine out of ten people agree that everyone in the UK should pay their tax on time. And nine out of ten people do pay on time.	8,524	3.6 % *
Additional information	You can pay by debit card, credit card or Direct Debit. You can also pay using internet and telephone banking. For more information on how to pay, go to www.hmrc.gov.uk/payinghmrc/ If you don't believe that this payment is overdue, please contact us on the number above.	8,499	3.5 % *
Interest	We are charging you interest on this amount	8,483	4.0 % *

An issue that has been highly prominent in the debate on behavioural public policy is the interpretation of effect size. The tax reminder letter experiments provide a nice example with which to illustrate. Proponents of behavioural science naturally focus on the positive effect that a simple, and essentially costless, change to the wording of a letter has on compliance. If there are around 100,000 people receive a reminder letter with an average debt of around £3000 each (Hallsworth et al. 2017) then a 5 % increase in repayment equates to around £15 million in extra revenue. This, and similar interventions, led to bold headlines on how much money the Nudge Unit was saving the government. Critics of behavioural science, however, highlight that the effect is relatively marginal given there is still around 60 % of debtors that do not pay by 23 days. Moreover, the natural escalation of debt recovery ultimately washes out the effect of the initial reminder letter meaning the overall savings are substantially less than £15 million.

Within this debate there is a natural middle ground (Halpern 2015). Behavioural interventions are, by their very nature likely to be relatively marginal. It is, for instance, a complex problem to recover outstanding debt and so it would be completely unrealistic to expect one sentence in a reminder letter to "solve the problem". While some behavioural interventions and nudges can have big effects (as we will discuss later with pension auto-enrolment) in most settings we should expect relatively small effects. Behavioural interventions, therefore, are not a panacea. That, however, is not a reason to downplay their importance. The tax authorities are sending out hundreds of thousands of letters every year and if a costless change in wording can have a positive benefit, then it is important to evaluate, account for, and analyse that effect.

The tax reminder letters are also a useful illustration of how behavioural public policy has led to increased utilisation of large, systematic randomised control trials to evaluate policy interventions. Pilot studies and trials have clearly been used in public policy for a long time. Their use, however, is somewhat limited in many economic settings by moral and ethical rules. For example, it would generally be considered unethical to randomise the fine that a debtor would receive from not filing their tax return on time. This would result in different material outcomes for debtors which would be hard to justify legally. Economic research is, therefore, often reliant on natural experiments in which, say, tax rules are changed sequentially in different regions (e.g. Feldstein 1995; Irani and Oesch 2013). Behavioural interventions raise fewer ethical objections because they do not directly lead to different material outcomes. For example, changing the wording of a reminder letter has no direct impact on the debtor and so would seem a relatively innocuous intervention. This opens the possibility for large-scale studies, such as Hallsworth et al. (2017). Studies still, however, need to be informed by economic theory and so we now turn our attention to methods that can be used to apply behavioural policy.

23.2 Methods of behavioural policy

We will begin by setting out the basic theory behind Nudge and libertarian paternalism. We will also discuss practical tools governments have available to apply behavioural insights, including the MINDSPACE and COM-B model. This discussion will highlight two distinct roles in which behavioural policy can be applied: (i) to create new policy ideas that use nudges, and (ii) to analyse the potential unintended behavioural consequences of policy. While attention has primarily focused on (i), it can be argued that (ii) is a particularly powerful avenue in which behavioural policy can be applied across government (Dolan et al. 2010). For instance, it has led to more attention around randomised control trials to test policy (Halpern 2015).

To explain the underlying ideas behind nudge let us return to the tax letter example. The framing of a tax letter does not, in any way, alter the choices available to recipient of the letter. The recipient can still pay the tax or not pay the tax. We have seen, however, that the framing of the letter can change the choices that people make in predictable ways. It is, thus, in the interests of the policymaker to frame choices in a way that "nudges" choice towards desirable outcomes. A *choice architect* is anyone responsible for framing a decision that others will take (Thaler and Sunstein 2009). Administrators and policymakers naturally play a role of choice architects in deciding how to frame tax letters and more generally frame interventions. A nudge, to quote from Thaler and Sunstein (2009, 6), is "any aspect of the choice architecture that alters people's behavior in a predictable way without forbidding any options or significantly changing their economic incentives. To count as a mere nudge, the intervention must be easy and cheap to avoid." Another example of a nudge, that we will consider in more detail below, is changing the default option. For instance, changing the default option to being automatically enrolled in a savings plan rather than having to opt in. The options and economic incentives remain exactly the same, irrespective of the default option. The choice architect has merely changed the framing of choices in a way that can influence behaviour.

Two inter-related questions to consider in applying nudges, or behavioural insights more generally, are: (i) in what settings are nudges likely to be most needed, and (ii) how we can design nudges to bring about the desired effect? We consider each question in turn.

At a basic level, nudges are most needed in settings where individuals are likely to make "wrong" choices, either for their own interest and/or that of society. For instance, delaying the payment of a tax bill harms the individual (because they will incur interest and additional hassle) and harms the taxpayer (who must fund debt recovery). Similarly, wasting energy heating a home harms the individual (who incurs larger bills) and society (who suffers from increased emissions). A particularly prominent example is that of saving for retirement. Abundant evidence shows that many individuals invest less in retirement savings than would be optimal (Benartzi 2012). This disadvantages the individual and creates an increased need for social insurance. Nudges can, therefore, be targeted at situations with the potential for a win–win, Pareto improvement (Sunstein 2016). In reality, things may not be this simple because, for example, a default savings plan may benefit one person but not be ideal for another (Madrian and Shea 2001). Even so, nudges are ideally directed to improve welfare.

Thaler and Sunstein (2009), drawing on the behavioural science literature, identify a range of factors that can lead to "wrong" choices. These include that the choice is complex, the individual has little experience in making similar choices, has to deal with uncertainty and lack of information, and makes choices their "future self" may regret. Saving for retirement is a choice where all these factors are relevant. The choice of a saving retirement plan is highly complex, must be made with large degrees of uncertainty and by the time the individual retires (and receives feedback on their choices) it is almost certainly too late to make any changes (Benartzi and Thaler 2007). From a policy perspective, "wrong" choices may also be identified from data and evidence. For instance, a government interested in reducing household energy consumption can identify areas in which individual choices can be nudged, whether that be investing in insulation, reducing the temperature on the thermostat, or similar (Zhou and Yang 2016).

We turn our attention next to the question of how nudges can be most effectively designed. In Table 23.2 we briefly set out the six principles Thaler and Sunstein (2009) suggest for a good choice architecture. The first principle on the list, incentives, is the focus of traditional economic policy intervention. For instance, the authorities may increase the interest rate on debt to encourage early repayment. The other five principles are driven by behavioural insights. They are principles to help guide the choice architecture with the objective of nudging individuals to make the "right" decision. Crucially, the principles point to potential pitfalls as well as opportunities. For instance, people are likely to stick with defaults and so it is vital the default is set in the right way. An opt-in saving scheme, for example, will encourage more people to save but can still be a bad choice architecture if the default is set at too low a savings rate (Madrian and Shea 2001).

Table 23.2: Principles for good choice architecture, spell NUDGES.

Principle	Description
iNcentives	People respond to incentives like price and cost, but only if these are salient.
Understand mappings	Help people to understand the consequences of choices for own welfare so that they can make a more informed decision.
Defaults	Defaults matter a lot because of present bias and choice overload, so think carefully about them.
Give feedback	People learn and so respond to feedback on when things are going well or badly.
Expect error	People make mistakes, so we need something that is as forgiving as possible to mistakes they may make.
Structure complex choices	The more complex the choice the more consideration needs to be given on how to structure the problem to help people make good choices.

Source: Thaler and Sunstein (2009).

Nudge sets out a framework for understanding and recognising the importance of behavioural interventions. Complimentary tools exist to guide the choice architect through the process of implementing behavioural interventions. One such tool is MINDSPACE (Dolan et al. 2010; Dolan et al. 2012). This tool provides a practical means to apply insights from behavioural economics and psychology in policymaking. Table 23.3 gives a brief overview of the main principles underlying MINDSPACE. The authors of MINDSPACE were clear to point out that it can serve different purposes (Dolan et al. 2010):

Enhance. MINDSPACE can help policymakers understand how current attempts to change behaviour could be improved.

Introduce. Some of the elements in MINDSPACE are not used extensively by policymakers, yet may have considerable impact.

Reassess. Government needs to understand ways it may be changing the behaviour of citizens unintentionally. It is quite possible that the state is producing unintended – and possibly unwanted – changes in behaviour.

Table 23.3: An overview of MINDSPACE.

Principle	Description
Messenger	We are heavily influenced by who communicates information
Incentives	Our responses to incentives are shaped by predictable mental shortcuts, such as strongly avoiding losses.
Norms	We are strongly influenced by what others do.
Defaults	We "go with the flow" of pre-set options.
Salience	Our attention is drawn to what is novel and seems relevant to us.
Priming	Our acts are often influenced by sub-conscious cues.
Affect	Our emotional associations can powerfully shape our actions.
Commitments	We seek to be consistent with our public promises, and reciprocate acts.
Ego	We act in ways that make us feel better about ourselves.

Source: Dolan et al. (2010)

The EAST framework provides a slightly simplified version of MINDSPACE taking on board the needs of analysts and policymakers working in government (Behavioural Insights Team 2014; Hallsworth et al. 2016). To quote Oliver Letwin, the then UK Minister for Government Policy, "Though we do not claim that EAST is a comprehensive summary of all there is to know about behavioural science, we do think that for busy policymakers, the EAST framework is an accessible, simple way to make more effective and efficient policy." EAST stands for Easy, Attractive, Social and Timely. The underlying logic is that people are more likely to adopt a behaviour if it is easy, their attention is attracted to it, they see others doing it or are encouraged by others to do it, and they are approached or encouraged at the right moment. The approach has been widely applied (Behavioural Insights Team 2014) although it could be seen to simplify the actual process of delivering on complex behavioural interventions (Feitsma 2019).

A final tool we will highlight is the COM-B model or behaviour change wheel (Michie et al. 2011). The model builds on the notion that policies influence behaviour through the interventions they enable or support. Interventions are thus seen as a layer between behaviour and policy. The main forms of intervention are identified as: restrictions, education, persuasion, incentivisation, coercion, training, enablement, modelling and environmental restructuring. This is related to the key policy categories of: environmental/social planning, communication and marketing, legislation, service provision, regulation, fiscal measures and guidelines. Linkages are then identified between behaviour, intervention and policy. For instance, incentivisation, coercion, training, environmental restructuring and enablement are identified as relating to fiscal measures. The COM-B model has been widely applied in studying health behaviours (Michie, Atkins, and West 2014) but is less widely used in economics. This partly reflects how behavioural public policy is in its infancy and so multiple co-existing frameworks have emerged. It also reflects that the COM-B model provides a very holistic model of behavioural intervention, while Nudge and MINDSPACE work with the idea that monetary incentives are still foremost in economic policymaking.

Underlying all the models discussed above is a strong focus on ethics. Some have argued that behaviour change is unethical because it involves "manipulation". This view, however, seems misjudged (Sunstein 2016). For instance, a theme in many behaviour change interventions is to increase the information individuals have, for example informing a taxpayer that nine out of ten people pay their taxes on time. Provided the information is factually correct it would seem ethically defensible to provide such information. Indeed, to argue that information should be "hidden" would seem harder to defend. Thus behavioural public policy is highlighting and identifying ethical issues that were previously ignored.

23.3 The application of behavioural public policy

We finish this chapter by discussing some examples of behavioural public policy and some of its limitations. The list of applications is far too wide to cover in any detail and so we pick out some highlights. There are many resources documenting the wider use of behavioural public policy (e.g. Halpern 2015; OECD 2017; Hallsworth and Kirkman 2020; Manning et al. 2020).

Recall that Nudge is particularly relevant in situations where individuals make "wrong" decisions in a manner that allows Pareto improvement. A prominent example, as already previewed, is saving for retirement. A number of behavioural interventions have been trialled and implemented to good success in this area. The Save More Tomorrow programme involves a worker committing that her retirement savings will automatically increase as her income rises (Benartzi 2012). This is a way for an individual to "procrastinate" on saving – the increase in saving is delayed – but in a way that is not particularly harmful, because saving will ultimately increase. The Save More Tomorrow programme has proved highly successful with dramatic increases in saving. Crucially, the programme does not in any way restrict or alter choice, it merely provides a good choice architecture to encourage saving.

Another example of good choice architecture is changing the default option. Several countries, beginning with New Zealand in 2006, implemented schemes in which workers are automatically enrolled in saving schemes (Rudolph 2019). Again, this qualifies as a nudge because only the default has changed and so a worker can freely opt out of the automatic enrolment. And, again, it has proved successful with dramatic increases in enrolment and saving. Some care, however, is needed in measuring success (Choi et al. 2003). For instance, if the automatic enrolment is into a scheme with a low savings rate and low interest rate that it may be sup-optimal. Indeed, for some, auto-enrolment may be worse than no enrolment because the default creates inertia.

Another setting in which behavioural interventions have been applied is in tackling consumer procrastination in switching to alternative, cheaper options, for insurance, energy supply, broadband packages etc. The novel aspect of this setting is how policy is designed to redress the choice architecture put in place by the private sector. A household energy supplier may, for instance, make it burdensome for consumers to switch providers. This choice architecture, called sludge, benefits the provider by discouraging switching (Thaler 2018). Policy can be designed to overcome such sludge. For instance, by facilitating easy comparison of providers and minimising the costs of switching (e.g. Tyers, Sweeney, and Moon 2019). These ideas can be applied to encourage switching in other aspects, such as energy home improvements (DellaValle and Sareen 2020).

The areas in which behavioural interventions have been applied is vast, including labour markets, environmental choices, and health and lifestyle choices. As we highlighted earlier, behavioural interventions are not a panacea for solving the world's problems. They are, though, changing the public policy landscape in a way that is encouraging the exploration of new solutions, and of systematically trialling and evaluating policy interventions. This was clear during the COVID-19 pandemic and is welcome in an era where we are seeing unprecedented amounts of data and pressing global problems such as climate change. Behavioural public policy is likely, therefore, to have a telling impact for the long term, particularly if we embrace a wide definition of behavioural public policy that is not solely focused on nudge (Ewert 2020).

We finish by highlighting an important challenge for the future of behavioural public policy, namely the extent to which it will become integrated within policy architecture. The current landscape is characterised by "nudge units" that sit somewhat independent and advise government. This includes nudge units from developed countries advising governments in less developed countries. As expertise and understanding grows it can be expected that behavioural public policy will become increasingly integrated within policymaking rather than sit alongside it (Gopalan and Pirog 2017).

References

Behavioural Insights Team. 2014. *EAST. Four Simple Ways to Apply Behavioural Insights*. https://www.bi.team/wp-content/uploads/2015/07/BIT-Publication-EAST_FA_WEB.pdf

Benartzi, S. 2012. *Save More Tomorrow: Practical Behavioral Finance Solutions to Improve 401 (K) Plans*. New York: Penguin.

Benartzi, S., and R. Thaler. 2007. "Heuristics and Biases in Retirement Savings Behavior." *Journal of Economic Perspectives* 21 (3), 81–104.

Bicchieri, C. 2016. *Norms in the Wild: How to Diagnose, Measure, and Change Social Norms*. Oxford: Oxford University Press.

Bobek, D. D., A. M. Hageman, and C. F. Kelliher. 2013. "Analyzing the Role of Social Norms in Tax Compliance Behavior." *Journal of Business Ethics* 115 (3), 451–468.

Bruni, L., and R. Sugden. 2007. "The Road Not Taken: How Psychology was Removed from Economics, and How It Might Be Brought Back." *The Economic Journal* 117 (516), 146–173.

Choi, J. J., D. Laibson, B. C. Madrian, and A. Metrick. 2003. "Optimal Defaults." *American Economic Review* 93 (2), 180–185.

DellaValle, N., and S. Sareen. 2020. "Nudging and Boosting for Equity? Towards a Behavioural Economics of Energy Justice." *Energy Research and Social Science* 68, 101589.

Dolan, P., M. Hallsworth, D. Halpern, D. King, and I. Vlaev. 2010. *MINDSPACE: Influencing Behaviour for Public Policy*. https://www.instituteforgovernment.org.uk/sites/default/files/publications/MINDSPACE.pdf

Dolan, P., M. Hallsworth, D. Halpern, D. King, R. Metcalfe, and I. Vlaev. 2012. "Influencing Behaviour: The Mindspace Way." *Journal of Economic Psychology* 33 (1), 264–277.

Dwenger, N., H. Kleven, I. Rasul, and J. Rincke. 2016. "Extrinsic and Intrinsic Motivations for Tax Compliance: Evidence from a Field Experiment in Germany." *American Economic Journal: Economic Policy* 8 (3), 203–232.

Ewert, B. 2020. "Moving Beyond the Obsession with Nudging Individual Behaviour: Towards a Broader Understanding of Behavioural Public Policy." *Public Policy and Administration* 35 (3), 337–360.

Farrow, K., G. Grolleau, and L. Ibanez. 2017. "Social Norms and Pro-Environmental Behavior: A Review of the Evidence." *Ecological Economics* 140, 1–13.

Feitsma, J. 2019. "Brokering Behaviour Change: The Work of Behavioural Insights Experts in Government." *Policy and Politics* 47 (1), 37–56.

Feldstein, M. 1995. "Behavioral Responses to Tax Rates: Evidence from the Tax Reform Act of 1986." *The American Economic Review* 85 (2), 170–174.

Gopalan, M., and M. A. Pirog. 2017. "Applying Behavioral Insights in Policy Analysis: Recent Trends in the United States." *Policy Studies Journal* 45 (S1), S82–S114.

Halpern, D. 2015. *Inside the Nudge Unit: How Small Changes Can Make A Big Difference*. London: W. H. Allen.

Halpern, D., and M. Sanders. 2016. "Nudging by Government: Progress, Impact, and Lessons Learned." *Behavioral Science and Policy* 2 (2), 52–65.

Hallsworth, M., and E. Kirkman. 2020. *Behavioral Insights*. Cambridge, MA: MIT Press.

Hallsworth, M., V. Snijders, H. Burd, J. Prestt, G. Judah, S. Huf, and D. Halpern. 2016. *Applying Behavioral Insights: Simple Ways to Improve Health Outcomes*. World Innovation Summit for Health, Doha, Qatar, 29–30 November. https://www.bi.team/wp-content/uploads/2016/11/WISH-2016_Behavioral_Insights_Report.pdf

Hallsworth, M., J. A. List, R. D. Metcalfe, and I. Vlaev. 2017. "The Behavioralist as Tax Collector: Using Natural Field Experiments to Enhance Tax Compliance." *Journal of Public Economics* 148, 14–31.

Haynes, L. C., D. P. Green, R. Gallagher, P. John, and D. J. Torgerson. 2013. "Collection of Delinquent Fines: An Adaptive Randomized Trial to Assess the Effectiveness of Alternative Text Messages." *Journal of Policy Analysis and Management* 32 (4), 718–730.

Hernandez, M., J. Jamison, E. Korczyc, N. Mazar, and R. Sormani. 2017. *Applying Behavioral Insights to Improve Tax Collection: Experimental Evidence from Poland*. Washington, D.C.: World Bank.

Irani, R. M., and D. Oesch. 2013. "Monitoring and Corporate Disclosure: Evidence from a Natural Experiment." *Journal of Financial Economics* 109 (2), 398–418.

Jacobson, R. P., C. R. Mortensen, and R. B. Cialdini. 2011. "Bodies Obliged and Unbound: Differentiated Response Tendencies for Injunctive and Descriptive Social Norms." *Journal of Personality and Social Psychology* 100 (3), 433–448.

Kettle, S., M. Hernandez, S. Ruda, and M. Sanders. 2016. *Behavioral Interventions in Tax Compliance: Evidence from Guatemala*. Washington, D.C.: The World Bank.

Madrian, B. C., and D. F. Shea. 2001. "The Power of Suggestion: Inertia in 401(k) Participation and Savings Behavior." *The Quarterly Journal of Economics* 116 (4), 1149–1187.

Manning, L, A. Dalton, A. Goodnow, A. Zeina, R. Vakis, and N. Faisal. 2020. *Behavioral Science Around the World: Volume Two – Profiles of 17 International Organizations*. eMBeD brief Washington, D.C.: World Bank Group.

Michie, S., M. M. Van Stralen, and R. West. 2011. "The Behaviour Change Wheel: A New Method for Characterising and Designing Behaviour Change Interventions." *Implementation Science* 6 (1), 1–12.

Michie, S., L. Atkins, and R. West. 2014. *The Behaviour Change Wheel. A Guide to Designing Interventions*. Sutton: Silverback Publishing.

OECD. 2017. *Behavioural Insights and Public Policy: Lessons from Around the World*, Paris: OECD Publishing.

OECD. 2019. *Tools and Ethics for Applied Behavioural Insights: The BASIC Toolkit*. Paris: OECD Publishing. https://doi.org/10.1787/9ea76a8f-en.

Oliver, A. (ed.) 2013. *Behavioural Public Policy*. Cambridge: Cambridge University Press.

Rudolph, H. P. 2019. "Pension Funds with Automatic Enrollment Schemes: Lessons for Emerging Economies." *World Bank Policy Research Working Paper* (8726). Washington, D.C.: World Bank. https://openknowledge.worldbank.org/handle/10986/31230

Sanders, M., V. Snijders, and M. Hallsworth. 2018. "Behavioural Science and Policy: Where Are We Now and Where Are We Going?" *Behavioural Public Policy* 2 (2), 144–167.

Straßheim, H. 2020. "The Rise and Spread of Behavioral Public Policy: An Opportunity for Critical Research and Self-Reflection." *International Review of Public Policy* 2 (1), 115–128.

Sunstein, C. R. 2016. *The Ethics of Influence: Government in the Age of Behavioral Science*. Cambridge: Cambridge University Press.

Thaler, R. H. 2015. *Misbehaving: The Making of Behavioral Economics*. London: Allen Lane.

Thaler, R. H. 2018. "Nudge, Not Sludge." *Science* 361 (6401), 431.

Thaler, R. H., and C. R. Sunstein. 2009. *Nudge: Improving Decisions About Health, Wealth, and Happiness*. New York: Penguin Books.

Tyers, R., M. Sweeney, and B. Moon. 2019. "Harnessing Behavioural Insights to Encourage Consumer Engagement in the British Energy Market: Results from a Field Trial." *Journal of Behavioral and Experimental Economics* 80, 162–176.

Wenzel, M. 2005. "Motivation or Rationalisation? Causal Relations Between Ethics, Norms and Tax Compliance." *Journal of Economic Psychology* 26 (4), 491–508.

Zhou, K., and S. Yang. 2016. "Understanding Household Energy Consumption Behavior: The Contribution of Energy Big Data Analytics." *Renewable and Sustainable Energy Reviews* 56, 810–819.

Tao Liu
24 North–South divide and global social policy

Abstract: Traditional research on the global North–South divide mainly focuses on the inequality of wealth distribution in northern and southern countries. This chapter assumes that the North–South divide in a global world includes inequality at the material and immaterial levels, including the level of uneven capacity to generate wealth and ideas. This article will explore the possibility of establishing a global redistribution mechanism under the increased global inequality. It mainly analyses which institutional conditions are conducive to and unfavourable for establishing a global redistribution mechanism including the paradoxical developments of strengthened global social cooperation on the one hand and the new trend of isolation and disentanglement of big powers on the other hand. It also analyses influential discourses and narratives at international level on eliminating the differences in redistribution of the material, institutional and symbolic resources between the North and the South such as the Tobin tax. In this process, the (dis-)integration of the European Union and the coordination of social policies within the EU framework could provide valuable and rich experiences for the discussion of a "cosmopolitan welfare state" beyond the welfare nationalism. Finally, this chapter will also attempt to propose some new schemes for global social policy and welfare.

Keywords: global, inequality, social policy, socio-material, immaterial, redistribution

24.1 Introduction

So far, most studies on social inequality have focused on the stratum inequality and regional inequality within nation states. However, it is an inescapable reality that social inequality, to a large extent, is not only a matter within national boundaries, since the most important and essential inequality on our planet is the inequality between countries and regions (Kreckel 2006). In other words, birthplaces and passports may be the biggest source of human inequality (Mau et al. 2015). For most people on earth, the country where they were born often fundamentally determines the material conditions and political, economic, cultural, social, and welfare rights. For example, two citizens born in Switzerland and in Swaziland may have completely different education, health, and welfare conditions since birth, and have completely different macro conditions to be defined as a social citizen or a non-social citizen. In this sense, social inequality more embodies social inequality on a scale beyond the scope of nation states, that is, the inequality and gap between the global North and South is essential and deterministic. The study of social inequality also needs to transcend the methodological

https://doi.org/10.1515/9783110721768-024

nationalism (in the sense of Ulrich Beck) (Weiss 2017), and it also needs to break through the container-model of the nation-states and open up new horizons for studying inequality through a global lens (Beck 2007).

In the existing research on world inequality, the research mainly focuses on the uneven distribution of material wealth and income in the world, which is undoubtedly an important part of the research. However, it is undeniable that the inequality of human society is not only in the material realm, but also in the social realm, especially in the realm of primary public services, such as the accessibility of medical and health services, as well as the right to education. Additionally, in the digital era, it also includes the digital ability and the so-called "digital literacy" which would further widen the gap in the world society. Moreover, the inequality of human society should also include the inequality in the spirit level, which is not only reflected in the unequal distribution of available cultural facilities in the world like bookstores and libraries, but also includes the ability to create world cultural and spiritual products. That means, in addition to the inequality in the realm of material wealth, the inequality in the immaterial, symbolic, and cultural realm is also one of the main sources of inequality. This paper mainly discusses the inequality in the world, including the inequality in the socio-material and immaterial realms, showing the gap between the global North and global South in many different sub-fields, such as economy, education, welfare, and culture, at the same time, it explores possible paths for redistribution on a global scale to bridge the gap between the North and South.

24.2 Global social inequality in socio-material and immaterial realms

When it comes to global inequality, theoretically we can first benefit from the world system theory in the field of sociology. According to the international industry and labour division, the world system theory divides the world market into three levels: centre, periphery, and semi-periphery (Wallerstein 1976). The centre is at the top of a global value chain and mainly exports industrial products to periphery countries. The periphery countries do not have basic industrial capacity, can only export raw materials and energy products to core countries, while semi-periphery countries can export some primary processed products to other parts of the world. Overall, periphery and semi-periphery countries are in a disadvantaged and marginalised position. They are exploited by the core countries in the uneven exchange relationship of a world market and are forced to exchange the manufacturing products of the central countries with raw materials with cheap prices. Therefore, inequality in the world is mainly reflected in the inequality of economic relations and international labour division. Although the world system theory constitutes a starting point for the study of social inequality in the world, it still fails to grasp and analyse various forms of inequality in the world more comprehensively, and only regards world inequality as the inequality in the world market. In the last two decades, some sociological studies have gradually begun to pay attention to inequality worldwide and believe that from the angle of a world society, social inequality must first be attributed to inequality caused by different regions and countries in the world (Milanovic 2006, 2013; Kreckel 2006; Weiss 2017; Greve 2010).

Most of the existing research on global social inequality and globalisation of inequality focus on several aspects related to the material reserves, especially the unequal distribution of material wealth in the world, such as the unequal distribution of income and assets between the North and South, the welfare state in the North and the marginalised economy and population in the South, etc. Economic capacity and strength as well as material wealth have become important means to compare the living standards of all countries in the world, but also to measure the North–South divide at a world scale. The gap between northern and southern states is first reflected in the huge gap in per capita GDP. At the same time, the human development index (HDI) developed by the United Nations is an important indicator to distinguish different levels of development between countries, as well as an important yardstick to measure the gap between the North and South. Other important indicators to measure global inequality include public service facilities, basic public services, such as the accessibility to primary public health care and public education and the coverage degree of these public services. Other common discussions and studies on global inequality also include the level of industrialisation, technological strength, and innovation ability. One indicator often used in the question of North–South divide is the indicator of digitalisation, which is usually called the digital and technological gap between North and South; it is mainly used to measure the number of internet users and the accessibility of broadband in each country. In these areas, there is a huge gap between the southern and northern countries.

This study links the existing research results and theories on global inequality and assumes that the indicators and indexes of previous studies on global inequality are of great relevance and cognitive significance. On this basis, the author advocates the establishment of multi-dimensional index system that identifies the North–South divide. In such a multidimensional inequality index complex, global inequality contains different levels of social facts and social phenomenon. Firstly, it includes inequality at the material level, which is also a domain we are familiar with, and it includes all the inequalities associated with the economic and wealth levels. The second level includes inequality at the social level, including inequality in the fields of life expectancy, per capita consumption, education, medicine, and social welfare which is closely related to the economic, monetary, and fiscal capacity of different national governments. The first two indicators can also be merged into a socio-material level of inequality, since such forms of inequality is tangible and accessible, and can be perceived and measured easily. The author assumes that there is also a widely neglected realm of global inequality, that is, the global inequality at the immaterial le-

vel, which includes the level of soft power including culture, political values and foreign policies, different countries have completely different cultural and ideological
strengths. The core countries can output their ruling ideas and thinking pattern to periphery countries through culture dissemination, while the periphery countries are culturally influenced, controlled and shaped by the core countries. The immaterial field
is important and indispensable because different cultural powers and capability of
creating discourse can put the leading countries in an advantageous position in constructing the international institutions, rules, and mechanisms, which is conducive to
the dominant position of the ruling countries, while the periphery southern countries
with low capacity of generating influential discourses and cultural goods are situated
in a disadvantaged position with fewer voices.

In terms of research methods, this paper adopts the research methods commonly
used in the neo-institutional "world polity" theory (Meyer et al. 1997; Meyer and
Jepperson 2000), that is, using the data of international governmental organisations
(IGOs) and international non-governmental organisations (INGOs) to show the deep
and insurmountable gap between the northern and southern countries in the socio-
material and immaterial realms. IGOs and INGOs are generally regarded as "disinter-
ested others" that possess high credibility in world society (Meyer et al. 1997), and
they are responsible for transmitting world cultural principles and ideas such as rationalisation, market economy, and human rights concepts to the rest of world. From another perspective, they also produce and publish standardised data in various realms
such as socio-material and immaterial realms (Berten and Leisering 2017). Through
the global accessibility and global sharing of these data produced by the World Bank,
UNDP, ILO, ISSA etc., we are able to construct an emerging world society and various
forms of inequality within the world society. Different from the trend of "isomorph-
ism" constructed by the theorists of the "world-polity" approach (Beckfield 2010), this
paper shows the heterogeneity and gap between the Global North and South through
these data provided by IGOs and INGOs. As sociologist Tobias Werron has concluded,
big data available in various fields has become an enabler of the competition in a cosmopolitan world (Werron 2014). It is precisely because of these data that we can create
a global comparison horizon to compare all kinds of economies and countries (Heintz
and Werron 2011) and more profoundly reveal the various forms of inequality in the
world society.

24.3 Constructing an uneven global society with multi-dimensional criteria

24.3.1 North–South divide in the socio-material realm

The gap between the North and South in the world is mainly described as a gap in the socio-material realm, and the most commonly used indicator is the one reflecting economic welfare and living standards. The classic indicator reflecting the world economy and the economic differences between the North and South is the per capita GDP provided by the World Bank annually, especially including the per capita PPP calculated according to the purchasing power of each country based on the exchange rate of each country's currency against the US dollar.[1] Whether based on per capita GDP or per capita PPP, the economic gap between the North and South of the world shows a similar dynamic with approximately the same granularity. The traditional European and North America without Mexico, together with Japan, South Korea, and Asian emerging economies, firmly occupy the top of the world economic pyramid, while most Asian countries, most Latin American countries, and African countries are at an absolute disadvantage in the world economy. According to data from the World Bank in 2015, the global absolute poverty population – that is, the population with daily income less than $1.9 is more than 700 million, all of which are distributed in the Global South.[2] The International Monetary Fund (IMF) provides similar indicators every year.[3] Another indicator that is very similar to GDP per capita is the World Bank's indicator for high-income and non-high-income economies, although the cluster group of non-high-income economy can be further subdivided into low-income, lower middle-income, and upper middle-income economies, however, the difference between high-income and non-high-income economies is a main indicator to divide core countries and those who are outside the exclusive elite group.[4] The boundary between North and South on the earth is also roughly the same as that of high-income and low-income economies. The Human Development Index (HDI) is an additional important indicator developed by the United Nations Development Programme (UNDP) to reflect a country's social and economic development and welfare status. It includes three sub-

---

1 See the data bank on GDP and PPP of all countries provided by the World Bank, available under https://data.worldbank.org/indicator/NY.GDP.MKTP.PP.CD.
2 See the report "Global Poverty Line Update" by the World Bank, available under https://www.worldbank.org/en/topic/poverty/brief/global-poverty-line-faq.
3 See the "world economic outlook database" provided by the IMF, available under https://www.imf.org/en/Publications/WEO/weo-database/2021/April/weo-report.
4 According to the data of the World Bank in 2019, high-income countries are those whose per capita GDP exceeds US $12535 per year, see the data bank of the World Bank, available under https://datahelpdesk.worldbank.org/knowledgebase/articles/906519#High_income.

indicators including (1) life expectancy, (2) years of schooling (including years of schooling completed and expected years of schooling after entering the education system) and (3) income per capita.[5] Thus, HDI involves three fields covering health, education, and economy, and it is often used to describe the global inequality and the North–South divide. The northern countries have higher HDI values, while the southern countries have lower HDI values. The value of 0.8 is a rough threshold and dividing line, which distinguishes the developed countries in the global North from the underdeveloped countries in the global South. Moreover, the socio-technical level of indicators also belongs to the socio-material realm in a broad sense. It is an indicator often used in the North–South divide in addition to social economy and social welfare. For example, the digital and technological divide is used to describe global inequality. The digital and technological gap usually includes the use and prevalence of the internet, the internet speed, the accessibility, and quality of broadband, etc. In the field of digital and communication technology, some emerging economies in Asia are catching up and have the potential to become leading countries in the future. However, it is undeniable that the differences in the digital and technological gap between the North and South continue to exist and tend to solidify for a long time. The international Telecommunication Union (ITU) is the most important information and data provider in this field.[6] According to the big data provided by ITU, researchers can track the gap of digital and communication technology in the global world for a long time.

Table 24.1: The North–South divide in a global world in the socio-material realm

Fields	Indicators or criteria	Producers of the world data	Functions
Economic field	GDP, GNP, PPP	World Bank, IMF	Distinguishing different cluster states with different economic capacities; distinguishing high-income and low- and middle-income countries
Social field	HDI	UNDP	Distinguishing different cluster states with different social, health and educational levels

---

5 See the website of UNDP on the Human Development Index (HDI), available under http://hdr.undp. org/en/content/human-development-index-hdi.
6 See the report "Measuring Digital Development: Facts and Figures 2020" by ITU, available under https://www.itu.int/en/ITU-D/Statistics/Pages/facts/default.aspx.

Table 24.1 (continued)

Fields	Indicators or criteria	Producers of the world data	Functions
Technical field	Global digital and tectological divide	The International Telecommunication Union (ITU)	Distinguishing different cluster states with different technological and digital capacities
Field of income distribution	Gini index at a world scale	The United Nations University World Institute	Demonstrating income inequality around the globe

Source: Author's own compilation

If the world is regarded as a country or a unified region, then the inequity of the world can also be measured by the Gini coefficient. So far, Gini coefficient is mainly used to measure the income inequality within a country, and it can also be used to measure the inequality of income distribution in a certain region of a country. Beyond the scope of nation-state, the United Nations University World Institute for development uses the world income inequality database (WIID) to measure the income inequality in the world. According to the data provided by the WIID, the relative Gini coefficient in the world decreased from 0.739 in 1975 to 0.631 in 2010,[7] income inequality around the world seems to be slowing at first glance. However, there are two explanations for this trend: (1) Gini coefficient of 0.613 is still high, which shows that although the income gap in the world has narrowed, we still live in a very unequal world with extremely uneven distribution of income. Commonly, if the Gini coefficient exceeds 0.4, it crosses the threshold of social instability for a society (Lyon, Cheung, and Gastwirth 2016); (2) The decline of Gini coefficient all over the world is especially due to the rapid economic development of China and India in the past three decades. The two countries with huge populations have lifted millions of residents out of poverty through rapid economic development. After deducting the successful factors of poverty alleviation in China and India, especially in China,[8] the inequality of income distribution in the world would be much higher. A flattened world that narrows the gap between the North and South is still far from us.

---

7 See the website of the United Nations University: https://unu.edu/media-relations/releases/global-income-inequality-unu-wider-press-release.html#info.
8 According to the data released by the World Bank in 2017, China's economic reform has lifted nearly 800 million people out of poverty, and China's development has greatly reduced the world's poor population, see the website of the World Bank: https://www.worldbank.org/en/news/speech/2017/12/07/from-local-to-global-china-role-global-poverty-reduction-future-of-development.

In addition to these general indicators, there are many sub-indicators in various fields that can show the huge gap between the world's North and South, such as access to clean drinking water, consumption of meat products, air quality, environmental quality, distribution of infectious diseases, etc. Whether an earth citizen is born in the global society of the North or the South will largely determine what kind of basic public goods and public services one obtains and what kind of environment one lives in, which is the essence of global inequality between core and periphery.

24.3.2 North–South divide in the immaterial realm

Until now, the study on global inequality has mainly focused on the socio-material realm, or the technical and digital realm, while global inequality in the immaterial realm is almost completely ignored. According to the neo-Gramscian approach, culture is the tool to safeguard the interests of the ruling class, and also an important way to create and legitimate the ruling hegemony in a society (Bieler et al. 2006). In a globalised world, the "dominant country" that holds the tools of cultural influences and discourse power can define rules and shape universal behaviour codes in global society, where cultural advantages and cultural dominance are also an essential manifestation of global inequality among countries and regions. From this point of view, countries with ideational capacity of creating universally recognised discourses in the field of public cultural products and social sciences have great power to influence the international norm system and international rules, so as to safeguard and consolidate the material interests of the dominant nation-states in general, like in the case of US influences on international relations (Krippendorf 1987). Here, the immaterial realm and the material realm of inequality are intricately linked. The world-polity theorists of Stanford University have concluded that the modern international organisation system and international belief system are based on the Western dominant culture through a lot of empirical research and theoretical construction. A "world culture" spreads all over the world through international governmental and non-governmental organisations, but its roots come from western culture, mainly including universalism, individualism, rationalism, and social progress ideas (Meyer et al. 1997; Boli and Thomas 1997). Here, the advantage of hard power is converted into the advantage of soft power.

From the angle of immaterial products, there is a deeper cultural gap between the northern and southern countries, in other words, the gap between the North and South in this realm is even greater than that in the socio-material realm. It is obvious that the social science theories we are now familiar with, whether they are theories of economics, politics, management, law, history, philosophy, social welfare, public administration, social policy, etc., are all from the West. Even the theories criticising western capitalist hegemony, such as the world system theory developed by Immanuel Wallerstein (Wallerstein 1979), also come from the West. The southern countries are completely passive and "voiceless" in theoretical discourses and theoretical creation. They can only follow the Western cultural tradition to establish their own academic disciplines. Southern countries rarely have influential social science theories in the world scientific community. In the field of public cultural products and social sciences, the northern countries occupy an absolute dominant position. From the perspective of the international system of the United Nations after World War II, the UN agencies and their symbolic power representing the world were also established by the victorious and powerful nations. Although a few non-western countries, such as Russia and China, were also among them, the international law system based on the United Nations was still established and dominated by the cluster countries of the Global North. Judging from these facts, the southern countries have almost no say in the international belief and organisational system owing to their weak discourse positions. Another indicator of cultural and ideological creativity is university rankings. In several international rankings,[9] the top 100 universities do not include any universities from Latin America and African countries. In Asian countries, only universities from Singapore, China, Japan, and South Korea are shortlisted, however, these East Asian and Southeast Asian countries have been included in the list of quasi-northern countries. The development level of university education and scientific research also reflects the huge gap between the southern countries and the northern countries in the world society. According to the soft power rankings developed by the two media companies Monocle and Portland to reflect cultural influence in 2018 and 2019, the 15 countries with the strongest soft power are northern countries, including the United States, European countries, Japan, and South Korea. The two different rankings are very consistent in showing the absolute supremacy and influence of the northern countries in the cultural field.[10]

24.4 The notion and concept of global redistribution – a utopian or post-utopian ideal type?

Because there is no global government or a world welfare state, there is no authoritative international entity with the prestige and legitimacy to implement a large-scale redistribution plan around the globe. However, there has never been a shortage of

---

9 They include four major ranking for education in the world, namely the USNEWS World University Rankings, QS World University Rankings, Times Higher Education World University Rankings, and ARWU World University Academic Rankings.
10 See Portland's Soft Power 30 report 2019, available under https://softpower30.com, and also see the Monocle's Soft Power Survey 2018/19, available under https://monocle.com/film/affairs/soft-power-survey-2018-19/.

creative ideas and innovative policy designs on a global scale for a worldwide redistribution. Tobin tax, which was proposed by the American economist James Tobin in 1972, advocates a global uniform tax on spot foreign exchange transactions. Its purpose is to reduce the market turbulence caused by speculative trading. The initiator of this idea believes that if this kind of tax system is adopted globally, it will reduce the volatility caused by speculation in the foreign exchange market and stabilise global trade. The tax revenues from the Tobin tax can be used as a global redistribution of income, invested in underdeveloped southern countries, and promote their economic development. Although the Tobin tax has triggered heated discussions around the world and has become an influential idea, it has remained in the discourse of the global left-wing for a long time, and there is still a lack of sufficient operation methods for real implementation at global and national level, so it is more like a utopian concept (Felix 1995; Johnson 1997).

In the post-utopian era, Robin Hood tax, the version 2.0 of Tobin tax, obtained a more realistic and operable scheme. In 2010, the Robin Hood tax campaign was jointly promoted by more than 50 charities and some international organisations, such as Comic Relief, Friends of the Earth, Greenpeace, Oxfam, and UNICEF. The campaign advocates a 0.05 % tax on global cross-border financial investment, especially on financial institutions, banks, and hedge funds, that means those special financial products and benefits from stocks, banks and hedge funds, real estate and financial derivatives will become major taxpayers. Half of the collected funds will go into the national budget, while the other half will be invested in international development aid. Therefore, the plan called for by the campaign has a strong global North–South redistribution feature. This plan immediately received a strong response in the United Kingdom, the United States, Canada, and European countries. In the post financial crisis era, it won the support of a large number of people in northern countries. Drawing lessons from the global financial crisis, the global redistribution plan gained greater popularity and legitimacy in 2010 and 2011(Sachs 2012; Franko, Tolbert, and Witko 2013).

This scheme has attracted great attention in the European Union and has become the main source of European Union Financial Transaction Tax. In 2012, some major powers within the EU, such as Germany, France, Italy, and Spain, were in favour of implementing the financial transaction tax, while some countries, such as Denmark, Czech Republic, and Luxembourg, were opposed to it, and some Central and Eastern European countries remained undecided. In 2014, 11 EU countries, including Germany and France, decided to levy Robin Hood tax from 2016.[11] According to this concept, every transaction of stocks, bonds, and financial derivatives of financial institutions in EU countries will be taxed, and the EU can levy 35 billion euros of tax every year.

---

[11] See the report form global tax news: https://www.tax-news.com/news/EU11_Scolded_For_Opa que_Financial_Transaction_Tax_Talks____64612.html.

However, the proposal met with opposition from some EU countries, such as the UK, the Netherlands, and Sweden. At that time, Britain, which was still a member of the European Union, strongly opposed the tax system. It was worried that more international capital would flow to countries and regions without this sort of tax, such as Singapore and Hong Kong. Once the financial transaction tax was implemented, it would bring huge financial losses to British and European household savings. Faced with the veto player's opposition, Europe's "Robin Hood tax" finally ran aground, but it is indeed the closest to a transnational and cross-border concept with global redistribution function in human history.

The different attitudes of EU countries towards "Robin Hood tax" also reflected the different economic structure and economic interests of member states. When a country's financial sector is larger, the transaction tax levied is higher, and when a country's manufacturing sector is large, it will pay less tax. Judging from the economic structure of EU countries at that time, France and Germany were the strongest advocators, which was also related to the high share of manufacturing industries in the two countries, while the UK was a firm opponent, which was related to the high proportion of financial sector in the UK. London Financial District was an eminent economic entity that 99 % relied on financial transactions. If the "Robin Hood tax" were to be passed, then the overall economic competitiveness of London would be seriously affected. This was also the main reason why Robin Hood's hometown opposed the "Robin Hood tax". Denmark and Sweden were also opposed to the "Robin Hood tax" because of the same doubts. In the 1980s, Sweden adopted a policy similar to the "Robin Hood tax", but this led to a large outflow of financial capital to London. The heterogeneity within the EU has affected the EU's actions. The shelving of "Robin Hood tax" in the European Union once again proves how difficult a supranational social policy of the European Union is. When it comes to the win–win situation of economic cooperation and market opening, nearly all EU member states are willing to join, and when it comes to redistribution and social policy, some member states will form an opposition alliance to block the social policy at the unified level of the EU. The heterogeneity within the EU is also the reason why it is difficult for the EU to effectively act in social policy.

24.5 Conclusion: global inequality needs new forms of global social policy

In the process of globalisation, the gap between the North and South is significant both in the socio-material realm and in the immaterial realm. Except for the emergence of a few emerging Asian economies as newly industrialised countries, the gap between the North and South is still difficult to bridge, which has become the biggest legitimacy issue of current global society. This paper argues that to understand global inequality, we need to understand it not only from the perspectives of economy, welfare, education, and life expectancy, but also from the perspectives of cultural products, public goods, and the output and diffusion capacity of knowledge. Only by understanding the gap from both the material and immaterial realm can we have a more complete understanding of global inequality. The typology of centre and periphery shall be redefined as an idea type based on uneven economic and cultural exchange, centre in the cultural sense relates to those cluster states who are able to generate global ideas, theories, and normative regulations to influence other countries, periphery in the cultural sense is related to the regions who are completely marginalised in global discourse-making.

The huge discrepancy between the North and South requires us to have creative ideas and innovative strategies to narrow the gap between the North and South. So far, the research on global social policy mainly focuses on how international governmental organisations and non-governmental organisations have shaped the social policymaking of nation states (Deacon 1997; Béland and Orenstein 2013). Some studies also involve the impact of international trade and globalisation on the internal social policy of the nation-state (Guan 2001; Dreher 2006), some focused upon ideas transfer and policy diffusion (Leisering, Liu, and Ten Brink 2017; Liu and Leisering 2018), but few studies involve the issue of global redistribution. In fact, global redistribution can be realised in various forms. For example, (1) a strong international organisation system, such as the United Nations organisation system or the G20, can levy taxes on cross-border financial transactions worldwide. The taxes should be mainly collected in high-income northern countries, and they will be mainly invested in low-income countries. (2) The economically powerful countries can imitate the "Marshall Plan" implemented by the United States after World War II, but this time the "Marshall Plan" will no longer aim at Western Europe and Japan, but rather at the third and fourth world countries. However, such a plan may lead the superpowers to pursue their geo-economic and geo-political interests, which may not be the optimal choice for global social policy. A better solution is (3) for international agencies to cooperate with the least developed countries (LDCs) to establish universal basic income in 46 countries with the least economic and productive capacity on earth. Because the social insurance system in the LDCs can only cover the workers with a formal employment relationship, which only accounts for a small part of the total population, the social insurance has only very limited function in eliminating the absolute poverty and famine. Additionally, the social assistance in the LDCs has the possibility of leakage and mistargeting, and it is difficult for the social assistance system to target the real poor in underdeveloped countries due to widespread nepotism and corruption. An unconditional basic income of the whole population will help to solve the above problems. Considering that most residents of the LDCs are poor, a simple and transparent system with less bureaucracy is better. Last but not at least, (4) a supranational social policy, such as the EU social policy, deserves further observation and exploration, because most countries in the world have joined at least one supranational organisation, such as the Association of Southeast Asian Nations (ASEAN), the African Union (AU), the League of Arab States (LAS), etc., and the EU is only one of them. In a supranational entity, there are developed and underdeveloped members, rich and poor members, and a unified economic policy also needs a unified social policy. The formation of a unified market is often the start of supranational social policy coordination, otherwise, even a unified economic policy is difficult to operate. Supranational social policy might be a relevant form of creating global social policy in future development.

References

Beck, U. 2007. "The Cosmopolitan Condition: Why Methodological Nationalism Fails." *Theory, Culture and Society* 24 (7–8), 286–290.

Beckfield, J. 2010. "The Social Structure of the World Polity." *American Journal of Sociology* 115 (4), 1018–1068.

Béland, D., and M. A. Orenstein. 2013. "International Organizations as Policy Actors: An Ideational Approach." *Global Social Policy* 13 (2), 125–143.

Berten, J., and L. Leisering. 2017. "Social Policy by Numbers. How International Organisations Construct Global Policy Proposals." *International Journal of Social Welfare* 26 (2), 151–167.

Bieler, A., W. Bonefeld, P. Burnham, and A. Morton. 2006. *Global Restructuring, State, Capital and Labour: Contesting Neo-Gramscian Perspectives*. Berlin: Springer.

Boli, J., and G. M. Thomas. 1997. "World Culture in the World Polity: A Century of International Non-Governmental Organization." *American Sociological Review* 62 (2), 171–190.

Deacon, B. 1997. *Global Social Policy: International Organizations and the Future of Welfare*. London: Sage.

Dreher, A. 2006. "The Influence of Globalization on Taxes and Social Policy: An Empirical Analysis for OECD Countries." *European Journal of Political Economy* 22 (1), 179–201.

Felix, D. 1995. "The Tobin Tax Proposal: Background, Issues and Prospects." *Futures* 27 (2), 195–208.

Franko, W., C. J. Tolbert, and C. Witko. 2013. "Inequality, Self-Interest, and Public Support for 'Robin Hood' Tax Policies." *Political Research Quarterly* 66 (4), 923–937.

Greve, J. 2010. "Globale Ungleichheit: Weltgesellschaftliche Perspektiven." *Berliner Journal für Soziologie* 20 (1), 65–87.

Guan, X. 2001. "Globalization, Inequality and Social Policy: China on the Threshold of Entry into the World Trade Organization." *Social Policy & Administration* 35 (3), 242–257.

Heintz, B., and T. Werron. 2011. "Wie ist Globalisierung möglich? Zur Entstehung globaler Vergleichshorizonte am Beispiel von Wissenschaft und Sport." *Kölner Zeitschrift für Soziologie und Sozialpsychologie* 63 (3), 359–394.

Johnson, R. 1997. "The Tobin Tax: Another Lost Opportunity?" *Development in Practice* 7 (2), 140–147.

Kreckel, R. 2006. "Soziologie der sozialen Ungleichheit im globalen Kontext." https://www2.soziologie.uni-halle.de/publikationen/pdf/0604.pdf.

Krippendorf, E. 1987. "The Dominance of American Approaches in International Relations." *Millennium* 16 (2), 207–214.

Leisering, L., T. Liu, and T. Ten Brink. 2017. "Synthesizing Disparate Ideas: How a Chinese Model of Social Assistance Was Forged." *Global Social Policy* 17 (3), 307–327.

Liu, T., and L. Leisering. 2017. "Protecting Injured Workers: How Global Ideas of Industrial Accident Insurance Travelled to China." *Journal of Chinese Governance* 2 (1), 106–123.

Lyon, M., L. C. Cheung, and J. L. Gastwirth. 2016. "The Advantages of Using Group Means in Estimating the Lorenz Curve and Gini Index from Grouped Data." *The American Statistician* 70 (1), 25–32.

Mau, S., F. Gülzau, L. Laube, and N. Zaun. 2015. "The Global Mobility Divide: How Visa Policies Have Evolved Over Time." *Journal of Ethnic and Migration Studies* 41 (8), 1192–1213.

Meyer, J. W., J. Boli, G. M. Thomas, and F. O. Ramirez. 1997. "World Society and the Nation-State." *American Journal of Sociology* 103 (1), 144–181.

Meyer, J. W., and R. L. Jepperson. 2000. "The 'Actors' of Modern Society: The Cultural Construction of Social Agency." *Sociological Theory* 18 (1), 100–120.

Milanovic, B. 2006. "Global Income Inequality." *World Economics* 7 (1), 131–157.

Milanovic, B. 2013. "Global Income Inequality in Numbers: In History and Now." *Global Policy* 4 (2), 198–208.

Sachs, J. 2010. "Robin Hood Tax's Time Has Come." *The Guardian*. https://www.theguardian.com/commentisfree/2010/mar/18/robin-hood-tax-benefits.

Wallerstein, I. 1976. "Semi-Peripheral Countries and the Contemporary World Crisis." *Theory and Society* 3 (4), 461–483.

Wallerstein, I. 1979. *The Capitalist World-Economy*. Cambridge: Cambridge University Press.

Weiss, A. 2017. *Soziologie globaler Ungleichheiten*. Berlin: Suhrkamp Verlag.

Werron, T. 2014. "On Public Forms of Competition." *Cultural Studies? Critical Methodologies* 14 (1), 62–76.

Young-Kyu Shin

25 Incentives-disincentives – the benefit side of the welfare states

Abstract: As welfare states need to provide the poor with benefits adequate to make a living and minimise the disincentive to employment implicitly accompanied by the provision of welfare benefits at the same time, a social security system must address a fundamental trade-off between the two factors. For this reason, incentives have been a central part of the discussions on the development and layout of welfare states and many researchers have analysed the interaction between a social security system and people's behaviour. The objective of this chapter is to review how different types of benefits have influenced incentives to work in welfare states. To answer the question, this chapter begins with how to evaluate work incentives resulting from a policy measure related to benefits. After that, the theoretical debate and empirical findings on the effect of unemployment insurance benefits on work incentives are addressed. In addition, in-work benefit schemes, which nowadays many welfare states have operated to encourage the unemployed to take a job, are explored, focusing on the features of such schemes and the empirical literature on their impact in different welfare states. Finally, given the situation that social investment policies have expanded, and dual-earner households have become dominant, this chapter reviews the studies to examine the association between childcare costs and work incentives.

Keywords: work incentives, unemployment insurance, in-work benefit schemes, childcare costs, net replacement rate, marginal effective tax rate, participation tax rate

25.1 Introduction

It is generally believed that welfare states need to provide poor people with benefits adequate to make a living and minimise the disincentive to employment implicitly accompanied by the provision of welfare benefits at the same time. Hence, incentives to work have been one of the core issues in the development of welfare states over several centuries. There has been much discussion about topics such as whether a social security system is equipped with sufficient incentives to encourage jobless people to take a job and whether a tax system could adversely affect people's behaviour related to labour market participation. For a long time the main target of the discussion has been unemployment insurance (UI), as the eligibility to receive it is directly associated with an individual's labour market status. On the other hand, since most welfare states introduced in-work benefits (IWBs) to conduct welfare reforms based on the idea of welfare-to-work in the late twentieth century, many studies have focused on the impacts of IWBs on work incentives. Recently, social investment policies have re-

https://doi.org/10.1515/9783110721768-025

ceived huge attention, particularly in European welfare states and studies on the relations between childcare costs and parents' work incentives have been performed.

The objective of this chapter is to review how the above-mentioned labour market and social policies are associated with work incentives. To achieve the goal, to begin with, section 25.2 introduces how to evaluate work incentives and commonly used measures. Section 25.3 reviews the discussion about UI schemes and work incentives and empirical findings concerning the impact of UI benefits on job search activities, while section 25.4 examines the characteristics of IWB schemes and investigates their effect on work incentives based on findings from single country case studies. Next, in section 25.5, net childcare costs in advanced welfare states are explored and the literature on how they can affect parents' labour market participation is surveyed. Finally, section 25.6 concludes this chapter with a summary and final remarks.

25.2 How to evaluate work incentives

In reality, no one knows what incentives should be offered to encourage people to actively search for a job. Therefore, researchers try to compare the relative degrees of work incentives designed by benefit schemes or examine whether or not a certain benefit actually caused the recipient to enter the labour market. In this context, the literature on the evaluation of the effects of benefits on financial incentives to work can be largely classified into two categories: ex-ante and ex-post approaches, although the specific tactics vary greatly depending on studies within this broad division (Laun 2019). Ex-ante approaches assess the strength of work incentives that policy measures related to benefits can create in a country, particularly in the situation where empirical analyses of their employment effects are not available. These methods usually employ a tax-benefit microsimulation model based on detailed country-specific register data. On the other hand, ex-post approaches evaluate to what extent financial incentives intended by benefit schemes contribute to employment increase by analysing how benefit recipients reacted to incentives. Many studies to estimate the employment effects of benefit schemes such as UI and IWBs before and after their introduction or expansion mainly adopt a "difference-in-differences" approach based on a quasi-experimental design (Laun 2019; Tatsiramos and van Ours 2014).

When it comes to ex-ante approaches, there are three commonly used measures of work incentives: the net replacement rate (NRR), the marginal effective tax rate (METR) and the participation tax rate (PTR). First, RRs imply an individual's out of work income as a percentage of their in work income (Adam and Browne 2010) and are calculated as follows:

$$NRR = \frac{net\ income\ out\ of\ work}{net\ income\ in\ work}$$

For example, if one were to receive €100 in benefits when out of work, and if they were to have a net income of €500 when in work, then the NRR is 0.20. As a result, the higher a NRR is, the weaker the scheme's work incentive is. The NRR is also widely used as an indicator to measure the generosity of UI benefits (Shin, Kemppainen, and Kuitto 2021).

Second, the METR quantifies the marginal increase in net income caused by a marginal increase in in work income (OECD 2018a). In other words, the METR describes what portion of an increase in gross family earnings is taken away through increased taxes and the reduction or loss of benefits (Brewer and Shaw 2018). The calculation of the MERT is made by the following formula:

$$METR = 1 - \frac{\Delta y_{net}}{\Delta y_{gross}} = 1 - \frac{y_{netNEW} - y_{netOLD}}{y_{grossNEW} - y_{grossOLD}}$$

Where Δy_{gross} is the additional earnings resulting from additional working hours and Δy_{net} means the change in net income gained after taxed and benefits. More specifically, $y_{grossOLD}$, $y_{grossNEW}$, y_{netOLD} and y_{netNEW} denote the gross earnings and net incomes in old and new labour market states respectively (Carone et al. 2004). For instance, a METR of 70 % at 25 working hours a week means that a worker will retain 30 % of the additional earnings and 70 % will be taxed away, if they increase the amount of working hours marginally above 25 hours. Usually, in the calculation, total taxes consist of national and local income tax and social security contributions paid by employees as well, while cash benefits include family benefits, social assistance, housing benefits and unemployment benefits. Thus, a high METR implies that the work incentive is weak. The degrees of METRs are more likely to influence the labour market attachment and working hours of people whose employment opportunities are limited and wages are low due to their low productivity (Carone et al. 2004).

The PTR can be understood as a version of METR for jobless individuals. The PTR demonstrates the proportion of additional earnings that will be taken away in either higher taxes or lower benefits after a jobless individual takes up a new job (Adam and Browne 2010; OECD 2018b).[1] The PTR for an individual is calculated as follows:

$$PTR = 1 - \frac{y_{netIW} - y_{netOW}}{y_{grossIW} - y_{grossOW}}$$

where $y_{grossIW}$ and $y_{grossOW}$ represents gross earnings of the individual when they are in work and out of work, while y_{netIW} and y_{netOW} denotes household disposable incomes when the individual in work and out of work, respectively. In case that a house-

---

1 Some studies call PTR the average effective tax rate (AETR) (see OECD 2018a).

hold has multiple earners, PTRs can be separately computed for each earner (Jara, Gasior, and Makovec 2017).

An important technical question concerning the calculations of NRRs, METRs and PTRs is who to compute them for. In this regard, most studies adopting those measures calculate all income measures at the household level, as the amounts of earnings, taxes and benefits depend on the size and composition of households and decisions about labour market participation are mainly made at the household level (Carone et al. 2004). In addition, the measures are calculated usually for several stylised types of families such as single adults with or without children and couples with or without children depending on the target groups and purposes of the evaluation.

25.3 Unemployment insurance and work incentives

UI provides unemployed people with benefits to guarantee income security and at the same time creates disincentives for them to try to find a new job. Thus, a UI scheme needs to be designed considering the trade-off between income support and incentives to work (Tatsiramos and van Ours 2014).

There are two major theoretical models to describe the disincentive to reemployment which UI benefits may cause: the labour-supply model and the job-search model. Moffitt and Nicholson's (1982) labour-supply model assumes that a newly unemployed person tends to plan their activities during their UI benefit period and accept a job offer after consuming a particular amount of leisure based on their own schedule. According to this model, UI benefit recipients are likely to become reemployed by the time they exhaust their benefits, as they are inclined to maximise their leisure time, as long as they do not lose income. On the other hand, the job-search model (Burdett 1979; Mortensen 1977) is premised on the assumption that unemployed individuals conduct a job search in the situation that they cannot expect what kind of wage they will be offered. In this model, such uncertainty makes them fix the degree of their search effort and the minimum salary they can accept. Consequently, unemployed workers will leave unemployment when they get an offer that is equivalent to or higher than their minimum acceptable wage. Given the situation, UI enables benefit recipients to diminish their job search activities or to increase their minimum acceptable salary, either of which leads to prolonging their unemployment periods (Decker 1997).

An important difference between the models is that the job-search model implies that the extension of unemployment period caused by UI can have a positive influence in the end. Because unemployed people can spend more time searching for a better position relying on the financial support that UI provides, it is probable that they would get more stable or higher paying jobs than they would not be protected by UI. As a result, from the perspective of job-search model, UI can be regarded as a support for job search activities rather than for leisure (Decker 1997).

Nowadays, because most welfare states operate mandatory UI schemes where every employee is obliged to join UI in principle, it is not practically beneficial to study the effect of UI membership on work incentives. Hence, studies have mainly analysed how the amount and duration of UI benefits affect work incentives. As UI acts as the key policy instrument to protect individuals against the income losses caused by unemployment (Lichter and Schiprowski 2021), the OECD tax-benefit data portal provides the NRRs and PTRs of UI benefits in member states on an annualised basis.

Figures 25.1 and 25.2 display the NRRs and PTRs of UI benefits at 67 % of the average wage for recipients of unemployment benefits in one-earner couples with two children after two months of unemployment in 2019, respectively. Because 67 % of the average wage mean a low level of income, the NRRs of all the countries in the analysis are at a high level, accounting for more than 65 %. The OECD average of NRRs is 78 %. Luxembourg (99 %) has a higher NRR than the other countries, followed by Norway (93 %), Germany (91 %) and Denmark (91 %). Next come South Korea (90 %) and Finland (90 %). In contrast, Australia shows the lowest NRR with 67 % and the UK has the second lowest number of NRR (68 %). The analysis shows that unemployed workers who had a low wage in Latvia and New Zealand also face a low net replacement rate of 70 %. When it comes to PTRs, the OECD average is 69 %. Luxembourg has the highest level (90 %) also in the comparison of PTRs. For Latvia, its PTR is at a very high level, accounting for 89 %, although its NRR is third lowest among. Next, Lithuania, Portugal, Belgium and the Netherlands also show a PTR higher than 80 %. On the other hand, Australia (45 %), Greece (46 %), New Zealand (48 %) and the UK (49 %) have a very low level of PTR.

The number of non-standard workers such as temporary workers and part-timers has continuously increased in the post-industrial labour market. Theoretically they can be protected by UI schemes as regular workers who have a standard employment contract, but they often fail to gain entitlements for unemployment benefits because the eligibility usually requires certain levels of wage, employment period and working hours (Matsaganis et al. 2016). As a result, given this situation, the work incentives of UI benefits may be meaningless to many non-standard workers in most OECD countries. Thus, it is necessary to improve UI schemes so that non-standard workers can be substantially protected by them.

While the OECD tax-benefit data have evaluated the work incentives of UI benefits in ex-ante approaches, many empirical studies have analysed their disincentive effect by investigating how UI affects reemployment in ex-post methods. The early literature tended to concentrate on the level of benefits (Tatsiramos and van Ours 2014), whereas recent analyses deal with not only the level but also the potential benefit duration of UI (Lichter and Schiprowski 2021). Although the theoretical models predict that generous UI benefits will delay benefit recipients' switch from unemployment to employment, empirical studies have provided mixed evidence with regard to benefit levels. Research findings for the US and the UK demonstrate that UI benefit level has a significant disincentive effect on reemployment, while case studies on continental

European countries and Nordic countries find insignificant or weak effects (Atkinson and Micklewright 1991; Pedersen and Westergård-Nielsen 1993; Røed, Jensen, and Thoursie 2007; Tatsiramos and van Ours 2014). On the other hand, empirical analyses focusing on benefit duration consistently display that a longer potential benefit duration discourages unemployed individuals to find a job at the early stage of unemployment and increase their UI benefit receipt period (De Groot and Van Der Klaauw 2019; Johnston and Mas 2018; Lichter and Schiprowski 2021; Schmieder, Von Wachter, and Bender 2012; Tatsiramos and van Ours 2014).

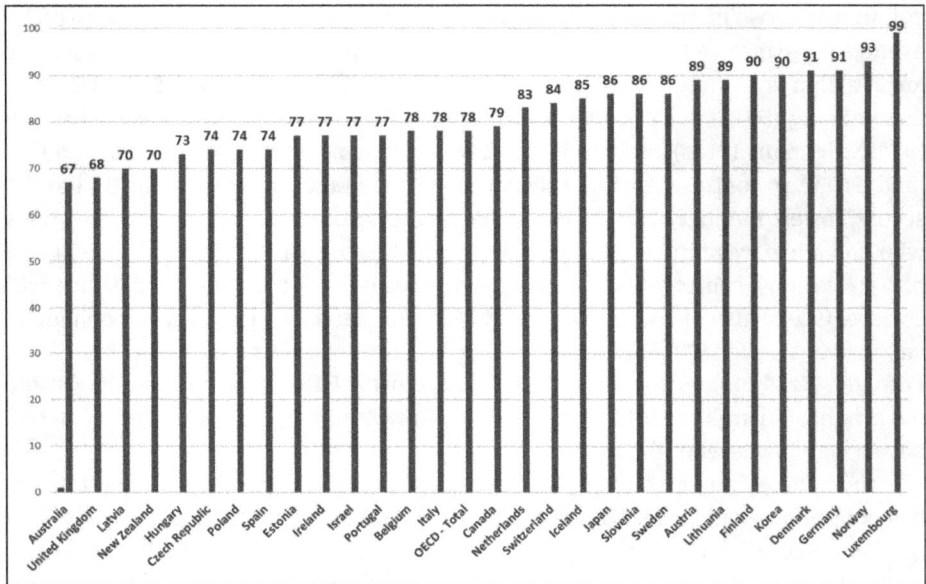

Figure 25.1: Net replacement rate of unemployment insurance benefits in 2019 (%).
Source: OECD statistics database, https://stats.oecd.org/Index.aspx?DataSetCode=NRR (accessed 11 October 2021)
Note: Net replacement rate of UI benefits at 67 % of the average wage for recipients of unemployment benefits in one-earner couple with two children after two months of unemployment. Social assistance and housing benefits are included.

As significant disincentive effects of potential benefit duration have been supported by empirical research, many recent studies show a tendency to emphasise the importance of interventions to encourage UI benefit recipients to be more active in seeking a job. These perspectives are mainly connected with arguments to support activation measures such as the establishment of minimum effort requirements to receive UI benefits (Arni and Schiprowski 2019; Graversen and Van Ours 2008; Lichter and Schiprowski 2021).

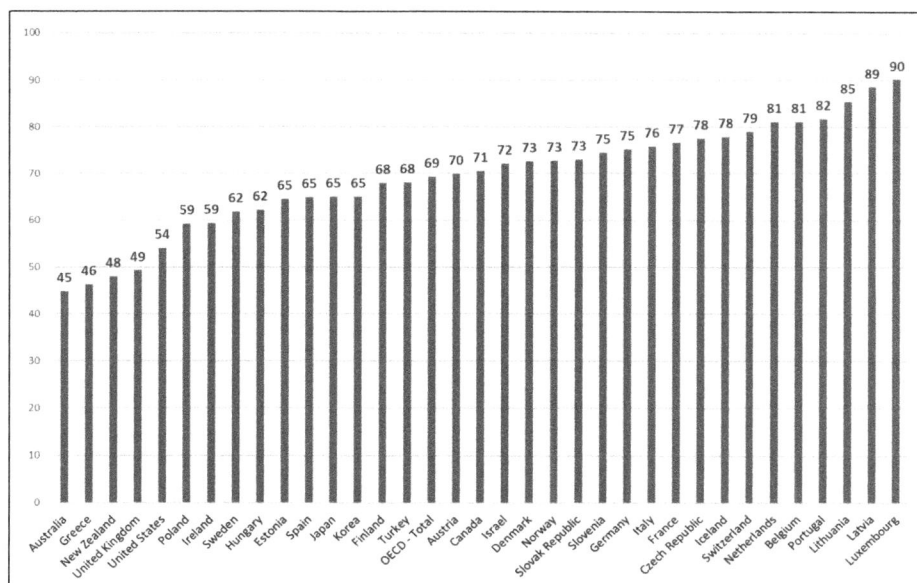

Figure 25.2: Participation tax rate of unemployment insurance benefits in 2019 (%).
Source: OECD statistics database, https://stats.oecd.org/Index.aspx?DataSetCode=NRR (accessed 11 October 2021)
Note: Participation tax rate of taking up work at 67 % of the average wage for recipients of unemployment benefits in one-earner couple with two children after two months of unemployment. Social assistance and housing benefits are included.

25.4 In-work benefits and work incentives

The origin of the IWB programme goes back to the 1970s and is known as the Family Income Supplement of the UK in 1971 and the Earned Income Tax Credit of the US in 1975, and many welfare states have introduced IWB schemes since the 1990s (Immervoll and Pearson 2009; OECD 2011). As the goals of IWB schemes are to enhance employment of vulnerable workers and improve the inclusiveness of the labour market (OECD 2018c), they are basically designed to create work incentives for disadvantaged groups and provide additional income to sustain their standard of living simultaneously (Vandelannoote and Verbist 2020). Thus, the essential part of IWB planning is to generate a significant gap in people's household incomes between when they are in work and when out of work.

Politically, a main reason IWB is currently a prominent measure across welfare states is that no political party ever shows a negative attitude towards the schemes. Both centre-right and centre-left parties have actively supported it as they are strong advocates of decreasing in-work poverty and increasing work incentives. Left parties are likely to prefer IWBs as a policy to alleviate in-work poverty, while right parties tend to have favourable attitudes towards the points that they reinforce work incentives and occasionally can be used as an easy way to reduce the generosity of social benefits (Clasen 2020). In addition, labour market dualisation is associated with the growth of IWBs. As the number of unemployed and precarious workers has gradually grown, IWB schemes are a useful policy measure that governments can adopt to subsidise low paid workers who are mainly in low skilled or part-time jobs (Clasen 2020).

As IWB designs vary considerably according to their target group, level and payment duration as well as the policy background in which they are introduced, the effect of IWBs on work incentives depends on how they are designed and operated (OECD 2018c; Vandelannoote and Verbist 2020). This makes it hard to conduct a cross-national comparison in terms of their effects or find out the associations between IWBs and work incentives. When the target groups are more sensitive to financial incentives, IWB schemes can be more effective in accentuating work incentives. As low-income workers are more responsive to financial incentives compared with middle- or high-income earners, most IWBs target at low-income workers or lone parents (Blundell et al. 2000; Chetty, Friedman, and Saez 2013). In addition, simply designed and transparently operated IWB schemes are more likely to achieve their objectives effectively, because potential recipients' understanding of the schemes is required to encourage their labour market participation via these policy measures (Chetty, Friedman, and Saez 2013). Finally, it is more efficient for IWBs to boost work incentives when earnings distribution in a country is more even. If the proportion of people with low earnings is high, the IWB costs would be also high because its target population is large (Immervoll and Pearson 2009).

When it comes to the actual effect of IWB on work incentives, most empirical studies on IWBs reveal that they have a significantly positive effect, meaning that the employment rate of IWB recipients increases as a result of IWB (Vandelannoote and Verbist 2020). In particular, an extensive amount of research has analysed the Earned Income Tax Credit (EITC) in the US and the Working Family Tax Credit (WFTC) in the UK. Laun (2019) sums up the findings concerning the work incentive effect of the EITC based on Hotz and Scholz (2003), Eissa and Hoynes (2006) and Nichols and Rothstein (2015), which includes an extensive review of the empirical literature on the EITC as follows: first, the EITC has increased the employment rate of single parents. Second, the effect of the EITC on the increase of working hours of employed people tends to be negative. Third, the EITC has a negative influence on secondary earners' work incentive because the benefit entitlement is decided depending on household income. Finally, the EITC also affects married women's labour market participation and working hours in a negative manner. Considering all the findings, Nichols and Rothstein (2015) conclude that the positive effects on single parents' labour supply exceeds the negative impacts on married women's working activities. It should be noted that this conclusion is only based on the US system of in-work benefits. No such effects are found in all countries which operate in-work benefits schemes. The evidence on the British WFTC has been reviewed by Blundell and Hoynes (2004), Blundell and Shephard

(2011) and Brewer et al. (2006). Overall, previous evidence reveals that the WFTC has positive labour supply effects, although their magnitudes tend to be smaller than those of the EITC in the US.

In addition to the US and UK cases, Laun (2019) gives an overview of the evidence on the effects of IWBs in seven European countries; France, Belgium, Denmark, Finland, Germany, the Netherlands and Sweden. According to the overview, it is difficult to conclude that IWBs schemes in those European countries are not always effective in increasing labour force participation because studies for some countries show mixed results and the evidence for the others is not convincing enough. However, as IWBs can have a positive effect on labour supply depending how the details are designed, all the countries have reformed and expanded their IWB systems without revoking them. The reforms should aim to overcome the lack of information, awareness and understanding about the design and reduce the level of bureaucracy which may negatively influence the operation of IWBs (Laun 2019).

25.5 Childcare costs and work incentives

Nowadays, most welfare states have extended social investment policies such as childcare, education and vocational training. These policies aim to improve human capital through education and training programmes and encourage both parents to participate in economic activity as well. Nevertheless, childcare costs impose a significant financial burden on working parents and sometimes eliminate the income from work in many welfare states (Browne and Neumann 2017). As a result, the heavy costs of non-parental childcare may act as a disincentive to labour force participation.

OECD (2020) displays net childcare costs for two children in full-time care in EU member states from various perspectives. Although a large majority of countries grant diverse types of financial support to reduce the high childcare costs, the level of net childcare costs varies across countries. Figure 25.3 shows net childcare costs, as percentage of women's median full-time earnings in 2019. The average of net childcare costs among EU countries is 14 % of female workers' median full-time earnings in the case of middle-income dual-earner households. This figure decreases to 12 % for low-income dual-earner couple, and to less than 10 % for single parents. The UK, Cyprus, Ireland and the Slovak Republic show the highest level of net childcare costs, where net childcare costs are higher than 25 % of women's median full-time earnings for most types of households included in the analysis. In contrast, the percentages in Malta, Italy and Germany are zero or near zero. On the other hand, Figure 25.4 presents net childcare costs in terms of the disposable household income. From this perspective, on average, net childcare costs account for about 9 % and 8 % for low- and middle-income families, respectively. However, the percentages vary widely across Europe depending on the types of families. Net childcare costs are zero in Malta and Italy, whereas those for a single-parent family in Cyprus and the Slovak Republic are higher than 35 %. It is noted that low-income single parents face much more difficulty affording non-parental childcare than other parents in some countries such as Slovak Republic, Cyprus and Romania.

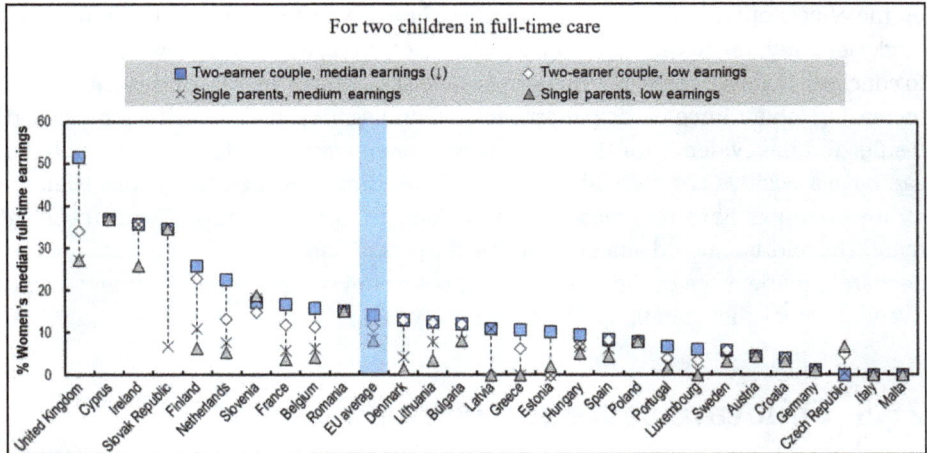

Figure 25.3: Net childcare costs, as percentage of women's median full-time earnings 2019. *Source*: OECD (2020, 16).

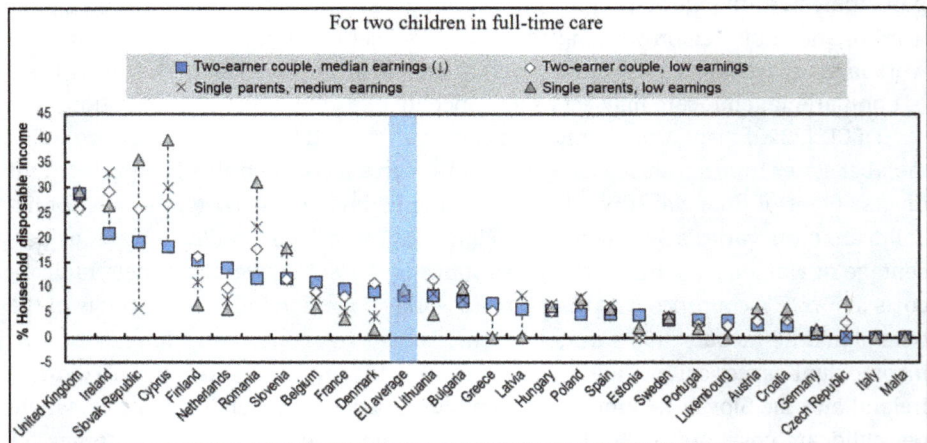

Figure 25.4: Net childcare costs, as percentage of household disposable income 2019. *Source*: OECD (2020, 35).

OECD (2020) examines the effect of net childcare costs on work incentives in European countries by calculating the PTR, which specifically means the percentage of income that is subtracted by increased taxes and reduced benefits including childcare costs when a parent starts a paid job. Figure 25.5 displays two versions of PTRs by country, which are calculated with and without considering childcare costs. First, it demonstrates that on average childcare costs elevate PTRs by about 12 percent points for a low-income single mother across EU countries. That is, they lose 53 % of their gross earnings before accounting for childcare costs, whereas the average loss with childcare costs increases to 65 % (Figure 25.5 – Panel A). For working mothers with a spouse or partner in full-time employment, their average loss of gross earning is 40 % and 55 %, before and after considering childcare costs, respectively (Figure 25.5 – Panel B).

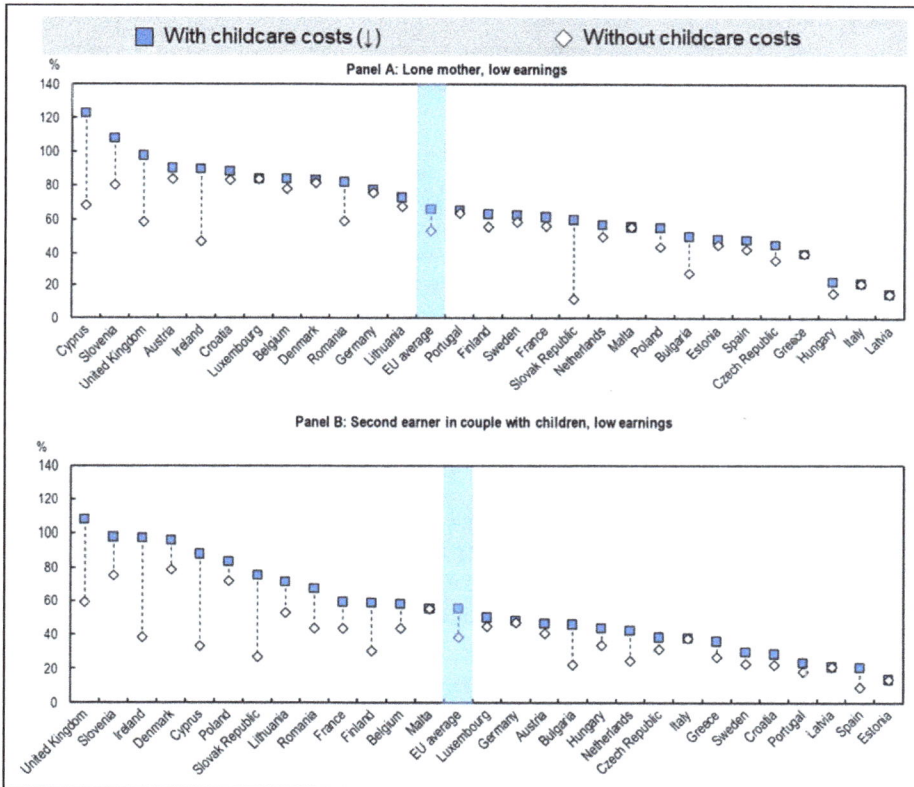

Figure 25.5: Participation tax rates of low earning mothers with and without childcare costs in European countries 2019.
Source: OECD (2020, 23).
Note: Calculations are for full-time care in a typical childcare centre for a two-child family, where both parents are in full-time employment and the children are aged two and three. Full-time care is defined as care for at least 40 hours per week. Low earnings refer to the 20th percentile, and median earnings to the 50th percentile, of the full-time gender-specific earnings distribution. Couples contain two earners, male and female; single parents are females. The original data came from the OECD tax-benefit model.

The figure also demonstrates that childcare costs have a larger impact on work incentives for low-income lone mothers in countries such as Cyprus, Ireland, Slovenia and the UK, where net childcare costs tend to show a high level. In these cases, it can be said that childcare costs contribute to weakening work incentives. On the contrary, in some countries such as Austria, Belgium, Denmark and Luxembourg, the effect of childcare costs on PTR is very low for single mother families, even though their PTRs are around 80 % or higher. This means that childcare costs are not the reason of weak work incentives in these nations. For second earners in couples, on the other hand, it is found that there is a correlation between childcare costs and the degree of work incentives, which implies that childcare costs play a significant role in accentuating work incentives for them (Browne and Neumann 2017).

25.6 Concluding remarks

This chapter explored how UI, IWBs and childcare costs can affect work incentives by reviewing the literature on the relevant evidence based on either ex-ante or ex-post approaches. Existing studies consistently indicate that a long potential duration of UI benefits acts as a disincentive for unemployed people to find jobs, which in turn leads to longer unemployment periods. On the other hand, for IWBs and childcare costs, it cannot simply be said that those policy measures improve work incentives, as previous research has illustrated that their effects depend on policy designs and operations as well as entire tax-benefit systems.

All the studies on work incentives which are reviewed in this chapter concentrate only on financial incentives. However, they do not consider the point that in fact jobless and marginally attached workers face various barriers to a decent job. These obstacles may include lack of adequate education or skills, health problems, care responsibilities, lack of transportation, lack of suitable information on job vacancies and so on (Fernandez et al. 2016; OECD 2015). Even if financial incentives of a policy scheme such as IWB are very strong, such people are still likely to have trouble entering the labour market in a situation where non-financial disincentives are still powerful. Moreover, benefit recipients often give up entering the labour market because they do not understand the work incentives provided. Such knowledge deficits are likely to be caused by the complexity of incentives rather than their lack of interest in working (Anderson 2002). Therefore, besides enhancing work incentives financially, it is necessary to deal with all employment barriers from a holistic perspective and provide the public with sufficient information about the incentives offered by benefit schemes in an easily understandable manner. As policies should ensure that work is accessible, attractive and sustainable to encourage vulnerable workers to continue to be in work, all obstacles to employment should be tackled via integrated measures that promote worker employability and job opportunities as well as work incentives (OECD 2018c).

References

Adam, S., and J. Browne. 2010. *Redistribution, Work Incentives and Thirty Years of UK Tax and Benefit Reform*, IFS Working Paper 10/24. https://ifs.org.uk/wps/wp1024.pdf.

Anderson, S. G. 2002. "Ensuring the Stability of Welfare-To-Work Exits: The Importance of Recipient Knowledge about Work Incentives." *Social Work* 47 (2), 162–170.

Arni, P., and A. Schiprowski. 2019. "Job Search Requirements, Effort Provision and Labor Market Outcomes." *Journal of Public Economics* 169, 65–88.

Atkinson, A. B., and J. Micklewright. 1991. "Unemployment Compensation and Labor Market Transitions: A Critical Review." *Journal of Economic Literature* 29 (4), 1679–1727.

Blundell, R., and H. W. Hoynes. 2004. "Has 'In-Work' Benefit Reform Helped the Labor Market?" In *Seeking a Premier Economy: The Economic Effects of British Economic Reforms, 1980–2000*, edited by D. Card, R. Blundell, and R. B. Freeman, 411–460. Chicago: University of Chicago Press.

Blundell, R., and A. Shephard. 2012. "Employment, Hours of Work and the Optimal Taxation of Low-Income Families." *The Review of Economic Studies* 79 (2), 481–510.

Blundell, R., A. Duncan, J. McCrae, and C. Meghir. 2000. "The Labour Market Impact of The Working Families' Tax Credit." *Fiscal Studies* 21 (1), 75–104.

Brewer, M., and J. Shaw. 2018. "How Taxes and Welfare Benefits Affect Work Incentives: A Life-Cycle Perspective." *Fiscal Studies* 39 (1), 5–38.

Brewer, M., A. Duncan, A. Shephard, and M. J. Suarez. 2006. "Did Working Families' Tax Credit Work? The Impact of In-Work Support on Labour Supply in Great Britain." *Labour Economics* 13 (6), 699–720.

Browne, J., and D. Neumann. 2017. *OECD Tax Wedge and Effective Tax Rates on Labour: Childcare Costs in 2015* (No. VS/2015/0427 (DI150030). OECD. https://taxben.oecd.org/tax-ben-resources/Childcare-costs-in-2015.pdf

Burdett, K. 1979. "Unemployment Insurance Payments as a Search Subsidy: A Theoretical Analysis." *Economic Inquiry* 17 (3), 333–343.

Carone, G., H. Immervoll, D. Paturot, and A. Salomäki. 2004. "Indicators of Unemployment and Low-Wage Traps: Marginal Effective Tax Rates on Employment Incomes." *OECD Social, Employment and Migration Working Papers* 18. Paris: OECD. https://www.oecd.org/social/soc/30975741.pdf.

Chetty, R., J. N. Friedman, and E. Saez. 2013. "Using Differences in Knowledge across Neighborhoods to Uncover the Impacts of the EITC on Earnings." *American Economic Review* 103 (7), 2683–2721.

Clasen, J. 2020. "Subsidizing Wages or Supplementing Transfers? The Politics and Ambiguity of In-Work Benefits." *Social Policy & Administration* 54 (1), 1–13.

de Groot, N., and B. van der Klaauw. 2019. The Effects of Reducing the Entitlement Period to Unemployment Insurance Benefits." *Labour Economics* 57, 195–208.

Decker, P. T. 1997. "Work Incentives and Disincentives." In *Unemployment Insurance in the United States: Analysis of Policy Issues*, edited by C. J. O'Leary and S. A. Wandner, 285–320. Kalamazoo, MI: W.E. Upjohn Institute for Employment Research.

Eissa, N., and H. W. Hoynes. 2006. "Behavioral Responses to Taxes: Lessons from the EITC and Labor Supply." *Tax Policy and the Economy* 20, 73–110.

Fernandez, R., H. Immervoll, D. Pacifico, and C. Thévenot. 2016. *Faces of Joblessness: Characterising Employment Barriers to Inform Policy*. OECD Social, Employment and Migration Working Paper 192. https://doi.org/10.1787/5jlwvz47xptj-en.

Graversen, B. K., and J. C. Van Ours. 2008. "How to Help Unemployed Find Jobs Quickly: Experimental Evidence from a Mandatory Activation Program." *Journal of Public Economics* 92 (10–11), 2020–2035.

Hotz, V. J., and J. K. Scholz. 2007. "The Earned Income Tax Credit." In *Means-Tested Transfer Programs in the United States*, edited by R. A. Moffitt, 141–197, Chicago: University of Chicago Press.

Immervoll, H., and M. Pearson. 2009. *A Good Time for Making Work Pay? Taking Stock of In-Work Benefits and Related Measures across the OECD*. IZA Policy Paper 3. Bonn: IZA. https://docs.iza.org/pp3.pdf.

Jara, H. X., K. Gasior, and M. Makovec. 2017. *Low Incentives to Work at the Extensive and Intensive Margin in Selected EU Countries*. EUROMOD Working Paper EM3/17. https://www.iser.essex.ac.uk/research/publications/working-papers/euromod/em3-17.pdf.

Johnston, A. C., and A. Mas. 2018. "Potential Unemployment Insurance Duration and Labor Supply: The Individual and Market-Level Response to a Benefit Cut." *Journal of Political Economy* 126 (6), 2480–2522.

Laun, L. 2019. *In-Work Benefits Across Europe*. Institute for Evaluation of Labour Market and Education Policy (IFAU) Working paper 2019:16, Uppsala, Sweden.

Lichter, A., and A. Schiprowski. 2021. "Benefit Duration, Job Search Behavior and Re-Employment." *Journal of Public Economics* 193, 104326.

Matsaganis, M., E. Özdemir, T. Ward, and A. Zavakou. 2016. *Non-Standard Employment and Access to Social Security Benefits*. Social Situation Monitor, Research Note, 8/2015. Brussels: European Commission. https://www.eurofound.europa.eu/data/platform-economy/records/non-standard-employment-and-access-to-social-security-benefits

Moffitt, R., and W. Nicholson. 1982. "The Effect of Unemployment Insurance on Unemployment: The Case of Federal Supplemental Benefits." *The Review of Economics and Statistics* 64 (1), 1–11.

Mortensen, D. T. 1977. "Unemployment Insurance and Job Search Decisions." *ILR Review* 30 (4), 505517.

Nichols, A., and J. Rothstein. 2015. *The Earned Income Tax Credit (EITC)* (NBER Working Paper w21211). National Bureau of Economic Research. https://www.nber.org/papers/w21211.

OECD. 2011. *Taxation and Employment*. OECD Tax Policy Studies No. 21. Paris: OECD.

OECD. 2015. *OECD Employment Outlook 2015*, Paris: OECD Publishing. https://doi.org/10.1787/empl_outlook-2015-en.

OECD. 2018a. *OECD Economic Surveys: Finland 2018*. Paris: OECD. https://doi.org/10.1787/eco_surveys-fin-2018-en.

OECD. 2018b. *Benefit Generosity and Work Incentives for Recipients of Disability Benefits in 12 EU Member States*. Paris: OECD.

OECD. 2018c. *Good Jobs for All in a Changing World of Work: The OECD Jobs Strategy*. Paris: OECD.

OECD. 2020. *Net Childcare Costs in EU Countries Impact on Family Incomes and Work Incentives, 2019*. Paris: OECD.

Pedersen, P. J., and N. Westergård-Nielsen. 1993. "Unemployment: A Review of the Evidence from Panel Data." *OECD Economic Studies* 20, 66–114.

Røed, K., P. Jensen, and A. Thoursie. 2008. "Unemployment Duration and Unemployment Insurance: A Comparative Analysis Based on Scandinavian Micro Data." *Oxford Economic Papers* 60 (2), 254–274.

Schmieder, J. F., T. Von Wachter, and S. Bender. 2012. "The Effects of Extended Unemployment Insurance over the Business Cycle: Evidence from Regression Discontinuity Estimates over 20 Years." *The Quarterly Journal of Economics* 127 (2), 701–752.

Shin, Y. K., T. Kemppainen, and K. Kuitto. 2021. "Precarious Work, Unemployment Benefit Generosity and Universal Basic Income Preferences: A Multilevel Study on 21 European Countries." *Journal of Social Policy* 50 (2), 323–345.

Tatsiramos, K., and J. C. Van Ours. 2014. "Labor Market Effects of Unemployment Insurance Design." *Journal of Economic Surveys* 28 (2), 284–311.

Vandelannoote, D., and G. Verbist. 2020. "The Impact of In-Work Benefits on Work Incentives and Poverty in Four European Countries." *Journal of European Social Policy* 30 (2), 144–157.

Part IV Future research needs

Bent Greve
26 The future of welfare states?

Abstract: This chapter attempts to condense the knowledge that can be deduced from the chapters in the book, combined with an interpretation of the key challenges for welfare states. There seems to be no doubt that there will still be a need for welfare states in one way or another, although the form, size and approach will continue to differ across countries – and in broader groups of welfare regimes.The challenges that are looked at in more detail in this chapter is: Technology, Demography, Financing, Inequality and Legitimacy. These five elements are often connected, although they are presented here separately.

Keywords: Technology, Demography, Financing, Inequality, Legitimacy, welfare state future, welfare state challenges

26.1 Introduction

Challenges, changes, new paths and differences are the elements that have characterised the previous chapters in this book. This last chapter attempts to condense the knowledge that can be deduced from the chapters, combined with an interpretation of the key challenges for welfare states.

There seems to be no doubt that there will still be a need for welfare states in one way or another, although the form, size and approach will continue to differ across countries – and in broader groups of welfare regimes.

The challenges that are looked at in more detail in this chapter can be summarised under the headings: Technology (section 26.2), Demography (section 26.3), Financing (section 26.4), Inequality (section 26.5) and Legitimacy (section 26.6). These five elements are often connected, although they are presented here separately. Section 26.7 then concludes the book. Given that this chapter is, at least partly, based on the information from other chapters, fewer references will be used than in other chapters.

26.2 Technology

Technology challenges welfare states, particularly because of its possible impact on the labour market (see especially Chapter 20), but also in a number of other areas (see for example Chapters 11 and 14, on health and long-term care), and it will also be able to affect the entire educational area. In the following, there will be a particular focus on employment.

https://doi.org/10.1515/9783110721768-026

A large number of studies (see, for example, Peralta-Alva and Roitman 2018; Georgieff and Milanez 2021; Lane and Saint-Martin 2021; Susskind 2020) have illustrated that there will be jobs that disappear completely, but at the same time there will be jobs where a number of functions disappear, and thus that fewer people can perform the same work. There will also be new jobs, and there can be discussions on whether the overall effects are positive or negative for employment (Greve 2017). The changes will, to a large extent, mainly affect countries with a high level of employment in more traditional production fields, but it will gradually also change employment in a number of areas with a high knowledge content, and therefore there will be significant changes in these areas. It also means that many will be challenged in their current job and some will lose their jobs completely. This has distributional consequences, and might imply a larger gap in society, cf. for example OECD (2019b).

It challenges welfare states if, as a result of technological change, there are growing tensions between those who are the core troops of the labour market and those who are on the periphery. This is because there might be a loss of self-esteem for those who lose their jobs and have difficulties after a long time on the labour market to be able to hold onto their jobs or get a new job if sacked. It may also (see below under Financing) have implications for the ability to fund welfare states. At the same time, technological development also plays a role in the need for changes in social security systems, both for those who are often outside the labour market, but also for the group of employees who have precarious working conditions.

This applies, for example, to those who work via platforms, and in a number of contexts are described as self-employed, the so-called solo-self-employed. They often have low incomes, no pension savings and often no access to social security schemes (Palier 2019; Greve 2019). The consequences are increased uncertainty for the individual, but also the risk of creating distortions of competition between companies that avoid having to contribute to financing social security, and those that have to, as well as if it means lower costs for some companies compared to others.

Technology thus presents very large challenges for welfare states and, at the same time, countries that do not take advantage of the new technological opportunities risk being weaker in their socio-economic development. There is therefore no doubt that technology will be used to solve some societal challenges, for example in the environmental field, but at the same time it can create questions in relation to distribution, employment and financing.

26.3 Demography

Demographic change has, for many years, been seen as one of the key challenges for welfare states. In short, the challenge is that as a result of us living longer, more and more elderly people need care and health treatment, while at the same time there are relatively more people outside the labour market who must be financed by those in the labour market.

What pulls in the opposite direction, however, is that the populations are probably getting older, but more people are also much healthier and more affluent than they were before, with the consequence that the need for care and treatment is pushed to a later point in life. However, this does not reduce the need in the long run, as health services are, to a large extent, something that most people need in the last years of their lives.

Since 2000, the average retirement age for men in the OECD area has grown from 63.1 to 65.4 and for women from 61.0 to 63.7 (OECD 2019a), which has reduced the pressure from demographic changes on welfare states' spending as well as revenue. Whether this continues given technological changes and is in line with citizens' expectations for a good life is another question.

At the same time, there will be a number of elements in addition to their health that may have an impact on whether people remain in the labour market, which will largely be about the working environment, including opportunities for a gradual withdrawal from the labour market. Raising the retirement age in a number of countries has also contributed to this, but at the same time it has challenged the more vulnerable groups in the labour market who, such as for health reasons, are not able to continue in a job.

26.4 Financing

Financing welfare states is, and will be, a challenge as there is not necessarily a connection between wishes for what welfare states must deliver and what it is possible to deliver. So, in this way, the challenge is not new. But it is sharpened by a number of the other elements included in this chapter. In addition, there will probably continue to be various external shocks, in line with the financial crisis in 2008/09 and the COVID-19 crisis. These crises require that there is an economic readiness to finance them, and thus that countries that have problems, such as large government deficits and government debt, will have more difficulty in tackling these types of crises in the future.

Combined with the risk of fewer jobs, the fact that there are activities in the economies (such as the platform economy) that are more difficult to tax and that there has been a tendency for tax competition between different countries means that financing can be a challenge. The use of tax havens and activities in the hidden economy are also challenges that need to be looked at (Zucman 2015). Internationally, work is under way to reduce this, but it takes time and means that, presumably, there will be less income available to fund welfare states than would otherwise be the case.

This is even truer if the countries, through trickle-down economic measures, have faith that by lowering taxes and duties they could boost the economy more, and then

subsequently have had difficulty raising taxation and duties to previous levels to reduce the general government deficits. The risk is thus that defunding in itself entails
demands for reductions in the expenditure of welfare states in the future, which may
also contribute to the expectations for welfare states not being met.

International agreements on a minimum level of taxation and the fight against tax
havens and tax evasion can thus be important aspects of being able to finance welfare
states in the coming years in a stable way.

26.5 Inequality

Regardless of how one measures inequality, and regardless of the uncertainty in calculating it, it seems clear that inequality has increased in relation to both income and
wealth (Stiglitz 2012; Piketty and Cantante 2018). In addition, there is strong inequality
on a wide range of other parameters, such as education, health and influence. Inequality is multidimensional (Greve 2021), and therefore it might not be sufficient to
look into just the economic aspect of inequality, albeit this is a central issue for welfare states to be aware of.

The schism here is that rising inequality can make it more difficult to find a financial basis for welfare states, while at the same time increasing the need for public initiatives for, for example, social security for people who lose their jobs.

Inequality can also increase the expectations of what welfare states should provide in terms of both cash and services, and thus increase pressure. At the same time
there may be less confidence that states will be able to solve these tasks, as has been
seen in particular in the more populist currents in a number of countries (see Chapter 22). Welfare states thus have some new balance points and possible conflicts between different groups in society that can reduce social cohesion.

Growing inequality may also help to explain the often-negative attitude towards
immigrants and others who are perceived as those who threaten one's own opportunities.

At the same time, it seems clear that rising inequality can be negative for economic growth (Berg and Ostry 2011; Aiyar and Ebeke 2020; Cingano 2014), and thus that
rising inequality not only creates contradictions between different population groups,
but can also have a direct counterproductive effect in trying to create economic opportunities for more people to have a better life.

One consequence of this is that welfare states will have a need to ensure that more
people are integrated into the development of society and that inequality becomes
smaller. There are a large number of instruments that can be used for this if desired.

26.6 Legitimacy

Legitimacy is an important aspect of the development of welfare states, as otherwise the necessary political support in democracies to finance public spending can be hard to find.

A problem for welfare states, also in relation to, for example, creating a higher degree of equality, will be that it is not given that there is an equal degree of legitimacy to support all parts of the welfare state, including the conditions for the receipt of public services. There is a difference in populations' assessments of who is deserving and who is not. Basically, the greatest support is for expenses in relation to health, long-term care and pensions, and to a lesser extent for income transfers to the unemployed and other people who cannot fully or partially support themselves, with people with different types of disabilities as an exception. This puts pressure on whether and how it is possible to ensure that welfare states can also more broadly ensure the inclusion of groups that do not necessarily have the same level of public support.

It increases the difficulty of prioritising in welfare states and increases the cross-pressure between the economic opportunities available and the expectation of voters of the tasks to be solved. This is also because within a number of areas there can be an expectation that, for example, new and better initiatives will happen as they become available, for example always the best, newest and thus often the most expensive treatment within the health area.

At the same time, however, there is widespread support for and the desire to be able to develop welfare states, and in most countries there is support for the public sector to play a central role in relation to a number of these tasks.

Who needs to do it – state, market and/or civil society – and who best can solve different tasks will also be an important element in the understanding of what there is support for in different welfare states. But, overall, it is important that there is support, as it ensures a more stable societal development.

26.7 Conclusion

Welfare states are, as they have probably always been, challenged to a greater or lesser degree, but hardly in crisis, as is often argued. They are challenged by the fact that there is a difference in support for different parts of welfare states, so that satisfaction also depends on new and better offers on the table, at the same time as there may be discussions about the scope and size of taxes and fees that the population is willing to finance.

It therefore also requires that welfare states ensure a healthy economy so that it cannot be so easily shaken when external crises have an impact on either expenditure or revenue in the individual country.

At the same time, there is no doubt that stable and well-functioning welfare states have a great impact on how happy a population is. In countries with well-functioning welfare states that ensure security and development opportunities, citizens are generally more satisfied with their lives. So, welfare states still have a role to play, and there is no indication that this will change in the coming years.

References

Aiyar, Shekhar, and Christian Ebeke. 2020. "Inequality of Opportunity, Inequality of Income and Economic Growth." *World Development* 136, 105115.

Berg, Andrew G., and Jonathan D. Ostry. 2011. "Inequality and Unsustainable Growth: Two Sides of the Same Coin?" IMF Staff Discussion Note. Washington, D.C.: International Monetary Fund.

Cingano, Federico. 2014. "Trends in Income Inequality and Its Impact on Economic Growth," no. 163. OECD. https://doi.org/10.1787/5jxrjncwxv6j-en.

Georgieff, Alexandre, and Anna Milanez. 2021. "What Happened to Jobs at High Risk of Automation?" OECD Social, Employment and Migration Working Papers, No. 255. Paris: OECD.

Greve, B. 2017. *Technology and the Future of Work. The Impact on Labour Markets and Welfare States*. Cheltenham: Edward Elgar.

Greve, B. 2019. "The Digital Economy and the Future of European Welfare States." *International Social Security Review* 72 (3), 79–94.

Greve, B. 2021. *Multidimensional Inequalities. International Perspectives Across Welfare States*. Berlin: De Gruyter.

Lane, Marguerita, and Anne Saint-Martin. 2021. "The Impact of Artificial Intelligence on the Labour Market: What Do We Know so Far?" 256. Social, Employment and Migration Working Papers No. 256. Paris: OECD.

OECD. 2019a. *Pensions at a Glance 2019*. Paris: OECD. https://doi.org/10.1787/b6d3dcfc-en.

OECD. 2019b. *Under Pressure: The Squeezed Middle Class*. Paris: OECD.

Palier, Bruno. 2019. "Work, Social Protection and the Middle Classes: What Future in the Digital Age?" *International Social Security Review* 72 (3), 113–133.

Peralta-Alva, A., and A. Roitman. 2018. "Technology and the Future of Work." WP/18/207. IMF Working Paper.

Piketty, T., and F. Cantante. 2018. "Wealth, Taxation and Inequality." In *Reducing Inequalities. A Challenge for the European Union*, edited by R. Carmo, C. Rio, and M. Medgyesi, 225–239. Cham: Palgrave Macmillan.

Stiglitz, Joseph E. 2012. *The Price of Inequality: How Today's Divided Society Endangers Our Future*. New York: WW Norton & Company.

Susskind, Daniel. 2020. *A World without Work: Technology, Automation and How We Should Respond*. London: Penguin UK.

Zucman, Gabriel. 2015. *The Hidden Wealth of Nations: The Scourge of Tax Havens*. Chicago: University of Chicago Press.

Contributors to this volume

Niklas Andreas Andersen is a Postdoctoral researcher in the research group WISER (Welfare, Inclusion, Social Work and Employment Relations) at the University of Aalborg with expertise in evidence-based Policymaking (EBPM), Governance, and Social and Employment policies. His research centres on understanding changes in the policy and governance of social and employment services with specific focus on the way evaluations, evidence and systems of monitoring act as drivers of change and/or stability. He is currently working with a number of Danish municipalities to enhance citizen involvement in the design and implementation of social and employment policies and services, as part of a four-year research project on citizen co-creation.

Fabrizio Antenucci holds a PhD in Economics and Quantitative Methods. He is a Research Fellow at the University of L'Aquila, and the local organiser of the EAEPE Summer School. His research interests include Labour Economics, Varieties of Capitalism, Economic Growth, International Economics.

Daniel Béland is Director of the McGill Institute for the Study of Canada and James McGill Professor in the Department of Political Science at McGill University (Montreal, Canada). A specialist of comparative fiscal and social policy, he has published 20 books and more than 160 articles in peer-reviewed journals such as *Comparative Political Studies*, *Social Policy & Administration*, *Governance*, *Journal of Public Policy*, *Journal of Social Policy*, *Policy Sciences*, and *Policy Studies Journal*.

Paul Bridgen is an Associate Professor of Social Policy in the School of Economic, Social and Political Sciences, University of Southampton, UK. He has published extensively on comparative social policy, often with Traute Meyer, with a particular focus on the UK and other liberal systems. He is currently working on the distributive impact of UK environmental taxation; domestic energy efficiency policy and fuel poverty; and the impact of welfare regimes on the development of eco-social policies.

Anna Cartwright is a Principal Lecturer in Economics at Oxford Brookes University and a RISCS Fellow in Quantification and Cyber Risk. She gained her PhD in Economics from the University of Southern Denmark and has previously worked at the University of Exeter, University of Kent and Coventry University. She has research expertise in industrial organisation, game theory and cyber security.

Edward Cartwright is a Professor of Economics at De Montfort University and Director of the Institute for Applied Economics and Social Value. He gained his PhD in Economics from Warwick University and has previously worked at the Paris School of Economics and the University of Kent. He has research expertise in game theory, public economics and cyber security.

https://doi.org/10.1515/9783110721768-027

Rossella Ciccia is Associate Professor of Social Policy at the Department of Social Policy and Intervention, University of Oxford, UK. Her research focuses on comparative social policy analysis in Europe and Latin America, with a particular emphasis on issues relating to gender, care and employment. Recent articles include "Protest and Social Policies for Outsiders: The Expansion of Social Pensions in Latin", *Journal of Social Policy* (together with Cesar Guzman-Concha) and "Unpacking Intersectional Solidarity: Dimensions of Power in Coalitions", *European Journal of Politics and Gender* (with Conny Roggeband).

Ivana Dobrotić is an Associate Professor of Comparative Social Policy at the University of Zagreb and Associate Member at the University of Oxford, Department of Social Policy and Intervention. Her research interest is in comparative social policy, with a particular interest in care and paid work, gender, social and spatial inequalities. She is a member of the International Network on Leave Policies & Research acting as co-editor of the *Annual International Review of Leave Policies & Related Research*, and a member of the steering committee of the ECPR Standing Group on Gender and Politics.

Fiona Dukelow is a Senior Lecturer in Social Policy at University College, Cork. Her research interests are in the areas of work and welfare, critical welfare theory and various aspects of historical and contemporary Irish social policy. She is co-author, with Mairéad Considine, of *Irish Social Policy: A Critical Introduction* (Policy Press, 2017) and co-editor, with Mary P. Murphy, of *The Irish Welfare State in the Twenty-First Century, Challenges and Change* (Palgrave, 2016).

Elke Heins is Senior Lecturer in Social Policy at the School of Social and Political Science, and Academic Co-convenor of the FUTURES Jean Monnet Centre of Excellence at the University of Edinburgh, UK. Her main research interests are comparative and European social policy. Recent publications include *European Futures – Challenges and Crossroads for the European Union of 2050* (Routledge, co-edited with Chad Damro and Drew Scott) and "Voices from the Past: Economic and Political Vulnerabilities in the Making of Next Generation EU" (*Comparative European Politics*, co-authored with Klaus Armingeon, Caroline de la Porte and Stefano Sacchi).

Maša Filipovič Hrast is an Associate Professor at the Faculty of Social Sciences, University of Ljubljana. She is Head of the Sociology Department and Head of Center for Welfare Studies. Her research topics include the development of the welfare state, social policy, housing policy, social inclusion, ageing and care policies. Her more recent publications include chapters in the following edited volumes: *Routledge Handbook of European Welfare States* (2020), *Attitudes, Aspirations and Welfare: Social Policy Directions in Uncertain Times* (Palgrave Macmillan, 2018), *After Austerity: Welfare State Transformation in Europe after the Great Recession* (Oxford University Press, 2017) and *Challenges to European Welfare Wystems* (Springer, 2016).

Gregor Fitzi is Research Fellow at the Department of Political Sciences of the University of Pisa and associated researcher at the Centre Georg Simmel, École des Hautes Études en Sciences Sociales, Paris. After his PhD in Sociology at the University of Bielefeld, he was assistant professor at the Institute of Sociology, University of Heidelberg, Interim Full Professor of Sociological Theory at the University of Bielefeld and Co-Director of the Centre for Citizenship, Social Pluralism and Religious Diversity, at University of Potsdam. Among his recent publications are: *The Challenge of Modernity. Simmel's Sociological Theory* (2019); with Jürgen Mackert and Bryan S. Turner (eds.), *Populism and the Crisis of Democracy*. 3 vols (Routledge, 2019); and with Bryan S. Turner. *Max Weber's Politics as a Profession*. Special Issue of the *Journal of Classical Sociology*, 4/2019.

Minna van Gerven is Professor of Social Policy at Tampere University, Finland. Her research interests include comparative and European social policy, welfare state change (design and implementation), and digitalisation. She has published in journals such as *Social Policy & Administration*, *Journal of Social Policy*, *Journal of Public Policy*, *Global Social Policy*, *Policy and Society*, *Policy and Politics*.

Bent Greve is Professor in Social Science with an emphasis on welfare state analysis at the University of Roskilde, Denmark. His research interest focuses on the welfare state, and social and labour market policy, often from a comparative perspective. He has published extensively on social and labour market policy, social security, tax expenditures, public sector expenditures and financing of the welfare state. He is editor of *Social Policy & Administration*. Recent books include *Myths, Narratives and the Welfare State* (Edward Elgar, 2020); *Austerity, Retrenchment and the Welfare State* (Edward Elgar, 2020); *Poverty. The Basics* (Routledge, 2020); *Routledge International Handbook of Poverty* (ed.) (Routledge, 2020); *Welfare, Populism and Welfare Chauvinism* (Policu Press, 2019); *Routledge Handbook of the Welfare State* (ed., 2nd edition) (Routledge, 2019); *Multidimensional Inequalities* (De Gruyter, 2021).

Ijin Hong is Associate Professor at the School of Government of Sun Yat-sen University (SYSU), P.R. China. She majored in Sociology and Political Institutions at La Sapienza University in Rome for her MA (2006), and in Social Welfare at Yonsei University, Seoul, for her PhD (2011). Her research involves social policies in Europe and East Asia from a comparative perspective, and she is interested in welfare state theory, health and social services, labour market and migration policies. Her work has appeared in *Social Policy & Administration*, *Journal of Comparative Policy Analysis*, *Political Quarterly*, *Stato e Mercato*, *Korean Journal of Social Policy* (한국사회정책학회). In 2017 she joined the East Asian Social Policy Network (EASP) as a member of the organizing committee.

M. Azhar Hussain is Professor of Economics at the University of Sharjah and Visiting Professor at Roskilde University. His research is focused on analyses of the empirical distribution of incomes and consumption, which includes a deeper understanding of inequality, poverty, deprivation, polarisation, and robust multidimensional rankings of welfare. The data materials behind the analyses mainly relate to the situation in Denmark, the European Union countries, and developing nations. He publishes both nationally and internationally in peer-reviewed journals and books.

Matteo Jessoula is Full Professor of Political Science and Director of the PhD programme in Political Studies at the Department of Social and Political Sciences of the University of Milan. He is national coordinator of the Italian team of ESPN-European Social Policy Network and co-Director of the International Observatory on Social Cohesion and Inclusion (OCIS) in Reggio Emilia; member of the Board of Espanet and Espanet Italia. Among his publications: *Labour Market Flexibility and Pension Reforms. Flexible Today, Secure Tomorrow?* (Palgrave, 2012; co-edited with K. Hinrichs); *Fighting Poverty and Social Exclusion in the EU. A Chance in Europe 2020*, (Routledge, 2018; co-edited with I. Madama); "Explaining Italian 'Exceptionalism' and its End: Minimum Income from Neglect to Hyper-Politicization (with M . Natili) in *Social Policy & Administration*, 2020.

Carlo Knotz is Associate Professor of Political Science at the University of Stavanger, Norway. His research is concerned with welfare state attitudes, labour markets, and labour market policies. His work has been published in, inter alia, the *European Sociological Review, Comparative Political Studies*, the *Journal of European Public Policy, Social Science & Medicine* and the *Journal of Social Policy*.

Bingqin Li is Professor at the Social Policy Research Centre at UNSW in Australia. She received her PhD in Social Policy from LSE and PhD in Economics from Nankai University, China. She had worked in LSE, Australian National University before moving to UNSW. Her research is on social policy and governance with a particular interest on China and China in comparison. Her on-going research includes the governance of complex social policy programmes in China, social inclusion and integration, social policy and development, social service delivery in multi-cultural society. Her research has been published in academic journals in social policy, urban studies and public policy. She is now an associate editor of the journal *Urban Governance*.

Tao Liu is a Professor in Social Policy at Zhejiang University in China and Professor in Sociology at the University Duisburg-Essen in Germany. His research focuses upon social policy, social protection, welfare states, pension insurance, long-term-care insurance, health governance in China, Germany and also in a global context. Recently he has published a few papers on social policy and labour protection for the crowdsourcing and gig economy in the digital age. He has published many peer-reviewed journal articles for social policy, social governance and policy learning in various international journals including *Global Social Policy*, *Social Policy & Administration*, *Journal of Aging and Social Policy*, *Urban Affairs Review*, *Environment and Urbanization*, *Journal of Asian Public Policy*, *Health Sociology Review* etc.

Amílcar Moreira is a Researcher SOCIUS, Research Centre in Economic and Organizational Sociology, and Guest Assistant Professor at the Lisbon School of Economics & Management, University of Lisbon. He specialises in comparative social policy, ageing, welfare-to-work policies and microsimulation, and has published books with international publishers such as Oxford University Press and Policy Press and articles in international peer-reviewed journals including as *Social Policy & Administration*, *European Journal of Social Security*, *Journal of Population Ageing* and the *European Journal of Ageing*.

Alexandra Lopes, Assistant Professor at the Department of Sociology of the University of Porto. She holds a PhD in Social Policy from the London School of Economics and Habilitation in Sociology from the University of Porto. Her research interests are primarily focused on LTC and institutional care arrangements. She works as an expert for the European Commission on these topics. She is the main scientific evaluator of the Portuguese branch of the Social Observatory of La Caixa Foundation and has authored several publications on LTC, familism and welfare arrangements in old age.

Philipp Lutz is an Assistant Professor in Political Science at the Vrije Universiteit in Amsterdam, Netherlands. His main research interests are the implications of migration for government policies and public opinion. His work has been published, inter alia, in the *British Journal of Political Science*, the *European Journal of Political Research*, the *Journal of European Public Policy*, *West European Politics* and the *International Studies Quarterly*.

Marcello Natili is Assistant Professor in Political Science at the Department of Social and Political Sciences of the University of Milan and a member of the Italian team of the European Social Policy Network. His work focuses on comparative welfare states research, and in particular minimum income schemes and European Social Governance. His publications include articles in *European Societies*, *Journal of European Social Policies*, *Journal of International and Comparative Social Policy*, *Journal of Social Policy* and *Social Policy & Administration*.

Virginija Poškutė is Associate Professor at the ISM University of Management and Economics in Vilnius, Lithuania. She is an economist and social policy analyst, studied at Vilnius University (Lithuania), Roskilde University (Denmark), University of Bath (UK) and Tilburg University (The Netherlands), and was Fulbright researcher at Darden Graduate School, University of Virginia (USA). Virginija has extensive international job experience (UNDP/Lithuania; International Master's Programme "European Social Policy Analysis" by CEPS/INSTEAD, Luxembourg and Leuven University, Belgium), has participated in various international consultancy projects for the World Bank, UN, UNDP, UNICEF, EIGE, European Commission, OECD as well as national projects on economic and social issues for the Ministry of Social Security and Labour, Ministry of Environment, Ministry of Economics and various NGOs. Virginija's main research interests are within social policy, welfare economics and competitiveness.

Luigi Salvati is PhD in Economics and an independent researcher. His research interests include Labour Economics, Economic Growth, Monetary and Fiscal Policy.

Mi Ah Schoyen is Senior Researcher at NOVA Norwegian Social Research, Oslo Metropolitan University. She works in the field of comparative welfare state research widely conceived. Her interests include the welfare mix, the politics and social consequences of welfare state reforms, intergenerational solidarity and the interplay between climate and social policy.

Young-Kyu Shin is an Associate Research Fellow at the Korea Institute for Health and Social Affairs (KIHASA) and visiting researcher at the Finnish Institute for Health and Welfare (THL). Prior to joining KIHASA, he worked as postdoctoral researcher at the University of Helsinki. His research interests lie in labour market policy, social benefits, in-work poverty and precarious work, particularly in a comparative perspective. He has published in the *Journal of Social Policy*, *Social Policy & Administration*, *Journal of European Social Policy*, and other international journals.

Kat Smith is a Professor of Public Health Policy at the University of Strathclyde (and Honorary Professor at the University of Edinburgh) with expertise in evidence use, public health and health inequalities, qualitative methods and evidence reviews. Her research centres on understanding, and working to improve, the use of evidence and expertise in policies impacting on people's health and wellbeing and on social inequalities. Kat has published over 65 peer-reviewed journal articles and five books. She is currently working with policy organisations in the UK to try to improve the way they use evidence in policymaking by employing complex systems modelling, as part of a five-year UKPRP Consortium award (www.sipher.ac.uk). She is Co-Editor-in-Chief of *Evidence & Policy* and the *Palgrave Studies in Science, Knowledge and Policy*.

Ron Thompson is a Principal Research Fellow in Education at the University of Huddersfield. He is currently co-directing a research project on interventions aimed at young people in England at risk of becoming early school leavers. His main research interests are in class-based educational inequalities, with a particular focus on marginalised young people. He has also written extensively on teacher education. His recent books include *Education, Work and Social Change*, published by Palgrave Macmillan, and *Education, Inequality and Social Class*, published by Routledge. Other work has appeared in a wide range of journals, including the *British Journal of Sociology of Education*, *Oxford Review of Education*, *Journal of Education and Work* and the *British Educational Research Journal*.

Philipp Trein is Assistant Professor of Public Administration and Policy at the University of Lausanne and a Senior Fellow at the Institute of European Studies at UC Berkeley. His research interests cover the coordination and integration of public policy, the politicisation of e-government, the politics of preventative health policies, the problem-solving capacity of multilevel systems, and crisis politics. His work is published in leading international and peer-reviewed journals in public administration, public policy, and political science. In 2018, his book *Healthy or Sick? Coevolution of Health Care and Public Health in a Comparative Perspective* was published with Cambridge University Press. More information can be found here: https://www.philipptrein.com/

Pasquale Tridico is Full Professor in Economic Policy at Roma Tre University, Co-ordinator of the Laurea Magistrale "Labour Market, Industrial Relations and Welfare Systems" at Roma Tre University, Director of the Centre of Excellence Jean Monnet "Labour, Welfare and Social Rights" (University Roma Tre). His research interests comprehend Labour Economics, Inequality, Varieties of capitalism, Transition and Emerging economies, Institutional Economics, Financial crisis and global governance, Economic development, EU integration and enlargement.

Athina Vlachantoni is Professor of Gerontology and Social Policy at the University of Southampton, UK. She holds a Bachelors in Politics and Social Policy (Royal Holloway, University of London), a Masters in Comparative Social Policy (University of Oxford) and a PhD in Social Policy (London School of Economics and Political Science). Her research interests are at the interface of population ageing and social policy, and she is currently Deputy Editor of the journal *Ageing & Society*, and a member of the Editorial Board of the *Journal of Social Policy*.

Tobias Wiß is Associate Professor in Political Science and leader of the research group "Socioeconomic Developments and Social Policy Reforms: The Moderating Role of Political Institutions" at the Johannes Kepler University Linz. His work focuses on comparative welfare state research and comparative political economy, in particular pensions and family policy. His work has been published in the *Journal of European Public Policy*, *Journal of European Social Policy*, *Social Policy & Administration* and *Journal of Comparative Policy Analysis*, among others.